CONTRACT LAW

Selected Source Materials
Annotated

2017 Edition

STEVEN J. BURTON
John F. Murray Professor of Law
University of Iowa

MELVIN A. EISENBERG
Jesse H. Choper Professor of Law Emeritus
University of California at Berkeley

WEST
ACADEMIC
PUBLISHING

COPYRIGHT © 1995, 1996 WEST PUBLISHING CO.
© West, a Thomson business, 1998–2008
© 2009–2012 Thomson Reuters
© 2013 LEG, Inc. d/b/a West Academic Publishing
© 2014–2016 LEG, Inc. d/b/a West Academic
© 2017 LEG, Inc. d/b/a West Academic
    444 Cedar Street, Suite 700
    St. Paul, MN 55101
    1-877-888-1330

Printed in the United States of America

ISBN: 978-1-68328-777-3

[No claim of copyright is made for official U.S. government statutes, rules or regulations.]

EDITORS' INTRODUCTION

Until the Twentieth Century, there were very few statutes governing contracts. Instead, judges made contract law through the common law process—on a case-by-case basis, bound by precedents. Today, much of contract law continues to be common law, but it is subject to many statutes, which are enacted by Congress and signed by the President or enacted by a state legislature and signed by a governor. There are four main drawbacks to the common law process insofar as contract law goes. First, judges normally are bound to follow precedent, which ties the law to the past. Consequently, the common law tends to change slowly. Second, because the common law is a matter of state law, the common law tends not to be uniform across different states. This diversity hampers transactions between parties in different states by making the law less predictable and contracting more costly. Third, courts cannot take the initiative to revise the common law; they can decide only the legal issues that litigating parties present to them. Fourth, also because courts only decide cases, they generally are not supposed to make laws by announcing new, broadly applicable rules. The common law consequently evolves on a piecemeal basis, by contrast with legislation. For these reasons, the common law can become outdated as contracting practices evolve. This, too, hampers transacting, makes contracting more costly, and also may fail to provide redress for new kinds of unfairness.

Several developments in the Twentieth Century led to the enactment of a number of important statutes and some landmark common law cases. Contracting between parties in different states increased. Mainly to promote greater uniformity, for example, the National Conference of Commissioners on Uniform State Laws (now called the "Uniform Law Commission") began proposing uniform laws for enactment by the states. The Uniform Commercial Code ("UCC") is among the most successful of their proposals. Upon enactment, it supplants the common law of contracts in a number of ways, including the law governing the sale of goods. Moreover, the American Law Institute ("ALI") developed and published the Restatement of Contracts (1932) and the Restatement (Second) of Contracts (1981). They state, and comment on, the common law in an effort to promote the law's uniformity, clarity, fairness, and relevance to current practices. Though the ALI is a private, non-profit organization that does not have the power to make law, both have been very influential with many courts. In addition, some contracts, such as those between merchants and consumers or employers and employees, were seen to be susceptible to unfairness. Several statutes and restatements, as well as a few landmark cases, responded with new laws and doctrines to correct for imbalances in the contracting process, contract terms, or both. Further, new technologies changed the contracting process in many ways, as by introducing contracting over the Internet. Statutes, restatements, and cases responded, again with new law. Finally, the globalization of the economy led to a burst of contracting across national borders. These contracts were governed by the laws of different nations, many of which differ fundamentally because they emerged from differing legal traditions. The lack of uniformity globally posed problems analogous to those that increased the costs of contracting between parties in different states of the United States. Several international conventions, and the UNIDROIT Principles of International Commercial Contracts, seek to ease these problems.

Contract law has changed considerably since the turn of the Twentieth Century. It will change more in the Twenty-First Century as change accelerates. This book includes legal documents that reflect the changes that already have occurred and several that may be harbingers of the future.

TABLE OF CONTENTS

TABLE OF CONTENTS

TABLES OF COMPARISON BETWEEN UCC, C.I.S.G., UNIDROIT PRINCIPLES, AND RESTATEMENT (SECOND) OF CONTRACTS

Table 1

U.C.C.	C.I.S.G.	UNIDROIT Principles
General Provisions		
§ 1–101		
§ 1–102		Preamble
§ 1–103(a)	Art. 7	Arts. 1, 6
§ 1–103(b)	Art. 7(2)	
§ 1–104		
§ 1–105		
§ 1–106		
§ 1–107		
§ 1–201		
§ 1–201(b)(46)	Art. 13	
§ 1–202	Art. 24	Art. 1.9
§ 1–203		
§ 1–204		
§ 1–205		
§ 1–206		
§ 1–301	Art. 1(1)	
§ 1–302	Art. 6	Art. 1.4
§ 1–303	Art. 9	Art. 1.8
§ 1–304	Art. 7(1)	Art. 1.7
§ 1–305	Arts. 5, 74	
§ 1–306		
§ 1–307		
§ 1–308		
§ 1–309		
§ 1–310		
Sales		
§ 2–101		
§ 2–102	Arts. 1, 2, 3, 4	
§ 2–103		
§ 2–104		
§ 2–105		
§ 2–106		
§ 2–106(3)–(4)	Art. 81	
§ 2–106(4)		Arts. 7.3.1, 7.3.5
§ 2–107		

TABLES OF COMPARISON

U.C.C.	C.I.S.G.	UNIDROIT Principles
§ 2–201	Art. 11	Art. 1.2
§ 2–202	Art. 11	Arts. 1.2, 2.17
§ 2–203		Art. 1.7
§ 2–204	Art. 23	Arts. 2.1, 2.2
§ 2–204(3)		Art. 2.14
§ 2–205	Art. 16(2)	Art. 2.4(2)
§ 2–206		Art. 2.6
§ 2–206(1)(a)		Art. 18(1)
§ 2–206(1)(b)–(c)		Art. 18(3)
§ 2–207	Art. 19	Arts. 2.11, 2.12, 2.22
§ 2–208	Art. 8	Art. 4.3
§ 2–209	Art. 29	Art. 2.18
§ 2–210		
§ 2–301	Arts. 30, 53, 54, 59	
§ 2–302		
§ 2–303		
§ 2–304		
§ 2–305		
§ 2–305(1)	Art. 55	Art. 5.7
§ 2–306		
§ 2–307		Arts. 6.1.2, 6.1.4
§ 2–308	Art. 31	Arts. 1.10, 6.1.6
§ 2–309(1)	Art. 33	Art. 6.1.1
§ 2–310	Arts. 57, 58	
§ 2–311	Arts. 60, 65	
§ 2–312	Arts. 41–43	
§ 2–313		
§ 2–314	Arts. 35, 36, 66	
§ 2–315		
§ 2–316		
§ 2–317		
§ 2–318		
§ 2–319	Art. 32	
§ 2–320	Art. 32	
§ 2–321		
§ 2–322		
§ 2–323		
§ 2–324		
§ 2–325		
§ 2–326		
§ 2–327		
§ 2–328	Art. 2(b)	

TABLES OF COMPARISON

U.C.C.	C.I.S.G.	Unidroit Principles
§ 2–401		
§ 2–402		
§ 2–403		Art. 3.3(2)
§ 2–501		
§ 2–502		
§ 2–503		
§ 2–504		
§ 2–505		
§ 2–506		
§ 2–507		
§ 2–508	Arts. 37, 48	Art. 7.1.4
§ 2–509	Arts. 67, 68, 69	
§ 2–510	Art. 36	
§ 2–511		Art. 6.1.7
§ 2–512		
§ 2–513	Art. 38	
§ 2–514	Art. 34	
§ 2–515		
§ 2–601	Art. 45	
§ 2–602	Arts. 39, 49(2)	
§ 2–603	Arts. 85, 86, 88	
§ 2–604	Art. 87	
§ 2–605		
§ 2–606		
§ 2–607		
§ 2–608		
§ 2–609	Arts. 71–72	Art. 7.3.4
§ 2–610	Arts. 71–72	Art. 7.3.3
§ 2–611	Art. 73	
§ 2–612		
§ 2–613		
§ 2–614		
§ 2–615	Art. 79	Art. 7.1.7
§ 2–616		
§ 2–701		
§ 2–702		
§ 2–703	Art. 61	
§ 2–704		
§ 2–705		
§ 2–706		Art. 7.4.5
§ 2–707		
§ 2–708	Arts. 74, 77	Art. 7.4

TABLES OF COMPARISON

U.C.C.	C.I.S.G.	UNIDROIT Principles
§ 2–709	Art. 62	Art. 7.2.1
§ 2–710		Art. 7.4.2
§ 2–711		
§ 2–712	Art. 75	Art. 7.4.5
§ 2–713	Art. 74	Art. 7.4.6
§ 2–714	Art. 74	
§ 2–715		Arts. 7.4.2, 7.4.4
§ 2–716	Art. 46(1)–(2)	Arts. 7.2.1, 7.2.2
§ 2–717	Art. 50	
§ 2–718		Arts. 7.4.13, 7.3.6
§ 2–719		
§ 2–720		
§ 2–721		
§ 2–722		
§ 2–723	Art. 76	Art. 7.4.6(2)
§ 2–724		
§ 2–725		

Table 2

U.C.C.	Restatement (Second) of Contracts	UNIDROIT Principles
	§ 1	Art. 1.3
	§§ 7, 85	Arts. 3.12–3.16
	§ 12	Art. 3.1
	§ 17	Art. 3.2
§ 2–204	§§ 19, 22	Art. 2.1
§ 2–204	§ 24	Art. 2.2
	§§ 26–27; cf. § 205	
	§ 27	Art. 2.13
§ 2–204(3)	§§ 33–34, 204	Art. 2.14
	§§ 35, 36(1)(c), 42, 43, 46	Arts. 2.3(2), 2.4(1)
	§§ 36(1)(b), 41	Arts. 2.7–2.8
	§§ 38, 40 Art.	Art. 2.5, 2.10
§ 2–207	§§ 39, 59	Art. 2.11(1)
§ 2–206	§§ 50, 53, 54–56, 69	Art. 2.6(1)
§ 2–206	§ 54	Art. 2.6(3)
§ 2–207	§ 61	Art. 2.11(2)
§ 1–207	§§ 63, 66–70	Arts. 1.9(2)–(3), 2.6(2)
§ 2–206	§§ 63, 66–70	Art. 2.6(2)
	§§ 63, 66–67, 70	Art. 2.9
	§§ 64–65	Art. 1.9(1)
	§ 77	Art. 7.1.6

TABLES OF COMPARISON

U.C.C.	Restatement (Second) of Contracts	UNIDROIT Principles
§ 2–201	Chapter 5 (§§ 110–150)	Art. 1.2
§ 2–209	§§ 148–150	Art. 2.18
	§ 151	Art. 3.4
	§§ 152–154, 201	Art. 3.5
	§ 152(2)	Art. 3.7
	§ 154(c)	Art. 3.6
	§§ 159–164	Art. 3.8
	§ 164	Art. 3.11
	§§ 175–176	Art. 3.9
	§ 177, § 79 (see Comment e)	Art. 3.10
§ 2–208	§§ 202–203	Arts. 4.1–4.4
	§ 202(1)	Art. 5.2(a)
	§§ 202(4)–(5), 222, 223	Art. 5.2(b)
	§ 203(d)	Art. 2.21
§§ 2–203, 1–102(3)	§ 205	Art. 1.7
	§ 203(a)	Art. 4.5
	§ 204	Art. 4.8
§ 2–305(1)	§ 204	Art. 5.7
	§ 205	Art. 5.2(c)–(d)
	§ 205	Art. 5.3
	§ 206	Art. 4.6
§ 2–202	§§ 209–210, 212–215	Art. 2.17
	§ 211(1)–(2)	Art. 2.19
	§ 211(3)	Art. 2.20
§ 2–207	§ 216	Art. 2.12
§ 1–303	§§ 219–223	Art. 1.8
	§ 230(2)(a)	Art. 7.1.2
§ 2–309(1)	§§ 233–234	Art. 6.1.1
§ 2–307	§ 233	Art. 6.1.2
§ 2–307	§ 234	Art. 6.1.4
	§ 235(2)	Art. 7.1.1
	§ 238	Art. 7.1.3
§ 2–106(4)	§ 241	Art. 7.3.1
	§ 240	Art. 6.1.3
§ 2–508	§ 241(d)	Art. 7.1.4
	§§ 241(d), 242	Art. 7.1.5
§ 2–610	§ 250	Art. 7.3.3
§ 2–609	§ 251	Art. 7.3.4
	§§ 261, 264	Art. 6.1.17
	§§ 261, 265–266	Arts. 6.2.1–6.2.2
§ 2–615	§§ 261–271	Art. 7.1.7
	§ 266	Art. 3.3(1)

TABLES OF COMPARISON

U.C.C.	Restatement (Second) of Contracts	UNIDROIT Principles
	§§ 267–268	Art. 6.2.3
§ 2–716(1)–(2)	§ 345(b)–(c)	Arts. 7.2.2–7.2.3
	§ 346	Art. 7.4.1
§ 2–708 (2), § 2–715	§ 347	Art. 7.4.2(1)
	§ 350	Arts. 7.4.7–7.4.8
§ 2–715	§ 351	Art. 7.4.4
	§ 352	Art. 7.4.3
§ 2–715	§§ 353, 355	Art. 7.4.2(2)
	§ 356	Art. 7.4.13
§ 2–718(2)	§§ 370–377	Art. 7.3.6
	§ 376	Art. 3.17

CONTRACT LAW

Selected Source Materials
Annotated

2017 Edition

PART I

UNIFORM COMMERCIAL CODE ARTICLE 1, ARTICLE 2, ARTICLE 3 (EXCERPTS), ARTICLE 9 (EXCERPTS)

UNIFORM COMMERCIAL CODE

[The National Conference of Commissioners on Uniform State Laws (now called the "Uniform Law Commission") and the American Law Institute ("ALI") initially proposed the Uniform Commercial Code ("UCC") in 1952. Upon enactment by a state, the UCC supplants the state's common law when that common law conflicts with the statute.

[In recent years, the Uniform Law Commission and the ALI have proposed various revisions and amendments to the UCC, many of which have been widely enacted by the states. The UCC now consists of ten main "Articles" on such topics as sales of goods, leases of goods, bank deposits and collections, funds transfers, letters of credit, and secured transactions. For a basic course in contracts, the most important Articles are Article 1, which contains general provisions that apply to any transaction governed by any other Article, and Article 2, which contains rules and standards that apply to transactions in goods. As of May 1, 2012, the version of Article 1 below had been enacted by 41 states, and Article 2 had been enacted by 49 states. Parts of Article 3, concerning commercial paper, and Article 9, concerning secured transactions, are also important. Accordingly, Part I of this pamphlet contains the entirety of Articles 1 and 2, and excerpts from Articles 3 and 9. In addition, Part II contains excerpts from an earlier version of Article 9, because though all 50 states have enacted a revision of Article 9, most of the cases addressing the relevant issues were decided before the revised version was proposed.

[Note that UCC § 1–201 contains a number of definitions that establish the meanings of many terms used in the statute. Sections 2–103 to 2–106 contain more definitions, which establish the meanings of many terms used in Article 2. When a statute defines a term, for the purposes of interpreting and applying that statute the term has the meaning as defined, not any other meaning. Note also that many of the Official Comments to specific sections include "definitional cross references" to definitions of terms used in that section but defined in another. In principle, this statute, like others, should be interpreted in accordance with these definitions as well, so as to further its purposes.]

ARTICLE 1

GENERAL PROVISIONS

PART 1. GENERAL PROVISIONS

PART 1

GENERAL PROVISIONS

§ 1–101. Short Titles.

(a) This [Act] may be cited as the Uniform Commercial Code.

(b) This article may be cited as Uniform Commercial Code—General Provisions.

§ 1–102.   Scope of Article.

This article applies to a transaction to the extent that it is governed by another article of [the Uniform Commercial Code].

§ 1–103.   Construction of [Uniform Commercial Code] to Promote Its Purposes and Policies; Applicability of Supplemental Principles of Law.

(a)   [The Uniform Commercial Code] must be liberally construed and applied to promote its underlying purposes and policies, which are:

     (1)   to simplify, clarify, and modernize the law governing commercial transactions;

     (2)   to permit the continued expansion of commercial practices through custom, usage, and agreement of the parties, and

     (3)   to make uniform the law among the various jurisdictions.

(b)   Unless displaced by the particular provisions of [the Uniform Commercial Code], the principles of law and equity, including the law merchant and the law relative to capacity to contract, principal and agent, estoppel, fraud, misrepresentation, duress, coercion, mistake, bankruptcy, and other validating or invalidating cause supplement its provisions.

§ 1–104.   Construction Against Implied Repeal.

[The Uniform Commercial Code] being a general act intended as a unified coverage of its subject matter, no part of it shall be deemed to be impliedly repealed by subsequent legislation if such construction can reasonably be avoided.

§ 1–105.   Severability.

If any provision or clause of [the Uniform Commercial Code] or its application to any person or circumstance is held invalid, the invalidity does not affect other provisions or applications of [the Uniform Commercial Code] which can be given effect without the invalid provision or application, and to this end the provisions of [the Uniform Commercial Code] are severable.

§ 1–106.   Use of Singular and Plural; Gender.

In [the Uniform Commercial Code], unless the statutory context otherwise requires:

     (1)   words in the singular number include the plural, and those in the plural include the singular; and

     (2)   words of any gender also refer to any other gender.

§ 1–107.   Section Captions.

Section captions are part of [the Uniform Commercial Code].

§ 1–108.   Relation to Electronic Signatures in Global and National Commerce Act.

This [Act] modifies, limits, and supersedes the federal Electronic Signatures in Global and National Commerce Act, (15 U.S.C. Section 7001, et. seq.) but does not modify, limit, or supersede Section 101(c) of that act (15 U.S.C. Section 7001(c)) or authorize electronic delivery of any of the notices described in Section 103 (b) of that act (15 U.S.C. Section 103(b)).

PART 2

GENERAL DEFINITIONS AND PRINCIPLES OF INTERPRETATION

§ 1–201.　General Definitions.

(a)　Unless the context otherwise requires, words or phrases defined in this section, or in the additional definitions contained in other articles of [the Uniform Commercial Code] that apply to particular articles or parts thereof, have the meanings stated.

(b)　Subject to definitions contained in other articles of [the Uniform Commercial Code] that apply to particular articles or parts thereof

(1)　"Action", in the sense of a judicial proceeding, includes recoupment, counterclaim, set-off, suit in equity, and any other proceeding in which rights are determined.

(2)　"Aggrieved party" means a party entitled to pursue a remedy.

(3)　"Agreement", as distinguished from "contract", means the bargain of the parties in fact, as found in their language or inferred from other circumstances, including course of performance, course of dealing, or usage of trade as provided in Section 1–303.

(4)　"Bank" means a person engaged in the business of banking and includes a savings bank, savings and loan association, credit union, and trust company.

(5)　"Bearer" means a person in control of a negotiable electronic document of title or a person in possession of a negotiable instrument, negotiable tangible document of title or certificated security that is payable to bearer or indorsed in blank.

(6)　"Bill of lading" means a document evidencing the receipt of goods for shipment issued by a person engaged in the business of transporting or forwarding goods.

(7)　"Branch" includes a separately incorporated foreign branch of a bank.

(8)　"Burden of establishing" a fact means the burden of persuading the trier of fact that the existence of the fact is more probable than its nonexistence.

(9)　"Buyer in ordinary course of business" means a person that buys goods in good faith, without knowledge that the sale violates the rights of another person in the goods, and in the ordinary course from a person, other than a pawnbroker, in the business of selling goods of that kind. A person buys goods in the ordinary course if the sale to the person comports with the usual or customary practices in the kind of business in which the seller is engaged or with the seller's own usual or customary practices. A person that sells oil, gas, or other minerals at the wellhead or minehead is a person in the business of selling goods of that kind. A buyer in ordinary course of business may buy for cash, by exchange of other property, or on secured or unsecured credit, and may acquire goods or documents of title under a preexisting contract for sale. Only a buyer that takes possession of the goods or has a right to recover the goods from the seller under Article 2 may be a buyer in ordinary course of business. "Buyer in ordinary course of business" does not include a person that acquires goods in a transfer in bulk or as security for or in total or partial satisfaction of a money debt.

(10)　"Conspicuous", with reference to a term, means so written, displayed, or presented that a reasonable person against which it is to operate ought to have noticed it. Whether a term is "conspicuous" or not is a decision for the court. Conspicuous terms include the following:

(A)　a heading in capitals equal to or greater in size than the surrounding text, or in contrasting type, font, or color to the surrounding text of the same or lesser size; and

(B)　language in the body of a record or display in larger type than the surrounding text, or in contrasting type, font, or color to the surrounding text of the same size, or set off

5

from surrounding text of the same size by symbols or other marks that call attention to the language.

(11) "Consumer" means an individual who enters into a transaction primarily for personal, family, or household purposes

(12) "Contract", as distinguished from "agreement", means the total legal obligation that results from the parties' agreement as determined by [the Uniform Commercial Code] as supplemented by any other applicable laws.

(13) "Creditor" includes a general creditor, a secured creditor, a lien creditor, and any representative of creditors, including an assignee for the benefit of creditors, a trustee in bankruptcy, a receiver in equity, and an executor or administrator of an insolvent debtor's or assignor's estate.

(14) "Defendant" includes a person in the position of defendant in a counterclaim, cross-claim, or third-party claim.

(15) "Delivery", with respect to an instrument, document of title, or chattel paper, means voluntary transfer of possession.

(16) "Document of title" includes bill of lading, dock warrant, dock receipt, warehouse receipt or order for the delivery of goods, and also any other document which in the regular course of business or financing is treated as adequately evidencing that the person in possession of it is entitled to receive, hold, and dispose of the document and the goods it covers. To be a document of title, a document must purport to be issued by or addressed to a bailee and purport to cover goods in the bailee's possession which are either identified or are fungible portions of an identified mass.

(17) "Fault" means a default, breach, or wrongful act or omission.

(18) "Fungible goods" means:

(A)   goods of which any unit, by nature or usage of trade, is the equivalent of any other like unit; or

(B)   goods that by agreement are treated as equivalent.

(19) "Genuine" means free of forgery or counterfeiting.

(20) "Good faith," except as otherwise provided in Article 5, means honesty in fact and the observance of reasonable commercial standards of fair dealing.

(21) "Holder" means:

(A)   the person in possession of a negotiable instrument that is payable either to bearer or to an identified person that is the person in possession; or

(B)   the person in possession of a document of title if the goods are deliverable either to bearer or to the order of the person in possession.

(22) "Insolvency proceeding" includes an assignment for the benefit of creditors or other proceeding intended to liquidate or rehabilitate the estate of the person involved.

(23) "Insolvent" means:

(A)   having generally ceased to pay debts in the ordinary course of business other than as a result of bona fide dispute;

(B)   being unable to pay debts as they become due; or

(C)   being insolvent within the meaning of federal bankruptcy law.

(24) "Money" means a medium of exchange currently authorized or adopted by a domestic or foreign government. The term includes a monetary unit of account established by an intergovernmental organization or by agreement between two or more countries.

(25) "Organization" means a person other than an individual.

(26) "Party", as distinguished from "third party", means a person that has engaged in a transaction or made an agreement subject to [the Uniform Commercial Code].

(27) "Person" means an individual, corporation, business trust, estate, trust, partnership, limited liability company, association, joint venture, government, governmental subdivision, agency, or instrumentality, public corporation, or any other legal or commercial entity.

(28) "Present value" means the amount as of a date certain of one or more sums payable in the future, discounted to the date certain by use of either an interest rate specified by the parties if that rate is not manifestly unreasonable at the time the transaction is entered into or, if an interest rate is not so specified, a commercially reasonable rate that takes into account the facts and circumstances at the time the transaction is entered into.

(29) "Purchase" means taking by sale, lease, discount, negotiation, mortgage, pledge, lien, security interest, issue or reissue, gift, or any other voluntary transaction creating an interest in property.

(30) "Purchaser" means a person that takes by purchase.

(31) "Record" means information that is inscribed on a tangible medium or that is stored in an electronic or other medium and is retrievable in perceivable form.

(32) "Remedy" means any remedial right to which an aggrieved party is entitled with or without resort to a tribunal.

(33) "Representative" means a person empowered to act for another, including an agent, an officer of a corporation or association, and a trustee, executor, or administrator of an estate.

(34) "Right" includes remedy.

(35) "Security interest" means an interest in personal property or fixtures which secures payment or performance of an obligation. "Security interest" includes any interest of a consignor and a buyer of accounts, chattel paper, a payment intangible, or a promissory note in a transaction that is subject to Article 9. "Security interest" does not include the special property interest of a buyer of goods on identification of those goods to a contract for sale under Section 2–401, but a buyer may also acquire a "security interest" by complying with Article 9. Except as otherwise provided in Section 2–505, the right of a seller or lessor of goods under Article 2 or 2A to retain or acquire possession of the goods is not a "security interest", but a seller or lessor may also acquire a "security interest" by complying with Article 9. The retention or reservation of title by a seller of goods notwithstanding shipment or delivery to the buyer under Section 2–401 is limited in effect to a reservation of a "security interest." Whether a transaction in the form of a lease creates a "security interest" is determined. pursuant to Section 1–203.

(36) "Send" in connection with a writing, record, or notice means:

    (A) to deposit in the mail or deliver for transmission by any other usual means of communication with postage or cost of transmission provided for and properly addressed and, in the case of an instrument, to an address specified thereon or otherwise agreed, or if there be none to any address reasonable under the circumstances; or

    (B) in any other way to cause to be received any record or notice within the time it would have arrived if properly sent.

(37) "Signed" includes using any symbol executed or adopted with present intention to adopt or accept a writing.

(38) "State" means a State of the United States, the District of Columbia, Puerto Rico, the United States Virgin Islands, or any territory or insular possession subject to the jurisdiction of the United States.

(39) "Surety" includes a guarantor or other secondary obligor.

(40) "Term" means a portion of an agreement that relates to a particular matter.

(41) "Unauthorized signature" means a signature made without actual, implied, or apparent authority. The term includes a forgery.

(42) "Warehouse receipt" means a receipt issued by a person engaged in the business of storing goods for hire.

(43) "Writing" includes printing, typewriting, or any other intentional reduction to tangible form. "Written" has a corresponding meaning.

Official Comments

. . .

10. "Conspicuous." Derived from former Section 1–201(10). This definition states the general standard that to be conspicuous a term ought to be noticed by a reasonable person. Whether a term is conspicuous is an issue for the court. Subparagraphs (A) and (B) set out several methods for making a term conspicuous. Requiring that a term be conspicuous blends a notice function (the term ought to be noticed) and a planning function (giving guidance to the party relying on the term regarding how that result can be achieved). Although these paragraphs indicate some of the methods for making a term attention-calling, the test is whether attention can reasonably be expected to be called to it. The statutory language should not be construed to permit a result that is inconsistent with that test. . . .

20. "Good faith." Former Section 1–201(19) defined "good faith" simply as honesty in fact; the definition contained no element of commercial reasonableness. Initially, that definition applied throughout the Code with only one exception. Former Section 2–103(1)(b) provided that "in this Article . . . good faith in the case of a merchant means honesty in fact and the observance of reasonable commercial standards of fair dealing in the trade." This alternative definition was limited in applicability in three ways. First, it applied only to transactions within the scope of Article 2. Second, it applied only to merchants. Third, strictly construed it applied only to uses of the phrase "good faith" in Article 2; thus, so construed it would not define "good faith" for its most important use—the obligation of good faith imposed by former Section 1–203.

Over time, however, amendments to the Uniform Commercial Code brought the Article 2 merchant concept of good faith (subjective honesty and objective commercial reasonableness) into other Articles. First, Article 2A explicitly incorporated the Article 2 standard. See Section 2A–103(7). Then, other Articles broadened the applicability of that standard by adopting it for all parties rather than just for merchants. See, e.g., Sections 3–103(a)(4), 4A–105(a)(6), 8–102(a)(10), and 9–102(a)(43). All of these definitions are comprised of two elements—honesty in fact and the observance of reasonable commercial standards of fair dealing. Only revised Article 5 defines "good faith" solely in terms of subjective honesty, and only Article 6 and Article 7 are without definitions of good faith. (It should be noted that, while revised Article 6 did not define good faith, Comment 2 to revised Section 6–102 states that "this Article adopts the definition of 'good faith' in Article 1 in all cases, even when the buyer is a merchant.") Given these developments, it is appropriate to move the broader definition of "good faith" to Article 1—of course, this definition is subject to the applicability of the narrower definition in revised Article 5. . . .

§ 1–202. Notice; Knowledge.

(a) Subject to subsection (f), a person has "notice" of a fact if the person:

    (1) has actual knowledge of it;

    (2) has received a notice or notification of it; or

(3) from all the facts and circumstances known to the person at the time in question, has reason to know that it exists.

(b) "Knowledge" means actual knowledge. "Knows" has a corresponding meaning.

(c) "Discover", "learn", or words of similar import refer to knowledge rather than to reason to know.

(d) A person "notifies" or "gives" a notice or notification to another person by taking such steps as may be reasonably required to inform the other person in ordinary course, whether or not the other person actually comes to know of it.

(e) Subject to subsection (f), a person "receives" a notice or notification when:

(1) it comes to that person's attention; or

(2) it is duly delivered in a form reasonable under the circumstances at the place of business through which the contract was made or at another location held out by that person as the place for receipt of such communications.

(f) Notice, knowledge, or a notice or notification received by an organization is effective for a particular transaction from the time it is brought to the attention of the individual conducting that transaction and, in any event, from the time it would have been brought to the individual's attention if the organization had exercised due diligence. An organization exercises due diligence if it maintains reasonable routines for communicating significant information to the person conducting the transaction and there is reasonable compliance with the routines. Due diligence does not require an individual acting for the organization to communicate information unless the communication is part of the individual's regular duties or the individual has reason to know of the transaction and that the transaction would be materially affected by the information.

§ 1–203. Lease Distinguished From Security Interest.

(a) Whether a transaction in the form of a lease creates a lease or security interest is determined by the facts of each case.

(b) A transaction in the form of a lease creates a security interest if the consideration that the lessee is to pay the lessor for the right to possession and use of the goods is an obligation for the term of the lease and is not subject to go termination by the lessee, and:

(1) the original term of the lease is equal to or greater than the remaining economic life of the goods;

(2) the lessee is bound to renew the lease for the remaining economic life of the goods or is bound to become the owner of the goods;

(3) the lessee has an option to renew the lease for the remaining economic life of the goods for no additional consideration or for nominal additional consideration upon compliance with the lease agreement; or

(4) the lessee has an option to become the owner of the goods for no additional consideration or for nominal additional consideration upon compliance with the lease agreement.

(c) A transaction in the form of a lease does not create a security interest merely because:

(1) the present value of the consideration the lessee is obligated to pay the lessor for the right to possession and use of the goods is substantially equal to or is greater than the fair market value of the goods at the time the lease is entered into;

(2) the lessee assumes risk of loss of the goods;

(3) the lessee agrees to pay, with respect to the goods, taxes, insurance, filing, recording, or registration fees, or service or maintenance costs;

     (4)   the lessee has an option to renew the lease or to become the owner of the goods;

     (5)   the lessee has an option to renew the lease for a fixed rent that is equal to or greater than the reasonably predictable fair market rent for the use of the goods for the term of the renewal at the time the option is to be performed; or

     (6)   the lessee has an option to become the owner of the goods for a fixed price that is equal to or greater than the reasonably predictable fair market value of the goods at the time the option is to be performed.

   (d)   Additional consideration is nominal if it is less than the lessee's reasonably predictable cost of performing under the lease agreement if the option is not exercised. Additional consideration is not nominal if

     (1)   when the option to renew the lease is granted to the lessee, the rent is stated to be the fair market rent for the use of the goods for the term of the renewal determined at the time the option is to be performed; or

     (2)   when the option to become the owner of the goods is granted to the lessee, the price is stated to be the fair market value of the goods determined at the time the option is to be performed.

   (e)   The "remaining economic life of the goods" and "reasonably predictable" fair market rent, fair market value, or cost of performing under the lease agreement must be determined with reference to the facts and circumstances at the time the transaction is entered into.

§ 1–204.   Value.

Except as otherwise provided in Articles 3, 4, [and] 5, [and 6], a person gives value for rights if the person acquires them:

     (1)   in return for a binding commitment to extend credit or for the extension of immediately available credit, whether or not drawn upon and whether or not a charge-back is provided for in the event of difficulties in collection;

     (2)   as security for, or in total or partial satisfaction of, a preexisting claim;

     (3)   by accepting delivery under a preexisting contract for purchase; or

     (4)   in return for any consideration sufficient to support a simple contract.

§ 1–205.   Reasonable Time; Seasonableness.

   (a)   Whether a time for taking an action required by [the Uniform Commercial Code] is reasonable depends on the nature, purpose, and circumstances of the action.

   (b)   An action is taken seasonably if it is taken at or within the time agreed or, if no time is agreed, at or within a reasonable time.

§ 1–206.   Presumptions.

Whenever [the Uniform Commercial Code] creates a "presumption" with respect to a fact, or provides that a fact is "presumed," the trier of fact must find the existence of the fact unless and until evidence is introduced that supports a finding of its nonexistence.

Legislative Note: Former Section 1–206, a Statute of Frauds for sales of "kinds of personal property not otherwise covered," has been deleted, The other articles of the Uniform Commercial Code make individual determinations as to requirements for memorializing transactions within their scope, so that the primary effect of former Section 1–206 was to impose a writing requirement on sales transactions not otherwise governed by the UCC. Deletion of former Section 1–206 does not constitute a recommendation to legislatures as to whether such sales transactions should be covered by a Statute of Frauds; rather, it reflects a determination that there is no need for uniform commercial law to resolve that issue.

PART 3

TERRITORIAL APPLICABILITY AND GENERAL RULES

§ 1–301. Territorial Applicability; Parties' Power to Choose Applicable Law [as amended in 2008].

(a) Except as otherwise provided in this section, when a transaction bears a reasonable relation to this state and also to another state or nation the parties may agree that the law either of this state or of such other state or nation shall govern their rights and duties.

(b) In the absence of an agreement effective under subsection (a), and except as provided in subsection (c), [the Uniform Commercial Code] applies to transactions bearing an appropriate relation to this state.

(c) If one of the following provisions of [the Uniform Commercial Code] specifies the applicable law, that provision governs and a contrary agreement is effective only to the extent permitted by the law so specified:

(1) Section 2–402.

. . .

§ 1–302. Variation by Agreement.

(a) Except as otherwise provided in subsection (b) or elsewhere in [the Uniform Commercial Code], the effect of provisions of [the Uniform Commercial Code] may be varied by agreement.

(b) The obligations of good faith, diligence, reasonableness, and care prescribed by [the Uniform Commercial Code] may not be disclaimed by agreement. The parties, by agreement, may determine the standards by which the performance of those obligations is to be measured if those standards are not manifestly unreasonable. Whenever [the Uniform Commercial Code] requires an action to be taken within a reasonable time, a time that is not manifestly unreasonable may be fixed by agreement.

(c) The presence in certain provisions of [the Uniform Commercial Code] of the phrase "unless otherwise agreed", or words of similar import, does not imply that the effect of other provisions may not be varied by agreement under this section.

Official Comments

. . .

1. Subsection (a) states affirmatively at the outset that freedom of contract is a principle of the Uniform Commercial Code: "the effect" of its provisions may be varied by "agreement." The meaning, of the statute itself must be found in its text, including its definitions, and in appropriate extrinsic aids; it cannot be varied by agreement. But the Uniform Commercial Code seeks to avoid the type of interference with evolutionary growth found in pre-Code cases such as Manhattan Co. v. Morgan, 242 N.Y. 38, 150 N.E. 594 (1926). Thus, private parties cannot make an instrument negotiable within the meaning of Article 3 except as provided in Section 3–104; nor can they change the meaning of such terms as "bona fide purchaser," "holder in due course," or "due negotiation," as used in the Uniform Commercial Code. But an agreement can change the legal consequences that would otherwise flow from the provisions of the Commercial Code. "Agreement" here includes the effect given to course of dealing, usage of trade and course of performance by Sections 1–201 and 1–303; the effect of an agreement on the rights of third parties is left to specific provisions of the Uniform Commercial Code and to supplementary principles applicable under Section 1–

103. The rights of third parties under Section 9–317 when a security interest is unperfected, for example, cannot be destroyed by a clause in the security agreement.

This principle of freedom of contract is subject to specific exceptions found elsewhere in the Uniform Commercial Code and to the general exception stated here. The specific exceptions vary in explicitness: the statute of frauds found in Section 2–201, for example, does not explicitly preclude oral waiver of the requirement of a writing, but a fair reading denies enforcement to such a waiver as part of the "contract" made unenforceable; Section 9–602, on the other hand, is a quite explicit limitation on freedom of contract. Under the exception for "the obligations of good faith, diligence, reasonableness and care prescribed by [the Uniform Commercial Code]," provisions of the Uniform Commercial Code prescribing such obligations are not to be disclaimed. However, the section also recognizes the prevailing practice of having agreements set forth standards by which due diligence is measured and explicitly provides that, in the absence of a showing that the standards manifestly are unreasonable, the agreement controls. In this connection, Section 1–303 incorporating into the agreement prior course of dealing and usages of trade is of particular importance.

Subsection (b) also recognizes that nothing is stronger evidence of a reasonable time than the fixing of such time by a fair agreement between the parties. However, provision is made for disregarding a clause which whether by inadvertence or overreaching fixes a time so unreasonable that it amounts to eliminating all remedy under the contract. The parties are not required to fix the most reasonable time but may fix any time which is not obviously unfair as judged by the time of contracting.

2.   An agreement that varies the effect of provisions of the Uniform Commercial Code may do so by stating the rules that will govern, in lieu of the provisions varied. Alternatively, the parties may vary the affect of such provisions by stating that their relationship will be governed by recognized bodies of rules or principles applicable to commercial transactions. Such bodies of rules or principles may include, for example, those that are promulgated by intergovernmental authorities such as UNCITRAL or UNIDROIT (see, e.g., UNIDROIT Principles of International Commercial Contracts), or non-legal codes such as trade codes.

3.   Subsection (c) is intended to make it clear that, as a matter of drafting phrases such as "unless otherwise agreed" have been used to avoid controversy as to whether the subject matter of a particular section does or does not fall within the exceptions to subsection (b), but absence of such words contains no negative implication since under subsection (b) the general and residual rule is that the effect of all provisions of the Uniform Commercial Code may be varied by agreement.

§ 1–303.   Course of Performance, Course of Dealing, and Usage of Trade.

(a)   A "course of performance" is a sequence of conduct between the parties to a particular transaction that exists if

    (1)   the agreement of the parties with respect to the transaction involves repeated occasions for performance by a party; and

    (2)   the other party, with knowledge of the nature of the performance and opportunity for objection to it, accepts the performance or acquiesces in it without objection.

(b)   A "course of dealing" is a sequence of conduct concerning previous transactions between the parties to a particular transaction that is fairly to be regarded as establishing a common basis of understanding for interpreting their expressions and other conduct.

(c)   A "usage of trade" is any practice or method of dealing having such regularity of observance in a place, vocation, or trade as to justify an expectation that it will be observed with respect to the transaction in question. The existence and scope of such a usage must be proved as facts. If it is established that such a usage is embodied in a trade code or similar record, the interpretation of the record is a question of law.

(d)   A course of performance or course of dealing between the parties or usage of trade in the vocation or trade in which they are engaged or of which they are or should be aware is relevant in ascertaining, the meaning of the parties' agreement, may give particular meaning to specific terms of the agreement, and may supplement or qualify the terms of the agreement. A usage of trade applicable in the place in which part of the performance under the agreement is to occur may be so utilized as to that part of the performance.

(e)   Except as otherwise provided in subsection (f), the express terms of an agreement and any applicable course of performance, course of dealing, or usage of trade must be construed whenever reasonable as consistent with each other. If such a construction is unreasonable:

    (1)   express terms prevail over course of performance, course of dealing, and usage of trade;

    (2)   course of performance prevails over course of dealing and usage of trade; and

    (3)   course of dealing prevails over usage of trade.

(f)   Subject to Section 2–209, a course of performance is relevant to show a waiver or modification of any term inconsistent with the course of performance.

(g)   Evidence of a relevant usage of trade offered by one party is not admissible unless that party has given the other party notice that the court finds sufficient to prevent unfair surprise to the other party.

Official Comment

. . .

Changes from former law. This section integrates the "course of performance" concept from Articles 2 and 2A into the principles of former Section 1–205, which deals with course of dealing and usage of trade. In so doing, the section slightly modifies the articulation of the course of performance rules to fit more comfortably with the approach and structure of former Section 1–205. There are also slight modifications to be more consistent with the definition of "agreement" in former Section 1–201(3). . . .

1.   The Uniform Commercial Code rejects both the "lay-dictionary" and the "conveyancer's" reading of a commercial agreement. Instead the meaning of the agreement of the parties is to be determined by the language used by them and by their action, read and interpreted in the light of commercial practices and other surrounding circumstances. The measure and background for interpretation are set by the commercial context, which may explain and supplement even the language of a formal or final writing.

2.   "Course of dealing," as defined in subsection (b), is restricted, literally, to a sequence of conduct between the parties previous to the agreement. A sequence of conduct after or under the agreement, however, is a "course of performance." "Course of dealing" may enter the agreement either by explicit provisions of the agreement or by tacit recognition.

3.   The Uniform Commercial Code deals with "usage of trade" as a factor in reaching the commercial meaning of the agreement that the parties have made. The language used is to be interpreted as meaning what it may fairly be expected to mean to parties involved in the particular commercial transaction in a given locality or in a given vocation or trade. By adopting in this context the term "usage of trade," the Uniform Commercial Code expresses its intent to reject those cases which see evidence of "custom" as representing an effort to displace or negate "established rules of law." A distinction is to be drawn between mandatory rules of law such as the Statute of Frauds provisions of Article 2 on Sales whose very office is to control and restrict the actions of the parties, and which cannot be abrogated by agreement, or by a usage of trade, and those rules of law (such as those in Part 3 of Article 2 on Sales) which fill in points which the parties have not considered and in fact agreed upon. The latter rules hold "unless otherwise agree" but yield to the contrary agreement of the parties. Part of the agreement of the parties to which such rules yield is to be sought for in the usages of trade which furnish the background and give particular meaning to the language used, and are the framework of common understanding controlling any general rules of law which hold only when there is no such understanding.

4.   A usage of trade under subsection (c) must have the "regularity of observance" specified. The ancient English tests for "custom" are abandoned in this connection. Therefore, it is not required that a usage of trade be "ancient or immemorial," "universal," or the like. Under the requirement of subsection (c) full recognition is thus available for new usages and for usages currently observed by the great majority of decent dealers, even though dissidents ready to cut corners do not agree. There is room also for proper recognition of usage agreed upon by merchants in trade codes.

5.   The policies of the Uniform Commercial Code controlling explicit unconscionable contracts and clauses (Sections 1–304, 2–302) apply to implicit clauses that rest on usage of trade and carry forward the policy underlying the ancient requirement that a custom or usage must be "reasonable." However, the emphasis is shifted. The very fact of commercial acceptance makes out a *prima facie* case that the usage is reasonable, and the burden is no longer on the usage to establish itself as being reasonable. But the anciently established policing of usage by the courts is continued to the extent necessary to cope with the situation arising if an unconscionable or dishonest practice should become standard.

6.   Subsection (d), giving the prescribed effect to usages "of which the parties are or should be aware," reinforces the provision of subsection (c) requiring not universality but only the described "regularity of observance" of the practice or method. This subsection also reinforces the point of subsection (c) that such usages may be either general to [a] trade or particular to a special branch of trade.

7.   Although the definition of "agreement" in Section 1–201 includes the elements of course of performance, course of dealing, and usage of trade, the fact that express reference is made in some sections to those elements is not to be construed as carrying a contrary intent or implication elsewhere. Compare Section 1–302(c).

8.   In cases of a well established line of usage varying from the general rules of the Uniform Commercial Code where the precise amount of the variation has not been worked out into a single standard, the party relying on the usage is entitled, in any event, to the minimum variation demonstrated. The whole is not to be disregarded because no particular line of detail has been established. In case a dominant pattern has been fairly evidenced, the party relying on the usage is entitled under this section to go to the trier of fact on the question of whether such dominant pattern has been incorporated into the agreement.

9.   Subsection (g) is intended to insure that this Act's liberal recognition of the needs of commerce in-regard to usage of trade shall not be made into an instrument of abuse.

§ 1–304.   Obligation of Good Faith.

Every contract or duty within [the Uniform Commercial Code] imposes an obligation of good faith in its performance and enforcement.

Official Comment

. . .

1.   This section sets forth a basic principle running throughout the Uniform Commercial Code. The principle is that in commercial transactions good faith is required in the performance and enforcement of all agreements or duties. While this duty is explicitly stated in some provisions of the Uniform Commercial Code, the applicability of the duty is broader than merely these situations and applies generally, as stated in this section, to the performance or enforcement of every contract or duty within this Act. It is further implemented by Section 1–303 on course of dealing course of performance, and usage of trade. This section does not support an independent cause of action for failure to perform or enforce in good faith. Rather, this section means that a failure to perform or enforce, in good faith, a specific duty or obligation under the contract, constitutes a breach of that contract or makes unavailable, under the particular circumstances, a remedial right or power. This distinction makes it clear that the doctrine of good faith merely directs a court towards interpreting contracts within the commercial context in which they are created, performed, and enforced, and does not create a separate duty of fairness and reasonableness which can be independently breached.

2.   "Performance and enforcement" of contracts and duties within the Uniform Commercial Code include the exercise of rights created by the Uniform Commercial Code.

§ 1–305.   Remedies to Be Liberally Administered.

(a)   The remedies provided by [the Uniform Commercial Code] must be liberally administered to the end that the aggrieved party maybe put in as good a position as if the other party had fully performed but neither-consequential or special damages nor penal damages may be had except as specifically provided in [the Uniform Commercial Code] or by other rule of law.

(b)   Any right or obligation declared by [the Uniform Commercial Code] is enforceable by action unless the provision declaring it specifies a different and limited effect.

§ 1–306.   Waiver or Renunciation of Claim or Right After Breach.

A claim or right arising out of an alleged breach may be discharged in whole or in part without consideration by agreement of the aggrieved party in an authenticated record.

§ 1–307.   Prima Facie Evidence by Third-Party Documents.

A document in due form purporting to be a bill of lading, policy or certificate of insurance, official weigher's or inspector's certificate, consular invoice, or any other document authorized or required by the contract to be issued by a third party is prima facie evidence of its own authenticity and genuineness and of the facts stated in the document by the third party.

§ 1–308.   Performance or Acceptance Under Reservation of Rights.

(a)   A party that with explicit reservation of rights performs or promises performance or assents to performance in a manner demanded or offered by the other party does not thereby prejudice the rights reserved. Such words as "without prejudice," "under protest," or the like are sufficient.

(b)   Subsection (a) does not apply to an accord and satisfaction.

Official Comment

1.   This section provides machinery for the continuation of performance along the lines contemplated by the contract despite a pending dispute, by adopting the mercantile device of going ahead with delivery, acceptance, or payment "without prejudice," "under protest," "under reserve," "with reservation of all our rights," and the like. All of these phrases completely reserve all rights within the meaning of this section. The section therefore contemplates that limited as well as general reservations and acceptance by a party may be made "subject to satisfaction of our purchaser," "subject to acceptance by our customers," or the like. . . .

3.   Subsection (b) states that this section does not apply to an accord and satisfaction. Section 3–311 governs if an accord and satisfaction is attempted by tender of a negotiable instrument as stated in that section. If Section 3–311 does not apply, the issue of whether an accord and satisfaction has been effected is determined by the law of contract. Whether or not Section 3–311 applies, this section has no application to an accord and satisfaction.

§ 1–309.   Option to Accelerate at Will.

A term providing that one party or that party's successor in interest may accelerate payment or performance or require collateral or additional collateral "at will" or when the party "deems itself insecure," or words of similar import, means that the party has power to do so only if that party in good faith believes that the prospect of payment or performance is impaired. The burden of establishing lack of good faith is on the party against which the power has been exercised.

§ 1–310.   Subordinated Obligations.

An obligation may be issued as subordinated to performance of another obligation of the person obligated, or a creditor may subordinate its right to performance of an obligation by agreement with either the person obligated or another creditor of the person obligated. Subordination does not create a security interest as against either the common debtor or a subordinated creditor.

ARTICLE 2

SALES

PART I

SHORT TITLE, GENERAL CONSTRUCTION AND SUBJECT MATTER

§ 2–101. Short Title.

This Article shall be known and may be cited as Uniform Commercial Code—Sales.

Official Comment

This Article is a complete revision and modernization of the Uniform Sales Act which was promulgated by the National Conference of Commissioners on Uniform State Laws in 1906 and has been adopted in [49] states and the District of Columbia.

The coverage of the present Article is much more extensive than that of the old Sales Act and extends to the various bodies of case law which have been developed both outside of and under the latter.

The arrangement of the present Article is in terms of contract for sale and the various steps of its performance. The legal consequences are stated as following directly from the contract and action taken under it without resorting to the idea of when property or title passed or was to pass as being the determining factor. The purpose is to avoid making practical issues between practical men turn upon the location of an intangible something, the passing of which no man can prove by evidence and to substitute for such abstractions proof of words and actions of a tangible character.

§ 2–102. Scope; Certain Security and Other Transactions Excluded From This Article.

Unless the context otherwise requires, this Article applies to transactions in goods; it does not apply to any transaction which although in the form of an unconditional contract to sell or present sale is intended to operate only as a security transaction nor does this Article impair or repeal any statute regulating sales to consumers, farmers or other specified classes of buyers.

Official Comment

. . .

Definitional Cross References:

"Contract". Section 1–201.

"Contract for sale". Section 2–106.

"Present sale". Section 2–106.

"Sale". Section 2–106.

§ 2–103. Definitions and Index of Definitions.

(1)   In this Article unless the context otherwise requires

    (a)   "Buyer" means a person who buys or contracts to buy goods.

    (b)   "Good faith" in the case of a merchant means honesty in fact and the observance of reasonable commercial standards of fair dealing in the trade.

    (c)   "Receipt" of goods means taking physical possession of them.

    (d)   "Seller" means a person who sells or contracts to sell goods.

(2)   Other definitions applying to this Article or to specified Parts thereof, and the sections in which they appear are:

"Acceptance". Section 2–606.

"Banker's credit". Section 2–325.

"Between merchants". Section 2–104.

"Cancellation". Section 2–106(4).

"Commercial unit". Section 2–105.

"Confirmed credit". Section 2–325.

"Conforming to contract". Section 2–106.

"Contract for sale". Section 2–106.

"Cover". Section 2–712.

"Entrusting". Section 2–403.

"Financing agency". Section 2–104.

"Future goods". Section 2–105.

"Goods". Section 2–105.

"Identification". Section 2–501.

"Installment contract". Section 2–612.

"Letter of Credit". Section 2–325.

"Lot". Section 2–105.

"Merchant". Section 2–104.

"Overseas". Section 2–323.

"Person in position of seller". Section 2–707.

"Present sale". Section 2–106.

"Sale". Section 2–106.

"Sale on approval". Section 2–326.

"Sale or return". Section 2–326.

"Termination". Section 2–106.

(3) The following definitions in other Articles apply to this Article:

"Check". Section 3–104.

"Consignee". Section 7–102.

"Consignor". Section 7–102.

"Consumer goods". Section 9–102.

"Dishonor". Section 3–502.

"Draft". Section 3–104.

(4) In addition Article 1 contains general definitions and principles of construction and interpretation applicable throughout this Article.

As amended in 1994.

Official Comment

. . .

Definitional Cross Reference:

"Person". Section 1–201.

§ 2–104. Definitions: "Merchant"; "Between Merchants"; "Financing Agency".

(1) "Merchant" means a person who deals in goods of the kind or otherwise by his occupation holds himself out as having knowledge or skill peculiar to the practices or goods involved in the transaction or to whom such knowledge or skill may be attributed by his employment of an agent or broker or other intermediary who by his occupation holds himself out as having such knowledge or skill.

(2) "Financing agency" means a bank, finance company or other person who in the ordinary course of business makes advances against goods or documents of title or who by arrangement with either the seller or the buyer intervenes in ordinary course to make or collect payment due or claimed under the contract for sale, as by purchasing or paying the seller's draft or making advances against it or by merely taking it for collection whether or not documents of title accompany the draft. "Financing agency" includes also a bank or other person who similarly intervenes between persons who are in the position of seller and buyer in respect to the goods (Section 2–707).

(3) "Between merchants" means in any transaction with respect to which both parties are chargeable with the knowledge or skill of merchants.

Official Comment

. . .

Purposes:

1.   This Article assumes that transactions between professionals in a given field require special and clear rules which may not apply to a casual or inexperienced seller or buyer. It thus adopts a policy of expressly stating rules applicable "between merchants" and "as against a merchant", wherever they are needed instead of making them depend upon the circumstances of each case as in the statutes cited above. . . .

2.   The term "merchant" as defined here roots in the "law merchant" concept of a professional in business. The professional status under the definition may be based upon specialized knowledge as to the goods, specialized knowledge as to business practices, or specialized knowledge as to both and which kind of specialized knowledge may be sufficient to establish the merchant status is indicated by the nature of the provisions.

The special provisions as to merchants appear only in this Article and they are of three kinds. Sections 2–201(2), 2–205, 2–207 and 2–209 dealing with the statute of frauds, firm offers, confirmatory memoranda and modification rest on normal business practices which are or ought to be typical of and familiar to any person in business. For purposes of these sections almost every person in business would, therefore, be deemed to be a "merchant" under the language "who . . . by his occupation holds himself out as having knowledge or skill peculiar to the practices . . . involved in the transaction . . . " since the practices involved in the transaction are non-specialized business practices such as answering mail. In this type of provision, banks or even universities, for example, well may be "merchants." But even these sections only apply to a merchant in his mercantile capacity; a lawyer or bank president buying fishing tackle for his own use is not a merchant.

On the other hand, in Section 2–314 on the warranty of merchantability, such warranty is implied only "if the seller is a merchant with respect to goods of that kind." Obviously this qualification restricts the implied warranty to a much smaller group than everyone who is engaged in business and requires a professional status as to particular kinds of goods. The exception in Section 2–402(2) for retention of possession by a merchant-seller falls in the same class; as does Section 2–403(2) on entrusting of possession to a merchant "who deals in goods of that kind".

A third group of sections includes 2–103(1)(b), which provides that in the case of a merchant "good faith" includes observance of reasonable commercial standards of fair dealing in the trade; 2–327(1)(c), 2–603 and 2–605, dealing with responsibilities of merchant buyers to follow seller's instructions, etc.; 2–509 on risk of loss, and 2–609 on adequate assurance of performance. This group of sections applies to persons who are merchants under either the "practices" or the "goods" aspect of the definition of merchant. . . .

Definitional Cross References:

"Bank". Section 1–201.

"Buyer". Section 2–103.

"Contract for sale". Section 2–106.

"Document of title". Section 1–201.

"Draft". Section 3–104.

"Goods". Section 2–105.

"Person". Section 1–201.

"Purchase". Section 1–201.

"Seller". Section 2–103.

§ 2–105. Definitions: Transferability; "Goods"; "Future" Goods; "Lot"; "Commercial Unit".

(1) "Goods" means all things (including specially manufactured goods) which are movable at the time of identification to the contract for sale other than the money in which the price is to be paid, investment securities (Article 8) and things in action. "Goods" also includes the unborn young of animals and growing crops and other identified things attached to realty as described in the section on goods to be severed from realty (Section 2–107).

(2) Goods must be both existing and identified before any interest in them can pass. Goods which are not both existing and identified are "future" goods. A purported present sale of future goods or of any interest therein operates as a contract to sell.

(3) There may be a sale of a part interest in existing identified goods.

(4) An undivided share in an identified bulk of fungible goods is sufficiently identified to be sold although the quantity of the bulk is not determined. Any agreed proportion of such a bulk or any quantity thereof agreed upon by number, weight or other measure may to the extent of the seller's interest in the bulk be sold to the buyer who then becomes an owner in common.

(5) "Lot" means a parcel or a single article which is the subject matter of a separate sale or delivery, whether or not it is sufficient to perform the contract.

(6) "Commercial unit" means such a unit of goods as by commercial usage is a single whole for purposes of sale and division of which materially impairs its character or value on the market or in use. A commercial unit may be a single article (as a machine) or a set of articles (as a suite of furniture or an assortment of sizes) or a quantity (as a bale, gross, or carload) or any other unit treated in use or in the relevant market as a single whole.

Official Comment

. . .

Purposes of Changes and New Matter:

1. Subsection (1) on "goods": The phraseology of the prior uniform statutory provision has been changed so that:

The definition of goods is based on the concept of movability and the term "chattels personal" is not used. It is not intended to deal with things which are not fairly identifiable as movables before the contract is performed.

Growing crops are included within the definition of goods since they are frequently intended for sale. The concept of "industrial" growing crops has been abandoned, for under modern practices fruit, perennial hay, nursery stock and the like must be brought within the scope of this Article. The young of animals are also included expressly in this definition since they, too, are frequently intended for sale and may be contracted for before birth. The period of gestation of domestic animals is such that the provisions of the section on identification can apply as in the case of crops to be planted. The reason of this definition also leads to the inclusion of a wool crop or the like as "goods" subject to identification under this Article.

The exclusion of "money in which the price is to be paid" from the definition of goods does not mean that foreign currency which is included in the definition of money may not be the subject matter of a sales transaction. Goods is intended to cover the sale of money when money is being treated as a commodity but not to include it when money is the medium of payment.

As to contracts to sell timber, minerals, or structures to be removed from the land Section 2–107(1) (Goods to be severed from realty: recording) controls.

The use of the word "fixtures" is avoided in view of the diversity of definitions of that term. This Article in including within its scope "things attached to realty" adds the further test that they must be capable of severance without material harm thereto. As between the parties any identified things which fall within that definition becomes "goods" upon the making of the contract for sale.

"Investment securities" are expressly excluded from the coverage of this Article. It is not intended by this exclusion, however, to prevent the application of a particular section of this Article by analogy to securities (as was done with the Original Sales Act in Agar v. Orda, 264 N.Y. 248, 190 N.E. 479, 99 A.L.R. 269 (1934)) when the reason of that section makes such application sensible and the situation involved is not covered by the Article of this Act dealing specifically with such securities (Article 8). . . .

Definitional Cross References:

"Buyer". Section 2–103.

"Contract". Section 1–201.

"Contract for sale". Section 2–106.

"Fungible". Section 1–201.

"Money". Section 1–201.

"Present sale". Section 2–106.

"Sale". Section 2–106.

"Seller". Section 2–103.

§ 2–106. Definitions: "Contract"; "Agreement"; "Contract for Sale"; "Sale"; "Present Sale"; "Conforming" to Contract; "Termination"; "Cancellation".

(1) In this Article unless the context otherwise requires "contract" and "agreement" are limited to those relating to the present or future sale of goods. "Contract for sale" includes both a present sale of goods and a contract to sell goods at a future time. A "sale" consists in the passing of title from the seller to the buyer for a price (Section 2–401). A "present sale" means a sale which is accomplished by the making of the contract.

(2) Goods or conduct including any part of a performance are "conforming" or conform to the contract when they are in accordance with the obligations under the contract.

(3) "Termination" occurs when either party pursuant to a power created by agreement or law puts an end to the contract otherwise than for its breach. On "termination" all obligations which are still executory on both sides are discharged but any right based on prior breach or performance survives.

(4) "Cancellation" occurs when either party puts an end to the contract for breach by the other and its effect is the same as that of "termination" except that the cancelling party also retains any remedy for breach of the whole contract or any unperformed balance.

Official Comment

. . .

Purposes of Changes and New Matter:

1. Subsection (1): "Contract for sale" is used as a general concept throughout this Article, but the rights of the parties do not vary according to whether the transaction is a present sale or a contract to sell unless the Article expressly so provides.

2. Subsection (2): It is in general intended to continue the policy of requiring exact performance by the seller of his obligations as a condition to his right to require acceptance. However, the seller is in part safeguarded against surprise as a result of sudden technicality on the buyer's part by the provisions of Section 2–508 on seller's cure of improper tender or delivery. Moreover usage of trade frequently permits commercial leeways in performance and the language of the agreement itself must be read in the light of

such custom or usage and also, prior course of dealing, and in a long term contract, the course of performance.

3.   Subsections (3) and (4): These subsections are intended to make clear the distinction carried forward throughout this Article between termination and cancellation.

. . .

Definitional Cross References:

"Agreement". Section 1–201.

"Buyer". Section 2–103.

"Contract". Section 1–201.

"Goods". Section 2–105.

"Party". Section 1–201.

"Remedy". Section 1–201.

"Rights". Section 1–201.

"Seller". Section 2–103.

§ 2–107.   Goods to Be Severed From Realty: Recording.

(1)   A contract for the sale of minerals or the like (including oil and gas) or a structure or its materials to be removed from realty is a contract for the sale of goods within this Article if they are to be severed by the seller but until severance a purported present sale thereof which is not effective as a transfer of an interest in land is effective only as a contract to sell.

(2)   A contract for the sale apart from the land of growing crops or other things attached to realty and capable of severance without material harm thereto but not described in subsection (1) or of timber to be cut is a contract for the sale of goods within this Article whether the subject matter is to be severed by the buyer or by the seller even though it forms part of the realty at the time of contracting, and the parties can by identification effect a present sale before severance.

(3)   The provisions of this section are subject to any third party rights provided by the law relating to realty records, and the contract for sale may be executed and recorded as a document transferring an interest in land and shall then constitute notice to third parties of the buyer's rights under the contract for sale.

Official Comment

. . .

Definitional Cross References:

"Buyer". Section 2–103.

"Contract". Section 1–201.

"Contract for sale". Section 2–106.

"Goods". Section 2–105.

"Party". Section 1–201.

"Present sale". Section 2–106.

"Rights". Section 1–201.

"Seller". Section 2–103.

PART II

FORM, FORMATION AND READJUSTMENT OF CONTRACT

§ 2–201.   Formal Requirements; Statute of Frauds.

(1)   Except as otherwise provided in this section a contract for the sale of goods for the price of $500 or more is not enforceable by way of action or defense unless there is some writing sufficient to indicate that a contract for sale has been made between the parties and signed by the party against whom enforcement is sought or by his authorized agent or broker. A writing is not insufficient because it omits or incorrectly states a term agreed upon but the contract is not enforceable under this paragraph beyond the quantity of goods shown in such writing.

(2)   Between merchants if within a reasonable time a writing in confirmation of the contract and sufficient against the sender is received and the party receiving it has reason to know its contents, it satisfies the requirements of subsection (1) against such party unless written notice of objection to its contents is given within 10 days after it is received.

(3)   A contract which does not satisfy the requirements of subsection (1) but which is valid in other respects is enforceable

(a)   if the goods are to be specially manufactured for the buyer and are not suitable for sale to others in the ordinary course of the seller's business and the seller, before notice of repudiation is received and under circumstances which reasonably indicate that the goods are for the buyer, has made either a substantial beginning of their manufacture or commitments for their procurement; or

(b)   if the party against whom enforcement is sought admits in his pleading, testimony or otherwise in court that a contract for sale was made, but the contract is not enforceable under this provision beyond the quantity of goods admitted; or

(c)   with respect to goods for which payment has been made and accepted or which have been received and accepted (Sec. 2–606).

Official Comment

. . .

Purposes of Changes: The changed phraseology of this section is intended to make it clear that:

1.   The required writing need not contain all the material terms of the contract and such material terms as are stated need not be precisely stated. All that is required is that the writing afford a basis for believing that the offered oral evidence rests on a real transaction. It may be written in lead pencil on a scratch pad. It need not indicate which party is the buyer and which the seller. The only term which must appear is the quantity term which need not be accurately stated but recovery is limited to the amount stated. The price, time and place of payment or delivery, the general quality of the goods, or any particular warranties may all be omitted.

Special emphasis must be placed on the permissibility of omitting the price term in view of the insistence of some courts on the express inclusion of this term even where the parties have contracted on the basis of a published price list. In many valid contracts for sale the parties do not mention the price in express terms, the buyer being bound to pay and the seller to accept a reasonable price which the trier of the fact may well be trusted to determine. Again, frequently the price is not mentioned since the parties have based their agreement on a price list or catalogue known to both of them and this list serves as an efficient safeguard against perjury. Finally, "market" prices and valuations that are current in the vicinity constitute a similar check. Thus if the price is not stated in the memorandum it can normally be supplied without danger of fraud. Of course if the "price" consists of goods rather than money the quantity of goods must be stated.

Only three definite and invariable requirements as to the memorandum are made by this subsection. First, it must evidence a contract for the sale of goods; second, it must be "signed", a word which includes any authentication which identifies the party to be charged; and third, it must specify a quantity.

2.   "Partial performance" as a substitute for the required memorandum can validate the contract only for the goods which have been accepted or for which payment has been made and accepted.

Receipt and acceptance either of goods or of the price constitutes an unambiguous overt admission by both parties that a contract actually exists. If the court can make a just apportionment, therefore, the agreed price of any goods actually delivered can be recovered without a writing or, if the price has been paid, the seller can be forced to deliver an apportionable part of the goods. The overt actions of the parties make admissible evidence of the other terms of the contract necessary to a just apportionment. This is true even though the actions of the parties are not in themselves inconsistent with a different transaction such as a consignment for resale or a mere loan of money.

Part performance by the buyer requires the delivery of something by him that is accepted by the seller as such performance. Thus, part payment may be made by money or check, accepted by the seller. If the agreed price consists of goods or services, then they must also have been delivered and accepted.

3.   Between merchants, failure to answer a written confirmation of a contract within ten days of receipt is tantamount to a writing under subsection (2) and is sufficient against both parties under subsection (1). The only effect, however, is to take away from the party who fails to answer the defense of the Statute of Frauds; the burden of persuading the trier of fact that a contract was in fact made orally prior to the written confirmation is unaffected. Compare the effect of a failure to reply under Section 2–207.

4.   Failure to satisfy the requirements of this section does not render the contract void for all purposes, but merely prevents it from being judicially enforced in favor of a party to the contract. For example, a buyer who takes possession of goods as provided in an oral contract which the seller has not meanwhile repudiated, is not a trespasser. Nor would the Statute of Frauds provisions of this section be a defense to a third person who wrongfully induces a party to refuse to perform an oral contract, even though the injured party cannot maintain an action for damages against the party so refusing to perform.

5.   The requirement of "signing" is discussed in the comment to Section 1–201.

6.   It is not necessary that the writing be delivered to anybody. It need not be signed or authenticated by both parties but it is, of course, not sufficient against one who has not signed it. Prior to a dispute no one can determine which party's signing of the memorandum may be necessary but from the time of contracting each party should be aware that to him it is signing by the other which is important.

7.   If the making of a contract is admitted in court, either in a written pleading, by stipulation or by oral statement before the court, no additional writing is necessary for protection against fraud. Under this section it is no longer possible to admit the contract in court and still treat the Statute as a defense. However, the contract is not thus conclusively established. The admission so made by a party is itself evidential against him of the truth of the facts so admitted and of nothing more; as against the other party, it is not evidential at all.

. . .

Definitional Cross References:

"Action". Section 1–201.

"Between merchants". Section 2–104.

"Buyer". Section 2–103.

"Contract". Section 1–201.

"Contract for sale". Section 2–106.

"Goods". Section 2–105.

"Notice". Section 1–201.

"Party". Section 1–201.

"Reasonable time". Section 1–204.

"Sale". Section 2–106.

"Seller". Section 2–103.

§ 2–202.   Final Written Expression: Parol or Extrinsic Evidence.

Terms with respect to which the confirmatory memoranda of the parties agree or which are otherwise set forth in a writing intended by the parties as a final expression of their agreement with respect to such terms as are included therein may not be contradicted by evidence of any prior agreement or of a contemporaneous oral agreement but may be explained or supplemented

(a)   by course of performance, course of dealing, or usage of trade (Section 1–303); and

(b)   by evidence of consistent additional terms unless the court finds the writing to have been intended also as a complete and exclusive statement of the terms of the agreement.

Official Comment

. . .

Purposes:

1.   This section definitely rejects:

(a)   Any assumption that because a writing has been worked out which is final on some matters, it is to be taken as including all the matters agreed upon;

(b)   The premise that the language used has the meaning attributable to such language by rules of construction existing in the law rather than the meaning which arises out of the commercial context in which it was used; and

(c)   The requirement that a condition precedent to the admissibility of the type of evidence specified in paragraph (a) is an original determination by the court that the language used is ambiguous.

2.   Paragraph (a) makes admissible evidence of course of dealing, usage of trade and course of performance to explain or supplement the terms of any writing stating the agreement of the parties in order that the true understanding of the parties as to the agreement may be reached. Such writings are to be read on the assumption that the course of prior dealings between the parties and the usages of trade were taken for granted when the document was phrased. Unless carefully negated they have become an element of the meaning of the words used. Similarly, the course of actual performance by the parties is considered the best indication of what they intended the writing to mean.

3.   Under paragraph (b) consistent additional terms, not reduced to writing, may be proved unless the court finds that the writing was intended by both parties as a complete and exclusive statement of all the terms. If the additional terms are such that, if agreed upon, they would certainly have been included in the document in the view of the court, then evidence of their alleged making must be kept from the trier of fact.

. . .

Definitional Cross References:

"Agreed" and "agreement". Section 1–201.

"Course of dealing". Section 1–303.

"Course of performance". Section 1–303.

"Party". Section 1–201.

"Term". Section 1–201.

"Usage of trade". Section 1–205.

"Written" and "writing". Section 1–201.

§ 2–203. Seals Inoperative.

The affixing of a seal to a writing evidencing a contract for sale or an offer to buy or sell goods does not constitute the writing a sealed instrument and the law with respect to sealed instruments does not apply to such a contract or offer.

Official Comment

. . .

Definitional Cross References:

"Contract for sale". Section 2–106.

"Goods". Section 2–105.

"Writing". Section 1–201.

§ 2–204. Formation in General.

(1)   A contract for sale of goods may be made in any manner sufficient to show agreement, including conduct by both parties which recognizes the existence of such a contract.

(2)   An agreement sufficient to constitute a contract for sale may be found even though the moment of its making is undetermined.

(3)   Even though one or more terms are left open a contract for sale does not fail for indefiniteness if the parties have intended to make a contract and there is a reasonably certain basis for giving an appropriate remedy.

Official Comment

. . .

Purposes of Changes:

Subsection (1) continues without change the basic policy of recognizing any manner of expression of agreement, oral, written or otherwise. The legal effect of such an agreement is, of course, qualified by other provisions of this Article.

Under subsection (1) appropriate conduct by the parties may be sufficient to establish an agreement. Subsection (2) is directed primarily to the situation where the interchanged correspondence does not disclose the exact point at which the deal was closed, but the actions of the parties indicate that a binding obligation has been undertaken.

Subsection (3) states the principle as to "open terms" underlying later sections of the Article. If the parties intend to enter into a binding agreement, this subsection recognizes that agreement as valid in law, despite missing terms, if there is any reasonably certain basis for granting a remedy. The test is not certainty as to what the parties were to do nor as to the exact amount of damages due the plaintiff. Nor is the fact that one or more terms are left to be agreed upon enough of itself to defeat an otherwise adequate agreement. Rather, commercial standards on the point of "indefiniteness" are intended to be applied, this Act making provision elsewhere for missing terms needed for performance, open price, remedies and the like.

The more terms the parties leave open, the less likely it is that they have intended to conclude a binding agreement, but their actions may be frequently conclusive on the matter despite the omissions.

. . .

Definitional Cross References:

"Agreement". Section 1–201.

"Contract". Section 1–201.

"Contract for sale". Section 2–106.

"Goods". Section 2–105.

"Party". Section 1–201.

"Remedy". Section 1–201.

"Term". Section 1–201.

§ 2–205.   Firm Offers.

An offer by a merchant to buy or sell goods in a signed writing which by its terms gives assurance that it will be held open is not revocable, for lack of consideration, during the time stated or if no time is stated for a reasonable time, but in no event may such period of irrevocability exceed three months; but any such term of assurance on a form supplied by the offeree must be separately signed by the offeror.

Official Comment

. . .

Purposes of Changes:

1.   This section is intended to modify the former rule which required that "firm offers" be sustained by consideration in order to bind, and to require instead that they must merely be characterized as such and expressed in signed writings.

2.   The primary purpose of this section is to give effect to the deliberate intention of a merchant to make a current firm offer binding. The deliberation is shown in the case of an individualized document by the merchant's signature to the offer, and in the case of an offer included on a form supplied by the other party to the transaction by the separate signing of the particular clause which contains the offer. "Signed" here also includes authentication but the reasonableness of the authentication herein allowed must be determined in the light of the purpose of the section. The circumstances surrounding the signing may justify something less than a formal signature or initialing but typically the kind of authentication involved here would consist of a minimum of initialing of the clause involved. . . . However, despite settled courses of dealing or usages of the trade whereby firm offers are made by oral communication and relied upon without more evidence, such offers remain revocable under this Article since authentication by a writing is the essence of this section. . . .

Definitional Cross References:

"Goods". Section 2–105.

"Merchant". Section 2–104.

"Signed". Section 1–201.

"Writing". Section 1–201.

§ 2–206.   Offer and Acceptance in Formation of Contract.

(1)   Unless otherwise unambiguously indicated by the language or circumstances

(a)   an offer to make a contract shall be construed as inviting acceptance in any manner and by any medium reasonable in the circumstances;

(b)   an order or other offer to buy goods for prompt or current shipment shall be construed as inviting acceptance either by a prompt promise to ship or by the prompt or current shipment of conforming or non-conforming goods, but such a shipment of non-conforming goods does not constitute an acceptance if the seller seasonably notifies the buyer that the shipment is offered only as an accommodation to the buyer.

(2) Where the beginning of a requested performance is a reasonable mode of acceptance an offeror who is not notified of acceptance within a reasonable time may treat the offer as having lapsed before acceptance.

Official Comment

. . .

Purposes of Changes: To make it clear that:

1. Any reasonable manner of acceptance is intended to be regarded as available unless the offeror has made quite clear that it will not be acceptable. Former technical rules as to acceptance, such as requiring that telegraphic offers be accepted by telegraphed acceptance, etc., are rejected and a criterion that the acceptance be "in any manner and by any medium reasonable under the circumstances," is substituted. This section is intended to remain flexible and its applicability to be enlarged as new media of communication develop or as the more time-saving present day media come into general use.

2. Either shipment or a prompt promise to ship is made a proper means of acceptance of an offer looking to current shipment. In accordance with ordinary commercial understanding the section interprets an order looking to current shipment as allowing acceptance either by actual shipment or by a prompt promise to ship and rejects the artificial theory that only a single mode of acceptance is normally envisaged by an offer. . . .

3. The beginning of performance by an offeree can be effective as acceptance so as to bind the offeror only if followed within a reasonable time by notice to the offeror. Such a beginning of performance must unambiguously express the offeree's intention to engage himself. For the protection of both parties it is essential that notice follow in due course to constitute acceptance. Nothing in this section however bars the possibility that under the common law performance begun may have an intermediate effect of temporarily barring revocation of the offer, or at the offeror's option, final effect in constituting acceptance. . . .

Definitional Cross References:

"Buyer". Section 2–103.

"Conforming". Section 2–106.

"Contract". Section 1–201.

"Goods". Section 2–105.

"Notifies". Section 1–201.

"Reasonable time". Section 1–204.

§ 2–207. Additional Terms in Acceptance or Confirmation.

(1) A definite and seasonable expression of acceptance or a written confirmation which is sent within a reasonable time operates as an acceptance even though it states terms additional to or different from those offered or agreed upon, unless acceptance is expressly made conditional on assent to the additional or different terms.

(2) The additional terms are to be construed as proposals for addition to the contract. Between merchants such terms become part of the contract unless:

(a) the offer expressly limits acceptance to the terms of the offer;

(b) they materially alter it; or

(c) notification of objection to them has already been given or is given within a reasonable time after notice of them is received.

(3)   Conduct by both parties which recognizes the existence of a contract is sufficient to establish a contract for sale although the writings of the parties do not otherwise establish a contract. In such case the terms of the particular contract consist of those terms on which the writings of the parties agree, together with any supplementary terms incorporated under any other provisions of this Act.

Official Comment

. . .

Purposes of Changes:

1.   This section is intended to deal with two typical situations. The one is the written confirmation, where an agreement has been reached either orally or by informal correspondence between the parties and is followed by one or both of the parties sending formal memoranda embodying the terms so far as agreed upon and adding terms not discussed. The other situation is offer and acceptance, in which a wire or letter expressed and intended as an acceptance or the closing of an agreement adds further minor suggestions or proposals such as "ship by Tuesday," "rush," "ship draft against bill of lading inspection allowed," or the like. A frequent example of the second situation is the exchange of printed purchase order and acceptance (sometimes called "acknowledgment") forms. Because the forms are oriented to the thinking of the respective drafting parties, the terms contained in them often do not correspond. Often the seller's form contains terms different from or additional to those set forth in the buyer's form. Nevertheless, the parties proceed with the transaction. [Comment 1 was amended in 1966.]

2.   Under this Article a proposed deal which in commercial understanding has in fact been closed is recognized as a contract. Therefore, any additional matter contained in the confirmation or in the acceptance falls within subsection (2) and must be regarded as a proposal for an added term unless the acceptance is made conditional on the acceptance of the additional or different terms. [Comment 2 was amended in 1966.]

3.   Whether or not additional or different terms will become part of the agreement depends upon the provisions of subsection (2). If they are such as materially to alter the original bargain, they will not be included unless expressly agreed to by the other party. If, however, they are terms which would not so change the bargain they will be incorporated unless notice of objection to them has already been given or is given within a reasonable time.

4.   Examples of typical clauses which would normally "materially alter" the contract and so result in surprise or hardship if incorporated without express awareness by the other party are: a clause negating such standard warranties as that of merchantability or fitness for a particular purpose in circumstances in which either warranty normally attaches; a clause requiring a guaranty of 90% or 100% deliveries in a case such as a contract by cannery, where the usage of the trade allows greater quantity leeways; a clause reserving to the seller the power to cancel upon the buyer's failure to meet any invoice when due; a clause requiring that complaints be made in a time materially shorter than customary or reasonable.

5.   Examples of clauses which involve no element of unreasonable surprise and which therefore are to be incorporated in the contract unless notice of objection is seasonably given are: a clause setting forth and perhaps enlarging slightly upon the seller's exemption due to supervening causes beyond his control, similar to those covered by the provision of this Article on merchant's excuse by failure of presupposed conditions or a clause fixing in advance any reasonable formula of proration under such circumstances; a clause fixing a reasonable time for complaints within customary limits, or in the case of a purchase for sub-sale, providing for inspection by the sub-purchaser; a clause providing for interest on overdue invoices or fixing the seller's standard credit terms where they are within the range of trade practice and do not limit any credit bargained for; a clause limiting the right of rejection for defects which fall within the customary trade tolerances for acceptance "with adjustment" or otherwise limiting remedy in a reasonable manner (see Sections 2–718 and 2–719).

6.   If no answer is received within a reasonable time after additional terms are proposed, it is both fair and commercially sound to assume that their inclusion has been assented to. Where clauses on confirming forms sent by both parties conflict each party must be assumed to object to a clause of the other conflicting with one on the confirmation sent by himself. As a result the requirement that there be notice of objection which is found in subsection (2) is satisfied and the conflicting terms do not become a part of the contract. The contract then consists of the terms originally expressly agreed to, terms on which the

confirmations agree, and terms supplied by this Act, including subsection (2). The written confirmation is also subject to Section 2–201. Under that section a failure to respond permits enforcement of a prior oral agreement; under this section a failure to respond permits additional terms to become part of the agreement. [Comment 6 was amended in 1966.]

7.　　In many cases, as where goods are shipped, accepted and paid for before any dispute arises, there is no question whether a contract has been made. In such cases, where the writings of the parties do not establish a contract, it is not necessary to determine which act or document constituted the offer and which the acceptance. See Section 2–204. The only question is what terms are included in the contract, and subsection (3) furnishes the governing rule. [Comment 7 was added in 1966.]

. . .

Definitional Cross References:

"Between merchants". Section 2–104.

"Contract". Section 1–201.

"Notification". Section 1–201.

"Reasonable time". Section 1–204.

"Seasonably". Section 1–204.

"Send". Section 1–201.

"Term". Section 1–201.

"Written". Section 1–201.

§ 2–208.   Course of Performance or Practical Construction.

(1)　　Where the contract for sale involves repeated occasions for performance by either party with knowledge of the nature of the performance and opportunity for objection to it by the other, any course of performance accepted or acquiesced in without objection shall be relevant to determine the meaning of the agreement.

(2)　　The express terms of the agreement and any such course of performance, as well as any course of dealing and usage of trade, shall be construed whenever reasonable as consistent with each other; but when such construction is unreasonable, express terms shall control course of performance and course of performance shall control both course of dealing and usage of trade (Section 1–205).

(3)　　Subject to the provisions of the next section on modification and waiver, such course of performance shall be relevant to show a waiver of modification of any term inconsistent with such course of performance.

§ 2–209.   Modification, Rescission and Waiver.

(1)　　An agreement modifying a contract within this Article needs no consideration to be binding.

(2)　　A signed agreement which excludes modification or rescission except by a signed writing cannot be otherwise modified or rescinded, but except as between merchants such a requirement on a form supplied by the merchant must be separately signed by the other party.

(3)　　The requirements of the statute of frauds section of this Article (Section 2–201) must be satisfied if the contract as modified is within its provisions.

(4)　　Although an attempt at modification or rescission does not satisfy the requirements of subsection (2) or (3) it can operate as a waiver.

(5)　　A party who has made a waiver affecting an executory portion of the contract may retract the waiver by reasonable notification received by the other party that strict performance will be required of any term waived, unless the retraction would be unjust in view of a material change of position in reliance on the waiver.

Official Comment

. . .

Purposes of Changes and New Matter:

1.　　This section seeks to protect and make effective all necessary and desirable modifications of sales contracts without regard to the technicalities which at present hamper such adjustments.

2.　　Subsection (1) provides that an agreement modifying a sales contract needs no consideration to be binding.

However, modifications made thereunder must meet the test of good faith imposed by this Act. The effective use of bad faith to escape performance on the original contract terms is barred, and the extortion of a "modification" without legitimate commercial reason is ineffective as a violation of the duty of good faith. Nor can a mere technical consideration support a modification made in bad faith.

The test of "good faith" between merchants or as against merchants includes "observance of reasonable commercial standards of fair dealing in the trade" (Section 2–103), and may in some situations require an objectively demonstrable reason for seeking a modification. But such matters as a market shift which makes performance come to involve a loss may provide such a reason even though there is no such unforeseen difficulty as would make out a legal excuse from performance under Sections 2–615 and 2–616.

. . .

Definitional Cross References:

"Agreement". Section 1–201.

"Between merchants". Section 2–104.

"Contract". Section 1–201.

"Notification". Section 1–201.

"Signed". Section 1–201.

"Term". Section 1–201.

"Writing". Section 1–201.

§ 2–210.　Delegation of Performance; Assignment of Rights.

(1)　　A party may perform his duty through a delegate unless otherwise agreed or unless the other party has a substantial interest in having his original promisor perform or control the acts required by the contract. No delegation of performance relieves the party delegating of any duty to perform or any liability for breach.

(2)　　Except as otherwise provided in Section 9–406, unless otherwise agreed, all rights of either seller or buyer can be assigned except where the assignment would materially change the duty of the other party, or increase materially the burden or risk imposed on him by his contract, or impair materially his chance of obtaining return performance. A right to damages for breach of the whole contract or a right arising out of the assignor's due performance of his entire obligation can be assigned despite agreement otherwise.

(3)　　The creation, attachment, perfection, or enforcement of a security interest in the seller's interest under a contract is not a transfer that materially changes the duty of or increases materially the burden or risk imposed on the buyer or impairs materially the buyer's chance of obtaining return performance within the purview of subsection (2) unless, and then only to the extent that, enforcement actually results in a delegation of material performance of the seller. Even in that event, the creation, attachment, perfection, and enforcement of the security interest remain effective, but (i) the seller is liable to the buyer for damages caused by the delegation to the extent that the damages could not reasonably be prevented by the buyer, and (ii) a court having jurisdiction may grant other appropriate relief, including cancellation of the contract for sale or an injunction against enforcement of the security interest or consummation of the enforcement.

(4)　Unless the circumstances indicate the contrary a prohibition of assignment of "the contract" is to be construed as barring only the delegation to the assignee of the assignor's performance.

(5)　An assignment of "the contract" or of "all my rights under the contract" or an assignment in similar general terms is an assignment of rights and unless the language or the circumstances (as in an assignment for security) indicate the contrary, it is a delegation of performance of the duties of the assignor and its acceptance by the assignee constitutes a promise by him to perform those duties. This promise is enforceable by either the assignor or the other party to the original contract.

(6)　The other party may treat any assignment which delegates performance as creating reasonable grounds for insecurity and may without prejudice to his rights against the assignor demand assurances from the assignee (Section 2–609).

Official Comment

. . .

Purposes:

1.　Generally, this section recognizes both delegation of performance and assignability as normal and permissible incidents of a contract for the sale of goods. . . .

3.　Under subsection (2) rights which are no longer executory such as a right to damages for breach may be assigned although the agreement prohibits assignment. In such cases no question of delegation of any performance is involved. Subsection (2) is subject to Section 9–406, which makes rights to payment for goods sold ("accounts"), whether or not earned, freely alienable notwithstanding a contrary agreement or rule of law.

4.　The nature of the contract or the circumstances of the case, however, may bar assignment of the contract even where delegation of performance is not involved. This Article and this section are intended to clarify this problem, particularly in cases dealing with output requirement and exclusive dealing contracts. In the first place the section on requirements and exclusive dealing removes from the construction of the original contract most of the "personal discretion" element by substituting the reasonably objective standard of good faith operation of the plant or business to be supplied. Secondly, the section on insecurity and assurances, which is specifically referred to in subsection (6) of this section, frees the other party from the doubts and uncertainty which may afflict him under an assignment of the character in question by permitting him to demand adequate assurance of due performance without which he may suspend his own performance. Subsection (6) is not in any way intended to limit the effect of the section on insecurity and assurances and the word "performance" includes the giving of orders under a requirements contract. Of course, in any case where a material personal discretion is sought to be transferred, effective assignment is barred by subsection (2). . . .

. . .

Definitional Cross References:

"Agreement". Section 1–201.

"Buyer". Section 2–103.

"Contract". Section 1–201.

"Party". Section 1–201.

"Rights". Section 1–201.

"Seller". Section 2–103.

"Term". Section 1–201.

PART III

GENERAL OBLIGATION AND CONSTRUCTION OF CONTRACT

§ 2–301. General Obligations of Parties.

The obligation of the seller is to transfer and deliver and that of the buyer is to accept and pay in accordance with the contract.

Official Comment

Definitional Cross References:

"Buyer". Section 2–103.

"Contract". Section 1–201.

"Party". Section 1–201.

"Seller". Section 2–103.

§ 2–302. Unconscionable Contract or Clause.

(1) If the court as a matter of law finds the contract or any clause of the contract to have been unconscionable at the time it was made the court may refuse to enforce the contract, or it may enforce the remainder of the contract without the unconscionable clause, or it may so limit the application of any unconscionable clause as to avoid any unconscionable result.

(2) When it is claimed or appears to the court that the contract or any clause thereof may be unconscionable the parties shall be afforded a reasonable opportunity to present evidence as to its commercial setting, purpose and effect to aid the court in making the determination.

Official Comment

. . .

1. This section is intended to make it possible for the courts to police explicitly against the contracts or clauses which they find to be unconscionable. In the past such policing has been accomplished by adverse construction of language, by manipulation of the rules of offer and acceptance or by determinations that the clause is contrary to public policy or to the dominant purpose of the contract. This section is intended to allow the court to pass directly on the unconscionability of the contract or particular clause therein and to make a conclusion of law as to its unconscionability. The basic test is whether, in the light of the general commercial background and the commercial needs of the particular trade or case, the clauses involved are so one-sided as to be unconscionable under the circumstances existing at the time of the making of the contract. Subsection (2) makes it clear that it is proper for the court to hear evidence upon these questions. The principle is one of the prevention of oppression and unfair surprise (Cf. Campbell Soup Co. v. Wentz, 172 F.2d 80, 3d Cir. 1948) and not of disturbance of allocation of risks because of superior bargaining power. The underlying basis of this section is illustrated by the results in cases such as the following:

Kansas City Wholesale Grocery Co. v. Weber Packing Corporation, 93 Utah 414, 73 P.2d 1272 (1937), where a clause limiting time for complaints was held inapplicable to latent defects in a shipment of catsup which could be discovered only by microscopic analysis; Hardy v. General Motors Acceptance Corporation, 38 Ga.App. 463, 144 S.E. 327 (1928), holding that a disclaimer of warranty clause applied only to express warranties, thus letting in a fair implied warranty; Andrews Bros. v. Singer & Co. (1934 CA) 1 K.B. 17, holding that where a car with substantial mileage was delivered instead of a "new" car, a disclaimer of warranties, including those "implied," left unaffected an "express obligation" on the description, even though the Sale of Goods Act called such an implied warranty; New Prague Flouring Mill Co. v. G. A. Spears, 194 Iowa 417, 189 N.W. 815 (1922), holding that a clause permitting the seller, upon the buyer's failure to supply shipping instructions, to cancel, ship, or allow delivery date to be indefinitely postponed 30 days at a time by the inaction, does not indefinitely postpone the date of measuring damages for the buyer's breach, to the seller's advantage; and Kansas Flour Mills Co. v. Dirks, 100 Kan. 376, 164 P. 273 (1917), where under a similar clause in a rising market the court permitted the buyer to measure his damages for non-delivery at the end of only one 30 day postponement; Green v. Arcos, Ltd. (1931 CA) 47 T.L.R. 336, where a blanket clause prohibiting rejection of shipments by the buyer was restricted to apply to shipments where discrepancies represented merely mercantile variations; Meyer v. Packard Cleveland Motor Co., 106 Ohio St. 328, 140 N.E. 118 (1922), in which the court held that a "waiver" of all agreements not specified did not preclude implied warranty of fitness of a rebuilt dump truck for ordinary use as a dump truck; Austin Co. v. J. H. Tillman Co., 104 Or. 541, 209 P. 131 (1922), where a clause limiting the buyer's remedy to return was held to be applicable only if the seller had delivered a machine needed for a construction job which reasonably met the contract description; Bekkevold v. Potts, 173 Minn. 87, 216 N.W. 790, 59 A.L.R. 1164 (1927), refusing to allow warranty of fitness for purpose imposed by law to be negated by clause excluding all warranties "made" by the seller; Robert A. Munroe & Co. v. Meyer (1930) 2 K.B. 312, holding that the warranty of description overrides a clause reading "with all faults and defects" where adulterated meat not up to the contract description was delivered.

2.   Under this section the court, in its discretion, may refuse to enforce the contract as a whole if it is permeated by the unconscionability, or it may strike any single clause or group of clauses which are so tainted or which are contrary to the essential purpose of the agreement, or it may simply limit unconscionable clauses so as to avoid unconscionable results.

3.   The present section is addressed to the court, and the decision is to be made by it. The commercial evidence referred to in subsection (2) is for the court's consideration, not the jury's. Only the agreement which results from the court's action on these matters is to be submitted to the general triers of the facts.

Definitional Cross Reference:

"Contract". Section 1–201.

§ 2–303.   Allocation or Division of Risks.

Where this Article allocates a risk or a burden as between the parties "unless otherwise agreed", the agreement may not only shift the allocation but may also divide the risk or burden.

Official Comment

. . .

Definitional Cross References:

"Party". Section 1–201.

"Agreement". Section 1–201.

§ 2–304.   Price Payable in Money, Goods, Realty, or Otherwise.

(1)   The price can be made payable in money or otherwise. If it is payable in whole or in part in goods each party is a seller of the goods which he is to transfer.

(2)   Even though all or part of the price is payable in an interest in realty the transfer of the goods and the seller's obligations with reference to them are subject to this Article, but not the transfer of the interest in realty or the transferor's obligations in connection therewith.

Official Comment

. . .

Definitional Cross References:

"Goods". Section 2–105.

"Money". Section 1–201.

"Party". Section 1–201.

"Seller". Section 2–103.

§ 2–305. Open Price Term.

(1)   The parties if they so intend can conclude a contract for sale even though the price is not settled. In such a case the price is a reasonable price at the time for delivery if

(a)   nothing is said as to price; or

(b)   the price is left to be agreed by the parties and they fail to agree; or

(c)   the price is to be fixed in terms of some agreed market or other standard as set or recorded by a third person or agency and it is not so set or recorded.

(2)   A price to be fixed by the seller or by the buyer means a price for him to fix in good faith.

(3)   When a price left to be fixed otherwise than by agreement of the parties fails to be fixed through fault of one party the other may at his option treat the contract as cancelled or himself fix a reasonable price.

(4)   Where, however, the parties intend not to be bound unless the price be fixed or agreed and it is not fixed or agreed there is no contract. In such a case the buyer must return any goods already received or if unable so to do must pay their reasonable value at the time of delivery and the seller must return any portion of the price paid on account.

Official Comment

. . .

Purposes of Changes:

1.   This section applies when the price term is left open on the making of an agreement which is nevertheless intended by the parties to be a binding agreement. This Article rejects in these instances the formula that "an agreement to agree is unenforceable" if the case falls within subsection (1) of this section, and rejects also defeating such agreements on the ground of "indefiniteness". Instead this Article recognizes the dominant intention of the parties to have the deal continue to be binding upon both. As to future performance, since this Article recognizes remedies such as cover (Section 2–712), resale (Section 2–706) and specific performance (Section 2–716) which go beyond any mere arithmetic as between contract price and market price, there is usually a "reasonably certain basis for granting an appropriate remedy for breach" so that the contract need not fail for indefiniteness.

2.   Under some circumstances the postponement of agreement on price will mean that no deal has really been concluded, and this is made express in the preamble of subsection (1) ("The parties *if they so intend*") and in subsection (4). Whether or not this is so is, in most cases, a question to be determined by the trier of fact.

3.   Subsection (2), dealing with the situation where the price is to be fixed by one party rejects the uncommercial idea that an agreement that the seller may fix the price means that he may fix any price he may wish by the express qualification that the price so fixed must be fixed in good faith. Good faith includes observance of reasonable commercial standards of fair dealing in the trade if the party is a merchant. (Section 2–103). But in the normal case a "posted price" or a future seller's or buyer's "given price," "price in effect," "market price," or the like satisfies the good faith requirement.

4.   The section recognizes that there may be cases in which a particular person's judgment is not chosen merely as a barometer or index of a fair price but is an essential condition to the parties' intent to make any contract at all. For example, the case where a known and trusted expert is to "value" a particular painting for which there is no market standard differs sharply from the situation where a named expert is to determine the grade of cotton, and the difference would support a finding that in the one the parties did not intend to make a binding agreement if that expert were unavailable whereas in the other they did so intend. Other circumstances would of course affect the validity of such a finding.

5.   Under subsection (3), wrongful interference by one party with any agreed machinery for price fixing in the contract may be treated by the other party as a repudiation justifying cancellation, or merely as a failure to take cooperative action thus shifting to the aggrieved party the reasonable leeway in fixing the price.

6.   Throughout the entire section, the purpose is to give effect to the agreement which has been made. That effect, however, is always conditioned by the requirement of good faith action which is made an inherent part of all contracts within this Act. (Section 1–203).

. . .

Definitional Cross References:

"Agreement". Section 1–201.

"Burden of establishing". Section 1–201.

"Buyer". Section 2–103.

"Cancellation". Section 2–106.

"Contract". Section 1–201.

"Contract for sale". Section 2–106.

"Fault". Section 1–201.

"Goods". Section 2–105.

"Party". Section 1–201.

"Receipt of goods". Section 2–103.

"Seller". Section 2–103.

"Term". Section 1–201.

§ 2–306.   Output, Requirements and Exclusive Dealings.

(1)   A term which measures the quantity by the output of the seller or the requirements of the buyer means such actual output or requirements as may occur in good faith, except that no quantity unreasonably disproportionate to any stated estimate or in the absence of a stated estimate to any normal or otherwise comparable prior output or requirements may be tendered or demanded.

(2)   A lawful agreement by either the seller or the buyer for exclusive dealing in the kind of goods concerned imposes unless otherwise agreed an obligation by the seller to use best efforts to supply the goods and by the buyer to use best efforts to promote their sale.

Official Comment

. . .

Purposes:

1.   Subsection (1) of this section, in regard to output and requirements, applies to this specific problem the general approach of this Act which requires the reading of commercial background and intent into the language of any agreement and demands good faith in the performance of that agreement. It applies to such contracts of nonproducing establishments such as dealers or distributors as well as to manufacturing concerns.

2.   Under this Article, a contract for output or requirements is not too indefinite since it is held to mean the actual good faith output or requirements of the particular party. Nor does such a contract lack mutuality of obligation since, under this section, the party who will determine quantity is required to operate his plant or conduct his business in good faith and according to commercial standards of fair dealing in the trade so that his output or requirements will approximate a reasonably foreseeable figure. Reasonable elasticity in the requirements is expressly envisaged by this section and good faith variations from prior

requirements are permitted even when the variation may be such as to result in discontinuance. A shut-down by a requirements buyer for lack of orders might be permissible when a shut-down merely to curtail losses would not. The essential test is whether the party is acting in good faith. Similarly, a sudden expansion of the plant by which requirements are to be measured would not be included within the scope of the contract as made but normal expansion undertaken in good faith would be within the scope of this section. One of the factors in an expansion situation would be whether the market price had risen greatly in a case in which the requirements contract contained a fixed price. Reasonable variation of an extreme sort is exemplified in Southwest Natural Gas Co. v. Oklahoma Portland Cement Co., 102 F.2d 630 (C.C.A.10, 1939). . . .

     3.   If an estimate of output or requirements is included in the agreement, no quantity unreasonably disproportionate to it may be tendered or demanded. Any minimum or maximum set by the agreement shows a clear limit on the intended elasticity. In similar fashion, the agreed estimate is to be regarded as a center around which the parties intend the variation to occur. . . .

     5.   Subsection (2), on exclusive dealing, makes explicit the commercial rule embodied in this Act under which the parties to such contracts are held to have impliedly, even when not expressly, bound themselves to use reasonable diligence as well as good faith in their performance of the contract. Under such contracts the exclusive agent is required, although no express commitment has been made, to use reasonable effort and due diligence in the expansion of the market or the promotion of the product, as the case may be. The principal is expected under such a contract to refrain from supplying any other dealer or agent within the exclusive territory. An exclusive dealing agreement brings into play all of the good faith aspects of the output and requirement problems of subsection (1). It also raises questions of insecurity and right to adequate assurance under this Article.

   . . .

Definitional Cross References:

    "Agreement". Section 1–201.

    "Buyer". Section 2–103.

    "Contract for sale". Section 2–106.

    "Good faith". Section 1–201.

    "Goods". Section 2–105.

    "Party". Section 1–201.

    "Term". Section 1–201.

    "Seller". Section 2–103.

§ 2–307.   Delivery in Single Lot or Several Lots.

    Unless otherwise agreed all goods called for by a contract for sale must be tendered in a single delivery and payment is due only on such tender but where the circumstances give either party the right to make or demand delivery in lots the price if it can be apportioned may be demanded for each lot.

Official Comment

   . . .

Definitional Cross References:

    "Contract for sale". Section 2–106.

    "Goods". Section 2–105.

    "Lot". Section 2–105.

    "Party". Section 1–201.

"Rights". Section 1–201.

§ 2–308. Absence of Specified Place for Delivery.

Unless otherwise agreed

(a) the place for delivery of goods is the seller's place of business or if he has none his residence; but

(b) in a contract for sale of identified goods which to the knowledge of the parties at the time of contracting are in some other place, that place is the place for their delivery; and

(c) documents of title may be delivered through customary banking channels.

Official Comment

. . .

Purposes of Change:

. . .

4.   The rules of this section apply only "unless otherwise agreed." The surrounding circumstances, usage of trade, course of dealing and course of performance, as well as the express language of the parties, may constitute an "otherwise agreement".

. . .

Definitional Cross References:

"Contract for sale". Section 2–106.

"Delivery". Section 1–201.

"Document of title". Section 1–201.

"Goods". Section 2–105.

"Party". Section 1–201.

"Seller". Section 2–103.

§ 2–309. Absence of Specific Time Provisions; Notice of Termination.

(1)   The time for shipment or delivery or any other action under a contract if not provided in this Article or agreed upon shall be a reasonable time.

(2)   Where the contract provides for successive performances but is indefinite in duration it is valid for a reasonable time but unless otherwise agreed may be terminated at any time by either party.

(3)   Termination of a contract by one party except on the happening of an agreed event requires that reasonable notification be received by the other party and an agreement dispensing with notification is invalid if its operation would be unconscionable.

Official Comment

. . .

Purposes of Changes and New Matter:

1.   Subsection (1) requires that all actions taken under a sales contract must be taken within a reasonable time where no time has been agreed upon. The reasonable time under this provision turns on the criteria as to "reasonable time" and on good faith and commercial standards set forth in Sections 1–203, 1–204 and 2–103. It thus depends upon what constitutes acceptable commercial conduct in view of the nature, purpose and circumstances of the action to be taken. Agreement as to a definite time, however, may be found in a term implied from the contractual circumstances, usage of trade or course of dealing or

performance as well as in an express term. Such cases fall outside of this subsection since in them the time for action is "agreed" by usage.

. . .

Definitional Cross References:

    "Agreement". Section 1–201.

    "Contract". Section 1–201.

    "Notification". Section 1–201.

    "Party". Section 1–201.

    "Reasonable time". Section 1–204.

    "Termination". Section 2–106.

§ 2–310.   Open Time for Payment or Running of Credit; Authority to Ship Under Reservation.

Unless otherwise agreed

(a)   payment is due at the time and place at which the buyer is to receive the goods even though the place of shipment is the place of delivery; and

(b)   if the seller is authorized to send the goods he may ship them under reservation, and may tender the documents of title, but the buyer may inspect the goods after their arrival before payment is due unless such inspection is inconsistent with the terms of the contract (Section 2–513); and

(c)   if delivery is authorized and made by way of documents of title otherwise than by subsection (b) then payment is due at the time and place at which the buyer is to receive the documents regardless of where the goods are to be received; and

(d)   where the seller is required or authorized to ship the goods on credit the credit period runs from the time of shipment but post-dating the invoice or delaying its dispatch will correspondingly delay the starting of the credit period.

Official Comment

. . .

Definitional Cross References:

    "Buyer". Section 2–103.

    "Delivery". Section 1–201.

    "Document of title". Section 1–201.

    "Goods". Section 2–105.

    "Receipt of goods". Section 2–103.

    "Seller". Section 2–103.

    "Send". Section 1–201.

    "Term". Section 1–201.

§ 2–311.   Options and Cooperation Respecting Performance.

(1)   An agreement for sale which is otherwise sufficiently definite (subsection (3) of Section 2–204) to be a contract is not made invalid by the fact that it leaves particulars of performance to be

specified by one of the parties. Any such specification must be made in good faith and within limits set by commercial reasonableness.

(2)   Unless otherwise agreed specifications relating to assortment of the goods are at the buyer's option and except as otherwise provided in subsections (1)(c) and (3) of Section 2–319 specifications or arrangements relating to shipment are at the seller's option.

(3)   Where such specification would materially affect the other party's performance but is not seasonably made or where one party's cooperation is necessary to the agreed performance of the other but is not seasonably forthcoming, the other party in addition to all other remedies

(a)   is excused for any resulting delay in his own performance; and

(b)   may also either proceed to perform in any reasonable manner or after the time for a material part of his own performance treat the failure to specify or to cooperate as a breach by failure to deliver or accept the goods.

Official Comment

. . .

Purposes:

1.   Subsection (1) permits the parties to leave certain detailed particulars of performance to be filled in by either of them without running the risk of having the contract invalidated for indefiniteness. The party to whom the agreement gives power to specify the missing details is required to exercise good faith and to act in accordance with commercial standards so that there is no surprise and the range of permissible variation is limited by what is commercially reasonable. The "agreement" which permits one party so to specify may be found as well in a course of dealing, usage of trade, or implication from circumstances as in explicit language used by the parties. . . .

3.   Subsection (3) applies when the exercise of an option or cooperation by one party is necessary to or materially affects the other party's performance, but it is not seasonably forthcoming; the subsection relieves the other party from the necessity for performance or excuses his delay in performance as the case may be. The contract-keeping party may at his option under this subsection proceed to perform in any commercially reasonable manner rather than wait. In addition to the special remedies provided, this subsection also reserves "all other remedies". The remedy of particular importance in this connection is that provided for insecurity. Request may also be made pursuant to the obligation of good faith for a reasonable indication of the time and manner of performance for which a party is to hold himself ready. . . .

. . .

Definitional Cross References:

"Agreement". Section 1–201.

"Buyer". Section 2–103.

"Contract for sale". Section 2–106.

"Goods". Section 2–105.

"Party". Section 1–201.

"Remedy". Section 1–201.

"Seasonably". Section 1–204.

"Seller". Section 2–103.

§ 2–312. Warranty of Title and Against Infringement; Buyer's Obligation Against Infringement.

(1)   Subject to subsection (2) there is in a contract for sale a warranty by the seller that

(a)   the title conveyed shall be good, and its transfer rightful; and

(b)   the goods shall be delivered free from any security interest or other lien or encumbrance of which the buyer at the time of contracting has no knowledge.

(2)   A warranty under subsection (1) will be excluded or modified only by specific language or by circumstances which give the buyer reason to know that the person selling does not claim title in himself or that he is purporting to sell only such right or title as he or a third person may have.

(3)   Unless otherwise agreed a seller who is a merchant regularly dealing in goods of the kind warrants that the goods shall be delivered free of the rightful claim of any third person by way of infringement or the like but a buyer who furnishes specifications to the seller must hold the seller harmless against any such claim which arises out of compliance with the specifications.

Official Comment

. . .

Definitional Cross References:

"Buyer". Section 2–103.

"Contract for sale". Section 2–106.

"Goods". Section 2–105.

"Person". Section 1–201.

"Right". Section 1–201.

"Seller". Section 2–103.

§ 2–313. Express Warranties by Affirmation, Promise, Description, Sample.

(1)   Express warranties by the seller are created as follows:

(a)   Any affirmation of fact or promise made by the seller to the buyer which relates to the goods and becomes part of the basis of the bargain creates an express warranty that the goods shall conform to the affirmation or promise.

(b)   Any description of the goods which is made part of the basis of the bargain creates an express warranty that the goods shall conform to the description.

(c)   Any sample or model which is made part of the basis of the bargain creates an express warranty that the whole of the goods shall conform to the sample or model.

(2)   It is not necessary to the creation of an express warranty that the seller use formal words such as "warrant" or "guarantee" or that he have a specific intention to make a warranty, but an affirmation merely of the value of the goods or a statement purporting to be merely the seller's opinion or commendation of the goods does not create a warranty.

Official Comment

. . .

Purposes of Changes: To consolidate and systematize basic principles with the result that:

1.   "Express" warranties rest on "dickered" aspects of the individual bargain, and go so clearly to the essence of that bargain that words of disclaimer in a form are repugnant to the basic dickered terms. "Implied" warranties rest so clearly on a common factual situation or set of conditions that no particular

language or action is necessary to evidence them and they will arise in such a situation unless unmistakably negated. . . .

2. Although this section is limited in its scope and direct purpose to warranties made by the seller to the buyer as part of a contract for sale, the warranty sections of this Article are not designed in any way to disturb those lines of case law growth which have recognized that warranties need not be confined either to sales contracts or to the direct parties to such a contract. They may arise in other appropriate circumstances such as in the case of bailments for hire, whether such bailment is itself the main contract or is merely a supplying of containers under a contract for the sale of their contents. . . .

3. The present section deals with affirmations of fact by the seller, descriptions of the goods or exhibitions of samples, exactly as any other part of a negotiation which ends in a contract is dealt with. No specific intention to make a warranty is necessary if any of these factors is made part of the basis of the bargain. In actual practice affirmations of fact made by the seller about the goods during a bargain are regarded as part of the description of those goods; hence no particular reliance on such statements need be shown in order to weave them into the fabric of the agreement. Rather, any fact which is to take such affirmations, once made, out of the agreement requires clear affirmative proof. The issue normally is one of fact.

4. In view of the principle that the whole purpose of the law of warranty is to determine what it is that the seller has in essence agreed to sell, the policy is adopted of those cases which refuse except in unusual circumstances to recognize a material deletion of the seller's obligation. Thus, a contract is normally a contract for a sale of something describable and described. A clause generally disclaiming "all warranties, express or implied" cannot reduce the seller's obligation with respect to such description and therefore cannot be given literal effect under Section 2–316.

This is not intended to mean that the parties, if they consciously desire, cannot make their own bargain as they wish. But in determining what they have agreed upon good faith is a factor and consideration should be given to the fact that the probability is small that a real price is intended to be exchanged for a pseudo-obligation.

5. Paragraph (1)(b) makes specific some of the principles set forth above when a description of the goods is given by the seller.

A description need not be by words. Technical specifications, blueprints and the like can afford more exact description than mere language and if made part of the basis of the bargain goods must conform with them. Past deliveries may set the description of quality, either expressly or impliedly by course of dealing. Of course, all descriptions by merchants must be read against the applicable trade usages with the general rules as to merchantability resolving any doubts.

6. The basic situation as to statements affecting the true essence of the bargain is no different when a sample or model is involved in the transaction. This section includes both a "sample" actually drawn from the bulk of goods which is the subject matter of the sale, and a "model" which is offered for inspection when the subject matter is not at hand and which has not been drawn from the bulk of the goods.

Although the underlying principles are unchanged, the facts are often ambiguous when something is shown as illustrative, rather than as a straight sample. In general, the presumption is that any sample or model just as any affirmation of fact is intended to become a basis of the bargain. But there is no escape from the question of fact. When the seller exhibits a sample purporting to be drawn from an existing bulk, good faith of course requires that the sample be fairly drawn. But in mercantile experience the mere exhibition of a "sample" does not of itself show whether it is merely intended to "suggest" or to "be" the character of the subject-matter of the contract. The question is whether the seller has so acted with reference to the sample as to make him responsible that the whole shall have at least the values shown by it. The circumstances aid in answering this question. If the sample has been drawn from an existing bulk, it must be regarded as describing values of the goods contracted for unless it is accompanied by an unmistakable denial of such responsibility. If, on the other hand, a model of merchandise not on hand is offered, the mercantile presumption that it has become a literal description of the subject matter is not so strong, and particularly so if modification on the buyer's initiative impairs any feature of the model.

7. The precise time when words of description or affirmation are made or samples are shown is not material. The sole question is whether the language or samples or models are fairly to be regarded as part

of the contract. If language is used after the closing of the deal (as when the buyer when taking delivery asks and receives an additional assurance), the warranty becomes a modification, and need not be supported by consideration if it is otherwise reasonable and in order (Section 2–209).

8.   Concerning affirmations of value or a seller's opinion or commendation under subsection (2), the basic question remains the same: What statements of the seller have in the circumstances and in objective judgment become part of the basis of the bargain? As indicated above, all of the statements of the seller do so unless good reason is shown to the contrary. The provisions of subsection (2) are included, however, since common experience discloses that some statements or predictions cannot fairly be viewed as entering into the bargain. Even as to false statements of value, however, the possibility is left open that a remedy may be provided by the law relating to fraud or misrepresentation.

. . .

Definitional Cross References:

"Buyer". Section 2–103.

"Conforming". Section 2–106.

"Goods". Section 2–105.

"Seller". Section 2–103.

§ 2–314.   Implied Warranty: Merchantability; Usage of Trade.

(1)   Unless excluded or modified (Section 2–316), a warranty that the goods shall be merchantable is implied in a contract for their sale if the seller is a merchant with respect to goods of that kind. Under this section the serving for value of food or drink to be consumed either on the premises or elsewhere is a sale.

(2)   Goods to be merchantable must be at least such as

(a)   pass without objection in the trade under the contract description; and

(b)   in the case of fungible goods, are of fair average quality within the description; and

(c)   are fit for the ordinary purposes for which such goods are used; and

(d)   run, within the variations permitted by the agreement, of even kind, quality and quantity within each unit and among all units involved; and

(e)   are adequately contained, packaged, and labeled as the agreement may require; and

(f)   conform to the promise or affirmations of fact made on the container or label if any.

(3)   Unless excluded or modified (Section 2–316) other implied warranties may arise from course of dealing or usage of trade.

Official Comment

. . .

Purposes of Changes:

This section, drawn in view of the steadily developing case law on the subject, is intended to make it clear that:

1.   The seller's obligation applies to present sales as well as to contracts to sell subject to the effects of any examination of specific goods. (Subsection (2) of Section 2–316). Also, the warranty of merchantability applies to sales for use as well as to sales for resale.

2.   The question when the warranty is imposed turns basically on the meaning of the terms of the agreement as recognized in the trade. Goods delivered under an agreement made by a merchant in a given line of trade must be of a quality comparable to that generally acceptable in that line of trade under the description or other designation of the goods used in the agreement.

3.   A specific designation of goods by the buyer does not exclude the seller's obligation that they be fit for the general purposes appropriate to such goods. A contract for the sale of second-hand goods, however, involves only such obligation as is appropriate to such goods for that is their contract description. A person making an isolated sale of goods is not a "merchant" within the meaning of the full scope of this section and, thus, no warranty of merchantability would apply. His knowledge of any defects not apparent on inspection would, however, without need for express agreement and in keeping with the underlying reason of the present section and the provisions on good faith, impose an obligation that known material but hidden defects be fully disclosed.

4.   Although a seller may not be a "merchant" as to the goods in question, if he states generally that they are "guaranteed" the provisions of this section may furnish a guide to the content of the resulting express warranty. This has particular significance in the case of second-hand sales, and has further significance in limiting the effect of fine-print disclaimer clauses where their effect would be inconsistent with large-print assertions of "guarantee." . . .

6.   Subsection (2) does not purport to exhaust the meaning of "merchantable" nor to negate any of its attributes not specifically mentioned in the text of the statute, but arising by usage of trade or through case law. The language used is "must be at least such as . . .," and the intention is to leave open other possible attributes of merchantability.

7.   Paragraphs (a) and (b) of subsection (2) are to be read together. Both refer, as indicated above, to the standards of that line of the trade which fits the transaction and the seller's business. "Fair average" is a term directly appropriate to agricultural bulk products and means goods centering around the middle belt of quality, not the least or the worst that can be understood in the particular trade by the designation, but such as can pass "without objection." Of course a fair percentage of the least is permissible but the goods are not "fair average" if they are all of the least or worst quality possible under the description. In cases of doubt as to what quality is intended, the price at which a merchant closes a contract is an excellent index of the nature and scope of his obligation under the present section.

8.   Fitness for the ordinary purposes for which goods of the type are used is a fundamental concept of the present section and is covered in paragraph (c). As stated above, merchantability is also a part of the obligation owing to the purchaser for use. Correspondingly, protection, under this aspect of the warranty, of the person buying for resale to the ultimate consumer is equally necessary, and merchantable goods must therefore be "honestly" resalable in the normal course of business because they are what they purport to be. . . .

12.   Subsection (3) is to make explicit that usage of trade and course of dealing can create warranties and that they are implied rather than express warranties and thus subject to exclusion or modification under Section 2–316. A typical instance would be the obligation to provide pedigree papers to evidence conformity of the animal to the contract in the case of a pedigreed dog or blooded bull. . . .

    . . .

Definitional Cross References:

    "Agreement". Section 1–201.

    "Contract". Section 1–201.

    "Contract for sale". Section 2–106.

    "Goods". Section 2–105.

    "Merchant". Section 2–104.

    "Seller". Section 2–103.

§ 2–315.   Implied Warranty: Fitness for Particular Purpose.

Where the seller at the time of contracting has reason to know any particular purpose for which the goods are required and that the buyer is relying on the seller's skill or judgment to select or furnish suitable goods, there is unless excluded or modified under the next section an implied warranty that the goods shall be fit for such purpose.

Official Comment

. . .

Purposes of Changes:

1.   Whether or not this warranty arises in any individual case is basically a question of fact to be determined by the circumstances of the contracting. Under this section the buyer need not bring home to the seller actual knowledge of the particular purpose for which the goods are intended or of his reliance on the seller's skill and judgment, if the circumstances are such that the seller has reason to realize the purpose intended or that the reliance exists. The buyer, of course, must actually be relying on the seller.

2.   A "particular purpose" differs from the ordinary purpose for which the goods are used in that it envisages a specific use by the buyer which is peculiar to the nature of his business whereas the ordinary purposes for which goods are used are those envisaged in the concept of merchantability and go to uses which are customarily made of the goods in question. For example, shoes are generally used for the purpose of walking upon ordinary ground, but a seller may know that a particular pair was selected to be used for climbing mountains.

A contract may of course include both a warranty of merchantability and one of fitness for a particular purpose.

The provisions of this Article on the cumulation and conflict of express and implied warranties must be considered on the question of inconsistency between or among warranties. In such a case any question of fact as to which warranty was intended by the parties to apply must be resolved in favor of the warranty of fitness for particular purpose as against all other warranties except where the buyer has taken upon himself the responsibility of furnishing the technical specifications. . . .

4.   . . . Although normally the [implied warranty of fitness for a particular purpose] will arise only where the seller is a merchant with the appropriate "skill or judgment," it can arise as to non-merchants where this is justified by the particular circumstances.

5.   . . . Under the present section the existence of a patent or other trade name and the designation of the article by that name, or indeed in any other definite manner, is only one of the facts to be considered on the question of whether the buyer actually relied on the seller, but it is not of itself decisive of the issue. If the buyer himself is insisting on a particular brand he is not relying on the seller's skill and judgment and so no warranty results. But the mere fact that the article purchased has a particular patent or trade name is not sufficient to indicate nonreliance if the article has been recommended by the seller as adequate for the buyer's purposes.

. . .

Definitional Cross References:

"Buyer". Section 2–103.

"Goods". Section 2–105.

"Seller". Section 2–103.

§ 2–316.   Exclusion or Modification of Warranties.

(1)   Words or conduct relevant to the creation of an express warranty and words or conduct tending to negate or limit warranty shall be construed wherever reasonable as consistent with each other; but subject to the provisions of this Article on parol or extrinsic evidence (Section 2–202) negation or limitation is inoperative to the extent that such construction is unreasonable.

(2)   Subject to subsection (3), to exclude or modify the implied warranty of merchantability or any part of it the language must mention merchantability and in case of a writing must be conspicuous, and to exclude or modify any implied warranty of fitness the exclusion must be by a writing and

conspicuous. Language to exclude all implied warranties of fitness is sufficient if it states, for example, that "There are no warranties which extend beyond the description on the face hereof."

(3)   Notwithstanding subsection (2)

(a)   unless the circumstances indicate otherwise, all implied warranties are excluded by expressions like "as is", "with all faults" or other language which in common understanding calls the buyer's attention to the exclusion of warranties and makes plain that there is no implied warranty; and

(b)   when the buyer before entering into the contract has examined the goods or the sample or model as fully as he desired or has refused to examine the goods there is no implied warranty with regard to defects which an examination ought in the circumstances to have revealed to him; and

(c)   an implied warranty can also be excluded or modified by course of dealing or course of performance or usage of trade.

(4)   Remedies for breach of warranty can be limited in accordance with the provisions of this Article on liquidation or limitation of damages and on contractual modification of remedy (Sections 2–718 and 2–719).

Official Comment

. . .

1.   This section is designed principally to deal with those frequent clauses in sales contracts which seek to exclude "all warranties, express or implied." It seeks to protect a buyer from unexpected and unbargained language of disclaimer by denying effect to such language when inconsistent with language of express warranty and permitting the exclusion of implied warranties only by conspicuous language or other circumstances which protect the buyer from surprise.

2.   . . . This Article treats the limitation or avoidance of consequential damages as a matter of limiting remedies for breach, separate from the matter of creation of liability under a warranty. If no warranty exists, there is of course no problem of limiting remedies for breach of warranty. Under subsection (4) the question of limitation of remedy is governed by the sections referred to rather than by this section. . . .

7.   Paragraph (a) of subsection (3) deals with general terms such as "as is," "as they stand," "with all faults," and the like. Such terms in ordinary commercial usage are understood to mean that the buyer takes the entire risk as to the quality of the goods involved. The terms covered by paragraph (a) are in fact merely a particularization of paragraph (c) which provides for exclusion or modification of implied warranties by usage of trade.

. . .

Definitional Cross References:

"Agreement". Section 1–201.

"Buyer". Section 2–103.

"Contract". Section 1–201.

"Course of dealing". Section 1–205.

"Goods". Section 2–105.

"Remedy". Section 1–201.

"Seller". Section 2–103.

"Usage of trade". Section 1–205.

§ 2–317.   Cumulation and Conflict of Warranties Express or Implied.

Warranties whether express or implied shall be construed as consistent with each other and as cumulative, but if such construction is unreasonable the intention of the parties shall determine which warranty is dominant. In ascertaining that intention the following rules apply:

(a) Exact or technical specifications displace an inconsistent sample or model or general language of description.

(b) A sample from an existing bulk displaces inconsistent general language of description.

(c) Express warranties displace inconsistent implied warranties other than an implied warranty of fitness for a particular purpose.

Official Comment

. . .

Purposes of Changes:

1. The present section rests on the basic policy of this Article that no warranty is created except by some conduct (either affirmative action or failure to disclose) on the part of the seller. Therefore, all warranties are made cumulative unless this construction of the contract is impossible or unreasonable. . . .

2. The rules of this section are designed to aid in determining the intention of the parties as to which of inconsistent warranties which have arisen from the circumstances of their transaction shall prevail. These rules of intention are to be applied only where factors making for an equitable estoppel of the seller do not exist and where he has in perfect good faith made warranties which later turn out to be inconsistent. To the extent that the seller has led the buyer to believe that all of the warranties can be performed, he is estopped from setting up any essential inconsistency as a defense.

. . .

Definitional Cross Reference:

"Party". Section 1–201.

§ 2–318.   Third Party Beneficiaries of Warranties Express or Implied.

Note: *If this Act is introduced in the Congress of the United States this section should be omitted. (States to select one alternative.)*

Alternative A

A seller's warranty whether express or implied extends to any natural person who is in the family or household of his buyer or who is a guest in his home if it is reasonable to expect that such person may use, consume or be affected by the goods and who is injured in person by breach of the warranty. A seller may not exclude or limit the operation of this section.

Alternative B

A seller's warranty whether express or implied extends to any natural person who may reasonably be expected to use, consume or be affected by the goods and who is injured in person by breach of the warranty. A seller may not exclude or limit the operation of this section.

Alternative C

A seller's warranty whether express or implied extends to any person who may reasonably be expected to use, consume or be affected by the goods and who is injured by breach of the warranty. A seller may not exclude or limit the operation of this section with respect to injury to the person of an individual to whom the warranty extends.

As amended in 1966.

Official Comment

. . .

Definitional Cross References:

"Buyer". Section 2–103.

"Goods". Section 2–105.

"Seller". Section 2–103.

§ 2–319.   F.O.B. and F.A.S. Terms.

(1) Unless otherwise agreed the term F.O.B. (which means "free on board") at a named place, even though used only in connection with the stated price, is a delivery term under which

(a) when the term is F.O.B. the place of shipment, the seller must at that place ship the goods in the manner provided in this Article (Section 2–504) and bear the expense and risk of putting them into the possession of the carrier; or

(b) when the term is F.O.B. the place of destination, the seller must at his own expense and risk transport the goods to that place and there tender delivery of them in the manner provided in this Article (Section 2–503);

(c) when under either (a) or (b) the term is also F.O.B. vessel, car or other vehicle, the seller must in addition at his own expense and risk load the goods on board. If the term is F.O.B. vessel the buyer must name the vessel and in an appropriate case the seller must comply with the provisions of this Article on the form of bill of lading (Section 2–323).

(2) Unless otherwise agreed the term F.A.S. vessel (which means "free alongside") at a named port, even though used only in connection with the stated price, is a delivery term under which the seller must

(a) at his own expense and risk deliver the goods alongside the vessel in the manner usual in that port or on a dock designated and provided by the buyer; and

(b) obtain and tender a receipt for the goods in exchange for which the carrier is under a duty to issue a bill of lading.

(3) Unless otherwise agreed in any case falling within subsection (1)(a) or (c) or subsection (2) the buyer must seasonably give any needed instructions for making delivery, including when the term is F.A.S. or F.O.B. the loading berth of the vessel and in an appropriate case its name and sailing date. The seller may treat the failure of needed instructions as a failure of cooperation under this Article (Section 2–311). He may also at his option move the goods in any reasonable manner preparatory to delivery or shipment.

(4) Under the term F.O.B. vessel or F.A.S. unless otherwise agreed the buyer must make payment against tender of the required documents and the seller may not tender nor the buyer demand delivery of the goods in substitution for the documents.

Official Comment

. . .

Definitional Cross References:

"Agreed". Section 1–201.

"Bill of lading". Section 1–201.

"Buyer". Section 2–103.

"Goods". Section 2–105.

"Seasonably". Section 1–204.

"Seller". Section 2–103.

"Term". Section 1–201.

§ 2–320.   C.I.F. and C. & F. Terms.

(1)   The term C.I.F. means that the price includes in a lump sum the cost of the goods and the insurance and freight to the named destination. The term C. & F. or C.F. means that the price so includes cost and freight to the named destination.

(2)   Unless otherwise agreed and even though used only in connection with the stated price and destination, the term C.I.F. destination or its equivalent requires the seller at his own expense and risk to

     (a)   put the goods into the possession of a carrier at the port for shipment and obtain a negotiable bill or bills of lading covering the entire transportation to the named destination; and

     (b)   load the goods and obtain a receipt from the carrier (which may be contained in the bill of lading) showing that the freight has been paid or provided for; and

     (c)   obtain a policy or certificate of insurance, including any war risk insurance, of a kind and on terms then current at the port of shipment in the usual amount, in the currency of the contract, shown to cover the same goods covered by the bill of lading and providing for payment of loss to the order of the buyer or for the account of whom it may concern; but the seller may add to the price the amount of the premium for any such war risk insurance; and

     (d)   prepare an invoice of the goods and procure any other documents required to effect shipment or to comply with the contract; and

     (e)   forward and tender with commercial promptness all the documents in due form and with any indorsement necessary to perfect the buyer's rights.

(3)   Unless otherwise agreed the term C. & F. or its equivalent has the same effect and imposes upon the seller the same obligations and risks as a C.I.F. term except the obligation as to insurance.

(4)   Under the term C.I.F. or C. & F. unless otherwise agreed the buyer must make payment against tender of the required documents and the seller may not tender nor the buyer demand delivery of the goods in substitution for the documents.

Official Comment

. . .

Definitional Cross References:

"Bill of lading". Section 1–201.

"Buyer". Section 2–103.

"Contract". Section 1–201.

"Goods". Section 2–105.

"Rights". Section 1–201.

"Seller". Section 2–103.

"Term". Section 1–201.

§ 2–321.   C.I.F. or C. & F.: "Net Landed Weights"; "Payment on Arrival"; Warranty of Condition on Arrival.

Under a contract containing a term C.I.F. or C. & F.

(1) Where the price is based on or is to be adjusted according to "net landed weights", "delivered weights", "out turn" quantity or quality or the like, unless otherwise agreed the seller must reasonably estimate the price. The payment due on tender of the documents called for by the contract is the amount so estimated, but after final adjustment of the price a settlement must be made with commercial promptness.

(2) An agreement described in subsection (1) or any warranty of quality or condition of the goods on arrival places upon the seller the risk of ordinary deterioration, shrinkage and the like in transportation but has no effect on the place or time of identification to the contract for sale or delivery or on the passing of the risk of loss.

(3) Unless otherwise agreed where the contract provides for payment on or after arrival of the goods the seller must before payment allow such preliminary inspection as is feasible; but if the goods are lost delivery of the documents and payment are due when the goods should have arrived.

Official Comment

. . .

Definitional Cross References:

"Agreement". Section 1–201.

"Contract". Section 1–201.

"Delivery". Section 1–201.

"Goods". Section 2–105.

"Seller". Section 2–103.

"Term". Section 1–201.

§ 2–322.   Delivery "Ex-ship".

(1) Unless otherwise agreed a term for delivery of goods "ex-ship" (which means from the carrying vessel) or in equivalent language is not restricted to a particular ship and requires delivery from a ship which has reached a place at the named port of destination where goods of the kind are usually discharged.

(2) Under such a term unless otherwise agreed

(a) the seller must discharge all liens arising out of the carriage and furnish the buyer with a direction which puts the carrier under a duty to deliver the goods; and

(b) the risk of loss does not pass to the buyer until the goods leave the ship's tackle or are otherwise properly unloaded.

Official Comment

. . .

Definitional Cross References:

"Buyer". Section 2–103.

"Goods". Section 2–105.

"Seller". Section 2–103.

"Term". Section 1–201.

§ 2–323.   Form of Bill of Lading Required in Overseas Shipment; "Overseas".

(1)   Where the contract contemplates overseas shipment and contains a term C.I.F. or C. & F. or F.O.B. vessel, the seller unless otherwise agreed must obtain a negotiable bill of lading stating that the goods have been loaded in board or, in the case of a term C.I.F. or C. & F., received for shipment.

(2)   Where in a case within subsection (1) a bill of lading has been issued in a set of parts, unless otherwise agreed if the documents are not to be sent from abroad the buyer may demand tender of the full set; otherwise only one part of the bill of lading need be tendered. Even if the agreement expressly requires a full set

    (a)   due tender of a single part is acceptable within the provisions of this Article on cure of improper delivery (subsection (1) of Section 2–508); and

    (b)   even though the full set is demanded, if the documents are sent from abroad the person tendering an incomplete set may nevertheless require payment upon furnishing an indemnity which the buyer in good faith deems adequate.

(3)   A shipment by water or by air or a contract contemplating such shipment is "overseas" insofar as by usage of trade or agreement it is subject to the commercial, financing or shipping practices characteristic of international deep water commerce.

Official Comment

. . .

Definitional Cross References:

    "Bill of lading". Section 1–201.

    "Buyer". Section 2–103.

    "Contract". Section 1–201.

    "Delivery". Section 1–201.

    "Financing agency". Section 2–104.

    "Person". Section 1–201.

    "Seller". Section 2–103.

    "Send". Section 1–201.

    "Term". Section 1–201.

§ 2–324.   "No Arrival, No Sale" Term.

Under a term "no arrival, no sale" or terms of like meaning, unless otherwise agreed,

    (a)   the seller must properly ship conforming goods and if they arrive by any means he must tender them on arrival but he assumes no obligation that the goods will arrive unless he has caused the non-arrival; and

    (b)   where without fault of the seller the goods are in part lost or have so deteriorated as no longer to conform to the contract or arrive after the contract time, the buyer may proceed as if there had been casualty to identified goods (Section 2–613).

Official Comment

. . .

Definitional Cross References:

"Buyer". Section 2–103.

"Conforming". Section 2–106.

"Contract". Section 1–201.

"Fault". Section 1–201.

"Goods". Section 2–105.

"Sale". Section 2–106.

"Seller". Section 2–103.

"Term". Section 1–201.

§ 2–325.   "Letter of Credit" Term; "Confirmed Credit".

(1) Failure of the buyer seasonably to furnish an agreed letter of credit is a breach of the contract for sale.

(2) The delivery to seller of a proper letter of credit suspends the buyer's obligation to pay. If the letter of credit is dishonored, the seller may on seasonable notification to the buyer require payment directly from him.

(3) Unless otherwise agreed the term "letter of credit" or "banker's credit" in a contract for sale means an irrevocable credit issued by a financing agency of good repute and, where the shipment is overseas, of good international repute. The term "confirmed credit" means that the credit must also carry the direct obligation of such an agency which does business in the seller's financial market.

Official Comment

. . .

Definitional Cross References:

"Buyer". Section 2–103.

"Contract for sale". Section 2–106.

"Draft". Section 3–104.

"Financing agency". Section 2–104.

"Notifies". Section 1–201.

"Overseas". Section 2–323.

"Purchaser". Section 1–201.

"Seasonably". Section 1–204.

"Seller". Section 2–103.

"Term". Section 1–201.

§ 2–326.   Sale on Approval and Sale or Return; Rights of Creditors.

(1) Unless otherwise agreed, if delivered goods may be returned by the buyer even though they conform to the contract, the transaction is

(a) a "sale on approval" if the goods are delivered primarily for use, and

(b)   a "sale or return" if the goods are delivered primarily for resale.

(2)   Goods held on approval are not subject to the claims of the buyer's creditors until acceptance; goods held on sale or return are subject to such claims while in the buyer's possession.

(3)   Any "or return" term of a contract for sale is to be treated as a separate contract for sale within the statute of frauds section of this Article (Section 2–201) and as contradicting the sale aspect of the contract within the provisions of this Article on parol or extrinsic evidence (Section 2–202).

Official Comment

1.   Both a "sale on approval" and a "sale or return" should be distinguished from other types of transactions with which they frequently have been confused. A "sale" on approval, "sometimes also called a sale 'on trial' or 'on satisfaction,' deals with a contract under which the seller undertakes a risk in order to satisfy its prospective buyer with the appearance or performance of the goods that are sold." The goods are delivered to the proposed purchaser but they remain the property of the seller until the buyer accepts them. The price has already been agreed. The buyer's willingness to receive and test the goods is the consideration for the seller's engagement to deliver and sell. A "sale or return," on the other hand, typically is a sale to a merchant whose unwillingness to buy is overcome by the seller's engagement to take back the goods (or any commercial unit of goods) in lieu of payment if they fail to be resold. A sale or return is a present sale of goods which may be undone at the buyer's option. Accordingly, subsection (2) provides that goods delivered on approval are not subject to the prospective buyer's creditors until acceptance, and goods delivered in a sale or return are subject to the buyer's creditors while in the buyer's possession.

These two transactions are so strongly delineated in practice and in general understanding that every presumption runs against a delivery to a consumer being a "sale or return" and against a delivery to a merchant for resale being a "sale on approval."

2.   The right to return goods for failure to conform to the contract of sale does not make the transaction a "sale on approval" or "sale or return" and has nothing to do with this section or Section 2–327. This section is not concerned with remedies for breach of contract. It deals instead with a power given by the contract to turn back the goods even though they are wholly as warranted. This section nevertheless presupposes that a contract for sale is contemplated by the parties, although that contract may be of the particular character that this section addresses (i.e., a sale on approval or a sale or return).

If a buyer's obligation as a buyer is conditioned not on its personal approval but on the article's passing a described objective test, the risk of loss by casualty pending the test is properly the seller's and proper return is at its expense. On the point of "satisfaction" as meaning "reasonable satisfaction" when an industrial machine is involved, this Article takes no position. . . .

§ 2–327.   Special Incidents of Sale on Approval and Sale or Return.

(1)   Under a sale on approval unless otherwise agreed

(a)   although the goods are identified to the contract the risk of loss and the title do not pass to the buyer until acceptance; and

(b)   use of the goods consistent with the purpose of trial is not acceptance but failure seasonably to notify the seller of election to return the goods is acceptance, and if the goods conform to the contract acceptance of any part is acceptance of the whole; and

(c)   after due notification of election to return, the return is at the seller's risk and expense but a merchant buyer must follow any reasonable instructions.

(2)   Under a sale or return unless otherwise agreed

(a)   the option to return extends to the whole or any commercial unit of the goods while in substantially their original condition, but must be exercised seasonably; and

(b)   the return is at the buyer's risk and expense.

Official Comment

. . .

Definitional Cross References:

"Agreed". Section 1–201.

"Buyer". Section 2–103.

"Commercial unit". Section 2–105.

"Conform". Section 2–106.

"Contract". Section 1–201.

"Goods". Section 2–105.

"Merchant". Section 2–104.

"Notifies". Section 1–201.

"Notification". Section 1–201.

"Sale on approval". Section 2–326.

"Sale or return". Section 2–326.

"Seasonably". Section 1–204.

"Seller". Section 2–103.

§ 2–328. Sale by Auction.

(1) In a sale by auction if goods are put up in lots each lot is the subject of a separate sale.

(2) A sale by auction is complete when the auctioneer so announces by the fall of the hammer or in other customary manner. Where a bid is made while the hammer is falling in acceptance of a prior bid the auctioneer may in his discretion reopen the bidding or declare the goods sold under the bid on which the hammer was falling.

(3) Such a sale is with reserve unless the goods are in explicit terms put up without reserve. In an auction with reserve the auctioneer may withdraw the goods at any time until he announces completion of the sale. In an auction without reserve, after the auctioneer calls for bids on an article or lot, that article or lot cannot be withdrawn unless no bid is made within a reasonable time. In either case a bidder may retract his bid until the auctioneer's announcement of completion of the sale, but a bidder's retraction does not revive any previous bid.

(4) If the auctioneer knowingly receives a bid on the seller's behalf or the seller makes or procures such a bid, and notice has not been given that liberty for such bidding is reserved, the buyer may at his option avoid the sale or take the goods at the price of the last good faith bid prior to the completion of the sale. This subsection shall not apply to any bid at a forced sale.

Official Comment

. . .

Definitional Cross References:

"Buyer". Section 2–103.

"Good faith". Section 1–201.

"Goods". Section 2–105.

"Lot". Section 2–105.

"Notice". Section 1–201.

"Sale". Section 2–106.

"Seller". Section 2–103.

PART IV

TITLE, CREDITORS AND GOOD FAITH PURCHASERS

§ 2–401. Passing of Title; Reservation for Security; Limited Application of This Section.

Each provision of this Article with regard to the rights, obligations and remedies of the seller, the buyer, purchasers or other third parties applies irrespective of title to the goods except where the provision refers to such title. Insofar as situations are not covered by the other provisions of this Article and matters concerning title become material the following rules apply:

(1) Title to goods cannot pass under a contract for sale prior to their identification to the contract (Section 2–501), and unless otherwise explicitly agreed the buyer acquires by their identification a special property as limited by this Act. Any retention or reservation by the seller of the title (property) in goods shipped or delivered to the buyer is limited in effect to a reservation of a security interest. Subject to these provisions and to the provisions of the Article on Secured Transactions (Article 9), title to goods passes from the seller to the buyer in any manner and on any conditions explicitly agreed on by the parties.

(2) Unless otherwise explicitly agreed title passes to the buyer at the time and place at which the seller completes his performance with reference to the physical delivery of the goods, despite any reservation of a security interest and even though a document of title is to be delivered at a different time or place; and in particular and despite any reservation of a security interest by the bill of lading

(a) if the contract requires or authorizes the seller to send the goods to the buyer but does not require him to deliver them at destination, title passes to the buyer at the time and place of shipment; but

(b) if the contract requires delivery at destination, title passes on tender there.

(3) Unless otherwise explicitly agreed where delivery is to be made without moving the goods,

(a) if the seller is to deliver a document of title, title passes at the time when and the place where he delivers such documents; or

(b) if the goods are at the time of contracting already identified and no documents are to be delivered, title passes at the time and place of contracting.

(4) A rejection or other refusal by the buyer to receive or retain the goods, whether or not justified, or a justified revocation of acceptance revests title to the goods in the seller. Such revesting occurs by operation of law and is not a "sale".

Official Comment

. . .

Definitional Cross References:

"Agreement". Section 1–201.

"Bill of lading". Section 1–201.

"Buyer". Section 2–103.

"Contract". Section 1–201.

"Contract for sale". Section 2–106.

"Delivery". Section 1–201.

"Document of title". Section 1–201.

"Good faith". Section 2–103.

"Goods". Section 2–105.

"Party". Section 1–201.

"Purchaser". Section 1–201.

"Receipt" of goods. Section 2–103.

"Remedy". Section 1–201.

"Rights". Section 1–201.

"Sale". Section 2–106.

"Security interest". Section 1–201.

"Seller". Section 2–103.

"Send". Section 1–201.

§ 2–402.   Rights of Seller's Creditors Against Sold Goods.

(1)   Except as provided in subsections (2) and (3), rights of unsecured creditors of the seller with respect to goods which have been identified to a contract for sale are subject to the buyer's rights to recover the goods under this Article (Sections 2–502 and 2–716).

(2)   A creditor of the seller may treat a sale or an identification of goods to a contract for sale as void if as against him a retention of possession by the seller is fraudulent under any rule of law of the state where the goods are situated, except that retention of possession in good faith and current course of trade by a merchant-seller for a commercially reasonable time after a sale or identification is not fraudulent.

(3)   Nothing in this Article shall be deemed to impair the rights of creditors of the seller

(a)   under the provisions of the Article on Secured Transactions (Article 9); or

(b)   where identification to the contract or delivery is made not in current course of trade but in satisfaction of or as security for a pre-existing claim for money, security or the like and is made under circumstances which under any rule of law of the state where the goods are situated would apart from this Article constitute the transaction a fraudulent transfer or voidable preference.

Official Comment

. . .

Definitional Cross References:

"Contract for sale". Section 2–106.

"Creditor". Section 1–201.

"Good faith". Section 2–103.

"Goods". Section 2–105.

"Merchant". Section 2–104.

"Money". Section 1–201.

"Reasonable time". Section 1–204.

"Rights". Section 1–201.

"Sale". Section 2–106.

"Seller". Section 2–103.

§ 2–403. Power to Transfer; Good Faith Purchase of Goods; "Entrusting".

(1) A purchaser of goods acquires all title which his transferor had or had power to transfer except that a purchaser of a limited interest acquires rights only to the extent of the interest purchased. A person with voidable title has power to transfer a good title to a good faith purchaser for value. When goods have been delivered under a transaction of purchase the purchaser has such power even though

(a) the transferor was deceived as to the identity of the purchaser, or

(b) the delivery was in exchange for a check which is later dishonored, or

(c) it was agreed that the transaction was to be a "cash sale", or

(d) the delivery was procured through fraud punishable as larcenous under the criminal law.

(2) Any entrusting of possession of goods to a merchant who deals in goods of that kind gives him power to transfer all rights of the entruster to a buyer in ordinary course of business.

(3) "Entrusting" includes any delivery and any acquiescence in retention of possession regardless of any condition expressed between the parties to the delivery or acquiescence and regardless of whether the procurement of the entrusting or the possessor's disposition of the goods have been such as to be larcenous under the criminal law. . . .

Official Comment

. . .

Definitional Cross References:

"Buyer in ordinary course of business". Section 1–201.

"Good faith". Sections 1–201 and 2–103.

"Goods". Section 2–105.

"Person". Section 1–201.

"Purchaser". Section 1–201.

"Signed". Section 1–201.

"Term". Section 1–201.

"Value". Section 1–201.

PART V

PERFORMANCE

§ 2–501. Insurable Interest in Goods; Manner of Identification of Goods.

(1) The buyer obtains a special property and an insurable interest in goods by identification of existing goods as goods to which the contract refers even though the goods so identified are nonconforming and he has an option to return or reject them. Such identification can be made at any time and in any manner explicitly agreed to by the parties. In the absence of explicit agreement identification occurs

(a) when the contract is made if it is for the sale of goods already existing and identified;

(b)   if the contract is for the sale of future goods other than those described in paragraph (c), when goods are shipped, marked or otherwise designated by the seller as goods to which the contract refers;

(c)   when the crops are planted or otherwise become growing crops or the young are conceived if the contract is for the sale of unborn young to be born within twelve months after contracting or for the sale of crops to be harvested within twelve months or the next normal harvest season after contracting whichever is longer.

(2)   The seller retains an insurable interest in goods so long as title to or any security interest in the goods remains in him and where the identification is by the seller alone he may until default or insolvency or notification to the buyer that the identification is final substitute other goods for those identified.

(3)   Nothing in this section impairs any insurable interest recognized under any other statute or rule of law.

Official Comment

. . .

Purposes:

1.   The present section deals with the manner of identifying goods to the contract so that an insurable interest in the buyer and the rights set forth in the next section will accrue. Generally speaking, identification may be made in any manner "explicitly agreed to" by the parties. The rules of paragraphs (a), (b) and (c) apply only in the absence of such "explicit agreement".

2.   In the ordinary case identification of particular existing goods as goods to which the contract refers is unambiguous and may occur in one of many ways. It is possible, however, for the identification to be tentative or contingent. In view of the limited effect given to identification by this Article, the general policy is to resolve all doubts in favor of identification. . . .

Definitional Cross References:

"Agreement". Section 1–201.

"Contract". Section 1–201.

"Contract for sale". Section 2–106.

"Future goods". Section 2–105.

"Goods". Section 2–105.

"Notification". Section 1–201.

"Party". Section 1–201.

"Sale". Section 2–106.

"Security interest". Section 1–201.

"Seller". Section 2–103.

§ 2–502.   Buyer's Right to Goods on Seller's Repudiation, Failure to Deliver, or Insolvency.

(1)   Subject to subsections (2) and (3) and even though the goods have not been shipped a buyer who has paid a part or all of the price of goods in which he has a special property under the provisions of the immediately preceding section may on making and keeping good a tender of any unpaid portion of their price recover them from the seller if:

(a)   in the case of goods bought for personal, family, or household purposes, the seller repudiates or fails to deliver as required by the contract; or

(b) in all cases, the seller becomes insolvent within ten days after receipt of the first installment on their price.

(2) The buyer's right to recover the goods under subsection (1)(a) vests upon acquisition of a special property, even if the seller had not then repudiated or failed to deliver.

(3) If the identification creating his special property has been made by the buyer he acquires the right to recover the goods only if they conform to the contract for sale.

§ 2–503. Manner of Seller's Tender of Delivery.

(1) Tender of delivery requires that the seller put and hold conforming goods at the buyer's disposition and give the buyer any notification reasonably necessary to enable him to take delivery. The manner, time and place for tender are determined by the agreement and this Article, and in particular

(a) tender must be at a reasonable hour, and if it is of goods they must be kept available for the period reasonably necessary to enable the buyer to take possession; but

(b) unless otherwise agreed the buyer must furnish facilities reasonably suited to the receipt of the goods.

(2) Where the case is within the next section respecting shipment tender requires that the seller comply with its provisions.

(3) Where the seller is required to deliver at a particular destination tender requires that he comply with subsection (1) and also in any appropriate case tender documents as described in subsections (4) and (5) of this section.

(4) Where goods are in the possession of a bailee and are to be delivered without being moved

(a) tender requires that the seller either tender a negotiable document of title covering such goods or procure acknowledgment by the bailee of the buyer's right to possession of the goods; but

(b) tender to the buyer of a non-negotiable document of title or of a written direction to the bailee to deliver is sufficient tender unless the buyer seasonably objects, and receipt by the bailee of notification of the buyer's rights fixes those rights as against the bailee and all third persons; but risk of loss of the goods and of any failure by the bailee to honor the non-negotiable document of title or to obey the direction remains on the seller until the buyer has had a reasonable time to present the document or direction, and a refusal by the bailee to honor the document or to obey the direction defeats the tender.

(5) Where the contract requires the seller to deliver documents

(a) he must tender all such documents in correct form, except as provided in this Article with respect to bills of lading in a set (subsection (2) of Section 2–323); and

(b) tender through customary banking channels is sufficient and dishonor of a draft accompanying the documents constitutes non-acceptance or rejection.

Official Comment

. . .

Purposes of Changes:

1. The major general rules governing the manner of proper or due tender of delivery are gathered in this section. The term "tender" is used in this Article in two different senses. In one sense it refers to "due tender" which contemplates an offer coupled with a present ability to fulfill all the conditions resting on the tendering party and must be followed by actual performance if the other party shows himself ready to proceed. Unless the context unmistakably indicates otherwise this is the meaning of "tender" in this Article

and the occasional addition of the word "due" is only for clarity and emphasis. At other times it is used to refer to an offer of goods or documents under a contract as if in fulfillment of its conditions even though there is a defect when measured against the contract obligation. Used in either sense, however, "tender" connotes such performance by the tendering party as puts the other party in default if he fails to proceed in some manner.

. . .

Definitional Cross References:

"Agreement". Section 1–201.

"Bill of lading". Section 1–201.

"Buyer". Section 2–103.

"Conforming". Section 2–106.

"Contract". Section 1–201.

"Delivery". Section 1–201.

"Dishonor". Section 3–508.

"Document of title". Section 1–201.

"Draft". Section 3–104.

"Goods". Section 2–105.

"Notification". Section 1–201.

"Reasonable time". Section 1–204.

"Receipt" of goods. Section 2–103.

"Rights". Section 1–201.

"Seasonably". Section 1–204.

"Seller". Section 2–103.

"Written". Section 1–201.

§ 2–504. Shipment by Seller.

Where the seller is required or authorized to send the goods to the buyer and the contract does not require him to deliver them at a particular destination, then unless otherwise agreed he must

(a) put the goods in the possession of such a carrier and make such a contract for their transportation as may be reasonable having regard to the nature of the goods and other circumstances of the case; and

(b) obtain and promptly deliver or tender in due form any document necessary to enable the buyer to obtain possession of the goods or otherwise required by the agreement or by usage of trade; and

(c) promptly notify the buyer of the shipment.

Failure to notify the buyer under paragraph (c) or to make a proper contract under paragraph (a) is a ground for rejection only if material delay or loss ensues.

Official Comment

. . .

Definitional Cross References:

"Agreement". Section 1–201.

"Buyer". Section 2–103.

"Contract". Section 1–201.

"Delivery". Section 1–201.

"Goods". Section 2–105.

"Notifies". Section 1–201.

"Seller". Section 2–103.

"Send". Section 1–201.

"Usage of trade". Section 1–205.

§ 2–505.   Seller's Shipment Under Reservation.

(1)   Where the seller has identified goods to the contract by or before shipment:

(a)   his procurement of a negotiable bill of lading to his own order or otherwise reserves in him a security interest in the goods. His procurement of the bill to the order of a financing agency or of the buyer indicates in addition only the seller's expectation of transferring that interest to the person named.

(b)   a non-negotiable bill of lading to himself or his nominee reserves possession of the goods as security but except in a case of conditional delivery (subsection (2) of Section 2–507) a non-negotiable bill of lading naming the buyer as consignee reserves no security interest even though the seller retains possession of the bill of lading.

(2)   When shipment by the seller with reservation of a security interest is in violation of the contract for sale it constitutes an improper contract for transportation within the preceding section but impairs neither the rights given to the buyer by shipment and identification of the goods to the contract nor the seller's powers as a holder of a negotiable document.

Official Comment

. . .

Definitional Cross References:

"Bill of lading". Section 1–201.

"Buyer". Section 2–103.

"Consignee". Section 7–102.

"Contract". Section 1–201.

"Contract for sale". Section 2–106.

"Delivery". Section 1–201.

"Financing agency". Section 2–104.

"Goods". Section 2–105.

"Holder". Section 1–201.

"Person". Section 1–201.

"Security interest". Section 1–201.

"Seller". Section 2–103.

§ 2–506.   Rights of Financing Agency.

(1)   A financing agency by paying or purchasing for value a draft which relates to a shipment of goods acquires to the extent of the payment or purchase and in addition to its own rights under the draft and any document of title securing it any rights of the shipper in the goods including the right to stop delivery and the shipper's right to have the draft honored by the buyer.

(2)   The right to reimbursement of a financing agency which has in good faith honored or purchased the draft under commitment to or authority from the buyer is not impaired by subsequent discovery of defects with reference to any relevant document which was apparently regular on its face.

Official Comment

. . .

Definitional Cross References:

"Buyer". Section 2–103.

"Document of title". Section 1–201.

"Draft". Section 3–104.

"Financing agency". Section 2–104.

"Good faith". Section 2–103.

"Goods". Section 2–105.

"Honor". Section 1–201.

"Purchase". Section 1–201.

"Rights". Section 1–201.

"Value". Section 1–201.

§ 2–507.   Effect of Seller's Tender; Delivery on Condition.

(1)   Tender of delivery is a condition to the buyer's duty to accept the goods and, unless otherwise agreed, to his duty to pay for them. Tender entitles the seller to acceptance of the goods and to payment according to the contract.

(2)   Where payment is due and demanded on the delivery to the buyer of goods or documents of title, his right as against the seller to retain or dispose of them is conditional upon his making the payment due.

Official Comment

. . .

Definitional Cross References:

"Buyer". Section 2–103.

"Contract". Section 1–201.

"Delivery". Section 1–201.

"Document of title". Section 1–201.

"Goods". Section 2–105.

"Rights". Section 1–201.

"Seller". Section 2–103.

§ 2–508. Cure by Seller of Improper Tender or Delivery; Replacement.

(1)   Where any tender or delivery by the seller is rejected because non-conforming and the time for performance has not yet expired, the seller may seasonably notify the buyer of his intention to cure and may then within the contract time make a conforming delivery.

(2)   Where the buyer rejects a non-conforming tender which the seller had reasonable grounds to believe would be acceptable with or without money allowance the seller may if he seasonably notifies the buyer have a further reasonable time to substitute a conforming tender.

Official Comment

. . .

Purposes:

1.   Subsection (1) permits a seller who has made a non-conforming tender in any case to make a conforming delivery within the contract time upon seasonable notification to the buyer. It applies even where the seller has taken back the non-conforming goods and refunded the purchase price. He may still make a good tender within the contract period. The closer, however, it is to the contract date, the greater is the necessity for extreme promptness on the seller's part in notifying of his intention to cure, if such notification is to be "seasonable" under this subsection.

The rule of this subsection, moreover, is qualified by its underlying reasons. Thus if, after contracting for June delivery, a buyer later makes known to the seller his need for shipment early in the month and the seller ships accordingly, the "contract time" has been cut down by the supervening modification and the time for cure of tender must be referred to this modified time term.

2.   Subsection (2) seeks to avoid injustice to the seller by reason of a surprise rejection by the buyer. However, the seller is not protected unless he had "reasonable grounds to believe" that the tender would be acceptable. Such reasonable grounds can lie in prior course of dealing, course of performance or usage of trade as well as in the particular circumstances surrounding the making of the contract. The seller is charged with commercial knowledge of any factors in a particular sales situation which require him to comply strictly with his obligations under the contract as, for example, strict conformity of documents in an overseas shipment or the sale of precision parts or chemicals for use in manufacture. Further, if the buyer gives notice either implicitly, as by a prior course of dealing involving rigorous inspections, or expressly, as by the deliberate inclusion of a "no replacement" clause in the contract, the seller is to be held to rigid compliance. If the clause appears in a "form" contract evidence that it is out of line with trade usage or the prior course of dealing and was not called to the seller's attention may be sufficient to show that the seller had reasonable grounds to believe that the tender would be acceptable.

3.   The words "a further reasonable time to substitute a conforming tender" are intended as words of limitation to protect the buyer. What is a "reasonable time" depends upon the attending circumstances. Compare Section 2–511 on the comparable case of a seller's surprise demand for legal tender.

4.   Existing trade usages permitting variations without rejection but with price allowance enter into the agreement itself as contractual limitations of remedy and are not covered by this section.

. . .

Definitional Cross References:

"Buyer". Section 2–103.

"Conforming". Section 2–106.

"Contract". Section 1–201.

"Money". Section 1–201.

"Notifies". Section 1–201.

"Reasonable time". Section 1–204.

"Seasonably". Section 1–204.

"Seller". Section 2–103.

§ 2–509.   Risk of Loss in the Absence of Breach.

(1)   Where the contract requires or authorizes the seller to ship the goods by carrier

(a)   if it does not require him to deliver them at a particular destination, the risk of loss passes to the buyer when the goods are duly delivered to the carrier even though the shipment is under reservation (Section 2–505); but

(b)   if it does require him to deliver them at a particular destination and the goods are there duly tendered while in the possession of the carrier, the risk of loss passes to the buyer when the goods are there duly so tendered as to enable the buyer to take delivery.

(2)   Where the goods are held by a bailee to be delivered without being moved, the risk of loss passes to the buyer

(a)   on his receipt of a negotiable document of title covering the goods; or

(b)   on acknowledgment by the bailee of the buyer's right to possession of the goods; or

(c)   after his receipt of a non-negotiable document of title or other written direction to deliver, as provided in subsection (4)(b) of Section 2–503.

(3)   In any case not within subsection (1) or (2), the risk of loss passes to the buyer on his receipt of the goods if the seller is a merchant; otherwise the risk passes to the buyer on tender of delivery.

(4)   The provisions of this section are subject to contrary agreement of the parties and to the provisions of this Article on sale on approval (Section 2–327) and on effect of breach on risk of loss (Section 2–510).

Official Comment

. . .

1.   The underlying theory of these sections on risk of loss is the adoption of the contractual approach rather than an arbitrary shifting of the risk with the "property" in the goods. The scope of the present section, therefore, is limited strictly to those cases where there has been no breach by the seller. Where for any reason his delivery or tender fails to conform to the contract, the present section does not apply and the situation is governed by the provisions on effect of breach on risk of loss. . . .

. . .

Definitional Cross References:

"Agreement". Section 1–201.

"Buyer". Section 2–103.

"Contract". Section 1–201.

"Delivery". Section 1–201.

"Document of title". Section 1–201.

"Goods". Section 2–105.

"Merchant". Section 2–104.

"Party". Section 1–201.

"Receipt" of goods. Section 2–103.

"Sale on approval". Section 2–326.

"Seller". Section 2–103.

§ 2–510.　Effect of Breach on Risk of Loss.

(1)　Where a tender or delivery of goods so fails to conform to the contract as to give a right of rejection the risk of their loss remains on the seller until cure or acceptance.

(2)　Where the buyer rightfully revokes acceptance he may to the extent of any deficiency in his effective insurance coverage treat the risk of loss as having rested on the seller from the beginning.

(3)　Where the buyer as to conforming goods already identified to the contract for sale repudiates or is otherwise in breach before risk of their loss has passed to him, the seller may to the extent of any deficiency in his effective insurance coverage treat the risk of loss as resting on the buyer for a commercially reasonable time.

Official Comment

. . .

Definitional Cross References:

"Buyer". Section 2–103.

"Conform". Section 2–106.

"Contract for sale". Section 2–106.

"Goods". Section 2–105.

"Seller". Section 2–103.

§ 2–511.　Tender of Payment by Buyer; Payment by Check.

(1)　Unless otherwise agreed tender of payment is a condition to the seller's duty to tender and complete any delivery.

(2)　Tender of payment is sufficient when made by any means or in any manner current in the ordinary course of business unless the seller demands payment in legal tender and gives any extension of time reasonably necessary to procure it.

(3)　Subject to the provisions of this Act on the effect of an instrument on an obligation (Section 3–310), payment by check is conditional and is defeated as between the parties by dishonor of the check on due presentment.

As amended in 1994.

Official Comment

. . .

Definitional Cross References:

"Buyer". Section 2–103.

"Check". Section 3–104.

"Dishonor". Section 3–508.

"Party". Section 1–201.

"Reasonable time". Section 1–204.

"Seller". Section 2–103.

§ 2–512.   Payment by Buyer Before Inspection.

(1)   Where the contract requires payment before inspection non-conformity of the goods does not excuse the buyer from so making payment unless

     (a)   the non-conformity appears without inspection; or

     (b)   despite tender of the required documents the circumstances would justify injunction against honor under the provisions of this Act (Section 5–114).

(2)   Payment pursuant to subsection (1) does not constitute an acceptance of goods or impair the buyer's right to inspect or any of his remedies.

Official Comment

. . .

Definitional Cross References:

     "Buyer". Section 2–103.

     "Conform". Section 2–106.

     "Contract". Section 1–201.

     "Financing agency". Section 2–104.

     "Goods". Section 2–105.

     "Remedy". Section 1–201.

     "Rights". Section 1–201.

§ 2–513.   Buyer's Right to Inspection of Goods.

(1)   Unless otherwise agreed and subject to subsection (3), where goods are tendered or delivered or identified to the contract for sale, the buyer has a right before payment or acceptance to inspect them at any reasonable place and time and in any reasonable manner. When the seller is required or authorized to send the goods to the buyer, the inspection may be after their arrival.

(2)   Expenses of inspection must be borne by the buyer but may be recovered from the seller if the goods do not conform and are rejected.

(3)   Unless otherwise agreed and subject to the provisions of this Article on C.I.F. contracts (subsection (3) of Section 2–321), the buyer is not entitled to inspect the goods before payment of the price when the contract provides

     (a)   for delivery "C.O.D." or on other like terms; or

     (b)   for payment against documents of title, except where such payment is due only after the goods are to become available for inspection.

(4)   A place or method of inspection fixed by the parties is presumed to be exclusive but unless otherwise expressly agreed it does not postpone identification or shift the place for delivery or for passing the risk of loss. If compliance becomes impossible, inspection shall be as provided in this section unless the place or method fixed was clearly intended as an indispensable condition failure of which avoids the contract.

Official Comment

. . .

Definitional Cross References:

"Buyer". Section 2–103.

"Conform". Section 2–106.

"Contract". Section 1–201.

"Contract for sale". Section 2–106.

"Document of title". Section 1–201.

"Goods". Section 2–105.

"Party". Section 1–201.

"Presumed". Section 1–201.

"Reasonable time". Section 1–204.

"Rights". Section 1–201.

"Seller". Section 2–103.

"Send". Section 1–201.

"Term". Section 1–201.

§ 2–514.   When Documents Deliverable on Acceptance; When on Payment.

Unless otherwise agreed documents against which a draft is drawn are to be delivered to the drawee on acceptance of the draft if it is payable more than three days after presentment; otherwise, only on payment.

Official Comment

. . .

Definitional Cross References:

"Delivery". Section 1–201.

"Draft". Section 3–104.

§ 2–515.   Preserving Evidence of Goods in Dispute.

In furtherance of the adjustment of any claim or dispute

(a) either party on reasonable notification to the other and for the purpose of ascertaining the facts and preserving evidence has the right to inspect, test and sample the goods including such of them as may be in the possession or control of the other; and

(b) the parties may agree to a third party inspection or survey to determine the conformity or condition of the goods and may agree that the findings shall be binding upon them in any subsequent litigation or adjustment.

Official Comment

. . .

Definitional Cross References:

"Conform". Section 2–106.

"Goods". Section 2–105.

"Notification". Section 1–201.

"Party". Section 1–201.

PART VI

BREACH, REPUDIATION AND EXCUSE

§ 2–601. Buyer's Rights on Improper Delivery.

Subject to the provisions of this Article on breach in installment contracts (Section 2–612) and unless otherwise agreed under the sections on contractual limitations of remedy (Sections 2–718 and 2–719), if the goods or the tender of delivery fail in any respect to conform to the contract, the buyer may

    (a)   reject the whole; or

    (b)   accept the whole; or

    (c)   accept any commercial unit or units and reject the rest.

Official Comment

. . .

Purposes of Changes: To make it clear that:

1.   A buyer accepting a non-conforming tender is not penalized by the loss of any remedy otherwise open to him. This policy extends to cover and regulate the acceptance of a part of any lot improperly tendered in any case where the price can reasonably be apportioned. Partial acceptance is permitted whether the part of the goods accepted conforms or not. The only limitation on partial acceptance is that good faith and commercial reasonableness must be used to avoid undue impairment of the value of the remaining portion of the goods. This is the reason for the insistence on the "commercial unit" in paragraph (c). In this respect, the test is not only what unit has been the basis of contract, but whether the partial acceptance produces so materially adverse an effect on the remainder as to constitute bad faith.

2.   Acceptance made with the knowledge of the other party is final. An original refusal to accept may be withdrawn by a later acceptance if the seller has indicated that he is holding the tender open. However, if the buyer attempts to accept, either in whole or in part, after his original rejection has caused the seller to arrange for other disposition of the goods, the buyer must answer for any ensuing damage since the next section provides that any exercise of ownership after rejection is wrongful as against the seller. Further, he is liable even though the seller may choose to treat his action as acceptance rather than conversion, since the damage flows from the misleading notice. Such arrangements for resale or other disposition of the goods by the seller must be viewed as within the normal contemplation of a buyer who has given notice of rejection. However, the buyer's attempts in good faith to dispose of defective goods where the seller has failed to give instructions within a reasonable time are not to be regarded as an acceptance.

. . .

Definitional Cross References:

    "Buyer". Section 2–103.

    "Commercial unit". Section 2–105.

"Conform". Section 2–106.

"Contract". Section 1–201.

"Goods". Section 2–105.

"Installment contract". Section 2–612.

"Rights". Section 1–201.

§ 2–602. Manner and Effect of Rightful Rejection.

(1) Rejection of goods must be within a reasonable time after their delivery or tender. It is ineffective unless the buyer seasonably notifies the seller.

(2) Subject to the provisions of the two following sections on rejected goods (Sections 2–603 and 2–604),

(a) after rejection any exercise of ownership by the buyer with respect to any commercial unit is wrongful as against the seller; and

(b) if the buyer has before rejection taken physical possession of goods in which he does not have a security interest under the provisions of this Article (subsection (3) of Section 2–711), he is under a duty after rejection to hold them with reasonable care at the seller's disposition for a time sufficient to permit the seller to remove them; but

(c) the buyer has no further obligations with regard to goods rightfully rejected.

(3) The seller's rights with respect to goods wrongfully rejected are governed by the provisions of this Article on Seller's remedies in general (Section 2–703).

Official Comment

. . .

Purposes of Changes: To make it clear that:

1. A tender or delivery of goods made pursuant to a contract of sale, even though wholly non-conforming, requires affirmative action by the buyer to avoid acceptance. Under subsection (1), therefore, the buyer is given a reasonable time to notify the seller of his rejection, but without such seasonable notification his rejection is ineffective. The sections of this Article dealing with inspection of goods must be read in connection with the buyer's reasonable time for action under this subsection. Contract provisions limiting the time for rejection fall within the rule of the section on "Time" and are effective if the time set gives the buyer a reasonable time for discovery of defects. What constitutes a due "notifying" of rejection by the buyer to the seller is defined in Section 1–201.

2. Subsection (2) lays down the normal duties of the buyer upon rejection, which flow from the relationship of the parties. Beyond his duty to hold the goods with reasonable care for the buyer's [seller's] disposition, this section continues the policy of . . . generally relieving the buyer from any duties with respect to them, except when the circumstances impose the limited obligation of salvage upon him under the next section.

3. The present section applies only to rightful rejection by the buyer. If the seller has made a tender which in all respects conforms to the contract, the buyer has a positive duty to accept and his failure to do so constitutes a "wrongful rejection" which gives the seller immediate remedies for breach. Subsection (3) is included here to emphasize the sharp distinction between the rejection of an improper tender and the non-acceptance which is a breach by the buyer.

4. The provisions of this section are to be appropriately limited or modified when a negotiation is in process.

. . .

Definitional Cross References:

"Buyer". Section 2–103.

"Commercial unit". Section 2–105.

"Goods". Section 2–105.

"Merchant". Section 2–104.

"Notifies". Section 1–201.

"Reasonable time". Section 1–204.

"Remedy". Section 1–201.

"Rights". Section 1–201.

"Seasonably". Section 1–204.

"Security interest". Section 1–201.

"Seller". Section 2–103.

§ 2–603. Merchant Buyer's Duties as to Rightfully Rejected Goods.

(1) Subject to any security interest in the buyer (subsection (3) of Section 2–711), when the seller has no agent or place of business at the market of rejection a merchant buyer is under a duty after rejection of goods in his possession or control to follow any reasonable instructions received from the seller with respect to the goods and in the absence of such instructions to make reasonable efforts to sell them for the seller's account if they are perishable or threaten to decline in value speedily. Instructions are not reasonable if on demand indemnity for expenses is not forthcoming.

(2) When the buyer sells goods under subsection (1), he is entitled to reimbursement from the seller or out of the proceeds for reasonable expenses of caring for and selling them, and if the expenses include no selling commission then to such commission as is usual in the trade or if there is none to a reasonable sum not exceeding ten per cent on the gross proceeds.

(3) In complying with this section the buyer is held only to good faith and good faith conduct hereunder is neither acceptance nor conversion nor the basis of an action for damages.

Official Comment

. . .

Purposes:

1. This section recognizes the duty imposed upon the merchant buyer by good faith and commercial practice to follow any reasonable instructions of the seller as to reshipping, storing, delivery to a third party, reselling or the like. Subsection (1) goes further and extends the duty to include the making of reasonable efforts to effect a salvage sale where the value of the goods is threatened and the seller's instructions do not arrive in time to prevent serious loss.

2. The limitations on the buyer's duty to resell under subsection (1) are to be liberally construed. The buyer's duty to resell under this section arises from commercial necessity and thus is present only when the seller has "no agent or place of business at the market of rejection". . . .

4. Since this section makes the resale of perishable goods an affirmative duty in contrast to a mere right to sell as under the case law, subsection (3) makes it clear that the buyer is liable only for the exercise of good faith in determining whether the value of the goods is sufficiently threatened to justify a quick resale or whether he has waited a sufficient length of time for instructions, or what a reasonable means and place of resale is.

5. A buyer who fails to make a salvage sale when his duty to do so under this section has arisen is subject to damages pursuant to the section on liberal administration of remedies.

. . .

Definitional Cross References:

"Buyer". Section 2–103.

"Good faith". Section 1–201.

"Goods". Section 2–105.

"Merchant". Section 2–104.

"Security interest". Section 1–201.

"Seller". Section 2–103.

§ 2–604.   Buyer's Options as to Salvage of Rightfully Rejected Goods.

Subject to the provisions of the immediately preceding section on perishables if the seller gives no instructions within a reasonable time after notification of rejection the buyer may store the rejected goods for the seller's account or reship them to him or resell them for the seller's account with reimbursement as provided in the preceding section. Such action is not acceptance or conversion.

Official Comment

. . .

Purposes:

The basic purpose of this section is twofold: on the one hand it aims at reducing the stake in dispute and on the other at avoiding the pinning of a technical "acceptance" on a buyer who has taken steps towards realization on or preservation of the goods in good faith. This section is essentially a salvage section and the buyer's right to act under it is conditioned upon (1) non-conformity of the goods, (2) due notification of rejection to the seller under the section on manner of rejection, and (3) the absence of any instructions from the seller which the merchant-buyer has a duty to follow under the preceding section.

This section is designed to accord all reasonable leeway to a rightfully rejecting buyer acting in good faith. The listing of what the buyer may do in the absence of instructions from the seller is intended to be not exhaustive but merely illustrative. This is not a "merchant's" section and the options are pure options given to merchant and nonmerchant buyers alike. The merchant-buyer, however, may in some instances be under a duty rather than an option to resell under the provisions of the preceding section.

. . .

Definitional Cross References:

"Buyer". Section 2–103.

"Notification". Section 1–201.

"Reasonable time". Section 1–204.

"Seller". Section 2–103.

§ 2–605.   Waiver of Buyer's Objections by Failure to Particularize.

(1) The buyer's failure to state in connection with rejection a particular defect which is ascertainable by reasonable inspection precludes him from relying on the unstated defect to justify rejection or to establish breach

(a) where the seller could have cured it if stated seasonably; or

(b) between merchants when the seller has after rejection made a request in writing for a full and final written statement of all defects on which the buyer proposes to rely.

(2)   Payment against documents made without reservation of rights precludes recovery of the payment for defects apparent on the face of the documents.

Official Comment

. . .

Purposes:

1.   The present section rests upon a policy of permitting the buyer to give a quick and informal notice of defects in a tender without penalizing him for omissions in his statement, while at the same time protecting a seller who is reasonably misled by the buyer's failure to state curable defects.

2.   Where the defect in a tender is one which could have been cured by the seller, a buyer who merely rejects the delivery without stating his objections to it is probably acting in commercial bad faith and seeking to get out of a deal which has become unprofitable. Subsection (1)(a), following the general policy of this Article which looks to preserving the deal wherever possible, therefore insists that the seller's right to correct his tender in such circumstances be protected.

3.   When the time for cure is past, subsection (1)(b) makes it plain that a seller is entitled upon request to a final statement of objections upon which he can rely. What is needed is that he make clear to the buyer exactly what is being sought. A formal demand under paragraph (b) will be sufficient in the case of a merchant-buyer.

4.   Subsection (2) applies to the particular case of documents the same principle which the section on effects of acceptance applies to the case of goods. . . .

. . .

Definitional Cross References:

"Between merchants". Section 2–104.

"Buyer". Section 2–103.

"Seasonably". Section 1–204.

"Seller". Section 2–103.

"Writing" and "written". Section 1–201.

§ 2–606.   What Constitutes Acceptance of Goods.

(1)   Acceptance of goods occurs when the buyer

(a)   after a reasonable opportunity to inspect the goods signifies to the seller that the goods are conforming or that he will take or retain them in spite of their non-conformity; or

(b)   fails to make an effective rejection (subsection (1) of Section 2–602), but such acceptance does not occur until the buyer has had a reasonable opportunity to inspect them; or

(c)   does any act inconsistent with the seller's ownership; but if such act is wrongful as against the seller it is an acceptance only if ratified by him.

(2)   Acceptance of a part of any commercial unit is acceptance of that entire unit.

Official Comment

. . .

Purposes of Changes and New Matter: To make it clear that:

1.   Under this Article "acceptance" as applied to goods means that the buyer, pursuant to the contract, takes particular goods which have been appropriated to the contract as his own, whether or not he is obligated to do so, and whether he does so by words, action, or silence when it is time to speak. If the

goods conform to the contract, acceptance amounts only to the performance by the buyer of one part of his legal obligation.

2.   Under this Article acceptance of goods is always acceptance of identified goods which have been appropriated to the contract or are appropriated by the contract. There is no provision for "acceptance of title" apart from acceptance in general, since acceptance of title is not material under this Article to the detailed rights and duties of the parties. (See Section 2–401). The refinements of the older law between acceptance of goods and of title become unnecessary in view of the provisions of the sections on effect and revocation of acceptance, on effects of identification and on risk of loss, and those sections which free the seller's and buyer's remedies from the complications and confusions caused by the question of whether title has or has not passed to the buyer before breach. . . .

Definitional Cross References:

"Buyer". Section 2–103.

"Commercial unit". Section 2–105.

"Goods". Section 2–105.

"Seller". Section 2–103.

§ 2–607.   Effect of Acceptance; Notice of Breach; Burden of Establishing Breach After Acceptance; Notice of Claim or Litigation to Person Answerable Over.

(1)   The buyer must pay at the contract rate for any goods accepted.

(2)   Acceptance of goods by the buyer precludes rejection of the goods accepted and if made with knowledge of a non-conformity cannot be revoked because of it unless the acceptance was on the reasonable assumption that the non-conformity would be seasonably cured but acceptance does not of itself impair any other remedy provided by this Article for non-conformity.

(3)   Where a tender has been accepted

(a)   the buyer must within a reasonable time after he discovers or should have discovered any breach notify the seller of breach or be barred from any remedy; and

(b)   if the claim is one for infringement or the like (subsection (3) of Section 2–312) and the buyer is sued as a result of such a breach he must so notify the seller within a reasonable time after he receives notice of the litigation or be barred from any remedy over for liability established by the litigation.

(4)   The burden is on the buyer to establish any breach with respect to the goods accepted.

(5)   Where the buyer is sued for breach of a warranty or other obligation for which his seller is answerable over

(a)   he may give his seller written notice of the litigation. If the notice states that the seller may come in and defend and that if the seller does not do so he will be bound in any action against him by his buyer by any determination of fact common to the two litigations, then unless the seller after seasonable receipt of the notice does come in and defend he is so bound.

(b)   if the claim is one for infringement or the like (subsection (3) of Section 2–312) the original seller may demand in writing that his buyer turn over to him control of the litigation including settlement or else be barred from any remedy over and if he also agrees to bear all expense and to satisfy any adverse judgment, then unless the buyer after seasonable receipt of the demand does turn over control the buyer is so barred.

(6)   The provisions of subsections (3), (4) and (5) apply to any obligation of a buyer to hold the seller harmless against infringement or the like (subsection (3) of Section 2–312).

Official Comment

. . .

Purposes of Changes: To continue the prior basic policies with respect to acceptance of goods while making a number of minor though material changes in the interest of simplicity and commercial convenience so that: . . .

4.   The time of notification [under subsection (3)(a)] is to be determined by applying commercial standards to a merchant buyer. "A reasonable time" for notification from a retail consumer is to be judged by different standards so that in his case it will be extended, for the rule of requiring notification is designed to defeat commercial bad faith, not to deprive a good faith consumer of his remedy.

The content of the notification need merely be sufficient to let the seller know that the transaction is still troublesome and must be watched. There is no reason to require that the notification which saves the buyer's rights under this section must include a clear statement of all the objections that will be relied on by the buyer, as under the section covering statements of defects upon rejection (Section 2–605). Nor is there reason for requiring the notification to be a claim for damages or of any threatened litigation or other resort to a remedy. The notification which saves the buyer's rights under this Article need only be such as informs the seller that the transaction is claimed to involve a breach, and thus opens the way for normal settlement through negotiation.

. . .

Definitional Cross References:

"Burden of establishing". Section 1–201.

"Buyer". Section 2–103.

"Conform". Section 2–106.

"Contract". Section 1–201.

"Goods". Section 2–105.

"Notifies". Section 1–201.

"Reasonable time". Section 1–204.

"Remedy". Section 1–201.

"Seasonably". Section 1–204.

§ 2–608.   Revocation of Acceptance in Whole or in Part.

(1)   The buyer may revoke his acceptance of a lot or commercial unit whose non-conformity substantially impairs its value to him if he has accepted it

(a)   on the reasonable assumption that its non-conformity would be cured and it has not been seasonably cured; or

(b)   without discovery of such non-conformity if his acceptance was reasonably induced either by the difficulty of discovery before acceptance or by the seller's assurances.

(2)   Revocation of acceptance must occur within a reasonable time after the buyer discovers or should have discovered the ground for it and before any substantial change in condition of the goods which is not caused by their own defects. It is not effective until the buyer notifies the seller of it.

(3)   A buyer who so revokes has the same rights and duties with regard to the goods involved as if he had rejected them.

Official Comment

. . .

Purposes of Changes: To make it clear that:

1.　Although the prior basic policy is continued, the buyer is no longer required to elect between revocation of acceptance and recovery of damages for breach. Both are now available to him. The non-alternative character of the two remedies is stressed by the terms used in the present section. The section no longer speaks of "rescission," a term capable of ambiguous application either to transfer of title to the goods or to the contract of sale and susceptible also of confusion with cancellation for cause of an executed or executory portion of the contract. The remedy under this section is instead referred to simply as "revocation of acceptance" of goods tendered under a contract for sale and involves no suggestion of "election" of any sort.

2.　Revocation of acceptance is possible only where the non-conformity substantially impairs the value of the goods to the buyer. For this purpose the test is not what the seller had reason to know at the time of contracting; the question is whether the non-conformity is such as will in fact cause a substantial impairment of value to the buyer though the seller had no advance knowledge as to the buyer's particular circumstances.

3.　"Assurances" by the seller under paragraph (b) of subsection (1) can rest as well in the circumstances or in the contract as in explicit language used at the time of delivery. The reason for recognizing such assurances is that they induce the buyer to delay discovery. These are the only assurances involved in paragraph (b). Explicit assurances may be made either in good faith or bad faith. In either case any remedy accorded by this Article is available to the buyer under the section on remedies for fraud.

. . .

Definitional Cross References:

"Buyer". Section 2–103.

"Commercial unit". Section 2–105.

"Conform". Section 2–106.

"Goods". Section 2–105.

"Lot". Section 2–105.

"Notifies". Section 1–201.

"Reasonable time". Section 1–204.

"Rights". Section 1–201.

"Seasonably". Section 1–204.

"Seller". Section 2–103.

§ 2–609.　Right to Adequate Assurance of Performance.

(1)　A contract for sale imposes an obligation on each party that the other's expectation of receiving due performance will not be impaired. When reasonable grounds for insecurity arise with respect to the performance of either party the other may in writing demand adequate assurance of due performance and until he receives such assurance may if commercially reasonable suspend any performance for which he has not already received the agreed return.

(2)　Between merchants the reasonableness of grounds for insecurity and the adequacy of any assurance offered shall be determined according to commercial standards.

(3)　Acceptance of any improper delivery or payment does not prejudice the aggrieved party's right to demand adequate assurance of future performance.

(4)   After receipt of a justified demand failure to provide within a reasonable time not exceeding thirty days such assurance of due performance as is adequate under the circumstances of the particular case is a repudiation of the contract.

Official Comment

. . .

Purposes:

1.   The section rests on the recognition of the fact that the essential purpose of a contract between commercial men is actual performance and they do not bargain merely for a promise, or for a promise plus the right to win a lawsuit and that a continuing sense of reliance and security that the promised performance will be forthcoming when due, is an important feature of the bargain. If either the willingness or the ability of a party to perform declines materially between the time of contracting and the time for performance, the other party is threatened with the loss of a substantial part of what he has bargained for. A seller needs protection not merely against having to deliver on credit to a shaky buyer, but also against having to procure and manufacture the goods, perhaps turning down other customers. Once he has been given reason to believe that the buyer's performance has become uncertain, it is an undue hardship to force him to continue his own performance. Similarly, a buyer who believes that the seller's deliveries have become uncertain cannot safely wait for the due date of performance when he has been buying to assure himself of materials for his current manufacturing or to replenish his stock of merchandise.

2.   Three measures have been adopted to meet the needs of commercial men in such situations. First, the aggrieved party is permitted to suspend his own performance and any preparation therefor, with excuse for any resulting necessary delay, until the situation has been clarified. "Suspend performance" under this section means to hold up performance pending the outcome of the demand, and includes also the holding up of any preparatory action. . . .

Secondly, the aggrieved party is given the right to require adequate assurance that the other party's performance will be duly forthcoming. This principle is reflected in the familiar clauses permitting the seller to curtail deliveries if the buyer's credit becomes impaired, which when held within the limits of reasonableness and good faith actually express no more than the fair business meaning of any commercial contract.

Third, and finally, this section provides the means by which the aggrieved party may treat the contract as broken if his reasonable grounds for insecurity are not cleared up within a reasonable time. This is the principle underlying the law of anticipatory breach, whether by way of defective part performance or by repudiation. The present section merges these three principles of law and commercial practice into a single theory of general application to all sales agreements looking to future performance.

3.   Subsection (2) of the present section requires that "reasonable" grounds and "adequate" assurance as used in subsection (1) be defined by commercial rather than legal standards. The express reference to commercial standards carries no connotation that the obligation of good faith is not equally applicable here.

Under commercial standards and in accord with commercial practice, a ground for insecurity need not arise from or be directly related to the contract in question. The law as to "dependence" or "independence" of promises within a single contract does not control the application of the present section.

Thus a buyer who falls behind in "his account" with the seller, even though the items involved have to do with separate and legally distinct contracts, impairs the seller's expectation of due performance. Again, under the same test, a buyer who requires precision parts which he intends to use immediately upon delivery, may have reasonable grounds for insecurity if he discovers that his seller is making defective deliveries of such parts to other buyers with similar needs. . . .

The nature of the sales contract enters also into the question of reasonableness. For example, a report from an apparently trustworthy source that the seller had shipped defective goods or was planning to ship them would normally give the buyer reasonable grounds for insecurity. But when the buyer has assumed the risk of payment before inspection of the goods, as in a sales contract on C.I.F. or similar cash against documents terms, that risk is not to be evaded by a demand for assurance. Therefore no ground for insecurity would exist under this section unless the report went to a ground which would excuse payment by the buyer.

4.   What constitutes "adequate" assurance of due performance is subject to the same test of factual conditions. For example, where the buyer can make use of a defective delivery, a mere promise by a seller of good repute that he is giving the matter his attention and that the defect will not be repeated, is normally sufficient. Under the same circumstances, however, a similar statement by a known corner-cutter might well be considered insufficient without the posting of a guaranty or, if so demanded by the buyer, a speedy replacement of the delivery involved. By the same token where a delivery has defects, even though easily curable, which interfere with easy use by the buyer, no verbal assurance can be deemed adequate which is not accompanied by replacement, repair, money-allowance, or other commercially reasonable cure. . . .

The entire foregoing discussion as to adequacy of assurance by way of explanation is subject to qualification when repeated occasions for the application of this section arise. This Act recognizes that repeated delinquencies must be viewed as cumulative. On the other hand, commercial sense also requires that if repeated claims for assurance are made under this section, the basis for these claims must be increasingly obvious.

5.   A failure to provide adequate assurance of performance and thereby to re-establish the security of expectation, results in a breach only "by repudiation" under subsection (4). Therefore, the possibility is continued of retraction of the repudiation under the section dealing with that problem, unless the aggrieved party has acted on the breach in some manner.

The thirty day limit on the time to provide assurance is laid down to free the question of reasonable time from uncertainty in later litigation.

6.   Clauses seeking to give the protected party exceedingly wide powers to cancel or readjust the contract when ground for insecurity arises must be read against the fact that good faith is a part of the obligation of the contract and not subject to modification by agreement and includes, in the case of a merchant, the reasonable observance of commercial standards of fair dealing in the trade. Such clauses can thus be effective to enlarge the protection given by the present section to a certain extent, to fix the reasonable time within which requested assurance must be given, or to define adequacy of the assurance in any commercially reasonable fashion. But any clause seeking to set up arbitrary standards for action is ineffective under this Article.

. . .

Definitional Cross References:

"Aggrieved party". Section 1–201.

"Between merchants". Section 2–104.

"Contract". Section 1–201.

"Contract for sale". Section 2–106.

"Party". Section 1–201.

"Reasonable time". Section 1–204.

"Rights". Section 1–201.

"Writing". Section 1–201.

§ 2–610.   Anticipatory Repudiation.

When either party repudiates the contract with respect to a performance not yet due the loss of which will substantially impair the value of the contract to the other, the aggrieved party may

     (a)   for a commercially reasonable time await performance by the repudiating party; or

     (b)   resort to any remedy for breach (Section 2–703 or Section 2–711), even though he has notified the repudiating party that he would await the latter's performance and has urged retraction; and

(c) in either case suspend his own performance or proceed in accordance with the provisions of this Article on the seller's right to identify goods to the contract notwithstanding breach or to salvage unfinished goods (Section 2–704).

Official Comment

. . .

Purposes: To make it clear that:

1. With the problem of insecurity taken care of by the preceding section and with provision being made in this Article as to the effect of a defective delivery under an installment contract, anticipatory repudiation centers upon an overt communication of intention or an action which renders performance impossible or demonstrates a clear determination not to continue with performance.

Under the present section when such a repudiation substantially impairs the value of the contract, the aggrieved party may at any time resort to his remedies for breach, or he may suspend his own performance while he negotiates with, or awaits performance by, the other party. But if he awaits performance beyond a commercially reasonable time he cannot recover resulting damages which he should have avoided.

2. It is not necessary for repudiation that performance be made literally and utterly impossible. Repudiation can result from action which reasonably indicates a rejection of the continuing obligation. And, a repudiation automatically results under the preceding section on insecurity when a party fails to provide adequate assurance of due future performance within thirty days after a justifiable demand therefor has been made. Under the language of this section, a demand by one or both parties for more than the contract calls for in the way of counter-performance is not in itself a repudiation nor does it invalidate a plain expression of desire for future performance. However, when under a fair reading it amounts to a statement of intention not to perform except on conditions which go beyond the contract, it becomes a repudiation.

3. The test chosen to justify an aggrieved party's action under this section is the same as that in the section on breach in installment contracts—namely the substantial value of the contract. . . .

. . .

Definitional Cross References:

"Aggrieved party". Section 1–201.

"Contract". Section 1–201.

"Party". Section 1–201.

"Remedy". Section 1–201.

§ 2–611. Retraction of Anticipatory Repudiation.

(1) Until the repudiating party's next performance is due he can retract his repudiation unless the aggrieved party has since the repudiation cancelled or materially changed his position or otherwise indicated that he considers the repudiation final.

(2) Retraction may be by any method which clearly indicates to the aggrieved party that the repudiating party intends to perform, but must include any assurance justifiably demanded under the provisions of this Article (Section 2–609).

(3) Retraction reinstates the repudiating party's rights under the contract with due excuse and allowance to the aggrieved party for any delay occasioned by the repudiation.

Official Comment

. . .

Purposes: To make it clear that: . . .

2.   Under subsection (2) an effective retraction must be accompanied by any assurances demanded under the section dealing with right to adequate assurance. A repudiation is of course sufficient to give reasonable ground for insecurity and to warrant a request for assurance as an essential condition of the retraction. However, after a timely and unambiguous expression of retraction, a reasonable time for the assurance to be worked out should be allowed by the aggrieved party before cancellation.

. . .

Definitional Cross References:

"Aggrieved party". Section 1–201.

"Cancellation". Section 2–106.

"Contract". Section 1–201.

"Party". Section 1–201.

"Rights". Section 1–201.

§ 2–612.   "Installment Contract"; Breach.

(1)   An "installment contract" is one which requires or authorizes the delivery of goods in separate lots to be separately accepted, even though the contract contains a clause "each delivery is a separate contract" or its equivalent.

(2)   The buyer may reject any installment which is non-conforming if the non-conformity substantially impairs the value of that installment and cannot be cured or if the non-conformity is a defect in the required documents; but if the non-conformity does not fall within subsection (3) and the seller gives adequate assurance of its cure the buyer must accept that installment.

(3)   Whenever non-conformity or default with respect to one or more installments substantially impairs the value of the whole contract there is a breach of the whole. But the aggrieved party reinstates the contract if he accepts a non-conforming installment without seasonably notifying of cancellation or if he brings an action with respect only to past installments or demands performance as to future installments.

Official Comment

. . .

Purposes of Changes:

. . .

3.   This Article rejects any approach which gives clauses such as "each delivery is a separate contract" their legalistically literal effect. Such contracts nonetheless call for installment deliveries. Even where a clause speaks of "a separate contract for all purposes", a commercial reading of the language under the section on good faith and commercial standards requires that the singleness of the document and the negotiation, together with the sense of the situation, prevail over any uncommercial and legalistic interpretation.

4.   One of the requirements for rejection under subsection (2) is non-conformity substantially impairing the value of the installment in question. However, an installment agreement may require accurate conformity in quality as a condition to the right to acceptance if the need for such conformity is made clear either by express provision or by the circumstances. In such a case the effect of the agreement is to define explicitly what amounts to substantial impairment of value impossible to cure. A clause requiring accurate compliance as a condition to the right to acceptance must, however, have some basis in

reason, must avoid imposing hardship by surprise and is subject to waiver or to displacement by practical construction.

Substantial impairment of the value of an installment can turn not only on the quality of the goods but also on such factors as time, quantity, assortment, and the like. It must be judged in terms of the normal or specifically known purposes of the contract. . . .

5.   Under subsection (2) an installment delivery must be accepted if the non-conformity is curable and the seller gives adequate assurance of cure. Cure of non-conformity of an installment in the first instance can usually be afforded by an allowance against the price, or in the case of reasonable discrepancies in quantity either by a further delivery or a partial rejection. This Article requires reasonable action by a buyer in regard to discrepant delivery and good faith requires that the buyer make any reasonable minor outlay of time or money necessary to cure an overshipment by severing out an acceptable percentage thereof. The seller must take over a cure which involves any material burden; the buyer's obligation reaches only to cooperation. Adequate assurance for purposes of subsection (2) is measured by the same standards as under the section on right to adequate assurance of performance.

6.   Subsection (3) is designed to further the continuance of the contract in the absence of an overt cancellation. The question arising when an action is brought as to a single installment only is resolved by making such action waive the right to cancellation. This involves merely a defect in one or more installments, as contrasted with the situation where there is a true repudiation within the section on anticipatory repudiation. Whether the non-conformity in any given installment justifies cancellation as to the future depends, not on whether such non-conformity indicates an intent or likelihood that the future deliveries will also be defective, but whether the non-conformity substantially impairs the value of the whole contract. If only the seller's security in regard to future installments is impaired, he has the right to demand adequate assurances of proper future performance but has not an immediate right to cancel the entire contract. It is clear under this Article, however, that defects in prior installments are cumulative in effect, so that acceptance does not wash out the defect "waived." Prior policy is continued, putting the rule as to buyer's default on the same footing as that in regard to seller's default. . . .

. . .

Definitional Cross References:

"Action". Section 1–201.

"Aggrieved party". Section 1–201.

"Buyer". Section 2–103.

"Cancellation". Section 2–106.

"Conform". Section 2–106.

"Contract". Section 1–201.

"Lot". Section 2–105.

"Notifies". Section 1–201.

"Seasonably". Section 1–204.

"Seller". Section 2–103.

§ 2–613.   Casualty to Identified Goods.

Where the contract requires for its performance goods identified when the contract is made, and the goods suffer casualty without fault of either party before the risk of loss passes to the buyer, or in a proper case under a "no arrival, no sale" term (Section 2–324) then

    (a)   if the loss is total the contract is avoided; and

    (b)   if the loss is partial or the goods have so deteriorated as no longer to conform to the contract the buyer may nevertheless demand inspection and at his option either treat the contract as avoided or accept the goods with due allowance from the contract price for the deterioration or the deficiency in quantity but without further right against the seller.

Official Comment

. . .

Definitional Cross References:

"Buyer". Section 2–103.

"Conform". Section 2–106.

"Contract". Section 1–201.

"Fault". Section 1–201.

"Goods". Section 2–105.

"Party". Section 1–201.

"Rights". Section 1–201.

"Seller". Section 2–103.

§ 2–614.   Substituted Performance.

(1)   Where without fault of either party the agreed berthing, loading, or unloading facilities fail or an agreed type of carrier becomes unavailable or the agreed manner of delivery otherwise becomes commercially impracticable but a commercially reasonable substitute is available, such substitute performance must be tendered and accepted.

(2)   If the agreed means or manner of payment fails because of domestic or foreign governmental regulation, the seller may withhold or stop delivery unless the buyer provides a means or manner of payment which is commercially a substantial equivalent. If delivery has already been taken, payment by the means or in the manner provided by the regulation discharges the buyer's obligation unless the regulation is discriminatory, oppressive or predatory.

Official Comment

. . .

Purposes:

1.   Subsection (1) requires the tender of a commercially reasonable substituted performance where agreed to facilities have failed or become commercially impracticable. Under this Article, in the absence of specific agreement, the normal or usual facilities enter into the agreement either through the circumstances, usage of trade or prior course of dealing.

This section appears between Section 2–613 on casualty to identified goods and the next section on excuse by failure of presupposed conditions, both of which deal with excuse and complete avoidance of the contract where the occurrence or non-occurrence of a contingency which was a basic assumption of the contract makes the expected performance impossible. The distinction between the present section and those sections lies in whether the failure or impossibility of performance arises in connection with an incidental matter or goes to the very heart of the agreement. The differing lines of solution are contrasted in a comparison of International Paper Co. v. Rockefeller, 161 App.Div. 180, 146 N.Y.S. 371 (1914) and Meyer v. Sullivan, 40 Cal.App. 723, 181 P. 847 (1919). In the former case a contract for the sale of spruce to be cut from a particular tract of land was involved. When a fire destroyed the trees growing on that tract the seller was held excused since performance was impossible. In the latter case the contract called for delivery of wheat "f.o.b. Kosmos Steamer at Seattle." The war led to cancellation of that line's sailing schedule after space had been duly engaged and the buyer was held entitled to demand substituted delivery at the warehouse on the line's loading dock. Under this Article, of course, the seller would also be entitled, had the market gone the other way, to make a substituted tender in that manner.

There must, however, be a true commercial impracticability to excuse the agreed to performance and justify a substituted performance. When this is the case a reasonable substituted performance tendered by either party should excuse him from strict compliance with contract terms which do not go to the essence of the agreement.

. . .

Definitional Cross References:

"Buyer". Section 2–103.

"Fault". Section 1–201.

"Party". Section 1–201.

"Seller". Section 2–103.

§ 2–615. Excuse by Failure of Presupposed Conditions.

Except so far as a seller may have assumed a greater obligation and subject to the preceding section on substituted performance:

(a) Delay in delivery or non-delivery in whole or in part by a seller who complies with paragraphs (b) and (c) is not a breach of his duty under a contract for sale if performance as agreed has been made impracticable by the occurrence of a contingency the non-occurrence of which was a basic assumption on which the contract was made or by compliance in good faith with any applicable foreign or domestic governmental regulation or order whether or not it later proves to be invalid.

(b) Where the causes mentioned in paragraph (a) affect only a part of the seller's capacity to perform, he must allocate production and deliveries among his customers but may at his option include regular customers not then under contract as well as his own requirements for further manufacture. He may so allocate in any manner which is fair and reasonable.

(c) The seller must notify the buyer seasonably that there will be delay or non-delivery and, when allocation is required under paragraph (b), of the estimated quota thus made available for the buyer.

Official Comment

. . .

Purposes:

. . .

2. The present section deliberately refrains from any effort at an exhaustive expression of contingencies and is to be interpreted in all cases sought to be brought within its scope in terms of its underlying reason and purpose.

3. The first test for excuse under this Article in terms of basic assumption is a familiar one. The additional test of commercial impracticability (as contrasted with "impossibility," "frustration of performance" or "frustration of the venture") has been adopted in order to call attention to the commercial character of the criterion chosen by this Article.

4. Increased cost alone does not excuse performance unless the rise in cost is due to some unforeseen contingency which alters the essential nature of the performance. Neither is a rise or a collapse in the market in itself a justification, for that is exactly the type of business risk which business contracts made at fixed prices are intended to cover. But a severe shortage of raw materials or of supplies due to a contingency such as war, embargo, local crop failure, unforeseen shutdown of major sources of supply or the like, which either causes a marked increase in cost or altogether prevents the seller from securing supplies necessary to his performance, is within the contemplation of this section. . . .

5.   Where a particular source of supply is exclusive under the agreement and fails through casualty, the present section applies rather than the provision on destruction or deterioration of specific goods. The same holds true where a particular source of supply is shown by the circumstances to have been contemplated or assumed by the parties at the time of contracting. (See Davis Co. v. Hoffmann-LaRoche Chemical Works, 178 App.Div. 855, 166 N.Y.S. 179 (1917) and International Paper Co. v. Rockefeller, 161 App.Div. 180, 146 N.Y.S. 371 (1914).) There is no excuse under this section, however, unless the seller has employed all due measures to assure himself that his source will not fail. (See Canadian Industrial Alcohol Co., Ltd., v. Dunbar Molasses Co., 258 N.Y. 194, 179 N.E. 383, 80 A.L.R. 1173 (1932) and Washington Mfg. Co. v. Midland Lumber Co., 113 Wash. 593, 194 P. 777 (1921).)

In the case of failure of production by an agreed source for causes beyond the seller's control, the seller should, if possible, be excused since production by an agreed source is without more a basic assumption of the contract. Such excuse should not result in relieving the defaulting supplier from liability nor in dropping into the seller's lap an unearned bonus of damages over. The flexible adjustment machinery of this Article provides the solution under the provision on the obligation of good faith. A condition to his making good the claim of excuse is the turning over to the buyer of his rights against the defaulting source of supply to the extent of the buyer's contract in relation to which excuse is being claimed.

6.   In situations in which neither sense nor justice is served by either answer when the issue is posed in flat terms of "excuse" or "no excuse," adjustment under the various provisions of this Article is necessary, especially the sections on good faith, on insecurity and assurance and on the reading of all provisions in the light of their purposes, and the general policy of this Act to use equitable principles in furtherance of commercial standards and good faith.

7.   The failure of conditions which go to convenience or collateral values rather than to the commercial practicability of the main performance does not amount to a complete excuse. However, good faith and the reason of the present section and of the preceding one may properly be held to justify and even to require any needed delay involved in a good faith inquiry seeking a readjustment of the contract terms to meet the new conditions.

8.   The provisions of this section are made subject to assumption of greater liability by agreement and such agreement is to be found not only in the expressed terms of the contract but in the circumstances surrounding the contracting, in trade usage and the like. Thus the exemptions of this section do not apply when the contingency in question is sufficiently foreshadowed at the time of contracting to be included among the business risks which are fairly to be regarded as part of the dickered terms, either consciously or as a matter of reasonable, commercial interpretation from the circumstances. . . .

9.   The case of a farmer who has contracted to sell crops to be grown on designated land may be regarded as falling either within the section on casualty to identified goods or this section, and he may be excused, when there is a failure of the specific crop, either on the basis of the destruction of identified goods or because of the failure of a basic assumption of the contract.

Exemption of the buyer in the case of a "requirements" contract is covered by the "Output and Requirements" section both as to assumption and allocation of the relevant risks. But when a contract by a manufacturer to buy fuel or raw material makes no specific reference to a particular venture and no such reference may be drawn from the circumstances, commercial understanding views it as a general deal in the general market and not conditioned on any assumption of the continuing operation of the buyer's plant. Even when notice is given by the buyer that the supplies are needed to fill a specific contract of a normal commercial kind, commercial understanding does not see such a supply contract as conditioned on the continuance of the buyer's further contract for outlet. On the other hand, where the buyer's contract is in reasonable commercial understanding conditioned on a definite and specific venture or assumption as, for instance, a war procurement subcontract known to be based on a prime contract which is subject to termination, or a supply contract for a particular construction venture, the reason of the present section may well apply and entitle the buyer to the exemption.

10.   Following its basic policy of using commercial practicability as a test for excuse, this section recognizes as of equal significance either a foreign or domestic regulation and disregards any technical distinctions between "law," "regulation," "order" and the like. Nor does it make the present action of the seller depend upon the eventual judicial determination of the legality of the particular governmental action. The seller's good faith belief in the validity of the regulation is the test under this Article and the best

evidence of his good faith is the general commercial acceptance of the regulation. However, governmental interference cannot excuse unless it truly "supervenes" in such a manner as to be beyond the seller's assumption of risk. And any action by the party claiming excuse which causes or colludes in inducing the governmental action preventing his performance would be in breach of good faith and would destroy his exemption.

11.   An excused seller must fulfill his contract to the extent which the supervening contingency permits, and if the situation is such that his customers are generally affected he must take account of all in supplying one. Subsections (a) and (b), therefore, explicitly permit in any proration a fair and reasonable attention to the needs of regular customers who are probably relying on spot orders for supplies. Customers at different stages of the manufacturing process may be fairly treated by including the seller's manufacturing requirements. A fortiori, the seller may also take account of contracts later in date than the one in question. The fact that such spot orders may be closed at an advanced price causes no difficulty, since any allocation which exceeds normal past requirements will not be reasonable. However, good faith requires, when prices have advanced, that the seller exercise real care in making his allocations, and in case of doubt his contract customers should be favored and supplies prorated evenly among them regardless of price. Save for the extra care thus required by changes in the market, this section seeks to leave every reasonable business leeway to the seller.

      . . .

Definitional Cross References:

      "Between merchants". Section 2–104.

      "Buyer". Section 2–103.

      "Contract". Section 1–201.

      "Contract for sale". Section 2–106.

      "Good faith". Section 1–201.

      "Merchant". Section 2–104.

      "Notifies". Section 1–201.

      "Seasonably". Section 1–201.

      "Seller". Section 2–103.

§ 2–616.   Procedure on Notice Claiming Excuse.

(1)   Where the buyer receives notification of a material or indefinite delay or an allocation justified under the preceding section he may by written notification to the seller as to any delivery concerned, and where the prospective deficiency substantially impairs the value of the whole contract under the provisions of this Article relating to breach of installment contracts (Section 2–612), then also as to the whole,

(a)   terminate and thereby discharge any unexecuted portion of the contract; or

(b)   modify the contract by agreeing to take his available quota in substitution.

(2)   If after receipt of such notification from the seller the buyer fails so to modify the contract within a reasonable time not exceeding thirty days the contract lapses with respect to any deliveries affected.

(3)   The provisions of this section may not be negated by agreement except in so far as the seller has assumed a greater obligation under the preceding section.

Official Comment

. . .

Definitional Cross References:

"Buyer". Section 2–103.

"Contract". Section 1–201.

"Installment contract". Section 2–612.

"Notification". Section 1–201.

"Reasonable time". Section 1–204.

"Seller". Section 2–103.

"Termination". Section 2–106.

"Written". Section 1–201.

PART VII

REMEDIES

§ 2–701. Remedies for Breach of Collateral Contracts Not Impaired.

Remedies for breach of any obligation or promise collateral or ancillary to a contract for sale are not impaired by the provisions of this Article.

Official Comment

. . .

Definitional Cross References:

"Contract for sale". Section 2–106.

"Remedy". Section 1–201.

§ 2–702. Seller's Remedies on Discovery of Buyer's Insolvency.

(1) Where the seller discovers the buyer to be insolvent he may refuse delivery except for cash including payment for all goods theretofore delivered under the contract, and stop delivery under this Article (Section 2–705).

(2) Where the seller discovers that the buyer has received goods on credit while insolvent he may reclaim the goods upon demand made within ten days after the receipt, but if misrepresentation of solvency has been made to the particular seller in writing within three months before delivery the ten day limitation does not apply. Except as provided in this subsection the seller may not base a right to reclaim goods on the buyer's fraudulent or innocent misrepresentation of solvency or of intent to pay.

(3) The seller's right to reclaim under subsection (2) is subject to the rights of a buyer in ordinary course or other good faith purchaser under this Article (Section 2–403). Successful reclamation of goods excludes all other remedies with respect to them.

As amended in 1966.

Official Comment

. . .

Definitional Cross References:

"Buyer". Section 2–103.

"Buyer in ordinary course of business". Section 1–201.

"Contract". Section 1–201.

"Good faith". Section 1–201.

"Goods". Section 2–105.

"Insolvent". Section 1–201.

"Person". Section 1–201.

"Purchaser". Section 1–201.

"Receipt" of goods. Section 2–103.

"Remedy". Section 1–201.

"Rights". Section 1–201.

"Seller". Section 2–103.

"Writing". Section 1–201.

§ 2–703. Seller's Remedies in General.

Where the buyer wrongfully rejects or revokes acceptance of goods or fails to make a payment due on or before delivery or repudiates with respect to a part or the whole, then with respect to any goods directly affected and, if the breach is of the whole contract (Section 2–612), then also with respect to the whole undelivered balance, the aggrieved seller may

(a) withhold delivery of such goods;

(b) stop delivery by any bailee as hereafter provided (Section 2–705);

(c) proceed under the next section respecting goods still unidentified to the contract;

(d) resell and recover damages as hereafter provided (Section 2–706);

(e) recover damages for non-acceptance (Section 2–708) or in a proper case the price (Section 2–709);

(f) cancel.

Official Comment

. . .

Purposes:

1. This section is an index section which gathers together in one convenient place all of the various remedies open to a seller for any breach by the buyer. This Article rejects any doctrine of election of remedy as a fundamental policy and thus the remedies are essentially cumulative in nature and include all of the available remedies for breach. Whether the pursuit of one remedy bars another depends entirely on the facts of the individual case. . . .

4. It should also be noted that this Act requires its remedies to be liberally administered and provides that any right or obligation which it declares is enforceable by action unless a different effect is specifically prescribed (Section 1–106).

. . .

Definitional Cross References:

"Aggrieved party". Section 1–201.

"Buyer". Section 2–103.

"Cancellation". Section 2–106.

"Contract". Section 1–201.

"Goods". Section 2–105.

"Remedy". Section 1–201.

"Seller". Section 2–103.

§ 2–704. Seller's Right to Identify Goods to the Contract Notwithstanding Breach or to Salvage Unfinished Goods.

(1) An aggrieved seller under the preceding section may

(a) identify to the contract conforming goods not already identified if at the time he learned of the breach they are in his possession or control;

(b) treat as the subject of resale goods which have demonstrably been intended for the particular contract even though those goods are unfinished.

(2) Where the goods are unfinished an aggrieved seller may in the exercise of reasonable commercial judgment for the purposes of avoiding loss and of effective realization either complete the manufacture and wholly identify the goods to the contract or cease manufacture and resell for scrap or salvage value or proceed in any other reasonable manner.

Official Comment

. . .

Purposes of Changes:

1. This section gives an aggrieved seller the right at the time of breach to identify to the contract any conforming finished goods, regardless of their resalability, and to use reasonable judgment as to completing unfinished goods. It thus makes the goods available for resale under the resale section, the seller's primary remedy, and in the special case in which resale is not practicable, allows the action for the price which would then be necessary to give the seller the value of his contract.

2. Under this Article the seller is given express power to complete manufacture or procurement of goods for the contract unless the exercise of reasonable commercial judgment as to the facts as they appear at the time he learns of the breach makes it clear that such action will result in a material increase in damages. The burden is on the buyer to show the commercially unreasonable nature of the seller's action in completing manufacture.

. . .

Definitional Cross References:

"Aggrieved party". Section 1–201.

"Conforming". Section 2–106.

"Contract". Section 1–201.

"Delivery". Section 2–103.

"Goods". Section 2–105.

"Rights". Section 1–201.

"Seller". Section 2–103.

§ 2–705.   Seller's Stoppage of Delivery in Transit or Otherwise.

(1)   The seller may stop delivery of goods in the possession of a carrier or other bailee when he discovers the buyer to be insolvent (Section 2–702) and may stop delivery of carload, truckload, planeload or larger shipments of express or freight when the buyer repudiates or fails to make a payment due before delivery or if for any other reason the seller has a right to withhold or reclaim the goods.

(2)   As against such buyer the seller may stop delivery until

(a)   receipt of the goods by the buyer; or

(b)   acknowledgment to the buyer by any bailee of the goods except a carrier that the bailee holds the goods for the buyer; or

(c)   such acknowledgment to the buyer by a carrier by reshipment or as warehouseman; or

(d)   negotiation to the buyer of any negotiable document of title covering the goods.

(3)(a)   To stop delivery the seller must so notify as to enable the bailee by reasonable diligence to prevent delivery of the goods.

(b)   After such notification the bailee must hold and deliver the goods according to the directions of the seller but the seller is liable to the bailee for any ensuing charges or damages.

(c)   If a negotiable document of title has been issued for goods the bailee is not obliged to obey a notification to stop until surrender of the document.

(d)   A carrier who has issued a non-negotiable bill of lading is not obliged to obey a notification to stop received from a person other than the consignor.

Official Comment

. . .

Definitional Cross References:

"Buyer". Section 2–103.

"Contract for sale". Section 2–106.

"Document of title". Section 1–201.

"Goods". Section 2–105.

"Insolvent". Section 1–201.

"Notification". Section 1–201.

"Receipt" of goods. Section 2–103.

"Rights". Section 1–201.

"Seller". Section 2–103.

§ 2–706.   Seller's Resale Including Contract for Resale.

(1)   Under the conditions stated in Section 2–703 on seller's remedies, the seller may resell the goods concerned or the undelivered balance thereof. Where the resale is made in good faith and in a commercially reasonable manner the seller may recover the difference between the resale price and the contract price together with any incidental damages allowed under the provisions of this Article (Section 2–710), but less expenses saved in consequence of the buyer's breach.

(2)   Except as otherwise provided in subsection (3) or unless otherwise agreed resale may be at public or private sale including sale by way of one or more contracts to sell or of identification to an existing contract of the seller. Sale may be as a unit or in parcels and at any time and place and on

any terms but every aspect of the sale including the method, manner, time, place and terms must be commercially reasonable. The resale must be reasonably identified as referring to the broken contract, but it is not necessary that the goods be in existence or that any or all of them have been identified to the contract before the breach.

(3) Where the resale is at private sale the seller must give the buyer reasonable notification of his intention to resell.

(4) Where the resale is at public sale

(a) only identified goods can be sold except where there is a recognized market for a public sale of futures in goods of the kind; and

(b) it must be made at a usual place or market for public sale if one is reasonably available and except in the case of goods which are perishable or threaten to decline in value speedily the seller must give the buyer reasonable notice of the time and place of the resale; and

(c) if the goods are not to be within the view of those attending the sale the notification of sale must state the place where the goods are located and provide for their reasonable inspection by prospective bidders; and

(d) the seller may buy.

(5) A purchaser who buys in good faith at a resale takes the goods free of any rights of the original buyer even though the seller fails to comply with one or more of the requirements of this section.

(6) The seller is not accountable to the buyer for any profit made on any resale. A person in the position of a seller (Section 2–707) or a buyer who has rightfully rejected or justifiably revoked acceptance must account for any excess over the amount of his security interest, as hereinafter defined (subsection (3) of Section 2–711).

Official Comment

. . .

Purposes of Changes: To simplify the prior statutory provision and to make it clear that: . . .

2. In order to recover the damages prescribed in subsection (1) the seller must act "in good faith and in a commercially reasonable manner" in making the resale. . . . Failure to act properly under this section deprives the seller of the measure of damages here provided and relegates him to that provided in Section 2–708. . . .

3. If the seller complies with the prescribed standard of duty in making the resale, he may recover from the buyer the damages provided for in subsection (1). Evidence of market or current prices at any particular time or place is relevant only on the question of whether the seller acted in a commercially reasonable manner in making the resale. . . .

4. Subsection (2) frees the remedy of resale from legalistic restrictions and enables the seller to resell in accordance with reasonable commercial practices so as to realize as high a price as possible in the circumstances. By "public" sale is meant a sale by auction. A "private" sale may be effected by solicitation and negotiation conducted either directly or through a broker. In choosing between a public and private sale the character of the goods must be considered and relevant trade practices and usages must be observed.

. . .

Definitional Cross References:

"Buyer". Section 2–103.

"Contract". Section 1–201.

"Contract for sale". Section 2–106.

"Good faith". Section 2–103.

"Goods". Section 2–105.

"Merchant". Section 2–104.

"Notification". Section 1–201.

"Person in position of seller". Section 2–707.

"Purchase". Section 1–201.

"Rights". Section 1–201.

"Sale". Section 2–106.

"Security interest". Section 1–201.

"Seller". Section 2–103.

§ 2–707. "Person in the Position of a Seller".

(1) A "person in the position of a seller" includes as against a principal an agent who has paid or become responsible for the price of goods on behalf of his principal or anyone who otherwise holds a security interest or other right in goods similar to that of a seller.

(2) A person in the position of a seller may as provided in this Article withhold or stop delivery (Section 2–705) and resell (Section 2–706) and recover incidental damages (Section 2–710).

Official Comment

. . .

Definitional Cross References:

"Consignee". Section 7–102.

"Consignor". Section 7–102.

"Goods". Section 2–105.

"Security interest". Section 1–201.

"Seller". Section 2–103.

§ 2–708. Seller's Damages for Non-Acceptance or Repudiation.

(1) Subject to subsection (2) and to the provisions of this Article with respect to proof of market price (Section 2–723), the measure of damages for non-acceptance or repudiation by the buyer is the difference between the market price at the time and place for tender and the unpaid contract price together with any incidental damages provided in this Article (Section 2–710), but less expenses saved in consequence of the buyer's breach.

(2) If the measure of damages provided in subsection (1) is inadequate to put the seller in as good a position as performance would have done then the measure of damages is the profit (including reasonable overhead) which the seller would have made from full performance by the buyer, together with any incidental damages provided in this Article (Section 2–710), due allowance for costs reasonably incurred and due credit for payments or proceeds of resale.

Official Comment

. . .

Purposes of Changes: To make it clear that: . . .

2. The provision of this section permitting recovery of expected profit including reasonable overhead where the standard measure of damages is inadequate, together with the new requirement that price actions

may be sustained only where resale is impractical, are designed to eliminate the unfair and economically wasteful results arising under the older law when fixed price articles were involved. This section permits the recovery of lost profits in all appropriate cases, which would include all standard priced goods. The normal measure there would be list price less cost to the dealer or list price less manufacturing cost to the manufacturer. It is not necessary to a recovery of "profit" to show a history of earnings, especially if a new venture is involved.

. . .

Definitional Cross References:

"Buyer". Section 2–103.

"Contract". Section 1–201.

"Seller". Section 2–103.

§ 2–709.   Action for the Price.

(1) When the buyer fails to pay the price as it becomes due the seller may recover, together with any incidental damages under the next section, the price

(a) of goods accepted or of conforming goods lost or damaged within a commercially reasonable time after risk of their loss has passed to the buyer; and

(b) of goods identified to the contract if the seller is unable after reasonable effort to resell them at a reasonable price or the circumstances reasonably indicate that such effort will be unavailing.

(2) Where the seller sues for the price he must hold for the buyer any goods which have been identified to the contract and are still in his control except that if resale becomes possible he may resell them at any time prior to the collection of the judgment. The net proceeds of any such resale must be credited to the buyer and payment of the judgment entitles him to any goods not resold.

(3) After the buyer has wrongfully rejected or revoked acceptance of the goods or has failed to make a payment due or has repudiated (Section 2–610), a seller who is held not entitled to the price under this section shall nevertheless be awarded damages for non-acceptance under the preceding section.

Official Comment

. . .

Purposes of Changes: To make it clear that: . . .

2. The action for the price is now generally limited to those cases where resale of the goods is impracticable except where the buyer has accepted the goods or where they have been destroyed after risk of loss has passed to the buyer. . . .

6. This section is intended to be exhaustive in its enumeration of cases where an action for the price lies.

. . .

Definitional Cross References:

"Action". Section 1–201.

"Buyer". Section 2–103.

"Conforming". Section 2–106.

"Contract". Section 1–201.

"Goods". Section 2–105.

"Seller". Section 2–103.

§ 2–710. Seller's Incidental Damages.

Incidental damages to an aggrieved seller include any commercially reasonable charges, expenses or commissions incurred in stopping delivery, in the transportation, care and custody of goods after the buyer's breach, in connection with return or resale of the goods or otherwise resulting from the breach.

Official Comment

. . .

Definitional Cross References:

"Aggrieved party". Section 1–201.

"Buyer". Section 2–103.

"Goods". Section 2–105.

"Seller". Section 2–103.

§ 2–711. Buyer's Remedies in General; Buyer's Security Interest in Rejected Goods.

(1) Where the seller fails to make delivery or repudiates or the buyer rightfully rejects or justifiably revokes acceptance then with respect to any goods involved, and with respect to the whole if the breach goes to the whole contract (Section 2–612), the buyer may cancel and whether or not he has done so may in addition to recovering so much of the price as has been paid

(a) "cover" and have damages under the next section as to all the goods affected whether or not they have been identified to the contract; or

(b) recover damages for non-delivery as provided in this Article (Section 2–713).

(2) Where the seller fails to deliver or repudiates the buyer may also

(a) if the goods have been identified recover them as provided in this Article (Section 2–502); or

(b) in a proper case obtain specific performance or replevy the goods as provided in this Article (Section 2–716).

(3) On rightful rejection or justifiable revocation of acceptance a buyer has a security interest in goods in his possession or control for any payments made on their price and any expenses reasonably incurred in their inspection, receipt, transportation, care and custody and may hold such goods and resell them in like manner as an aggrieved seller (Section 2–706).

Official Comment

. . .

Purposes of Changes:

1. To index in this section the buyer's remedies, subsection (1) covering those remedies permitting the recovery of money damages, and subsection (2) covering those which permit reaching the goods themselves. The remedies listed here are those available to a buyer who has not accepted the goods or who has justifiably revoked his acceptance. The remedies available to a buyer with regard to goods finally accepted appear in [§ 2–714] dealing with breach in regard to accepted goods. . . .

3.   It should also be noted that this Act requires its remedies to be liberally administered and provides that any right or obligation which it declares is enforceable by action unless a different effect is specifically prescribed (Section 1–106).

. . .

Definitional Cross References:

"Aggrieved party". Section 1–201.

"Buyer". Section 2–103.

"Cancellation". Section 2–106.

"Contract". Section 1–201.

"Cover". Section 2–712.

"Goods". Section 2–105.

"Notifies". Section 1–201.

"Receipt" of goods. Section 2–103.

"Remedy". Section 1–201.

"Security interest". Section 1–201.

"Seller". Section 2–103.

§ 2–712.   "Cover"; Buyer's Procurement of Substitute Goods.

(1)   After a breach within the preceding section the buyer may "cover" by making in good faith and without unreasonable delay any reasonable purchase of or contract to purchase goods in substitution for those due from the seller.

(2)   The buyer may recover from the seller as damages the difference between the cost of cover and the contract price together with any incidental or consequential damages as hereinafter defined (Section 2–715), but less expenses saved in consequence of the seller's breach.

(3)   Failure of the buyer to effect cover within this section does not bar him from any other remedy.

Official Comment

. . .

Purposes:

1.   This section provides the buyer with a remedy aimed at enabling him to obtain the goods he needs thus meeting his essential need. This remedy is the buyer's equivalent of the seller's right to resell.

2.   The definition of "cover" under subsection (1) envisages a series of contracts or sales, as well as a single contract or sale; goods not identical with those involved but commercially usable as reasonable substitutes under the circumstances of the particular case; and contracts on credit or delivery terms differing from the contract in breach, but again reasonable under the circumstances. The test of proper cover is whether at the time and place the buyer acted in good faith and in a reasonable manner, and it is immaterial that hindsight may later prove that the method of cover used was not the cheapest or most effective.

The requirement that the buyer must cover "without unreasonable delay" is not intended to limit the time necessary for him to look around and decide as to how he may best effect cover. The test here is similar to that generally used in this Article as to reasonable time and seasonable action.

3.   Subsection (3) expresses the policy that cover is not a mandatory remedy for the buyer. The buyer is always free to choose between cover and damages for non-delivery under the next section.

However, this subsection must be read in conjunction with the section which limits the recovery of consequential damages to such as could not have been obviated by cover. . . .

4.   This section does not limit cover to merchants, in the first instance. It is the vital and important remedy for the consumer buyer as well. Both are free to use cover: the domestic or non-merchant consumer is required only to act in normal good faith while the merchant buyer must also observe all reasonable commercial standards of fair dealing in the trade, since this falls within the definition of good faith on his part.

. . .

Definitional Cross References:

"Buyer". Section 2–103.

"Contract". Section 1–201.

"Good faith". Section 2–103.

"Goods". Section 2–105.

"Purchase". Section 1–201.

"Remedy". Section 1–201.

"Seller". Section 2–103.

§ 2–713.   Buyer's Damages for Non-Delivery or Repudiation.

(1)   Subject to the provisions of this Article with respect to proof of market price (Section 2–723), the measure of damages for non-delivery or repudiation by the seller is the difference between the market price at the time when the buyer learned of the breach and the contract price together with any incidental and consequential damages provided in this Article (Section 2–715), but less expenses saved in consequence of the seller's breach.

(2)   Market price is to be determined as of the place for tender or, in cases of rejection after arrival or revocation of acceptance, as of the place of arrival.

Official Comment

. . .

Purposes of Changes: To clarify the former rule so that:

1.   The general baseline adopted in this section uses as a yardstick the market in which the buyer would have obtained cover had he sought that relief. So the place for measuring damages is the place of tender (or the place of arrival if the goods are rejected or their acceptance is revoked after reaching their destination) and the crucial time is the time at which the buyer learns of the breach.

2.   The market or current price to be used in comparison with the contract price under this section is the price for goods of the same kind and in the same branch of trade. . . .

5.   The present section provides a remedy which is completely alternative to cover under the preceding section and applies only when and to the extent that the buyer has not covered.

. . .

Definitional Cross References:

"Buyer". Section 2–103.

"Contract". Section 1–201.

"Seller". Section 2–103.

§ 2–714. Buyer's Damages for Breach in Regard to Accepted Goods.

(1)   Where the buyer has accepted goods and given notification (subsection (3) of Section 2–607) he may recover as damages for any non-conformity of tender the loss resulting in the ordinary course of events from the seller's breach as determined in any manner which is reasonable.

(2)   The measure of damages for breach of warranty is the difference at the time and place of acceptance between the value of the goods accepted and the value they would have had if they had been as warranted, unless special circumstances show proximate damages of a different amount.

(3)   In a proper case any incidental and consequential damages under the next section may also be recovered.

Official Comment

. . .

Definitional Cross References:

"Buyer". Section 2–103.

"Conform". Section 2–106.

"Goods". Section 1–201.

"Notification". Section 1–201.

"Seller". Section 2–103.

§ 2–715. Buyer's Incidental and Consequential Damages.

(1)   Incidental damages resulting from the seller's breach include expenses reasonably incurred in inspection, receipt, transportation and care and custody of goods rightfully rejected, any commercially reasonable charges, expenses or commissions in connection with effecting cover and any other reasonable expense incident to the delay or other breach.

(2)   Consequential damages resulting from the seller's breach include

(a)   any loss resulting from general or particular requirements and needs of which the seller at the time of contracting had reason to know and which could not reasonably be prevented by cover or otherwise; and

(b)   injury to person or property proximately resulting from any breach of warranty.

Official Comment

. . .

Purposes of Changes and New Matter:

1.   Subsection (1) is intended to provide reimbursement for the buyer who incurs reasonable expenses in connection with the handling of rightfully rejected goods or goods whose acceptance may be justifiably revoked, or in connection with effecting cover where the breach of the contract lies in non-conformity or non-delivery of the goods. The incidental damages listed are not intended to be exhaustive but are merely illustrative of the typical kinds of incidental damage.

2.   Subsection (2) operates to allow the buyer, in an appropriate case, any consequential damages which are the result of the seller's breach. The "tacit agreement" test for the recovery of consequential damages is rejected. Although the older rule at common law which made the seller liable for all consequential damages of which he had "reason to know" in advance is followed, the liberality of that rule is modified by refusing to permit recovery unless the buyer could not reasonably have prevented the loss by cover or otherwise. Subparagraph (2) carries forward the provisions of the prior uniform statutory provision as to consequential damages resulting from breach of warranty, but modifies the rule by requiring first that the buyer attempt to minimize his damages in good faith, either by cover or otherwise.

3.   In the absence of excuse under the section on merchant's excuse by failure of presupposed conditions, the seller is liable for consequential damages in all cases where he had reason to know of the buyer's general or particular requirements at the time of contracting. It is not necessary that there be a conscious acceptance of an insurer's liability on the seller's part, nor is his obligation for consequential damages limited to cases in which he fails to use due effort in good faith.

Particular needs of the buyer must generally be made known to the seller while general needs must rarely be made known to charge the seller with knowledge.

Any seller who does not wish to take the risk of consequential damages has available the section on contractual limitation of remedy.

4.   The burden of proving the extent of loss incurred by way of consequential damage is on the buyer, but the section on liberal administration of remedies rejects any doctrine of certainty which requires almost mathematical precision in the proof of loss. Loss may be determined in any manner which is reasonable under the circumstances.

5.   Subsection (2)(b) states the usual rule as to breach of warranty, allowing recovery for injuries "proximately" resulting from the breach. Where the injury involved follows the use of goods without discovery of the defect causing the damage, the question of "proximate" cause turns on whether it was reasonable for the buyer to use the goods without such inspection as would have revealed the defects. If it was not reasonable for him to do so, or if he did in fact discover the defect prior to his use, the injury would not proximately result from the breach of warranty. . . .

. . .

Definitional Cross References:

"Cover". Section 2–712.

"Goods". Section 1–201.

"Person". Section 1–201.

"Receipt" of goods. Section 2–103.

"Seller". Section 2–103.

§ 2–716. Buyer's Right to Specific Performance or Replevin.

(1)   Specific performance may be decreed where the goods are unique or in other proper circumstances.

(2)   The decree for specific performance may include such terms and conditions as to payment of the price, damages, or other relief as the court may deem just.

(3)   The buyer has a right of replevin for goods identified to the contract if after reasonable effort he is unable to effect cover for such goods or the circumstances reasonably indicate that such effort will be unavailing or if the goods have been shipped under reservation and satisfaction of the security interest in them has been made or tendered. In the case of goods bought for personal, family, or household purposes, the buyer's right of replevin vests upon acquisition of a special property, even if the seller had not then repudiated or failed to deliver.

Official Comment

. . .

Purposes of Changes: To make it clear that:

1.   The present section continues in general prior policy as to specific performance and injunction against breach. However, without intending to impair in any way the exercise of the court's sound discretion in the matter, this Article seeks to further a more liberal attitude than some courts have shown in connection with the specific performance of contracts of sale.

2.   In view of this Article's emphasis on the commercial feasibility of replacement, a new concept of what are "unique" goods is introduced under this section. Specific performance is no longer limited to goods which are already specific or ascertained at the time of contracting. The test of uniqueness under this section must be made in terms of the total situation which characterizes the contract. Output and requirements contracts involving a particular or peculiarly available source or market present today the typical commercial specific performance situation, as contrasted with contracts for the sale of heirlooms or priceless works of art which were usually involved in the older cases. However, uniqueness is not the sole basis of the remedy under this section for the relief may also be granted "in other proper circumstances" and inability to cover is strong evidence of "other proper circumstances".

3.   The legal remedy of replevin is given to the buyer in cases in which cover is reasonably unavailable and goods have been identified to the contract. This is in addition to the buyer's right to recover identified goods under Section 2–502. For consumer goods, the buyer's right to replevin vests upon the buyer's acquisition of a special property, which occurs upon identification of the goods to the contract. See Section 2–501. Inasmuch as a secured party normally acquires no greater rights in its collateral that its debtor had or had power to convey, see Section 2–403(1) (first sentence), a buyer who acquires a right of replevin under subsection (3) will take free of a security interest created by the seller if it attaches to the goods after the goods have been identified to the contract. The buyer will take free, even if the buyer does not buy in ordinary course and even if the security interest is perfected. Of course, to the extent that the buyer pays the price after the security interest attaches, the payments will constitute proceeds of the security interest.

4.   This section is intended to give the buyer rights to the goods comparable to the seller's rights to the price. . . .

. . .

Definitional Cross References:

"Buyer". Section 2–103.

"Goods". Section 1–201.

"Rights". Section 1–201.

§ 2–717. Deduction of Damages From the Price.

The buyer on notifying the seller of his intention to do so may deduct all or any part of the damages resulting from any breach of the contract from any part of the price still due under the same contract.

Official Comment

. . .

Purposes:

1.   This section permits the buyer to deduct from the price damages resulting from any breach by the seller and does not limit the relief to cases of breach of warranty as did the prior uniform statutory provision. To bring this provision into application the breach involved must be of the same contract under which the price in question is claimed to have been earned.

2.   The buyer, however, must give notice of his intention to withhold all or part of the price if he wishes to avoid a default within the meaning of the section on insecurity and right to assurances. In conformity with the general policies of this Article, no formality of notice is required and any language which reasonably indicates the buyer's reason for holding up his payment is sufficient.

. . .

Definitional Cross References:

"Buyer". Section 2–103.

"Notifies". Section 1–201.

§ 2–718.   Liquidation or Limitation of Damages; Deposits.

(1)   Damages for breach by either party may be liquidated in the agreement but only at an amount which is reasonable in the light of the anticipated or actual harm caused by the breach, the difficulties of proof of loss, and the inconvenience or nonfeasibility of otherwise obtaining an adequate remedy. A term fixing unreasonably large liquidated damages is void as a penalty.

(2)   Where the seller justifiably withholds delivery of goods because of the buyer's breach, the buyer is entitled to restitution of any amount by which the sum of his payments exceeds

(a)   the amount to which the seller is entitled by virtue of terms liquidating the seller's damages in accordance with subsection (1), or

(b)   in the absence of such terms, twenty per cent of the value of the total performance for which the buyer is obligated under the contract or $500, whichever is smaller.

(3)   The buyer's right to restitution under subsection (2) is subject to offset to the extent that the seller establishes

(a)   a right to recover damages under the provisions of this Article other than subsection (1), and

(b)   the amount or value of any benefits received by the buyer directly or indirectly by reason of the contract.

(4)   Where a seller has received payment in goods their reasonable value or the proceeds of their resale shall be treated as payments for the purposes of subsection (2); but if the seller has notice of the buyer's breach before reselling goods received in part performance, his resale is subject to the conditions laid down in this Article on resale by an aggrieved seller (Section 2–706).

Official Comment

. . .

Purposes:

1.   Under subsection (1) liquidated damage clauses are allowed where the amount involved is reasonable in the light of the circumstances of the case. The subsection sets forth explicitly the elements to be considered in determining the reasonableness of a liquidated damage clause. A term fixing unreasonably large liquidated damages is expressly made void as a penalty. An unreasonably small amount would be subject to similar criticism and might be stricken under the section on unconscionable contracts or clauses.

2.   Subsection (2) refuses to recognize a forfeiture unless the amount of the payment so forfeited represents a reasonable liquidation of damages as determined under subsection (1). A special exception is made in the case of small amounts (20% of the price or $500, whichever is smaller) deposited as security. No distinction is made between cases in which the payment is to be applied on the price and those in which it is intended as security for performance. Subsection (2) is applicable to any deposit or down or part payment. In the case of a deposit or [trade] in of goods resold before the breach, the amount actually received on the resale is to be viewed as the deposit rather than the amount allowed the buyer for the trade in. However, if the seller knows of the breach prior to the resale of the goods [traded] in, he must make reasonable efforts to realize their true value, and this is assured by requiring him to comply with the conditions laid down in the section on resale by an aggrieved seller.

Definitional Cross References:

"Aggrieved party". Section 1–201.

"Agreement". Section 1–201.

"Buyer". Section 2–103.

"Goods". Section 2–105.

"Notice". Section 1–201.

"Party". Section 1–201.

"Remedy". Section 1–201.

"Seller". Section 2–103.

"Term". Section 1–201.

§ 2–719. Contractual Modification or Limitation of Remedy.

(1) Subject to the provisions of subsections (2) and (3) of this section and of the preceding section on liquidation and limitation of damages,

    (a) the agreement may provide for remedies in addition to or in substitution for those provided in this Article and may limit or alter the measure of damages recoverable under this Article, as by limiting the buyer's remedies to return of the goods and repayment of the price or to repair and replacement of non-conforming goods or parts; and

    (b) resort to a remedy as provided is optional unless the remedy is expressly agreed to be exclusive, in which case it is the sole remedy.

(2) Where circumstances cause an exclusive or limited remedy to fail of its essential purpose, remedy may be had as provided in this Act.

(3) Consequential damages may be limited or excluded unless the limitation or exclusion is unconscionable. Limitation of consequential damages for injury to the person in the case of consumer goods is prima facie unconscionable but limitation of damages where the loss is commercial is not.

Official Comment

. . .

Purposes:

1. Under this section parties are left free to shape their remedies to their particular requirements and reasonable agreements limiting or modifying remedies are to be given effect.

However, it is of the very essence of a sales contract that at least minimum adequate remedies be available. If the parties intend to conclude a contract for sale within this Article they must accept the legal consequence that there be at least a fair quantum of remedy for breach of the obligations or duties outlined in the contract. Thus any clause purporting to modify or limit the remedial provisions of this Article in an unconscionable manner is subject to deletion and in that event the remedies made available by this Article are applicable as if the stricken clause had never existed. Similarly, under subsection (2), where an apparently fair and reasonable clause because of circumstances fails in its purpose or operates to deprive either party of the substantial value of the bargain, it must give way to the general remedy provisions of this Article.

2. Subsection (1)(b) creates a presumption that clauses prescribing remedies are cumulative rather than exclusive. If the parties intend the term to describe the sole remedy under the contract, this must be clearly expressed.

3. Subsection (3) recognizes the validity of clauses limiting or excluding consequential damages but makes it clear that they may not operate in an unconscionable manner. Actually such terms are merely an allocation of unknown or undeterminable risks. The seller in all cases is free to disclaim warranties in the manner provided in Section 2–316.

. . .

Definitional Cross References:

"Agreement". Section 1–201.

"Buyer". Section 2–103.

"Conforming". Section 2–106.

"Contract". Section 1–201.

"Goods". Section 2–105.

"Remedy". Section 1–201.

"Seller". Section 2–103.

§ 2–720.   Effect of "Cancellation" or "Rescission" on Claims for Antecedent Breach.

Unless the contrary intention clearly appears, expressions of "cancellation" or "rescission" of the contract or the like shall not be construed as a renunciation or discharge of any claim in damages for an antecedent breach.

Official Comment

. . .

Definitional Cross References:

"Cancellation". Section 2–106.

"Contract". Section 1–201.

§ 2–721.   Remedies for Fraud.

Remedies for material misrepresentation or fraud include all remedies available under this Article for non-fraudulent breach. Neither rescission or a claim for rescission of the contract for sale nor rejection or return of the goods shall bar or be deemed inconsistent with a claim for damages or other remedy.

Official Comment

. . .

Definitional Cross References:

"Contract for sale". Section 2–106.

"Goods". Section 1–201.

"Remedy". Section 1–201.

§ 2–722.   Who Can Sue Third Parties for Injury to Goods.

Where a third party so deals with goods which have been identified to a contract for sale as to cause actionable injury to a party to that contract

(a) a right of action against the third party is in either party to the contract for sale who has title to or a security interest or a special property or an insurable interest in the goods; and if the goods have been destroyed or converted a right of action is also in the party who either bore the risk of loss under the contract for sale or has since the injury assumed that risk as against the other;

(b) if at the time of the injury the party plaintiff did not bear the risk of loss as against the other party to the contract for sale and there is no arrangement between them for disposition of the recovery, his suit or settlement is, subject to his own interest, as a fiduciary for the other party to the contract;

(c) either party may with the consent of the other sue for the benefit of whom it may concern.

Official Comment

. . .

Definitional Cross References:

"Action". Section 1–201.

"Buyer". Section 2–103.

"Contract for sale". Section 2–106.

"Goods". Section 2–105.

"Party". Section 1–201.

"Rights". Section 1–201.

"Security interest". Section 1–201.

§ 2–723. Proof of Market Price: Time and Place.

(1) If an action based on anticipatory repudiation comes to trial before the time for performance with respect to some or all of the goods, any damages based on market price (Section 2–708 or Section 2–713) shall be determined according to the price of such goods prevailing at the time when the aggrieved party learned of the repudiation.

(2) If evidence of a price prevailing at the times or places described in this Article is not readily available the price prevailing within any reasonable time before or after the time described or at any other place which in commercial judgment or under usage of trade would serve as a reasonable substitute for the one described may be used, making any proper allowance for the cost of transporting the goods to or from such other place.

(3) Evidence of a relevant price prevailing at a time or place other than the one described in this Article offered by one party is not admissible unless and until he has given the other party such notice as the court finds sufficient to prevent unfair surprise.

Official Comment

. . .

Purposes: To eliminate the most obvious difficulties arising in connection with the determination of market price, when that is stipulated as a measure of damages by some provision of this Article. Where the appropriate market price is not readily available the court is here granted reasonable leeway in receiving evidence of prices current in other comparable markets or at other times comparable to the one in question. In accordance with the general principle of this Article against surprise, however, a party intending to offer evidence of such a substitute price must give suitable notice to the other party.

This section is not intended to exclude the use of any other reasonable method of determining market price or of measuring damages if the circumstances of the case make this necessary.

Definitional Cross References:

"Action". Section 1–201.

"Aggrieved party". Section 1–201.

"Goods". Section 2–105.

"Notifies". Section 1–201.

"Party". Section 1–201.

"Reasonable time". Section 1–204.

"Usage of trade". Section 1–205.

§ 2–724. Admissibility of Market Quotations.

Whenever the prevailing price or value of any goods regularly bought and sold in any established commodity market is in issue, reports in official publications or trade journals or in newspapers or periodicals of general circulation published as the reports of such market shall be admissible in evidence. The circumstances of the preparation of such a report may be shown to affect its weight but not its admissibility.

Official Comment

. . .

Definitional Cross Reference:

"Goods". Section 2–105.

§ 2–725. Statute of Limitations in Contracts for Sale.

(1) An action for breach of any contract for sale must be commenced within four years after the cause of action has accrued. By the original agreement the parties may reduce the period of limitation to not less than one year but may not extend it.

(2) A cause of action accrues when the breach occurs, regardless of the aggrieved party's lack of knowledge of the breach. A breach of warranty occurs when tender of delivery is made, except that where a warranty explicitly extends to future performance of the goods and discovery of the breach must await the time of such performance the cause of action accrues when the breach is or should have been discovered.

(3) Where an action commenced within the time limited by subsection (1) is so terminated as to leave available a remedy by another action for the same breach such other action may be commenced after the expiration of the time limited and within six months after the termination of the first action unless the termination resulted from voluntary discontinuance or from dismissal for failure or neglect to prosecute.

(4) This section does not alter the law on tolling of the statute of limitations nor does it apply to causes of action which have accrued before this Act becomes effective.

Official Comment

. . .

Definitional Cross References:

"Action". Section 1–201.

"Aggrieved party". Section 1–201.

"Agreement". Section 1–201.

"Contract for sale". Section 2–106.

"Goods". Section 2–105.

"Party". Section 1–201.

"Remedy". Section 1–201.

"Term". Section 1–201.

"Termination". Section 2–106.

ARTICLE 3

COMMERCIAL PAPER

(Excerpts)

PART I. SHORT TITLE, FORM AND INTERPRETATION

PART I

SHORT TITLE, FORM AND INTERPRETATION

§ 3–103. Definitions.

(a)   In this Article

. . .

(4)   "Good faith" means honesty in fact and the observance of reasonable commercial standards of fair dealing. . . .

§ 3–104. Negotiable Instrument.

(a)   Except as provided in subsections (c) and (d), "negotiable instrument" means an unconditional promise or order to pay a fixed amount of money, with or without interest or other charges described in the promise or order, if it:

(1)   is payable to bearer or to order at the time it is issued or first comes into possession of a holder;

(2)   is payable on demand or at a definite time; and

(3)   does not state any other undertaking or instruction by the person promising or ordering payment to do any act in addition to the payment of money, but the promise or order may contain (i) an undertaking or power to give, maintain, or protect collateral to secure payment, (ii) an authorization or power to the holder to confess judgment or realize on or dispose of collateral, or (iii) a waiver of the benefit of any law intended for the advantage or protection of an obligor.

(b)   "Instrument" means a negotiable instrument.

(c)   An order that meets all of the requirements of subsection (a), except paragraph (1), and otherwise falls within the definition of "check" in subsection (f) is a negotiable instrument and a check.

107

(d)   A promise or order other than a check is not an instrument if, at the time it is issued or first comes into possession of a holder, it contains a conspicuous statement, however expressed, to the effect that the promise or order is not negotiable or is not an instrument governed by this Article. . . .

§ 3–106.   Unconditional Promise or Order.

(a)   Except as provided in this section, for the purposes of Section 3–104(a), a promise or order is unconditional unless it states (i) an express condition to payment, (ii) that the promise or order is subject to or governed by another writing, or (iii) that rights or obligations with respect to the promise or order are stated in another writing. A reference to another writing does not of itself make the promise or order conditional.

(b)   A promise or order is not made conditional (i) by a reference to another writing for a statement of rights with respect to collateral, prepayment, or acceleration, or (ii) because payment is limited to resort to a particular fund or source.

(c)   If a promise or order requires, as a condition to payment, a countersignature by a person whose specimen signature appears on the promise or order, the condition does not make the promise or order conditional for the purposes of Section 3–104(a). If the person whose specimen signature appears on an instrument fails to countersign the instrument, the failure to countersign is a defense to the obligation of the issuer, but the failure does not prevent a transferee of the instrument from becoming a holder of the instrument.

(d)   If a promise or order at the time it is issued or first comes into possession of a holder contains a statement, required by applicable statutory or administrative law, to the effect that the rights of a holder or transferee are subject to claims or defenses that the issuer could assert against the original payee, the promise or order is not thereby made conditional for the purposes of Section 3–104(a); but if the promise or order is an instrument, there cannot be a holder in due course of the instrument.

§ 3–201.   Negotiation.

(a)   "Negotiation" means a transfer of possession, whether voluntary or involuntary, of an instrument by a person other than the issuer to a person who thereby becomes its holder.

(b)   Except for negotiation by a remitter, if an instrument is payable to an identified person, negotiation requires transfer of possession of the instrument and its indorsement by the holder. If an instrument is payable to bearer, it may be negotiated by transfer of possession alone.

§ 3–302.   Holder in Due Course.

(a)   Subject to subsection (c) and Section 3–106(d), "holder in due course" means the holder of an instrument if:

(1)   the instrument when issued or negotiated to the holder does not bear such apparent evidence of forgery or alteration or is not otherwise so irregular or incomplete as to call into question its authenticity; and

(2)   the holder took the instrument (i) for value, (ii) in good faith, (iii) without notice that the instrument is overdue or has been dishonored or that there is an uncured default with respect to payment of another instrument issued as part of the same series, (iv) without notice that the instrument contains an unauthorized signature or has been altered, (v) without notice of any claim to the instrument described in Section 3–306, and (vi) without notice that any party has a defense or claim in recoupment described in Section 3–305(a).

(b)   Notice of discharge of a party, other than discharge in an insolvency proceeding, is not notice of a defense under subsection (a), but discharge is effective against a person who became a holder in due course with notice of the discharge. Public filing or recording of a document does not of itself constitute notice of a defense, claim in recoupment, or claim to the instrument.

(c) Except to the extent a transferor or predecessor in interest has rights as a holder in due course, a person does not acquire rights of a holder in due course of an instrument taken (i) by legal process or by purchase in an execution, bankruptcy, or creditor's sale or similar proceeding, (ii) by purchase as part of a bulk transaction not in ordinary course of business of the transferor, or (iii) as the successor in interest to an estate or other organization.

(d) If, under Section 3–303(a)(1), the promise of performance that is the consideration for an instrument has been partially performed, the holder may assert rights as a holder in due course of the instrument only to the fraction of the amount payable under the instrument equal to the value of the partial performance divided by the value of the promised performance.

(e) If (i) the person entitled to enforce an instrument has only a security interest in the instrument and (ii) the person obliged to pay the instrument has a defense, claim in recoupment, or claim to the instrument that may be asserted against the person who granted the security interest, the person entitled to enforce the instrument may assert rights as a holder in due course only to an amount payable under the instrument which, at the time of enforcement of the instrument, does not exceed the amount of the unpaid obligation secured.

(f) To be effective, notice must be received at a time and in a manner that gives a reasonable opportunity to act on it.

(g) This section is subject to any law limiting status as a holder in due course in particular classes of transactions.

§ 3–303. Value and Consideration.

(a) An instrument is issued or transferred for value if:

(1) the instrument is issued or transferred for a promise of performance, to the extent the promise has been performed;

(2) the transferee acquires a security interest or other lien in the instrument other than a lien obtained by judicial proceeding;

(3) the instrument is issued or transferred as payment of, or as security for, an antecedent claim against any person, whether or not the claim is due;

(4) the instrument is issued or transferred in exchange for a negotiable instrument; or

(5) the instrument is issued or transferred in exchange for the incurring of an irrevocable obligation to a third party by the person taking the instrument.

(b) "Consideration" means any consideration sufficient to support a simple contract. The drawer or maker of an instrument has a defense if the instrument is issued without consideration. If an instrument is issued for a promise of performance, the issuer has a defense to the extent performance of the promise is due and the promise has not been performed. If an instrument is issued for value as stated in subsection (a), the instrument is also issued for consideration.

§ 3–305. Defenses and Claims in Recoupment.

(a) Except as stated in subsection (b), the right to enforce the obligation of a party to pay an instrument is subject to the following:

(1) a defense of the obligor based on (i) infancy of the obligor to the extent it is a defense to a simple contract, (ii) duress, lack of legal capacity, or illegality of the transaction which, under other law, nullifies the obligation of the obligor, (iii) fraud that induced the obligor to sign the instrument with neither knowledge nor reasonable opportunity to learn of its character or its essential terms, or (iv) discharge of the obligor in insolvency proceedings;

(2) a defense of the obligor stated in another section of this Article or a defense of the obligor that would be available if the person entitled to enforce the instrument were enforcing a right to payment under a simple contract; and

(3) a claim in recoupment of the obligor against the original payee of the instrument if the claim arose from the transaction that gave rise to the instrument; but the claim of the obligor may be asserted against a transferee of the instrument only to reduce the amount owing on the instrument at the time the action is brought.

(b) The right of a holder in due course to enforce the obligation of a party to pay the instrument is subject to defenses of the obligor stated in subsection (a)(1), but is not subject to defenses of the obligor stated in subsection (a)(2) or claims in recoupment stated in subsection (a)(3) against a person other than the holder.

(c) Except as stated in subsection (d), in an action to enforce the obligation of a party to pay the instrument, the obligor may not assert against the person entitled to enforce the instrument a defense, claim in recoupment, or claim to the instrument (Section 3–306) of another person, but the other person's claim to the instrument may be asserted by the obligor if the other person is joined in the action and personally asserts the claim against the person entitled to enforce the instrument. An obligor is not obliged to pay the instrument if the person seeking enforcement of the instrument does not have rights of a holder in due course and the obligor proves that the instrument is a lost or stolen instrument.

(d) In an action to enforce the obligation of an accommodation party to pay an instrument, the accommodation party may assert against the person entitled to enforce the instrument any defense or claim in recoupment under subsection (a) that the accommodated party could assert against the person entitled to enforce the instrument, except the defenses of discharge in insolvency proceedings, infancy, and lack of legal capacity.

§ 3–311. Accord and Satisfaction by Use of Instrument.

(a) If a person against whom a claim is asserted proves that (i) that person in good faith tendered an instrument to the claimant as full satisfaction of the claim, (ii) the amount of the claim was unliquidated or subject to a bona fide dispute, and (iii) the claimant obtained payment of the instrument, the following subsections apply.

(b) Unless subsection (c) applies, the claim is discharged if the person against whom the claim is asserted proves that the instrument or an accompanying written communication contained a conspicuous statement to the effect that the instrument was tendered as full satisfaction of the claim.

(c) Subject to subsection (d), a claim is not discharged under subsection (b) if either of the following applies:

(1) The claimant, if an organization, proves that (i) within a reasonable time before the tender, the claimant sent a conspicuous statement to the person against whom the claim is asserted that communications concerning disputed debts, including an instrument tendered as full satisfaction of a debt, are to be sent to a designated person, office, or place, and (ii) the instrument or accompanying communication was not received by that designated person, office, or place.

(2) The claimant, whether or not an organization, proves that within 90 days after payment of the instrument, the claimant tendered repayment of the amount of the instrument to the person against whom the claim is asserted. This paragraph does not apply if the claimant is an organization that sent a statement complying with paragraph (1)(i).

(d) A claim is discharged if the person against whom the claim is asserted proves that within a reasonable time before collection of the instrument was initiated, the claimant, or an agent of the claimant having direct responsibility with respect to the disputed obligation, knew that the instrument was tendered in full satisfaction of the claim.

Official Comment

. . .

3.   As part of the revision of Article 3, Section 1–207 has been amended to add subsection (2) stating that Section 1–207 "does not apply to an accord and satisfaction." Because of that amendment and revised Article 3, Section 3–311 governs full satisfaction checks. Section 3–311 follows the common law rule with some minor variations to reflect modern business conditions. . . .

4.   Subsection (a) states three requirements for application of Section 3–311. "Good faith" in subsection (a)(i) is defined in Section 3–103(a)(4) as not only honesty in fact, but the observance of reasonable commercial standards of fair dealing. The meaning of "fair dealing" will depend upon the facts in the particular case. For example, suppose an insurer tenders a check in settlement of a claim for personal injury in an accident clearly covered by the insurance policy. The claimant is necessitous and the amount of the check is very small in relationship to the extent of the injury and the amount recoverable under the policy. If the trier of fact determines that the insurer was taking unfair advantage of the claimant, an accord and satisfaction would not result from payment of the check because of the absence of good faith by the insurer in making the tender. Another example of lack of good faith is found in the practice of some business debtors in routinely printing full satisfaction language on their check stocks so that all or a large part of the debts of the debtor are paid by checks bearing the full satisfaction language, whether or not there is any dispute with the creditor. Under such a practice the claimant cannot be sure whether a tender in full satisfaction is or is not being made. Use of a check on which full satisfaction language was affixed routinely pursuant to such a business practice may prevent an accord and satisfaction on the ground that the check was not tendered in good faith under subsection (a)(i).

Section 3–311 does not apply to cases in which the debt is a liquidated amount and not subject to a bona fide dispute. Subsection (a)(ii). Other law applies to cases in which a debtor is seeking discharge of such a debt by paying less than the amount owed. For the purpose of subsection (a)(iii) obtaining acceptance of a check is considered to be obtaining payment of the check. . . .

5.   Subsection (c)(1) is a limitation on subsection (b) in cases in which the claimant is an organization. It is designed to protect the claimant against inadvertent accord and satisfaction. If the claimant is an organization payment of the check might be obtained without notice to the personnel of the organization concerned with the disputed claim. Some business organizations have claims against very large numbers of customers. Examples are department stores, public utilities and the like. These claims are normally paid by checks sent by customers to a designated office at which clerks employed by the claimant or a bank acting for the claimant process the checks and record the amounts paid. If the processing office is not designed to deal with communications extraneous to recording the amount of the check and the account number of the customer, payment of a full satisfaction check can easily be obtained without knowledge by the claimant of the existence of the full satisfaction statement. This is particularly true if the statement is written on the reverse side of the check in the area in which indorsements are usually written. Normally, the clerks of the claimant have no reason to look at the reverse side of checks. Indorsement by the claimant normally is done by mechanical means or there may be no indorsement at all. . . . Subsection (c)(1) allows the claimant to protect itself by advising customers by a conspicuous statement that communications regarding disputed debts must be sent to a particular person, office, or place. The statement must be given to the customer within a reasonable time before the tender is made. This requirement is designed to assure that the customer has reasonable notice that the full satisfaction check must be sent to a particular place. The reasonable time requirement could be satisfied by a notice on the billing statement sent to the customer. If the full satisfaction check is sent to the designated destination and the check is paid, the claim is discharged. If the claimant proves that the check was not received at the designated destination the claim is not discharged unless subsection (d) applies.

6.   Subsection (c)(2) is also designed to prevent inadvertent accord and satisfaction. It can be used by a claimant other than an organization or by a claimant as an alternative to subsection (c)(1). Some organizations may be reluctant to use subsection (c)(1) because it may result in confusion of customers that causes checks to be routinely sent to the special designated person, office, or place. Thus, much of the benefit of rapid processing of checks may be lost. An organization that chooses not to send a notice complying with subsection (c)(1)(i) may prevent an inadvertent accord and satisfaction by complying with subsection (c)(2). If the claimant discovers that it has obtained payment of a full satisfaction check, it may prevent an accord

and satisfaction if, within 90 days of the payment of the check, the claimant tenders repayment of the amount of the check to the person against whom the claim is asserted.

7.   Subsection (c) is subject to subsection (d). If a person against whom a claim is asserted proves that the claimant obtained payment of a check known to have been tendered in full satisfaction of the claim by "the claimant or an agent of the claimant having direct responsibility with respect to the disputed obligation," the claim is discharged even if (i) the check was not sent to the person, office, or place required by a notice complying with subsection (c)(1), or (ii) the claimant tendered repayment of the amount of the check in compliance with subsection (c)(2). . . .

ARTICLE 9

SECURED TRANSACTIONS*

(2000)

PART 1. GENERAL PROVISIONS

[SUBPART 1. SHORT TITLE, DEFINITIONS, AND GENERAL CONCEPTS]

PART 2. EFFECTIVENESS OF SECURITY AGREEMENT; ATTACHMENT OF SECURITY INTEREST; RIGHTS OF PARTIES TO SECURITY AGREEMENT

[SUBPART 2. EFFECTIVENESS AND ATTACHMENT]

PART 3. PERFECTION AND PRIORITY

[SUBPART 2. PERFECTION]

[SUBPART 3. PRIORITY]

---

*   Article 9 has been adopted by all 50 states in its 2000 version, excerpts from which are set forth here. In 2010, however, the Uniform Law Commission adopted some amendments. The states are expected to enact these amendments within a few years and the version of Article 9 set forth in this pamphlet includes those amendments. Most of the cases decided under Article 9 were decided under a pre-2000 version of the Article. For this reason, Part II of this pamphlet contains excerpts from that version.

PART 1

GENERAL PROVISION

[SUBPART 1. SHORT TITLE, DEFINITIONS, AND GENERAL CONCEPTS]

§ 9–101.   Short Title.

This article may be cited as Uniform Commercial Code—Secured Transactions.

§ 9–102.   Definitions and Index of Definitions.

(a)   **[Article 9 definitions.]** In this article:

(1)   "Accession" means goods that are physically united with other goods in such a manner that the identity of the original goods is not lost.

(2)   "Account", except as used in "account for", means a right to payment of a monetary obligation, whether or not earned by performance, (i) for property that has been or is to be sold, leased, licensed, assigned, or otherwise disposed of, (ii) for services rendered or to be rendered, (iii) for a policy of insurance issued or to be issued, (iv) for a secondary obligation incurred or to be incurred, (v) for energy provided or to be provided, (vi) for the use or hire of a vessel under a charter or other contract, (vii) arising out of the use of a credit or charge card or information contained on or for use with the card, or (viii) as winnings in a lottery or other game of chance operated or sponsored by a State, governmental unit of a State, or person licensed or authorized to operate the game by a State or governmental unit of a State. The term includes health-care-insurance receivables. The term does not include (i) rights to payment evidenced by chattel paper or an instrument, (ii) commercial tort claims, (iii) deposit accounts, (iv) investment property, (v) letter-of-credit rights or letters of credit, or (vi) rights to payment for money or funds advanced or sold, other than rights arising out of the use of a credit or charge card or information contained on or for use with the card.

(3)   "Account debtor" means a person obligated on an account, chattel paper, or general intangible. The term does not include persons obligated to pay a negotiable instrument, even if the instrument constitutes part of chattel paper. . . .

(7)   "Authenticate" means:

(A)   to sign; or

(B)   with present intent to adopt or accept a record, to attach to or logically associate with the record an electronic sound, symbol, or process. . . .

(11)   "Chattel paper" means a record or records that evidence both a monetary obligation and a security interest in specific goods, a security interest in specific goods and software used in the goods, a lease of specific goods, or a lease of specific goods and license of software used in the

goods. In this paragraph, "monetary obligation" means a monetary obligation secured by the goods or owed under a lease of the goods and includes a monetary obligation with respect to software used in the goods. The term does not include charters or other contracts involving the use or hire of a vessel. If a transaction is evidenced by records that include an instrument or series of instruments, the group of records taken together constitutes chattel paper.

(12) "Collateral" means the property subject to a security interest or agricultural lien. The term includes:

(A) proceeds to which a security interest attaches;

(B) accounts, chattel paper, payment intangibles, and promissory notes that have been sold; and

(C) goods that are the subject of a consignment.

(13) "Commercial tort claim" means a claim arising in tort with respect to which:

(A) the claimant is an organization; or

(B) the claimant is an individual and the claim:

(i) arose in the course of the claimant's business or profession; and

(ii) does not include damages arising out of personal injury to or the death of an individual.

(14) "Commodity account" means an account maintained by a commodity intermediary in which a commodity contract is carried for a commodity customer. . . .

(15) "Commodity contract" means a commodity futures contract, an option on a commodity futures contract, a commodity option, or another contract if the contract or option is:

(A) traded on or subject to the rules of a board of trade that has been designated as a contract market for such a contract pursuant to federal commodities laws; or

(B) traded on a foreign commodity board of trade, exchange, or market, and is carried on the books of a commodity intermediary for a commodity customer. . . .

(22) "Consumer debtor" means a debtor in a consumer transaction.

(23) "Consumer goods" means goods that are used or bought for use primarily for personal, family, or household purposes.

(24) "Consumer-goods transaction" means a consumer transaction in which:

(A) an individual incurs an obligation primarily for personal, family, or household purposes; and

(B) a security interest in consumer goods secures the obligation.

(25) "Consumer obligor" means an obligor who is an individual and who incurred the obligation as part of a transaction entered into primarily for personal, family, or household purposes.

(26) "Consumer transaction" means a transaction in which (i) an individual incurs an obligation primarily for personal, family, or household purposes, (ii) a security interest secures the obligation, and (iii) the collateral is held or acquired primarily for personal, family, or household purposes. The term includes consumer-goods transactions. . . .

(29) "Deposit account" means a demand, time, savings, passbook, or similar account maintained with a bank. The term does not include investment property or accounts evidenced by an instrument.

(30) "Document" means a document of title or a receipt of the type described in § 7–201(2).

(31) "Electronic chattel paper" means chattel paper evidenced by a record or records consisting of information stored in an electronic medium.

(32) "Encumbrance" means a right, other than an ownership interest, in real property. The term includes mortgages and other liens on real property. . . .

(37) "Filing office" means an office designated in § 9–501 as the place to file a financing statement. . . .

(39) "Financing statement" means a record or records composed of an initial financing statement and any filed record relating to the initial financing statement. . . .

(42) "General intangible" means any personal property, including things in action, other than accounts, chattel paper, commercial tort claims, deposit accounts, documents, goods, instruments, investment property, letter-of-credit rights, letters of credit, money, and oil, gas, or other minerals before extraction. The term includes payment intangibles and software.

(43) [Reserved.]

(44) "Goods" means all things that are movable when a security interest attaches. The term includes (i) fixtures, (ii) standing timber that is to be cut and removed under a conveyance or contract for sale, (iii) the unborn young of animals, (iv) crops grown, growing, or to be grown, even if the crops are produced on trees, vines, or bushes, and (v) manufactured homes. The term also includes a computer program embedded in goods and any supporting information provided in connection with a transaction relating to the program if (i) the program is associated with the goods in such a manner that it customarily is considered part of the goods, or (ii) by becoming the owner of the goods, a person acquires a right to use the program in connection with the goods. The term does not include a computer program embedded in goods that consist solely of the medium in which the program is embedded. The term also does not include accounts, chattel paper, commercial tort claims, deposit accounts, documents, general intangibles, instruments, investment property, letter-of-credit rights, letters of credit, money, or oil, gas, or other minerals before extraction. . . .

(46) "Health-care-insurance receivable" means an interest in or claim under a policy of insurance, which is a right to payment of a monetary obligation for health-care goods or services provided.

(47) "Instrument" means a negotiable instrument or any other writing that evidences a right to the payment of a monetary obligation, is not itself a security agreement or lease, and is of a type that in ordinary course of business is transferred by delivery with any necessary endorsement or assignment. The term does not include (i) investment property, (ii) letters of credit, or (iii) writings that evidence a right to payment arising out of the use of a credit or charge card or information contained on or for use with the card.

(48) "Inventory" means goods, other than farm products, which:

(A) are leased by a person as lessor;

(B) are held by a person for sale or lease or to be furnished under a contract of service;

(C) are furnished by a person under a contract of service; or

(D) consist of raw materials, work in process, or materials used or consumed in a business.

(49) "Investment property" means a security, whether certificated or uncertificated, security entitlement, securities account, commodity contract, or commodity account. . . .

(51) "Letter-of-credit right" means a right to payment or performance under a letter of credit, whether or not the beneficiary has demanded or is at the time entitled to demand payment or performance. The term does not include the right of a beneficiary to demand payment or performance under a letter of credit.

(52) "Lien creditor" means:

    (A)   a creditor that has acquired a lien on the property involved by attachment, levy, or the like;

    (B)   an assignee for benefit of creditors from the time of assignment;

    (C)   a trustee in bankruptcy from the date of the filing of the petition; or

    (D)   a receiver in equity from the time of appointment. . . .

(56) "New debtor" means a person that becomes bound as debtor under § 9–203(d) by a security agreement previously entered into by another person.

(57) "New value" means (i) money, (ii) money's worth in property, services, or new credit, or (iii) release by a transferee of an interest in property previously transferred to the transferee. The term does not include an obligation substituted for another obligation. . . .

(59) "Obligor" means a person that, with respect to an obligation secured by a security interest in or an agricultural lien on the collateral, (i) owes payment or other performance of the obligation, (ii) has provided property other than the collateral to secure payment or other performance of the obligation, or (iii) is otherwise accountable in whole or in part for payment or other performance of the obligation. The term does not include issuers or nominated persons under a letter of credit.

(60) "Original debtor" means a person that, as debtor, entered into a security agreement to which a new debtor has become bound under § 9–203(d).

(61) "Payment intangible" means a general intangible under which the account debtor's principal obligation is a monetary obligation.

(62) "Person related to", with respect to an individual, means:

    (A)   the spouse of the individual;

    (B)   a brother, brother-in-law, sister, or sister-in-law of the individual;

    (C)   an ancestor or lineal descendant of the individual or the individual's spouse; or

    (D)   any other relative, by blood or marriage, of the individual or the individual's spouse who shares the same home with the individual. . . .

(63) "Person related to", with respect to an organization, means:

    (A)   a person directly or indirectly controlling, controlled by, or under common control with the organization;

    (B)   an officer or director of, or a person performing similar functions with respect to, the organization;

    (C)   an officer or director of, or a person performing similar functions with respect to, a person described in subparagraph (A);

    (D)   the spouse of an individual described in subparagraph (A), (B), or (C); or

    (E)   an individual who is related by blood or marriage to an individual described in subparagraph (A), (B), (C), or (D) and shares the same home with the individual. . . .

(65) "Promissory note" means an instrument that evidences a promise to pay a monetary obligation, does not evidence an order to pay, and does not contain an acknowledgment by a bank that the bank has received for deposit a sum of money or funds. . . .

(70) "Record", except as used in "for record", "of record", "record or legal title", and "record owner", means information that is inscribed on a tangible medium or which is stored in an electronic or other medium and is retrievable in perceivable form. . . .

(73) "Secured party" means:

(A) a person in whose favor a security interest is created or provided for under a security agreement, whether or not any obligation to be secured is outstanding;

(B) a person that holds an agricultural lien;

(C) a consignor;

(D) a person to which accounts, chattel paper, payment intangibles, or promissory notes have been sold;

(E) a trustee, indenture trustee, agent, collateral agent, or other representative in whose favor a security interest or agricultural lien is created or provided for; or

(F) a person that holds a security interest arising under § 2–401, 2–505, 2–711(3), 2A–508(5), 4–210, or 5–118.

(74) "Security agreement" means an agreement that creates or provides for a security interest.

(75) "Send", in connection with a record or notification, means:

(A) to deposit in the mail, deliver for transmission, or transmit by any other usual means of communication, with postage or cost of transmission provided for, addressed to any address reasonable under the circumstances; or

(B) to cause the record or notification to be received within the time that it would have been received if properly sent under subparagraph (A). . . .

(c) **[Article 1 definitions and principles.]** Article 1 contains general definitions and principles of construction and interpretation applicable throughout this article.

[SUBPART 2. APPLICABILITY OF ARTICLE]

§ 9–109. Scope.

(a) **[General scope of article.]** Except as otherwise provided in subsection (c) and (d), this article applies to:

(1) a transaction, regardless of its form, that creates a security interest in personal property or fixtures by contract;

(2) an agricultural lien;

(3) a sale of accounts, chattel paper, payment intangibles, or promissory notes. . . .

(5) a security interest arising under § 2–401, 2–505, 2–711(3), or 2A–508(5), as provided in § 9–110; and

(6) a security interest arising under § 4–210 or 5–118. . . .

(d) **[Inapplicability of article.]** This article does not apply to:

(1) a landlord's lien, other than an agriculture lien;

(2) a lien, other than an agriculture lien, given by statute or other rule of law for services or materials, but Section 9–333 applies with respect to priority of the lien;

(3) an assignment of a claim for wages, salary, or other compensation of an employee;

(4) a sale of accounts, chattel paper, payment intangibles, or promissory notes as part of a sale of the business out of which they arose;

(5) an assignment of accounts, chattel paper, payment intangibles, or promissory notes which is for the purpose of collection only;

(6)　an assignment of a right to payment under a contract to an assignee that is also obligated to perform under the contract;

(7)　an assignment of a single account, payment intangible, or promissory note to an assignee in full or partial satisfaction of a preexisting indebtedness; . . .

(9)　an assignment of a right represented by a judgment, other than a judgment taken on a right to payment that was collateral; . . .

(12)　an assignment of a claim arising in tort, other than a commercial tort claim, but Sections 9–315 and 9–322 apply with respect to proceeds and priorities in proceeds. . . .

PART 2

EFFECTIVENESS OF SECURITY AGREEMENT; ATTACHMENT OF SECURITY INTEREST; RIGHTS OF PARTIES TO SECURITY AGREEMENT

[SUBPART 2. EFFECTIVENESS AND ATTACHMENT]

§ 9–201.　General Validity of Security Agreement.

(a)　**[General effectiveness.]** Except as otherwise provided in [the Uniform Commercial Code], a security agreement is effective according to its terms between the parties, against purchasers of the collateral, and against creditors. . . .

§ 9–203.　Attachment and Enforceability of Security Interest; Proceeds; Supporting Obligations; Formal Requisites.

(a)　**[Attachment.]** A security interest attaches to collateral when it becomes enforceable against the debtor with respect to the collateral, unless an agreement expressly postpones the time of attachment.

(b)　**[Enforceability.]** Except as otherwise provided in subsections (c) through (i), a security interest is enforceable against the debtor and third parties with respect to the collateral only if:

(1)　value has been given;

(2)　the debtor has rights in the collateral or the power to transfer rights in the collateral to a secured party; and

(3)　one of the following conditions is met:

(A)　the debtor has authenticated a security agreement that provides a description of the collateral and, if the security interest covers timber to be cut, a description of the land concerned;

(B)　the collateral is not a certificated security and is in the possession of the secured party under § 9–313 pursuant to the debtor's security agreement;

(C)　the collateral is a certificated security in registered form and the security certificate has been delivered to the secured party under § 8–301 pursuant to the debtor's security agreement; or

(D)　the collateral is deposit accounts, electronic chattel paper, investment property, or letter-of-credit rights, and the secured party has control under § 9–104, 9–105, 9–106, or 9–107 pursuant to the debtor's security agreement. . . .

(e)　**[Effect of new debtor becoming bound.]** If a new debtor becomes bound as debtor by a security agreement entered into by another person:

(1) the agreement satisfies subsection (b)(3) with respect to existing or after-acquired property of the new debtor to the extent the property is described in the agreement; and

(2) another agreement is not necessary to make a security interest in the property enforceable.

(f) **[Proceeds and supporting obligations.]** The attachment of a security interest in collateral gives the secured party the rights to proceeds provided by § 9–315 and is also attachment of a security interest in a supporting obligation for the collateral.

(g) **[Lien securing right to payment.]** The attachment of a security interest in a right to payment or performance secured by a security interest or other lien on personal or real property is also attachment of a security interest in the security interest, mortgage, or other lien. . . .

§ 9–204. After-Acquired Property; Future Advances.

(a) **[After-acquired collateral.]** Except as otherwise provided in subsection (b), a security agreement may create or provide for a security interest in after-acquired collateral.

(b) **[When after-acquired property clause not effective.]** A security interest does not attach under a term constituting an after-acquired property clause to:

(1) consumer goods, other than an accession when given as additional security, unless the debtor acquires rights in them within 10 days after the secured party gives value; or

(2) a commercial tort claim.

(c) **[Future advances and other value.]** A security agreement may provide that collateral secures, or that accounts, chattel paper, payment intangibles, or promissory notes are sold in connection with, future advances or other value, whether or not the advances or value are given pursuant to commitment.

PART 3

PERFECTION AND PRIORITY

[SUBPART 2. PERFECTION]

§ 9–308. When Security Interest or Agricultural Lien is Perfected; Continuity of Perfection.

(a) **[Perfection of security interest.]** Except as otherwise provided in this section and § 9–309, a security interest is perfected if it has attached and all of the applicable requirements for perfection in § 9–310 through 9–316 have been satisfied. A security interest is perfected when it attaches if the applicable requirements are satisfied before the security interest attaches.

(b) **[Perfection of agricultural lien.]** An agricultural lien is perfected if it has become effective and all of the applicable requirements for perfection in § 9–310 have been satisfied. An agricultural lien is perfected when it becomes effective if the applicable requirements are satisfied before the agricultural lien becomes effective.

(c) **[Continuous perfection; perfection by different methods.]** A security interest or agricultural lien is perfected continuously if it is originally perfected by one method under this article and is later perfected by another method under this article, without an intermediate period when it was unperfected.

(d) **[Supporting obligation.]** Perfection of a security interest in collateral also perfects a security interest in a supporting obligation for the collateral.

(e)   **[Lien securing right to payment.]** Perfection of a security interest in a right to payment or performance also perfects a security interest in a security interest, mortgage, or other lien on personal or real property securing the right.

(f)   **[Security entitlement carried in securities account.]** Perfection of a security interest in a securities account also perfects a security interest in the security entitlements carried in the securities account.

(g)   **[Commodity contract carried in commodity account.]** Perfection of a security interest in a commodity account also perfects a security interest in the commodity contracts carried in the commodity account.

§ 9–309.   Security Interest Perfected Upon Attachment.

The following security interests are perfected when they attach:

(1)   a purchase-money security interest in consumer goods, except as otherwise provided in § 9–311(b) with respect to consumer goods that are subject to a statute or treaty described in § 9–311(a);

(2)   an assignment of accounts or payment intangibles which does not by itself or in conjunction with other assignments to the same assignee transfer a significant part of the assignor's outstanding accounts or payment intangibles;

(3)   a sale of a payment intangible;

(4)   a sale of a promissory note. . . .

(12) an assignment for the benefit of all creditors of the transferor and subsequent transfers by the assignee thereunder; and

(13) a security interest created by an assignment of a beneficial interest in a decedent's estate.

§ 9–310.   When Filing Required to Perfect Security Interest or Agricultural Lien; Security Interests and Agricultural Liens to Which Filing Provisions Do Not Apply.

(a)   **[General rule: perfection by filing.]** Except as otherwise provided in subsection (b) and § 9–312(b), a financing statement must be filed to perfect all security interests and agricultural liens.

(b)   **[Exceptions: filing not necessary.]** The filing of a financing statement is not necessary to perfect a security interest:

(1)   that is perfected under § 9–308(d), (e), (f), or (g);

(2)   that is perfected under § 9–309 when it attaches;

(3)   in property subject to a statute, regulation, or treaty described in § 9–311(a);

(4)   in goods in possession of a bailee which is perfected under § 9–312(d)(1) or (2);

(5)   in certificated securities, documents, goods, or instruments which is perfected without filing or possession under § 9–312(e), (f), or (g);

(6)   in collateral in the secured party's possession under § 9–313;

(7)   in a certificated security which is perfected by delivery of the security certificate to the secured party under § 9–313;

(8)   in deposit accounts, electronic chattel paper, investment property, or letter-of-credit rights which is perfected by control under § 9–314;

(9)   in proceeds which is perfected under § 9–315; or

(10)   that is perfected under § 9–316.

(c)   **[Assignment of perfected security interest.]** If a secured party assigns a perfected security interest or agricultural lien, a filing under this article is not required to continue the perfected status of the security interest against creditors of and transferees from the original debtor.

§ 9–312.   Perfection of Security Interests in Chattel Paper, Deposit Accounts, Documents, Goods Covered by Documents, Instruments, Investment Property, Letter-of-Credit Rights, and Money; Perfection by Permissive Filing; Temporary Perfection Without Filing or Transfer of Possession.

(a)   **[Perfection by filing permitted.]** A security interest in chattel paper, negotiable documents, instruments, or investment property may be perfected by filing.

(b)   **[Control or possession of certain collateral.]** Except as otherwise provided in § 9–315(c) and (d) for proceeds:

(1)   a security interest in a deposit account may be perfected only by control under § 9–314;

(2)   and except as otherwise provided in § 9–308(d), a security interest in a letter-of-credit right may be perfected only by control under § 9–314; and

(3)   a security interest in money may be perfected only by the secured party's taking possession under § 9–313.

(c)   **[Goods covered by negotiable document.]** While goods are in the possession of a bailee that has issued a negotiable document covering the goods:

(1)   a security interest in the goods may be perfected by perfecting a security interest in the document; and

(2)   a security interest perfected in the document has priority over any security interest that becomes perfected in the goods by another method during that time.

(d)   **[Goods covered by nonnegotiable document.]** While goods are in the possession of a bailee that has issued a nonnegotiable document covering the goods, a security interest in the goods may be perfected by:

(1)   issuance of a document in the name of the secured party;

(2)   the bailee's receipt of notification of the secured party's interest; or

(3)   filing as to the goods.

§ 9–313.   When Possession by or Delivery to Secured Party Perfects Security Interest Without Filing.

(a)   **[Perfection by possession or delivery.]** Except as otherwise provided in subsection (b), a secured party may perfect a security interest in negotiable documents, goods, instruments, money, or tangible chattel paper by taking possession of the collateral. A secured party may perfect a security interest in certificated securities by taking delivery of the certificated securities under § 8–301.

(b)   **[Goods covered by certificate of title.]** With respect to goods covered by a certificate of title issued by this State, a secured party may perfect a security interest in the goods by taking possession of the goods only in the circumstances described in § 9–316(d).

(c)   **[Collateral in possession of person other than debtor.]** With respect to collateral other than certificated securities and goods covered by a document, a secured party takes possession of collateral in the possession of a person other than the debtor, the secured party, or a lessee of the collateral from the debtor in the ordinary course of the debtor's business, when:

(1)　the person in possession authenticates a record acknowledging that it holds possession of the collateral for the secured party's benefit; or

(2)　the person takes possession of the collateral after having authenticated a record acknowledging that it will hold possession of collateral for the secured party's benefit.

(d)　**[Time of perfection by possession; continuation of perfection.]** If perfection of a security interest depends upon possession of the collateral by a secured party, perfection occurs no earlier than the time the secured party takes possession and continues only while the secured party retains possession.

(e)　**[Time of perfection by delivery; continuation of perfection.]** A security interest in a certificated security in registered form is perfected by delivery when delivery of the certificated security occurs under § 8–301 and remains perfected by delivery until the debtor obtains possession of the security certificate. . . .

[SUBPART 3. PRIORITY]

§ 9–317.　Interests That Take Priority Over or Take Free of Security Interest or Agricultural Lien.

(a)　**[Conflicting security interests and rights of lien creditors.]** A security interest or agricultural lien is subordinate to the rights of:

(1)　a person entitled to priority under § 9–322; and

(2)　except as otherwise provided in subsection (e), a person that becomes a lien creditor before the earlier of the time the security interest or agricultural lien is perfected or a financing statement covering the collateral is filed.

(b)　**[Buyers that receive delivery.]** Except as otherwise provided in subsection (e), a buyer, other than a secured party, of tangible chattel paper, documents, goods, instruments, or a certificated security takes free of a security interest or agricultural lien if the buyer gives value and receives delivery of the collateral without knowledge of the security interest or agricultural lien and before it is perfected.

(c)　**[Lessees that receive delivery.]** Except as otherwise provided in subsection (e), a lessee of goods takes free of a security interest or agricultural lien if the lessee gives value and receives delivery of the collateral without knowledge of the security interest or agricultural lien and before it is perfected.

(d)　**[Licensees and buyers of certain collateral.]** A licensee of a general intangible or a buyer, other than a secured party, of collateral other than tangible chattel paper, tangible documents, goods, instruments, or a certificated security takes free of a security interest if the licensee or buyer gives value without knowledge of the security interest and before it is perfected.

(e)　**[Purchase-money security interest.]** Except as otherwise provided in sections 9–320 and 9–321, if a person files a financing statement with respect to a purchase-money security interest before or within 20 days after the debtor receives delivery of the collateral, the security interest takes priority over the rights of a buyer, lessee, or lien creditor which arise between the time the security interest attaches and the time of filing.

§ 9–322.　Priorities Among Conflicting Security Interests in and Agricultural Liens on Same Collateral.

(a)　**[General priority rules.]** Except as otherwise provided in this section, priority among conflicting security interests and agricultural liens in the same collateral is determined according to the following rules:

(1)　Conflicting perfected security interests and agricultural liens rank according to priority in time of filing or perfection. Priority dates from the earlier of the time a filing covering the collateral is first made or the security interest or agricultural lien is first perfected, if there is no period thereafter when there is neither filing nor perfection.

(2)　A perfected security interest or agricultural lien has priority over a conflicting unperfected security interest or agricultural lien.

(3)　The first security interest or agricultural lien to attach or become effective has priority if conflicting security interests and agricultural liens are unperfected.

(b)　**[Time of perfection: proceeds and supporting obligations.]** For the purposes of subsection (a)(1):

(1)　the time of filing or perfection as to a security interest in collateral is also the time of filing or perfection as to a security interest in proceeds; and

(2)　the time of filing or perfection as to a security interest in collateral supported by a supporting obligation is also the time of filing or perfection as to a security interest in the supporting obligation.

(c)　**[Special priority rules: proceeds and supporting obligations.]** Except as otherwise provided in subsection (f), a security interest in collateral which qualifies for priority over a conflicting security interest under § 9–327, 9–328, 9–329, 9–330, or 9–331 also has priority over a conflicting security interest in:

(1)　any supporting obligation for the collateral; and

(2)　proceeds of the collateral if:

(A)　the security interest in proceeds is perfected;

(B)　the proceeds are cash proceeds or of the same type as the collateral; and

(C)　in the case of proceeds that are proceeds of proceeds, all intervening proceeds are cash proceeds, proceeds of the same type as the collateral, or an account relating to the collateral. . . .

(d)　**[First-to-file priority rule for certain collateral.]** Subject to subsection (e) and except as otherwise provided in subsection (f), if a security interest in chattel paper, deposit accounts, negotiable documents, instruments, investment property, or letter-of-credit rights is perfected by a method other than filing, conflicting perfected security interests in proceeds of the collateral rank according to priority in time of filing.

(e)　**[Applicability of subsection (d).]** Subsection (d) applies only if the proceeds of the collateral are not cash proceeds, chattel paper, negotiable documents, instruments, investment property, or letter-of-credit rights.

§ 9–323.　Future Advances.

(a)　**[When priority based on time of advance.]** Except as otherwise provided in subsection (c), for purposes of determining the priority of a perfected security interest under § 9–322(a)(1), perfection of the security interest dates from the time an advance is made to the extent that the security interest secures an advance that:

   (1)   is made while the security interest is perfected only:

      (A)   under § 9–309 when it attaches; or

      (B)   temporarily under § 9–312(e), (f), or (g); and

   (2)   is not made pursuant to a commitment entered into before or while the security interest is perfected by a method other than under § 9–309 or 9–312(e), (f), or (g).

(b) **[Lien creditor.]** Except as otherwise provided in subsection (c), a security interest is subordinate to the rights of a person that becomes a lien creditor to the extent that the security interest secures an advance made more than 45 days after the person becomes a lien creditor unless the advance is made:

   (1)   without knowledge of the lien; or

   (2)   pursuant to a commitment entered into without knowledge of the lien.

(c) **[Buyer of receivables.]** Subsections (a) and (b) do not apply to a security interest held by a secured party that is a buyer of accounts, chattel paper, payment intangibles, or promissory notes or a consignor.

(d) **[Buyer of goods.]** Except as otherwise provided in subsection (e), a buyer of goods other than a buyer in ordinary course of business takes free of a security interest to the extent that it secures advances made after the earlier of:

   (1)   the time the secured party acquires knowledge of the buyer's purchase; or

   (2)   45 days after the purchase.

(e) **[Advances made pursuant to commitment: priority of buyer of goods.]** Subsection (d) does not apply if the advance is made pursuant to a commitment entered into without knowledge of the buyer's purchase and before the expiration of the 45-day period.

(f) **[Lessee of goods.]** Except as otherwise provided in subsection (g), a lessee of goods, other than a lessee in ordinary course of business, takes the leasehold interest free of a security interest to the extent that it secures advances made after the earlier of:

   (1)   the time the secured party acquires knowledge of the lease; or

   (2)   45 days after the lease contract becomes enforceable.

(g) **[Advances made pursuant to commitment: priority of lessee of goods.]** Subsection (f) does not apply if the advance is made pursuant to a commitment entered into without knowledge of the lease and before the expiration of the 45-day period.

§ 9–324.   Priority of Purchase-Money Security Interests.

(a) **[General rule: purchase-money priority.]** Except as otherwise provided in subsection (g), a perfected purchase-money security interest in goods other than inventory or livestock has priority over a conflicting security interest in the same goods, and, except as otherwise provided in § 9–327, a perfected security interest in its identifiable proceeds also has priority, if the purchase-money security interest is perfected when the debtor receives possession of the collateral or within 20 days thereafter.

(b) **[Inventory purchase-money priority.]** Subject to subsection (c) and except as otherwise provided in subsection (g), a perfected purchase-money security interest in inventory has priority over a conflicting security interest in the same inventory, has priority over a conflicting security interest in chattel paper or an instrument constituting proceeds of the inventory and in proceeds of the chattel paper, if so provided in § 9–330, and, except as otherwise provided in § 9–327, also has priority in identifiable cash proceeds of the inventory to the extent the identifiable cash proceeds are received on or before the delivery of the inventory to a buyer, if:

(1) the purchase-money security interest is perfected when the debtor receives possession of the inventory;

(2) the purchase-money secured party sends an authenticated notification to the holder of the conflicting security interest;

(3) the holder of the conflicting security interest receives the notification within five years before the debtor receives possession of the inventory; and

(4) the notification states that the person sending the notification has or expects to acquire a purchase-money security interest in inventory of the debtor and describes the inventory.

(c) **[Holders of conflicting inventory security interests to be notified.]** Subsections (b)(2) through (4) apply only if the holder of the conflicting security interest had filed a financing statement covering the same types of inventory:

(1) if the purchase-money security interest is perfected by filing, before the date of the filing; or

(2) if the purchase-money security interest is temporarily perfected without filing or possession under § 9–312(f), before the beginning of the 20-day period thereunder.

(d) **[Livestock purchase-money priority.]** Subject to subsection (e) and except as otherwise provided in subsection (g), a perfected purchase-money security interest in livestock that are farm products has priority over a conflicting security interest in the same livestock, and, except as otherwise provided in § 9–327, a perfected security interest in their identifiable proceeds and identifiable products in their unmanufactured states also has priority, if:

(1) the purchase-money security interest is perfected when the debtor receives possession of the livestock;

(2) the purchase-money secured party sends an authenticated notification to the holder of the conflicting security interest;

(3) the holder of the conflicting security interest receives the notification within six months before the debtor receives possession of the livestock; and

(4) the notification states that the person sending the notification has or expects to acquire a purchase-money security interest in livestock of the debtor and describes the livestock.

(e) **[Holders of conflicting livestock security interests to be notified.]** Subsections (d)(2) through (4) apply only if the holder of the conflicting security interest had filed a financing statement covering the same types of livestock:

(1) if the purchase-money security interest is perfected by filing, before the date of the filing; or

(2) if the purchase-money security interest is temporarily perfected without filing or possession under § 9–312(f), before the beginning of the 20-day period thereunder.

(f) **[Software purchase-money priority.]** Except as otherwise provided in subsection (g), a perfected purchase-money security interest in software has priority over a conflicting security interest in the same collateral, and, except as otherwise provided in § 9–327, a perfected security interest in its identifiable proceeds also has priority, to the extent that the purchase-money security interest in the goods in which the software was acquired for use has priority in the goods and proceeds of the goods under this section.

(g) **[Conflicting purchase-money security interests.]** If more than one security interest qualifies for priority in the same collateral under subsection (a), (b), (d), or (f):

(1) a security interest securing an obligation incurred as all or part of the price of the collateral has priority over a security interest securing an obligation incurred for value given to enable the debtor to acquire rights in or the use of collateral; and

(2) in all other cases, § 9–322(a) applies to the qualifying security interests.

§ 9–325. Priority of Security Interests in Transferred Collateral.

(a) **[Subordination of security interest in transferred collateral.]** Except as otherwise provided in subsection (b), a security interest created by a debtor is subordinate to a security interest in the same collateral created by another person if:

(1) the debtor acquired the collateral subject to the security interest created by the other person;

(2) the security interest created by the other person was perfected when the debtor acquired the collateral; and

(3) there is no period thereafter when the security interest is unperfected.

(b) **[Limitation of subsection (a) subordination.]** Subsection (a) subordinates a security interest only if the security interest:

(1) otherwise would have priority solely under § 9–322(a) or 9–324; or

(2) arose solely under § 2–711(3) or 2A–508(5).

PART 4

RIGHTS OF THIRD PARTIES

§ 9–403. Agreement Not to Assert Defenses Against Assignee.

(a) **["Value."]** In this section, "value" has the meaning provided in § 3–303(a).

(b) **[Agreement not to assert claim or defense.]** Except as otherwise provided in this section, an agreement between an account debtor and an assignor not to assert against an assignee any claim or defense that the account debtor may have against the assignor is enforceable by an assignee that takes an assignment:

(1) for value;

(2) in good faith;

(3) without notice of a claim of a property or possessory right to the property assigned; and

(4) without notice of a defense or claim in recoupment of the type that may be asserted against a person entitled to enforce a negotiable instrument under § 3–305(a).

(c) **[When subsection (b) not applicable.]** Subsection (b) does not apply to defenses of a type that may be asserted against a holder in due course of a negotiable instrument under § 3–305(b).

(d) **[Omission of required statement in consumer transaction.]** In a consumer transaction, if a record evidences the account debtor's obligation, law other than this article requires that the record include a statement to the effect that the rights of an assignee are subject to claims or defenses that the account debtor could assert against the original obligee, and the record does not include such a statement:

(1) the record has the same effect as if the record included such a statement; and

(2) the account debtor may assert against an assignee those claims and defenses that would have been available if the record included such a statement.

(e) **[Rule for individual under other law.]** This section is subject to law other than this article which establishes a different rule for an account debtor who is an individual and who incurred the obligation primarily for personal, family, or household purposes.

(f) **[Other law not displaced.]** Except as otherwise provided in subsection (d), this section does not displace law other than this article which gives effect to an agreement by an account debtor not to assert a claim or defense against an assignee.

§ 9–404. Rights Acquired by Assignee; Claims and Defenses Against Assignee.

(a) **[Assignee's rights subject to terms, claims, and defenses; exceptions.]** Unless an account debtor has made an enforceable agreement not to assert defenses or claims, and subject to subsections (b) through (e), the rights of an assignee are subject to:

(1) all terms of the agreement between the account debtor and assignor and any defense or claim in recoupment arising from the transaction that gave rise to the contract; and

(2) any other defense or claim of the account debtor against the assignor which accrues before the account debtor receives a notification of the assignment authenticated by the assignor or the assignee.

(b) **[Account debtor's claim reduces amount owed to assignee.]** Subject to subsection (c) and except as otherwise provided in subsection (d), the claim of an account debtor against an assignor may be asserted against an assignee under subsection (a) only to reduce the amount the account debtor owes.

(c) **[Rule for individual under other law.]** This section is subject to law other than this article which establishes a different rule for an account debtor who is an individual and who incurred the obligation primarily for personal, family, or household purposes.

(d) **[Omission of required statement in consumer transaction.]** In a consumer transaction, if a record evidences the account debtor's obligation, law other than this article requires that the record include a statement to the effect that the account debtor's recovery against an assignee with respect to claims and defenses against the assignor may not exceed amounts paid by the account debtor under the record, and the record does not include such a statement, the extent to which a claim of an account debtor against the assignor may be asserted against an assignee is determined as if the record included such a statement.

(e) **[Inapplicability to health-care-insurance receivable.]** This section does not apply to an assignment of a health-care-insurance receivable.

§ 9–405. Modification of Assigned Contract.

(a) **[Effect of modification on assignee.]** A modification of or substitution for an assigned contract is effective against an assignee if made in good faith. The assignee acquires corresponding rights under the modified or substituted contract. The assignment may provide that the modification or substitution is a breach of contract by the assignor. This subsection is subject to subsections (b) through (d).

(b) **[Applicability of subsection (a).]** Subsection (a) applies to the extent that:

(1) the right to payment or a part thereof under an assigned contract has not been fully earned by performance; or

(2) the right to payment or a part thereof has been fully earned by performance and the account debtor has not received notification of the assignment under § 9–406(a).

(c) **[Rule for individual under other law.]** This section is subject to law other than this article which establishes a different rule for an account debtor who is an individual and who incurred the obligation primarily for personal, family, or household purposes.

(d) **[Inapplicability to health-care-insurance receivable.]** This section does not apply to an assignment of a health-care-insurance receivable.

§ 9–406.   Discharge of Account Debtor; Notification of Assignment; Identification and Proof of Assignment; Restrictions on Assignment of Accounts, Chattel Paper, Payment Intangibles, and Promissory Notes Ineffective.

(a)   **[Discharge of account debtor; effect of notification.]** Subject to subsections (b) through (i), an account debtor on an account, chattel paper, or a payment intangible may discharge its obligation by paying the assignor until, but not after, the account debtor receives a notification, authenticated by the assignor or the assignee, that the amount due or to become due has been assigned and that payment is to be made to the assignee. After receipt of the notification, the account debtor may discharge its obligation by paying the assignee and may not discharge the obligation by paying the assignor.

(b)   **[When notification ineffective.]** Subject to subsection (h), notification is ineffective under subsection (a):

(1)   if it does not reasonably identify the rights assigned;

(2)   to the extent that an agreement between an account debtor and a seller of a payment intangible limits the account debtor's duty to pay a person other than the seller and the limitation is effective under law other than this article; or

(3)   at the option of an account debtor, if the notification notifies the account debtor to make less than the full amount of any installment or other periodic payment to the assignee, even if:

(A)   only a portion of the account, chattel paper, or general intangible has been assigned to that assignee;

(B)   a portion has been assigned to another assignee; or

(C)   the account debtor knows that the assignment to that assignee is limited.

(c)   **[Proof of assignment.]** Subject to subsection (h), if requested by the account debtor, an assignee shall seasonably furnish reasonable proof that the assignment has been made. Unless the assignee complies, the account debtor may discharge its obligation by paying the assignor, even if the account debtor has received a notification under subsection (a).

(d)   **[Term restricting assignment generally ineffective.]** Except as otherwise provided in subsection (e) and sections 2A–303 and 9–407, and subject to subsection (h), a term in an agreement between an account debtor and an assignor or in a promissory note is ineffective to the extent that it:

(1)   prohibits, restricts, or requires the consent of the account debtor or person obligated on the promissory note to the assignment or transfer of, or the creation, attachment, perfection, or enforcement of a security interest in, the account, chattel paper, payment intangible, or promissory note; or

(2)   provides that the assignment or transfer or the creation, attachment, perfection, or enforcement of the security interest may give rise to a default, breach, right of recoupment, claim, defense, termination, right of termination, or remedy under the account, chattel paper, payment intangible, or promissory note.

(e)   **[Inapplicability of subsection (d) to certain sales.]** Subsection (d) does not apply to the sale of a payment intangible or promissory note, other than a sale pursuant to a disposition under Section 9–610 or an acceptance of collateral under Section 9–620.

(f)   **[Legal restrictions on assignment generally ineffective.]** Except as otherwise provided in sections 2A–303 and 9–407 and subject to subsections (h) and (i), a rule of law, statute, or regulation that prohibits, restricts, or requires the consent of a government, governmental body or official, or account debtor to the assignment or transfer of, or creation of a security interest in, an account or chattel paper is ineffective to the extent that the rule of law, statute, or regulation:

(1)　prohibits, restricts, or requires the consent of the government, governmental body or official, or account debtor to the assignment or transfer of, or the creation, attachment, perfection, or enforcement of a security interest in the account or chattel paper; or

(2)　provides that the assignment or transfer or the creation, attachment, perfection, or enforcement of the security interest may give rise to a default, breach, right of recoupment, claim, defense, termination, right of termination, or remedy under the account or chattel paper.

(g)　**[Subsection (b)(3) not waivable.]** Subject to subsection (h), an account debtor may not waive or vary its option under subsection (b)(3).

(h)　**[Rule for individual under other law.]** This section is subject to law other than this article which establishes a different rule for an account debtor who is an individual and who incurred the obligation primarily for personal, family, or household purposes.

(i)　**[Inapplicability to health-care-insurance receivable.]** This section does not apply to an assignment of a health-care-insurance receivable.

(j)　**[Section prevails over specified inconsistent law.]** This section prevails over any inconsistent provisions of the following statutes, rules, and regulations: [List here any statutes, rules, and regulations containing provisions inconsistent with this section.]

PART II
PRE-2000 VERSION OF ARTICLE 9

INTRODUCTORY NOTE

[As discussed in the Introductory Note to Part I, NCCUSL and the ALI have approved revisions of various UCC Articles in recent years, including Article 9. The revised version of Article 9 has been widely enacted, and is set out in Part I of this book. Part II of this book includes excerpts from the prior version of Article 9, because most of the cases under Article 9 have been decided under the prior version, since the revised version is so new.]

PRE-2000 VERSION OF ARTICLE 9

SECURED TRANSACTIONS; SALES OF ACCOUNTS AND CHATTEL PAPER

PART I. SHORT TITLE, APPLICABILITY AND DEFINITIONS

PART I

SHORT TITLE, APPLICABILITY AND DEFINITIONS

§ 9–101. Short Title.

This Article shall be known and may be cited as Uniform Commercial Code—Secured Transactions.

§ 9–102. Policy and Subject Matter of Article.

(1)   Except as otherwise provided in Section 9–104 on excluded transactions, this Article applies

(a)   to any transaction (regardless of its form) which is intended to create a security interest in personal property or fixtures including goods, documents, instruments, general intangibles, chattel paper or accounts; and also

(b)   to any sale of accounts or chattel paper.

(2)   This Article applies to security interests created by contract including pledge, assignment, chattel mortgage, chattel trust, trust deed, factor's lien, equipment trust, conditional sale, trust receipt, other lien or title retention contract and lease or consignment intended as security. This Article does not apply to statutory liens except as provided in Section 9–310.

(3)   The application of this Article to a security interest in a secured obligation is not affected by the fact that the obligation is itself secured by a transaction or interest to which this Article does not apply.

§ 9–104.   Transactions Excluded From Article.

This Article does not apply

(a)   to a security interest subject to any statute of the United States, to the extent that such statute governs the rights of parties to and third parties affected by transactions in particular types of property; or

(b)   to a landlord's lien; or

(c)   to a lien given by statute or other rule of law for services or materials except as provided in Section 9–310 on priority of such liens; or

(d)   to a transfer of a claim for wages, salary or other compensation of an employee; or

(e)   to a transfer by a government or governmental subdivision or agency; or

(f)   to a sale of accounts or chattel paper as part of a sale of the business out of which they arose, or an assignment of accounts or chattel paper which is for the purpose of collection only, or a transfer of a right to payment under a contract to an assignee who is also to do the performance under the contract or a transfer of a single account to an assignee in whole or partial satisfaction of a preexisting indebtedness; or

(g)   to a transfer of an interest in or claim in or under any policy of insurance, except as provided with respect to proceeds (Section 9–306) and priorities in proceeds (Section 9–312); or

(h)   to a right represented by a judgment (other than a judgment taken on a right to payment which was collateral); or

(i)   to any right of set-off; or

(j)   except to the extent that provision is made for fixtures in Section 9–313, to the creation or transfer of an interest in or lien on real estate, including a lease or rents thereunder; or

(k)   to a transfer in whole or in part of any claim arising out of tort; or

(*l*)   to a transfer of an interest in any deposit account (subsection (1) of Section 9–105), except as provided with respect to proceeds (Section 9–306) and priorities in proceeds (Section 9–312).

§ 9–105.   Definitions and Index of Definitions.

(1)   In this Article unless the context otherwise requires:

(a)   "Account debtor" means the person who is obligated on an account, chattel paper or general intangible;

(b)   "Chattel paper" means a writing or writings which evidence both a monetary obligation and a security interest in or a lease of specific goods, but a charter or other contract involving the use or hire of a vessel is not chattel paper. When a transaction is evidenced both by such a security agreement or a lease and by an instrument or a series of instruments, the group of writings taken together constitutes chattel paper;

(c) "Collateral" means the property subject to a security interest, and includes accounts and chattel paper which have been sold;

(d) "Debtor" means the person who owes payment or other performance of the obligation secured, whether or not he owns or has rights in the collateral, and includes the seller of accounts or chattel paper. Where the debtor and the owner of the collateral are not the same person, the term "debtor" means the owner of the collateral in any provision of the Article dealing with the collateral, the obligor in any provision dealing with the obligation, and may include both where the context so requires;

(e) "Deposit account" means a demand, time, savings, passbook or like account maintained with a bank, savings and loan association, credit union or like organization, other than an account evidenced by a certificate of deposit;

(f) "Document" means document of title as defined in the general definitions of Article 1 (Section 1–201), and a receipt of the kind described in subsection (2) of Section 7–201;

(g) "Encumbrance" includes real estate mortgages and other liens on real estate and all other rights in real estate that are not ownership interests;

(h) "Goods" includes all things which are movable at the time the security interest attaches or which are fixtures (Section 9–313), but does not include money, documents, instruments, investment property, accounts, chattel paper, general intangibles, or minerals or the like (including oil and gas) before extraction. "Goods" also includes standing timber which is to be cut and removed under a conveyance or contract for sale, the unborn young of animals, and growing crops;

(i) "Instrument" means a negotiable instrument (defined in Section 3–104), or any other writing which evidences a right to the payment of money and is not itself a security agreement or lease and is of a type which is in ordinary course of business transferred by delivery with any necessary indorsement or assignment. The term does not include investment property;

(j) "Mortgage" means a consensual interest created by a real estate mortgage, a trust deed on real estate, or the like;

(k) An advance is made "pursuant to commitment" if the secured party has bound himself to make it, whether or not a subsequent event of default or other event not within his control has relieved or may relieve him from his obligation;

(l) "Security agreement" means an agreement which creates or provides for a security interest;

(m) "Secured party" means a lender, seller or other person in whose favor there is a security interest, including a person to whom accounts or chattel paper have been sold. When the holders of obligations issued under an indenture of trust, equipment trust agreement or the like are represented by a trustee or other person, the representative is the secured party;

(n) "Transmitting utility" means any person primarily engaged in the railroad, street railway or trolley bus business, the electric or electronics communications transmission business, the transmission of goods by pipeline, or the transmission or the production and transmission of electricity, steam, gas or water, or the provision of sewer service. . . .

(4) In addition Article 1 contains general definitions and principles of construction and interpretation applicable throughout this Article.

§ 9–106. Definitions: "Account"; "General Intangibles".

"Account" means any right to payment for goods sold or leased or for services rendered which is not evidenced by an instrument or chattel paper, whether or not it has been earned by performance. "General intangibles" means any personal property (including things in action) other than goods, accounts, chattel paper, documents, instruments, investment property, and money. All rights to payment earned or unearned under a charter or other contract involving the use or hire of a vessel and all rights incident to the charter or contract are accounts.

§ 9–109. Classification of Goods: "Consumer Goods"; "Equipment"; "Farm Products"; "Inventory".

Goods are

(1) "consumer goods" if they are used or bought for use primarily for personal, family or household purposes;

(2) "equipment" if they are used or bought for use primarily in business (including farming or a profession) or by a debtor who is a non-profit organization or a governmental subdivision or agency or if the goods are not included in the definitions of inventory, farm products or consumer goods;

(3) "farm products" if they are crops or livestock or supplies used or produced in farming operations or if they are products of crops or livestock in their unmanufactured states (such as ginned cotton, wool-clip, maple syrup, milk and eggs), and if they are in the possession of a debtor engaged in raising, fattening, grazing or other farming operations. If goods are farm products they are neither equipment nor inventory;

(4) "inventory" if they are held by a person who holds them for sale or lease or to be furnished under contracts of service or if he has so furnished them, or if they are raw materials, work in process or materials used or consumed in a business. Inventory of a person is not to be classified as his equipment.

PART II

VALIDITY OF SECURITY AGREEMENT AND RIGHTS OF PARTIES THERETO

§ 9–201. General Validity of Security Agreement.

Except as otherwise provided by this Act a security agreement is effective according to its terms between the parties, against purchasers of the collateral and against creditors. Nothing in this Article validates any charge or practice illegal under any statute or regulation thereunder governing usury, small loans, retail installment sales, or the like, or extends the application of any such statute or regulation to any transaction not otherwise subject thereto.

§ 9–203. Attachment and Enforceability of Security Interest; Proceeds; Formal Requisites.

(1) Subject to the provisions of Section 4–210 on the security interest of a collecting bank, Sections 9–115 and 9–116 on security interests in investment property, and Section 9–113 on a security interest arising under the Articles on Sales and Leases, a security interest is not enforceable against the debtor or third parties with respect to the collateral and does not attach unless:

(a) the collateral is in the possession of the secured party pursuant to agreement, the collateral is investment property and the secured party has control pursuant to agreement, or the debtor has signed a security agreement which contains a description of the collateral and in addition, when the security interest covers crops growing or to be grown or timber to be cut, a description of the land concerned;

(b) value has been given; and

(c) the debtor has rights in the collateral.

136

(2)   A security interest attaches when it becomes enforceable against the debtor with respect to the collateral. Attachment occurs as soon as all of the events specified in subsection (1) have taken place unless explicit agreement postpones the time of attaching.

(3)   Unless otherwise agreed a security agreement gives the secured party the rights to proceeds provided by Section 9–306.

(4)   A transaction, although subject to this Article, is also subject to _____,* and in the case of conflict between the provisions of this Article and any such statute, the provisions of such statute control. Failure to comply with any applicable statute has only the effect which is specified therein.

§ 9–204.   After-Acquired Property; Future Advances.

(1)   Except as provided in subsection (2), a security agreement may provide that any or all obligations covered by the security agreement are to be secured by after-acquired collateral.

(2)   No security interest attaches under an after-acquired property clause to consumer goods other than accessions (Section 9–314) when given as additional security unless the debtor acquires rights in them within ten days after the secured party gives value.

(3)   Obligations covered by a security agreement may include future advances or other value whether or not the advances or value are given pursuant to commitment (subsection (1) of Section 9–105).

§ 9–206.   Agreement Not to Assert Defenses Against Assignee; Modification of Sales Warranties Where Security Agreement Exists.

(1)   Subject to any statute or decision which establishes a different rule for buyers or lessees of consumer goods, an agreement by a buyer or lessee that he will not assert against an assignee any claim or defense which he may have against the seller or lessor is enforceable by an assignee who takes his assignment for value, in good faith and without notice of a claim or defense, except as to defenses of a type which may be asserted against a holder in due course of a negotiable instrument under the Article on Negotiable Instruments (Article 3). A buyer who as part of one transaction signs both a negotiable instrument and a security agreement makes such an agreement.

(2)   When a seller retains a purchase money security interest in goods the Article on Sales (Article 2) governs the sale and any disclaimer, limitation or modification of the seller's warranties.

PART III

RIGHTS OF THIRD PARTIES; PERFECTED AND UNPERFECTED SECURITY INTERESTS; RULES OF PRIORITY

§ 9–301.   Persons Who Take Priority Over Unperfected Security Interests; Rights of "Lien Creditor".

(1)   Except as otherwise provided in subsection (2), an unperfected security interest is subordinate to the rights of

(a)   persons entitled to priority under Section 9–312;

(b)   a person who becomes a lien creditor before the security interest is perfected;

(c)   in the case of goods, instruments, documents, and chattel paper, a person who is not a secured party and who is a transferee in bulk or other buyer not in ordinary course of

---

*   **Note:** *At* * *in subsection (4) insert reference to any local statute regulating small loans, retail installment sales and the like. . . .*

business or is a buyer of farm products in ordinary course of business, to the extent that he gives value and receives delivery of the collateral without knowledge of the security interest and before it is perfected;

(d)　　in the case of accounts, general intangibles, and investment property, a person who is not a secured party and who is a transferee to the extent that he gives value without knowledge of the security interest and before it is perfected.

(2)　　If the secured party files with respect to a purchase money security interest before or within ten days after the debtor receives possession of the collateral, he takes priority over the rights of a transferee in bulk or of a lien creditor which arise between the time the security interest attaches and the time of filing.

(3)　　A "lien creditor" means a creditor who has acquired a lien on the property involved by attachment, levy or the like and includes an assignee for benefit of creditors from the time of assignment, and a trustee in bankruptcy from the date of the filing of the petition or a receiver in equity from the time of appointment.

(4)　　A person who becomes a lien creditor while a security interest is perfected takes subject to the security interest only to the extent that it secures advances made before he becomes a lien creditor or within 45 days thereafter or made without knowledge of the lien or pursuant to a commitment entered into without knowledge of the lien.

. . .

§ 9–302. When Filing Is Required to Perfect Security Interest; Security Interests to Which Filing Provisions of This Article Do Not Apply.

(1)　　A financing statement must be filed to perfect all security interests except the following:

(a)　　a security interest in collateral in possession of the secured party under Section 9–305;

(b)　　a security interest temporarily perfected in instruments, certificated securities, or documents without delivery under Section 9–304 or in proceeds for a 10 day period under Section 9–306;

(c)　　a security interest created by an assignment of a beneficial interest in a trust or a decedent's estate;

(d)　　a purchase money security interest in consumer goods; but filing is required for a motor vehicle required to be registered; and fixture filing is required for priority over conflicting interests in fixtures to the extent provided in Section 9–313;

(e)　　an assignment of accounts which does not alone or in conjunction with other assignments to the same assignee transfer a significant part of the outstanding accounts of the assignor;

(f)　　a security interest of a collecting bank (Section 4–210) or arising under the Articles on Sales and Leases (see Section 9–113) or covered in subsection (3) of this section;

(g)　　an assignment for the benefit of all the creditors of the transferor, and subsequent transfers by the assignee thereunder.

(h)　　a security interest in investment property which is perfected without filing under Section 9–115 or Section 9–116.

(2)　　If a secured party assigns a perfected security interest, no filing under this Article is required in order to continue the perfected status of the security interest against creditors of and transferees from the original debtor.

(3)　　The filing of a financing statement otherwise required by this Article is not necessary or effective to perfect a security interest in property subject to

(a)   a statute or treaty of the United States which provides for a national or international registration or a national or international certificate of title or which specifies a place of filing different from that specified in this Article for filing of the security interest; or

(b)   the following statutes of this state; [list any certificate of title statute covering automobiles, trailers, mobile homes, boats, farm tractors, or the like, and any central filing statute.]; but during any period in which collateral is inventory held for sale by a person who is in the business of selling goods of that kind, the filing provisions of this Article (Part 4) apply to a security interest in that collateral created by him as debtor; or

(c)   a certificate of title statute of another jurisdiction under the law of which indication of a security interest on the certificate is required as a condition of perfection (subsection (2) of Section 9–103).

(4)   Compliance with a statute or treaty described in subsection (3) is equivalent to the filing of a financing statement under this Article, and a security interest in property subject to the statute or treaty can be perfected only by compliance therewith except as provided in Section 9–103 on multiple state transactions. Duration and renewal of perfection of a security interest perfected by compliance with the statute or treaty are governed by the provisions of the statute or treaty; in other respects the security interest is subject to this Article.

§ 9–303.   When Security Interest Is Perfected; Continuity of Perfection.

(1)   A security interest is perfected when it has attached and when all of the applicable steps required for perfection have been taken. Such steps are specified in Sections 9–115, 9–302, 9–304, 9–305 and 9–306. If such steps are taken before the security interest attaches, it is perfected at the time when it attaches.

(2)   If a security interest is originally perfected in any way permitted under this Article and is subsequently perfected in some other way under this Article, without an intermediate period when it was unperfected, the security interest shall be deemed to be perfected continuously for the purposes of this Article.

§ 9–305.   When Possession by Secured Party Perfects Security Interest Without Filing.

A security interest in letters of credit and advices of credit (subsection (2)(a) of Section 5–116), goods, instruments, money, negotiable documents, or chattel paper may be perfected by the secured party's taking possession of the collateral. If such collateral other than goods covered by a negotiable document is held by a bailee, the secured party is deemed to have possession from the time the bailee receives notification of the secured party's interest. A security interest is perfected by possession from the time possession is taken without a relation back and continues only so long as possession is retained, unless otherwise specified in this Article. The security interest may be otherwise perfected as provided in this Article before or after the period of possession by the secured party.

§ 9–312.   Priorities Among Conflicting Security Interests in the Same Collateral.

(1)   The rules of priority stated in other sections of this Part and in the following sections shall govern when applicable: Section 4–210 with respect to the security interests of collecting banks in items being collected, accompanying documents and proceeds; Section 9–103 on security interests related to other jurisdictions; Section 9–114 on consignments; Section 9–115 on security interests in investment property.

(2)   A perfected security interest in crops for new value given to enable the debtor to produce the crops during the production season and given not more than three months before the crops become growing crops by planting or otherwise takes priority over an earlier perfected security interest to the

extent that such earlier interest secures obligations due more than six months before the crops become growing crops by planting or otherwise, even though the person giving new value had knowledge of the earlier security interest.

(3)   A perfected purchase money security interest in inventory has priority over a conflicting security interest in the same inventory and also has priority in identifiable cash proceeds received on or before the delivery of the inventory to a buyer if

(a)   the purchase money security interest is perfected at the time the debtor receives possession of the inventory; and

(b)   the purchase money secured party gives notification in writing to the holder of the conflicting security interest if the holder had filed a financing statement covering the same types of inventory (i) before the date of the filing made by the purchase money secured party, or (ii) before the beginning of the 21 day period where the purchase money security interest is temporarily perfected without filing or possession (subsection (5) of Section 9–304); and

(c)   the holder of the conflicting security interest receives the notification within five years before the debtor receives possession of the inventory; and

(d)   the notification states that the person giving the notice has or expects to acquire a purchase money security interest in inventory of the debtor, describing such inventory by item or type.

(4)   A purchase money security interest in collateral other than inventory has priority over a conflicting security interest in the same collateral or its proceeds if the purchase money security interest is perfected at the time the debtor receives possession of the collateral or within ten days thereafter.

(5)   In all cases not governed by other rules stated in this section (including cases of purchase money security interests which do not qualify for the special priorities set forth in subsections (3) and (4) of this section), priority between conflicting security interests in the same collateral shall be determined according to the following rules:

(a)   Conflicting security interests rank according to priority in time of filing or perfection. Priority dates from the time a filing is first made covering the collateral or the time the security interest is first perfected, whichever is earlier, provided that there is no period thereafter when there is neither filing nor perfection.

(b)   So long as conflicting security interests are unperfected, the first to attach has priority.

(6)   For the purposes of subsection (5) a date of filing or perfection as to collateral is also a date of filing or perfection as to proceeds.

(7)   If future advances are made while a security interest is perfected by filing, the taking of possession, or under Section 9–115 or Section 9–116 on investment property, the security interest has the same priority for the purposes of subsection (5) or Section 9–115(5) with respect to the future advances as it does with respect to the first advance. If a commitment is made before or while the security interest is so perfected, the security interest has the same priority with respect to advances made pursuant thereto. In other cases a perfected security interest has priority from the date the advance is made.

§ 9–318.   Defenses Against Assignee; Modification of Contract After Notification of Assignment; Term Prohibiting Assignment Ineffective; Identification and Proof of Assignment.

(1)   Unless an account debtor has made an enforceable agreement not to assert defenses or claims arising out of a sale as provided in Section 9–206 the rights of an assignee are subject to

(a)   all the terms of the contract between the account debtor and assignor and any defense or claim arising therefrom; and

(b)   any other defense or claim of the account debtor against the assignor which accrues before the account debtor receives notification of the assignment.

(2)   So far as the right to payment or a part thereof under an assigned contract has not been fully earned by performance, and notwithstanding notification of the assignment, any modification of or substitution for the contract made in good faith and in accordance with reasonable commercial standards is effective against an assignee unless the account debtor has otherwise agreed but the assignee acquires corresponding rights under the modified or substituted contract. The assignment may provide that such modification or substitution is a breach by the assignor.

(3)   The account debtor is authorized to pay the assignor until the account debtor receives notification that the amount due or to become due has been assigned and that payment is to be made to the assignee. A notification which does not reasonably identify the rights assigned is ineffective. If requested by the account debtor, the assignee must seasonably furnish reasonable proof that the assignment has been made and unless he does so the account debtor may pay the assignor.

(4)   A term in any contract between an account debtor and an assignor is ineffective if it prohibits assignment of an account or prohibits creation of a security interest in a general intangible for money due or to become due or requires the account debtor's consent to such assignment or security interest.

Official Comment

. . .

Purposes:

1.   Subsection (1) makes no substantial change in prior law. An assignee has traditionally been subject to defenses or setoffs existing before an account debtor is notified of the assignment. When the account debtor's defenses on an assigned claim arise from the contract between him and the assignor, it makes no difference whether the breach giving rise to the defense occurs before or after the account debtor is notified of the assignment (paragraph (1)(a)). The account debtor may also have claims against the assignor which arise independently of that contract: an assignee is subject to all such claims which accrue before, and free of all those which accrue after, the account debtor is notified (paragraph (1)(b)). The account debtor may waive his right to assert claims or defenses against an assignee to the extent provided in Section 9–206.

2.   Prior law was in confusion as to whether modification of an executory contract by account debtor and assignor without the assignee's consent was possible after notification of an assignment. Subsection (2) makes good faith modifications by assignor and account debtor without the assignee's consent effective against the assignee even after notification. This rule may do some violence to accepted doctrines of contract law. Nevertheless it is a sound and indeed a necessary rule in view of the realities of large scale procurement. When for example it becomes necessary for a government agency to cut back or modify existing contracts, comparable arrangements must be made promptly in hundreds and even thousands of subcontracts lying in many tiers below the prime contract. Typically the right to payments under these subcontracts will have been assigned. The government, as sovereign, might have the right to amend or terminate existing contracts apart from statute. This subsection gives the prime contractor (the account debtor) the right to make the required arrangements directly with his subcontractors without undertaking the task of procuring assents from the many banks to whom rights under the contracts may have been assigned. Assignees are protected by the provision which gives them automatically corresponding rights under the modified or substituted contract. Notice that subsection (2) applies only so far as the right to payment has not been earned by performance, and therefore its application ends entirely when the work is done or the goods furnished. . . .

4.   Subsection (4) breaks sharply with the older contract doctrines by denying effectiveness to contractual terms prohibiting assignment of sums due and to become due under contracts of sale, construction contracts and the like. Under the rule as stated, an assignment would be effective even if made to an assignee who took with full knowledge that the account debtor had sought to prohibit or restrict assignment of the claims.

It is only for the past hundred years that our law has recognized the possibility of assigning choses in action. The history of this development, at law and equity, is in broad outline well known. Lingering traces of the absolute common law prohibition have survived almost to our own day.

There can be no doubt that a term prohibiting assignment of proceeds was effective against an assignee with notice through the nineteenth century and well into the twentieth. Section 151 of the Restatement, Contracts (1932) so states the law without qualification, but the changing character of the law is shown in the proposed Section [322] of the Restatement, Second, Contracts.

The original rule of law has been progressively undermined by a process of erosion which began much earlier than the cited section of the Restatement, Contracts would suggest. The cases are legion in which courts have construed the heart out of prohibitory or restrictive terms and held the assignment good. The cases are not lacking where courts have flatly held assignments valid without bothering to construe away the prohibition. See 4 Corbin on Contracts (1951) §§ 872, 873. Such cases as Allhusen v. Caristo Const. Corp., 303 N.Y. 446, 103 N.E.2d 891 (1952), are rejected by this subsection.

This gradual and largely unacknowledged shift in legal doctrine has taken place in response to economic need: as accounts and other rights under contracts have become the collateral which secures an ever increasing number of financing transactions, it has been necessary to reshape the law so that these intangibles, like negotiable instruments and negotiable documents of title, can be freely assigned.

Subsection (4) thus states a rule of law which is widely recognized in the cases and which corresponds to current business practices. It can be regarded as a revolutionary departure only by those who still cherish the hope that we may yet return to the views entertained some two hundred years ago by the Court of King's Bench. . . .

PART III
RESTATEMENT (SECOND) OF CONTRACTS

RESTATEMENT (SECOND) OF CONTRACTS*

(1981)

[The American Law Institute (ALI) is a private, but publicly oriented, organization composed of lawyers, judges, and legal academics. Its objective is to promote the clarification and simplification of the law and its better adaptation to social needs. It has sought to achieve this objective in part by preparing "Restatements" of various branches of the common law, including Contracts. The Restatements consist of statements of legal rules and standards (the "black letter law"), comments that explain each rule or standard and illustrate its application, and reporter's notes that refer to the main precedents and scholarly works upon which the rules, standards, comments, and illustrations were based. The ALI, however, has no law-making power. Its Restatements are only persuasive authorities—not binding authorities—until a court adopts one or more provisions as common law in the relevant jurisdiction. Nonetheless, many of the Restatements, especially the Restatement [First] of Contracts (1932) and much of the Restatement (Second) of Contracts (1981), have been highly influential in the courts. But the Restatements, convenient though they are, are not substitutes for the statutes and precedents that constitute the law in the relevant jurisdiction.

[The theory of the Restatements has changed somewhat over time. The introduction to the Restatement [First] of Contracts stated that "The function of the Institute is to state clearly and precisely in the light of the [courts'] decisions the principles and rules of the common law." The present theory is that the ALI "should feel obliged in [its] deliberations to give weight to all of the considerations that the courts, under a proper view of the judicial function, deem it right to weigh in theirs." Wechsler, *The Course of the Restatements*, 55 A.B.A.J. 147, 156 (1969).

[The complete Restatement (Second) of Contracts takes up three large volumes. This pamphlet contains the sections and comments, and a few illustrations, that should be most helpful to students in a basic course in contracts. Note that the Restatement (Second)'s rules and standards are stated as though they applied to all contracts. This is a bit misleading. When the Uniform Commercial Code ("UCC") or another statute applies, the rules of the statute override any inconsistent common law rules as the ALI restates them or otherwise. It is important to bear this in mind, especially when the transaction in question involves goods and, therefore, Article 2 of the UCC applies. In addition, the ALI has published several new Restatements, in final or draft form, whose subject matters partially overlap that of the Restatement (Second) of Contracts, including the Restatement (Third) of Employment Law (Tent. Draft No. 2, 2009), the Restatement (Third) of Restitution and Unjust Enrichment (2011), and the ALI Principles of the Law of Software Contracts (2010). Parts IV and V of this pamphlet contain relevant excerpts from these documents.]

CHAPTER 1. MEANING OF TERMS

CHAPTER 2. FORMATION OF CONTRACTS—PARTIES AND CAPACITY

CHAPTER 3. FORMATION OF CONTRACTS—MUTUAL ASSENT

TOPIC 1. IN GENERAL

TOPIC 2. MANIFESTATION OF ASSENT IN GENERAL

TOPIC 3. MAKING OF OFFERS

TOPIC 4. DURATION OF THE OFFEREE'S POWER OF ACCEPTANCE

CHAPTER 7. MISREPRESENTATION, DURESS AND UNDUE INFLUENCE

TOPIC 1. MISREPRESENTATION

TOPIC 2. DURESS AND UNDUE INFLUENCE

CHAPTER 8. UNENFORCEABILITY ON GROUNDS OF PUBLIC POLICY

TOPIC 1. UNENFORCEABILITY IN GENERAL

TOPIC 2. RESTRAINT OF TRADE

TOPIC 3. IMPAIRMENT OF FAMILY RELATIONS

TOPIC 4. INTERFERENCE WITH OTHER PROTECTED INTERESTS

CHAPTER 10. PERFORMANCE AND NON-PERFORMANCE

TOPIC 1. PERFORMANCES TO BE EXCHANGED UNDER AN EXCHANGE OF PROMISES

TOPIC 2. EFFECT OF PERFORMANCE AND NON-PERFORMANCE

TOPIC 3. EFFECT OF PROSPECTIVE NON-PERFORMANCE

TOPIC 4. APPLICATION OF PERFORMANCES

CHAPTER 11. IMPRACTICABILITY OF PERFORMANCE AND FRUSTRATION OF PURPOSE

CHAPTER 12. DISCHARGE BY ASSENT OR ALTERATION

TOPIC 1. THE REQUIREMENT OF CONSIDERATION

TOPIC 2. SUBSTITUTED PERFORMANCE, SUBSTITUTED CONTRACT, ACCORD AND ACCOUNT STATED

TOPIC 3. AGREEMENT OF RESCISSION, RELEASE AND CONTRACT NOT TO SUE

TOPIC 4. ALTERATION

CHAPTER 13. JOINT AND SEVERAL PROMISORS AND PROMISEES

TOPIC 1. JOINT AND SEVERAL PROMISORS

TOPIC 2. JOINT AND SEVERAL PROMISEES

CHAPTER 1

MEANING OF TERMS

§ 1.   Contract Defined.

A contract is a promise or a set of promises for the breach of which the law gives a remedy, or the performance of which the law in some way recognizes as a duty.

Comment

a.   Other meanings. The word "contract" is often used with meanings different from that given here. It is sometimes used as a synonym for "agreement" or "bargain." It may refer to legally ineffective agreements, or to wholly executed transactions such as conveyances; it may refer indifferently to the acts of the parties, to a document which evidences those acts, or to the resulting legal relations. In a statute the word may be given still other meanings by context or explicit definition. As is indicated in the Introductory Note to the Restatement of this Subject, definition in terms of "promise" excludes wholly executed transactions in which no promises are made; such a definition also excludes analogous obligations imposed by law rather than by virtue of a promise.

b.   Act and resulting legal relations. As the term is used in the Restatement of this Subject, "contract," like "promise," denotes the act or acts of promising. But, unlike the term "promise," "contract" applies only to those acts which have legal effect as stated in the definition given. Thus the word "contract" is commonly and quite properly also used to refer to the resulting legal obligation, or to the entire resulting complex of legal relations. Compare Uniform Commercial Code § 1–201(11), defining "contract" in terms of "the total legal obligation which results from the parties' agreement."

§ 2.   Promise; Promisor; Promisee; Beneficiary.

(1)   A promise is a manifestation of intention to act or refrain from acting in a specified way, so made as to justify a promisee in understanding that a commitment has been made.

(2)   The person manifesting the intention is the promisor.

(3)   The person to whom the manifestation is addressed is the promisee.

(4)   Where performance will benefit a person other than the promisee, that person is a beneficiary.

Comment

a.   Acts and resulting relations. "Promise" as used in the Restatement of this Subject denotes the act of the promisor. If by virtue of other operative facts there is a legal duty to perform, the promise is a contract; but the word "promise" is not limited to acts having legal effect. Like "contract," however, the word "promise" is commonly and quite properly also used to refer to the complex of human relations which results from the promisor's words or acts of assurance, including the justified expectations of the promisee and any moral or legal duty which arises to make good the assurance by performance. The performance may be specified either in terms describing the action of the promisor or in terms of the result which that action or inaction is to bring about.

b.   Manifestation of intention. Many contract disputes arise because different people attach different meanings to the same words and conduct. The phrase "manifestation of intention" adopts an external or objective standard for interpreting conduct; it means the external expression of intention as distinguished from undisclosed intention. A promisor manifests an intention if he believes or has reason to believe that the promisee will infer that intention from his words or conduct. Rules governing cases where the promisee could reasonably draw more than one inference as to the promisor's intention are stated in connection with the acceptance of offers (see §§ 19 and 20), and the scope of contractual obligations (see §§ 201, 219).

§ 3.   Agreement Defined; Bargain Defined.

An agreement is a manifestation of mutual assent on the part of two or more persons. A bargain is an agreement to exchange promises or to exchange a promise for a performance or to exchange performances.

Comment

Agreement distinguished from bargain. Agreement has in some respects a wider meaning than contract, bargain or promise. On the other hand, there are contracts which do not require agreement. See, e.g., §§ 82–90, 94, 104. The word "agreement" contains no implication that legal consequences are or are not produced. It applies to transactions executed on one or both sides, and also to those that are wholly executory. The word contains no implication of mental agreement. Such agreement usually but not always exists where the parties manifest assent to a transaction. . . .

§ 4.   How a Promise May Be Made.

A promise may be stated in words either oral or written, or may be inferred wholly or partly from conduct.

§ 5.   Terms of Promise, Agreement, or Contract.

(1)   A term of a promise or agreement is that portion of the intention or assent manifested which relates to a particular matter.

(2)   A term of a contract is that portion of the legal relations resulting from the promise or set of promises which relates to a particular matter, whether or not the parties manifest an intention to create those relations.

§ 6.   Formal Contracts.

The following types of contracts are subject in some respects to special rules that depend on their formal characteristics and differ from those governing contracts in general:

    (a)   Contracts under seal,

    (b)   Recognizances,

    (c)   Negotiable instruments and documents,

    (d)   Letters of credit.

§ 7.   Voidable Contracts.

A voidable contract is one where one or more parties have the power, by a manifestation of election to do so, to avoid the legal relations created by the contract, or by ratification of the contract to extinguish the power of avoidance.

§ 8.   Unenforceable Contracts.

An unenforceable contract is one for the breach of which neither the remedy of damages nor the remedy of specific performance is available, but which is recognized in some other way as creating a duty of performance, though there has been no ratification.

CHAPTER 2

FORMATION OF CONTRACTS—
PARTIES AND CAPACITY

§ 9. Parties Required.

There must be at least two parties to a contract, a promisor and a promisee, but there may be any greater number.

§ 10. Multiple Promisors and Promisees of the Same Performance.

(1) Where there are more promisors than one in a contract, some or all of them may promise the same performance, whether or not there are also promises of separate performances.

(2) Where there are more promisees than one in a contract, a promise may be made to some or all of them as a unit, whether or not the same or another performance is separately promised to one or more of them.

§ 11. When a Person May Be Both Promisor and Promisee.

A contract may be formed between two or more persons acting as a unit and one or more but fewer than all of these persons, acting either singly or with other persons.

§ 12. Capacity to Contract.

(1) No one can be bound by contract who has not legal capacity to incur at least voidable contractual duties. Capacity to contract may be partial and its existence in respect of a particular transaction may depend upon the nature of the transaction or upon other circumstances.

(2) A natural person who manifests assent to a transaction has full legal capacity to incur contractual duties thereby unless he is

    (a) under guardianship, or

    (b) an infant, or

    (c) mentally ill or defective, or

    (d) intoxicated.

Comment

. . .

c. *Inability to manifest assent.* In order to incur a contractual duty, a party must make a promise, manifesting his intention; in most cases he must manifest assent to a bargain. See §§ 2, 17, 18. The conduct of a party is not effective as a manifestation of his assent unless he intends to engage in the conduct. See § 19. Hence if physical disability prevents a person from acting, or if mental disability is so extreme that he cannot form the necessary intent, there is no contract. Similarly, even if he intends to engage in the conduct, there is no contract if the other party knows or has reason to know that he does not intend the resulting appearance of assent. See § 20. In such cases it is proper to say that incapacity prevents the formation of a contract. . . .

§ 13. Persons Affected by Guardianship.

A person has no capacity to incur contractual duties if his property is under guardianship by reason of an adjudication of mental illness or defect.

§ 14.   Infants.

Unless a statute provides otherwise, a natural person has the capacity to incur only voidable contractual duties until the beginning of the day before the person's eighteenth birthday.

Comment

. . .

c.   *Restoration of consideration.* An infant need not take any action to disaffirm his contracts until he comes of age. If sued upon the contract, he may defend on the ground of infancy without returning the consideration received. His disaffirmance revests in the other party the title to any property received by the infant under the contract. If the consideration received by the infant has been dissipated by him, the other party is without remedy unless the infant ratifies the contract after coming of age or is under some non-contractual obligation. But some states, by statute or decision, have restricted the power of disaffirmance, either generally or under particular circumstances, by requiring restoration of the consideration received. Where the infant seeks to enforce the contract, the conditions of the other party's promise must be fulfilled. The problems arising when an infant seeks to disaffirm a conveyance or executed contract are beyond the scope of the Restatement of this Subject, whether the disaffirmance is attempted before or after he comes of age. As to what constitutes ratification, see § 85.

§ 15.   Mental Illness or Defect.

(1)   A person incurs only voidable contractual duties by entering into a transaction if by reason of mental illness or defect

     (a)   he is unable to understand in a reasonable manner the nature and consequences of the transaction,

or

     (b)   he is unable to act in a reasonable manner in relation to the transaction and the other party has reason to know of his condition.

(2)   Where the contract is made on fair terms and the other party is without knowledge of the mental illness or defect, the power of avoidance under Subsection (1) terminates to the extent that the contract has been so performed in whole or in part or the circumstances have so changed that avoidance would be unjust. In such a case a court may grant relief as justice requires.

Comment

a.   *Rationale.* A contract made by a person who is mentally incompetent requires the reconciliation of two conflicting policies: the protection of justifiable expectations and of the security of transactions, and the protection of persons unable to protect themselves against imposition. Each policy has sometimes prevailed to a greater extent than is stated in this Section. At one extreme, it has been said that a lunatic has no capacity to contract because he has no mind; this view has given way to a better understanding of mental phenomena and to the doctrine that contractual obligation depends on manifestation of assent rather than on mental assent. See §§ 2, 19. At the other extreme, it has been asserted that mental incompetency has no effect on a contract unless other grounds of avoidance are present, such as fraud, undue influence, or gross inadequacy of consideration; it is now widely believed that such a rule gives inadequate protection to the incompetent and his family, particularly where the contract is entirely executory. . . .

§ 16.   Intoxicated Persons.

A person incurs only voidable contractual duties by entering into a transaction if the other party has reason to know that by reason of intoxication

     (a)   he is unable to understand in a reasonable manner the nature and consequences of the transaction,

or

     (b)   he is unable to act in a reasonable manner in relation to the transaction.

Comment

a.   *Rationale.* Compulsive alcoholism may be a form of mental illness; and when a guardian is appointed for the property of a habitual drunkard, his transactions are treated like those of a person under guardianship by reason of mental illness. See §§ 13, 15. If drunkenness is so extreme as to prevent any manifestation of assent, there is no capacity to contract. See §§ 2, 12, 19. It would be possible to treat voluntary intoxication as a temporary mental disorder in all cases, but voluntary intoxication not accompanied by any other disability has been thought less excusable than mental illness. Compare Model Penal Code § 2.08 and Comment. Hence a contract made by an intoxicated person is enforceable by the other party even though entirely executory, unless the other person has reason to know that the intoxicated person lacks capacity. Elements of overreaching or other unfair advantage may be relevant on the issues of competency, of the other party's reason to know, and of the appropriate remedy. . . . Use of drugs may raise similar problems.

b.   *What contracts are voidable.* The standard of competency in intoxication cases is the same as that in cases of mental illness. If the intoxication is so extreme as to prevent any manifestation of assent, there is no contract. Otherwise the other party is affected only by intoxication of which he has reason to know. A contract made by a person who is so drunk he does not know what he is doing is voidable if the other party has reason to know of the intoxication. Where there is some understanding of the transaction despite intoxication, avoidance depends on a showing that the other party induced the drunkenness or that the consideration was inadequate or that the transaction departed from the normal pattern of similar transactions; if the particular transaction in its result is one which a reasonably competent person might have made, it cannot be avoided even though entirely executory. . . .

CHAPTER 3

FORMATION OF CONTRACTS—MUTUAL ASSENT

TOPIC 1. IN GENERAL

§ 17.   Requirement of a Bargain.

(1)   Except as stated in Subsection (2), the formation of a contract requires a bargain in which there is a manifestation of mutual assent to the exchange and a consideration.

(2)   Whether or not there is a bargain a contract may be formed under special rules applicable to formal contracts or under the rules stated in §§ 82–94.

Comment

a.   Formal contracts. The types of contracts listed in § 6 are not necessarily subject to the requirements of manifestation of assent and consideration. Where contracts under seal still have their common-law effect, neither manifestation of assent by the promisee nor consideration is essential. See §§ 95, 104(1). Under Uniform Commercial Code § 3–408, a negotiable instrument may be binding without consideration in some cases. Under Uniform Commercial Code §§ 5–105, 5–106, neither manifestation of assent by the customer or the beneficiary nor consideration is necessary to the establishment of a letter of credit. . . .

c.   "Meeting of the minds." The element of agreement is sometimes referred to as a "meeting of the minds." The parties to most contracts give actual as well as apparent assent, but it is clear that a mental reservation of a party to a bargain does not impair the obligation he purports to undertake. The phrase used here, therefore, is "manifestation of mutual assent," as in the definition of "agreement" in § 3. . . . Topics 2–5, §§ 18–70, explain this requirement.

d.   "Sufficient consideration." The element of exchange is embodied in the concept of consideration. In some cases a promise is not binding for want of consideration, despite the presence of an element of exchange. "Consideration" has sometimes been used to refer to the element of exchange, without regard to whether it is sufficient to make an informal promise legally binding; the consideration which satisfies the legal requirement has then been called "sufficient consideration." As the term "consideration" is used here, however, it refers to an element of exchange which is legally sufficient, and the word "sufficient" would therefore be redundant. The requirement of consideration is the subject of §§ 71–81. . . .

e.   Informal contract without bargain. There are numerous atypical cases where informal promises are binding though not made as part of a bargain. In such cases it is often said that there is consideration by virtue of reliance on the promise or by virtue of some circumstance, such as a "past consideration," which does not involve the element of exchange. In this Restatement, however, "consideration" is used only to refer to the element of exchange, and contracts not involving that element are described as promises binding without consideration. There is no requirement of agreement for such contracts. They are the subject of §§ 82–94.

TOPIC 2. MANIFESTATION OF ASSENT IN GENERAL

§ 18.   Manifestation of Mutual Assent.

Manifestation of mutual assent to an exchange requires that each party either make a promise or begin or render a performance.

Comment

. . .

c.   *Sham or jest.* Where all the parties to what would otherwise be a bargain manifest an intention that the transaction is not to be taken seriously, there is no such manifestation of assent to the exchange as is required by this Section. In some cases the setting makes it clear that there is no contract, as where a business transaction is simulated on a stage during a dramatic performance. In other cases, there may be doubt as to whether there is a joke, or one of the parties may take the joke seriously. If one party is deceived and has no reason to know of the joke the law takes the joker at his word. Even if the deceived party had reason to know of the joke, there may be a claim for fraud or unjust enrichment by virtue of the promise made. Where the parties to a sham transaction intend to deceive third parties, considerations of public policy may sometimes preclude a defense of sham. . . .

§ 19.   Conduct as Manifestation of Assent.

(1)   The manifestation of assent may be made wholly or partly by written or spoken words or by other acts or by failure to act.

(2)   The conduct of a party is not effective as a manifestation of his assent unless he intends to engage in the conduct and knows or has reason to know that the other party may infer from his conduct that he assents.

(3)   The conduct of a party may manifest assent even though he does not in fact assent. In such cases a resulting contract may be voidable because of fraud, duress, mistake, or other invalidating cause.

Comment

. . .

b.   *"Reason to know."* A person has reason to know a fact, present or future, if he has information from which a person of ordinary intelligence would infer that the fact in question does or will exist. A person of superior intelligence has reason to know a fact if he has information from which a person of his intelligence would draw the inference. There is also reason to know if the inference would be that there is such a substantial chance of the existence of the fact that, if exercising reasonable care with reference to the matter in question, the person would predicate his action upon the assumption of its possible existence.

Reason to know is to be distinguished from knowledge and from "should know." Knowledge means conscious belief in the truth of a fact; reason to know need not be conscious. "Should know" imports a duty to others to ascertain facts; the words "reason to know" are used both where the actor has a duty to another and where he would not be acting adequately in the protection of his own interests were he not acting with reference to the facts which he has reason to know. . . . Uniform Commercial Code § 1–201(25). . . .

§ 20.   Effect of Misunderstanding.

(1)   There is no manifestation of mutual assent to an exchange if the parties attach materially different meanings to their manifestations and

     (a)   neither party knows or has reason to know the meaning attached by the other; or

     (b)   each party knows or each party has reason to know the meaning attached by the other.

(2)   The manifestations of the parties are operative in accordance with the meaning attached to them by one of the parties if

     (a)   that party does not know of any different meaning attached by the other, and the other knows the meaning attached by the first party; or

     (b)   that party has no reason to know of any different meaning attached by the other, and the other has reason to know the meaning attached by the first party.

Comment

. . .

b. The need for interpretation. The meaning given to words or other conduct depends to a varying extent on the context and on the prior experience of the parties. Almost never are all the connotations of a bargain exactly identical for both parties; it is enough that there is a core of common meaning sufficient to determine their performances with reasonable certainty or to give a reasonably certain basis for an appropriate legal remedy. See § 33. . . .

c. Interpretation and agreement. There is a problem of interpretation in determining whether a contract has been made as well as in determining what obligations a contract imposes. Where one party makes a precise and detailed offer and the other accepts it, or where both parties sign the same written agreement, there may be an "integrated" agreement (see § 209) and the problem is then one of interpreting the offer or written agreement. In other cases agreement may be found in a jumble of letters, telegrams, acts and spoken words. In either type of case, the parties may have different understandings, intentions and meanings. Even though the parties manifest mutual assent to the same words of agreement, there may be no contract because of a material difference of understanding as to the terms of the exchange. . . .

§ 21. Intention to Be Legally Bound.

Neither real nor apparent intention that a promise be legally binding is essential to the formation of a contract, but a manifestation of intention that a promise shall not affect legal relations may prevent the formation of a contract.

§ 22. Mode of Assent: Offer and Acceptance.

(1) The manifestation of mutual assent to an exchange ordinarily takes the form of an offer or proposal by one party followed by an acceptance by the other party or parties.

(2) A manifestation of mutual assent may be made even though neither offer nor acceptance can be identified and even though the moment of formation cannot be determined.

§ 23. Necessity That Manifestations Have Reference to Each Other.

It is essential to a bargain that each party manifest assent with reference to the manifestation of the other.

TOPIC 3. MAKING OF OFFERS

§ 24. Offer Defined.

An offer is the manifestation of willingness to enter into a bargain, so made as to justify another person in understanding that his assent to that bargain is invited and will conclude it.

Comment

a. Offer as promise. An offer may propose an executed sale or barter rather than a contract, or it may propose the exchange of a promise for a performance or an exchange of promises, or it may propose two or more such transactions in combination or in the alternative. In the normal case of an offer of an exchange of promises, or in the case of an offer of a promise for an act, the offer itself is a promise, revocable until accepted. There may also be an offer of a performance, to be exchanged either for a return promise (§ 55) or for a return performance; in such cases the offer is not necessarily a promise, but there are often warranties or other incidental promises. . . .

b. Proposal of contingent gift. A proposal of a gift is not an offer within the present definition; there must be an element of exchange. Whether or not a proposal is a promise, it is not an offer unless it specifies a promise or performance by the offeree as the price or consideration to be given by him. It is not enough that there is a promise performable on a certain contingency. . . .

§ 25. Option Contracts.

An option contract is a promise which meets the requirements for the formation of a contract and limits the promisor's power to revoke an offer.

§ 26. Preliminary Negotiations.

A manifestation of willingness to enter into a bargain is not an offer if the person to whom it is addressed knows or has reason to know that the person making it does not intend to conclude a bargain until he has made a further manifestation of assent.

Comment

. . .

b. *Advertising.* Business enterprises commonly secure general publicity for the goods or services they supply or purchase. Advertisements of goods by display, sign, handbill, newspaper, radio or television are not ordinarily intended or understood as offers to sell. The same is true of catalogues, price lists and circulars, even though the terms of suggested bargains may be stated in some detail. It is of course possible to make an offer by an advertisement directed to the general public (see § 29), but there must ordinarily be some language of commitment or some invitation to take action without further communication. . . .

c. *Quotation of price.* A "quotation" of price is usually a statement of price per unit of quantity; it may omit the quantity to be sold, time and place of delivery, terms of payment, and other terms. It is sometimes associated with a price list or circular, but the word "quote" is commonly understood as inviting an offer rather than as making one, even when directed to a particular customer. But just as the word "offer" does not necessarily mean that an offer is intended, so the word "quote" may be used in an offer. In determining whether an offer is made relevant factors include the terms of any previous inquiry, the completeness of the terms of the suggested bargain, and the number of persons to whom a communication is addressed. . . .

d. *Invitation of bids or other offers.* Even though terms are specified in detail, it is common for one party to request the other to make an offer. The words "Make me an offer" would normally indicate that no offer is being made, and other conduct such as the announcement of an auction may have similar effect. See § 28. A request for bids on a construction project is similar, even though the practice may be to accept the lowest bid conforming to specifications and other requirements. And forms used or statements made by a traveling salesman may make it clear that the customer is making an offer to be accepted at the salesman's home office. See § 69. . . .

§ 27. Existence of Contract Where Written Memorial Is Contemplated.

Manifestations of assent that are in themselves sufficient to conclude a contract will not be prevented from so operating by the fact that the parties also manifest an intention to prepare and adopt a written memorial thereof; but the circumstances may show that the agreements are preliminary negotiations.

Comment

a. Parties who plan to make a final written instrument as the expression of their contract necessarily discuss the proposed terms of the contract before they enter into it and often, before the final writing is made, agree upon all the terms which they plan to incorporate therein. This they may do orally or by exchange of several writings. It is possible thus to make a contract the terms of which include an obligation to execute subsequently a final writing which shall contain certain provisions. If parties have definitely agreed that they will do so, and that the final writing shall contain these provisions and no others, they have then concluded the contract.

b. On the other hand, if either party knows or has reason to know that the other party regards the agreement as incomplete and intends that no obligation shall exist until other terms are assented to or until the whole has been reduced to another written form, the preliminary negotiations and agreements do not constitute a contract.

c. Among the circumstances which may be helpful in determining whether a contract has been concluded are the following: the extent to which express agreement has been reached on all the terms to be included, whether the contract is of a type usually put in writing, whether it needs a formal writing for its full expression, whether it has few or many details, whether the amount involved is large or small, whether it is a common or unusual contract, whether a standard form of contract is widely used in similar transactions, and whether either party takes any action in preparation for performance during the negotiations. Such circumstances may be shown by oral testimony or by correspondence or other preliminary or partially complete writings.

d. Even though a binding contract is made before a contemplated written memorial is prepared and adopted, the subsequent written document may make a binding modification of the terms previously agreed to.

§ 28. Auctions.

(1) At an auction, unless a contrary intention is manifested,

     (a) the auctioneer invites offers from successive bidders which he may accept or reject;

     (b) when goods are put up without reserve, the auctioneer makes an offer to sell at any price bid by the highest bidder, and after the auctioneer calls for bids the goods cannot be withdrawn unless no bid is made within a reasonable time;

     (c) whether or not the auction is without reserve, a bidder may withdraw his bid until the auctioneer's announcement of completion of the sale, but a bidder's retraction does not revive any previous bid.

(2) Unless a contrary intention is manifested, bids at an auction embody terms made known by advertisement, posting or other publication of which bidders are or should be aware, as modified by any announcement made by the auctioneer when the goods are put up.

Comment

a. Manifestation of contrary intention. The rules stated in this Section reflect the usual understanding at an auction sale. Established auctions often have their own customary rules, made known by publication or by announcement at the commencement of the auction. Such rules prevail even though they are contrary to the rules stated here. Compare the phrase, "unless otherwise agreed," explained in the Introductory Note to this Restatement; see Uniform Commercial Code §§ 1–102, 1–205, 2–328. But where an auction is held pursuant to statute or court order, there may be requirements or terms which cannot be varied by private agreement.

b. Auction with reserve. An auction as ordinarily conducted furnishes an illustration of the principle stated in § 26. The auctioneer, by beginning to auction property, does not impliedly say: "I offer to sell this property to which ever of you makes the highest bid," but rather requests that the bidders make offers to him, as indeed he frequently states in his remarks to those before him. Hence, it is understood that he may reject all bids and withdraw the goods from sale until he announces completion of the sale. Similarly, under § 42, a bidder may withdraw his bid at any time before the announcement of completion. See Uniform Commercial Code § 2–328(3).

§ 29. To Whom an Offer Is Addressed.

(1) The manifested intention of the offeror determines the person or persons in whom is created a power of acceptance.

(2) An offer may create a power of acceptance in a specified person or in one or more of a specified group or class of persons, acting separately or together, or in anyone or everyone who makes a specified promise or renders a specified performance.

§ 30. Form of Acceptance Invited.

(1) An offer may invite or require acceptance to be made by an affirmative answer in words, or by performing or refraining from performing specified act, or may empower the offeree to make a selection of terms in his acceptance.

(2) Unless otherwise indicated by the language or the circumstances, an offer invites acceptance in any manner and by any medium reasonable in the circumstances.

§ 31. Offer Proposing a Single Contract or a Number of Contracts.

An offer may propose the formation of a single contract by a single acceptance or the formation of a number of contracts by successive acceptances from time to time.

§ 32. Invitation of Promise or Performance.

In case of doubt an offer is interpreted as inviting the offeree to accept either by promising to perform what the offer requests or by rendering the performance, as the offeree chooses.

Comment

a. *Promise or performance.* In the ordinary commercial bargain a party expects to be bound only if the other party either renders the return performance or binds himself to do so either by express words or by part performance or other conduct. Unless the language or the circumstances indicate that one party is to have an option, therefore, the usual offer invites an acceptance which either amounts to performance or constitutes a promise. The act of acceptance may be merely symbolic of assent and promise, or it may also be part or all of the performance bargained for. See §§ 2, 4, 18, 19. In either case notification of the offeror may be necessary. See §§ 54, 56.

The rule of this Section is a particular application of the rule stated in § 30(2). The offeror is often indifferent as to whether acceptance takes the form of words of promise or acts of performance, and his words literally referring to one are often intended and understood to refer to either. Where performance takes time, however, the beginning of performance may constitute a promise to complete it. See § 62. . . .

b. *Offer limited to acceptance by performance only.* Language or circumstances sometimes make it clear that the offeree is not to bind himself in advance of performance. His promise may be worthless to the offeror, or the circumstances may make it unreasonable for the offeror to expect a firm commitment from the offeree. In such cases, the offer does not invite a promissory acceptance, and a promise is ineffective as an acceptance. Examples are found in offers of reward or of prizes in a contest, made to a large number of people but to be accepted by only one. See § 29. Non-commercial arrangements among relatives and friends. . . and offers which leave important terms to be fixed by the offeree in the course of performance (see §§ 33, 34) provide other examples.

It is a separate question whether the offeree undertakes any responsibility to complete performance once begun, or whether he takes any responsibility for the quality of the performance when completed. . . .

§ 33. Certainty.

(1) Even though a manifestation of intention is intended to be understood as an offer, it cannot be accepted so as to form a contract unless the terms of the contract are reasonably certain.

(2) The terms of a contract are reasonably certain if they provide a basis for determining the existence of a breach and for giving an appropriate remedy.

(3) The fact that one or more terms of a proposed bargain are left open or uncertain may show that a manifestation of intention is not intended to be understood as an offer or as an acceptance.

Comment

a. *Certainty of terms.* It is sometimes said that the agreement must be capable of being given an exact meaning and that all the performances to be rendered must be certain. Such statements may be appropriate in determining whether a manifestation of intention is intended to be understood as an offer.

But the actions of the parties may show conclusively that they have intended to conclude a binding agreement, even though one or more terms are missing or are left to be agreed upon. In such cases courts endeavor, if possible, to attach a sufficiently definite meaning to the bargain. . . .

   b.   *Certainty in basis for remedy.* The rule stated in Subsection (2) reflects the fundamental policy that contracts should be made by the parties, not by the courts, and hence that remedies for breach of contract must have a basis in the agreement of the parties. . . . [T]he degree of certainty required may be affected by the dispute which arises and by the remedy sought. Courts decide the disputes before them, not other hypothetical disputes which might have arisen. . . .

§ 34.   Certainty and Choice of Terms; Effect of Performance or Reliance.

   (1)   The terms of a contract may be reasonably certain even though it empowers one or both parties to make a selection of terms in the course of performance.

   (2)   Part performance under an agreement may remove uncertainty and establish that a contract enforceable as a bargain has been formed.

   (3)   Action in reliance on an agreement may make a contractual remedy appropriate even though uncertainty is not removed.

TOPIC 4. DURATION OF THE OFFEREE'S POWER OF ACCEPTANCE

§ 35.   The Offeree's Power of Acceptance.

   (1)   An offer gives to the offeree a continuing power to complete the manifestation of mutual assent by acceptance of the offer.

   (2)   A contract cannot be created by acceptance of an offer after the power of acceptance has been terminated in one of the ways listed in § 36.

§ 36.   Methods of Termination of the Power of Acceptance.

   (1)   An offeree's power of acceptance may be terminated by

      (a)   rejection or counter-offer by the offeree, or

      (b)   lapse of time, or

      (c)   revocation by the offeror, or

      (d)   death or incapacity of the offeror or offeree.

   (2)   In addition, an offeree's power of acceptance is terminated by the non-occurrence of any condition of acceptance under the terms of the offer.

§ 37.   Termination of Power of Acceptance Under Option Contract.

   Notwithstanding §§ 38–49, the power of acceptance under an option contract is not terminated by rejection or counter-offer, by revocation, or by death or incapacity of the offeror, unless the requirements are met for the discharge of a contractual duty.

§ 38.   Rejection.

   (1)   An offeree's power of acceptance is terminated by his rejection of the offer, unless the offeror has manifested a contrary intention.

   (2)   A manifestation of intention not to accept an offer is a rejection unless the offeree manifests an intention to take it under further advisement.

Comment

a. *The probability of reliance.* The legal consequences of a rejection rest on its probable effect on the offeror. An offeror commonly takes steps to prepare for performance in the event that the offer is accepted. If the offeree states in effect that he declines to accept the offer, it is highly probable that the offeror will change his plans in reliance on the statement. . . . To protect the offeror in such reliance, the power of acceptance is terminated without proof of reliance. . . .

b. *Contrary statement of offeror or offeree.* The rule of this Section is designed to give effect to the intentions of the parties, and a manifestation of intention on the part of either that the offeree's power of acceptance is to continue is effective. . . .

§ 39. Counter-Offers.

(1) A counter-offer is an offer made by an offeree to his offeror relating to the same matter as the original offer and proposing a substituted bargain differing from that proposed by the original offer.

(2) An offeree's power of acceptance is terminated by his making of a counter-offer, unless the offeror has manifested a contrary intention or unless the counter-offer manifests a contrary intention of the offeree.

Comment

a. *Counter-offer as rejection.* It is often said that a counter-offer is a rejection, and it does have the same effect in terminating the offeree's power of acceptance. But in other respects a counter-offer differs from a rejection. A counter-offer must be capable of being accepted; it carries negotiations on rather than breaking them off. The termination of the power of acceptance by a counter-offer merely carries out the usual understanding of bargainers that one proposal is dropped when another is taken under consideration; if alternative proposals are to be under consideration at the same time, warning is expected. . . .

Illustration

1. A offers B to sell him a parcel of land for $5,000, stating that the offer will remain open for thirty days. B replies, "I will pay $4800 for the parcel," and on A's declining that, B writes, within the thirty day period, "I accept your offer to sell for $5,000." There is no contract unless A's offer was [an option supported by consideration], or unless A's reply to the counter-offer manifested an intention to renew his original offer.

b. *Qualified acceptance, inquiry or separate offer.* A common type of counter-offer is the qualified or conditional acceptance, which purports to accept the original offer but makes acceptance expressly conditional on assent to additional or different terms. See § 59. Such a counter-offer must be distinguished from an unqualified acceptance which is accompanied by a proposal for modification of the agreement or for a separate agreement. A mere inquiry regarding the possibility of different terms, a request for a better offer, or a comment upon the terms of the offer, is ordinarily not a counter-offer. Such responses to an offer may be too tentative or indefinite to be offers of any kind; or they may deal with new matters rather than a substitution for the original offer; or their language may manifest an intention to keep the original offer under consideration.

Illustration

2. A makes the same offer to B as that stated in Illustration 1, and B replies, "Won't you take less?" A answers, "No." An acceptance thereafter by B within the thirty-day period is effective. B's inquiry was not a counter-offer, and A's original offer stands.

c. *Contrary statement of offeror or offeree.* An offeror may state in his offer that it shall continue for a stated time in any event and that in the meanwhile he will be glad to receive counter-offers. Likewise an offeree may state that he is holding the offer under advisement, but that if the offeror desires to close a bargain at once the offeree makes a specific counter-offer. Such an answer will not extend the time that the original offer remains open, but will not cut that time short. . . .

Illustration

3.   A makes the same offer to B as that stated in Illustration 1. B replies "I am keeping your offer under advisement, but if you wish to close the matter at once I will give you $4800." A does not reply, and within the thirty-day period B accepts the original offer. B's acceptance is effective.

§ 40. Time When Rejection or Counter-Offer Terminates the Power of Acceptance.

Rejection or counter-offer by mail or telegram does not terminate the power of acceptance until received by the offeror, but limits the power so that a letter or telegram of acceptance started after the sending of an otherwise effective rejection or counter-offer is only a counter-offer unless the acceptance is received by the offeror before he receives the rejection or counter-offer.

§ 41. Lapse of Time.

(1)   An offeree's power of acceptance is terminated at the time specified in the offer, or, if no time is specified, at the end of a reasonable time.

(2)   What is a reasonable time is a question of fact, depending on all the circumstances existing when the offer and attempted acceptance are made.

(3)   Unless otherwise indicated by the language or the circumstances, and subject to the rule stated in § 49, an offer sent by mail is seasonably accepted if an acceptance is mailed at any time before midnight on the day on which the offer is received.

Comment

. . .

b.   *Reasonable time.* . . . The circumstances to be considered have a wide range: they include the nature of the proposed contract, the purposes of the parties, the course of dealing between them, and any relevant usages of trade. In general, the question is what time would be thought satisfactory to the offeror by a reasonable man in the position of the offeree. . . .

d.   *Direct negotiations.* Where the parties bargain face to face or over the telephone, the time for acceptance does not ordinarily extend beyond the end of the conversation unless a contrary intention is indicated. A contrary intention may be indicated either by express words or by the circumstances. For example, the delivery of a written offer to the offeree, or an expectation that some action will be taken before acceptance, may indicate that a delayed acceptance is invited. . . .

f.   *Speculative transactions.* The rule that an offer becomes irrevocable when an acceptance is mailed (§§ 42, 63) in effect imposes a risk of commitment on the offeror during the period required for communication of the acceptance, although during that period the offeror has no assurance that the bargain has been concluded. The rule that the power of acceptance is terminated by the lapse of a reasonable time serves to limit this risk. The more significant the risk, the greater is the need for limitation, and hence the shorter is the time which is reasonable.

These considerations have their principal application in the sale of property which may be subject to rapid fluctuation in value, such as commodities, securities or land. The value of such property, however, may be stable for substantial periods of time, particularly in the case of land. Absence of actual fluctuation during the period before acceptance is a factor tending to indicate that acceptance occurred within a reasonable time. Similarly, delay in acceptance of an offer to insure may not be unreasonable if there is no change in the risk or in the applicable insurance rates.

The reasonable time for acceptance in a speculative transaction is brief not only because the offeror does not ordinarily intend to assume an extended risk without compensation but also because he does not intend to give the offeree an extended opportunity for speculation at the offeror's expense. If the offeree makes use for speculative purposes of time allowed for communication, there may be a lack of good faith, and an acceptance may not be timely even though it arrives within the time contemplated by the offeror. Compare Uniform Commercial Code §§ 1–203, 2–103.

§ 42.   Revocation by Communication From Offeror Received by Offeree.

An offeree's power of acceptance is terminated when the offeree receives from the offeror a manifestation of an intention not to enter into the proposed contract.

§ 43.   Indirect Communication of Revocation.

An offeree's power of acceptance is terminated when the offeror takes definite action inconsistent with an intention to enter into the proposed contract and the offeree acquires reliable information to that effect.

§ 44.   Effect of Deposit on Revocability of Offer.

An offeror's power of revocation is not limited by the deposit of money or other property to be forfeited in the event of revocation, but the deposit may be forfeited to the extent that it is not a penalty.

§ 45.   Option Contract Created by Part Performance or Tender.

(1)   Where an offer invites an offeree to accept by rendering a performance and does not invite a promissory acceptance, an option contract is created when the offeree tenders or begins the invited performance or tenders a beginning of it.

(2)   The offeror's duty of performance under any option contract so created is conditional on completion or tender of the invited performance in accordance with the terms of the offer.

Comment

. . .

b.   Manifestation of contrary intention. The rule of this Section is designed to protect the offeree in justifiable reliance on the offeror's promise, and the rule yields to a manifestation of intention which makes reliance unjustified. A reservation of power to revoke after performance has begun means that as yet there is no promise and no offer. . . .

d.   Beginning to perform. If the invited performance takes time, the invitation to perform necessarily includes an invitation to begin performance. In most such cases the beginning of performance carries with it an express or implied promise to complete performance. See § 62. In the less common case where the offer does not contemplate or invite a promise by the offeree, the beginning of performance nevertheless completes the manifestation of mutual assent and furnishes consideration for an option contract. . . .

e.   Completion of performance. Where part performance or tender by the offeree creates an option contract, the offeree is not bound to complete performance. The offeror alone is bound, but his duty of performance is conditional on completion of the offeree's performance. . . .

f.   Preparations for performance. What is begun or tendered must be part of the actual performance invited in order to preclude revocation under this Section. Beginning preparations, though they may be essential to carrying out the contract or to accepting the offer, is not enough. Preparations to perform may, however, constitute justifiable reliance sufficient to make the offeror's promise binding under § 87(2).

In many cases what is invited depends on what is a reasonable mode of acceptance. See § 30. The distinction between preparing for performance and beginning performance in such cases may turn on many factors: the extent to which the offeree's conduct is clearly referable to the offer, the definite and substantial character of that conduct, and the extent to which it is of actual or prospective benefit to the offeror rather than the offeree, as well as the terms of the communications between the parties, their prior course of dealing, and any relevant usages of trade. . . .

§ 46.   Revocation of General Offer.

Where an offer is made by advertisement in a newspaper or other general notification to the public or to a number of persons whose identity is unknown to the offeror, the offeree's power of acceptance is terminated when a notice of termination is given publicity by advertisement or other general notification equal to that given to the offer and no better means of notification is reasonably available.

§ 47.   Revocation of Divisible Offer.

An offer contemplating a series of independent contracts by separate acceptances may be effectively revoked so as to terminate the power to create future contracts, though one or more of the proposed contracts have already been formed by the offeree's acceptance.

§ 48.   Death or Incapacity of Offeror or Offeree.

An offeree's power of acceptance is terminated when the offeree or offeror dies or is deprived of legal capacity to enter into the proposed contract.

Comment

a.   Death of offeror. The offeror's death terminates the power of the offeree without notice to him. This rule seems to be a relic of the obsolete view that a contract requires a "meeting of minds," and it is out of harmony with the modern doctrine that a manifestation of assent is effective without regard to actual mental assent. . . .

§ 49.   Effect of Delay in Communication of Offer.

If communication of an offer to the offeree is delayed, the period within which a contract can be created by acceptance is not thereby extended if the offeree knows or has reason to know of the delay, though it is due to the fault of the offeror; but if the delay is due to the fault of the offeror or to the means of transmission adopted by him, and the offeree neither knows nor has reason to know that there has been delay, a contract can be created by acceptance within the period which would have been permissible if the offer had been dispatched at the time that its arrival seems to indicate.

TOPIC 5. ACCEPTANCE OF OFFERS

§ 50.   Acceptance of Offer Defined; Acceptance by Performance; Acceptance by Promise.

(1)   Acceptance of an offer is a manifestation of assent to the terms thereof made by the offeree in a manner invited or required by the offer.

(2)   Acceptance by performance requires that at least part of what the offer requests be performed or tendered and includes acceptance by a performance which operates as a return promise.

(3)   Acceptance by a promise requires that the offeree complete every act essential to the making of the promise.

Comment

. . .

b.   Acceptance by performance. Where the offer requires acceptance by performance and does not invite a return promise, as in the ordinary case of an offer of a reward, a contract can be created only by the offeree's performance. . . . In such cases the act requested and performed as consideration for the offeror's promise ordinarily also constitutes acceptance; under § 45 the beginning of performance or the tender of part performance of what is requested may both indicate assent and furnish consideration for an option contract. In some other cases the offeree may choose to create a contract either by making a promise or by rendering or tendering performance; in most such cases the beginning of performance or a tender of part performance operates as a promise to render complete performance. See §§ 32, 62. Mere preparation to perform, however, is not acceptance, although in some cases preparation may make the offeror's promise binding under § 87(2). . . .

c. *Acceptance by promise.* The typical contract consists of mutual promises and is formed by an acceptance constituting a return promise by the offeree. A promissory acceptance may be explicitly required by the offer, or may be the only type of acceptance which is reasonable under the circumstances, or the offeree may choose to accept by promise an offer which invites acceptance either by promise or by performance. See §§ 30, 32. The promise may be made in words or other symbols of assent, or it may be implied from conduct, other than acts of performance, provided only that it is in a form invited or required by the offer. An act of performance may also operate as a return promise, but the acceptance in such a case is treated as an acceptance by performance rather than an acceptance by promise; thus the requirement of notification is governed by § 54 rather than by § 56. As appears from § 63, acceptance by promise may be effective when a written promise is started on its way, but the offeree must complete the acts necessary on his part to constitute a promise by him. Similarly, in cases where communication to the offeror is unnecessary under § 69, the acts constituting the promise must be complete. . . .

§ 51. Effect of Part Performance Without Knowledge of Offer.

Unless the offeror manifests a contrary intention, an offeree who learns of an offer after he has rendered part of the performance requested by the offer may accept by completing the requested performance.

§ 52. Who May Accept an Offer.

An offer can be accepted only by a person whom it invites to furnish the consideration.

§ 53. Acceptance by Performance; Manifestation of Intention Not to Accept.

(1) An offer can be accepted by the rendering of a performance only if the offer invites such an acceptance.

(2) Except as stated in § 69, the rendering of a performance does not constitute an acceptance if within a reasonable time the offeree exercises reasonable diligence to notify the offeror of non-acceptance.

(3) Where an offer of a promise invites acceptance by performance and does not invite a promissory acceptance, the rendering of the invited performance does not constitute an acceptance if before the offeror performs his promise the offeree manifests an intention not to accept.

§ 54. Acceptance by Performance; Necessity of Notification to Offeror.

(1) Where an offer invites an offeree to accept by rendering a performance, no notification is necessary to make such an acceptance effective unless the offer requests such a notification.

(2) If an offeree who accepts by rendering a performance has reason to know that the offeror has no adequate means of learning of the performance with reasonable promptness and certainty, the contractual duty of the offeror is discharged unless

(a) the offeree exercises reasonable diligence to notify the offeror of acceptance, or

(b) the offeror learns of the performance within a reasonable time, or

(c) the offer indicates that notification of acceptance is not required.

§ 55. Acceptance of Non-Promissory Offers.

Acceptance by promise may create a contract in which the offeror's performance is completed when the offeree's promise is made.

§ 56. Acceptance by Promise; Necessity of Notification to Offeror.

Except as stated in § 69 or where the offer manifests a contrary intention, it is essential to an acceptance by promise either that the offeree exercise reasonable diligence to notify the offeror of acceptance or that the offeror receive the acceptance seasonably.

Comment

a. Necessity of notification. Where the offeree has performed in whole or in part, notification to the offeror is not essential to acceptance, although failure to notify may discharge the offeror's duty of performance. See § 54. Similarly, where the offeror has rendered a performance and the offeree has taken the benefit of that performance, the offeree may be bound without notification to the offeror. See § 69. In such cases the enforcement of the promise rests in part on a change of position in justifiable reliance on a promise, often reinforced by a corresponding benefit received by the promisor. . . .

Illustrations

2.   A makes written application for life insurance through an agent for B Insurance Company, pays the first premium, and is given a receipt stating that the insurance "shall take effect as of the date of approval of the application" at B's home office. Approval at the home office in accordance with B's usual practice is an acceptance of A's offer even though no steps are taken to notify A.

§ 57.   Effect of Equivocal Acceptance.

Where notification is essential to acceptance by promise, the offeror is not bound by an acceptance in equivocal terms unless he reasonably understands it as an acceptance.

§ 58.   Necessity of Acceptance Complying With Terms of Offer.

An acceptance must comply with the requirements of the offer as to the promise to be made or the performance to be rendered.

Comment

a. Scope. This rule applies to the substance of the bargain the basic principle that the offeror is the master of his offer. . . . That principle rests on the concept of private autonomy underlying contract law. It is mitigated by the interpretation of offers, in accordance with common understanding, as inviting acceptance in any reasonable manner unless there is contrary indication. . . .

§ 59.   Purported Acceptance Which Adds Qualifications.

A reply to an offer which purports to accept it but is conditional on the offeror's assent to terms additional to or different from those offered is not an acceptance but is a counter-offer.

Comment

a. Qualified acceptance. A qualified or conditional acceptance proposes an exchange different from that proposed by the original offeror. Such a proposal is a counter-offer and ordinarily terminates the power of acceptance of the original offeree. See § 39. The effect of the qualification or condition is to deprive the purported acceptance of effect. But a definite and seasonable expression of acceptance is operative despite the statement of additional or different terms if the acceptance is not made to depend on assent to the additional or different terms. See § 61; Uniform Commercial Code § 2–207(1). The additional or different terms are then to be construed as proposals for modification of the contract. See Uniform Commercial Code § 2–207(2). Such proposals may sometimes be accepted by the silence of the original offeror. See § 69. . . .

b. Statement of conditions implied in offer. To accept, the offeree must assent unconditionally to the offer as made, but the fact that the offeree makes a conditional promise is not sufficient to show that his acceptance is conditional. The offer itself may either expressly or by implication propose that the offeree make a conditional promise as his part of the exchange. By assenting to such a proposal the offeree makes a conditional promise, but his acceptance is unconditional. The offeror's promise may also be conditional on the same or a different fact or event. . . .

§ 60.   Acceptance of Offer Which States Place, Time or Manner of Acceptance.

If an offer prescribes the place, time or manner of acceptance its terms in this respect must be complied with in order to create a contract. If an offer merely suggests a permitted place, time or manner of acceptance, another method of acceptance is not precluded.

Comment

a.   *Interpretation of offer.* If the offeror prescribes the only way in which his offer may be accepted, an acceptance in any other way is a counter-offer. But frequently in regard to the details of methods of acceptance, the offeror's language, if fairly interpreted, amounts merely to a statement of a satisfactory method of acceptance, without positive requirement that this method shall be followed. . . .

§ 61.   Acceptance Which Requests Change of Terms.

An acceptance which requests a change or addition to the terms of the offer is not thereby invalidated unless the acceptance is made to depend on an assent to the changed or added terms.

§ 62.   Effect of Performance by Offeree Where Offer Invites Either Performance or Promise.

(1)   Where an offer invites an offeree to choose between acceptance by promise and acceptance by performance, the tender or beginning of the invited performance or a tender of a beginning of it is an acceptance by performance.

(2)   Such an acceptance operates as a promise to render complete performance.

Comment

a.   *The offeree's power to choose.* The offeror normally invites a promise by the offeree for the purpose of obtaining performance of the promise. Full performance fulfills that purpose more directly than the promise invited, and hence constitutes a reasonable mode of acceptance. The offeror can insist on any mode of acceptance, but ordinarily he invites acceptance in any reasonable manner; in case of doubt, an offer is interpreted as inviting the offeree to choose between acceptance by promise and acceptance by performance. See §§ 30, 32, 58.

b.   *Part performance or tender.* Where acceptance by performance is invited and no promise is invited, the beginning of performance or the tender of part performance creates an option contract and renders the offer irrevocable. See §§ 37, 45. Under Subsection (1) of this Section the offer is similarly rendered irrevocable where it invites the offeree to choose between acceptance by promise and acceptance by performance. In both types of cases, if the invited performance takes time, the invitation to perform necessarily includes an invitation to begin performance; if performance requires cooperation by the offeror, there is an offer only if acceptance can be completed by tender of performance. But unless an option contract is contemplated, the offeree is expected to be bound as well as the offeror, and Subsection (2) of this Section states the implication of promise which results from that expectation. . . . In such standard cases as the shipment of goods in response to an order, the acceptance will come to the offeror's attention in normal course; in other cases, the rule of § 54(2) ordinarily requires prompt notification. . . .

d.   *Preparations for performance.* As under § 45, what is begun or tendered must be part of the actual performance invited, rather than preparation for performance, in order to make the rule of this Section applicable. See Comment *f* to § 45. But preparations to perform may bring the case within § 87(2) on justifiable reliance.

Illustrations

1.   A, a merchant, mails B, a carpenter in the same city, an offer to employ B to fit up A's office in accordance with A's specifications and B's estimate previously submitted, the work to be completed in two weeks. The offer says, "You may begin at once," and B immediately buys lumber and begins to work on it in his own shop. The next day, before B has sent a notice of acceptance or begun work at A's

office or rendered the lumber unfit for other jobs, A revokes the offer. The revocation is timely, since B has not begun to perform.

    2.   A, a regular customer of B, orders fragile goods from B which B carries in stock and ships in his own trucks. Following his usual practice, B selects the goods ordered, tags them as A's, crates them and loads them on a truck at substantial expense. Performance has begun, and A's offer is irrevocable. See Uniform Commercial Code § 2–206 and Comment 2.

§ 63.   Time When Acceptance Takes Effect.

Unless the offer provides otherwise,

    (a)   an acceptance made in a manner and by a medium invited by an offer is operative and completes the manifestation of mutual assent as soon as put out of the offeree's possession, without regard to whether it ever reaches the offeror; but

    (b)   an acceptance under an option contract is not operative until received by the offeror.

Comment

    . . .

    b.   In the interest of simplicity and clarity, the rule [that an acceptance is effective on dispatch] has been extended [in section 63] to cases where an acceptance is lost or delayed in the course of transmission. The convenience of the rule is less clear in such cases than in cases of attempted revocation of the offer, however, and the language of the offer is often properly interpreted as making the offeror's duty of performance conditional upon receipt of the acceptance. Indeed, where the receipt of notice is essential to enable the offeror to perform, such a condition is normally implied. . . .

    c.   *Revocation of acceptance.* The fact that the offeree has power to reclaim his acceptance from the post office or telegraph company does not prevent the acceptance from taking effect on dispatch. Nor, in the absence of additional circumstances, does the actual recapture of the acceptance deprive it of legal effect, though as a practical matter the offeror cannot assert his rights unless he learns of them. An attempt to revoke the acceptance by an overtaking communication is similarly ineffective, even though the revocation is received before the acceptance is received. After mailing an acceptance of a revocable offer, the offeree is not permitted to speculate at the offeror's expense during the time required for the letter to arrive.

    A purported revocation of acceptance may, however, affect the rights of the parties. It may amount to an offer to rescind the contract or to a repudiation of it, or it may bar the offeree by estoppel from enforcing it. . . .

§ 64.   Acceptance by Telephone or Teletype.

Acceptance given by telephone or other medium of substantially instantaneous two-way communication is governed by the principles applicable to acceptances where the parties are in the presence of each other.

§ 65.   Reasonableness of Medium of Acceptance.

Unless circumstances known to the offeree indicate otherwise, a medium of acceptance is reasonable if it is the one used by the offeror or one customary in similar transactions at the time and place the offer is received.

Comment

    a.   *Significance of use of reasonable medium.* Under § 30 an offer invites acceptance by any reasonable medium unless there is contrary indication; under § 63 an acceptance so invited is ordinarily effective upon dispatch. If an unreasonable medium of acceptance is used, on the other hand, the governing rule is that stated in § 67. . . .

§ 66.   Acceptance Must Be Properly Dispatched.

An acceptance sent by mail or otherwise from a distance is not operative when dispatched, unless it is properly addressed and such other precautions taken as are ordinarily observed to insure safe transmission of similar messages.

§ 67.   Effect of Receipt of Acceptance Improperly Dispatched.

Where an acceptance is seasonably dispatched but the offeree uses means of transmission not invited by the offer or fails to exercise reasonable diligence to insure safe transmission, it is treated as operative upon dispatch if received within the time in which a properly dispatched acceptance would normally have arrived.

§ 68.   What Constitutes Receipt of Revocation, Rejection, or Acceptance.

A written revocation, rejection, or acceptance is received when the writing comes into the possession of the person addressed, or of some person authorized by him to receive it for him, or when it is deposited in some place which he has authorized as the place for this or similar communications to be deposited for him.

§ 69.   Acceptance by Silence or Exercise of Dominion.

(1)   Where an offeree fails to reply to an offer, his silence and inaction operate as an acceptance in the following cases only:

(a)   Where an offeree takes the benefit of offered services with reasonable opportunity to reject them and reason to know that they were offered with the expectation of compensation.

(b)   Where the offeror has stated or given the offeree reason to understand that assent may be manifested by silence or inaction, and the offeree in remaining silent and inactive intends to accept the offer.

(c)   Where because of previous dealings or otherwise, it is reasonable that the offeree should notify the offeror if he does not intend to accept.

(2)   An offeree who does any act inconsistent with the offeror's ownership of offered property is bound in accordance with the offered terms unless they are manifestly unreasonable. But if the act is wrongful as against the offeror it is an acceptance only if ratified by him.

Comment

. . .

c.   *Intent to accept.* The mere fact that an offeror states that silence will constitute acceptance does not deprive the offeree of his privilege to remain silent without accepting. But the offeree is entitled to rely on such a statement if he chooses. The case for acceptance is strongest when the reliance is definite and substantial or when the intent to accept is objectively manifested though not communicated to the offeror. Compare §§ 54, 87(2). Even though the intent to accept is manifested only by silent inaction, however, the offeror who has invited such an acceptance cannot complain of the resulting uncertainty in his position. . . .

d.   *Prior conduct of the offeree.* Explicit statement by the offeree, usage of trade, or a course of dealing between the parties may give the offeror reason to understand that silence will constitute acceptance. In such a situation the offer may tacitly incorporate that understanding, and if the offeree intends to accept the case then falls within Subsection (1)(b). Under Subsection (1)(c) the offeree's silence is acceptance, regardless of his actual intent, unless both parties understand that no acceptance is intended. See § 20. . . .

§ 70.   Effect of Receipt by Offeror of a Late or Otherwise Defective Acceptance.

A late or otherwise defective acceptance may be effective as an offer to the original offeror, but his silence operates as an acceptance in such a case only as stated in § 69.

CHAPTER 4

FORMATION OF CONTRACTS—CONSIDERATION

TOPIC 1. THE REQUIREMENT OF CONSIDERATION

§ 71. Requirement of Exchange; Types of Exchange.

(1) To constitute consideration, a performance or a return promise must be bargained for.

(2) A performance or return promise is bargained for if it is sought by the promisor in exchange for his promise and is given by the promisee in exchange for that promise.

(3) The performance may consist of

    (a) an act other than a promise, or

    (b) a forbearance, or

    (c) the creation, modification, or destruction of a legal relation.

(4) The performance or return promise may be given to the promisor or to some other person. It may be given by the promisee or by some other person.

Comment

. . .

b. *"Bargained for."* In the typical bargain, the consideration and the promise bear a reciprocal relation of motive or inducement: the consideration induces the making of the promise and the promise induces the furnishing of the consideration. Here, as in the matter of mutual assent, the law is concerned with the external manifestation rather than the undisclosed mental state: it is enough that one party manifests an intention to induce the other's response and to be induced by it and that the other responds in accordance with the inducement. . . . But it is not enough that the promise induces the conduct of the promisee or that the conduct of the promisee induces the making of the promise; both elements must be present, or there is no bargain. Moreover, a mere pretense of bargain does not suffice, as where there is a false recital of consideration or where the purported consideration is merely nominal. . . .

§ 72. Exchange of Promise for Performance.

Except as stated in §§ 73 and 74, any performance which is bargained for is consideration.

Comment

. . .

b. *Substantive bases for enforcement; the half-completed exchange.* Bargains are widely believed to be beneficial to the community in the provision of opportunities for freedom of individual action and exercise of judgment and as a means by which productive energy and product are apportioned in the economy. The enforcement of bargains rests in part on the common belief that enforcement enhances that utility. Where one party has performed, there are additional grounds for enforcement. Where, for example, one party has received goods from the other and has broken his promise to pay for them, enforcement of the promise not only encourages the making of socially useful bargains; it also reimburses the seller for a loss incurred in reliance on the promise and prevents the unjust enrichment of the buyer at the seller's expense. Each of these three grounds of enforcement, bargain, reliance and unjust enrichment, has independent force, but the bargain element alone satisfies the requirement of consideration except in the cases covered by §§ 73, 74, 76 and 77. Cases of promises binding by virtue of reliance or unjust enrichment are dealt with in §§ 82–94.

c.   *Formality.* Consideration furnishes a substantive rather than a formal basis for the enforcement of a promise. Many bargains, particularly when fully performed on one side, involve acts in the course of performance which satisfy some or all of the functions of form and thus may be thought of as natural formalities. Four principal functions have been identified which legal formalities in general may serve: the *evidentiary* function, to provide evidence of the existence and terms of the contract; the *cautionary* function, to guard the promisor against ill-considered action; the *deterrent* function, to discourage transactions of doubtful utility; and the *channeling* or signalizing function, to distinguish a particular type of transaction from other types and from tentative or exploratory expressions of intention in the way that coinage distinguishes money from other metal. But formality is not essential to consideration; nor does formality supply consideration where the element of exchange is absent. Rules under which formality makes binding a promise not supported by consideration are stated in §§ 82–94. . . .

§ 73.   Performance of Legal Duty.

Performance of a legal duty owed to a promisor which is neither doubtful nor the subject of honest dispute is not consideration; but a similar performance is consideration if it differs from what was required by the duty in a way which reflects more than a pretense of bargain.

Comment

a.   *Rationale.* A claim that the performance of a legal duty furnished consideration for a promise often raises a suspicion that the transaction was gratuitous or mistaken or unconscionable. . . . Mistake, misrepresentation, duress, undue influence, or public policy may invalidate the transaction even though there is consideration. See Chapters 6–8. But the rule of this Section renders unnecessary any inquiry into the existence of such an invalidating cause, and denies enforcement to some promises which would otherwise be valid. Because of the likelihood that the promise was obtained by an express or implied threat to withhold performance of a legal duty, the promise does not have the presumptive social utility normally found in a bargain. Enforcement must therefore rest on some substantive or formal basis other than the mere fact of bargain. . . .

b.   *Public duties; torts and crimes.* A legal duty may be owed to the promisor as a member of the public, as when the promisee is a public official. In such cases there is often no direct sanction available to a member of the public to compel performance of the duty, and the danger of express or implied threats to withhold performance affects public as well as private interests. A bargain by a public official to obtain private advantage for performing his duty is therefore unenforceable as against public policy. . . . And under this section performance of the duty is not consideration for a promise.

Similar reasoning may apply to duties of public utilities, duties of fiduciaries, and in some cases to duties of citizens generally. Thus a bargain to pay a witness for testimony may be unenforceable as against public policy. . . .

In applying this Section it is first necessary to define the legal duty. The requirement of consideration is satisfied if the duty is doubtful or is the subject of honest dispute, or if the consideration includes a performance in addition to or materially different from the performance of the duty. Whether such facts eliminate duress or violation of public policy or other invalidating cause depends on the circumstances. Ordinarily a mere formality such as the affixing of a seal, though sufficient to render consideration unnecessary, does not cure such defects. In some situations, however, where there is no other invalidating cause but lack of consideration, the bargain may be enforceable by virtue of reliance or unjust enrichment or formality. See §§ 82–109. . . .

c.   *Contractual duty to the promisor.* Legal remedies for breach of contract ordinarily involve delay and expense and rarely put the promisee in fully as good a position as voluntary performance. It is therefore often to a promisee's advantage to offer a bonus to a recalcitrant promisor to induce performance without legal proceedings, and an unscrupulous promisor may threaten breach in order to obtain such a bonus. In extreme cases, a bargain for additional compensation under such circumstances may be voidable for duress. See §§ 175–76. And the lack of social utility in such bargains provides what modern justification there is for the rule that performance of a contractual duty is not consideration for a new promise.

But the rule has not been limited to cases where there was a possibility of unfair pressure, and it has been much criticized as resting on scholastic logic. Slight variations of circumstance are commonly held to take a case out of the rule, particularly where the parties have made an equitable adjustment in the course of performance of a continuing contract, or where an impecunious debtor has paid part of his debt in satisfaction of the whole. See §§ 89, 273–77. And in some states the rule has simply been repudiated. . . .

d.   *Contractual duty to third person.* The rule that performance of legal duty is not consideration for a promise has often been applied in cases involving a contractual duty owed to a person other than the promisor. In such cases, however, there is less likelihood of economic coercion or other unfair pressure than there is if the duty is owed to the promisee. In some cases consideration can be found in the fact that the promisee gives up his right to propose to the third person the rescission or modification of the contractual duty. But the tendency of the law has been simply to hold that performance of contractual duty can be consideration if the duty is not owed to the promisor. Relief may still be given to the promisor in appropriate cases under the rules governing duress and other invalidating causes. . . .

e.   *Voidable and unenforceable duties.* The duty referred to in the Section is confined to a duty for which any remedy ordinarily allowed by the law for that kind of duty is still available. One who may at will avoid a legal relation or refrain from any performance without legal consequences, or against whom all remedies appropriate to the enforcement of his duty have become barred, is not under a duty within the meaning of the Section. . . .

f.   *Doubtful, disputed and unliquidated duties.* Such duties are not within this Section. They are the subject of § 74.

§ 74.   Settlement of Claims.

(1)   Forbearance to assert or the surrender of a claim or defense which proves to be invalid is not consideration unless

     (a)   the claim or defense is in fact doubtful because of uncertainty as to the facts or the law, or

     (b)   the forbearing or surrendering party believes that the claim or defense may be fairly determined to be valid.

(2)   The execution of a written instrument surrendering a claim or defense by one who is under no duty to execute it is consideration if the execution of the written instrument is bargained for even though he is not asserting the claim or defense and believes that no valid claim or defense exists.

Comment

a.   *Relation to legal-duty rule.* Subsection (1) elaborates a limitation on the scope of the legal-duty rule stated in § 73. That limitation is based on the traditional policy of favoring compromises of disputed claims in order to reduce the volume of litigation. . . .

c.   *Unliquidated obligations.* An undisputed obligation may be unliquidated, that is, uncertain or disputed in amount. The settlement of such a claim is governed by the same principles as settlement of a claim the existence of which is doubtful or disputed. The payment of any definite sum of money on account of a single claim which is entirely unliquidated is consideration for a return promise. An admission by the obligor that a minimum amount is due does not liquidate the claim even partially unless he is contractually bound to the admission. But payment of less than is admittedly due may in some circumstances tend to show that a partial defense or offset was not asserted in good faith.

Payment of an obligation which is liquidated and undisputed is not consideration for a promise to surrender an unliquidated claim which is wholly distinct. See § 73. Whether in a particular case there is a single unliquidated claim or a combination of separate claims, some liquidated and some not, depends on the circumstances and the agreements of the parties. If there are no circumstances of unfair pressure or economic coercion and a disputed item is closely related to an undisputed item, the two are treated as making up a single unliquidated claim; and payment of the amount admittedly due can be consideration for a promise to surrender the entire claim.

e. *Execution of release or quit-claim deed.* Subsection (2) provides for the situation where the party who would be subject to a claim or defense, if one existed, wants assurance of its non-existence. Such assurance may be useful, for example, to enable him to obtain credit or to sell property. Although surrender of a non-existent claim by one who knows he has no claim is not consideration for a promise, the execution of an instrument of surrender may be consideration if there is no improper pressure or deception. . . . But there is no consideration if the surrendering party is under a duty to execute the instrument. . . .

§ 75. Exchange of Promise for Promise.

Except as stated in §§ 76 and 77, a promise which is bargained for is consideration if, but only if, the promised performance would be consideration.

Comment

a. *The executory exchange.* In modern times the enforcement of bargains is not limited to those partly completed, but is extended to the wholly executory exchange in which promise is exchanged for promise. In such a case the element of unjust enrichment is not present; the element of reliance, if present at all, is less tangible and direct than in the case of the half-completed exchange. The promise is enforced by virtue of the fact of bargain, without more. Since the principle that bargains are binding is widely understood and is reinforced in many situations by custom and convention, the fact of bargain also tends to satisfy the cautionary and channeling functions of form. . . .

§ 76. Conditional Promise.

(1) A conditional promise is not consideration if the promisor knows at the time of making the promise that the condition cannot occur.

(2) A promise conditional on a performance by the promisor is a promise of alternative performances within § 77 unless occurrence of the condition is also promised.

§ 77. Illusory and Alternative Promises.

A promise or apparent promise is not consideration if by its terms the promisor or purported promisor reserves a choice of alternative performances unless

(a) each of the alternative performances would have been consideration if it alone had been bargained for; or

(b) one of the alternative performances would have been consideration and there is or appears to the parties to be a substantial possibility that before the promisor exercises his choice events may eliminate the alternatives which would not have been consideration.

Comment

a. *Illusory promises.* Words of promise which by their terms make performance entirely optional with the "promisor" do not constitute a promise. See Comment e to § 2; compare § 76. In such cases there might theoretically be a bargain to pay for the utterance of the words, but in practice it is performance which is bargained for. Where the apparent assurance of performance is illusory, it is not consideration for a return promise. A different rule applies, however, where performance is optional, not by the terms of the agreement, but by virtue of a rule of law. See § 5 (defining "term"), § 78. . . .

§ 78. Voidable and Unenforceable Promises.

The fact that a rule of law renders a promise voidable or unenforceable does not prevent it from being consideration.

§ 79. Adequacy of Consideration; Mutuality of Obligation.

If the requirement of consideration is met, there is no additional requirement of

    (a)   a gain, advantage, or benefit to the promisor or a loss, disadvantage, or detriment to the promisee; or

    (b)   equivalence in the values exchanged; or

    (c)   "mutuality of obligation."

Comment

. . .

    c.   *Exchange of unequal values.* To the extent that the apportionment of productive energy and product in the economy are left to private action, the parties to transactions are free to fix their own valuations. The resolution of disputes often requires a determination of value in the more general sense of market value, and such values are commonly fixed as an approximation based on a multitude of private valuations. But in many situations there is no reliable external standard of value, or the general standard is inappropriate to the precise circumstances of the parties. Valuation is left to private action in part because the parties are thought to be better able than others to evaluate the circumstances of particular transactions. . . .

    d.   *Pretended exchange.* Disparity in value, with or without other circumstances, sometimes indicates that the purported consideration was not in fact bargained for but was a mere formality or pretense. Such a sham or "nominal" consideration does not satisfy the requirement of § 71. . . .

    e.   *Effects of gross inadequacy.* Although the requirement of consideration may be met despite a great difference in the values exchanged, gross inadequacy of consideration may be relevant in the application of other rules. Inadequacy "such as shocks the conscience" is often said to be a "badge of fraud," justifying a denial of specific performance. . . . Inadequacy may also help to justify rescission or cancelation on the ground of lack of capacity . . . mistake, misrepresentation, duress or undue influence. . . . Unequal bargains are also limited by the statutory law of usury . . . and by special rules developed for the sale of an expectation of inheritance, for contractual penalties and forfeitures . . . and for agreements between secured lender and borrower. . . .

§ 80. Multiple Exchanges.

    (1)   There is consideration for a set of promises if what is bargained for and given in exchange would have been consideration for each promise in the set if exchanged for that promise alone.

    (2)   The fact that part of what is bargained for would not have been consideration if that part alone had been bargained for does not prevent the whole from being consideration.

§ 81. Consideration as Motive or Inducing Cause.

    (1)   The fact that what is bargained for does not of itself induce the making of a promise does not prevent it from being consideration for the promise.

    (2)   The fact that a promise does not of itself induce a performance or return promise does not prevent the performance or return promise from being consideration for the promise.

TOPIC 2. CONTRACTS WITHOUT CONSIDERATION

§ 82. Promise to Pay Indebtedness; Effect on the Statute of Limitations.

    (1)   A promise to pay all or part of an antecedent contractual or quasi-contractual indebtedness owed by the promisor is binding if the indebtedness is still enforceable or would be except for the effect of a statute of limitations.

(2) The following facts operate as such a promise unless other facts indicate a different intention:

(a) A voluntary acknowledgment to the obligee, admitting the present existence of the antecedent indebtedness; or

(b) A voluntary transfer of money, a negotiable instrument, or other thing by the obligor to the obligee, made as interest on or part payment of or collateral security for the antecedent indebtedness; or

(c) A statement to the obligee that the statute of limitations will not be pleaded as a defense.

Comment

a. Requirement of a writing. Statutes enacted in most States provide that a promise included in the Section is not binding unless it is in writing and signed by or on behalf of the promisor, except where the promise is inferred from part payment or from the giving of a negotiable instrument or collateral security as stated in Subsection (2)(b). . . . In a few States, no writing is required in any case. In a few other States, the rule is more stringent than that generally prevailing and even part payment or giving of security imposes no promissory duty on a debtor unless there is also a signed writing. Most of the statutes requiring a writing are inapplicable to promises supported by consideration or made enforceable by reliance. See § 90. . . .

§ 83. Promise to Pay Indebtedness Discharged in Bankruptcy.

An express promise to pay all or part of an indebtedness of the promisor, discharged or dischargeable in bankruptcy proceedings begun before the promise is made, is binding.

Comment

a. Rationale. The early history of the rule of this Section is the same as that of the rule of § 82, relating to the statute of limitations, and the two rules are similar in many respects. But only a few States have enacted statutes requiring the promises described in this Section to be in writing. In modern times discharge in bankruptcy has been thought to reflect a somewhat stronger public policy than the statute of limitations, and a promise implied from acknowledgment or part payment does not revive a debt discharged in bankruptcy. Although in the absence of a statute an oral promise is effective, the courts have insisted on the formality of express promise, denying effect to expressions of expectation or of good intention. . . .

§ 84. Promise to Perform a Duty in Spite of Non-Occurrence of a Condition.

(1) Except as stated in Subsection (2), a promise to perform all or part of a conditional duty under an antecedent contract in spite of the non-occurrence of the condition is binding, whether the promise is made before or after the time for the condition to occur, unless

(a) occurrence of the condition was a material part of the agreed exchange for the performance of the duty and the promisee was under no duty that it occur; or

(b) uncertainty of the occurrence of the condition was an element of the risk assumed by the promisor.

(2) If such a promise is made before the time for the occurrence of the condition has expired and the condition is within the control of the promisee or a beneficiary, the promisor can make his duty again subject to the condition by notifying the promisee or beneficiary of his intention to do so if

(a) the notification is received while there is still a reasonable time to cause the condition to occur under the antecedent terms or an extension given by the promisor; and

(b) reinstatement of the requirement of the condition is not unjust because of a material change of position by the promisee or beneficiary; and

(c) the promise is not binding apart from the rule stated in Subsection (1).

Comment

a.   Rationale. Like the rules stated in §§ 82 and 83, the rule of Subsection (1) can be thought of in terms of waiver of a defense not addressed to the merits, and rests in large part on the policies against forfeiture and unjust enrichment. Where the waiver is made before the time for the occurrence of the condition, it may induce non-occurrence of the condition, and enforcement may also rest on reliance or on excuse by prevention or hindrance. See §§ 89, 90. But a waiver made after the original duty has been discharged, though it is sometimes said to "reinstate" the duty, in fact creates a new duty unqualified by the condition. . . .

c.   Conditions material to the exchange or risk. A promise is often conditional on the receipt of some performance regarded as the equivalent of the performance promised, as in the case of an option contract to sell a horse if the promisee pays $500 for him. A promise may also be conditional on a fortuitous event, and the risk or burden assumed by the promisor may depend on the probability that the condition will occur, as in a promise to insure a house against fire. In both types of cases, where a promise to disregard the non-occurrence of the condition materially affects the value received by the promisor or the burden or risk assumed by him, the promise is not binding under Subsection (1). Such a promise may be binding by virtue of reliance or for some other reason. See §§ 89, 90. See also § 246. But a waiver of the price of a horse or of the fire required by an insurance policy is not within this Section.

d.   Conditions which may be waived. The rule of Subsection (1) applies primarily to conditions which may be thought of as procedural or technical, or to instances in which the non-occurrence of condition is comparatively minor. Examples are conditions which merely relate to the time or manner of the return performance or provide for the giving of notice or the supplying of proofs. Insurance policies ordinarily contain conditions of notice and proof of loss and of time for suit; and guarantors, indorsers and other sureties may be discharged by an agreement varying the duty of the principal debtor, by failure of diligence in presentment or prosecution, or by failure to give a required notice. In such cases, even though a promise to disregard the non-occurrence of the condition subjects the promisor to a new duty, the new duty is not regarded as significantly different from the old and the promise is binding without consideration, reliance, or formality. See, e.g., Uniform Commercial Code § 3–606, Comment 2. . . .

Illustrations

. . .

3.   A employs B to build a house, promising to pay therefor $10,000 on the production of a certificate from A's architect, C, stating that the work has been satisfactorily completed. B builds the house but the work is defective in certain trivial particulars. C refuses to give B a certificate. A says to B, "My architect rightfully refuses to give you a certificate but the defects are not serious; I will pay you the full price which I promised." A is bound to do so, and has no power to restore the requirement of the condition.

4.   A, an insurance company, insures B's house for $5000 against loss by fire. The insurance policy provides that it shall be payable only if B gives written notification of any loss within thirty days after its occurrence. An insured loss occurs and B gives only oral notification thereof within thirty days. A tells him, either before or after the lapse of thirty days from the loss, that this notification is sufficient. A cannot thereafter rely upon B's failure to give written notification as an excuse for failure to pay for the loss. . . .

f.   Reinstatement after waiver. If the requirement of a condition has been eliminated from a contract by an agreement supported by consideration it cannot be reinstated by unilateral action of the promisor. Nor can it be reinstated if a new unconditional duty has been created by a promise made after the original duty was discharged by non-occurrence of the condition, or if reinstatement would be unjust in view of a change of position by the other party. Compare Uniform Commercial Code § 2–209(5); Restatement of Restitution § 142. But where the requirement of a condition is waived in advance, the promisor may reinstate the requirement by giving notice to the other party before the latter has materially changed his position. Whether delay alone makes reinstatement unjust depends upon the circumstances: in some cases a reasonable extension of time sufficiently protects the other party; in others the extension may be required to be both definite and reasonable; in some no extension can put him in as good a position to perform as before the waiver. . . .

Illustration

6.   In Illustration 4, A can restore the requirement of the condition by notifying B of his intention to do so if there still remains a reasonable time for the occurrence of the condition before the expiration of the thirty-day period, unless such action would be unjust in view of a material change of position by B in reliance on A's waiver. If a reasonable time does not remain, A cannot restore the requirement of the condition by extending the time.

§ 85.   Promise to Perform a Voidable Duty.

Except as stated in § 93, a promise to perform all or part of an antecedent contract of the promisor, previously voidable by him, but not avoided prior to the making of the promise, is binding.

§ 86.   Promise for Benefit Received.

(1)   A promise made in recognition of a benefit previously received by the promisor from the promisee is binding to the extent necessary to prevent injustice.

(2)   A promise is not binding under Subsection (1)

     (a)   if the promisee conferred the benefit as a gift or for other reasons the promisor has not been unjustly enriched; or

     (b)   to the extent that its value is disproportionate to the benefit.

Comment

a.   *"Past consideration;" "moral obligation."* Enforcement of promises to pay for benefit received has sometimes been said to rest on "past consideration" or on the "moral obligation" of the promisor, and there are statutes in such terms in a few states. Those terms are not used here: "past consideration" is inconsistent with the meaning of consideration stated in § 71, and there seems to be no consensus as to what constitutes a "moral obligation." The mere fact of promise has been thought to create a moral obligation, but it is clear that not all promises are enforced. Nor are moral obligations based solely on gratitude or sentiment sufficient of themselves to support a subsequent promise.

Illustrations

1.   A gives emergency care to B's adult son while the son is sick and without funds far from home. B subsequently promises to reimburse A for his expenses. The promise is not binding under this Section.

2.   A lends money to B, who later dies. B's widow promises to pay the debt. The promise is not binding under this Section. . . .

b.   *Rationale.* Although in general a person who has been unjustly enriched at the expense of another is required to make restitution, restitution is denied in many cases in order to protect persons who have had benefits thrust upon them. . . . In other cases restitution is denied by virtue of rules designed to guard against false claims, stale claims, claims already litigated, and the like. In many such cases a subsequent promise to make restitution removes the reason for the denial of relief, and the policy against unjust enrichment then prevails. . . .

d.   *Emergency services and necessaries.* The law of restitution in the absence of promise severely limits recovery for necessaries furnished to a person under disability and for emergency services. . . . A subsequent promise in such a case may remove doubt as to the reality of the benefit and as to its value, and may negate any danger of imposition or false claim. A positive showing that payment was expected is not then required; an intention to make a gift must be shown to defeat restitution.

Illustration

. . .

6.   A finds B's escaped bull and feeds and cares for it. B's subsequent promise to pay reasonable compensation to A is binding. . . .

f.   Benefit conferred pursuant to contract. By virtue of the policy of enforcing bargains, the enrichment of one party as a result of an unequal exchange is not regarded as unjust, and this Section has no application to a promise to pay or perform more or to accept less than is called for by a preexisting bargain between the same parties. Compare §§ 79, 89. Similarly, if a third person receives a benefit as a result of the performance of a bargain, this Section does not make binding the subsequent promise of the third person to pay extra compensation to the performing party. But a promise to pay in substitution for the return performance called for by the bargain may be binding under this Section.

i.   Partial enforcement. . . . [W]here a benefit received is a liquidated sum of money, a promise is not enforceable under this Section beyond the amount of the benefit. Where the value of the benefit is uncertain, a promise to pay the value is binding and a promise to pay a liquidated sum may serve to fix the amount due if in all the circumstances it is not disproportionate to the benefit. A promise which is excessive may sometimes be enforced to the extent of the value of the benefit, and the remedy may be thought of as quasi-contractual rather than contractual. . . .

Illustrations

. . .

12.   A, a married woman of sixty, has rendered household services without compensation over a period of years for B, a man of eighty living alone and having no close relatives. B has a net worth of three million dollars and has often assured A that she will be well paid for her services, whose reasonable value is not in excess of $6,000. B executes and delivers to A a written promise to pay A $25,000 "to be taken from my estate." The promise is binding.

13.   The facts being otherwise as stated in Illustration 12, B's promise is made orally and is to leave A his entire estate. A cannot recover more than the reasonable value of her services.

§ 87. Option Contract.

(1)   An offer is binding as an option contract if it

(a)   is in writing and signed by the offeror, recites a purported consideration for the making of the offer, and proposes an exchange on fair terms within a reasonable time; or

(b)   is made irrevocable by statute.

(2)   An offer which the offeror should reasonably expect to induce action or forbearance of a substantial character on the part of the offeree before acceptance and which does induce such action or forbearance is binding as an option contract to the extent necessary to avoid injustice.

Comment

a.   Consideration and form. The traditional common-law devices for making a firm offer or option contract are the giving of consideration and the affixing of a seal. See §§ 25, 95. But the firm offer serves a useful purpose even though no preliminary bargain is made: it is often a necessary step in the making of the main bargain proposed, and it partakes of the natural formalities inherent in business transactions. The erosion of the formality of the seal has made it less and less satisfactory as a universal formality. As literacy has spread, the personal signature has become the natural formality and the seal has become more and more anachronistic. The rules stated in this section reflect the judicial and legislative response to this situation. . . .

b.   Nominal consideration. . . . [A] comparatively small payment may furnish consideration for the irrevocability of an offer proposing a transaction involving much larger sums. . . . [S]uch a nominal consideration is regularly held sufficient to support a short-time option proposing an exchange on fair terms. The fact that the option is an appropriate preliminary step in the conclusion of a socially useful transaction provides a sufficient substantive basis for enforcement, and a signed writing taking a form appropriate to a bargain satisfies the desiderata of form. . . .

e.   Reliance. Subsection (2) states the application of § 90 to reliance on an unaccepted offer, with qualifications which would not be appropriate in some other types of cases covered by § 90. It is important chiefly in cases of reliance that is not part performance. If the beginning of performance is a reasonable mode of acceptance, it makes the offer fully enforceable under § 45 or § 62; if not, the offeror commonly has no reason to expect part performance before acceptance. But circumstances may be such that the offeree must undergo substantial expense, or undertake substantial commitments, or forego alternatives, in order to put himself in a position to accept by either promise or performance. The offer may be made expressly irrevocable in contemplation of reliance by the offeree. If reliance follows in such cases, justice may require a remedy. Compare Restatement, Second, Torts § 325; Restatement, Second, Agency § 378. But the reliance must be substantial as well as foreseeable.

Full-scale enforcement of the offered contract is not necessarily appropriate in such cases. Restitution of benefits conferred may be enough, or partial or full reimbursement of losses may be proper. Various factors may influence the remedy: the formality of the offer, its commercial or social context, the extent to which the offeree's reliance was understood to be at his own risk, the relative competence and the bargaining position of the parties, the degree of fault on the part of the offeror, the ease and certainty of proof of particular items of damage and the likelihood that unprovable damages have been suffered. . . .

§ 88.   Guaranty.

A promise to be surety for the performance of a contractual obligation, made to the obligee, is binding if

    (a)   the promise is in writing and signed by the promisor and recites a purported consideration; or

    (b)   the promise is made binding by statute; or

    (c)   the promisor should reasonably expect the promise to induce action or forbearance of a substantial character on the part of the promisee or a third person, and the promise does induce such action or forbearance.

§ 89.   Modification of Executory Contract.

A promise modifying a duty under a contract not fully performed on either side is binding

    (a)   if the modification is fair and equitable in view of circumstances not anticipated by the parties when the contract was made; or

    (b)   to the extent provided by statute; or

    (c)   to the extent that justice requires enforcement in view of material change of position in reliance on the promise.

Comment

a.   *Rationale.* This Section relates primarily to adjustments in on-going transactions. Like offers and guaranties, such adjustments are ancillary to exchanges and have some of the same presumptive utility. See §§ 72, 87, 88. Indeed, paragraph (a) deals with bargains which are without consideration only because of the rule that performance of a legal duty to the promisor is not consideration. See § 73. This Section is also related to § 84 on waiver of conditions: it may apply to cases in which § 84 is inapplicable because a condition is material to the exchange or risk. As in cases governed by § 84, relation to a bargain tends to satisfy the cautionary and channeling functions of legal formalities. See Comment *c* to § 72. The Statute of Frauds may prevent enforcement in the absence of reliance. See §§ 149–50. Otherwise formal requirements are at a minimum.

b.   *Performance of legal duty.* The rule of § 73 finds its modern justification in cases of promises made by mistake or induced by unfair pressure. Its application to cases where those elements are absent has been much criticized and is avoided if paragraph (a) of this Section is applicable. The limitation to a modification which is "fair and equitable" goes beyond absence of coercion and requires an objectively demonstrable reason for seeking a modification. Compare Uniform Commercial Code § 2–209 Comment. The reason for modification must rest in circumstances not "anticipated" as part of the context in which the contract was made, but a frustrating event may be unanticipated for this purpose if it was not adequately covered, even though it was foreseen as a remote possibility. When such a reason is present, the relative financial strength of the parties, the formality with which the modification is made, the extent to which it is performed or relied on and other circumstances may be relevant to show or negate imposition or unfair surprise.

The same result called for by paragraph (a) is sometimes reached on the ground that the original contract was "rescinded" by mutual agreement and that new promises were then made which furnished consideration for each other. That theory is rejected here because it is fictitious when the "rescission" and new agreement are simultaneous, and because if logically carried out it might uphold unfair and inequitable modifications. . . .

d.   Reliance. Paragraph (c) states the application of § 90 to modification of an executory contract in language adapted from Uniform Commercial Code § 2–209. Even though the promise is not binding when made, it may become binding in whole or in part by reason of action or forbearance by the promisee or third persons in reliance on it. In some cases the result can be viewed as based either on estoppel to contradict a representation of fact or on reliance on a promise. Ordinarily reliance by the promisee is reasonably foreseeable and makes the modification binding with respect to performance by the promisee under it and any return performance owed by the promisor. But as under § 84 the original terms can be reinstated for the future by reasonable notification received by the promisee unless reinstatement would be unjust in view of a change of position on his part. Compare Uniform Commercial Code § 2–209(5). . . .

§ 90.   Promise Reasonably Inducing Action or Forbearance.

(1)   A promise which the promisor should reasonably expect to induce action or forbearance on the part of the promisee or a third person and which does induce such action or forbearance is binding if injustice can be avoided only by enforcement of the promise. The remedy granted for breach may be limited as justice requires.

(2)   A charitable subscription or a marriage settlement is binding under Subsection (1) without proof that the promise induced action or forbearance.

Comment

a.   Relation to other rules. . . . It is fairly arguable that the enforcement of informal contracts in the action of assumpsit rested historically on justifiable reliance on a promise. Certainly reliance is one of the main bases for enforcement of the half-completed exchange, and the probability of reliance lends support to the enforcement of the executory exchange. See Comments to §§ 72, 75. This Section thus states a basic principle which often renders inquiry unnecessary as to the precise scope of the policy of enforcing bargains. Sections 87–89 state particular applications of the same principle to promises ancillary to bargains, and it also applies in a wide variety of non-commercial situations. . . .

b.   Character of reliance protected. The principle of this Section is flexible. The promisor is affected only by reliance which he does or should foresee, and enforcement must be necessary to avoid injustice. Satisfaction of the latter requirement may depend on the reasonableness of the promisee's reliance, on its definite and substantial character in relation to the remedy sought, on the formality with which the promise is made, on the extent to which the evidentiary, cautionary, deterrent and channeling functions of form are met by the commercial setting or otherwise, and on the extent to which such other policies as the enforcement of bargains and the prevention of unjust enrichment are relevant. Compare Comment to § 72. . . .

d.   Partial enforcement. A promise binding under this section is a contract, and full-scale enforcement by normal remedies is often appropriate. But the same factors which bear on whether any relief should be granted also bear on the character and extent of the remedy. In particular, relief may sometimes be limited to restitution or to damages or specific relief measured by the extent of the promisee's reliance rather than by the terms of the promise. . . .

§ 91.   Effect of Promises Enumerated in §§ 82–90 When Conditional.

If a promise within the terms of §§ 82–90 is in terms conditional or performable at a future time the promisor is bound thereby, but performance becomes due only upon the occurrence of the condition or upon the arrival of the specified time.

§ 92.   To Whom Promises Enumerated in §§ 82–85 Must Be Made.

The new promise referred to in §§ 82–85 is not binding unless it is made to a person who is then an obligee of the antecedent duty.

§ 93.   Promises Enumerated in §§ 82–85 Made in Ignorance of Facts.

A promise within the terms of §§ 82–85 is not binding unless the promisor knew or had reason to know the essential facts of the previous transaction to which the promise relates, but his knowledge of the legal effect of the facts is immaterial.

§ 94.   Stipulations.

A promise or agreement with reference to a pending judicial proceeding, made by a party to the proceeding or his attorney, is binding without consideration. By statute or rule of court such an agreement is generally binding only

(a)   if it is in writing and signed by the party or attorney, or

(b)   if it is made or admitted in the presence of the court, or

(c)   to the extent that justice requires enforcement in view of material change of position in reliance on the promise or agreement.

§ 95.   Requirements for Sealed Contract or Written Contract or Instrument.

(1)   In the absence of statute a promise is binding without consideration if

(a)   it is in writing and sealed; and

(b)   the document containing the promise is delivered; and

(c)   the promisor and promisee are named in the document or so described as to be capable of identification when it is delivered.

(2)   When a statute provides in effect that a written contract or instrument is binding without consideration or that lack of consideration is an affirmative defense to an action on a written contract or instrument, in order to be subject to the statute a promise must either

(a)   be expressed in a document signed or otherwise assented to by the promisor and delivered; or

(b)   be expressed in a writing or writings to which both promisor and promisee manifest assent.

§ 96.   What Constitutes a Seal.

(1)   A seal is a manifestation in tangible and conventional form of an intention that a document be sealed.

(2)   A seal may take the form of a piece of wax, a wafer or other substance affixed to the document or of an impression made on the document.

(3)   By statute or decision in most States in which the seal retains significance a seal may take the form of a written or printed seal, word, scrawl or other sign.

TOPIC 3. CONTRACTS UNDER SEAL; WRITING AS A STATUTORY SUBSTITUTE FOR THE SEAL

§ 97.   When a Promise Is Sealed.

A written promise is sealed if the promisor affixes or impresses a seal on the document or adopts a seal already thereon.

§ 98. Adoption of a Seal by Delivery.

Unless extrinsic circumstances manifest a contrary intention, the delivery of a written promise by the promisor amounts to the adoption of any seal then on the document which has apparent reference to his signature or to the signature of another party to the document.

§ 99. Adoption of the Same Seal by Several Parties.

Any number of parties to the same instrument may adopt one seal.

§ 100. Recital of Sealing or Delivery.

A recital of the sealing or of the delivery of a written promise is not essential to its validity as a contract under seal and is not conclusive of the fact of sealing or delivery unless a statute makes a recital of sealing the equivalent of a seal.

§ 101. Delivery.

A written promise, sealed or unsealed, may be delivered by the promisor in escrow, conditionally to the promisee, or unconditionally.

§ 102. Unconditional Delivery.

A written promise is delivered unconditionally when the promisor puts it out of his possession and manifests an intention that it is to take effect at once according to its terms.

§ 103. Delivery in Escrow; Conditional Delivery to the Promisee.

(1)   A written promise is delivered in escrow by the promisor when he puts it into the possession of a person other than the promisee without reserving a power of revocation and manifests an intention that the document is to take effect according to its terms upon the occurrence of a stated condition but not otherwise.

(2)   A written promise is delivered conditionally to the promisee when the promisor puts it into the possession of the promisee without reserving a power of revocation and manifests an intention that the document is to take effect according to its terms upon the occurrence of a stated condition but not otherwise.

(3)   Delivery of a written promise in escrow or its conditional delivery to the promisee has the same effect as unconditional delivery would have if the requirement of the condition were expressed in the writing.

(4)   In the absence of a statute modifying the significance of a seal, delivery of a sealed promise in escrow or its conditional delivery to the promisee is irrevocable for the time specified by the promisor for the occurrence of the condition, or, if no time is specified, for a reasonable time.

§ 104. Acceptance or Disclaimer by the Promisee.

(1)   Neither acceptance by the promisee nor knowledge by him of the existence of a promise is essential to the formation of a contract by the delivery of a written promise which is binding without consideration.

(2)   A promisee who has not manifested assent to a written promise may, within a reasonable time after learning of its existence and terms, render it inoperative by disclaimer.

(3)   Acceptance or disclaimer is irrevocable.

§ 105. Acceptance Where Return Promise Is Contemplated.

Where a conveyance or a document containing a promise also purports to contain a return promise by the grantee or promisee, acceptance by the grantee or promisee is essential to create any contractual obligation other than an option contract binding on the grantor or promisor.

§ 106. What Amounts to Acceptance of Instrument.

Acceptance of a conveyance or of a document containing a promise is a manifestation of assent to the terms thereof made, either before or after delivery, in accordance with any requirements imposed by the grantor or promisor. If the acceptance occurs before delivery and is not binding as an option contract, it is revocable until the moment of delivery.

§ 107. Creation of Unsealed Contract by Acceptance by Promisee.

Where a grantee or promisee accepts a sealed document which purports to contain a return promise by him, he makes the return promise. But if he does not sign or seal the document his promise is not under seal, and whether it is binding depends on the rules governing unsealed contracts.

§ 108. Requirement of Naming or Describing Promisor and Promisee.

A promise under seal is not binding without consideration unless both the promisor and the promisee are named in the document or so described as to be capable of identification when it is delivered.

§ 109. Enforcement of a Sealed Contract by Promisee Who Does Not Sign or Seal It.

The promisee of a promise under seal is not precluded from enforcing it as a sealed contract because he has not signed or sealed the document, unless his doing so was a condition of the delivery, whether or not the document contains a promise by him.

CHAPTER 5

THE STATUTE OF FRAUDS

§ 110. Classes of Contracts Covered.

(1)   The following classes of contracts are subject to a statute, commonly called the Statute of Frauds, forbidding enforcement unless there is a written memorandum or an applicable exception:

(a)   a contract of an executor or administrator to answer for a duty of his decedent (the executor-administrator provision);

(b)   a contract to answer for the duty of another (the suretyship provision);

(c)   a contract made upon consideration of marriage (the marriage provision);

(d)   a contract for the sale of an interest in land (the land contract provision);

(e)   a contract that is not to be performed within one year from the making thereof (the one-year provision).

. . .

(5)   In many states other classes of contracts are subject to a requirement of a writing.

TOPIC 1. THE EXECUTOR-ADMINISTRATOR PROVISION

§ 111. Contract of Executor or Administrator.

A contract of an executor or administrator to answer personally for a duty of his decedent is within the Statute of Frauds if a similar contract to answer for the duty of a living person would be within the Statute as a contract to answer for the duty of another.

TOPIC 2. THE SURETYSHIP PROVISION

§ 112. Requirement of Suretyship.

A contract is not within the Statute of Frauds as a contract to answer for the duty of another unless the promisee is an obligee of the other's duty, the promisor is a surety for the other, and the promisee knows or has reason to know of the suretyship relation.

§ 113. Promises of the Same Performance for the Same Consideration.

Where promises of the same performance are made by two persons for a consideration which inures to the benefit of only one of them, the promise of the other is within the Statute of Frauds as a contract to answer for the duty of another, whether or not the promise is in terms conditional on default by the one to whose benefit the consideration inures, unless

(a)   the other is not a surety for the one to whose benefit the consideration inures; or

(b)   the promises are in terms joint and do not create several duties or joint and several duties; or

(c)   the promisee neither knows nor has reason to know that the consideration does not inure to the benefit of both promisors.

§ 114. Independent Duty of Promisor.

A contract to perform or otherwise to satisfy all or part of a duty of a third person to the promisee is not within the Statute of Frauds as a contract to answer for the duty of another if, by the terms of the promise when it is made, performance thereof can involve no more than

(a) the application of funds or property held by the promisor for the purpose, or

(b) performance of any other duty owing, irrespective of his promise, by the promisor to the promisee, or

(c) performance of a duty which is either owing, irrespective of his promise, by the promisor to the third person, or which the promisee reasonably believes to be so owing.

§ 115. Novation.

A contract that is itself accepted in satisfaction of a previously existing duty of a third person to the promisee is not within the Statute of Frauds as a contract to answer for the duty of another.

§ 116. Main Purpose; Advantage to Surety.

A contract that all or part of a duty of a third person to the promisee shall be satisfied is not within the Statute of Frauds as a promise to answer for the duty of another if the consideration for the promise is in fact or apparently desired by the promisor mainly for his own economic advantage, rather than in order to benefit the third person. If, however, the consideration is merely a premium for insurance, the contract is within the Statute.

§ 117. Promise to Sign a Written Contract of Suretyship.

A promise to sign a written contract as a surety for the performance of a duty owed to the promisee or to sign a negotiable instrument for the accommodation of a person other than the promisee is within the Statute of Frauds.

§ 118. Promise to Indemnify a Surety.

A promise to indemnify against liability or loss made to induce the promisee to become a surety is not within the Statute of Frauds as a contract to answer for the duty of another.

§ 119. Assumption of Duty by Another.

A contract not within the Statute of Frauds as a contract to answer for the duty of another when made is not brought within it by a subsequent promise of another person to assume performance of the duty as principal obligor.

§ 120. Obligations on Negotiable Instruments.

(1) An obligation on a negotiable instrument or a guaranty written on the instrument is not within the Statute of Frauds.

(2) A promise to pay a negotiable instrument, made by a party to it who has been or may be discharged by the holder's failure or delay in making presentment or giving notice of dishonor or in making protest, is not within the Statute of Frauds.

§ 121. Contract of Assignor or Factor.

(1) A contract by the assignor of a right that the obligor of the assigned right will perform his duty is not within the Statute of Frauds as a contract to answer for the duty of another.

(2) A contract by an agent with his principal that a purchaser of the principal's goods through the agent will pay their price to the principal is not within the Statute of Frauds as a contract to answer for the duty of another.

§ 122. Contract to Buy a Right From the Obligee.

A contract to purchase a right which the promisee has or may acquire against a third person is not within the Statute of Frauds as a contract to answer for the duty of another.

§ 123. Contract to Discharge the Promisee's Duty.

A contract to discharge a duty owed by the promisee to a third person is not within the Statute of Frauds as a contract to answer for the duty of another.

TOPIC 3. THE MARRIAGE PROVISION

§ 124. Contract Made Upon Consideration of Marriage.

A promise for which all or part of the consideration is either marriage or a promise to marry is within the Statute of Frauds, except in the case of an agreement which consists only of mutual promises of two persons to marry each other.

TOPIC 4. THE LAND CONTRACT PROVISION

§ 125. Contract to Transfer, Buy, or Pay for an Interest in Land.

(1) A promise to transfer to any person any interest in land is within the Statute of Frauds.

(2) A promise to buy any interest in land is within the Statute of Frauds, irrespective of the person to whom the transfer is to be made.

(3) When a transfer of an interest in land has been made, a promise to pay the price, if originally within the Statute of Frauds, ceases to be within it unless the promised price is itself in whole or in part an interest in land.

(4) Statutes in most states except from the land contract and one-year provisions of the Statute of Frauds short-term leases and contracts to lease, usually for a term not longer than one year.

§ 126. Contract to Procure Transfer or to Act as Agent.

(1) A contract to procure the transfer of an interest in land by a person other than the promisor is within the Statute of Frauds.

(2) A contract to act as agent for another in endeavoring to procure the transfer of any interest in land by someone other than the promisor is not within the Statute of Frauds as a contract for the sale of an interest in land.

§ 127. Interest in Land.

An interest in land within the meaning of the Statute is any right, privilege, power or immunity, or combination thereof, which is an interest in land under the law of property and is not "goods" within the Uniform Commercial Code.

§ 128. Boundary and Partition Agreements.

(1) A contract between owners of adjoining tracts of land fixing a dividing boundary is within the Statute of Frauds but if the location of the boundary was honestly disputed the contract becomes enforceable notwithstanding the Statute when the agreed boundary has been marked or has been recognized in the subsequent use of the tracts.

(2) A contract by joint tenants or tenants in common to partition land into separate tracts for each tenant is within the Statute of Frauds but becomes enforceable notwithstanding the Statute as to each tract when possession of it is taken in severalty in accordance with the agreement.

§ 129. Action in Reliance; Specific Performance.

A contract for the transfer of an interest in land may be specifically enforced notwithstanding failure to comply with the Statute of Frauds if it is established that the party seeking enforcement, in reasonable reliance on the contract and on the continuing assent of the party against whom enforcement is sought, has so changed his position that injustice can be avoided only by specific enforcement.

TOPIC 5. THE ONE-YEAR PROVISION

§ 130. Contract Not to Be Performed Within a Year.

(1)   Where any promise in a contract cannot be fully performed within a year from the time the contract is made, all promises in the contract are within the Statute of Frauds until one party to the contract completes his performance.

(2)   When one party to a contract has completed his performance, the one-year provision of the Statute does not prevent enforcement of the promises of other parties.

Comment

a.   Possibility of performance within one year. The English Statute of Frauds applied to an action "upon any agreement that is not to be performed within the space of one year from the making thereof." The design was said to be not to trust to the memory of witnesses for a longer time than one year, but the statutory language was not appropriate to carry out that purpose. The result has been a tendency to construction narrowing the application of the statute. Under the prevailing interpretation, the enforceability of a contract under the one-year provision does not turn on the actual course of subsequent events, nor on the expectations of the parties as to the probabilities. Contracts of uncertain duration are simply excluded; the provision covers only those contracts whose performance cannot possibly be completed within a year. . . .

TOPIC 6. SATISFACTION OF THE STATUTE BY A MEMORANDUM

§ 131. General Requisites of a Memorandum.

Unless additional requirements are prescribed by the particular statute, a contract within the Statute of Frauds is enforceable if it is evidenced by any writing, signed by or on behalf of the party to be charged, which

(a)   reasonably identifies the subject matter of the contract,

(b)   is sufficient to indicate that a contract with respect thereto has been made between the parties or offered by the signer to the other party, and

(c)   states with reasonable certainty the essential terms of the unperformed promises in the contract.

Comment

. . .

c.   Rationale. The primary purpose of the Statute is evidentiary, to require reliable evidence of the existence and terms of the contract and to prevent enforcement through fraud or perjury of contracts never in fact made. The contents of the writing must be such as to make successful fraud unlikely, but the possibility need not be excluded that some other subject matter or person than those intended will also fall within the words of the writing. Where only an evidentiary purpose is served, the requirement of a memorandum is read in the light of the dispute which arises and the admissions of the party to be charged; there is no need for evidence on points not in dispute.

§ 132. Several Writings.

The memorandum may consist of several writings if one of the writings is signed and the writings in the circumstances clearly indicate that they relate to the same transaction.

§ 133. Memorandum Not Made as Such.

Except in the case of a writing evidencing a contract upon consideration of marriage, the Statute may be satisfied by a signed writing not made as a memorandum of a contract.

§ 134. Signature.

The signature to a memorandum may be any symbol made or adopted with an intention, actual or apparent, to authenticate the writing as that of the signer.

§ 135. Who Must Sign.

Where a memorandum of a contract within the Statute is signed by fewer than all parties to the contract and the Statute is not otherwise satisfied, the contract is enforceable against the signers but not against the others.

§ 136. Time of Memorandum.

A memorandum sufficient to satisfy the Statute may be made or signed at any time before or after the formation of the contract.

§ 137. Loss or Destruction of a Memorandum.

The loss or destruction of a memorandum does not deprive it of effect under the Statute.

TOPIC 7. CONSEQUENCES OF NON-COMPLIANCE

§ 138. Unenforceability.

Where a contract within the Statute of Frauds is not enforceable against the party to be charged by an action against him, it is not enforceable by a set-off or counterclaim in an action brought by him, or as a defense to a claim by him.

§ 139. Enforcement by Virtue of Action in Reliance.

(1) A promise which the promisor should reasonably expect to induce action or forbearance on the part of the promisee or a third person and which does induce the action or forbearance is enforceable notwithstanding the Statute of Frauds if injustice can be avoided only by enforcement of the promise. The remedy granted for breach is to be limited as justice requires.

(2) In determining whether injustice can be avoided only by enforcement of the promise, the following circumstances are significant:

(a) the availability and adequacy of other remedies, particularly cancellation and restitution;

(b) the definite and substantial character of the action or forbearance in relation to the remedy sought;

(c) the extent to which the action or forbearance corroborates evidence of the making and terms of the promise, or the making and terms are otherwise established by clear and convincing evidence;

(d) the reasonableness of the action or forbearance;

(e) the extent to which the action or forbearance was foreseeable by the promisor.

Comment

a. Relation to other rules. This Section is complementary to § 90, which dispenses with the requirement of consideration if the same conditions are met, but it also applies to promises supported by consideration. Like § 90, this Section overlaps in some cases with rules based on estoppel or fraud; it states a basic principle which sometimes renders inquiry unnecessary as to the precise scope of other policies. . . .

b. Avoidance of injustice. Like § 90 this Section states a flexible principle, but the requirement of consideration is more easily displaced than the requirement of a writing. . . . Subsection (2) lists some of the relevant factors in applying the latter requirement. Each factor relates either to the extent to which reliance furnishes a compelling substantive basis for relief in addition to the expectations created by the promise or to the extent to which the circumstances satisfy the evidentiary purpose of the Statute and fulfill any cautionary, deterrent and channeling functions it may serve.

§ 140. Defense of Failure to Perform.

The Statute of Frauds does not invalidate defenses based on the plaintiff's failure to perform a condition of his claim or defenses based on his present or prospective breach of the contract he seeks to enforce.

§ 141. Action for Value of Performance Under Unenforceable Contract.

(1) In an action for the value of performance under a contract, except as stated in Subsection (2), the Statute of Frauds does not invalidate any defense which would be available if the contract were enforceable against both parties.

(2) Where a party to a contract which is unenforceable against him refuses either to perform the contract or to sign a sufficient memorandum, the other party is justified in suspending any performance for which he has not already received the agreed return, and such a suspension is not a defense in an action for the value of performance rendered before the suspension.

§ 142. Tort Liability for Acts Under Unenforceable Contract.

Where because of the existence of a contract conduct would not be tortious, unenforceability of the contract under the Statute of Frauds does not make the conduct tortious if it occurs without notice of repudiation of the contract.

§ 143. Unenforceable Contract as Evidence.

The Statute of Frauds does not make an unenforceable contract inadmissible in evidence for any purpose other than its enforcement in violation of the Statute.

§ 144. Effect of Unenforceable Contract as to Third Parties.

Only a party to a contract or a transferee or successor of a party to the contract can assert that the contract is unenforceable under the Statute of Frauds.

§ 145. Effect of Full Performance.

Where the promises in a contract have been fully performed by all parties, the Statute of Frauds does not affect the legal relations of the parties.

§ 146. Rights of Competing Transferees of Property.

(1) Where a contract to transfer property or a transfer was unenforceable against the transferor under the Statute of Frauds but subsequently becomes enforceable, the contract or transfer has whatever priority it would have had aside from the Statute of Frauds over an intervening contract by the transferor to transfer the same property to a third person.

(2) If the third person obtains title to the property by an enforceable transaction before the prior contract becomes enforceable, the prior contract is unenforceable against him and does not affect his title.

§ 147. Contract Containing Multiple Promises.

(1) Where performance of the promises in a contract which subject it to the Statute of Frauds is exclusively beneficial to one party, that party by agreeing to forego the performance may render the remainder of the contract enforceable, but this rule does not apply to a contract to transfer property on the promisor's death.

(2) Where the promises in a contract which subject it to the Statute have become enforceable or where the duty to perform them has been discharged by performance or otherwise, the Statute does not prevent enforcement of the remaining promises.

(3) Except as stated in this Section, where some of the unperformed promises in a contract are unenforceable against a party under the Statute of Frauds, all the promises in the contract are unenforceable against him.

§ 148. Rescission by Oral Agreement.

Notwithstanding the Statute of Frauds, all unperformed duties under an enforceable contract may be discharged by an oral agreement of rescission. The Statute may, however, apply to a contract to rescind a transfer of property.

§ 149. Oral Modification.

(1) For the purpose of determining whether the Statute of Frauds applies to a contract modifying but not rescinding a prior contract, the second contract is treated as containing the originally agreed terms as modified. The Statute may, however, apply independently of the original terms to a contract to modify a transfer of property.

(2) Where the second contract is unenforceable by virtue of the Statute of Frauds and there has been no material change of position in reliance on it, the prior contract is not modified.

§ 150. Reliance on Oral Modification.

Where the parties to an enforceable contract subsequently agree that all or part of a duty need not be performed or of a condition need not occur, the Statute of Frauds does not prevent enforcement of the subsequent agreement if reinstatement of the original terms would be unjust in view of a material change of position in reliance on the subsequent agreement.

CHAPTER 6

MISTAKE

§ 151. Mistake Defined.

A mistake is a belief that is not in accord with the facts.

§ 152. When Mistake of Both Parties Makes a Contract Voidable.

(1)   Where a mistake of both parties at the time a contract was made as to a basic assumption on which the contract was made has a material effect on the agreed exchange of performances, the contract is voidable by the adversely affected party unless he bears the risk of the mistake under the rule stated in § 154.

(2)   In determining whether the mistake has a material effect on the agreed exchange of performances, account is taken of any relief by way of reformation, restitution, or otherwise.

Comment

. . .

b.   *Basic assumption*. A mistake of both parties does not make the contract voidable unless it is one as to a basic assumption on which both parties made the contract. The term "basic assumption" has the same meaning here as it does in Chapter 11 in connection with impracticability (§§ 261, 266(1)) and frustration (§§ 265, 266(2)). See Uniform Commercial Code § 2–615(a). For example, market conditions and the financial situation of the parties are ordinarily not such assumptions, and, generally, just as shifts in market conditions or financial ability do not effect discharge under the rules governing impracticability, mistakes as to market conditions or financial ability do not justify avoidance under the rules governing mistake. . . . The parties may have had such a "basic assumption," even though they were not conscious of alternatives. . . . Where, for example, a party purchases an annuity on the life of another person, it can be said that it was a basic assumption that the other person was alive at the time, even though the parties never consciously addressed themselves to the possibility that he was dead. . . .

g.   *Relation to breach of warranty*. The rule stated in this Section has a close relationship to the rules governing warranties [in a] sale by a seller of goods or of other kinds of property. A buyer usually finds it more advantageous to rely on the law of warranty than on the law of mistake. Because of the broad scope of a seller's warranties, a buyer is more often entitled to relief based on a claim of breach of warranty than on a claim based on mistake. Furthermore, because relief for breach of warranty is generally based on the value that the property would have had if it had been as warranted (see Uniform Commercial Code § 2–714(2)), it is ordinarily more extensive than that afforded if he merely seeks to avoid the contract on the ground of mistake. Nevertheless, . . . warranties are not necessarily exclusive and, even absent a warranty, a buyer may be able to avoid on the ground of mistake if he brings himself within the rule stated in this Section. The effect, on a buyer's claim of mistake, of language purporting to disclaim the seller's responsibility for the goods is governed by the rules on interpretation stated in Chapter 9. . . .

h.   *Mistakes as to different assumptions*. The rule stated in this Section applies only where both parties are mistaken as to the same basic assumption. Their mistakes need not be, and often they will not be, identical. If, however, the parties are mistaken as to different assumptions, the rule stated in § 153, rather than that stated in this Section, applies.

§ 153. When Mistake of One Party Makes a Contract Voidable.

Where a mistake of one party at the time a contract was made as to a basic assumption on which he made the contract has a material effect on the agreed exchange of performances that is adverse to him, the contract is voidable by him if he does not bear the risk of the mistake under the rule stated in § 154, and

(a)   the effect of the mistake is such that enforcement of the contract would be unconscionable, or

(b)   the other party had reason to know of the mistake or his fault caused the mistake.

Comment

a.   Rationale. Courts have traditionally been reluctant to allow a party to avoid a contract on the ground of mistake, even as to a basic assumption, if the mistake was not shared by the other party. Nevertheless, relief has been granted where the other party actually knew (see §§ 160, 161) or had reason to know of the mistake at the time the contract was made or where his fault caused the mistake. There has, in addition, been a growing willingness to allow avoidance where the consequences of the mistake are so grave that enforcement of the contract would be unconscionable. This Section states a rule that permits avoidance on this latter basis, as well as on the more traditional grounds. The rules stated in this Section also apply to option contracts, under which a party's offer is irrevocable either under a statute, such as one applying to bids for public works, or on other grounds. The parol evidence rule does not preclude the use of prior or contemporaneous agreements or negotiations to establish that a party was mistaken. See § 214(d). Nevertheless, because mistakes are the exception rather than the rule, the trier of the facts should examine the evidence with particular care when a party attempts to avoid liability by proving mistake. See Comment c to § 155. The rule stated in this Section is subject to that stated in § 157 on fault of the party seeking relief. It is also subject to the rules on exercise of the power of avoidance stated in §§ 380–85.

b.   Similarity to rule where both are mistaken. In order for a party to have the power to avoid a contract for a mistake that he alone made, he must at least meet the same requirements that he would have had to meet had both parties been mistaken (§ 152). The mistake must be one as to a basic assumption on which the contract was made; it must have a material effect on the agreed exchange of performances; and the mistaken party must not bear the risk of the mistake. The most common sorts of such mistakes occur in bids on construction contracts and result from clerical errors in the computation of the price or in the omission of component items. . . . The rule stated in this Section is not, however, limited to such cases. It also applies, for example, to a misreading of specifications . . . or such misunderstanding as does not prevent a manifestation of mutual assent. . . . Where only one party is mistaken, however, he must meet either the additional requirement stated in Subparagraph (a) or one of the additional requirements stated in Subparagraph (b).

c.   Additional requirement of unconscionability. Under Subparagraph (a), the mistaken party must in addition show that enforcement of the contract would be unconscionable. The reason for this additional requirement is that, if only one party was mistaken, avoidance of the contract will more clearly disappoint the expectations of the other party than if he too was mistaken. . . . Although § 208, Unconscionable Contract or Term, is not itself applicable to such cases since the unconscionability does not appear at the time the contract is made, the standards of unconscionability in such cases are similar to those under § 208 (see Comment c to § 208). The mistaken party bears the substantial burden of establishing unconscionability and must ordinarily show not only the position he would have been in had the facts been as he believed them to be but also the position in which he finds himself as a result of his mistake. For example, in the typical case of a mistake as to the price in a bid, the builder must show the profit or loss that will result if he is required to perform, as well as the profit that he would have made had there been no mistake.

§ 154. When a Party Bears the Risk of a Mistake.

A party bears the risk of a mistake when

(a)   the risk is allocated to him by agreement of the parties, or

(b)   he is aware, at the time the contract is made, that he has only limited knowledge with respect to the facts to which the mistake relates but treats his limited knowledge as sufficient, or

(c)   the risk is allocated to him by the court on the ground that it is reasonable in the circumstances to do so.

Comment

a.   *Rationale.* . . . A party . . . bears the risk of many mistakes as to existing circumstances even though they upset basic assumptions and unexpectedly affect the agreed exchange of performances. For example, it is commonly understood that the seller of farm land generally cannot avoid the contract of sale upon later discovery by both parties that the land contains valuable mineral deposits, even though the price was negotiated on the basic assumption that the land was suitable only for farming and the effect on the agreed exchange of performances is material. In such a case a court will ordinarily allocate the risk of the mistake to the seller, so that he is under a duty to perform regardless of the mistake. . . .

b.   *Allocation by agreement.* The most obvious case of allocation of the risk of a mistake is one in which the parties themselves provide for it by their agreement. . . .

c.   *Conscious ignorance.* Even though the mistaken party did not agree to bear the risk, he may have been aware when he made the contract that his knowledge with respect to the facts to which the mistake relates was limited. If he was not only so aware that his knowledge was limited but undertook to perform in the face of that awareness, he bears the risk of the mistake. It is sometimes said in such a situation that, in a sense, there was not mistake but "conscious ignorance." . . .

§ 155. When Mistake of Both Parties as to Written Expression Justifies Reformation.

Where a writing that evidences or embodies an agreement in whole or in part fails to express the agreement because of a mistake of both parties as to the contents or effect of the writing, the court may at the request of a party reform the writing to express the agreement, except to the extent that rights of third parties such as good faith purchasers for value will be unfairly affected.

§ 156. Mistake as to Contract Within the Statute of Frauds.

If reformation of a writing is otherwise appropriate, it is not precluded by the fact that the contract is within the Statute of Frauds.

§ 157. Effect of Fault of Party Seeking Relief.

A mistaken party's fault in failing to know or discover the facts before making the contract does not bar him from avoidance or reformation under the rules stated in this Chapter, unless his fault amounts to a failure to act in good faith and in accordance with reasonable standards of fair dealing.

Comment

a.   *Rationale.* The mere fact that a mistaken party could have avoided the mistake by the exercise of reasonable care does not preclude either avoidance (§§ 152, 153) or reformation (§ 155). Indeed, since a party can often avoid a mistake by the exercise of such care, the availability of relief would be severely circumscribed if he were to be barred by his negligence. Nevertheless, in extreme cases the mistaken party's fault is a proper ground for denying him relief for a mistake that he otherwise could have avoided. Although the critical degree of fault is sometimes described as "gross" negligence, that term is not well defined and is avoided in this Section as it is in the Restatement, Second, of Torts. Instead, the rule is stated in terms of good faith and fair dealing. The general duty of good faith and fair dealing, imposed under the rule stated in § 205, extends only to the performance and enforcement of a contract and does not apply to the negotiation stage prior to the formation of the contract. See Comment c to § 205. Therefore, a failure to act in good faith and in accordance with reasonable standards of fair dealing during pre-contractual negotiations does not amount to a breach. Nevertheless, under the rule stated in this Section, the failure bars a mistaken party from relief based on a mistake that otherwise would not have been made. During the negotiation stage each party is held to a degree of responsibility appropriate to the justifiable expectations of the other. The terms "good faith" and "fair dealing" are used, in this context, in much the same sense as in § 205 and Uniform Commercial Code [§ 1–304].

§ 158. Relief Including Restitution.

(1) In any case governed by the rules stated in this Chapter, either party may have a claim for relief including restitution under the rules stated in §§ 240 and 376.

(2) In any case governed by the rules stated in this Chapter, if those rules together with the rules stated in Chapter 16 will not avoid injustice, the court may grant relief on such terms as justice requires including protection of the parties' reliance interests.

Comment

a. Scope. A court may use several techniques to adjust the rights of the parties after discovery of a mistake. Subsection (1) speaks to claims for relief such as that provided by the rule on part performances as agreed equivalents stated in § 240 and those on restitution and other relief stated in Chapter 16. Subsection (2) speaks to supplying a term to avoid injustice. See the analogous rule stated in § 272.

b. Relief including restitution. Avoidance of a contract ideally involves a reversal of any steps that the parties may have taken by way of performance, so that each party returns such benefit as he may have received. This is not, however, possible in all cases. Occasionally a party who has performed may be entitled to recover on the contract for the part that he has performed under the rule on part performances as agreed equivalents (§ 240). Even where this is not so, it may be appropriate to permit avoidance coupled with a money claim for restitution to the extent that one party's performance has benefited the other. Such claims are governed by the rules stated in §§ 370–77. A party may also have a claim that goes beyond mere restitution and includes elements of reliance by the claimant. . . .

c. Supplying a term to avoid injustice. Under the rule stated in § 204, when the parties have not agreed with respect to a term that is essential to a determination of their rights and duties, the court will supply a term that is reasonable in the circumstances. Ordinarily the rules stated in this Chapter, coupled with those stated in Chapter 16, will be adequate to allow the court to arrive at a just result. See Subsection (1). If, however, these rules will not suffice to avoid injustice, the court may supply a term just as it may in cases of impracticability of performance and frustration of purpose. See § 272(2) and Comment c to that section. Here, as there, a particularly significant application occurs when the just solution is to "sever" the agreement and require that some unexecuted part of it be performed on both sides, rather than to relieve both parties of all their duties. The situation differs from that envisioned in § 240, under which the court merely allows recovery at the contract rate for performance that has already been rendered. The question under this Section is whether the court can salvage a part of the agreement that is still executory on both sides. . . .

Sometimes the party who is not adversely affected by a mistake can, by assenting to a modification of the contract, eliminate the effect of the mistake on the agreed exchange. He should generally be allowed to do so and thereby to preclude avoidance by the party who would otherwise be adversely affected. A court may, under Subsection (2), grant the party who has not been adversely affected what is, in effect, an option to enforce the contract on new terms. . . .

The Court may also exercise its discretion under Subsection (2) where both parties have been responsible for the mistake. It may do so, for example, where a mistake of one party resulted both from his failure to act in good faith and in accordance with reasonable standards of fair dealing (§ 157) and from the fault of the other party (§ 153(b)). See Comment f to § 153. Furthermore, for the sake of simplicity, the rules stated in this Chapter have been formulated in terms of the typical contract based on an exchange of consideration by two parties, and it does not, therefore, deal exhaustively with problems of mistake involving several parties (§ 9) including intended beneficiaries (§ 302), promises enforceable because of reliance (§ 90), promises enforceable because under seal (§ 95), and other less typical situations. In such cases, the court will apply rules analogous to those stated in this Chapter. See Comments b, d, and e to § 155. The situations dealt with in Subsection (2) are to be distinguished from those envisioned by § 155, where a writing is reformed to carry out the intentions of the parties.

CHAPTER 7

MISREPRESENTATION, DURESS AND UNDUE INFLUENCE

TOPIC 1. MISREPRESENTATION

§ 159. Misrepresentation Defined.

A misrepresentation is an assertion that is not in accord with the facts.

§ 160. When Action Is Equivalent to an Assertion (Concealment).

Action intended or known to be likely to prevent another from learning a fact is equivalent to an assertion that the fact does not exist.

§ 161. When Non-Disclosure Is Equivalent to an Assertion.

A person's non-disclosure of a fact known to him is equivalent to an assertion that the fact does not exist in the following cases only:

    (a) where he knows that disclosure of the fact is necessary to prevent some previous assertion from being a misrepresentation or from being fraudulent or material.

    (b) where he knows that disclosure of the fact would correct a mistake of the other party as to a basic assumption on which that party is making the contract and if non-disclosure of the fact amounts to a failure to act in good faith and in accordance with reasonable standards of fair dealing.

    (c) where he knows that disclosure of the fact would correct a mistake of the other party as to the contents or effect of a writing, evidencing or embodying an agreement in whole or in part.

    (d) where the other person is entitled to know the fact because of a relation of trust and confidence between them.

Comment

a. Concealment distinguished. Like concealment, non-disclosure of a fact may be equivalent to a misrepresentation. Concealment necessarily involves an element of non-disclosure, but it is the act of preventing another from learning of a fact that is significant and this act is always equivalent to a misrepresentation (§ 160). Non-disclosure without concealment is equivalent to a misrepresentation only in special situations. A party making a contract is not expected to tell all that he knows to the other party, even if he knows that the other party lacks knowledge on some aspects of the transaction. His nondisclosure, as such, has no legal effect except in the situations enumerated in this Section. He may not, of course, tell half-truths and his assertion of only some of the facts without the inclusion of such additional matters as he knows or believes to be necessary to prevent it from being misleading is itself a misrepresentation. . . . In contrast to the rule applicable to liability in tort for misrepresentation, it is not enough, where disclosure is expected, merely to make reasonable efforts to disclose the relevant facts. Actual disclosure is required. Compare Restatement, Second, Torts § 551, Comment d. . . .

c. Failure to correct. One who has made an assertion that is neither a fraudulent nor a material misrepresentation may subsequently acquire knowledge that bears significantly on his earlier assertion. He is expected to speak up and correct the earlier assertion in three cases. First, if his assertion was not a misrepresentation because it was true, he may later learn that it is no longer true. . . . Second, his assertion may have been a misrepresentation but may not have been fraudulent. If this was because he believed that it was true, he may later learn that it was not true. . . . Third, if his assertion was a misrepresentation but was not material because he had no reason to know of the other's special characteristics that made reliance likely, he may later learn of such characteristics. If a person fails to correct his earlier assertion in these situations, the result is the same as it would have been had he had his newly acquired knowledge at the time he made the assertion. The rule stated in Clause (a), like that stated in Clause (d), extends to non-disclosure by persons who are not parties to the transaction. . . .

    d.   *Known mistake as to a basic assumption.* In many situations, if one party knows that the other is mistaken as to a basic assumption, he is expected to disclose the fact that would correct the mistake. A seller of real or personal property is, for example, ordinarily expected to disclose a known latent defect of quality or title that is of such a character as would probably prevent the buyer from buying at the contract price. An owner is ordinarily expected to disclose a known error in a bid that he has received from a contractor. See Comment e to § 153. The mistake must be as to a basic assumption, as is also required by the rules on mistake stated in § 152 . . . and § 153. . . . The rule stated in Clause (b), is, however, broader than these rules for mistake because it does not require a showing of a material effect on the agreed exchange and is not affected by the fact that the party seeking relief bears the risk of the mistake (§ 154). Nevertheless, a party need not correct all mistakes of the other and is expected only to act in good faith and in accordance with reasonable standards of fair dealing, as reflected in prevailing business ethics. A party may, therefore, reasonably expect the other to take normal steps to inform himself and to draw his own conclusions. If the other is indolent, inexperienced or ignorant, or if his judgment is bad or he lacks access to adequate information, his adversary is not generally expected to compensate for these deficiencies. A buyer of property, for example, is not ordinarily expected to disclose circumstances that make the property more valuable than the seller supposes. . . . In contrast to the rules stated in Clauses (a) and (d), that stated in Clause (b) is limited to non-disclosure by a party to the transaction. Actual knowledge is required for the application of the rule stated in Clause (b). The case of a party who does not know but has reason to know of a mistake is governed by the rule stated in § 153(b). As to knowledge in the case of an organization, see the analogous rule in Uniform Commercial Code § 1–201(27). . . .

Illustrations

    7.   A, seeking to induce B to make a contract to sell land, knows that B does not know that the land has appreciably increased in value because of a proposed shopping center but does not disclose this to B. B makes the contract. Since B's mistake is not one as to a basic assumption . . . A's non-disclosure is not equivalent to an assertion that the value of the land has not appreciably increased. . . . The contract is not voidable by B. . . .

    10.   A, seeking to induce B to make a contract to sell A land, learns from government surveys that the land contains valuable mineral deposits and knows that B does not know this, but does not disclose this to B. B makes the contract. A's non-disclosure does not amount to a failure to act in good faith and in accordance with reasonable standards of fair dealing and is therefore not equivalent to an assertion that the land does not contain valuable mineral deposits. The contract is not voidable by B.

    11.   The facts being otherwise as stated in Illustration 10, A learns of the valuable mineral deposits from trespassing on B's land and not from government surveys. A's non-disclosure is equivalent to an assertion that the land does not contain valuable mineral deposits, and this assertion is a misrepresentation. . . .

    f.   *Relation of trust and confidence.* The rule stated in Clause (d) supplements that stated in § 173 with respect to contracts between parties in a fiduciary relation. Where the latter rule applies, as in the case of a trustee, an agent, a guardian, or an executor or administrator, its more stringent requirements govern. Even where a party is not, strictly speaking, a fiduciary, he may stand in such a relation of trust and confidence to the other as to give the other the right to expect disclosure. Such a relationship normally exists between members of the same family and may arise, in other situations as, for example, between physician and patient. In addition, some types of contracts, such as those of suretyship or guaranty, marine insurance and joint adventure, are recognized as creating in themselves confidential relations and hence as requiring the utmost good faith and full and fair disclosure. As to contracts of suretyship, see Restatement of Security § 124. . . .

§ 162. When a Misrepresentation Is Fraudulent or Material.

    (1)   A misrepresentation is fraudulent if the maker intends his assertion to induce a party to manifest his assent and the maker

206

(a) knows or believes that the assertion is not in accord with the facts, or

(b) does not have the confidence that he states or implies in the truth of the assertion, or

(c) knows that he does not have the basis that he states or implies for the assertion.

(2) A misrepresentation is material if it would be likely to induce a reasonable person to manifest his assent, or if the maker knows that it would be likely to induce the recipient to do so.

§ 163. When a Misrepresentation Prevents Formation of a Contract.

If a misrepresentation as to the character or essential terms of a proposed contract induces conduct that appears to be a manifestation of assent by one who neither knows nor has reasonable opportunity to know of the character or essential terms of the proposed contract, his conduct is not effective as a manifestation of assent.

§ 164. When a Misrepresentation Makes a Contract Voidable.

(1) If a party's manifestation of assent is induced by either a fraudulent or a material misrepresentation by the other party upon which the recipient is justified in relying, the contract is voidable by the recipient.

(2) If a party's manifestation of assent is induced by either a fraudulent or a material misrepresentation by one who is not a party to the transaction upon which the recipient is justified in relying, the contract is voidable by the recipient, unless the other party to the transaction in good faith and without reason to know of the misrepresentation either gives value or relies materially on the transaction.

§ 165. Cure by Change of Circumstances.

If a contract is voidable because of a misrepresentation and, before notice of an intention to avoid the contract, the facts come into accord with the assertion, the contract is no longer voidable unless the recipient has been harmed by relying on the misrepresentation.

§ 166. When a Misrepresentation as to a Writing Justifies Reformation.

If a party's manifestation of assent is induced by the other party's fraudulent misrepresentation as to the contents or effect of a writing evidencing or embodying in whole or in part an agreement, the court at the request of the recipient may reform the writing to express the terms of the agreement as asserted,

(a) if the recipient was justified in relying on the misrepresentation, and

(b) except to the extent that rights of third parties such as good faith purchasers for value will be unfairly affected.

§ 167. When a Misrepresentation Is an Inducing Cause.

A misrepresentation induces a party's manifestation of assent if it substantially contributes to his decision to manifest his assent.

§ 168. Reliance on Assertions of Opinion.

(1) An assertion is one of opinion if it expresses only a belief, without certainty, as to the existence of a fact or expresses only a judgment as to quality, value, authenticity, or similar matters.

(2) If it is reasonable to do so, the recipient of an assertion of a person's opinion as to facts not disclosed and not otherwise known to the recipient may properly interpret it as an assertion

(a) that the facts known to that person are not incompatible with his opinion, or

(b) that he knows facts sufficient to justify him in forming it.

§ 169. When Reliance on an Assertion of Opinion Is Not Justified.

To the extent that an assertion is one of opinion only, the recipient is not justified in relying on it unless the recipient

(a) stands in such a relation of trust and confidence to the person whose opinion is asserted that the recipient is reasonable in relying on it, or

(b) reasonably believes that, as compared with himself, the person whose opinion is asserted has special skill, judgment or objectivity with respect to the subject matter, or

(c) is for some other special reason particularly susceptible to a misrepresentation of the type involved.

§ 170. Reliance on Assertions as to Matters of Law.

If an assertion is one as to a matter of law, the same rules that apply in the case of other assertions determine whether the recipient is justified in relying on it.

§ 171. When Reliance on an Assertion of Intention Is Not Justified.

(1) To the extent that an assertion is one of intention only, the recipient is not justified in relying on it if in the circumstances a misrepresentation of intention is consistent with reasonable standards of dealing.

(2) If it is reasonable to do so, the promisee may properly interpret a promise as an assertion that the promisor intends to perform the promise.

§ 172. When Fault Makes Reliance Unjustified.

A recipient's fault in not knowing or discovering the facts before making the contract does not make his reliance unjustified unless it amounts to a failure to act in good faith and in accordance with reasonable standards of fair dealing.

§ 173. When Abuse of a Fiduciary Relation Makes a Contract Voidable.

If a fiduciary makes a contract with his beneficiary relating to matters within the scope of the fiduciary relation, the contract is voidable by the beneficiary, unless

(a) it is on fair terms, and

(b) all parties beneficially interested manifest assent with full understanding of their legal rights and of all relevant facts that the fiduciary knows or should know.

TOPIC 2. DURESS AND UNDUE INFLUENCE

§ 174. When Duress by Physical Compulsion Prevents Formation of a Contract.

If conduct that appears to be a manifestation of assent by a party who does not intend to engage in that conduct is physically compelled by duress, the conduct is not effective as a manifestation of assent.

§ 175. When Duress by Threat Makes a Contract Voidable.

(1) If a party's manifestation of assent is induced by an improper threat by the other party that leaves the victim no reasonable alternative, the contract is voidable by the victim.

(2) If a party's manifestation of assent is induced by one who is not a party to the transaction, the contract is voidable by the victim unless the other party to the transaction in good faith and without reason to know of the duress either gives value or relies materially on the transaction.

§ 176. When a Threat Is Improper.

(1)   A threat is improper if

    (a)   what is threatened is a crime or a tort, or the threat itself would be a crime or a tort if it resulted in obtaining property,

    (b)   what is threatened is a criminal prosecution,

    (c)   what is threatened is the use of civil process and the threat is made in bad faith, or

    (d)   the threat is a breach of the duty of good faith and fair dealing under a contract with the recipient.

(2)   A threat is improper if the resulting exchange is not on fair terms, and

    (a)   the threatened act would harm the recipient and would not significantly benefit the party making the threat,

    (b)   the effectiveness of the threat inducing the manifestation of assent is significantly increased by prior unfair dealing by the party making the threat, or

    (c)   what is threatened is otherwise a use of power for illegitimate ends.

Comment

a.   Rationale. An ordinary offer to make a contract commonly involves an implied threat by one party, the offeror, not to make the contract unless his terms are accepted by the other party, the offeree. Such threats are an accepted part of the bargaining process. A threat does not amount to duress unless it is so improper as to amount to an abuse of that process. Courts first recognized as improper threats of physical violence and later included wrongful seizure or detention of goods. Modern decisions have recognized as improper a much broader range of threats, notably those to cause economic harm. . . .

e.   Breach of contract. A threat by a party to a contract not to perform his contractual duty is not, of itself, improper. Indeed, a modification induced by such a threat may be binding, even in the absence of consideration, if it is fair and equitable in view of unanticipated circumstances. See § 89. The mere fact that the modification induced by the threat fails to meet this test does not mean that the threat is necessarily improper. However, the threat is improper if it amounts to a breach of the duty of good faith and fair dealing imposed by the contract. See § 205. As under the Uniform Commercial Code, the "extortion of a 'modification' without legitimate commercial reason is ineffective as a violation of the duty of good faith. . . . The test of 'good faith' between merchants or as against merchants includes 'observance of reasonable commercial standards of fair dealing in the trade' (Section 2–103), and may in some situations require an objectively demonstrable reason for seeking a modification. But such matters as a market shift which makes performance come to involve a loss may provide such a reason even though there is no such unforeseen difficulty as would make out a legal excuse from performance under Sections 2–615 and 2–616." Comment 2 to Uniform Commercial Code § 2–209. . . .

f.   Other improper threats. The proper limits of bargaining are difficult to define with precision. Hard bargaining between experienced adversaries of relatively equal power ought not to be discouraged. Parties are generally held to the resulting agreement, even though one has taken advantage of the other's adversity, as long as the contract has been dictated by general economic forces. See Illustration 14. Where, however, a party has been induced to make a contract by some power exercised by the other for illegitimate ends, the transaction is suspect. For example, absent statute, a threat of refusal to deal with another party is ordinarily not duress, but if other factors are present an agreement that results from such a threat may be called into question. Subsection (2) deals with threats that are improper if the resulting exchange is not on fair terms. Clause (a) is concerned with cases in which a party threatens to do an act that would not significantly benefit him but would harm the other party. If, on the recipient's refusal to contract, the maker of the threat were to do the threatened act, it would therefore be done maliciously and unconscionably, out of pure vindictiveness. A typical example is a threat to make public embarrassing information concerning the recipient unless he makes a proposed contract. See Illustration 12 and Model Penal Code § 223.4(g). Clause (b) is concerned with cases in which the party making the threat has by unfair dealing achieved an advantage over the recipient that makes his threat unusually effective. Typical examples involve manipulative conduct during the bargaining stage that leaves one person at the mercy of the other. . . .

Clause (c) is concerned with other cases in which the threatened act involves the use of power for illegitimate ends. Many of the situations encompassed by clauses (1)(b), (1)(c), (2)(a) and (2)(b) involve extreme applications of this general rule, but it is more broadly applicable to analogous cases. . . . If, in any of these cases, the threat comes within Subsection (1), as where the threatened act or the threat itself is criminal or tortious (Clause (1)(a)), it is improper without an inquiry into the fairness of the resulting exchange under Subsection 2. See Comment *a*. . . .

Illustration

16.   A, a municipal water company seeking to induce B, a developer outside the city limits, to make a contract for water at rates greatly in excess of those similarly situated, threatens to refuse to supply to B unless B makes the contract. B, having no reasonable alternative, makes the contract. Because the threat amounts to a use for illegitimate ends of A's power not to supply water, the contract is voidable by B. . . .

§ 177. When Undue Influence Makes a Contract Voidable.

(1)   Undue influence is unfair persuasion of a party who is under the domination of the person exercising the persuasion or who by virtue of the relation between them is justified in assuming that that person will not act in a manner inconsistent with his welfare.

(2)   If a party's manifestation of assent is induced by undue influence by the other party, the contract is voidable by the victim.

(3)   If a party's manifestation of assent is induced by one who is not a party to the transaction, the contract is voidable by the victim unless the other party to the transaction in good faith and without reason to know of the undue influence either gives value or relies materially on the transaction.

Comment

a.   *Required domination or relation.* The rule stated in this Section protects a person only if he is under the domination of another or is justified, by virtue of his relation with another in assuming that the other will not act inconsistently with his welfare. Relations that often fall within the rule include those of parent and child, husband and wife, clergyman and parishioner, and physician and patient. In each case it is a question of fact whether the relation is such as to give undue weight to the other's attempts at persuasion. The required relation may be found in situations other than those enumerated. However, the mere fact that a party is weak, infirm or aged does not of itself suffice, although it may be a factor in determining whether the required relation existed.

b.   *Unfair persuasion.* Where the required domination or relation is present, the contract is voidable if it was induced by any unfair persuasion on the part of the stronger party. The law of undue influence therefore affords protection in situations where the rules on duress and misrepresentation give no relief. The degree of persuasion that is unfair depends on a variety of circumstances. The ultimate question is whether the result was produced by means that seriously impaired the free and competent exercise of judgment. Such factors as the unfairness of the resulting bargain, the unavailability of independent advice, and the susceptibility of the person persuaded are circumstances to be taken into account in determining whether there was unfair persuasion, but they are not in themselves controlling. Compare § 173.

CHAPTER 8

UNENFORCEABILITY ON GROUNDS OF PUBLIC POLICY

TOPIC 1. UNENFORCEABILITY IN GENERAL

§ 178. When a Term Is Unenforceable on Grounds of Public Policy.

(1)   A promise or other term of an agreement is unenforceable on grounds of public policy if legislation provides that it is unenforceable or the interest in its enforcement is clearly outweighed in the circumstances by a public policy against the enforcement of such terms.

(2)   In weighing the interest in the enforcement of a term, account is taken of

    (a)   the parties' justified expectations,

    (b)   any forfeiture that would result if enforcement were denied, and

    (c)   any special public interest in the enforcement of the particular term.

(3)   In weighing a public policy against enforcement of a term, account is taken of

    (a)   the strength of that policy as manifested by legislation or judicial decisions,

    (b)   the likelihood that a refusal to enforce the term will further that policy,

    (c)   the seriousness of any misconduct involved and the extent to which it was deliberate, and

    (d)   the directness of the connection between that misconduct and the term.

Comment

. . .

b.   Balancing of interests. Only infrequently does legislation, on grounds of public policy, provide that a term is unenforceable. When a court reaches that conclusion, it usually does so on the basis of a public policy derived either from its own perception of the need to protect some aspect of the public welfare or from legislation that is relevant to that policy although it says nothing explicitly about unenforceability. See § 179. In some cases the contravention of public policy is so grave, as when an agreement involves a serious crime or tort, that unenforceability is plain. In other cases the contravention is so trivial as that it plainly does not preclude enforcement. In doubtful cases, however, a decision as to enforceability is reached only after a careful balancing, in the light of all the circumstances, of the interest in the enforcement of the particular promise against the policy against the enforcement of such terms. . . .

§ 179. Bases of Public Policies Against Enforcement.

A public policy against the enforcement of promises or other terms may be derived by the court from

    (a)   legislation relevant to such a policy, or

    (b)   the need to protect some aspect of the public welfare, as is the case for the judicial policies against, for example,

        (i)   restraint of trade (§§ 186–188),

        (ii)   impairment of family relations (§§ 189–191), and

        (iii)   interference with other protected interests (§§ 192–196, 356).

§ 180. Effect of Excusable Ignorance.

If a promisee is excusably ignorant of facts or of legislation of a minor character, of which the promisor is not excusably ignorant and in the absence of which the promise would be enforceable, the promisee has a claim for damages for its breach but cannot recover damages for anything that he has done after he learns of the facts or legislation.

§ 181. Effect of Failure to Comply With Licensing or Similar Requirement.

If a party is prohibited from doing an act because of his failure to comply with a licensing, registration or similar requirement, a promise in consideration of his doing that act or of his promise to do it is unenforceable on grounds of public policy if

    (a)   the requirement has a regulatory purpose, and

    (b)   the interest in the enforcement of the promise is clearly outweighed by the public policy behind the requirement.

§ 182. Effect of Performance if Intended Use Is Improper.

If the promisee has substantially performed, enforcement of a promise is not precluded on grounds of public policy because of some improper use that the promisor intends to make of what he obtains unless the promisee

    (a)   acted for the purpose of furthering the improper use, or

    (b)   knew of the use and the use involves grave social harm.

§ 183. When Agreement Is Enforceable as to Agreed Equivalents.

If the parties' performances can be apportioned into corresponding pairs of part performances so that the parts of each pair are properly regarded as agreed equivalents and one pair is not offensive to public policy, that portion of the agreement is enforceable by a party who did not engage in serious misconduct.

§ 184. When Rest of Agreement Is Enforceable.

(1)   If less than all of an agreement is unenforceable under the rule stated in § 178, a court may nevertheless enforce the rest of the agreement in favor of a party who did not engage in serious misconduct if the performance as to which the agreement is unenforceable is not an essential part of the agreed exchange.

(2)   A court may treat only part of a term as unenforceable under the rule stated in Subsection (1) if the party who seeks to enforce the term obtained it in good faith and in accordance with reasonable standards of fair dealing.

§ 185. Excuse of a Condition on Grounds of Public Policy.

To the extent that a term requiring the occurrence of a condition is unenforceable under the rule stated in § 178, a court may excuse the non-occurrence of the condition unless its occurrence was an essential part of the agreed exchange.

TOPIC 2. RESTRAINT OF TRADE

§ 186. Promise in Restraint of Trade.

(1)   A promise is unenforceable on grounds of public policy if it is unreasonably in restraint of trade.

(2)   A promise is in restraint of trade if its performance would limit competition in any business or restrict the promisor in the exercise of a gainful occupation.

§ 187. Non-Ancillary Restraints on Competition.

A promise to refrain from competition that imposes a restraint that is not ancillary to an otherwise valid transaction or relationship is unreasonably in restraint of trade.

§ 188. Ancillary Restraints on Competition.

(1)   A promise to refrain from competition that imposes a restraint that is ancillary to an otherwise valid transaction or relationship is unreasonably in restraint of trade if

(a)   the restraint is greater than is needed to protect the promisee's legitimate interest, or

(b)   the promisee's need is outweighed by the hardship to the promisor and the likely injury to the public.

(2)   Promises imposing restraints that are ancillary to a valid transaction or relationship include the following:

(a)   a promise by the seller of a business not to compete with the buyer in such a way as to injure the value of the business sold;

(b)   a promise by an employee or other agent not to compete with his employer or other principal;

(c)   a promise by a partner not to compete with the partnership.

TOPIC 3. IMPAIRMENT OF FAMILY RELATIONS

§ 189. Promise in Restraint of Marriage.

A promise is unenforceable on grounds of public policy if it is unreasonably in restraint of marriage.

§ 190. Promise Detrimental to Marital Relationship.

(1)   A promise by a person contemplating marriage or by a married person, other than as part of an enforceable separation agreement, is unenforceable on grounds of public policy if it would change some essential incident of the marital relationship in a way detrimental to the public interest in the marriage relationship. A separation agreement is unenforceable on grounds of public policy unless it is made after separation or in contemplation of an immediate separation and is fair in the circumstances.

(2)   A promise that tends unreasonably to encourage divorce or separation is unenforceable on grounds of public policy.

§ 191. Promise Affecting Custody.

A promise affecting the right of custody of a minor child is unenforceable on grounds of public policy unless the disposition as to custody is consistent with the best interest of the child.

TOPIC 4. INTERFERENCE WITH OTHER PROTECTED INTERESTS

§ 192. Promise Involving Commission of a Tort.

A promise to commit a tort or to induce the commission of a tort is unenforceable on grounds of public policy.

§ 193. Promise Inducing Violation of Fiduciary Duty.

A promise by a fiduciary to violate his fiduciary duty or a promise that tends to induce such a violation is unenforceable on grounds of public policy.

§ 194. Promise Interfering With Contract With Another.

A promise that tortiously interferes with performance of a contract with a third person or a tortiously induced promise to commit a breach of contract is unenforceable on grounds of public policy.

§ 195. Term Exempting From Liability for Harm Caused Intentionally, Recklessly or Negligently.

(1) A term exempting a party from tort liability for harm caused intentionally or recklessly is unenforceable on grounds of public policy.

(2) A term exempting a party from tort liability for harm caused negligently is unenforceable on grounds of public policy if

(a) the term exempts an employer from liability to an employee for injury in the course of his employment;

(b) the term exempts one charged with a duty of public service from liability to one to whom that duty is owed for compensation for breach of that duty, or

(c) the other party is similarly a member of a class protected against the class to which the first party belongs.

(3) A term exempting a seller of a product from his special tort liability for physical harm to a user or consumer is unenforceable on grounds of public policy unless the term is fairly bargained for and is consistent with the policy underlying that liability.

§ 196. Term Exempting From Consequences of Misrepresentation.

A term unreasonably exempting a party from the legal consequences of a misrepresentation is unenforceable on grounds of public policy.

TOPIC 5. RESTITUTION

§ 197. Restitution Generally Unavailable.

Except as stated in §§ 198 and 199, a party has no claim in restitution for performance that he has rendered under or in return for a promise that is unenforceable on grounds of public policy unless denial of restitution would cause disproportionate forfeiture.

§ 198. Restitution in Favor of Party Who Is Excusably Ignorant or Is Not Equally in the Wrong.

A party has a claim in restitution for performance that he has rendered under or in return for a promise that is unenforceable on grounds of public policy if

(a) he was excusably ignorant of the facts or of legislation of a minor character, in the absence of which the promise would be enforceable, or

(b) he was not equally in the wrong with the promisor.

§ 199. Restitution Where Party Withdraws or Situation Is Contrary to Public Interest.

A party has a claim in restitution for performance that he has rendered under or in return for a promise that is unenforceable on grounds of public policy if he did not engage in serious misconduct and

(a) he withdraws from the transaction before the improper purpose has been achieved, or

(b) allowance of the claim would put an end to a continuing situation that is contrary to the public interest.

CHAPTER 9

THE SCOPE OF CONTRACTUAL OBLIGATIONS

TOPIC 1. THE MEANING OF AGREEMENTS

§ 200. Interpretation of Promise or Agreement.

Interpretation of a promise or agreement or a term thereof is the ascertainment of its meaning.

Comment

. . .

b. *Manifestation of intention.* As is made clear in Chapter 3, particularly §§ 17–20, the intention of a party that is relevant to formation of a contract is the intention manifested by him rather than any different undisclosed intention. The definitions of "promise," "agreement," and "term" in §§ 2, 3 and 5 also refer to "manifestation of intention." It follows that the meaning of the words or other conduct of a party is not necessarily the meaning he expects or understands. He is not bound by a meaning unless he has reason to know of it, but the expectation and understanding of the other party must also be taken into account. See § 201. . . .

c. *Interpretation and legal operation.* Interpretation is not a determination of the legal effect of words or other conduct. Properly interpreted, an agreement may not be enforceable as a contract, or a term such as a promise to pay a penalty may be denied legal effect, or it may have a legal effect different from that agreed upon, as in a case of employment at less than a statutory minimum wage.

§ 201. Whose Meaning Prevails.

(1) Where the parties have attached the same meaning to a promise or agreement or a term thereof, it is interpreted in accordance with that meaning.

(2) Where the parties have attached different meanings to a promise or agreement or a term thereof, it is interpreted in accordance with the meaning attached by one of them if at the time the agreement was made

(a) that party did not know of any different meaning attached by the other, and the other knew the meaning attached by the first party; or

(b) that party had no reason to know of any different meaning attached by the other, and the other had reason to know the meaning attached by the first party.

(3) Except as stated in this Section, neither party is bound by the meaning attached by the other, even though the result may be a failure of mutual assent.

Comment

a. *The meaning of words.* Words are used as conventional symbols of mental states, with standardized meanings based on habitual or customary practice. Unless a different intention is shown, language is interpreted in accordance with its generally prevailing meaning. See § 202(3). Usages of varying degrees of generality are recorded in dictionaries, but there are substantial differences between English and American usages and between usages in different parts of the United States. Differences of usage also exist in various localities and in different social, economic, religious and ethnic groups. All these usages change over time, and persons engaged in transactions with each other often develop temporary usages peculiar to themselves. Moreover, most words are commonly used in more than one sense.

b. *The problem of context.* Uncertainties in the meaning of words are ordinarily greatly reduced by the context in which they are used. The same is true of other conventional symbols, and the meaning of conduct not used as a conventional symbol is even more dependent on its setting. But the context of words and other conduct is seldom exactly the same for two different people, since connotations depend on the entire past experience and the attitudes and expectations of the person whose understanding is in question. In general, the context relevant to interpretation of a bargain is the context common to both parties. More precisely, the question of meaning in cases of misunderstanding depends on an inquiry into what each party knew or had reason to know, as stated in Subsections (2) and (3). See § 20 and Illustrations. Ordinarily a party has reason to know of meanings in general usage.

c. Mutual understanding. Subsection (1) makes it clear that the primary search is for a common meaning of the parties, not a meaning imposed on them by the law. . . . The objective of interpretation in the general law of contracts is to carry out the understanding of the parties rather than to impose obligations on them contrary to their understanding: "the courts do not make a contract for the parties." Ordinarily, therefore, the mutual understanding of the parties prevails even where the contractual term has been defined differently by statute or administrative regulation. But parties who used a standardized term in an unusual sense obviously run the risk that their agreement will be misinterpreted in litigation. . . .

§ 202. Rules in Aid of Interpretation.

(1) Words and other conduct are interpreted in the light of all the circumstances, and if the principal purpose of the parties is ascertainable it is given great weight.

(2) A writing is interpreted as a whole, and all writings that are part of the same transaction are interpreted together.

(3) Unless a different intention is manifested,

(a) where language has a generally prevailing meaning, it is interpreted in accordance with that meaning;

(b) technical terms and words of art are given their technical meaning when used in a transaction within their technical field.

(4) Where an agreement involves repeated occasions for performance by either party with knowledge of the nature of the performance and opportunity for objection to it by the other, any course of performance accepted or acquiesced in without objection is given great weight in the interpretation of the agreement.

(5) Wherever reasonable, the manifestations of intention of the parties to a promise or agreement are interpreted as consistent with each other and with any relevant course of performance, course of dealing, or usage of trade.

Comment

a. Scope of special rules. The rules in this Section are applicable to all manifestations of intention and all transactions. The rules are general in character, and serve merely as guides in the process of interpretation. They do not depend upon any determination that there is an ambiguity, but are used in determining what meanings are reasonably possible as well as in choosing among possible meanings.

b. Circumstances. The meaning of words and other symbols commonly depends on their context; the meaning of other conduct is even more dependent on the circumstances. In interpreting the words and conduct of the parties to a contract, a court seeks to put itself in the position they occupied at the time the contract was made. When the parties have adopted a writing as a final expression of their agreement, interpretation is directed to the meaning of that writing in the light of the circumstances. See §§ 209, 212. The circumstances for this purpose include the entire situation, as it appeared to the parties, and in appropriate cases may include facts known to one party of which the other had reason to know. See § 201. . . .

c. Principal purpose. The purposes of the parties to a contract are not always identical; particularly in business transactions, the parties often have divergent or even conflicting interests. But up to a point they commonly join in a common purpose of attaining a specific factual or legal result which each regards as necessary to the attainment of his ultimate purposes. Moreover, one party may know or have reason to know the purpose of the other and thus that his meaning is one consistent with that purpose. Determination that the parties have a principal purpose in common requires interpretation, but if such a purpose is disclosed further interpretation is guided by it. Even language which is otherwise explicit may be read with a modification needed to make it consistent with such a purpose. . . .

d. Interpretation of the whole. Meaning is inevitably dependent on context. A word changes meaning when it becomes part of a sentence, the sentence when it becomes part of a paragraph. A longer writing similarly affects the paragraph, other related writings affect the particular writing, and the circumstances affect the whole. Where the whole can be read to give significance to each part, that reading is preferred; if such a reading would be unreasonable, a choice must be made. See § 203. To fit the immediate verbal context or the more remote total context particular words or punctuation may be disregarded or supplied; clerical or grammatical errors may be corrected; singular may be treated as plural or plural as singular. . . .

    e.   *General usage.* In the United States the English language is used far more often in a sense which would be generally understood throughout the country than in a sense peculiar to some locality or group. In the absence of some contrary indication, therefore, English words are read as having the meaning given them by general usage, if there is one. This rule is a rule of interpretation in the absence of contrary evidence, not a rule excluding contrary evidence. It may also yield to internal indications such as inconsistency, absurdity, or departure from normal grammar, punctuation, or word order. . . .

    f.   *Technical terms.* Parties to an agreement often use the vocabulary of a particular place, vocation or trade, in which new words are coined and common words are assigned new meanings. But technical terms are often misused, and it may be shown that a technical word or phrase was used in a non-technical sense. Moreover, the same word may have a variety of technical and other meanings. "Mules" may mean animals, shoes or machines; a "ram" may mean an animal or a hydraulic ram; "zebra" may refer to a mammal, a butterfly, a lizard, a fish, a type of plant, tree or wood, or merely to the letter "Z". . . .

§ 203. Standards of Preference in Interpretation.

    In the interpretation of a promise or agreement or a term thereof, the following standards of preference are generally applicable:

    (a)   an interpretation which gives a reasonable, lawful, and effective meaning to all the terms is preferred to an interpretation which leaves a part unreasonable, unlawful, or of no effect;

    (b)   express terms are given greater weight than course of performance, course of dealing, and usage of trade, course of performance is given greater weight than course of dealing or usage of trade, and course of dealing is given greater weight than usage of trade;

    (c)   specific terms and exact terms are given greater weight than general language;

    (d)   separately negotiated or added terms are given greater weight than standardized terms or other terms not separately negotiated.

Comment

    a.   *Scope.* The rules of this Section are applicable to all manifestations of intention and all transactions. They apply only in choosing among reasonable interpretations. They do not override evidence of the meaning of the parties, but aid in determining meaning or prescribe legal effect when meaning is in doubt. . . .

    f.   *Superseded standard terms.* The rule stated in Subsection (d) has frequent application in cases of standardized documents. Printed forms are often misused, and there may be a question whether the parties manifested assent to a printed term on a writing. A printed provision that is clearly part of an integrated contract is normally to be interpreted as consistent with other terms, but in cases of inconsistency a handwritten or typewritten term inserted in connection with the particular transaction ordinarily prevails. Similarly, a typewritten term may be superseded by drawing a line through it, modified by interlineation, or controlled by an inconsistent handwritten insertion in another part of the agreement. It is sometimes said generally that handwritten terms control typewritten and printed terms, and typewritten control printed. . . . But the rule yields to manifestation of a contrary intention.

§ 204. Supplying an Omitted Essential Term.

    When the parties to a bargain sufficiently defined to be a contract have not agreed with respect to a term which is essential to a determination of their rights and duties, a term which is reasonable in the circumstances is supplied by the court.

Comment

. . .

c.   *Interpretation and omission.* Interpretation may be necessary to determine that the parties have not agreed with respect to a particular term, but the supplying of an omitted term is not within the definition of interpretation in § 200. . . .

d.   *Supplying a term.* The process of supplying an omitted term has sometimes been disguised as a literal or a purposive reading of contract language directed to a situation other than the situation that arises. Sometimes it is said that the search is for the term the parties would have agreed to if the question had been brought to their attention. Both the meaning of the words used and the probability that a particular term would have been used if the question had been raised may be factors in determining what term is reasonable in the circumstances. But where there is in fact no agreement, the court should supply a term which comports with community standards of fairness and policy rather than analyze a hypothetical model of the bargaining process.

Thus where a contract calls for a single performance such as the rendering of a service or the delivery of goods, the parties are most unlikely to agree explicitly that performance will be rendered within a "reasonable time;" but if no time is specified, a term calling for performance within a reasonable time is supplied. . . .

TOPIC 2. CONSIDERATIONS OF FAIRNESS AND THE PUBLIC INTEREST

§ 205. Duty of Good Faith and Fair Dealing.

Every contract imposes upon each party a duty of good faith and fair dealing in its performance and its enforcement.

Comment

a.   *Meanings of "good faith."* Good faith is defined in Uniform Commercial Code § 1–201(19) as "honesty in fact in the conduct or transaction concerned." "In the case of a merchant" Uniform Commercial Code § 2–103(1)(b) provides that good faith means "honesty in fact and the observance of reasonable commercial standards of fair dealing in the trade." The phrase "good faith" is used in a variety of contexts, and its meaning varies somewhat with the context. Good faith performance or enforcement of a contract emphasizes faithfulness to an agreed common purpose and consistency with the justified expectations of the other party; it excludes a variety of types of conduct characterized as involving "bad faith" because they violate community standards of decency, fairness or reasonableness. The appropriate remedy for a breach of the duty of good faith also varies with the circumstances.

b.   *Good faith purchase.* In many situations a good faith purchaser of property for value can acquire better rights in the property than his transferor had. See, e.g., § 342. In this context "good faith" focuses on the honesty of the purchaser, as distinguished from his care or negligence. Particularly in the law of negotiable instruments inquiry may be limited to "good faith" under what has been called "the rule of the pure heart and the empty head." When diligence or inquiry is a condition of the purchaser's right, it is said that good faith is not enough. This focus on honesty is appropriate to cases of good faith purchase; it is less so in cases of good faith performance.

c.   *Good faith in negotiation.* This Section, like **Uniform Commercial Code § 1–203**, does not deal with good faith in the formation of a contract. Bad faith in negotiation, although not within the scope of this Section, may be subject to sanctions. Particular forms of bad faith in bargaining are the subjects of rules as to capacity to contract, mutual assent and consideration and of rules as to invalidating causes such as fraud and duress. See, for example, §§ 90 and 208. Moreover, remedies for bad faith in the absence of agreement are found in the law of torts or restitution. For examples of a statutory duty to bargain in good faith, see, e.g., National Labor Relations Act § 8(d) and the federal Truth in Lending Act. In cases of negotiation for modification of an existing contractual relationship, the rule stated in this Section may overlap with more specific rules requiring negotiation in good faith. See §§ 73, 89; Uniform Commercial Code § 2–209 and Comment.

d. Good faith performance. Subterfuges and evasions violate the obligation of good faith in performance even though the actor believes his conduct to be justified. But the obligation goes further: bad faith may be overt or may consist of inaction, and fair dealing may require more than honesty. A complete catalogue of types of bad faith is impossible, but the following types are among those which have been recognized in judicial decisions: evasion of the spirit of the bargain, lack of diligence and slacking off, willful rendering of imperfect performance, abuse of a power to specify terms, and interference with or failure to cooperate in the other party's performance.

§ 206. Interpretation Against the Draftsman.

In choosing among the reasonable meanings of a promise or agreement or a term thereof, that meaning is generally preferred which operates against the party who supplies the words or from whom a writing otherwise proceeds.

Comment

a. Rationale. Where one party chooses the terms of a contract, he is likely to provide more carefully for the protection of his own interests than for those of the other party. He is also more likely than the other party to have reason to know of uncertainties of meaning. Indeed, he may leave meaning deliberately obscure, intending to decide at a later date what meaning to assert. In cases of doubt, therefore, so long as other factors are not decisive, there is substantial reason for preferring the meaning of the other party. The rule is often invoked in cases of standardized contracts and in cases where the drafting party has the stronger bargaining position, but it is not limited to such cases. It is in strictness a rule of legal effect, sometimes called construction, as well as interpretation: its operation depends on the positions of the parties as they appear in litigation, and sometimes the result is hard to distinguish from a denial of effect to an unconscionable clause. . . .

§ 207. Interpretation Favoring the Public.

In choosing among the reasonable meanings of a promise or agreement or a term thereof, a meaning that serves the public interest is generally preferred.

§ 208. Unconscionable Contract or Term.

If a contract or term thereof is unconscionable at the time the contract is made a court may refuse to enforce the contract, or may enforce the remainder of the contract without the unconscionable term, or may so limit the application of any unconscionable term as to avoid any unconscionable result.

Comment

a. Scope. . . . The determination that a contract or term is or is not unconscionable is made in the light of its setting, purpose and effect. Relevant factors include weaknesses in the contracting process like those involved in more specific rules as to contractual capacity, fraud, and other invalidating causes; the policy also overlaps with rules which render particular bargains or terms unenforceable on grounds of public policy. Policing against unconscionable contracts or terms has sometimes been accomplished "by adverse construction of language, by manipulation of the rules of offer and acceptance or by determinations that the clause is contrary to public policy or to the dominant purpose of the contract." Uniform Commercial Code § 2–302 Comment 1. Particularly in the case of standardized agreements, the rule of this Section permits the court to pass directly on the unconscionability of the contract or clause rather than to avoid unconscionable results by interpretation. Compare § 211. . . .

c. Overall imbalance. Inadequacy of consideration does not of itself invalidate a bargain, but gross disparity in the values exchanged may be an important factor in a determination that a contract is unconscionable and may be sufficient ground, without more, for denying specific performance. . . . Such a disparity may also corroborate indications of defects in the bargaining process. . . . Theoretically it is possible for a contract to be oppressive taken as a whole, even though there is no weakness in the bargaining process and no single term which is in itself unconscionable. Ordinarily, however, an unconscionable contract involves other factors as well as overall imbalance. . . .

d.   Weakness in the bargaining process. A bargain is not unconscionable merely because the parties to it are unequal in bargaining position, nor even because the inequality results in an allocation of risks to the weaker party. But gross inequality of bargaining power, together with terms unreasonably favorable to the stronger party, may confirm indications that the transaction involved elements of deception or compulsion, or may show that the weaker party had no meaningful choice, no real alternative, or did not in fact assent or appear to assent to the unfair terms. Factors which may contribute to a finding of unconscionability in the bargaining process include the following: belief by the stronger party that there is no reasonable probability that the weaker party will fully perform the contract; knowledge of the stronger party that the weaker party will be unable to receive substantial benefits from the contract; knowledge of the stronger party that the weaker party is unable reasonably to protect his interests by reason of physical or mental infirmities, ignorance, illiteracy or inability to understand the language of the agreement, or similar factors. See Uniform Consumer Credit Code § 6.111.

TOPIC 3. EFFECT OF ADOPTION OF A WRITING

§ 209. Integrated Agreements.

(1)   An integrated agreement is a writing or writings constituting a final expression of one or more terms of an agreement.

(2)   Whether there is an integrated agreement is to be determined by the court as a question preliminary to determination of a question of interpretation or to application of the parol evidence rule.

(3)   Where the parties reduce an agreement to a writing which in view of its completeness and specificity reasonably appears to be a complete agreement, it is taken to be an integrated agreement unless it is established by other evidence that the writing did not constitute a final expression.

Comment

c.   Proof of integration. Whether a writing has been adopted as an integrated agreement is a question of fact to be determined in accordance with all relevant evidence. . . . Ordinarily the issue whether there is an integrated agreement is determined by the trial judge in the first instance as a question preliminary to an interpretative ruling or to the application of the parol evidence rule. . . .

§ 210. Completely and Partially Integrated Agreements.

(1)   A completely integrated agreement is an integrated agreement adopted by the parties as a complete and exclusive statement of the terms of the agreement.

(2)   A partially integrated agreement is an integrated agreement other than a completely integrated agreement.

(3)   Whether an agreement is completely or partially integrated is to be determined by the court as a question preliminary to determination of a question of interpretation or to application of the parol evidence rule.

Comment

a.   Complete integration. The definition in Subsection (1) is to be read with the definition of integrated agreement in § 209, to reject the assumption sometimes made that because a writing has been worked out which is final on some matters, it is to be taken as including all the matters agreed upon. Even though there is an integrated agreement, consistent additional terms not reduced to writing may be shown, unless the court finds that the writing was assented to by both parties as a complete and exclusive statement of all the terms. . . .

b.   Proof of complete integration. That a writing was or was not adopted as a completely integrated agreement may be proved by any relevant evidence. A document in the form of a written contract, signed by both parties and apparently complete on its face, may be decisive of the issue in the absence of credible contrary evidence. But a writing cannot of itself prove its own completeness, and wide latitude must be allowed for inquiry into circumstances bearing on the intention of the parties. . . .

§ 211. Standardized Agreements.

(1)   Except as stated in Subsection (3), where a party to an agreement signs or otherwise manifests assent to a writing and has reason to believe that like writings are regularly used to embody terms of agreements of the same type, he adopts the writing as an integrated agreement with respect to the terms included in the writing.

(2)   Such a writing is interpreted wherever reasonable as treating alike all those similarly situated, without regard to their knowledge or understanding of the standard terms of the writing.

(3)   Where the other party has reason to believe that the party manifesting such assent would not do so if he knew that the writing contained a particular term, the term is not part of the agreement.

Comment

. . .

b.   *Assent to unknown terms.* A party who makes regular use of a standardized form of agreement does not ordinarily expect his customers to understand or even to read the standard terms. One of the purposes of standardization is to eliminate bargaining over details of individual transactions, and that purpose would not be served if a substantial number of customers retained counsel and reviewed the standard terms. Employees regularly using a form often have only a limited understanding of its terms and limited authority to vary them. Customers do not in fact ordinarily understand or even read the standard terms. They trust to the good faith of the party using the form and to the tacit representation that like terms are being accepted regularly by others similarly situated. But they understand that they are assenting to the terms not read or not understood, subject to such limitations as the law may impose.

c.   *Review of unfair terms.* . . . The obvious danger of overreaching has resulted in government regulation of insurance policies, bills of lading, retail installment sales, small loans, and other particular types of contracts. . . . Apart from such regulation, standard terms imposed by one party are enforced. But standard terms may be superseded by separately negotiated or added terms . . ., they are construed against the draftsman . . ., and they are subject to the overriding obligation of good faith . . . and to the power of the court to refuse to enforce an unconscionable contract or term (§ 208). . . .

d.   *Non-contractual documents.* The same document may serve both contractual and other purposes, and a party may assent to it for other purposes without understanding that it embodies contract terms. He may nevertheless be bound if he has reason to know that it is used to embody contract terms. Insurance policies, steamship tickets, bills of lading, and warehouse receipts are commonly so obviously contractual in form as to give the customer reason to know their character. But baggage checks or automobile parking lot tickets may appear to be mere identification tokens, and a party without knowledge or reason to know that the token purports to be a contract is then not bound by terms printed on the token. Documents such as invoices, instructions for use, and the like, delivered after a contract is made, may raise similar problems. . . .

f.   *Terms excluded.* Subsection (3) applies to standardized agreements the general principles stated in §§ 20 and 201. Although customers typically adhere to standardized agreements and are bound by them without even appearing to know the standard terms in detail, they are not bound to unknown terms which are beyond the range of reasonable expectation. A debtor who delivers a check to his creditor with the amount blank does not authorize the insertion of an infinite figure. Similarly, a party who adheres to the other party's standard terms does not assent to a term if the other party has reason to believe that the adhering party would not have accepted the agreement if he had known that the agreement contained the particular term. Such a belief or assumption may be shown by the prior negotiations or inferred from the circumstances. Reason to believe may be inferred from the fact that the term is bizarre or oppressive, from the fact that it eviscerates the non-standard terms explicitly agreed to, or from the fact that it eliminates the dominant purpose of the transaction. The inference is reinforced if the adhering party never had an opportunity to read the term, or if it is illegible or otherwise hidden from view. This rule is closely related to the policy against unconscionable terms and the rule of interpretation against the draftsman. . . .

§ 212. Interpretation of Integrated Agreement.

(1)   The interpretation of an integrated agreement is directed to the meaning of the terms of the writing or writings in the light of the circumstances, in accordance with the rules stated in this Chapter.

(2) A question of interpretation of an integrated agreement is to be determined by the trier of fact if it depends on the credibility of extrinsic evidence or on a choice among reasonable inferences to be drawn from extrinsic evidence. Otherwise a question of interpretation of an integrated agreement is to be determined as a question of law.

Comment

. . .

b. . . . It is sometimes said that extrinsic evidence cannot change the plain meaning of a writing, but meaning can almost never be plain except in a context. Accordingly, the rule stated in Subsection (1) is not limited to cases where it is determined that the language used is ambiguous. Any determination of meaning or ambiguity should only be made in the light of the relevant evidence of the situation and relations of the parties, the subject matter of the transaction, preliminary negotiations and statements made therein, usages of trade, and the course of dealing between the parties.

§ 213. Effect of Integrated Agreement on Prior Agreements (Parol Evidence Rule).

(1) A binding integrated agreement discharges prior agreements to the extent that it is inconsistent with them.

(2) A binding completely integrated agreement discharges prior agreements to the extent that they are within its scope.

(3) An integrated agreement that is not binding or that is voidable and avoided does not discharge a prior agreement. But an integrated agreement, even though not binding, may be effective to render inoperative a term which would have been part of the agreement if it had not been integrated.

Comment

a. *Parol evidence rule.* This Section states what is commonly known as the parol evidence rule. It is not a rule of evidence but a rule of substantive law. Nor is it a rule of interpretation; it defines the subject matter of interpretation. It renders inoperative prior written agreements as well as prior oral agreements. . . .

§ 214. Evidence of Prior or Contemporaneous Agreements and Negotiations.

Agreements and negotiations prior to or contemporaneous with the adoption of a writing are admissible in evidence to establish

    (a) that the writing is or is not an integrated agreement;

    (b) that the integrated agreement, if any, is completely or partially integrated;

    (c) the meaning of the writing, whether or not integrated;

    (d) illegality, fraud, duress, mistake, lack of consideration, or other invalidating cause;

    (e) ground for granting or denying rescission, reformation, specific performance, or other remedy.

§ 215. Contradiction of Integrated Terms.

Except as stated in the preceding Section, where there is a binding agreement, either completely or partially integrated, evidence of prior or contemporaneous agreements or negotiations is not admissible in evidence to contradict a term of the writing.

Comment

a. *Relation to other rules.* Like § 216, this Section states an evidentiary consequence of § 213. A binding integrated agreement discharges inconsistent prior agreements, and evidence of a prior agreement is therefore irrelevant to the rights of the parties when offered to contradict a term of the writing. The same evidence may be properly considered on the preliminary issues whether there is an integrated agreement and whether it is completely or partially integrated. See §§ 209, 210. If there is a finding that there is an integrated agreement or a completely integrated agreement, the evidence may nevertheless be relevant to a question of interpretation, to a question of invalidating cause, or to a question of remedy. See § 214. But the earlier agreement, no matter how clear, cannot override a later agreement which supersedes or amends it. . . .

§ 216. Consistent Additional Terms.

(1)   Evidence of a consistent additional term is admissible to supplement an integrated agreement unless the court finds that the agreement was completely integrated.

(2)   An agreement is not completely integrated if the writing omits a consistent additional agreed term which is

    (a)   agreed to for separate consideration, or

    (b)   such a term as in the circumstances might naturally be omitted from the writing.

Comment

a.   *Relation to other rules.* Like § 215, this Section states an evidentiary consequence of § 213. It also limits the concept of a completely integrated agreement set forth in § 210. Compare Uniform Commercial Code § 2–202(b). Where the limitation is not applicable, the court must decide whether the agreement is completely integrated on the basis of all relevant evidence, including the evidence of consistent additional terms.

b.   *Consistency.* Terms of prior agreements are superseded to the extent that they are inconsistent with an integrated agreement, and evidence of them is not admissible to contradict a term of the integration. See §§ 213, 215. The determination whether an alleged additional term is consistent or inconsistent with the integrated agreement requires interpretation of the writing in the light of all the circumstances, including the evidence of the additional term. For this purpose, the meaning of the writing includes not only the terms explicitly stated but also those fairly implied as part of the bargain of the parties in fact. It does not include a term supplied by a rule of law designed to fill gaps where the parties have not agreed otherwise, unless it can be inferred that the parties contracted with reference to the rule of law. There is no clear line between implications of fact and rules of law filling gaps; although fairly clear examples of each can be given, other cases will involve almost imperceptible shadings. See § 204.

§ 217. Integrated Agreement Subject to Oral Requirement of a Condition.

Where the parties to a written agreement agree orally that performance of the agreement is subject to the occurrence of a stated condition, the agreement is not integrated with respect to the oral condition.

§ 218. Untrue Recitals; Evidence of Consideration.

(1)   A recital of a fact in an integrated agreement may be shown to be untrue.

(2)   Evidence is admissible to prove whether or not there is consideration for a promise, even though the parties have reduced their agreement to a writing which appears to be a completely integrated agreement.

TOPIC 4. SCOPE AS AFFECTED BY USAGE

§ 219. Usage.

Usage is habitual or customary practice.

§ 220. Usage Relevant to Interpretation.

(1)   An agreement is interpreted in accordance with a relevant usage if each party knew or had reason to know of the usage and neither party knew or had reason to know that the meaning attached by the other was inconsistent with the usage.

(2) When the meaning attached by one party accorded with a relevant usage and the other knew or had reason to know of the usage, the other is treated as having known or had reason to know the meaning attached by the first party.

Comment

. . .

b. *Interpretation of language.* An agreement may have a legal effect not intended by either party, but interpretation is limited to meanings intended by at least one party. Neither party is bound by a meaning unless he knows or has reason to know of it. See §§ 200, 201. Usage is subject to the same rule: a party is not bound by a usage unless he knows or has reason to know of it. Hence a party who asserts a meaning based on usage must show either that the other party knew of the usage or that the other party had reason to know of it. Analytically, the meaning of language is a question of fact, but in the absence of extrinsic evidence the meaning of language in an integrated writing is to be determined as a question of law. See § 212. Where a usage of words is sufficiently well known, a court will take judicial cognizance of it without proof; otherwise the burden of establishing a usage is on the party asserting it. See § 202. Ordinarily there is no requirement that a usage relevant to the interpretation of language be pleaded, but a party against whom evidence of usage is offered may be entitled to a continuance or to notice sufficient to prevent unfair surprise. See Uniform Commercial Code § 1–205(6). . . .

c. *Agreed but unstated terms.* An agreement or term thereof need not be stated in words if the parties manifest assent to it by other conduct, and such assent is often manifested by conduct in accordance with usage. Where there is an integrated agreement, an agreed but unstated term may be annexed by usage on the same principle which controls consistent additional terms generally. See § 216. But it is so common to contract with reference to usage, leaving the usage unstated, that no inquiry is necessary as to whether it is natural in the particular circumstances to omit the term from the writing. See Uniform Commercial Code § 2–202(a). Where it is claimed that the usage contradicts the express terms, the issue is resolved as a question of interpretation. See § 203(b). Whether a usage is reasonable may bear on the issue whether the parties contracted with reference to it, but if they did they are not in general forbidden to make agreements which seem unreasonable to others. . . .

d. *Ambiguity and contradiction.* Language and conduct are in general given meaning by usage rather than by the law, and ambiguity and contradiction likewise depend upon usage. Hence usage relevant to interpretation is treated as part of the context of an agreement in determining whether there is ambiguity or contradiction as well as in resolving ambiguity or contradiction. There is no requirement that an ambiguity be shown before usage can be shown, and no prohibition against showing that language or conduct have a different meaning in the light of usage from the meaning they might have apart from the usage. The normal effect of a usage on a written contract is to vary its meaning from the meaning it would otherwise have. . . .

§ 221. Usage Supplementing an Agreement.

An agreement is supplemented or qualified by a reasonable usage with respect to agreements of the same type if each party knows or has reason to know of the usage and neither party knows or has reason to know that the other party has an intention inconsistent with the usage.

Comment

a. *Agreed terms and omitted terms.* . . . This Section [applies] to cases where the parties did not advert to the problem with which the usage deals, or where one or each separately foresaw the problem but failed to manifest any intention with respect to it. In such cases, in the absence of usage, the court would supply a reasonable term. . . . But if there is a reasonable usage which supplies an omitted term and the parties know or have reason to know of the usage, it is a surer guide than the court's own judgment of what is reasonable. Thus a usage may make it unnecessary to inquire into or prove what the actual intentions of the parties were with respect to an unstated term. . . .

Illustrations

. . .

2.   A, an ordained rabbi, is employed by B, an orthodox Jewish congregation, to officiate as cantor at specified religious services. At the time the contract is made, it is the practice of such congregations to seat men and women separately at services, and a contrary practice would violate A's religious beliefs. At a time when it is too late for A to obtain substitute employment, B adopts a contrary practice. A refuses to officiate. The practice is part of the contract, and A is entitled to the agreed compensation.

§ 222. Usage of Trade.

(1)   A usage of trade is a usage having such regularity of observance in a place, vocation, or trade as to justify an expectation that it will be observed with respect to a particular agreement. It may include a system of rules regularly observed even though particular rules are changed from time to time.

(2)   The existence and scope of a usage of trade are to be determined as questions of fact. If a usage is embodied in a written trade code or similar writing the interpretation of the writing is to be determined by the court as a question of law.

(3)   Unless otherwise agreed, a usage of trade in the vocation or trade in which the parties are engaged or a usage of trade of which they know or have reason to know gives meaning to or supplements or qualifies their agreement.

Comment

. . .

b.   *Regularity of observance.* A usage of trade need not be "ancient or immemorial," "universal," or the like. Unless agreed to in fact, it must be reasonable, but commercial acceptance by regular observance makes out a prima facie case that a usage of trade is reasonable. There is no requirement that an agreement be ambiguous before evidence of a usage of trade can be shown, nor is it required that the usage of trade be consistent with the meaning the agreement would have apart from the usage. When the usage consists of a system of rules, the parties need not be aware of a particular rule if they know or have reason to know the system and the particular rule is within the scheme of the system. A change within the system may have effect promptly, even though there has been no time for regular observance of the change. . . .

Illustrations

1.   A contracts to sell B 10,000 shingles. By usage of the lumber trade, in which both are engaged, two packs of a certain size constitute 1,000, though not containing that exact number. Unless otherwise agreed, 1,000 in the contract means two packs.

2.   A contracts to sell B 1,000 feet of San Domingo mahogany. By usage of dealers in mahogany, known to A and B, good figured mahogany of a certain density is known as San Domingo mahogany, though it does not come from San Domingo. Unless otherwise agreed, the usage is part of the contract. . . .

3.   A and B enter into a contract for the purchase and sale of "No. 1 heavy book paper guaranteed free from ground wood." Usage in the paper trade may show that this means paper not containing over 3% ground wood.

§ 223. Course of Dealing.

(1)   A course of dealing is a sequence of previous conduct between the parties to an agreement which is fairly to be regarded as establishing a common basis of understanding for interpreting their expressions and other conduct.

(2)   Unless otherwise agreed, a course of dealing between the parties gives meaning to or supplements or qualifies their agreement.

Comment

a. *Relation to other rules.* This Section follows Uniform Commercial Code § 1–205 and states a particular application of the rules stated in §§ 220 and 221. As to conflict between course of dealing and express terms, course of performance or usage of trade, see § 203.

b. *Common basis of understanding.* Course of dealing may become part of an agreement either by explicit provision or by tacit recognition, or it may guide the court in supplying an omitted term. Like usage of trade, it may determine the meaning of language or it may annex an agreed but unstated term. There is no requirement that an agreement be ambiguous before evidence of a course of dealing can be shown, nor is it required that the course of dealing be consistent with the meaning the agreement would have apart from the course of dealing.

TOPIC 5. CONDITIONS AND SIMILAR EVENTS

§ 224. Condition Defined.

A condition is an event, not certain to occur, which must occur, unless its non-occurrence is excused, before performance under a contract becomes due.

§ 225. Effects of the Non-Occurrence of a Condition.

(1) Performance of a duty subject to a condition cannot become due unless the condition occurs or its non-occurrence is excused.

(2) Unless it has been excused, the non-occurrence of a condition discharges the duty when the condition can no longer occur.

(3) Non-occurrence of a condition is not a breach by a party unless he is under a duty that the condition occur.

§ 226. How an Event May Be Made a Condition.

An event may be made a condition either by the agreement of the parties or by a term supplied by the court.

Comment

a. *By agreement of the parties.* No particular form of language is necessary to make an event a condition, although such words as "on condition that," "provided that" and "if" are often used for this purpose. . . .

c. *By a term supplied by court.* When the parties have omitted a term that is essential to a determination of their rights and duties, the court may supply a term which is reasonable in the circumstances (§ 204). Where that term makes an event a condition, it is often described as a "constructive" (or "implied in law") condition. This serves to distinguish it from events which are made conditions by the agreement of the parties, either by their words or by other conduct, and which are described as "express" and as "implied in fact" (inferred from fact) conditions. . . .

§ 227. Standards of Preference With Regard to Conditions.

(1) In resolving doubts as to whether an event is made a condition of an obligor's duty, and as to the nature of such an event, an interpretation is preferred that will reduce the obligee's risk of forfeiture, unless the event is within the obligee's control or the circumstances indicate that he has assumed the risk.

(2) Unless the contract is of a type under which only one party generally undertakes duties, when it is doubtful whether

    (a) a duty is imposed on an obligee that an event occur, or

    (b) the event is made a condition of the obligor's duty, or

226

(c)   the event is made a condition of the obligor's duty and a duty is imposed on the obligee that the event occur,

the first interpretation is preferred if the event is within the obligee's control. . . .

Comment

. . .

b.   *Condition or not.* The non-occurrence of a condition of an obligor's duty may cause the obligee to lose his right to the agreed exchange after he has relied substantially on the expectation of that exchange, as by preparation or performance. The word "forfeiture" is used in this Restatement to refer to the denial of compensation that results in such a case. The policy favoring freedom of contract requires that, within broad limits . . . the agreement of the parties should be honored even though forfeiture results. When, however, it is doubtful whether or not the agreement makes an event a condition of an obligor's duty, an interpretation is preferred that will reduce the risk of forfeiture. . . . When the nature of the condition is such that the uncertainty as to the event will be resolved before either party has relied on its anticipated occurrence, both parties can be entirely relieved of their duties, and the obligee risks only the loss of his expectations. When, however, the nature of the condition is such that the uncertainty is not likely to be resolved until after the obligee has relied by preparing to perform or by performing at least in part, he risks forfeiture. If the event is within his control, he will often assume this risk. If it is not within his control, it is sufficiently unusual for him to assume the risk that, in case of doubt, an interpretation is preferred under which the event is not a condition. The rule is, of course, subject to a showing of a contrary intention, and even without clear language, circumstances may show that he assumed the risk of its non-occurrence.

Although the rule is consistent with a policy of avoiding forfeiture and unjust enrichment, it is not directed at the avoidance of actual forfeiture and unjust enrichment. Since the intentions of the parties must be taken as of the time the contract was made, the test is whether a particular interpretation would have avoided the risk of forfeiture viewed as of that time, not whether it will avoid actual forfeiture in the resolution of a dispute that has arisen later. . . .

c.   *Nature of Event.* In determining the nature of the event that is made a condition by the agreement, as in determining whether the agreement makes an event a condition in the first place . . ., it will not ordinarily be supposed that a party has assumed the risk of forfeiture. Where the language is doubtful, an interpretation is generally preferred that will avoid this risk. This standard of preference finds an important application in the case of promises to pay for work done if some independent third party, such as an architect, surveyor or engineer, is satisfied with it, where the risk of forfeiture in the case of a judgment that is dishonest or based on a gross mistake as to the facts is substantial. The standard does not, however, help a party if the condition is within his control or if the circumstances otherwise indicate that he assumed that risk.

Illustrations

. . .

5.   A contracts with B to repair B's building for $20,000, payment to be made "on the satisfaction of C, B's architect, and the issuance of his certificate." A makes the repairs, but C refuses to issue his certificate, and explains why he is not satisfied. Other experts in the field consider A's performance to be satisfactory and disagree with C's explanation. A has no claim against B. . . . If C is honestly not satisfied, B is under no duty to pay A, and it makes no difference if his dissatisfaction was not reasonable.

6.   The facts being otherwise as stated in Illustration 5, C refuses to issue his certificate although he admits that he is satisfied. A has a claim against B for $20,000. The quoted language will be interpreted so that the requirement of the certificate is merely evidentiary and the condition occurs when there is, as here, adequate evidence that C is honestly satisfied.

7.   The facts being otherwise as stated in Illustration 5, C does not make a proper inspection of the work and gives no reasons for his dissatisfaction. A has a claim against B for $20,000. In using the quoted language, A and B assumed that C would exercise an honest judgment and by failing to make a proper inspection, C did not exercise such a judgment. . . .

8.   The facts being otherwise as stated in Illustration 5, C makes a gross mistake with reference to the facts on which his refusal to give a certificate is based. A has a claim against B for $20,000. In using the quoted language, A and B assumed that C would exercise his judgment without a gross mistake as to the facts. . . .

§ 228. Satisfaction of the Obligor as a Condition.

When it is a condition of an obligor's duty that he be satisfied with respect to the obligee's performance or with respect to something else, and it is practicable to determine whether a reasonable person in the position of the obligor would be satisfied, an interpretation is preferred under which the condition occurs if such a reasonable person in the position of the obligor would be satisfied.

§ 229. Excuse of a Condition to Avoid Forfeiture.

To the extent that the non-occurrence of a condition would cause disproportionate forfeiture, a court may excuse the non-occurrence of that condition unless its occurrence was a material part of the agreed exchange.

Comment

a. Relation to other rules. Although both this Section and § 208, on unconscionable contract or term, limit freedom of contract, they are designed to reach different types of situations. While § 208 speaks of unconscionability "at the time the contract is made," this Section is concerned with forfeiture that would actually result if the condition were not excused. It is intended to deal with a term that does not appear to be unconscionable at the time the contract is made but that would, because of ensuing events, cause forfeiture.

b. Disproportionate forfeiture. The rule stated in the present Section is, of necessity, a flexible one, and its application is within the sound discretion of the court. Here, as in § 227(1), "forfeiture" is used to refer to the denial of compensation that results when the obligee loses his right to the agreed exchange after he has relied substantially, as by preparation or performance on the expectation of that exchange. See Comment b to § 227. The extent of the forfeiture in any particular case will depend on the extent of that denial of compensation. In determining whether the forfeiture is "disproportionate," a court must weigh the extent of the forfeiture by the obligee against the importance to the obligor of the risk from which he sought to be protected and the degree to which that protection will be lost if the non-occurrence of the condition is excused to the extent required to prevent forfeiture. The character of the agreement may, as in the case of insurance agreements, affect the rigor with which the requirement is applied. . . .

Illustrations

1.   A contracts to build a house for B, using pipe of Reading manufacture. In return, B agrees to pay $75,000 in progress payments, each payment to be made "on condition that no pipe other than that of Reading manufacture has been used." Without A's knowledge, a subcontractor mistakenly uses pipe of Cohoes manufacture which is identical in quality and is distinguishable only by the name of the manufacturer which is stamped on it. The mistake is not discovered until the house is completed, when replacement of the pipe will require destruction of substantial parts of the house. B refuses to pay the unpaid balance of $10,000. A court may conclude that the use of Reading rather than Cohoes pipe is so relatively unimportant to B that the forfeiture that would result from denying A the entire balance would be disproportionate, and may allow recovery by A subject to any claim for damages for A's breach of his duty to use Reading pipe.

2.   A, an ocean carrier, carries B's goods under a contract providing that it is a condition of A's liability for damage to cargo that "written notice of claim for loss or damage must be given within 10 days after removal of goods." B's cargo is damaged during carriage and A knows of this. On removal of the goods, B notes in writing on the delivery record that the cargo is damaged, and five days later informs A over the telephone of a claim for that damage and invites A to participate in an inspection within the ten day period. A inspects the goods within the period, but B does not give written notice of its claim until 25 days after removal of the goods. Since the purpose of requiring the condition of written notice is to alert the carrier and enable it to make a prompt investigation, and since this purpose had

been served by the written notice of damage and the oral notice of claim, the court may excuse the non-occurrence of the condition to the extent required to allow recovery by B.

CHAPTER 10

PERFORMANCE AND NON-PERFORMANCE

TOPIC 1. PERFORMANCES TO BE EXCHANGED
UNDER AN EXCHANGE OF PROMISES

§ 230. Event That Terminates a Duty.

(1)   Except as stated in Subsection (2), if under the terms of the contract the occurrence of an event is to terminate an obligor's duty of immediate performance or one to pay damages for breach, that duty is discharged if the event occurs.

(2)   The obligor's duty is not discharged if occurrence of the event

(a)   is the result of a breach by the obligor of his duty of good faith and fair dealing, or

(b)   could not have been prevented because of impracticability and continuance of the duty does not subject the obligor to a materially increased burden. . . .

Illustrations

1.   A, an insurance company, insures the property of B under a policy providing that no recovery can be had if suit is not brought on the policy within two years after a loss. A loss occurs and B lets two years pass before bringing suit. A's duty to pay B for the loss is discharged and B cannot maintain the action on the policy.

2.   The facts being otherwise as stated in Illustration 1, B lives in a foreign country and is prevented by the outbreak of war from bringing suit against A for two years. A's duty to pay B for the loss is not discharged and B can maintain an action on the policy when the war is ended.

§ 231. Criterion for Determining When Performances Are to Be Exchanged Under an Exchange of Promises.

Performances are to be exchanged under an exchange of promises if each promise is at least part of the consideration for the other and the performance of each promise is to be exchanged at least in part for the performance of the other.

Comment

a.   Expectation of an exchange of performances. Agreements involving an exchange of promises play a vital role in an economically advanced society. Ordinarily when parties make such an agreement, they not only regard the promises themselves as the subject of an exchange (§ 71(2)), but they also intend that the performances of those promises shall subsequently be exchanged for each other. Even without a showing of such an actual intention, a court will often, out of a sense of fairness, assume that it was their expectation that there would be a subsequent exchange of the performance of each party for that of the other. Cf. 204. This Chapter consists, in substantial part, of rules designed to secure that expectation of a subsequent exchange of performances. . . .

§ 232. When It Is Presumed That Performances Are to Be Exchanged Under an Exchange of Promises.

Where the consideration given by each party to a contract consists in whole or in part of promises, all the performances to be rendered by each party taken collectively are treated as performances to be exchanged under an exchange of promises, unless a contrary intention is clearly manifested.

§ 233. Performance at One Time or in Installments.

(1) Where performances are to be exchanged under an exchange of promises, and the whole of one party's performance can be rendered at one time, it is due at one time, unless the language or the circumstances indicate the contrary.

(2) Where only a part of one party's performance is due at one time under Subsection (1), if the other party's performance can be so apportioned that there is a comparable part that can also be rendered at that time, it is due at that time, unless the language or the circumstances indicate the contrary.

§ 234. Order of Performances.

(1) Where all or part of the performances to be exchanged under an exchange of promises can be rendered simultaneously, they are to that extent due simultaneously, unless the language or the circumstances indicate the contrary.

(2) Except to the extent stated in Subsection (1), where the performance of only one party under such an exchange requires a period of time, his performance is due at an earlier time than that of the other party, unless the language or the circumstances indicate the contrary.

Comment

a. Advantages of simultaneous performance. A requirement that the parties perform simultaneously where their performances are to be exchanged under an exchange of promises is fair for two reasons. First, it offers both parties maximum security against disappointment of their expectations of a subsequent exchange of performances by allowing each party to defer his own performance until he has been assured that the other will perform. . . . Second, it avoids placing on either party the burden of financing the other before the latter has performed. . . .

b. When simultaneous performance possible under agreement. . . . Cases in which simultaneous performance is possible under the terms of the contract can be grouped into five categories: (1) where the same time is fixed for the performance of each party; (2) where a time is fixed for the performance of one of the parties and no time is fixed for the other; (3) where no time is fixed for the performance of either party; (4) where the same period is fixed within which each party is to perform; (5) where different periods are fixed within which each party is to perform. The requirement of simultaneous performance applies to the first four categories. The requirement does not apply to the fifth category, even if simultaneous performance is possible, because in fixing different periods for performance the parties must have contemplated the possibility of performance at different times under their agreement. Therefore in cases in the fifth category the circumstances show an intention contrary to the rule stated in Subsection (1). . . .

Illustrations

1. A promises to sell land to B, delivery of the deed to be on July 1. B promises to pay A $50,000, payment to be made on July 1. Delivery of the deed and payment of the price are due simultaneously.

2. A promises to sell land to B, the deed to be delivered on July 1. B promises to pay A $50,000, no provision being made for the time of payment. Delivery of the deed and payment of the price are due simultaneously.

3. A promises to sell land to B and B promises to pay A $50,000, no provision being made for the time either of delivery of the deed or of payment. Delivery of the deed and payment of the price are due simultaneously.

4. A promises to sell land to B, delivery of the deed to be on or before July 1. B promises to pay A $50,000, payment to be on or before July 1. Delivery of the deed and payment of the price are due simultaneously.

5. A promises to sell land to B, delivery of the deed to be on or before July 1. B promises to pay A $50,000, payment to be on or before August 1. Delivery of the deed and payment of the [price] are not due simultaneously. . . .

e. Where performance requires a period of time. Where the performance of one party requires a period of time and the performance of the other party does not, their performance can not be simultaneous. Since one of the parties must perform first, he must forego the security that a requirement of simultaneous performance affords against disappointment of his expectation of an exchange of performances, and he must bear the burden of financing the other party before the latter has performed. See Comment *a*. Of course the parties can by express provision mitigate the harshness of a rule that requires that one completely perform before the other perform at all. They often do this, for example, in construction contracts by stating a formula under which payment is to be made at stated intervals as work progresses. But it is not feasible for courts to devise such formulas for the wide variety of such cases that come before them in which the parties have made no provision. . . .

f. Applicability of rule. The rule stated in Subsection (2) usually finds its application to contracts involving services, such as construction and employment contracts. The common practice of making express provision for progress payments has diminished its importance with regard to the former, and the widespread enactment of state wage statutes giving the employee a right to the frequent periodic payment of wages has lessened its significance with regard to the latter. Nevertheless, it is a helpful rule for residual cases not otherwise provided for. . . .

Illustration

9. A contracts to do the concrete work on a building being constructed by B for $10 a cubic yard. In the absence of language or circumstances indicating the contrary, payment by B is not due until A has finished the concrete work. . . .

TOPIC 2. EFFECT OF PERFORMANCE AND NON-PERFORMANCE

§ 235. Effect of Performance as Discharge and of Non-Performance as Breach.

(1) Full performance of a duty under a contract discharges the duty.

(2) When performance of a duty under a contract is due any non-performance is a breach.

§ 236. Claims for Damages for Total and for Partial Breach.

(1) A claim for damages for total breach is one for damages based on all of the injured party's remaining rights to performance.

(2) A claim for damages for partial breach is one for damages based on only part of the injured party's remaining rights to performance.

§ 237. Effect on Other Party's Duties of a Failure to Render Performance.

Except as stated in § 240, it is a condition of each party's remaining duties to render performances to be exchanged under an exchange of promises that there be no uncured material failure by the other party to render any such performance due at an earlier time.

Comment

a. Effect of non-occurrence of condition. . . . A material failure of performance has, under this Section, these effects on the other party's remaining duties of performance with respect to the exchange. It prevents performance of those duties from becoming due, at least temporarily, and it discharges those duties if it has not been cured during the time in which performance can occur. The occurrence of conditions of the type dealt with in this Section is required out of a sense of fairness rather than as a result of the agreement of the parties. Such conditions are therefore sometimes referred to as "constructive conditions of exchange." Cf. § 204. . . .

§ 238. Effect on Other Party's Duties of a Failure to Offer Performance.

Where all or part of the performances to be exchanged under an exchange of promises are due simultaneously, it is a condition of each party's duties to render such performance that the other party either render or, with manifested present ability to do so, offer performance of his part of the simultaneous exchange.

§ 239. Effect on Other Party's Duties of a Failure Justified by Non-Occurrence of a Condition.

(1)   A party's failure to render or to offer performance may, except as stated in Subsection (2), affect the other party's duties under the rules stated in §§ 237 and 238 even though failure is justified by the non-occurrence of a condition.

(2)   The rule stated in Subsection (1) does not apply if the other party assumed the risk that he would have to perform in spite of such a failure.

§ 240. Part Performances as Agreed Equivalents.

If the performances to be exchanged under an exchange of promises can be apportioned into corresponding pairs of part performances so that the parts of each pair are properly regarded as agreed equivalents, a party's performance of his part of such a pair has the same effect on the other's duties to render performance of the agreed equivalent as it would have if only that pair of performances had been promised.

§ 241. Circumstances Significant in Determining Whether a Failure Is Material.

In determining whether a failure to render or to offer performance is material, the following circumstances are significant:

(a)   the extent to which the injured party will be deprived of the benefit which he reasonably expected;

(b)   the extent to which the injured party can be adequately compensated for the part of that benefit of which he will be deprived;

(c)   the extent to which the party failing to perform or to offer to perform will suffer forfeiture;

(d)   the likelihood that the party failing to perform or to offer to perform will cure his failure, taking account of all the circumstances including any reasonable assurances;

(e)   the extent to which the behavior of the party failing to perform or to offer to perform comports with standards of good faith and fair dealing.

Comment

a. Nature of significant circumstances. The application of the rules stated in §§ 237 and 238 turns on a standard of materiality that is necessarily imprecise and flexible. . . . It is to be applied in the light of the facts of each case in such a way as to further the purpose of securing for each party his expectation of an exchange of performances. . . .

b. Loss of benefit to injured party. Since the purpose of the rules stated in §§ 237 and 238 is to secure the parties' expectation of an exchange of performances, an important circumstance in determining whether a failure is material is the extent to which the injured party will be deprived of the benefit which he reasonably expected from the exchange (Subsection (a)). If the consideration given by either party consists partly of some performance and only partly of a promise (see Comment a to § 232), regard must be had to the entire exchange, including that performance, in applying this criterion. Although the relationship between the monetary loss to the injured party as a result of the failure and the contract price may be significant, no simple rule based on the ratio of the one to the other can be laid down, and here, as elsewhere under this Section, all relevant circumstances must be considered. In construction contracts, for example, defects affecting structural soundness are ordinarily regarded as particularly significant. In the sale of goods a particularly exacting standard has evolved. There it has long been established that, in the absence of a showing of a contrary intention, a buyer is entitled to expect strict performance of the contract, and Uniform Commercial Code § 2–601 carries forward this expectation by allowing the buyer to reject "if the goods or the tender of delivery fail in any respect to conform to the contract." The Code, however, compensates to some extent for the severity of this standard by extending the seller's right to cure beyond the point when the time for performance has expired in some instances (§ 2–508(2)), by allowing revocation of acceptance only if a nonconformity "substantially impairs" the value of the goods to the buyer (§ 2–608(1)), and by allowing the injured party to treat a nonconformity or default as to one installment under an installment contract as a breach of the whole only if it "substantially impairs" the value of the whole (§ 2–612(3)).

    c.   Adequacy of compensation for loss. The second circumstance, the extent to which the injured party can be adequately compensated for his loss of benefit (Subsection (b)), is a corollary of the first. Difficulty that he may have in proving with sufficient certainty the amount of that loss will affect the adequacy of compensation. If the failure is a breach, the injured party always has a claim for damages, and the question becomes one of the adequacy of that claim to compensate him for the lost benefit. Where the failure is not a breach, the question becomes one of the adequacy of any claim, such as one in restitution, to which the injured party may be entitled. This is a particularly important circumstance when the party in breach seeks specific performance. Such relief may be granted if damages can adequately compensate the injured party for the defect in performance. See Comment c to § 242.

    d.   Forfeiture by party who fails. Because a material failure acts as the non-occurrence of a condition, the same risk of forfeiture obtains as in the case of conditions generally if the party who fails to perform or tender has relied substantially on the expectation of the exchange, as through preparation or performance. Therefore a third circumstance is the extent to which the party failing to perform or to make an offer to perform will suffer forfeiture if the failure is treated as material. For this reason a failure is less likely to be regarded as material if it occurs late, after substantial preparation or performance, and more likely to be regarded as material if it occurs early, before such reliance. For the same reason the failure is more likely to be regarded as material if such preparation or performance as has taken place can be returned to and salvaged by the party failing to perform or tender, and less likely to be regarded as material if it cannot. These factors argue against a finding of material failure and in favor of one of substantial performance where a builder has completed performance under a construction contract and, because the building is on the owner's land, can salvage nothing if he is denied recovery of the balance of the price. Even in such a case, however, the potential forfeiture may be mitigated if the builder has a claim in restitution (§§ 370–77, especially § 374) or if he has already received progress payments under a provision of the contract. The same factors argue for a finding of material failure where a seller tenders goods and can salvage them by resale to others if they are rejected and he is denied recovery of the price. This helps to explain the severity of the rule as applied to the sale of goods. See Comment b. Even in such a case, however, the potential forfeiture may be aggravated if the seller has manufactured the goods specially for the buyer or has spent substantial sums in shipment. . . .

    e.   Uncertainty. A material failure by one party gives the other party the right to withhold further performance as a means of securing his expectation of an exchange of performances. To the extent that that expectation is already reasonably secure, in spite of the failure, there is less reason to conclude that the failure is material. The likelihood that the failure will be cured is therefore a significant circumstance in determining whether it is material (Subsection (d)). The fact that the injured party already has some security for the other party's performance argues against a determination that the failure is material. So do reasonable assurances of performance given by the other party after his failure. So does a shift in the market that makes performance of the contract more favorable to the other party. On the other hand, defaults by the other party under other contracts or as to other installments under the same contract argue for a determination of materiality. So does such financial weakness of the other party as suggests an inability to cure. This circumstance differs from the notion of reasonable grounds for insecurity (§ 251), in that the former can become relevant only after there has been an actual failure to perform or to tender. On discharge by repudiation, see § 253(2). . . .

    f.   Absence of good faith or fair dealing. A party's adherence to standards of good faith and fair dealing (§ 205) will not prevent his failure to perform a duty from amounting to a breach (§ 236(2)). Nor will his adherence to such standards necessarily prevent his failure from having the effect of the non-occurrence of a condition (§ 237; cf. § 238). The extent to which the behavior of the party failing to perform or to offer to perform comports with standards of good faith and fair dealing is, however, a significant circumstance in determining whether the failure is material (Subsection (e)). In giving weight to this factor courts have often used such less precise terms as "wilful." Adherence to the standards stated in Subsection (e) is not conclusive, since other circumstances may cause a failure to be material in spite of such adherence. Nor is non-adherence conclusive, and other circumstances may cause a failure not to be material in spite of such non-adherence.

§ 242. Circumstances Significant in Determining When Remaining Duties Are Discharged.

In determining the time after which a party's uncured material failure to render or to offer performance discharges the other party's remaining duties to render performance under the rules stated in §§ 237 and 238, the following circumstances are significant:

    (a)   those stated in § 241;

    (b)   the extent to which it reasonably appears to the injured party that delay may prevent or hinder him in making reasonable substitute arrangements;

    (c)   the extent to which the agreement provides for performance without delay, but a material failure to perform or to offer to perform on a stated day does not of itself discharge the other party's remaining duties unless the circumstances, including the language of the agreement, indicate that performance or an offer to perform by that day is important.

Comment

a.   Cure. . . . [A] party's uncured material failure to perform or to offer to perform not only has the effect of suspending the other party's duties . . . but, when it is too late for the performance or the offer to perform to occur, the failure also has the effect of discharging those duties. . . . Ordinarily there is some period of time between suspension and discharge, and during this period a party may cure his failure. Even then, since any breach gives rise to a claim, a party who has cured a material breach has still committed a breach, by his delay, for which he is liable in damages. Furthermore, in some instances timely performance is so essential that any delay immediately results in discharge and there is no period of time during which the injured party's duties are merely suspended and the other party can cure his failure. . . .

d.   Effect of agreement. . . . It is, of course, open to the parties to make performance or tender by a stated date a condition by their agreement, in which event, absent excuse . . . delay beyond that date results in discharge. . . . Such stock phrases as "time is of the essence" do not necessarily have this effect, although under Subsection (c) they are to be considered along with other circumstances in determining the effect of delay.

§ 243. Effect of a Breach by Non-Performance as Giving Rise to a Claim for Damages for Total Breach.

    (1)   With respect to performances to be exchanged under an exchange of promises, a breach by non-performance gives rise to a claim for damages for total breach only if it discharges the injured party's remaining duties to render such performance, other than a duty to render an agreed equivalent under § 240.

    (2)   Except as stated in Subsection (3), a breach by non-performance accompanied or followed by a repudiation gives rise to a claim for damages for total breach.

    (3)   Where at the time of the breach the only remaining duties of performance are those of the party in breach and are for the payment of money in installments not related to one another, his breach by non-performance as to less than the whole, whether or not accompanied or followed by a repudiation, does not give rise to a claim for damages for total breach.

    (4)   In any case other than those stated in the preceding subsections, a breach by non-performance gives rise to a claim for total breach only if it so substantially impairs the value of the contract to the injured party at the time of the breach that it is just in the circumstances to allow him to recover damages based on all his remaining rights to performance.

§ 244. Effect of Subsequent Events on Duty to Pay Damages.

A party's duty to pay damages for total breach by non-performance is discharged if it appears after the breach that there would have been a total failure by the injured party to perform his return promise.

§ 245. Effect of a Breach by Non-Performance as Excusing the Non-Occurrence of a Condition.

Where a party's breach by non-performance contributes materially to the non-occurrence of a condition of one of his duties, the non-occurrence is excused.

§ 246. Effect of Acceptance as Excusing the Non-Occurrence of a Condition.

(1) Except as stated in Subsection (2), an obligor's acceptance or his retention for an unreasonable time of the obligee's performance, with knowledge of or reason to know of the non-occurrence of a condition of the obligor's duty, operates as a promise to perform in spite of that non-occurrence, under the rules stated in § 84.

(2) If at the time of its acceptance or retention the obligee's performance involves such attachment to the obligor's property that removal would cause material loss, the obligor's acceptance or retention of that performance operates as a promise to perform in spite of the non-occurrence of the condition, under the rules stated in § 84, only if the obligor with knowledge of or reason to know of the defects manifests assent to the performance.

§ 247. Effect of Acceptance of Part Performance as Excusing the Subsequent Non-Occurrence of a Condition.

An obligor's acceptance of part of the obligee's performance, with knowledge or reason to know of the non-occurrence of a condition of the obligor's duty, operates as a promise to perform in spite of a subsequent non-occurrence of the condition under the rules stated in § 84 to the extent that it justifies the obligee in believing that subsequent performances will be accepted in spite of that non-occurrence.

§ 248. Effect of Insufficient Reason for Rejection as Excusing the Non-Occurrence of a Condition.

Where a party rejecting a defective performance or offer of performance gives an insufficient reason for rejection, the non-occurrence of a condition of his duty is excused only if he knew or had reason to know of that non-occurrence and then only to the extent that the giving of an insufficient reason substantially contributes to a failure by the other party to cure.

§ 249. When Payment Other Than by Legal Tender Is Sufficient.

Where the payment or offer of payment of money is made a condition of an obligor's duty, payment or offer of payment in any manner current in the ordinary course of business satisfies the requirement unless the obligee demands payment in legal tender and gives any extension of time reasonably necessary to procure it.

TOPIC 3. EFFECT OF PROSPECTIVE NON-PERFORMANCE

§ 250. When a Statement or an Act Is a Repudiation.

A repudiation is

(a) a statement by the obligor to the obligee indicating that the obligor will commit a breach that would of itself give the obligee a claim for damages for total breach under § 243, or

(b) a voluntary affirmative act which renders the obligor unable or apparently unable to perform without such a breach.

Comment

　　a.　Consequences of repudiation. A statement by a party to the other that he will not or cannot perform without a breach, or a voluntary affirmative act that renders him unable or apparently unable to perform without a breach may impair the value of the contract to the other party. It may have several consequences under this Restatement. If it accompanies a breach by non-performance that would otherwise give rise to only a claim for damages for partial breach, it may give rise to a claim for damages for total breach instead (§ 243). Even if it occurs before any breach by non-performance, it may give rise to a claim for damages for total breach (§ 253(1)), discharge the other party's duties (§ 253(2)), or excuse the non-occurrence of a condition (§ 255).

　　b.　Nature of statement. In order to constitute a repudiation, a party's language must be sufficiently positive to be reasonably interpreted to mean that the party will not or cannot perform. Mere expression of doubt as to his willingness or ability to perform is not enough to constitute a repudiation, although such an expression may give an obligee reasonable grounds to believe that the obligor will commit a serious breach and may ultimately result in a repudiation under the rule stated in § 251. However, language that under a fair reading "amounts to a statement of intention not to perform except on conditions which go beyond the contract" constitutes a repudiation. Comment 2 to Uniform Commercial Code § 2–610. Language that is accompanied by a breach by non-performance may amount to a repudiation even though, standing alone, it would not be sufficiently positive. See § 243(2). . . .

§ 251. When a Failure to Give Assurance May Be Treated as a Repudiation.

　　(1)　Where reasonable grounds arise to believe that the obligor will commit a breach by non-performance that would of itself give the obligee a claim for damages for total breach under § 243, the obligee may demand adequate assurance of due performance and may, if reasonable, suspend any performance for which he has not already received the agreed exchange until he receives such assurance.

　　(2)　The obligee may treat as a repudiation the obligor's failure to provide within a reasonable time such assurance of due performance as is adequate in the circumstances of the particular case.

Comment

　　a.　Rationale. Ordinarily an obligee has no right to demand reassurance by the obligor that the latter will perform when his performance is due. However, a contract "imposes an obligation on each party that the other's expectation of receiving due performance will not be impaired." Uniform Commercial Code § 2–609(1). When, therefore, an obligee reasonably believes that the obligor will commit a breach by non-performance that would of itself give him a claim for damages for total breach (§ 243), he may, under the rule stated in this Section, be entitled to demand assurance of performance. . . .

　　c.　Reasonable grounds for belief. . . . Conduct by a party that indicates his doubt as to his willingness or ability to perform but that is not sufficiently positive to amount to a repudiation . . . may give reasonable grounds for [an obligee's belief that there will be a breach]. And events that indicate a party's apparent inability, but do not amount to a repudiation because they are not voluntary acts, may also give reasonable grounds for such a belief. . . .

§ 252. Effect of Insolvency.

　　(1)　Where the obligor's insolvency gives the obligee reasonable grounds to believe that the obligor will commit a breach under the rule stated in § 251, the obligee may suspend any performance for which he has not already received the agreed exchange until he receives assurance in the form of performance itself, an offer of performance, or adequate security.

　　(2)　A person is insolvent who either has ceased to pay his debts in the ordinary course of business or cannot pay his debts as they become due or is insolvent within the meaning of the federal bankruptcy law.

§ 253. Effect of a Repudiation as a Breach and on Other Party's Duties.

(1)   Where an obligor repudiates a duty before he has committed a breach by non-performance and before he has received all of the agreed exchange for it, his repudiation alone gives rise to a claim for damages for total breach.

(2)   Where performances are to be exchanged under an exchange of promises, one party's repudiation of a duty to render performance discharges the other party's remaining duties to render performance.

Comment

a.   *Breach.* An obligee under a contract is ordinarily entitled to the protection of his expectation that the obligor will perform. For this reason, a repudiation by the obligor under § 250 or § 251 generally gives rise to a claim for damages for total breach even though it is not accompanied or preceded by a breach by non-performance. Such a repudiation is sometimes elliptically called an "anticipatory breach," meaning a breach by anticipatory repudiation, because it occurs before there is any breach by non-performance. . . .

§ 254. Effect of Subsequent Events on Duty to Pay Damages.

(1)   A party's duty to pay damages for total breach by repudiation is discharged if it appears after the breach that there would have been a total failure by the injured party to perform his return promise.

(2)   A party's duty to pay damages for total breach by repudiation is discharged if it appears after the breach that the duty that he repudiated would have been discharged by impracticability or frustration before any breach by non-performance.

§ 255. Effect of a Repudiation as Excusing the Non-Occurrence of a Condition.

Where a party's repudiation contributes materially to the non-occurrence of a condition of one of his duties, the non-occurrence is excused.

§ 256. Nullification of Repudiation or Basis for Repudiation.

(1)   The effect of a statement as constituting a repudiation under § 250 or the basis for a repudiation under § 251 is nullified by a retraction of the statement if notification of the retraction comes to the attention of the injured party before he materially changes his position in reliance on the repudiation or indicates to the other party that he considers the repudiation to be final.

(2)   The effect of events other than a statement as constituting a repudiation under § 250 or the basis for a repudiation under § 251 is nullified if, to the knowledge of the injured party, those events have ceased to exist before he materially changes his position in reliance on the repudiation or indicates to the other party that he considers the repudiation to be final.

Comment

. . .

c.   *Time for nullification.* Once the injured party has materially changed his position in reliance on the repudiation, nullification would clearly be unjust. In the interest of certainty, however, it is undesirable to make the injured party's rights turn exclusively on such a vague criterion, and he may therefore prevent subsequent nullification by indicating to the other party that he considers the repudiation final. . . .

§ 257. Effect of Urging Performance in Spite of Repudiation.

The injured party does not change the effect of a repudiation by urging the repudiator to perform in spite of his repudiation or to retract his repudiation.

TOPIC 4. APPLICATION OF PERFORMANCES

§ 258. Obligor's Direction of Application.

(1) Except as stated in Subsection (2), as between two or more contractual duties owed by an obligor to the same obligee, a performance is applied according to a direction made by the obligor to the obligee at or before the time of performance.

(2) If the obligor is under a duty to a third person to devote a performance to the discharge of a particular duty that the obligor owes to the obligee and the obligee knows or has reason to know this, the obligor's performance is applied to that duty.

§ 259. Creditor's Application.

(1) Except as stated in Subsections (2) and (3), if the debtor has not directed application of a payment as between two or more matured debts, the payment is applied according to a manifestation of intention made within a reasonable time by the creditor to the debtor.

(2) A creditor cannot apply such a payment to a debt if

     (a)   the debtor could not have directed its application to that debt, or

     (b)   a forfeiture would result from a failure to apply it to another debt and the creditor knows or has reason to know this, or

     (c)   the debt is disputed or is unenforceable on grounds of public policy.

(3) If a creditor is owed one such debt in his own right and another in a fiduciary capacity, he cannot, unless empowered to do so by the beneficiary, effectively apply to the debt in his own right a greater proportion of a payment than that borne by the unsecured portion of that debt to the unsecured portions of both claims.

§ 260. Application of Payments Where Neither Party Exercises His Power.

(1) If neither the debtor nor the creditor has exercised his power with respect to the application of a payment as between two or more matured debts, the payment is applied to debts to which the creditor could have applied it with just regard to the interests of third persons, the debtor and the creditor.

(2) In applying payments under the rule stated in Subsection (1), a payment is applied to the earliest matured debt and ratably among debts of the same maturity, except that preference is given

     (a)   to a debt that the debtor is under a duty to a third person to pay immediately, and

     (b)   if he is not under such a duty,

         (i)   to overdue interest rather than principal, and

         (ii)   to an unsecured or precarious debt rather than one that is secured or certain of payment.

CHAPTER 11

IMPRACTICABILITY OF PERFORMANCE AND FRUSTRATION OF PURPOSE

§ 261. Discharge by Supervening Impracticability.

Where, after a contract is made, a party's performance is made impracticable without his fault by the occurrence of an event the non-occurrence of which was a basic assumption on which the contract was made, his duty to render that performance is discharged, unless the language or the circumstances indicate the contrary.

§ 262. Death or Incapacity of Person Necessary for Performance.

If the existence of a particular person is necessary for the performance of a duty, his death or such incapacity as makes performance impracticable is an event the non-occurrence of which was a basic assumption on which the contract was made.

§ 263. Destruction, Deterioration or Failure to Come Into Existence of Thing Necessary for Performance.

If the existence of a specific thing is necessary for the performance of a duty, its failure to come into existence, destruction, or such deterioration as makes performance impracticable is an event the non-occurrence of which was a basic assumption on which the contract was made.

§ 264. Prevention by Governmental Regulation or Order.

If the performance of a duty is made impracticable by having to comply with a domestic or foreign governmental regulation or order, that regulation or order is an event the non-occurrence of which was a basic assumption on which the contract was made.

§ 265. Discharge by Supervening Frustration.

Where, after a contract is made, a party's principal purpose is substantially frustrated without his fault by the occurrence of an event the non-occurrence of which was a basic assumption on which the contract was made, his remaining duties to render performance are discharged, unless the language or the circumstances indicate the contrary.

§ 266. Existing Impracticability or Frustration.

(1) Where, at the time a contract is made, a party's performance under it is impracticable without his fault because of a fact of which he has no reason to know and the non-existence of which is a basic assumption on which the contract is made, no duty to render that performance arises, unless the language or circumstances indicate the contrary.

(2) Where, at the time a contract is made, a party's principal purpose is substantially frustrated without his fault by a fact of which he has no reason to know and the non-existence of which is a basic assumption on which the contract is made, no duty of that party to render performance arises, unless the language or circumstances indicate the contrary.

§ 267. Effect on Other Party's Duties of a Failure Justified by Impracticability or Frustration.

(1) A party's failure to render or to offer performance may, except as stated in Subsection (2), affect the other party's duties under the rules stated in §§ 237 and 238 even though the failure is justified under the rules stated in this Chapter.

(2) The rule stated in Subsection (1) does not apply if the other party assumed the risk that he would have to perform despite such a failure.

§ 268. Effect on Other Party's Duties of a Prospective Failure Justified by Impracticability or Frustration.

(1) A party's prospective failure of performance may, except as stated in Subsection (2), discharge the other party's duties or allow him to suspend performance under the rules stated in §§ 251(1) and 253(2) even though the failure would be justified under the rules stated in this Chapter.

(2) The rule stated in Subsection (1) does not apply if the other party assumed the risk that he would have to perform in spite of such a failure.

§ 269. Temporary Impracticability or Frustration.

Impracticability of performance or frustration of purpose that is only temporary suspends the obligor's duty to perform while the impracticability or frustration exists but does not discharge his duty or prevent it from arising unless his performance after the cessation of the impracticability or frustration would be materially more burdensome than had there been no impracticability or frustration.

§ 270. Partial Impracticability.

Where only part of an obligor's performance is impracticable, his duty to render the remaining part is unaffected if

(a) it is still practicable for him to render performance that is substantial, taking account of any reasonable substitute performance that he is under a duty to render; or

(b) the obligee, within a reasonable time, agrees to render any remaining performance in full and to allow the obligor to retain any performance that has already been rendered.

§ 271. Impracticability as Excuse for Non-Occurrence of a Condition.

Impracticability excuses the non-occurrence of a condition if the occurrence of the condition is not a material part of the agreed exchange and forfeiture would otherwise result. . . .

Illustrations

1. A contracts with B to repair B's building for $20,000, payment to be made "on the satisfaction of C, B's architect, and the issuance of his certificate." A properly makes the repairs, but C dies before he is able to give a certificate. Since presentation of the architect's certificate is not a material part of the agreed exchange and forfeiture would otherwise result, the occurrence of the condition is excused, and A has a claim against B for $20,000. . . .

2. A, an insurance company, issues to B a policy of accidental injury insurance which provides that notice within 14 days of an accident is a condition of A's duty. B is injured as a result of an accident covered by the policy but is so mentally deranged that he is unable to give notice for 20 days. B gives notice as soon as he is able. Since the giving of notice within 14 days is not a material part of the agreed exchange, and forfeiture would otherwise result, the non-occurrence of the condition is excused and B has a claim against A under the policy.

§ 272. Relief Including Restitution.

(1) In any case governed by the rules stated in this Chapter, either party may have a claim for relief including restitution under the rules stated in §§ 240 and 377.

(2) In any case governed by the rules stated in this Chapter, if those rules together with the rules stated in Chapter 16 will not avoid injustice, the court may grant relief on such terms as justice requires including protection of the parties' reliance interests.

CHAPTER 12

DISCHARGE BY ASSENT OR ALTERATION

TOPIC 1. THE REQUIREMENT OF CONSIDERATION

§ 273. Requirement of Consideration or a Substitute.

Except as stated in §§ 274–77, an obligee's manifestation of assent to a discharge is not effective unless

    (a)   it is made for consideration,

    (b)   it is made in circumstances in which a promise would be enforceable without consideration, or

    (c)   it has induced such action or forbearance as would make a promise enforceable.

§ 274. Cancellation, Destruction or Surrender of a Writing.

An obligee's cancellation, destruction or surrender to the obligor of a writing of a type customarily accepted as a symbol or as evidence of his right discharges without consideration the obligor's duty if it is done with the manifested intention to discharge it.

§ 275. Assent to Discharge Duty of Return Performance.

If a party, before he has fully performed his duty under a contract, manifests to the other party his assent to discharge the other party's duty to render part or all of the agreed exchange, the duty is to that extent discharged without consideration.

§ 276. Assent to Discharge Duty to Transfer Property.

A duty of an obligor in possession of identified personal property to transfer an interest in that property is discharged without consideration if the obligee manifests to the obligor his assent to the discharge of that duty.

§ 277. Renunciation.

(1)   A written renunciation signed and delivered by the obligee discharges without consideration a duty arising out of a breach of contract.

(2)   A renunciation by the obligee on his acceptance from the obligor of some performance under a contract discharges without consideration a duty to pay damages for a breach that gives rise only to a claim for damages for partial breach of contract.

§ 278. Substituted Performance.

(1)   If an obligee accepts in satisfaction of the obligor's duty a performance offered by the obligor that differs from what is due, the duty is discharged.

(2)   If an obligee accepts in satisfaction of the obligor's duty a performance offered by a third person, the duty is discharged, but an obligor who has not previously assented to the performance for his benefit may in a reasonable time after learning of it render the discharge inoperative from the beginning by disclaimer.

§ 279. Substituted Contract.

(1)   A substituted contract is a contract that is itself accepted by the obligee in satisfaction of the obligor's existing duty.

(2)   The substituted contract discharges the original duty and breach of the substituted contract by the obligor does not give the obligee a right to enforce the original duty.

§ 280. Novation.

A novation is a substituted contract that includes as a party one who was neither the obligor nor the obligee of the original duty.

§ 281. Accord and Satisfaction.

(1)   An accord is a contract under which an obligee promises to accept a stated performance in satisfaction of the obligor's existing duty. Performance of the accord discharges the original duty.

(2)   Until performance of the accord, the original duty is suspended unless there is such a breach of the accord by the obligor as discharges the new duty of the obligee to accept the performance in satisfaction. If there is such a breach, the obligee may enforce either the original duty or any duty under the accord.

(3)   Breach of the accord by the obligee does not discharge the original duty, but the obligor may maintain a suit for specific performance of the accord, in addition to any claim for damages for partial breach.

TOPIC 2. SUBSTITUTED PERFORMANCE, SUBSTITUTED CONTRACT, ACCORD AND ACCOUNT STATED

§ 282. Account Stated.

(1)   An account stated is a manifestation of assent by debtor and creditor to a stated sum as an accurate computation of an amount due the creditor. A party's retention without objection for an unreasonably long time of a statement of account rendered by the other party is a manifestation of assent.

(2)   The account stated does not itself discharge any duty but is an admission by each party of the facts asserted and a promise by the debtor to pay according to its terms.

TOPIC 3. AGREEMENT OF RESCISSION, RELEASE AND CONTRACT NOT TO SUE

§ 283. Agreement of Rescission.

(1)   An agreement of rescission is an agreement under which each party agrees to discharge all of the other party's remaining duties of performance under an existing contract.

(2)   An agreement of rescission discharges all remaining duties of performance of both parties. It is a question of interpretation whether the parties also agree to make restitution with respect to performance that has been rendered.

§ 284. Release.

(1)   A release is a writing providing that a duty owed to the maker of the release is discharged immediately or on the occurrence of a condition.

(2)   The release takes effect on delivery as stated in §§ 101–03 and, subject to the occurrence of any condition, discharges the duty.

§ 285. Contract Not to Sue.

(1)   A contract not to sue is a contract under which the obligee of a duty promises never to sue the obligor or a third person to enforce the duty or not to do so for a limited time.

(2)   Except as stated in Subsection (3), a contract never to sue discharges the duty and a contract not to sue for a limited time bars an action to enforce the duty during that time.

(3)   A contract not to sue one co-obligor bars levy of execution on the property of the promisee during the agreed time but does not bar an action or the recovery of judgment against any co-obligor.

TOPIC 4. ALTERATION

§ 286. Alteration of Writing.

(1) If one to whom a duty is owed under a contract alters a writing that is an integrated agreement or that satisfies the Statute of Frauds with respect to that contract, the duty is discharged if the alteration is fraudulent and material.

(2) An alteration is material if it would, if effective, vary any party's legal relations with the maker of the alteration or adversely affect that party's legal relations with a third person. The unauthorized insertion in a blank space in a writing is an alteration.

§ 287. Assent to or Forgiveness of Alteration.

(1) If a party, knowing of an alteration that discharges his duty, manifests assent to the altered terms, his manifestation is equivalent to an acceptance of an offer to substitute those terms.

(2) If a party, knowing of an alteration that discharges his duty, asserts a right under the original contract or otherwise manifests a willingness to remain subject to the original contract or to forgive the alteration, the original contract is revived.

CHAPTER 13

JOINT AND SEVERAL PROMISORS AND PROMISEES

TOPIC 1. JOINT AND SEVERAL PROMISORS

§ 288. Promises of the Same Performance.

(1) Where two or more parties to a contract make a promise or promises to the same promisee, the manifested intention of the parties determines whether they promise that the same performance or separate performances shall be given.

(2) Unless a contrary intention is manifested, a promise by two or more promisors is a promise that the same performance shall be given.

§ 289. Joint, Several, and Joint and Several Promisors of the Same Performance.

(1) Where two or more parties to a contract promise the same performance to the same promisee, each is bound for the whole performance thereof, whether his duty is joint, several, or joint and several.

(2) Where two or more parties to a contract promise the same performance to the same promisee, they incur only a joint duty unless an intention is manifested to create several duties or joint and several duties.

(3) By statute in most states some or all promises which would otherwise create only joint duties create joint and several duties.

§ 290. Compulsory Joinder of Joint Promisors.

(1) By statute in most states where the distinction between joint duties and joint and several duties retains significance, an action can be maintained against one or more promisors who incur only a joint duty, even though other promisors subject to the same duty are not served with process.

(2) In the absence of statute, an action can be maintained against promisors who incur only a joint duty without joinder of those beyond the jurisdiction of the court, the representatives of deceased promisors, or those against whom the duty is not enforceable at the time of suit.

§ 291. Judgment in an Action Against Co-Promisors.

In an action against promisors of the same performance, whether their duties are joint, several, or joint and several, judgment can properly be entered for or against one even though no judgment or a different judgment is entered with respect to another, except that judgment for one and against another is improper where there has been a determination on the merits and the liability of one cannot exist without the liability of the other.

§ 292. Effect of Judgment for or Against Co-Promisors.

(1) A judgment against one or more promisors does not discharge other promisors of the same performance unless joinder of the other promisors is required by the rule stated in § 290. By statute in most states judgment against one promisor does not discharge co-promisors even where such joinder is required.

(2) The effect of judgment for one or more promisors of the same performance is determined by the rules of res judicata relating to suretyship or vicarious liability.

§ 293. Effect of Performance or Satisfaction on Co-Promisors.

Full or partial performance or other satisfaction of the contractual duty of a promisor discharges the duty to the obligee of each other promisor of the same performance to the extent of the amount or value applied to the discharge of the duty of the promisor who renders it.

§ 294. Effect of Discharge on Co-Promisors.

(1) Except as stated in § 295, where the obligee of promises of the same performance discharges one promisor by release, rescission or accord and satisfaction,

(a) co-promisors who are bound only by a joint duty are discharged unless the discharged promisor is a surety for the co-promisor;

(b) co-promisors who are bound by joint and several duties or by several duties are not discharged except to the extent required by the law of suretyship.

(2) By statute in many states a discharge of one promisor does not discharge other promisors of the same performance except to the extent required by the law of suretyship.

(3) Any consideration received by the obligee for discharge of one promisor discharges the duty of each other promisor of the same performance to the extent of the amount or value received. An agreement to the contrary is not effective unless it is made with a surety and expressly preserves the duty of his principal.

§ 295. Effect of Contract Not to Sue; Reservation of Rights.

(1) Where the obligee of promises of the same performance contracts not to sue one promisor, the other promisors are not discharged except to the extent required by the law of suretyship.

(2) Words which purport to release or discharge a promisor and also to reserve rights against other promisors of the same performance have the effect of a contract not to sue rather than a release or discharge.

(3) Any consideration received by the obligee for a contract not to sue one promisor discharges the duty of each other promisor of the same performance to the extent of the amount or value received. An agreement to the contrary is not effective unless it is made with a surety and expressly preserves the duty of his principal.

§ 296. Survivorship of Joint Duties.

On the death of one of two or more promisors of the same performance in a contract, the estate of the deceased promisor is bound by the contract, whether the duty was joint, several, or joint and several.

TOPIC 2. JOINT AND SEVERAL PROMISEES

§ 297. Obligees of the Same Promised Performance.

(1) Where a party to a contract makes a promise to two or more promisees or for the benefit of two or more beneficiaries, the manifested intention of the parties determines whether he promises the same performance to all, a separate performance to each, or some combination.

(2) Except to the extent that a different intention is manifested or that the interests of the obligees in the performance or in the remedies for breach are distinct, the rights of obligees of the same performance are joint.

§ 298. Compulsory Joinder of Joint Obligees.

(1) In an action based on a joint right created by a promise, the promisor by making appropriate objection can prevent recovery of judgment against him unless there are joined either as plaintiffs or as defendants all the surviving joint obligees.

(2) Except in actions on negotiable instruments and except as stated in § 300, any joint obligee unless limited by agreement may sue in the name of all the joint obligees for the enforcement of the promise by a money judgment.

§ 299. Discharge by or Tender to One Joint Obligee.

Except where the promise is made in a negotiable instrument and except as stated in § 300, any joint obligee, unless limited by agreement, has power to discharge the promisor by receipt of the promised performance or by release or otherwise, and tender to one joint obligee is equivalent to a tender to all.

§ 300. Effect of Violation of Duty to a Co-Obligee.

(1) If an obligee attempts or threatens to discharge the promisor in violation of his duty to a co-obligee of the same performance, the co-obligee may obtain an injunction forbidding the discharge.

(2) A discharge of the promisor by an obligee in violation of his duty to a co-obligee of the same performance is voidable to the extent necessary to protect the co-obligee's interest in the performance, except to the extent that the promisor has given value or otherwise changed his position in good faith and without knowledge or reason to know of the violation.

§ 301. Survivorship of Joint Rights.

On the death of a joint obligee, unless a contrary intention was manifested, the surviving obligees are solely entitled as against the promisor to receive performance, to discharge the promisor, or to sue for the enforcement of the promise by a money judgment. On the death of the last surviving obligee, only his estate is so entitled.

CHAPTER 14

CONTRACT BENEFICIARIES

§ 302. Intended and Incidental Beneficiaries.

(1)   Unless otherwise agreed between promisor and promisee, a beneficiary of a promise is an intended beneficiary if recognition of a right to performance in the beneficiary is appropriate to effectuate the intention of the parties and either

(a)   the performance of the promise will satisfy an obligation of the promisee to pay money to the beneficiary; or

(b)   the circumstances indicate that the promisee intends to give the beneficiary the benefit of the promised performance.

(2)   An incidental beneficiary is a beneficiary who is not an intended beneficiary.

Comment

. . .

d.   *Other intended beneficiaries.* Either a promise to pay the promisee's debt to a beneficiary or a gift promise involves a manifestation of intention by the promisee and promisor sufficient, in a contractual setting, to make reliance by the beneficiary both reasonable and probable. Other cases may be quite similar in this respect. Examples are a promise to perform a supposed or asserted duty of the promisee, a promise to discharge a lien on the promisee's property, or a promise to satisfy the duty of a third person. In such cases, if the beneficiary would be reasonable in relying on the promise as manifesting an intention to confer a right on him, he is an intended beneficiary. Where there is doubt whether such reliance would be reasonable, considerations of procedural convenience and other factors not strictly dependent on the manifested intention of the parties may affect the question whether under Subsection (1) recognition of a right in the beneficiary is appropriate. In some cases an overriding policy, which may be embodied in a statute, requires recognition of such a right without regard to the intention of the parties. . . .

e.   *Incidental beneficiaries.* Performance of a contract will often benefit a third person. But unless the third person is an intended beneficiary as here defined, no duty to him is created. See § 315.

Illustrations

16.   B contracts with A to erect an expensive building on A's land. C's adjoining land would be enhanced in value by the performance of the contract. C is [only] an incidental beneficiary [and cannot bring suit under the contract].

17.   B contracts with A to buy a new car manufactured by C. C is [only] an incidental beneficiary [and cannot bring suit under the contract], even though the promise can only be performed if money is paid to C.

18.   A, a labor union, promises B, a trade association, not to strike against any member of B during a certain period. One of the members of B charters a ship from C on terms under which such a strike would cause financial loss to C. C is [only] an incidental beneficiary of A's promise [and cannot bring suit under the contract].

19.   A contracts to erect a building for C. B then contracts with A to supply lumber needed for the building. C is [only] an incidental beneficiary of B's promise, and B is [only] an incidental beneficiary of C's promise to pay A for the building [and neither can bring suit under the other's contract].

§ 303. Conditional Promises; Promises Under Seal.

The statements in this Chapter are applicable to both conditional and unconditional promises and to sealed and unsealed promises.

§ 304. Creation of Duty to Beneficiary.

A promise in a contract creates a duty in the promisor to any intended beneficiary to perform the promise, and the intended beneficiary may enforce the duty.

§ 305. Overlapping Duties to Beneficiary and Promisee.

(1) A promise in a contract creates a duty in the promisor to the promisee to perform the promise even though he also has a similar duty to an intended beneficiary.

(2) Whole or partial satisfaction of the promisor's duty to the beneficiary satisfies to that extent the promisor's duty to the promisee.

§ 306. Disclaimer by a Beneficiary.

A beneficiary who has not previously assented to the promise for his benefit may in a reasonable time after learning of its existence and terms render any duty to himself inoperative from the beginning by disclaimer.

§ 307. Remedy of Specific Performance.

Where specific performance is otherwise an appropriate remedy, either the promisee or the beneficiary may maintain a suit for specific enforcement of a duty owed to an intended beneficiary.

Comment

. . .

b. *Suit by promisee.* Even though a contract creates a duty to a beneficiary, the promisee has a right to performance. . . . The promisee cannot recover damages suffered by the beneficiary, but the promisee is a proper party to sue for specific performance if that remedy is otherwise appropriate. . . .

d. *Gift promise.* Where the promisee intends to make a gift of the promised performance to the beneficiary, the beneficiary ordinarily has an economic interest in the performance but the promisee does not. Thus the promisee may suffer no damages as the result of breach by the promisor. In such cases the promisee's remedy in damages is not an adequate remedy . . . and specific performance may be appropriate. . . . The court may of course so fashion its decree as to protect the interests of the promisee and beneficiary without unnecessary injury to the promisor or innocent third persons. . . .

§ 308. Identification of Beneficiaries.

It is not essential to the creation of a right in an intended beneficiary that he be identified when a contract containing the promise is made.

§ 309. Defenses Against the Beneficiary.

(1) A promise creates no duty to a beneficiary unless a contract is formed between the promisor and the promisee; and if a contract is voidable or unenforceable at the time of its formation the right of any beneficiary is subject to the infirmity.

(2) If a contract ceases to be binding in whole or in part because of impracticability, public policy, non-occurrence of a condition, or present or prospective failure of performance, the right of any beneficiary is to that extent discharged or modified.

(3) Except as stated in Subsections (1) and (2) and in § 311 or as provided by the contract, the right of any beneficiary against the promisor is not subject to the promisor's claims or defenses against the promisee or to the promisee's claims or defenses against the beneficiary.

(4) A beneficiary's right against the promisor is subject to any claim or defense arising from his own conduct or agreement.

§ 310. Remedies of the Beneficiary of a Promise to Pay the Promisee's Debt; Reimbursement of Promisee.

(1) Where an intended beneficiary has an enforceable claim against the promisee, he can obtain a judgment or judgments against either the promisee or the promisor or both based on their respective duties to him. Satisfaction in whole or in part of either of these duties, or of a judgment thereon, satisfies to that extent the other duty or judgment, subject to the promisee's right of subrogation.

(2) To the extent that the claim of an intended beneficiary is satisfied from assets of the promisee, the promisee has a right of reimbursement from the promisor, which may be enforced directly and also, if the beneficiary's claim is fully satisfied, by subrogation to the claim of the beneficiary against the promisor, and to any judgment thereon and to any security therefor.

§ 311. Variation of a Duty to a Beneficiary.

(1) Discharge or modification of a duty to an intended beneficiary by conduct of the promisee or by a subsequent agreement between promisor and promisee is ineffective if a term of the promise creating the duty so provides.

(2) In the absence of such a term, the promisor and promisee retain power to discharge or modify the duty by subsequent agreement.

(3) Such a power terminates when the beneficiary, before he receives notification of the discharge or modification, materially changes his position in justifiable reliance on the promise or brings suit on it or manifests assent to it at the request of the promisor or promisee.

(4) If the promisee receives consideration for an attempted discharge or modification of the promisor's duty which is ineffective against the beneficiary, the beneficiary can assert a right to the consideration so received. The promisor's duty is discharged to the extent of the amount received by the beneficiary.

Comment

. . .

g. *Reliance.* In the absence of some contrary indication, an intended beneficiary is justified in relying on the promise. It is immaterial whether he learns of the promise from the promisor, the promisee or a third party, and whether the promise is one to satisfy the promisee's duty or is a gift promise or is neither. If there is a material change of position in justifiable reliance on the promise, the change of position precludes discharge or modification of the contract without the beneficiary's consent. . . .

h. *Assent.* Even though there is no novation and no change of position by the beneficiary, the power of promisor and promisee to vary the promisor's duty to an intended beneficiary is terminated when the beneficiary manifests assent to the promise in a manner invited by the promisor or promisee. This rule rests in part on an analogy to the law of offer and acceptance and in part on the probability that the beneficiary will rely in ways difficult or impossible to prove. The bringing of suit against the promisor is a sufficient manifestation of assent to preclude discharge or modification. . . .

§ 312. Mistake as to Duty to Beneficiary.

The effect of an erroneous belief of the promisor or promisee as to the existence or extent of a duty owed to an intended beneficiary is determined by the rules making contracts voidable for mistake.

§ 313. Government Contracts.

(1) The rules stated in this Chapter apply to contracts with a government or governmental agency except to the extent that application would contravene the policy of the law authorizing the contract or prescribing remedies for its breach.

(2) In particular, a promisor who contracts with a government or governmental agency to do an act for or render a service to the public is not subject to contractual liability to a member of the public for consequential damages resulting from performance or failure to perform unless

(a) the terms of the promise provide for such liability; or

(b) the promisee is subject to liability to the member of the public for the damages and a direct action against the promisor is consistent with the terms of the contract and with the policy of the law authorizing the contract and prescribing remedies for its breach.

§ 314. Suretyship Defenses.

An intended beneficiary who has an enforceable claim against the promisee is affected by the incidents of the suretyship of the promisee from the time he has knowledge of it.

§ 315. Effect of a Promise of Incidental Benefit.

An incidental beneficiary acquires by virtue of the promise no right against the promisor or the promisee.

CHAPTER 15

ASSIGNMENT AND DELEGATION

§ 316. Scope of This Chapter.

(1)   In this Chapter, references to assignment of a right or delegation of a duty or condition, to the obligee or obligor of an assigned right or delegated duty, or to an assignor or assignee, are limited to rights, duties, and conditions arising under a contract or for breach of a contract.

(2)   The statements in this Chapter are qualified in some respects by statutory and other rules governing negotiable instruments and documents, relating to interests in land, and affecting other classes of contracts.

TOPIC 1. WHAT CAN BE ASSIGNED OR DELEGATED

§ 317. Assignment of a Right.

(1)   An assignment of a right is a manifestation of the assignor's intention to transfer it by virtue of which the assignor's right to performance by the obligor is extinguished in whole or in part and the assignee acquires a right to such performance.

(2)   A contractual right can be assigned unless

(a)   the substitution of a right of the assignee for the right of the assignor would materially change the duty of the obligor, or materially increase the burden or risk imposed on him by his contract, or materially impair his chance of obtaining return performance, or materially reduce its value to him, or

(b)   the assignment is forbidden by statute or is otherwise inoperative on grounds of public policy, or

(c)   assignment is validly precluded by contract.

§ 318. Delegation of Performance of Duty.

(1)   An obligor can properly delegate the performance of his duty to another unless the delegation is contrary to public policy or the terms of his promise.

(2)   Unless otherwise agreed, a promise requires performance by a particular person only to the extent that the obligee has a substantial interest in having that person perform or control the acts promised.

(3)   Unless the obligee agrees otherwise, neither delegation of performance nor a contract to assume the duty made with the obligor by the person delegated discharges any duty or liability of the delegating obligor.

Comment

. . .

c.   *Non-delegable duties.* Delegation of performance is a normal and permissible incident of many types of contract. See Uniform Commercial Code § 2–210, Comment. The principal exceptions relate to contracts for personal services and to contracts for the exercise of personal skill or discretion. . . . Even where delegation is normal, a particular contract may call for personal performance. . . . In the absence of contrary agreement, Subsection (2) precludes delegation only where a substantial reason is shown why delegated performance is not as satisfactory as personal performance.

Illustrations

5.   A, a teacher employed in a public or private school, attempts to delegate the performance of his duties to B, a competent person. An offer by B to perform A's duties need not be accepted, and actual performance by B without the assent of the employer will create no right in either A or B to the salary stated in A's contract.

6.   A contracts with B, a corporation, to sing three songs over the radio as part of an advertisement of B's product. A's performance is not delegable unless B assents.

7.   A contracts with B that A will personally cut the grass on B's meadow. A cannot effectively delegate performance of the duty to C, however competent C may be.

§ 319. Delegation of Performance of Condition.

(1)   Where a performance by a person is made a condition of a duty, performance by a person delegated by his satisfies that requirement unless the delegation is contrary to public policy or the terms of the agreement.

(2)   Unless otherwise agreed, an agreement requires performance of a condition by a particular person only to the extent that the obligor has a substantial interest in having that person perform or control the acts required.

§ 320. Assignment of Conditional Rights.

The fact that a right is created by an option contract or is conditional on the performance of a return promise or is otherwise conditional does not prevent its assignment before the condition occurs.

§ 321. Assignment of Future Rights.

(1)   Except as otherwise provided by statute, an assignment of a right to payment expected to arise out of an existing employment or other continuing business relationship is effective in the same way as an assignment of an existing right.

(2)   Except as otherwise provided by statute and as stated in Subsection (1), a purported assignment of a right expected to arise under a contract not in existence operates only as a promise to assign the right when it arises and as a power to enforce it.

§ 322. Contractual Prohibition of Assignment.

(1)   Unless the circumstances indicate the contrary, a contract term prohibiting assignment of "the contract" bars only the delegation to an assignee of the performance by the assignor of a duty or condition.

(2)   A contract term prohibiting assignment of rights under the contract, unless a different intention is manifested,

(a)   does not forbid assignment of a right to damages for breach of the whole contract or a right arising out of the assignor's due performance of his entire obligation;

(b)   gives the obligor a right to damages for breach of the terms forbidding assignment but does not render the assignment ineffective;

(c)   is for the benefit of the obligor, and does not prevent the assignee from acquiring rights against the assignor or the obligor from discharging his duty as if there were no such prohibition.

Comment

a.   *Rationale.* In the absence of statute or other contrary public policy, the parties to a contract have power to limit the rights created by their agreement. The policy against restraints on the alienation of property has limited application to contractual rights. . . .

Illustrations

1.   A holds a policy of industrial insurance issued to him by the B Insurance Company. After lapse for failure to pay premiums, B refuses to pay the "cash surrender value" provided for in the policy. A and others similarly situated assign their claims to C for collection. The assignment is effective without regard to any contractual prohibition of assignment.

2.   A and B contract for the sale of land by B to A. A fully performs the contract, becomes entitled to specific performance on B's refusal to convey the land, and then assigns his rights to C. C is entitled to specific performance against B without regard to any contractual prohibition of assignment. . . .

§ 323. Obligor's Assent to Assignment or Delegation.

(1)   A term of a contract manifesting an obligor's assent to the future assignment of a right or an obligee's assent to the future delegation of the performance of a duty or condition is effective despite any subsequent objection.

(2)   A manifestation of such assent after the formation of a contract is similarly effective if made for consideration or in circumstances in which a promise would be binding without consideration, or if a material change of position takes place in reliance on the manifestation.

TOPIC 2. MODE OF ASSIGNMENT OR DELEGATION

§ 324. Mode of Assignment in General.

It is essential to an assignment of a right that the obligee manifest an intention to transfer the right to another person without further action or manifestation of intention by the obligee. The manifestation may be made to the other or to a third person on his behalf and, except as provided by statute or by contract, may be made either orally or by a writing.

§ 325. Order as Assignment.

(1)   A written order drawn upon an obligor and signed and delivered to another person by the obligee is an assignment if it is conditional on the existence of a duty of the drawee to the drawer to comply with the order and the drawer manifests an intention that a person other than the drawer is to retain the performance.

(2)   An order which directs the drawee to render a performance without reference to any duty of the drawee is not of itself an assignment, even though the drawee is under a duty to the drawer to comply with the order and even though the order indicates a particular account to be debited or any other fund or source from which reimbursement is expected.

§ 326. Partial Assignment.

(1)   Except as stated in Subsection (2), an assignment of a part of a right, whether the part is specified as a fraction, as an amount, or otherwise, is operative as to that part to the same extent and in the same manner as if the part had been a separate right.

(2)   If the obligor has not contracted to perform separately the assigned part of a right, no legal proceeding can be maintained by the assignor or assignee against the obligor over his objection, unless all the persons entitled to the promised performance are joined in the proceeding, or unless joinder is not feasible and it is equitable to proceed without joinder.

§ 327. Acceptance or Disclaimer by the Assignee.

(1)   A manifestation of assent by an assignee to the assignment is essential to make it effective unless

(a)   a third person gives consideration for the assignment, or

(b)   the assignment is irrevocable by virtue of the delivery of a writing to a third person.

(2)   An assignee who has not manifested assent to an assignment may, within a reasonable time after learning of its existence and terms, render it inoperative from the beginning by disclaimer.

§ 328. Interpretation of Words of Assignment; Effect of Acceptance of Assignment.

(1)   Unless the language or the circumstances indicate the contrary, as in an assignment for security, an assignment of "the contract" or of "all my rights under the contract" or an assignment in similar general terms is an assignment of the assignor's rights and a delegation of his unperformed duties under the contract.

(2)   Unless the language or the circumstances indicate the contrary, the acceptance by an assignee of such an assignment operates as a promise to the assignor to perform the assignor's unperformed duties, and the obligor of the assigned rights is an intended beneficiary of the promise.

Caveat: The Institute expresses no opinion as to whether the rule stated in Subsection (2) applies to an assignment by a purchaser of his rights under a contract for the sale of land.

Comment

. . .

   c.   *Land contracts.* By virtue of the right of either party to obtain specific performance of a contract for the sale of land, such contracts are treated for many purposes as creating a property interest in the purchaser and thus as partially executed. The vendor's interest resembles the interest of a mortgagee under a mortgage given as security for the purchase price. An assignment of the vendor's rights under the contract is similar to an assignment of a right to payment for goods or services: ordinarily no assumption of the vendor's duties by the assignee is implied merely from the acceptance of the assignment.

   When the purchaser under a land contract assigns his rights, the assignment has commonly been treated like a sale of land "subject to" a mortgage. In this view acceptance of the assignment does not amount to an assumption of the assignor's duties unless the contract of assignment so provides either expressly or by implication. . . . Decisions refusing to infer an assumption of duties by the assignee have been influenced by doctrinal difficulties in the recognition of rights of assignees and beneficiaries. Those difficulties have now been overcome, and it is doubtful whether adherence to such decisions carries out the probable intention of the parties in the usual case. But since the shift in doctrine has not yet produced any definite change in the body of decisions, the Institute expresses no opinion on the application of Subsection (2) to an assignment by a purchaser under a land contract. . . .

§ 329. Repudiation by Assignor and Novation With Assignee.

   (1)   The legal effect of a repudiation by an assignor of his duty to the obligor of the assigned right is not limited by the fact that the assignee is a competent person and has promised to perform the duty.

   (2)   If the obligor, with knowledge of such a repudiation, accepts any performance from the assignee without reserving his rights against the assignor, a novation arises by which the duty of the assignor is discharged and a similar duty of the assignee is substituted.

§ 330. Contracts to Assign in the Future, or to Transfer Proceeds to Be Received.

   (1)   A contract to make a future assignment of a right, or to transfer proceeds to be received in the future by the promisor, is not an assignment.

   (2)   Except as provided by statute, the effect of such a contract on the rights and duties of the obligor and third persons is determined by the rules relating to specific performance of contracts.

TOPIC 3. EFFECT BETWEEN ASSIGNOR AND ASSIGNEE

§ 331. Partially Effective Assignments.

   An assignment may be conditional, revocable, or voidable by the assignor, or unenforceable by virtue of a Statute of Frauds.

§ 332. Revocability of Gratuitous Assignments.

   (1)   Unless a contrary intention is manifested, a gratuitous assignment is irrevocable if

      (a)   the assignment is in a writing either signed or under seal that is delivered by the assignor; or

      (b)   the assignment is accompanied by delivery of a writing of a type customarily accepted as a symbol or as evidence of the right assigned.

   (2)   Except as stated in this Section, a gratuitous assignment is revocable and the right of the assignee is terminated by the assignor's death or incapacity, by a subsequent assignment by the assignor, or by notification from the assignor received by the assignee or by the obligor.

(3)   A gratuitous assignment ceases to be revocable to the extent that before the assignee's right is terminated he obtains

    (a)   payment or satisfaction of the obligation, or

    (b)   judgment against the obligor, or

    (c)   a new contract of the obligor by novation.

(4)   A gratuitous assignment is irrevocable to the extent necessary to avoid injustice where the assignor should reasonably expect the assignment to induce action or forbearance by the assignee or a subassignee and the assignment does induce such action or forbearance.

(5)   An assignment is gratuitous unless it is given or taken

    (a)   in exchange for a performance or return promise that would be consideration for a promise; or

    (b)   as security for or in total or partial satisfaction of a pre-existing debt or other obligation.

§ 333. Warranties of an Assignor.

(1)   Unless a contrary intention is manifested, one who assigns or purports to assign a right by assignment under seal or for value warrants to the assignee

    (a)   that he will do nothing to defeat or impair the value of the assignment and has no knowledge of any fact which would do so;

    (b)   that the right, as assigned, actually exists and is subject to no limitations or defenses good against the assignor other than those stated or apparent at the time of the assignment;

    (c)   that any writing evidencing the right which is delivered to the assignee or exhibited to him to induce him to accept the assignment is genuine and what it purports to be.

(2)   An assignment does not of itself operate as a warranty that the obligor is solvent or that he will perform his obligation.

(3)   An assignor is bound by affirmations and promises to the assignee with reference to the right assigned in the same way and to the same extent that one who transfers goods is bound in like circumstances.

(4)   An assignment of a right to a subassignee does not operate as an assignment of the assignee's rights under his assignor's warranties unless an intention is manifested to assign the rights under the warranties.

TOPIC 4. EFFECT ON THE OBLIGOR'S DUTY

§ 334. Variation of Obligor's Duty by Assignment.

(1)   If the obligor's duty is conditional on the personal cooperation of the original obligee or another person, an assignee's right is subject to the same condition.

(2)   If the obligor's duty is conditional on cooperation which the obligee could properly delegate to an agent, the condition may occur if there is similar cooperation by an assignee.

§ 335. Assignment by a Joint Obligee.

A joint obligee may effectively assign his right, but the assignee can enforce it only in the same manner and to the same extent as the assignor could have enforced it.

§ 336. Defenses Against an Assignee.

(1)   By an assignment the assignee acquires a right against the obligor only to the extent that the obligor is under a duty to the assignor; and if the right of the assignor would be voidable by the obligor or unenforceable against him if no assignment had been made, the right of the assignee is subject to the infirmity.

(2)   The right of an assignee is subject to any defense or claim of the obligor which accrues before the obligor receives notification of the assignment, but not to defenses or claims which accrue thereafter except as stated in this Section or as provided by statute.

(3)   Where the right of an assignor is subject to discharge or modification in whole or in party by impracticability, public policy, non-occurrence of a condition, or present or prospective failure of performance by an obligee, the right of the assignee is to that extent subject to discharge or modification even after the obligor receives notification of the assignment.

(4)   An assignee's right against the obligor is subject to any defense or claim arising from his conduct or to which he was subject as a party or a prior assignee because he had notice.

§ 337. Elimination of Defenses by Subsequent Events.

Where the right of an assignor is limited or voidable or unenforceable or subject to discharge or modification, subsequent events which would eliminate the limitation or defense have the same effect on the right of the assignee.

§ 338. Discharge of an Obligor After Assignment.

(1)   Except as stated in this Section, notwithstanding an assignment, the assignor retains his power to discharge or modify the duty of the obligor to the extent that the obligor performs or otherwise gives value until but not after the obligor receives notification that the right has been assigned and that performance is to be rendered to the assignee.

(2)   So far as an assigned right is conditional on the performance of a return promise, and notwithstanding notification of the assignment, any modification of or substitution for the contract made by the assignor and obligor in good faith and in accordance with reasonable commercial standards is effective against the assignee. The assignee acquires corresponding rights under the modified or substituted contract.

(3)   Notwithstanding a defect in the right of an assignee, he has the same power his assignor had to discharge or modify the duty of the obligor to the extent that the obligor gives value or otherwise changes his position in good faith and without knowledge or reason to know of the defect.

(4)   Where there is a writing of a type customarily accepted as a symbol or as evidence of the right assigned, a discharge or modification is not effective

    (a)   against the owner or an assignor having a power of avoidance, unless given by him or by a person in possession of the writing with his consent and any necessary indorsement or assignment;

    (b)   against a subsequent assignee who takes possession of the writing and gives value in good faith and without knowledge or reason to know of the discharge or modification.

§ 339. Protection of Obligor in Cases of Adverse Claims.

Where a claim adverse to that of an assignee subjects the obligor to a substantial risk beyond that imposed on him by his contract, the obligor will be granted such relief as is equitable in the circumstances.

TOPIC 5. PRIORITIES BETWEEN ASSIGNEE AND ADVERSE CLAIMANTS

§ 340. Effect of Assignment on Priority and Security.

(1)   An assignee is entitled to priority of payment from the obligor's insolvent estate to the extent that the assignor would have been so entitled in the absence of assignment.

(2)   Where an assignor holds collateral as security for the assigned right and does not effectively transfer the collateral to the assignee, the assignor is a constructive trustee of the collateral for the assignee in accordance with the rules stated for pledges in §§ 29–34 of the Restatement of Security.

§ 341. Creditors of an Assignor.

(1)   Except as provided by statute, the right of an assignee is superior to a judicial lien subsequently obtained against the property of the assignor, unless the assignment is ineffective or revocable or is voidable by the assignor or by the person obtaining the lien or is in fraud of creditors.

(2)   Notwithstanding the superiority of the right of an assignee, an obligor who does not receive notification of the assignment until after he has lost his opportunity to assert the assignment as a defense in the proceeding in which the judicial lien was obtained is discharged from his duty to the assignee to the extent of his satisfaction of the lien.

§ 342. Successive Assignees From the Same Assignor.

Except as otherwise provided by statute, the right of an assignee is superior to that of a subsequent assignee of the same right from the same assignor, unless

(a)   the first assignment is ineffective or revocable or is voidable by the assignor or by the subsequent assignee; or

(b)   the subsequent assignee in good faith and without knowledge or reason to know of the prior assignment gives value and obtains

(i)   payment or satisfaction of the obligation,

(ii)   judgment against the obligor,

(iii)   a new contract with the obligor by novation, or

(iv)   possession of a writing of a type customarily accepted as a symbol or as evidence of the right assigned.

§ 343. Latent Equities.

If an assignor's right against the obligor is held in trust or constructive trust for or subject to a right of avoidance or equitable lien of another than the obligor, an assignee does not so hold it if he gives value and becomes an assignee in good faith and without notice of the right of the other.

CHAPTER 16

REMEDIES

TOPIC 1. IN GENERAL

§ 344. Purposes of Remedies.

Judicial remedies under the rules stated in this Restatement serve to protect one or more of the following interests of a promisee:

    (a) his "expectation interest," which is his interest in having the benefit of his bargain by being put in as good a position as he would have been in had the contract been performed,

    (b) his "reliance interest," which is his interest in being reimbursed for loss caused by reliance on the contract by being put in as good a position as he would have been in had the contract not been made, or

    (c) his "restitution interest," which is his interest in having restored to him any benefit that he has conferred on the other party.

Comment

    a. *Three interests.* The law of contract remedies implements the policy in favor of allowing individuals to order their own affairs by making legally enforceable promises. Ordinarily, when a court concludes that there has been a breach of contract, it enforces the broken promise by protecting the expectation that the injured party had when he made the contract. It does this by attempting to put him in as good a position as he would have been in had the contract been performed, that is, had there been no breach. The interest protected in this way is called the "expectation interest." It is sometimes said to give the injured party the "benefit of the bargain." This is not, however, the only interest that may be protected.

    The promisee may have changed his position in reliance on the contract by, for example, incurring expenses in preparing to perform, in performing, or in foregoing opportunities to make other contracts. In that case, the court may recognize a claim based on his reliance rather than on his expectation. It does this by attempting to put him back in the position in which he would have been had the contract not been made. The interest protected in this way is called "reliance interest." Although it may be equal to the expectation interest, it is ordinarily smaller because it does not include the injured party's lost profit.

    In some situations a court will recognize yet a third interest and grant relief to prevent unjust enrichment. This may be done if a party has not only changed his own position in reliance on the contract but has also conferred a benefit on the other party by, for example, making a part payment or furnishing services under the contract. The court may then require the other party to disgorge the benefit that he has received by returning it to the party who conferred it. The interest of the claimant protected in this way is called the "restitution interest." Although it may be equal to the expectation or reliance interest, it is ordinarily smaller because it includes neither the injured party's lost profit nor that part of his expenditures in reliance that resulted in no benefit to the other party. . . .

    b. *Expectation interest.* In principle, at least, a party's expectation interest represents the actual worth of the contract to him rather than to some reasonable third person. Damages based on the expectation interest therefore take account of any special circumstances that are peculiar to the situation of the injured party, including his personal values and even his idiosyncrasies, as well as his own needs and opportunities. . . . In practice, however, the injured party is often held to a more objective valuation of his expectation interest because he may be barred from recovering for loss resulting from such special circumstances on the ground that it was not foreseeable or cannot be shown with sufficient certainty. See §§ 351 and 352. Furthermore, since he cannot recover for loss that he could have avoided by arranging a substitute transaction on the market (§ 350), his recovery is often limited by the objective standard of market price. . . . The expectation interest is not based on the injured party's hopes when he made the contract but on the actual value that the contract would have had to him had it been performed. . . . It is therefore based on the circumstances at the time for performance and not those at the time of the making of the contract. . . .

§ 345. Judicial Remedies Available.

The judicial remedies available for the protection of the interests stated in § 344 include a judgment or order

- (a)   awarding a sum of money due under the contract or as damages,
- (b)   requiring specific performance of a contract or enjoining its non-performance,
- (c)   requiring restoration of a specific thing to prevent unjust enrichment,
- (d)   awarding a sum of money to prevent unjust enrichment,
- (e)   declaring the rights of the parties, and
- (f)   enforcing an arbitration award.

TOPIC 2. ENFORCEMENT BY AWARD OF DAMAGES

§ 346. Availability of Damages.

(1)   The injured party has a right to damages for any breach by a party against whom the contract is enforceable unless the claim for damages has been suspended or discharged.

(2)   If the breach caused no loss or if the amount of the loss is not proved under the rules stated in this Chapter, a small sum fixed without regard to the amount of loss will be awarded as nominal damages.

§ 347. Measure of Damages in General.

Subject to the limitations stated in §§ 350–53, the injured party has a right to damages based on his expectation interest as measured by

- (a)   the loss in the value to him of the other party's performance caused by its failure or deficiency, plus
- (b)   any other loss, including incidental or consequential loss, caused by the breach, less
- (c)   any cost or other loss that he has avoided by not having to perform.

Comment

   a.   *Expectation interest.* Contract damages are ordinarily based on the injured party's expectation interest and are intended to give him the benefit of his bargain by awarding him a sum of money that will, to the extent possible, put him in as good a position as he would have been in had the contract been performed. See § 344(1)(a). In some situations the sum awarded will do this adequately as, for example, where the injured party has simply had to pay an additional amount to arrange a substitute transaction and can be adequately compensated by damages based on that amount. In other situations the sum awarded cannot adequately compensate the injured party for his disappointed expectation as, for example, where a delay in performance has caused him to miss an invaluable opportunity. The measure of damages stated in this Section is subject to the agreement of the parties, as where they provide for liquidated damages (§ 356) or exclude liability for consequential damages. . . .

   f.   *Lost volume.* Whether a subsequent transaction is a substitute for the broken contract sometimes raises difficult questions of fact. If the injured party could and would have entered into the subsequent contract, even if the contract had not been broken, and could have had the benefit of both, he can be said to have "lost volume" and the subsequent transaction is not a substitute for the broken contract. The injured party's damages are then based on the net profit that he has lost as a result of the broken contract. Since entrepreneurs try to operate at optimum capacity, however, it is possible that an additional transaction would not have been profitable and that the injured party would not have chosen to expand his business by undertaking it had there been no breach. It is sometimes assumed that he would have done so, but the question is one of fact to be resolved according to the circumstances of each case. . . . See also Uniform Commercial Code § 2–708(2). . . .

§ 348. Alternatives to Loss in Value of Performance.

(1) If a breach delays the use of property and the loss in value to the injured party is not proved with reasonable certainty, he may recover damages based on the rental value of the property or on interest on the value of the property.

(2) If a breach results in defective or unfinished construction and the loss in value to the injured party is not proved with sufficient certainty, he may recover damages based on.

(a) the diminution in the market price of the property caused by the breach, or

(b) the reasonable cost of completing performance or of remedying the defects if that cost is not clearly disproportionate to the probable loss in value to him.

(3) If a breach is of a promise conditioned on a fortuitous event and it is uncertain whether the event would have occurred had there been no breach, the injured party may recover damages based on the value of the conditional right at the time of breach.

Comment

a. *Reason for alternative bases.* Although in principle the injured party is entitled to recover based on the loss in value to him caused by the breach, in practice he may be precluded from recovery on this basis because he cannot show the loss in value to him with sufficient certainty. See § 352. In such a case, if there is a reasonable alternative to loss in value, he may claim damages based on that alternative. . . .

c. *Incomplete or defective performance.* If the contract is one for construction, including repair or similar performance affecting the condition of property, and the work is not finished, the injured party will usually find it easier to prove what it would cost to have the work completed by another contractor than to prove the difference between the values to him of the finished and the unfinished performance. Since the cost to complete is usually less than the loss in value to him, he is limited by the rule on avoidability to damages based on cost to complete. See § 350(1). If he has actually had the work completed, damages will be based on his expenditures if he comes within the rule stated in § 350(2). . . .

Sometimes, however, such a large part of the cost to remedy the defects consists of the cost to undo what has been improperly done that the cost to remedy the defects will be clearly disproportionate to the probable loss in value to the injured party. Damages based on the cost to remedy the defects would then give the injured party a recovery greatly in excess of the loss in value to him and result in a substantial windfall. Such an award will not be made. . . .

§ 349. Damages Based on Reliance Interest.

As an alternative to the measure of damages stated in § 347, the injured party has a right to damages based on his reliance interest, including expenditures made in preparation for performance or in performance, less any loss that the party in breach can prove with reasonable certainty the injured party would have suffered had the contract been performed.

Comment

a. *Reliance interest where profit uncertain.* . . . Under the rule stated in this Section, the injured party may, if he chooses, ignore the element of profit and recover as damages his expenditures in reliance. He may choose to do this if he cannot prove his profit with reasonable certainty. He may also choose to do this in the case of a losing contract, one under which he would have had a loss rather than a profit. In that case, however, it is open to the party in breach to prove the amount of the loss, to the extent that he can do so with reasonable certainty under the standard stated in § 352, and have it subtracted from the injured party's damages. The resulting damages will then be the same as those under the rule stated in § 347. . . .

§ 350. Avoidability as a Limitation on Damages.

(1) Except as stated in Subsection (2), damages are not recoverable for loss that the injured party could have avoided without undue risk, burden or humiliation.

(2) The injured party is not precluded from recovery by the rule stated in Subsection (1) to the extent that he has made reasonable but unsuccessful efforts to avoid loss.

§ 351. Unforeseeability and Related Limitations on Damages.

(1) Damages are not recoverable for loss that the party in breach did not have reason to foresee as a probable result of the breach when the contract was made.

(2) Loss may be foreseeable as a probable result of a breach because it follows from the breach

    (a) in the ordinary course of events, or

    (b) as a result of special circumstances, beyond the ordinary course of events, that the party in breach had reason to know.

(3) A court may limit damages for foreseeable loss by excluding recovery for loss of profits, by allowing recovery only for loss incurred in reliance, or otherwise if it concludes that in the circumstances justice so requires in order to avoid disproportionate compensation.

Comment

a. Requirement of foreseeability. A contracting party is generally expected to take account of those risks that are foreseeable at the time he makes the contract. He is not, however, liable in the event of breach for loss that he did not at the time of contracting have reason to foresee as a probable result of such a breach. The mere circumstance that some loss was foreseeable, or even that some loss of the same general kind was foreseeable, will not suffice if the loss that actually occurred was not foreseeable. It is enough, however, that the loss was foreseeable as a probable, as distinguished from a necessary, result of his breach. Furthermore, the party in breach need not have made a "tacit agreement" to be liable for the loss. Nor must he have had the loss in mind when making the contract, for the test is an objective one based on what he had reason to foresee. There is no requirement of foreseeability with respect to the injured party. In spite of these qualifications, the requirement of foreseeability is a more severe limitation of liability than is the requirement of substantial or "proximate" cause in the case of an action in tort or for breach of warranty. Compare Restatement, Second, Torts § 431; Uniform Commercial Code § 2–715(2)(b). Although the recovery that is precluded by the limitation of foreseeability is usually based on the expectation interest and takes the form of lost profits. . ., the limitation may also preclude recovery based on the reliance interest. . . .

f. Other limitations on damages. It is not always in the interest of justice to require the party in breach to pay damages for all of the foreseeable loss that he has caused. There are unusual instances in which it appears from the circumstances either that the parties assumed that one of them would not bear the risk of a particular loss or that, although there was no such assumption, it would be unjust to put the risk on that party. One such circumstance is an extreme disproportion between the loss and the price charged by the party whose liability for that loss is in question. The fact that the price is relatively small suggests that it was not intended to cover the risk of such liability. Another such circumstance is an informality of dealing, including the absence of a detailed written contract, which indicates that there was no careful attempt to allocate all of the risks. The fact that the parties did not attempt to delineate with precision all of the risks justifies a court in attempting to allocate them fairly. The limitations dealt with in this Section are more likely to be imposed in connection with contracts that do not arise in a commercial setting. Typical examples of limitations imposed on damages under this discretionary power involve the denial of recovery for loss of profits and the restriction of damages to loss incurred in reliance on the contract. Sometimes these limits are covertly imposed, by means of an especially demanding requirement of foreseeability or of certainty. The rule stated in this Section recognizes that what is done in such cases is the imposition of a limitation in the interests of justice.

Illustrations

17. A, a private trucker, contracts with B to deliver to B's factory a machine that has just been repaired and without which B's factory, as A knows, cannot reopen. Delivery is delayed because A's truck breaks down. In an action by B against A for breach of contract the court may, after taking into consideration such factors as the absence of an elaborate written contract and the extreme

disproportion between B's loss of profits during the delay and the price of the trucker's services, exclude recovery for loss of profits.

18. A, a retail hardware dealer, contracts to sell B an inexpensive lighting attachment, which, as A knows, B needs in order to use his tractor at night on his farm. A is delayed in obtaining the attachment and, since no substitute is available, B is unable to use the tractor at night during the delay. In an action by B against A for breach of contract, the court may, after taking into consideration such factors as the absence of an elaborate written contract and the extreme disproportion between B's loss of profits during the delay and the price of the attachment, exclude recovery for loss of profits.

§ 352. Uncertainty as a Limitation on Damages.

Damages are not recoverable for loss beyond an amount that the evidence permits to be established with reasonable certainty.

§ 353. Loss Due to Emotional Disturbance.

Recovery for emotional disturbance will be excluded unless the breach also caused bodily harm or the contract or the breach is of such a kind that serious emotional disturbance was a particularly likely result.

Comment

a. Emotional disturbance. Damages for emotional disturbance are not ordinarily allowed. Even if they are foreseeable, they are often particularly difficult to establish and to measure. There are, however, two exceptional situations where such damages are recoverable. In the first, the disturbance accompanies a bodily injury. In such cases the action may nearly always be regarded as one in tort. . . . In the second exceptional situation, the contract or the breach is of such a kind that serious emotional disturbance was a particularly likely result. Common examples are contracts of carriers and innkeepers with passengers and guests, contracts for the carriage or proper disposition of dead bodies, and contracts for the delivery of messages concerning death. Breach of such a contract is particularly likely to cause serious emotional disturbance. Breach of other types of contracts, resulting for example in sudden impoverishment or bankruptcy, may by chance cause even more severe emotional disturbance, but, if the contract is not one where this was a particularly likely risk, there is no recovery for such disturbance. . . .

§ 354. Interest as Damages.

(1) If the breach consists of a failure to pay a definite sum in money or to render a performance with fixed or ascertainable monetary value, interest is recoverable from the time for performance on the amount due less all deductions to which the party in breach is entitled.

(2) In any other case, such interest may be allowed as justice requires on the amount that would have been just compensation had it been paid when performance was due.

§ 355. Punitive Damages.

Punitive damages are not recoverable for a breach of contract unless the conduct constituting the breach is also a tort for which punitive damages are recoverable.

§ 356. Liquidated Damages and Penalties.

(1) Damages for breach by either party may be liquidated in the agreement but only at an amount that is reasonable in the light of the anticipated or actual loss caused by the breach and the difficulties of proof of loss. A term fixing unreasonably large liquidated damages is unenforceable on grounds of public policy as a penalty.

(2) A term in a bond providing for an amount of money as a penalty for non-occurrence of the condition of the bond is unenforceable on grounds of public policy to the extent that the amount exceeds the loss caused by such non-occurrence.

Comment

a. *Liquidated damages or penalty.* The parties to a contract may effectively provide in advance the damages that are to be payable in the event of breach as long as the provision does not disregard the principle of compensation. . . . However, the parties to a contract are not free to provide a penalty for its breach. The central objective behind the system of contract remedies is compensatory, not punitive. Punishment of a promisor for having broken his promise has no justification on either economic or other grounds and a term providing such a penalty is unenforceable on grounds of public policy. . . .

TOPIC 3. ENFORCEMENT BY SPECIFIC PERFORMANCE AND INJUNCTION

§ 357. Availability of Specific Performance and Injunction.

(1) Subject to the rules stated in §§ 359–69, specific performance of a contract duty will be granted in the discretion of the court against a party who has committed or is threatening to commit a breach of the duty.

(2) Subject to the rules stated in §§ 359–69, an injunction against breach of a contract duty will be granted in the discretion of the court against a party who has committed or is threatening to commit a breach of the duty if

(a) the duty is one of forbearance, or

(b) the duty is one to act and specific performance would be denied only for reasons that are inapplicable to an injunction.

§ 358. Form of Order and Other Relief.

(1) An order of specific performance or an injunction will be so drawn as best to effectuate the purposes for which the contract was made and on such terms as justice requires. It need not be absolute in form and the performance that it requires need not be identical with that due under the contract.

(2) If specific performance or an injunction is denied as to part of the performance that is due, it may nevertheless be granted as to the remainder.

(3) In addition to specific performance or an injunction, damages and other relief may be awarded in the same proceeding and an indemnity against future harm may be required.

§ 359. Effect of Adequacy of Damages.

(1) Specific performance or an injunction will not be ordered if damages would be adequate to protect the expectation interest of the injured party.

(2) The adequacy of the damage remedy for failure to render one part of the performance due does not preclude specific performance or injunction as to the contract as a whole.

(3) Specific performance or an injunction will not be refused merely because there is a remedy for breach other than damages, but such a remedy may be considered in exercising discretion under the rule stated in § 357.

Comment

a. *Bases for requirement.* The underlying objective in choosing the form of relief to be granted is to select a remedy that will adequately protect the legally recognized interest of the injured party. If, as is usually the case, that interest is the expectation interest, the remedy may take the form either of damages or of specific performance or an injunction. As to the situation in which the interest to be protected is the restitution interest, see § 373.

During the development of the jurisdiction of courts of equity, it came to be recognized that equitable relief would not be granted if the award of damages at law was adequate to protect the interests of the injured party. There is, however, a tendency to liberalize the granting of equitable relief by enlarging the classes of cases in which damages are not regarded as an adequate remedy. This tendency has been encouraged by the adoption of the Uniform Commercial Code, which "seeks to further a more liberal attitude than some courts have shown in connection with the specific performance of contracts of sale." Comment 1 to Uniform Commercial Code § 2–716. In accordance with this tendency, if the adequacy of the damage remedy is uncertain, the combined effect of such other factors as uncertainty of terms (§ 362), insecurity as to the agreed exchange (§ 363) and difficulty of enforcement (§ 366) should be considered. Adequacy is to some extent relative, and the modern approach is to compare remedies to determine which is more effective in serving the ends of justice. Such a comparison will often lead to the granting of equitable relief. Doubts should be resolved in favor of the granting of specific performance or injunction. . . .

§ 360. Factors Affecting Adequacy of Damages.

In determining whether the remedy in damages would be adequate, the following circumstances are significant:

    (a)   the difficulty of proving damages with reasonable certainty,

    (b)   the difficulty of procuring a suitable substitute performance by means of money awarded as damages, and

    (c)   the likelihood that an award of damages could not be collected.

Comment

. . .

b.   *Difficulty in proving damages.* The damage remedy may be inadequate to protect the injured party's expectation interest because the loss caused by the breach is too difficult to estimate with reasonable certainty. . . . If the injured party has suffered loss but cannot sustain the burden of proving it, only nominal damages will be awarded. If he can prove some but not all of his loss, he will not be compensated in full. In either case damages are an inadequate remedy. Some types of interests are by their very nature incapable of being valued in money. Typical examples include heirlooms, family treasures and works of art that induce a strong sentimental attachment. Examples may also be found in contracts of a more commercial character. The breach of a contract to transfer shares of stock may cause a loss in control over the corporation. The breach of a contract to furnish an indemnity may cause the sacrifice of property and financial ruin. The breach of a covenant not to compete may cause the loss of customers of an unascertainable number or importance. The breach of a requirements contract may cut off a vital supply of raw materials. In such situations, equitable relief is often appropriate. . . .

c.   *Difficulty of obtaining substitute.* If the injured party can readily procure by the use of money a suitable substitute for the promised performance, the damage remedy is ordinarily adequate. Entering into a substitute transaction is generally a more efficient way to prevent injury than is a suit for specific performance or an injunction and there is a sound economic basis for limiting the injured party to damages in such a case. Furthermore, the substitute transaction affords a basis for proving damages with reasonable certainty, eliminating the factor stated in Paragraph (a). . . .

§ 361. Effect of Provision for Liquidated Damages.

Specific performance or an injunction may be granted to enforce a duty even though there is a provision for liquidated damages for breach of that duty.

§ 362. Effect of Uncertainty of Terms.

Specific performance or an injunction will not be granted unless the terms of the contract are sufficiently certain to provide a basis for an appropriate order.

§ 363. Effect of Insecurity as to the Agreed Exchange.

Specific performance or an injunction may be refused if a substantial part of the agreed exchange for the performance to be compelled is unperformed and its performance is not secured to the satisfaction of the court.

§ 364. Effect of Unfairness.

(1) Specific performance or an injunction will be refused if such relief would be unfair because

    (a)   the contract was induced by mistake or by unfair practices,

    (b)   the relief would cause unreasonable hardship or loss to the party in breach or to third persons, or

    (c)   the exchange is grossly inadequate or the terms of the contract are otherwise unfair.

(2) Specific performance or an injunction will be granted in spite of a term of the agreement if denial of such relief would be unfair because it would cause unreasonable hardship or loss to the party seeking relief or to third persons.

Comment

a. Types of unfairness. Courts have traditionally refused equitable relief on grounds of unfairness . . . in situations where they would not necessarily refuse to award damages. Some of these situations involve . . . elements of substantive unfairness in the exchange itself or in its terms that fall short of what is required for unenforceability on grounds of unconscionability. . . .

b. Unfairness in the exchange. Unfairness in the exchange does not of itself make an agreement unenforceable. . . . If it is extreme, however, it may be a sufficient ground, without more, for denying specific performance or an injunction. . . .

§ 365. Effect of Public Policy.

Specific performance or an injunction will not be granted if the act or forbearance that would be compelled or the use of compulsion is contrary to public policy.

§ 366. Effect of Difficulty in Enforcement or Supervision.

A promise will not be specifically enforced if the character and magnitude of the performance would impose on the court burdens in enforcement or supervision that are disproportionate to the advantages to be gained from enforcement and to the harm to be suffered from its denial.

§ 367. Contracts for Personal Service or Supervision.

(1) A promise to render personal service will not be specifically enforced.

(2) A promise to render personal service exclusively for one employer will not be enforced by an injunction against serving another if its probable result will be to compel a performance involving personal relations the enforced continuance of which is undesirable or will be to leave the employee without other reasonable means of making a living.

§ 368. Effect of Power of Termination.

(1) Specific performance or an injunction will not be granted against a party who can substantially nullify the effect of the order by exercising a power of termination or avoidance.

(2) Specific performance or an injunction will not be denied merely because the party seeking relief has a power to terminate or avoid his duty unless the power could be used, in spite of the order, to deprive the other party of reasonable security for the agreed exchange for his performance.

§ 369. Effect of Breach by Party Seeking Relief.

Specific performance or an injunction may be granted in spite of a breach by the party seeking relief, unless the breach is serious enough to discharge the other party's remaining duties of performance.

TOPIC 4. RESTITUTION

§ 370. Requirement That Benefit Be Conferred.

A party is entitled to restitution under the rules stated in this Restatement only to the extent that he has conferred a benefit on the other party by way of part performance or reliance. . . .

Illustrations

2. A contracts to sell B a machine for $100,000. After A has spent $40,000 on the manufacture of the machine but before its completion, B repudiates the contract. A cannot get restitution of the $40,000 because no benefit was conferred on B. . . .

5. A, a social worker, promises B to render personal services to C in return for B's promise to educate A's children. B repudiates the contract after A has rendered part of the services. A can get restitution from B for the services, even though they were not rendered to B, because they conferred a benefit on B. . . .

§ 371. Measure of Restitution Interest.

If a sum of money is awarded to protect a party's restitution interest, it may as justice requires be measured by either

(a) the reasonable value to the other party of what he received in terms of what it would have cost him to obtain it from a person in the claimant's position, or

(b) the extent to which the other party's property has been increased in value or his other interests advanced.

Comment

a. Measurement of benefit. Under the rules stated in §§ 344 and 370, a party who is liable in restitution for a sum of money must pay an amount equal to the benefit that has been conferred upon him. If the benefit consists simply of a sum of money received by the party from whom restitution is sought, there is no difficulty in determining this amount. If the benefit consists of something else, however, such as services or property, its measurement in terms of money may pose serious problems. . . .

A particularly significant circumstance is whether the benefit has been conferred by way of performance or by way of reliance in some other way. . . . Recovery is ordinarily more generous for a benefit that has been conferred by performance. To the extent that the benefit may reasonably be measured in different ways, the choice is within the discretion of the court. Thus a court may take into account the value of opportunities for benefit even if they have not been fully realized in the particular case.

An especially important choice is that between the reasonable value to a party of what he received in terms of what it would have cost him to obtain it from a person in the claimant's position and the addition to the wealth of that party as measured by the extent to which his property has been increased in value or his other interests advanced. In practice, the first measure is usually based on the market price of such a substitute. Under the rule stated in this Section, the court has considerable discretion in making the choice between these two measures of benefit. Under either choice, the court may properly consider the purposes of the recipient of the benefit when he made the contract, even if those purposes were later frustrated or abandoned.

b. Choice of measure. The reasonable value to the party against whom restitution is sought (Paragraph (a)) is ordinarily less than the cost to the party seeking restitution, since his expenditures are excluded to the extent that they conferred no benefit. See Comment *a* to § 344. Nor can the party against whom restitution is sought reduce the amount for which he may himself be liable by subtracting such expenditures from the amount of the benefit that he has received. . . . The reasonable value to the party from whom restitution is sought (Paragraph (a)), is, however, usually greater than the addition to his wealth (Paragraph (b)). If this is so, a party seeking restitution for part performance is commonly allowed the more generous measure of reasonable value, unless that measure is unduly difficult to apply, except when he is in breach (§ 374). . . . In the case of services rendered in an emergency or to save life, however, restitution based on addition to wealth will greatly exceed that based on expense saved and recovery is invariably limited to the smaller amount. See Illustration 2. In the case of services rendered to a third party as the intended beneficiary of a gift promise, restitution from the promisee based on his enrichment is generally not susceptible of measurement and recovery based on reasonable value is appropriate. . . .

Illustrations

1.   A, a carpenter, contracts to repair B's roof for $3,000. A does part of the work at a cost of $2,000, increasing the market price of B's house by $1,200. The market price to have a similar carpenter do the work done by A is $1,800. A's restitution interest is equal to the benefit conferred on B. That benefit may be measured either by the addition to B's wealth from A's services in terms of the $1,200 increase in the market price of B's house or the reasonable value to B of A's services in terms of the $1,800 that it would have cost B to engage a similar carpenter to do the same work. If the work was not completed because of a breach by A . . . $1,200 is appropriate. If the work was not completed because of a breach by B . . . $1,800 is appropriate. . . .

§ 372. Specific Restitution.

(1)   Specific restitution will be granted to a party who is entitled to restitution, except that:

    (a)   specific restitution based on a breach by the other party under the rule stated in § 373 may be refused in the discretion of the court if it would unduly interfere with the certainty of title to land or otherwise cause injustice, and

    (b)   specific restitution in favor of the party in breach under the rule stated in § 374 will not be granted.

(2)   A decree of specific restitution may be made conditional on return of or compensation for anything that the party claiming restitution has received.

(3)   If specific restitution, with or without a sum of money, will be substantially as effective as restitution in money in putting the party claiming restitution in the position he was in before rendering any performance, the other party can discharge his duty by tendering such restitution before suit is brought and keeping his tender good.

§ 373. Restitution When Other Party Is in Breach.

(1)   Subject to the rule stated in Subsection (2), on a breach by non-performance that gives rise to a claim for damages for total breach or on a repudiation, the injured party is entitled to restitution for any benefit that he has conferred on the other party by way of part performance or reliance.

(2)   The injured party has no right to restitution if he has performed all of his duties under the contract and no performance by the other party remains due other than payment of a definite sum of money for that performance.

§ 374. Restitution in Favor of Party in Breach.

(1)   Subject to the rule stated in Subsection (2), if a party justifiably refuses to perform on the ground that his remaining duties of performance have been discharged by the other party's breach, the party in breach is entitled to restitution for any benefit that he has conferred by way of part performance or reliance in excess of the loss that he has caused by his own breach.

(2)   To the extent that, under the manifested assent of the parties, a party's performance is to be retained in the case of breach, that party is not entitled to restitution if the value of the performance as liquidated damages is reasonable in the light of the anticipated or actual loss caused by the breach and the difficulties of proof of loss.

§ 375. Restitution When Contract Is Within Statute of Frauds.

A party who would otherwise have a claim in restitution under a contract is not barred from restitution for the reason that the contract is unenforceable by him because of the Statute of Frauds unless the Statute provides otherwise or its purpose would be frustrated by allowing restitution.

§ 376. Restitution When Contract Is Voidable.

A party who has avoided a contract on the ground of lack of capacity, mistake, misrepresentation, duress, undue influence or abuse of a fiduciary relation is entitled to restitution for any benefit that he has conferred on the other party by way of part performance or reliance.

§ 377. Restitution in Cases of Impracticability, Frustration, Non-Occurrence of Condition or Disclaimer by Beneficiary.

A party whose duty of performance does not arise or is discharged as a result of impracticability of performance, frustration of purpose, non-occurrence of a condition or disclaimer by a beneficiary is entitled to restitution for any benefit that he has conferred on the other party by way of part performance or reliance.

TOPIC 5. PRECLUSION BY ELECTION AND AFFIRMANCE

§ 378. Election Among Remedies.

If a party has more than one remedy under the rules stated in this Chapter, his manifestation of a choice of one of them by bringing suit or otherwise is not a bar to another remedy unless the remedies are inconsistent and the other party materially changes his position in reliance on the manifestation.

§ 379. Election to Treat Duties of Performance Under Aleatory Contract as Discharged.

If a right or duty of the injured party is conditional on an event that is fortuitous or is supposed by the parties to be fortuitous, he cannot treat his remaining duties to render performance as discharged on the ground of the other party's breach by non-performance if he does not manifest to the other party his intention to do so before any adverse change in the situation of the injured party resulting from the occurrence of that event or a material change in the probability of its occurrence.

§ 380. Loss of Power of Avoidance by Affirmance.

(1) The power of a party to avoid a contract for incapacity, duress, undue influence or abuse of a fiduciary relation is lost if, after the circumstances that made the contract voidable have ceased to exist, he manifests to the other party his intention to affirm it or acts with respect to anything that he has received in a manner inconsistent with disaffirmance.

(2) The power of a party to avoid a contract for mistake or misrepresentation is lost if after he knows or has reason to know of the mistake or of the misrepresentation if it is non-fraudulent or knows of the misrepresentation if it is fraudulent, he manifests to the other party his intention to affirm it or acts with respect to anything that he has received in a manner inconsistent with disaffirmance.

(3) If the other party rejects an offer by the party seeking avoidance to return what he has received, the party seeking avoidance if entitled to restitution can, after the lapse of a reasonable time, enforce a lien on what he has received by selling it and crediting the proceeds toward his claim in restitution.

§ 381. Loss of Power of Avoidance by Delay.

(1) The power of a party to avoid a contract for incapacity, duress, undue influence or abuse of a fiduciary relation is lost if, after the circumstances that made it voidable have ceased to exist, he does not within a reasonable time manifest to the other party his intention to avoid it.

(2) The power of a party to avoid a contract for misrepresentation or mistake is lost if after he knows of a fraudulent misrepresentation or knows or has reason to know of a non-fraudulent misrepresentation or mistake he does not within a reasonable time manifest to the other party his intention to avoid it. The power of a party to avoid a contract for non-fraudulent misrepresentation or mistake is also lost if the contract has been so far performed or the circumstances have otherwise so changed that avoidance would be inequitable and if damages will be adequate compensation.

(3)   In determining what is a reasonable time, the following circumstances are significant:

(a)   the extent to which the delay enabled or might have enabled the party with the power of avoidance to speculate at the other party's risk;

(b)   the extent to which the delay resulted or might have resulted in justifiable reliance by the other party or by third persons;

(c)   the extent to which the ground for avoidance was the result of any fault by either party; and

(d)   the extent to which the other party's conduct contributed to the delay.

(4)   If a right or duty of the party who has the power of avoidance for non-fraudulent misrepresentation or mistake is conditional on an event that is fortuitous or is supposed by the parties to be fortuitous, a manifestation of intention under Subsection (1) or (2) is not effective unless it is made before any adverse change in his situation resulting from the occurrence of that event or a material change in the probability of its occurrence.

§ 382. Loss of Power to Affirm by Prior Avoidance.

(1) If a party has effectively exercised his power of avoidance, a subsequent manifestation of intent to affirm is inoperative unless the other party manifests his assent to affirmance by refusal to accept a return of his performance or otherwise.

(2)   A party has not exercised his power of avoidance under the rule stated in Subsection (1) until

(a)   he has regained all or a substantial part of what he would be entitled to by way of restitution on avoidance,

(b)   he has obtained a final judgment of or based on avoidance, or

(c)   the other party has materially relied on or manifested his assent to a statement of disaffirmance.

§ 383. Avoidance in Part.

A contract cannot be avoided in part except that where one or more corresponding pairs of part performances have been fully performed by one or both parties the rest of the contract can be avoided.

§ 384. Requirement That Party Seeking Restitution Return Benefit.

(1)   Except as stated in Subsection (2), a party will not be granted restitution unless

(a)   he returns or offers to return, conditional on restitution, any interest in property that he has received in exchange in substantially as good condition as when it was received by him, or

(b)   the court can assure such return in connection with the relief granted.

(2)   The requirement stated in Subsection (1) does not apply to property

(a)   that was worthless when received or that has been destroyed or lost by the other party or as a result of its own defects,

(b)   that either could not from the time of receipt have been returned or has been used or disposed of without knowledge of the grounds for restitution if justice requires that compensation be accepted in its place and the payment of such compensation can be assured, or

(c)   as to which the contract apportions the price if that part of the price is not included in the claim for restitution.

§ 385. Effect of Power of Avoidance on Duty of Performance or on Duty Arising Out of Breach.

(1)   Unless an offer to restore performance received is a condition of avoidance, a party has no duty of performance while his power of avoidance exists.

(2) If an offer to restore performance received is a condition of avoidance, a duty to pay damages is terminated by such an offer made before the power of avoidance is lost.

PART IV

RESTATEMENT OF THE LAW (THIRD) EMPLOYMENT LAW (2014) (EXCERPTS)

RESTATEMENT OF THE LAW (THIRD)
EMPLOYMENT LAW*

(2014)

(Excerpts)

[Many federal and state statutes regulate aspects of relationships between employees and their employers. The minimum wage statutes, for example, establish floors for the price terms in employment contracts. Nonetheless, the common law continues to govern the unregulated terms of the relationship. There have been dramatic changes in this body of law over the last few decades, especially with respect to an employer's right to terminate an employee. These changes, however, are not uniform from state to state. Even within a state, the highest court may not yet have fully developed the implications of the changes. Employment law, consequently, is not as clear as it could be in important respects, which can result in avoidable uncertainty in the law.

[In 2000, the American Law Institute ("ALI") began work on a Restatement of the Law (Third), Employment Law. Its aim is to clarify the common law of employment by, among other things, restating the law to reflect, and detail the implications of, the recent changes. The following excerpts, concerning termination qualify the traditional common law default rule, which provides that in the absence of a fixed contractual duration, either party may terminate an employment relationship at will, with or without a reason. The Restatement lays out several significant exceptions to this rule. Most notable among these exceptions are the effect of statutes and public policy, and the ways in which an employer's employment-policy statements can become binding on the employer, and can be changed, without complying with the traditional common law rules of contract formation, modification, and consideration.]

---

§ 2.01. Default Rule of an At-Will Employment Relationship.

Either party may terminate an employment relationship with or without cause unless the right to do so is limited by a statute, other law or public policy, of a § 2.02 agreement, binding employer promise, or binding employer statement.

§ 2.02. Agreements and Binding Employer Promises or Statements Providing for Terms Other Than At-Will Employment.

The employment relationship is not terminable at will by an employer if:

(a)   an agreement between the employer and the employee provides for (1) a definite term of employment, or (2) an indefinite term of employment and requires cause (defined in § 2.04) to terminate the employment (§ 2.03); or

(b)   a promise by the employer to limit termination of employment reasonably induces detrimental reliance by the employee (§ 2.02, Comment *c*); or

(c)   a policy statement made by the employer limits termination of employment (§ 2.05); or

(d)   the implied duty of good faith and fair dealing applicable to all employment; (§ 2.07) limits termination of employment; or

(e)   any other principle recognized in the general law of contracts limit termination of employment (§ 2.02, comment *d*).

---

§ 2.03. Agreements for a Definite or Indefinite Term.

(a)   An employer must have cause (§ 2.04) for termination of

   (1)   an unexpired agreement for a definite term of employment, or

   (2)   an agreement for an indefinite term of employment requiring cause for termination.

   (b)   In the absence of an express agreement otherwise by an employee, the employee is under no reciprocal obligation to have cause to terminate the employment relationship.

§ 2.04. Cause for Termination of Employment Agreements.

Unless otherwise provided for in the agreement:

   (a)   An employer has cause for early termination of an agreement for a definite term of employment if the employee has engaged in misconduct, other malfeasance, or other material breach of the agreement, such as persistent neglect of duties, gross negligence, or failure to perform the duties of the position due to a permanent disability.

   (b)   An employer has cause for terminating an agreement for an indefinite term of employment requiring cause for termination if, in addition to the grounds stated in § 2.04(a), if because of a significant change in the employer's economic circumstances, the employer no longer needs the services that the employee is providing.

§ 2.05. Binding Employer Policy Statements.

Policy statements by an employer in such documents as employee manuals, personnel handbooks, and employment-policy directives that are provided or made accessible to employees, whether by physical or electronic means, and that, reasonably read in context, establish limits on the employer's power to terminate the employment relationship are binding on the employer until modified or revoked (as provided in § 2.06).

§ 2.06. Modification or Revocation of Binding Employer Policy Statements.

   (a)   An employer may prospectively modify or revoke its binding policy statement by providing reasonable advance notice of the modified statement or revocation to the affected employees.

   (b)   Modifications and revocations apply to all employees hired, and all employees who continue working, after the effective date of the notice of modification or revocation.

   (c)   Modifications and revocations cannot adversely affect vested or accrued employee rights that may have been created by the statement, an agreement based on the statement (covered by § 2.03), or reasonable detrimental reliance on a promise in the statement (covered by § 2.02, Comment c).

§ 2.07. Implied Duty of Good Faith and Fair Dealing.

   (a)   Each party to an employment contract, including at-will employment, owes a nonwaivable duty of good faith and fair dealing to each other party, which includes an agreement by each not to hinder the other's performance under, or to deprive the other of the benefit of, the contract.

   (b)   In at-will employment, the implied duty of good faith and fair dealing must be read consistently with the at-will nature of the relationship such that it cannot be used to require cause for termination in an employment agreement otherwise terminable at will.

   (c)   In any employment relationship, including at-will employment, the employer's implied duty of good faith and fair dealing includes the duty not to terminate or seek to terminate the employment relationship for the purpose of

   (1)   preventing the vesting or accrual of an employee right or benefit, or

   (2)   retaliating against the employee for performing the employee's obligations under the employment contract or law.

PART V

RESTATEMENT OF THE LAW CONSUMER CONTRACTS

*Discussion Draft**

(2017)

(Excerpts)

[The American Law Institute has commissioned an all-new Restatement of the Law, Consumer Contracts. It seeks to clarify how the courts have applied the principles embodied in the Restatement Second of Contracts and the Uniform Commercial Code to transactions that either were not contemplated at the time those projects were completed (and therefore not addressed), like the purchase of software licenses and all online transactions, or that became a more significant part of the economy since that time. In this regard, two concepts have proven to be particularly challenging—assent and unconscionability—and the Restatement has devoted significant attention to these matters.

[Excerpts from the April 17, 2017 Discussion Draft follow. This draft was for discussion at the ALI's 2017 Council Meeting. It bears emphasis that the ALI has not (yet) approved it. Accordingly, it does not represent the views of the ALI at this time.]

SUBJECTS COVERED

---

*   © 2017 by The American Law Institute.

§ 1.   Definitions and Scope

(a)   Definitions

     (1)   "Consumer"—An individual acting primarily for personal, family, or household purposes.

     (2)   "Business"—An individual or entity other than a consumer that regularly participates in or solicits, directly or indirectly, transactions with consumers.

     (3)   "Contract"—A promise or set of promises for the breach of which the law gives a remedy, or the performance of which the law in some way recognizes as a duty.

     (4)   "Consumer Contract"—A contract between a business and a consumer other than an employment contract.

     (5)   "Standard Contract Terms"—Terms in a consumer contract that have been drafted prior to the transaction by any party other than the consumer and govern transactions between the business and multiple consumers.

     (6)   "Affirmation or promise"—Any communication about the transaction, including but not limited to communications about quantity, quality, characteristics, utility, price, discount, comparative cost, service, and remedy, intended to reach consumers, including in negotiations, advertising, brochures, or labels, or in any record accompanying the transaction, but excluding communications that are reasonably understood as "puffing" or statements of opinion.

     (7)   "Good faith"—honesty in fact and the observance of reasonable commercial standards of fair dealing.

(b)   Scope: This Restatement applies to Consumer Contracts.

§ 2.   Adoption of Standard Contract Terms

(a)   A standard contract term is adopted as part of a consumer contract if, after receiving reasonable notice of the standard contract term and a reasonable opportunity to review it, the consumer signifies assent to the transaction.

(b)   When a standard contract term is available for review only after the consumer signifies assent to the transaction, the standard contract term is adopted as part of the consumer contract if

     (1)   the consumer receives reasonable notice regarding the existence of the standard contract term before signifying assent to the transaction, and

     (2)   the consumer has a reasonable opportunity to terminate the transaction after the standard contract term is made available for review, and does not exercise that power.

(c)   If the consumer signifies assent to the transaction, a contract exists even if some of the standard contract terms are not adopted. In such case, the terms of the contract are those adopted under subsection (a) or (b), along with any terms supplied by law.

Comments

. . .

     4.   *Relation to other Sections.* The adoption rules in this Section represent a reality in which consent to the standard contract terms is rarely informed. In classic contract law, the requirement of assent was regarded as a meaningful measure that protects the contracting party, under the premise that this party would signify assent only to a contract that promotes its interests. The length and complexity of standard-form contracts has diluted the effectiveness and plausibility of this front-end self-protection. As courts have moved to permit the more lenient adoption procedures, they have simultaneously recognized the importance of other safeguards in consumer-contract law that place mandatory restrictions over permissible contracting. At the center of this alternative mode of consumer protection stand rules that strike down unconscionable terms and provisions that undermine consumers' benefit of the bargain (§ 5). Adding to the

protection afforded by the unconscionability doctrine are the good-faith duties that govern contract modification and open discretion terms (§§ 3–4) and rules that police deception and enforce precontractual affirmations and promises (§§ 6–8). If consumers are not expected to scrutinize the legal terms up front, courts should scrutinize them ex post. The ex post scrutiny is intended to uproot terms that are so extreme that they would be unlikely to survive in an environment of meaningful assent, or that peel off the value that consumers bargained for.

Thus, the "grand bargain" that the common law of consumer contracts reflects allows for relatively permissive adoption of the standard contract terms that businesses draft, balanced by a set of substantive boundary restrictions that prohibit businesses from going too far. One of the Restatement's methodological cornerstones is the commitment, throughout, to reflect this fundamental tradeoff: as assent rules shift to the more permissive end of the continuum, courts have perceived greater need and justification for mandatory restrictions and ex post scrutiny of abusive terms. The two stand-alone regulatory techniques—mutual assent and mandatory restrictions—are independent legal doctrines, but their optimal scope developed within a unified hydraulic framework, whereby shifts within one doctrine inform the scope of the other.

. . .

14. *Relation to the Uniform Commercial Code and to the Restatement Second of Contracts.* The rules restated herein are consistent with, and elaborate on, the general principles of contract formation, as articulated in UCC § 2–204 and in Restatement Second of Contracts, Chapter 3. With respect to post-affirmation adoption of terms (subsection (b)), some courts have interpreted UCC § 2–207 to deny adoption of these terms as part of the consumer contract. Most courts, however, reject the application of UCC § 2–207 and, as no other provisions of Article 2 address the question which post-purchase terms become part of the contract, apply instead UCC § 2–204 and—through the gateway provided by UCC § 1–103(b)—general common-law principles.

. . . .

§ 3.   Modification of Standard Contract Terms

(a) Modified standard contract terms are adopted under the same rules that apply to original standard contract terms under § 2, but only if the consumer has received a reasonable notice of the proposed modification and a reasonable opportunity to reject the modified terms.

(b) A modification of the standard contract terms is enforceable only if made in good faith.

Comments

. . .

3. *Notice and opportunity to reject.* Modified terms are adopted only if the consumer receives a notice of the new terms and has a meaningful right to reject them. If there is no notice or no reasonable opportunity to reject, there is no reason to infer that the consumer's decision to continue the service signifies acceptance of the new terms. A meaningful opportunity to reject requires that the business either give the consumer the option to continue the relationship without the new terms, or a reasonable opportunity to terminate the contractual relationship altogether. If termination of the contractual relationship by the consumer is not feasible or practicable—for example, because such termination would impose a loss of value acquired by the consumer prior to the proposed modification—then the consumer does not have a meaningful opportunity to reject. In such case, the modified terms are not adopted, even if the consumer signified assent to the modification.

There is a close conceptual relationship between adoption of standard terms after the consumer signifies assent to the transaction under § 2(b) and modification of standard terms under § 3—in both settings the standard contract terms are presented to the consumer after the original decision to enter into the transaction was already made. Indeed, the adoption of the standard contract terms in both settings has to satisfy a similar requirement—the existence of a reasonable opportunity to reject the transaction (which, in turn, requires affording the consumer a reasonable time period in which to exercise such rejection). But a reasonable right to reject the modification under § 3 requires more than the opportunity to avoid the transaction under § 2(b). It requires that such rejection would not force the consumer to squander value already acquired prior to the modification.

    . . . .

    4.   *Good faith.* Modifications do not require "fresh" consideration. But they must be made in good faith. Compare U.C.C. § 2–209. See also Restatement Second, Contracts § 89 (adopting the related "fair and equitable" test for modifications that are not supported by fresh bargained-for consideration). The duty of good faith applies generally in contract law (see U.C.C. § 1–304 and Restatement Second, Contracts § 205). It is emphasized here, because of the central role that it plays in policing modifications—preventing opportunistic modifications that take advantage of locked-in consumers, who have already invested in the relationship with the business. Thus, some terms that may be acceptable if presented as part of the original contract may not satisfy the good-faith requirement if presented as part of the modification. A modification is more likely to satisfy the good-faith test if the modified terms are simultaneously being offered, as original terms, to new customers. Then, there is less concern that the modification takes advantage of consumers who are locked in by the switching costs. Further, the good-faith test will generally bar the modification of short-term contracts, such as a one-shot purchase-of-product contract, unless circumstances not anticipated by the parties when the contract was made are present.

§ 4.   Discretionary Obligations

(a)   A contract or any term that grants the business discretion to determine its contractual rights and obligations means such discretion as exercised in good faith.

(b)   A term in a contract that purports to grant the business discretion to determine its contractual rights and obligations in violation of the good-faith restriction of subsection (a) is unenforceable by the business.

§ 5.   Unconscionability

(a)   An unconscionable contract or term is unenforceable.

(b)   A contract or a term is unconscionable if it is

    (1)   Substantively unconscionable, namely fundamentally unfair or unreasonably one-sided, and

    (2)   Procedurally unconscionable, amounting to unfair surprise or depriving the consumer of meaningful choice.

(c)   In determining that a contract or a term is unconscionable, a greater degree of one of the elements in subsection (b) may offset a lesser degree of the other element. In appropriate circumstances, a high degree of substantive unconscionability is sufficient to make a standard contract term unconscionable.

(d)   Without limiting the scope of subsection (b)(1), a contract term is presumed to be substantively unconscionable if its effect is to:

    (1)   Exclude or limit the business's liability or the consumer's remedies that would otherwise be applicable for

        (A)   Death or personal injury for which, in the absence of a contractual provision in the consumer contract, the business would be liable, or

        (B)   Any loss to the consumer caused by an intentional or negligent act or omission of the business, or

    (2)   Unreasonably expand the consumer's liability, the business's remedies, or the business's enforcement powers, that would otherwise be applicable, or

    (3)   Unreasonably limit the consumer's ability to pursue a complaint or seek reasonable redress for a violation of a legal right.

(e)   When it is claimed or appears to the court that the contract or any term may be unconscionable, the parties shall be afforded a reasonable opportunity to present evidence as to its commercial setting, purpose, and effect.

Comments

. . .

2.   *The two prongs of unconscionability.* The doctrine of unconscionability has the primary goal of protecting contracting parties against fundamentally unfair and unreasonably one-sided terms. It thus represents a main component in the "grand bargain" that this Restatement and the underlying case law reflect. Because consumers rarely read or review the non-core standard contract terms, and because such faintly reviewed terms may nevertheless be adopted under §§ 2–3 of the Restatement, the doctrine of unconscionability is a primary tool against the inclusion of intolerable terms in the consumer contract. While the principal element of the unconscionability doctrine is the substantive prong that identifies such intolerable terms, the doctrine recognizes that sometimes consumers may choose to accept harsh terms in exchange for another benefit (such as low price). The doctrine asks whether consumers in fact meaningfully chose to accept a harsh term by also requiring (except in rare circumstances) a showing of some quantum of procedural unconscionability. In determining whether a contract or a term is unconscionable, a court has to examine their expected effects as they appear at the time that the contract was made (compare U.C.C. § 2–302 and Restatement Second, Contracts § 208).

3.   *Sliding scale.* In general, both the substantive and the procedural prongs are necessary for a finding of unconscionability. But they need not be present in the same degree. Under § 5(c), the two prongs are viewed in tandem and a sliding-scale approach is applied: a large quantum of one prong of unconscionability may offset a relatively small quantum of the other. Because the ultimate goal of the unconscionability doctrine is to deny enforcement to contract terms that are fundamentally unfair, in appropriate circumstances a high degree of substantive unconscionability is sufficient to find that a standard contract term, ordinarily not one of the "core" terms of the deal of which most consumers are ordinarily aware, is unconscionable. Conversely, because contract law seeks to deny enforcement to agreements that are adopted via fundamentally defective processes of formation, in appropriate circumstances severe procedural problems are sufficient to render an agreement unenforceable, e.g., under the doctrines of duress or misrepresentation, even when the terms of that agreement are not substantively unconscionable.

4.   *Substantive unconsciona*bility. The substantive-unconscionability test in subsection (b)(1) addresses the unfairness and one-sidedness of a contract term that potentially undermine the consumer's benefit from the bargain, and for which the business cannot show a reasonable justification. There are various ways to characterize the required severity of the substantive unconscionability—e.g., "shock the conscience," "oppressive," or "fundamentally unfair." These tests, as articulated in the UCC and by courts, are all intended to capture a limiting criterion, that the doctrine is to be used only when the one-sidedness of a term in the contract is extreme.

In general, it is impossible to evaluate the one-sidedness of a particular term without looking at the contract as a whole, including the price. What might appear as unfair may be merely a bargain-basement deal in which the pro-business term is matched by a pro-consumer price or other consumer advantage. Thus, for example, a contract that provides few rights to a consumer may not be problematic if a low price reflects those minimal rights, but might be problematic without the corresponding benefit of a low price. While the presence of a competitive market environment may suggest that, in ordinary commerce, pro-business terms would lead to more favorable prices for consumers, it does not preclude a legal finding that a term is substantively unconscionable. Specifically, if a term does not affect consumers' contracting decisions (see Comment 6 below on procedural unconscionability), the business may inefficiently reduce the quality of the term, and then use the cost savings (from the reduced quality) to offer a pro-consumer price. In such cases, economic analysis suggests that the resulting term-price combination would not generally be optimal, implying that the pro-consumer price might not outweigh the anti-consumer effect of the unconscionable term.

. . .

7.   *Procedural unconscionability.* The procedural prong of the unconscionability doctrine refers to some defects with the bargaining process, like a surprising and unexpected term, or lack of meaningful choice. Presenting the terms in standard-form, nonnegotiable format does not in itself render a term procedurally unconscionable, even though it is exceedingly common for consumers to be unaware of the language, meaning, and effect of the standard contract terms. Courts finding that a standard contract term contains a large quantum of substantive unconscionability may provide redress to the consumer by using the "sliding scale" methodology (see Comment 2). They either require no additional showing of procedural unconscionability, or, more often, regard the standard-form delivery itself procedurally unconscionable. Note, however, that if the finding of procedural unconscionability is based solely on the use of standard-form presentation, this low quantum of procedural unconscionability would have to be matched with a high degree of substantive unconscionability to render the contract or term unenforceable.

The procedural-unconscionability test may look to consumer awareness of the term in a market context. The question would be whether an ordinary consumer would be aware of the term, or could expect its inclusion. When consumers expect or are aware of a term, it can affect their contracting decisions. In these situations, the reasons for intervention in the substance of the deal are diminished. The question, then, in applying the procedural unconscionability test, is whether a term can affect the contracting decisions of a large enough number of consumers. (If the market is segmented, the question is whether a term can affect the contracting decisions of consumers in the relevant segment.) A term that does not affect the contracting decisions of a substantial number of consumers is presumed to be procedurally unconscionable.

A term that can affect the contracting decisions of a substantial number of consumers is subject to forces of market competition, even if it is not negotiated and even if it appears in the contracts of all businesses in the relevant market. Such a term is policed by market forces, and so policing by courts—through the unconscionability doctrine—is both unnecessary and leads to undesirable results, including a reduction in consumer choice. On the other hand, when drafting terms do not affect consumers' contracting decisions, the business is not subject to market discipline, and so the unconscionability doctrine can be usefully applied to police such terms. The prevalence, in the relevant market, of a pro-business term does not negate a finding of unconscionability. Indeed, if a term does not affect consumers' contracting decisions, all businesses might be tempted to draft this term in a one-sided, pro-business fashion.

It is presumed that non-core standard contract terms do not affect the contracting decisions of a substantial number of consumers. This presumption applies most forcefully when the standard contract term is part of a long list of fine-print terms; it is rebutted when the standard contract term is part of the "core" of the transaction, e.g., a bottom-line price or delivery fee. The presumption that non-core standard contract terms do not affect the contracting decisions of consumers is not rebutted even if they are presented in larger font or in a conspicuous place in the form contract, because it is exceedingly common for consumers to be unaware even of such bolstered disclosure. This presumption that standard contract terms do not affect the contracting decisions of a substantial number of consumers can be rebutted by the business using survey evidence (as commonly used in litigation involving aspects of unfair competition), or by any other indicia suggesting that the affected term was a salient part of the precontractual representations. (See also Comment [11] below on "Burden of proof.")

Note that a term may affect the purchasing decisions of many consumers, and yet be misunderstood by (imperfectly rational) consumers who misinterpret the effect of the term to increase, rather than decrease, their benefit of the bargain. This term would affect the purchasing decisions of many consumers, but in the wrong direction. Courts may find such terms procedurally unconscionable. Such terms may also be policed under § 6 (Deception).

. . . .

11.   *Burden of proof.* If a term is presumed to be substantively unconscionable under subsection (d), the burden is on the business to prove that the presumption is rebutted in the particular case. In addition, if a standard contract term is substantively unconscionable, the burden is on the business to prove that there is no procedural unconscionability (namely, that the term can affect the contracting decisions of a substantial number of consumers). As noted in Comment 6, it is presumed that standard contract terms do not affect the contracting decisions of a substantial number of consumers and are, therefore, procedurally

286

unconscionable. The burden is on the business to rebut the presumption and prove that the standard contract terms were presented in a way that affected consumers' contracting decisions.

§ 6.   Deception

(a) A contract or a term agreed to as a result of a deceptive act or practice is voidable by the consumer.

(b) Without limiting the scope of subsection (a), the following acts or practices are presumptively deceptive:

    (1) Making a material affirmation of fact or promise that is contradicted by or unreasonably limited in the standard contract terms;

    (2) Obscuring a charge to be paid by the consumer.

Comments

. . .

7. *Effects of deception.* The ordinary consequence of a conflict between an affirmation of fact or promise and a standard contract term under this Section is the removal of the standard contract term from the agreement, to the extent necessary to avoid the conflict. If severance of specific standard contract terms is not sufficient to undo the conflict with the affirmation of fact or promise, the consumer may avoid the contract in its entirety. Any terms avoided under this Section are replaced by provisions consistent with the affirmation of fact or promise made to the consumer and, if necessary, by gap-fillers in accordance with the guidelines in § 9 to this Restatement.

. . . .

§ 7.   Affirmations and Promises Not Part of the Standard Contract Terms

(a) An affirmation or promise made by the business, which is made part of the basis of the bargain, becomes part of the consumer contract.

(b) An affirmation or promise made by a third party, which is made part of the basis of the bargain between the business and the consumer,

    (1) Becomes part of the contract between the business and the consumer, if

        (i) the business knew or reasonably should have known of it, and

        (ii) the consumer could have reasonably believed that the business intended to stand behind the affirmation or promise; and

    (2) Creates a contractual obligation between the third party and the consumer, even if that party did not transact directly with the consumer, so long as the third party has an appreciable financial interest in the contract between the business and the consumer.

(c) Standard contract terms that purport to negate or limit the effect of subsections (a) and (b) are not enforceable.

. . . .

§ 8.   Integrated Agreements

(a) Standard contract terms presumptively constitute an integrated agreement with respect to these terms.

(b) Standard contract terms containing an express complete-integration clause presumptively constitute a completely integrated agreement with respect to the transaction.

(c)   The presumptions in subsections (a) and (b) are rebutted when the standard contract terms contradict or unreasonably limit an affirmation or promise that is made part of the basis of the bargain between the business and the consumer.

. . . .

§ 9.   Effects of Derogation from Mandatory Rules

(a)   If the court finds that a contract or any term excludes, limits, or violates any mandatory rule, the court may refuse to enforce the contract, or it may enforce the remainder of the contract without the derogating term, or it may limit the application of the derogating term.

(b)   If the court enforces the remainder of the contract without the derogating term, the court may replace the derogating term with

   (1)   A term that is reasonable in the circumstances, or

   (2)   A term that effects the minimal correction necessary to bring the contract into compliance with the mandatory rule, or

   (3)   A term that operates against the business, if the derogating term was inserted by the business in bad faith.

. . . .

PART VI

RESTATEMENT (THIRD) OF RESTITUTION AND UNJUST ENRICHMENT

RESTATEMENT (THIRD) OF RESTITUTION AND UNJUST ENRICHMENT

(2011)

(Excerpts)

TOPIC 1
RESTITUTION TO A PERFORMING PARTY
WITH NO CLAIM ON THE CONTRACT

Sec.

---

§ 31.   Unenforceability.

(1)   A person who renders performance under an agreement that cannot be enforced against the recipient by reason of

(a)   indefiniteness, or

(b)   the failure to satisfy an extrinsic requirement of enforceability such as the Statute of Frauds, has a claim in restitution against the recipient as necessary to prevent unjust enrichment. There is no unjust enrichment if the claimant receives the counterperformance specified by the parties' unenforceable agreement.

(2)   There is no claim under this section if enforcement of the agreement is barred by the applicable statute of limitations, nor in any other case in which the allowance of restitution would defeat the policy of the law that makes the agreement unenforceable. Restitution is appropriate except to the extent that forfeiture is an intended or acceptable consequence of unenforceability.

§ 32.   Illegality.

A person who renders performance under an agreement that is illegal or otherwise unenforceable for reasons of public policy may obtain restitution from the recipient in accordance with the following rules:

(1)   Restitution will be allowed, whether or not necessary to prevent unjust enrichment, if restitution is required by the policy of the underlying prohibition.

(2)   Restitution will also be allowed, as necessary to prevent unjust enrichment, if the allowance of restitution will not defeat or frustrate the policy of the underlying prohibition. There is no unjust enrichment if the claimant receives the counterperformance specified by the parties' unenforceable agreement.

(3)   Restitution will be denied, notwithstanding the enrichment of the defendant at the claimant's expense, if a claim under subsection (2) is foreclosed by the claimant's inequitable conduct. . . .

§ 33.   Incapacity of Recipient.

(1)   A person who renders performance under an agreement that is unenforceable by reason of the other party's legal incapacity has a claim in restitution against the recipient as necessary to prevent unjust enrichment. There is no unjust enrichment if the claimant receives the counterperformance specified by the parties' unenforceable agreement.

(2) Restitution under this section is available only to a person who has dealt with the recipient in good faith on reasonable terms.

(3) Notwithstanding the unjust enrichment of the recipient, restitution may be limited or denied if it would be inconsistent with the protection that the doctrine of incapacity is intended to afford in the circumstances of the case.

§ 34. Mistake or Supervening Change of Circumstances.

(1) A person who renders performance under a contract that is subject to avoidance by reason of mistake or supervening change of circumstances has a claim in restitution to recover the performance or its value, as necessary to prevent unjust enrichment. . . .

(2) For purposes of subsection (1):

(a) the value of a nonreturnable contractual performance is measured by reference to the recipient's contractual expectations; and

(b) the recipient's liability in restitution may be reduced to allow for loss incurred in reliance on the contract.

§ 35. Performance of Disputed Obligation.

(1) If one party to a contract demands from the other a performance that is not in fact due by the terms of their agreement, under circumstances making it reasonable to accede to the demand rather than to insist on an immediate test of the disputed obligation, the party on whom the demand is made may render such performance under protest or with reservation of rights, preserving a claim in restitution to recover the value of the benefit conferred in excess of the recipient's contractual entitlement.

(2) The claim described in subsection (1) is available only to a party acting in good faith and in the reasonable protection of its own interests. It is not available where there has been an accord and satisfaction, or where a performance with reservation of rights is inadequate to discharge the claimant's obligation to the recipient.

§ 36. Restitution to a Party in Default.

(1) A performing party whose material breach prevents a recovery on the contract has a claim in restitution against the recipient of performance, as necessary to prevent unjust enrichment.

(2) Enrichment from receipt of an incomplete or defective contractual performance is measured by comparison to the recipient's position had the contract been fully performed. The claimant has the burden of establishing the fact and amount of any net benefit conferred.

(3) A claim under this section may be displaced by a valid agreement of the parties establishing their rights and remedies in the event of default.

(4) If the claimant's default involves fraud or other inequitable conduct, restitution may on that account be denied. . . .

TOPIC 2
ALTERNATIVE REMEDIES FOR BREACH
OF AN ENFORCEABLE CONTRACT

§ 37. Rescission for Material Breach.

(1) Except as provided in subsection (2), a plaintiff who is entitled to a remedy for the defendant's material breach or repudiation may choose rescission as an alternative to enforcement if the further requirements of § 54 can be met.

(2) Rescission as a remedy for breach of contract is not available against a defendant whose defaulted obligation is exclusively an obligation to pay money.

§ 38. Performance-Based Damages.

(1) As an alternative to damages based on the expectation interest . . ., a plaintiff who is entitled to a remedy for material breach or repudiation may recover damages measured by the cost or value of the plaintiff's performance.

(2) Performance-based damages are measured by

(a) uncompensated expenditures made in reasonable reliance on the contract, including expenditures made in preparation for performance or in performance, less any loss the defendant can prove with reasonable certainty the plaintiff would have suffered had the contract been performed . . .; or

(b) the market value of the plaintiff's uncompensated contractual performance, not exceeding the price of such performance as determined by reference to the parties' agreement.

(3) A plaintiff whose damages are measured by the rules of subsection (2) may also recover for any other loss, including incidental or consequential loss, caused by the breach.

§ 39. Profit From Opportunistic Breach.

(1) If a deliberate breach of contract results in profit to the defaulting promisor and the available damage remedy affords inadequate protection to the promisee's contractual entitlement, the promisee has a claim to restitution of the profit realized by the promisor as a result of the breach. Restitution by the rule of this section is an alternative to a remedy in damages.

(2) A case in which damages afford inadequate protection to the promisee's contractual entitlement is ordinarily one in which damages will not permit the promisee to acquire a full equivalent to the promised performance in a substitute transaction.

(3) Breach of contract is profitable when it results in gains to the defendant (net of potential liability in damages) greater than the defendant would have realized from performance of the contract. Profits from breach include saved expenditure and consequential gains that the defendant would not have realized but for the breach, as measured by the rules that apply in other cases of disgorgement. . . .

PART VII
ELECTRONIC CONTRACTING

UNIFORM ELECTRONIC TRANSACTIONS ACT

(Excerpts)

[The National Conference of Commissioners on Uniform State Laws ("NCCUSL," now the Uniform Law Commission) proposed the Uniform Electronic Transactions Act ("UETA") in 1999. Forty-seven states, the District of Columbia, and the Virgin Islands have enacted it. (Other states, notably New York and Illinois, have similar statutes.) Prior to enactment, state statutes of frauds provided that, generally speaking, an action could not be brought on certain types of contracts unless the contract was in writing and signed by the party to be charged. UETA removes the resulting barriers to electronic commerce, including contracting by email, over the Internet, between computers without human intervention, and by using a wide variety of other electronic means. UETA applies when parties have agreed to conduct their transaction in electronic form, UETA § 5(b), although whether the parties have so agreed is to be determined from the context and other surrounding circumstances, including the conduct of the parties. UETA establishes that electronic records and signatures generally are equivalent to paper writings and manual signatures, thereby displacing statutes of frauds in a great many cases. UETA must be construed and applied to further its purposes—"(1) to facilitate electronic transactions consistent with other applicable law; (2) to be consistent with reasonable practices concerning electronic transactions and with the continued expansion of those practices; and (3) to effectuate its general purpose to make uniform the law with respect to the subject of [the Act] among States enacting it." *Id.* at § 6.

[Where enacted, UETA is state law. In 2000, just a year after NCCUSL proposed UETA, Congress enacted a federal statute, the Electronic Signatures in Global Commerce Act ("E-Sign"), below. E-Sign's purposes are essentially the same as UETA's. This development raised a question whether E-Sign "preempts"—supersedes—UETA, because federal statutes are "the supreme law of the land," U.S. Const., Art. VI(2), and E-Sign applies very broadly to "any transaction in or affecting interstate or foreign commerce." 15 U.S.C. § 7001(a). However, E-Sign provides that under most circumstances it does not preempt UETA (and some other state statutes with similar effect). 15 U.S.C. § 7002(a).

[UETA addresses some issues that E-Sign does not mention, and it treats a few issues differently. Consequently, UETA and E-Sign are both important parts of the law governing contracts.]

Table of Contents

§ 1.   Short Title.

This [Act] may be cited as the Uniform Electronic Transactions Act.

§ 2.   Definitions.

In this [Act]:

(1) "Agreement" means the bargain of the parties in fact, as found in their language or inferred from other circumstances and from rules, regulations, and procedures given the effect of agreements under laws otherwise applicable to a particular transaction.

(2) "Automated transaction" means a transaction conducted or performed, in whole or in part, by electronic means or electronic records, in which the acts or records of one or both parties are not reviewed by an individual in the ordinary course in forming a contract, performing under an existing contract, or fulfilling an obligation required by the transaction.

(3) "Computer program" means a set of statements or instructions to be used directly or indirectly in an information processing system in order to bring about a certain result.

(4) "Contract" means the total legal obligation resulting from the parties' agreement as affected by this [Act] and other applicable law.

(5) "Electronic" means relating to technology having electrical, digital, magnetic, wireless, optical, electromagnetic, or similar capabilities.

(6) "Electronic agent" means a computer program or an electronic or other automated means used independently to initiate an action or respond to electronic records or performances in whole or in part, without review or action by an individual.

(7) "Electronic record" means a record created, generated, sent, communicated, received, or stored by electronic means.

(8) "Electronic signature" means an electronic sound, symbol, or process attached to or logically associated with a record and executed or adopted by a person with the intent to sign the record.

(9) "Governmental agency" means an executive, legislative, or judicial agency, department, board, commission, authority, institution, or instrumentality of the federal government or of a State or of a county, municipality, or other political subdivision of a State.

(10) "Information" means data, text, images, sounds, codes, computer programs, software, databases, or the like.

(11) "Information processing system" means an electronic system for creating, generating, sending, receiving, storing, displaying, or processing information.

(12) "Person" means an individual, corporation, business trust, estate, trust, partnership, limited liability company, association, joint venture, governmental agency, public corporation, or any other legal or commercial entity.

(13) "Record" means information that is inscribed on a tangible medium or that is stored in an electronic or other medium and is retrievable in perceivable form.

(14) "Security procedure" means a procedure employed for the purpose of verifying that an electronic signature, record, or performance is that of a specific person or for detecting changes or errors in the information in an electronic record. The term includes a procedure that requires the use of algorithms or other codes, identifying words or numbers, encryption, or callback or other acknowledgment procedures.

(15) "State" means a State of the United States, the District of Columbia, Puerto Rico, the United States Virgin Islands, or any territory or insular possession subject to the jurisdiction of the United States. The term includes an Indian tribe or band, or Alaskan native village, which is recognized by federal law or formally acknowledged by a State.

(16) "Transaction" means an action or set of actions occurring between two or more persons relating to the conduct of business, commercial, or governmental affairs.

Comment

1. "Agreement."

Whether the parties have reached an agreement is determined by their express language and all surrounding circumstances. The Restatement 2d Contracts § 3 provides that, "An agreement is a manifestation of mutual assent on the part of two or more persons." See also Restatement 2d Contracts, Section 2, Comment b. The Uniform Commercial Code specifically includes in the circumstances from which an agreement may be inferred "course of performance, course of dealing and usage of trade . . ." as defined in the UCC. Although the definition of agreement in this Act does not make specific reference to usage of trade and other party conduct, this definition is not intended to affect the construction of the parties' agreement under the substantive law applicable to a particular transaction. Where that law takes account of usage and conduct in informing the terms of the parties' agreement, the usage or conduct would be relevant as "other circumstances" included in the definition under this Act.

Where the law applicable to a given transaction provides that system rules and the like constitute part of the agreement of the parties, such rules will have the same effect in determining the parties agreement under this Act. For example, UCC Article 4 (Section 4–103(b)) provides that Federal Reserve regulations and operating circulars and clearinghouse rules have the effect of agreements. Such agreements by law properly would be included in the definition of agreement in this Act.

The parties' agreement is relevant in determining whether the provisions of this Act have been varied by agreement. In addition, the parties' agreement may establish the parameters of the parties' use of electronic records and signatures, security procedures and similar aspects of the transaction. See Model Trading Partner Agreement, 45 Business Lawyer Supp. Issue (June 1990). See Section 5(b) and Comments thereto.

2. "Automated Transaction."

An automated transaction is a transaction performed or conducted by electronic means in which machines are used without human intervention to form contracts and perform obligations under existing contracts. Such broad coverage is necessary because of the diversity of transactions to which this Act may apply.

As with electronic agents, this definition addresses the circumstance where electronic records may result in action or performance by a party although no human review of the electronic records is anticipated. Section 14 provides specific rules to assure that where one or both parties do not review the electronic records, the resulting agreement will be effective.

The critical element in this definition is the lack of a human actor on one or both sides of a transaction. For example, if one orders books from Bookseller.com through Bookseller's website, the transaction would be an automated transaction because Bookseller took and confirmed the order via its machine. Similarly, if Automaker and supplier do business through Electronic Data Interchange, Automaker's computer, upon receiving information within certain pre-programmed parameters, will send an electronic order to supplier's computer. If Supplier's computer confirms the order and processes the shipment because the order falls within pre-programmed parameters in Supplier's computer, this would be a fully automated transaction. If, instead, the Supplier relies on a human employee to review, accept, and process the Buyer's order, then only the Automaker's side of the transaction would be automated. In either case, the entire transaction falls within this definition.

3.   **"Computer program."**

This definition refers to the functional and operating aspects of an electronic, digital system. It relates to operating instructions used in an electronic system such as an electronic agent. (See definition of "Electronic Agent.")

4.   **"Electronic."**

The basic nature of most current technologies and the need for a recognized, single term warrants the use of "electronic" as the defined term. The definition is intended to assure that the Act will be applied broadly as new technologies develop. The term must be construed broadly in light of developing technologies in order to fulfill the purpose of this Act to validate commercial transactions regardless of the medium used by the parties. Current legal requirements for "writings" can be satisfied by almost any tangible media, whether paper, other fibers, or even stone. The purpose and applicability of this Act covers intangible media which are technologically capable of storing, transmitting and reproducing information in human perceivable form, but which lack the tangible aspect of paper, papyrus or stone.While not all technologies listed are technically "electronic" in nature (e.g., optical fiber technology), the term "electronic" is the most descriptive term available to describe the majority of current technologies. For example, the development of biological and chemical processes for communication and storage of data, while not specifically mentioned in the definition, are included within the technical definition because such processes operate on electromagnetic impulses. However, whether a particular technology may be characterized as technically "electronic," i.e., operates on electromagnetic impulses, should not be determinative of whether records and signatures created, used and stored by means of a particular technology are covered by this Act. This Act is intended to apply to all records and signatures created, used and stored by any medium which permits the information to be retrieved in perceivable form.

5.   **"Electronic agent."**

This definition establishes that an electronic agent is a machine. As the term "electronic agent" has come to be recognized, it is limited to a tool function. The effect on the party using the agent is addressed in the operative provisions of the Act (e.g., Section 14).An electronic agent, such as a computer program or other automated means employed by a person, is a tool of that person. As a general rule, the employer of a tool is responsible for the results obtained by the use of that tool since the tool has no independent volition of its own. However, an electronic agent, by definition, is capable within the parameters of its programming, of initiating, responding or interacting with other parties or their electronic agents once it has been activated by a party, without further attention of that party.

While this Act proceeds on the paradigm that an electronic agent is capable of performing only within the technical strictures of its preset programming, it is conceivable that, within the useful life of this Act, electronic agents may be created with the ability to act autonomously, and not just automatically. That is, through developments in artificial intelligence, a computer may be able to "learn through experience, modify the instructions in their own programs, and even devise new instructions." Allen and Widdison, "Can Computers Make Contracts?" *9 Harv. J.L. & Tech 25* (Winter, 1996). If such developments occur, courts may construe the definition of electronic agent accordingly, in order to recognize such new capabilities.

The examples involving Bookseller.com and Automaker in the Comment to the definition of Automated Transaction are equally applicable here. Bookseller acts through an electronic agent in processing an order for books. Automaker and the supplier each act through electronic agents in facilitating and effectuating the just-in-time inventory process through EDI.

6.   **"Electronic record."**

An electronic record is a subset of the broader defined term "record." It is any record created, used or stored in a medium other than paper (see definition of electronic). The defined term is also used in this Act as a limiting definition in those provisions in which it is used.Information processing systems, computer equipment and programs, electronic data interchange, electronic mail, voice mail, facsimile, telex, telecopying, scanning, and similar technologies all qualify as electronic under this Act. Accordingly information stored on a computer hard drive or floppy disc, facsimiles, voice mail messages, messages on a telephone answering machine, audio and video tape recordings, among other records, all would be electronic records under this Act.

7. **"Electronic signature."**

The idea of a signature is broad and not specifically defined. Whether any particular record is "signed" is a question of fact. Proof of that fact must be made under other applicable law. This Act simply assures that the signature may be accomplished through electronic means. No specific technology need be used in order to create a valid signature. One's voice on an answering machine may suffice if the requisite intention is present. Similarly, including one's name as part of an electronic mail communication also may suffice, as may the firm name on a facsimile. It also may be shown that the requisite intent was not present and accordingly the symbol, sound or process did not amount to a signature. One may use a digital signature with the requisite intention, or one may use the private key solely as an access device with no intention to sign, or otherwise accomplish a legally binding act. In any case the critical element is the intention to execute or adopt the sound or symbol or process for the purpose of signing the related record.

The definition requires that the signer execute or adopt the sound, symbol, or process with the intent to sign the record. The act of applying a sound, symbol or process to an electronic record could have differing meanings and effects. The consequence of the act and the effect of the act as a signature are determined under other applicable law. However, the essential attribute of a signature involves applying a sound, symbol or process with an intent to do a legally significant act. It is that intention that is understood in the law as a part of the word "sign", without the need for a definition.

This Act establishes, to the greatest extent possible, the equivalency of electronic signatures and manual signatures. Therefore the term "signature" has been used to connote and convey that equivalency. The purpose is to overcome unwarranted biases against electronic methods of signing and authenticating records. The term "authentication," used in other laws, often has a narrower meaning and purpose than an electronic signature as used in this Act. However, an authentication under any of those other laws constitutes an electronic signature under this Act.

The precise effect of an electronic signature will be determined based on the surrounding circumstances under Section 9(b).

This definition includes as an electronic signature the standard webpage click through process. For example, when a person orders goods or services through a vendor's website, the person will be required to provide information as part of a process which will result in receipt of the goods or services. When the customer ultimately gets to the last step and clicks "I agree," the person has adopted the process and has done so with the intent to associate the person with the record of that process. The actual effect of the electronic signature will be determined from all the surrounding circumstances[. However,] the person adopted a process which the circumstances indicate s/he intended to have the effect of getting the goods/services and being bound to pay for them. The adoption of the process carried the intent to do a legally significant act, the hallmark of a signature.

Another important aspect of this definition lies in the necessity that the electronic signature be linked or logically associated with the record. In the paper world, it is assumed that the symbol adopted by a party is attached to or located somewhere in the same paper that is intended to be authenticated, e.g., an allonge firmly attached to a promissory note, or the classic signature at the end of a long contract. These tangible manifestations do not exist in the electronic environment, and accordingly, this definition expressly provides that the symbol must in some way be linked to, or connected with, the electronic record being signed. This linkage is consistent with the regulations promulgated by the Food and Drug Administration. 21 CFR Part 11 (March 20, 1997).

A digital signature using public key encryption technology would qualify as an electronic signature, as would the mere inclusion of one's name as a part of an e-mail message—so long as in each case the signer executed or adopted the symbol with the intent to sign. . . .

9. **"Information processing system."**

This definition is consistent with the UNCITRAL Model Law on Electronic Commerce. The term includes computers and other information systems. It is principally used in Section 15 in connection with the sending and receiving of information. In that context, the key aspect is that the information enter a system from which a person can access it.

10. "Record."

This is a standard definition designed to embrace all means of communicating or storing information except human memory. It includes any method for storing or communicating information, including "writings." A record need not be indestructible or permanent, but the term does not include oral or other communications which are not stored or preserved by some means. Information that has not been retained other than through human memory does not qualify as a record. As in the case of the terms "writing" or "written," the term "record" does not establish the purposes, permitted uses or legal effect which a record may have under any particular provision of substantive law. ABA Report on Use of the Term "Record," October 1, 1996.

11. "Security procedure."

A security procedure may be applied to verify an electronic signature, verify the identity of the sender, or assure the informational integrity of an electronic record. The definition does not identify any particular technology. This permits the use of procedures which the parties select or which are established by law. It permits the greatest flexibility among the parties and allows for future technological development.

The definition in this Act is broad and is used to illustrate one way of establishing attribution or content integrity of an electronic record or signature. The use of a security procedure is not accorded operative legal effect, through the use of presumptions or otherwise, by this Act. In this Act, the use of security procedures is simply one method for proving the source or content of an electronic record or signature.

A security procedure may be technologically very sophisticated, such as an asymmetric cryptographic system. At the other extreme the security procedure may be as simple as a telephone call to confirm the identity of the sender through another channel of communication. It may include the use of a mother's maiden name or a personal identification number (PIN). Each of these examples is a method for confirming the identity of a person or accuracy of a message.

12. "Transaction."

The definition has been limited to actions between people taken in the context of business, commercial or governmental activities. The term includes all interactions between people for business, commercial, including specifically consumer, or governmental purposes. However, the term does not include unilateral or non-transactional actions. As such it provides a structural limitation on the scope of the Act as stated in the next section. It is essential that the term commerce and business be understood and construed broadly to include commercial and business transactions involving individuals who may qualify as "consumers" under other applicable law. If Alice and Bob agree to the sale of Alice's car to Bob for $2000 using an internet auction site, that transaction is fully covered by this Act. Even if Alice and Bob each qualify as typical "consumers" under other applicable law, their interaction is a transaction in commerce. Accordingly their actions would be related to commercial affairs, and fully qualify as a transaction governed by this Act.

Other transaction types include:

1.   A single purchase by an individual from a retail merchant, which may be accomplished by an order from a printed catalog sent by facsimile, or by exchange of electronic mail.

2.   Recurring orders on a weekly or monthly basis between large companies which have entered into a master trading partner agreement to govern the methods and manner of their transaction parameters.

3.   A purchase by an individual from an online internet retail vendor. Such an arrangement may develop into an ongoing series of individual purchases, with security procedures and the like, as a part of doing ongoing business.

4.   The closing of a business purchase transaction via facsimile transmission of documents or even electronic mail. In such a transaction, all parties may participate through electronic conferencing technologies. At the appointed time all electronic records are executed electronically and transmitted to the other party. In such a case, the electronic records and electronic signatures are validated under this Act, obviating the need for "in person" closings.

A transaction must include interaction between two or more persons. Consequently, to the extent that the execution of a will, trust, or a health care power of attorney or similar health care designation does not involve another person and is a unilateral act, it would not be covered by this Act because not occurring as a part of a transaction as defined in this Act. However, this Act *does* apply to all electronic records and signatures *related* to a transaction, and so does cover, for example, internal auditing and accounting records related to a transaction.

§ 3.   Scope.

(a)   Except as otherwise provided in subsection (b), this [Act] applies to electronic records and electronic signatures relating to a transaction.

(b)   This [Act] does not apply to a transaction to the extent it is governed by:

     (1)   a law governing the creation and execution of wills, codicils, or testamentary trusts;

     (2)   [The Uniform Commercial Code other than Sections 1–107 and 1–206, Article 2, and Article 2A];

     (3)   [the Uniform Computer Information Transactions Act]; and

     (4)   [other laws, if any, identified by State].

(c)   This [Act] applies to an electronic record or electronic signature otherwise excluded from the application of this [Act] under subsection (b) to the extent it is governed by a law other than those specified in subsection (b).

(d)   A transaction subject to this [Act] is also subject to other applicable substantive law.

§ 4.   Prospective Application.

This [Act] applies to any electronic record or electronic signature created, generated, sent, communicated, received, or stored on or after the effective date of this [Act].

§ 5.   Use of Electronic Records and Electronic Signatures; Variation by Agreement.

(a)   This [Act] does not require a record or signature to be created, generated, sent, communicated, received, stored, or otherwise processed or used by electronic means or in electronic form.

(b)   This [Act] applies only to transactions between parties each of which has agreed to conduct transactions by electronic means. Whether the parties agree to conduct a transaction by electronic means is determined from the context and surrounding circumstances, including the parties' conduct.

(c)   A party that agrees to conduct a transaction by electronic means may refuse to conduct other transactions by electronic means. The right granted by this subsection may not be waived by agreement.

(d)   Except as otherwise provided in this [Act], the effect of any of its provisions may be varied by agreement. The presence in certain provisions of this [Act] of the words "unless otherwise agreed", or words of similar import, does not imply that the effect of other provisions may not be varied by agreement.

(e)   Whether an electronic record or electronic signature has legal consequences is determined by this [Act] and other applicable law.

Comment

This section limits the applicability of this Act to transactions which parties have agreed to conduct electronically. Broad interpretation of the term agreement is necessary to assure that this Act has the widest possible application consistent with its purpose of removing barriers to electronic commerce.

1.   This section makes clear that this Act is intended to facilitate the use of electronic means, but does not require the use of electronic records and signatures. This fundamental principle is set forth in

subsection (a) and elaborated by subsections (b) and (c), which require an intention to conduct transactions electronically and preserve the right of a party to refuse to use electronics in any subsequent transaction.

2.   The paradigm of this Act is two willing parties doing transactions electronically. It is therefore appropriate that the Act is voluntary and preserves the greatest possible party autonomy to refuse electronic transactions. The requirement that party agreement be found from all the surrounding circumstances is a limitation on the scope of this Act.

3.   If this Act is to serve to facilitate electronic transactions, it must be applicable under circumstances not rising to a full fledged contract to use electronics. While absolute certainty can be accomplished by obtaining an explicit contract before relying on electronic transactions, such an explicit contract should not be necessary before one may feel safe in conducting transactions electronically. Indeed, such a requirement would itself be an unreasonable barrier to electronic commerce, at odds with the fundamental purpose of this Act. Accordingly, the requisite agreement, express or implied, must be determined from all available circumstances and evidence.

4.   Subsection (b) provides that the Act applies to transactions in which the parties have agreed to conduct the transaction electronically. In this context it is essential that the parties' actions and words be broadly construed in determining whether the requisite agreement exists. Accordingly, the Act expressly provides that the party's agreement is to be found from all circumstances, including the parties' conduct. The critical element is the intent of a party to conduct a transaction electronically. Once that intent is established, this Act applies. See Restatement 2d Contracts, Sections 2, 3, and 19.

Examples of circumstances from which it may be found that parties have reached an agreement to conduct transactions electronically include the following:

A.   Automaker and supplier enter into a Trading Partner Agreement setting forth the terms, conditions and methods for the conduct of business between them electronically.

B.   Joe gives out his business card with his business e-mail address. It may be reasonable, under the circumstances, for a recipient of the card to infer that Joe has agreed to communicate electronically for business purposes. However, in the absence of additional facts, it would not necessarily be reasonable to infer Joe's agreement to communicate electronically for purposes outside the scope of the business indicated by use of the business card.

C.   Sally may have several e-mail addresses—home, main office, office of a non-profit organization on whose board Sally sits. In each case, it may be reasonable to infer that Sally is willing to communicate electronically with respect to business related to the business/purpose associated with the respective e-mail addresses. However, depending on the circumstances, it may not be reasonable to communicate with Sally for purposes other than those related to the purpose for which she maintained a particular e-mail account.

D.   Among the circumstances to be considered in finding an agreement would be the time when the assent occurred relative to the timing of the use of electronic communications. If one orders books from an on-line vendor, such as Bookseller.com, the intention to conduct that transaction and to receive any correspondence related to the transaction electronically can be inferred from the conduct. Accordingly, as to information related to that transaction it is reasonable for Bookseller to deal with the individual electronically.

The examples noted above are intended to focus the inquiry on the party's agreement to conduct a transaction electronically. Similarly, if two people are at a meeting and one tells the other to send an e-mail to confirm a transaction—the requisite agreement under subsection (b) would exist. In each case, the use of a business card, statement at a meeting, or other evidence of willingness to conduct a transaction electronically must be viewed in light of all the surrounding circumstances with a view toward broad validation of electronic transactions.

5.   Just as circumstances may indicate the existence of agreement, express or implied from surrounding circumstances, circumstances may also demonstrate the absence of true agreement. For example:

A.   If Automaker, Inc. were to issue a recall of automobiles via its Internet website, it would not be able to rely on this Act to validate that notice in the case of a person who never logged on to the website, or indeed, had no ability to do so, notwithstanding a clause in a paper purchase contract by which the buyer agreed to receive such notices in such a manner.

B. Buyer executes a standard form contract in which an agreement to receive all notices electronically in set forth on page 3 in the midst of other fine print. Buyer has never communicated with Seller electronically, and has not provided any other information in the contract to suggest a willingness to deal electronically. Not only is it unlikely that any but the most formalistic of agreements may be found, but nothing in this Act prevents courts from policing such form contracts under common law doctrines relating to contract formation, unconscionability and the like.

6. Subsection (c) has been added to make clear the ability of a party to refuse to conduct a transaction electronically, even if the person has conducted transactions electronically in the past. The effectiveness of a party's refusal to conduct a transaction electronically will be determined under other applicable law in light of all surrounding circumstances. Such circumstances must include an assessment of the transaction involved.

A party's right to decline to act electronically under a specific contract, on the ground that each action under that contract amounts to a separate "transaction," must be considered in light of the purpose of the contract and the action to be taken electronically. For example, under a contract for the purchase of goods, the giving and receipt of notices electronically, as provided in the contract, should not be viewed as discreet transactions. Rather such notices amount to separate actions which are part of the "transaction" of purchase evidenced by the contract. Allowing one party to require a change of medium in the middle of the transaction evidenced by that contract is not the purpose of this subsection. Rather this subsection is intended to preserve the party's right to conduct the next purchase in a non-electronic medium.

7. Subsection (e) is an essential provision in the overall scheme of this Act. While this Act validates and effectuates electronic records and electronic signatures, the legal effect of such records and signatures is left to existing substantive law outside this Act except in very narrow circumstances. . . . Even when this Act operates to validate records and signatures in an electronic medium, it expressly preserves the substantive rules of other law applicable to such records. See, e.g., Section 11.

For example, beyond validation of records, signatures and contracts based on the medium used, Section 7(a) and (b) should not be interpreted as establishing the legal effectiveness of any given record, signature or contract. Where a rule of law requires that the record contain minimum substantive content, the legal effect of such a record will depend on whether the record meets the substantive requirements of other applicable law.

Section 8 expressly preserves a number of legal requirements in currently existing law relating to the presentation of information in writing. Although this Act now would allow such information to be presented in an electronic record, Section 8 provides that the other substantive requirements of law must be satisfied in the electronic medium as well.

§ 6.   Construction and Application.

This [Act] must be construed and applied:

    (1)   to facilitate electronic transactions consistent with other applicable law;

    (2)   to be consistent with reasonable practices concerning electronic transactions and with the continued expansion of those practices; and

    (3)   to effectuate its general purpose to make uniform the law with respect to the subject of this [Act] among States enacting it.

§ 7.   Legal Recognition of Electronic Records, Electronic Signatures, and Electronic Contracts.

(a)   A record or signature may not be denied legal effect or enforceability solely because it is in electronic form.

(b)   A contract may not be denied legal effect or enforceability solely because an electronic record was used in its formation.

(c)   If a law requires a record to be in writing, an electronic record satisfies the law.

(d)   If a law requires a signature, an electronic signature satisfies the law.

Comment

1.   This section sets forth the fundamental premise of this Act: namely, that the medium in which a record, signature, or contract is created, presented or retained does not affect it's legal significance. Subsections (a) and (b) are designed to eliminate the single element of medium as a reason to deny effect or enforceability to a record, signature, or contract. The fact that the information is set forth in an electronic, as opposed to paper, record is irrelevant.

2.   Under Restatement 2d Contracts Section 8, a contract may have legal effect and yet be unenforceable. Indeed, one circumstance where a record or contract may have effect but be unenforceable is in the context of the Statute of Frauds. Though a contract may be unenforceable, the records may have collateral effects, as in the case of a buyer that insures goods purchased under a contract unenforceable under the Statute of Frauds. The insurance company may not deny a claim on the ground that the buyer is not the owner, though the buyer may have no direct remedy against seller for failure to deliver. See Restatement 2d Contracts, Section 8, Illustration 4.

While this section would validate an electronic record for purposes of a statute of frauds, if an agreement to conduct the transaction electronically cannot reasonably be found (see Section 5(b)) then a necessary predicate to the applicability of this Act would be absent and this Act would not validate the electronic record. Whether the electronic record might be valid under other law is not addressed by this Act.

3.   Subsections (c) and (d) provide the positive assertion that electronic records and signatures satisfy legal requirements for writings and signatures. The provisions are limited to requirements in laws that a record be in writing or be signed. This section does not address requirements imposed by other law in addition to requirements for writings and signatures. See, e.g., Section 8.

Subsections (c) and (d) are particularized applications of subsection (a). The purpose is to validate and effectuate electronic records and signatures as the equivalent of writings, subject to all of the rules applicable to the efficacy of a writing, except as such other rules are modified by the more specific provisions of this Act.

Illustration 1: A sends the following e-mail to B: "I hereby offer to buy widgets from you, delivery next Tuesday. /s/ A." B responds with the following e-mail: "I accept your offer to buy widgets for delivery next Tuesday. /s/ B." The e-mails may not be denied effect solely because they are electronic. In addition, the e-mails do qualify as records under the Statute of Frauds. However, because there is no quantity stated in either record, the parties' agreement would be unenforceable under existing UCC Section 2–201(1).

Illustration 2: A sends the following e-mail to B: "I hereby offer to buy 100 widgets for $1000, delivery next Tuesday. /s/ A." B responds with the following e-mail: "I accept your offer to purchase 100 widgets for $1000, delivery next Tuesday. /s/ B." In this case the analysis is the same as in Illustration 1 except that here the records otherwise satisfy the requirements of UCC Section 2–201(1). The transaction may not be denied legal effect solely because there is not a pen and ink "writing" or "signature".

4.   Section 8 addresses additional requirements imposed by other law which may affect the legal effect or enforceability of an electronic record in a particular case. For example, in Section 8(a) the legal requirement addressed is *the provision of information* in writing. The section then sets forth the standards to be applied in determining whether the provision of information by an electronic record is the equivalent of the provision of information in writing. The requirements in Section 8 are in addition to the bare validation that occurs under this section.

5.   Under the substantive law applicable to a particular transaction within this Act, the legal effect of an electronic record may be separate from the issue of whether the record contains a signature. For example, where notice must be given as part of a contractual obligation, the effectiveness of the notice will turn on whether the party provided the notice regardless of whether the notice was signed (see Section 15).

An electronic record attributed to a party under Section 9 and complying with the requirements of Section 15 would suffice in that case, notwithstanding that it may not contain an electronic signature.

§ 8.   Provision of Information in Writing; Presentation of Records.

(a) If parties have agreed to conduct a transaction by electronic means and a law requires a person to provide, send, or deliver information in writing to another person, the requirement is satisfied if the information is provided, sent, or delivered, as the case may be, in an electronic record capable of retention by the recipient at the time of receipt. An electronic record is not capable of retention by the recipient if the sender or its information processing system inhibits the ability of the recipient to print or store the electronic record.

(b) If a law other than this [Act] requires a record (i) to be posted or displayed in a certain manner, (ii) to be sent, communicated, or transmitted by a specified method, or (iii) to contain information that is formatted in a certain manner, the following rules apply:

(1) The record must be posted or displayed in the manner specified in the other law.

(2) Except as otherwise provided in subsection (d)(2), the record must be sent, communicated, or transmitted by the method specified in the other law.

(3) The record must contain the information formatted in the manner specified in the other law.

(c) If a sender inhibits the ability of a recipient to store or print an electronic record, the electronic record is not enforceable against the recipient.

(d) The requirements of this section may not be varied by agreement, but:

(1) to the extent a law other than this [Act] requires information to be provided, sent, or delivered in writing but permits that requirement to be varied by agreement, the requirement under subsection (a) that the information be in the form of an electronic record capable of retention may also be varied by agreement; and

(2) a requirement under a law other than this [Act] to send, communicate, or transmit a record by [first-class mail, postage prepaid] [regular United States mail], may be varied by agreement to the extent permitted by the other law.

§ 9.   Attribution and Effect of Electronic Record and Electronic Signature.

(a) An electronic record or electronic signature is attributable to a person if it was the act of the person. The act of the person may be shown in any manner, including a showing of the efficacy of any security procedure applied to determine the person to which the electronic record or electronic signature was attributable.

(b) The effect of an electronic record or electronic signature attributed to a person under subsection (a) is determined from the context and surrounding circumstances at the time of its creation, execution, or adoption, including the parties' agreement, if any, and otherwise as provided by law.

Comment

1. Under subsection (a), so long as the electronic record or electronic signature resulted from a person's action it will be attributed to that person—the legal effect of that attribution is addressed in subsection (b). This section does not alter existing rules of law regarding attribution. The section assures that such rules will be applied in the electronic environment. A person's actions include actions taken by human agents of the person, as well as actions taken by an electronic agent, i.e., the tool, of the person. Although the rule may appear to state the obvious, it assures that the record or signature is not ascribed to a machine, as opposed to the person operating or programing the machine.

In each of the following cases, both the electronic record and electronic signature would be attributable to a person under subsection (a):

A.   The person types his/her name as part of an e-mail purchase order;

B.   The person's employee, pursuant to authority, types the person's name as part of an e-mail purchase order;

C.   The person's computer, programmed to order goods upon receipt of inventory information within particular parameters, issues a purchase order which includes the person's name, or other identifying information, as part of the order.

In each of the above cases, law other than this Act would ascribe both the signature and the action to the person if done in a paper medium. Subsection (a) expressly provides that the same result will occur when an electronic medium is used.

2.   Nothing in this section affects the use of a signature as a device for attributing a record to a person. Indeed, a signature is often the primary method for attributing a record to a person. In the foregoing examples, once the electronic signature is attributed to the person, the electronic record would also be attributed to the person, unless the person established fraud, forgery, or other invalidating cause. However, a signature is not the only method for attribution.

3.   The use of facsimile transmissions provides a number of examples of attribution using information other than a signature. A facsimile may be attributed to a person because of the information printed across the top of the page that indicates the machine from which it was sent. Similarly, the transmission may contain a letterhead which identifies the sender. Some cases have held that the letterhead actually constituted a signature because it was a symbol adopted by the sender with intent to authenticate the facsimile. However, the signature determination resulted from the necessary finding of intention in that case. Other cases have found facsimile letterheads NOT to be signatures because the requisite intention was not present. The critical point is that with or without a signature, information within the electronic record may well suffice to provide the facts resulting in attribution of an electronic record to a particular party.

In the context of attribution of records, normally the content of the record will provide the necessary information for a finding of attribution. It is also possible that an established course of dealing between parties may result in a finding of attribution Just as with a paper record, evidence of forgery or counterfeiting may be introduced to rebut the evidence of attribution.

4.   Certain information may be present in an electronic environment that does not appear to attribute but which clearly links a person to a particular record. Numerical codes, personal identification numbers, public and private key combinations all serve to establish the party to whom an electronic record should be attributed. Of course security procedures will be another piece of evidence available to establish attribution.

The inclusion of a specific reference to security procedures as a means of proving attribution is salutary because of the unique importance of security procedures in the electronic environment. In certain processes, a technical and technological security procedure may be the best way to convince a trier of fact that a particular electronic record or signature was that of a particular person. In certain circumstances, the use of a security procedure to establish that the record and related signature came from the person's business might be necessary to overcome a claim that a hacker intervened. The reference to security procedures is not intended to suggest that other forms of proof of attribution should be accorded less persuasive effect. It is also important to recall that the particular strength of a given procedure does not affect the procedure's status as a security procedure, but only affects the weight to be accorded the evidence of the security procedure as tending to establish attribution.

5.   This section does apply in determining the effect of a "click-through" transaction. A "click-through" transaction involves a process which, if executed with an intent to "sign," will be an electronic signature. See definition of Electronic Signature. In the context of an anonymous "click-through," issues of proof will be paramount. This section will be relevant to establish that the resulting electronic record is attributable to a particular person upon the requisite proof, including security procedures which may track the source of the click-through.

6.   Once it is established that a record or signature is attributable to a particular party, the effect of a record or signature must be determined in light of the context and surrounding circumstances, including the parties' agreement, if any. Also informing the effect of any attribution will be other legal requirements considered in light of the context. Subsection (b) addresses the effect of the record or signature once attributed to a person.

§ 10.   Effect of Change or Error.

If a change or error in an electronic record occurs in a transmission between parties to a transaction, the following rules apply:

(1)   If the parties have agreed to use a security procedure to detect changes or errors and one party has conformed to the procedure, but the other party has not, and the nonconforming party would have detected the change or error had that party also conformed, the conforming party may avoid the effect of the changed or erroneous electronic record.

(2)   In an automated transaction involving an individual, the individual may avoid the effect of an electronic record that resulted from an error made by the individual in dealing with the electronic agent of another person if the electronic agent did not provide an opportunity for the prevention or correction of the error and, at the time the individual learns of the error, the individual:

(A)   promptly notifies the other person of the error and that the individual did not intend to be bound by the electronic record received by the other person;

(B)   takes reasonable steps, including steps that conform to the other person's reasonable instructions, to return to the other person or, if instructed by the other person, to destroy the consideration received, if any, as a result of the erroneous electronic record; and

(C)   has not used or received any benefit or value from the consideration, if any, received from the other person.

(3)   If neither paragraph (1) nor paragraph (2) applies, the change or error has the effect provided by other law, including the law of mistake, and the parties' contract, if any.

(4)   Paragraphs (2) and (3) may not be varied by agreement.

§ 11.   Notarization and Acknowledgment.

If a law requires a signature or record to be notarized, acknowledged, verified, or made under oath, the requirement is satisfied if the electronic signature of the person authorized to perform those acts, together with all other information required to be included by other applicable law, is attached to or logically associated with the signature or record.

§ 12.   Retention of Electronic Records; Originals.

(a)   If a law requires that a record be retained, the requirement is satisfied by retaining an electronic record of the information in the record which:

(1)   accurately reflects the information set forth in the record after it was first generated in its final form as an electronic record or otherwise; and

(2)   remains accessible for later reference.

(b)   A requirement to retain a record in accordance with subsection (a) does not apply to any information the sole purpose of which is to enable the record to be sent, communicated, or received.

(c)   A person may satisfy subsection (a) by using the services of another person if the requirements of that subsection are satisfied.

(d)   If a law requires a record to be presented or retained in its original form, or provides consequences if the record is not presented or retained in its original form, that law is satisfied by an electronic record retained in accordance with subsection (a).

(e)   If a law requires retention of a check, that requirement is satisfied by retention of an electronic record of the information on the front and back of the check in accordance with subsection (a).

(f)   A record retained as an electronic record in accordance with subsection (a) satisfies a law requiring a person to retain a record for evidentiary, audit, or like purposes, unless a law enacted after the effective date of this [Act] specifically prohibits the use of an electronic record for the specified purpose.

(g)   This section does not preclude a governmental agency of this State from specifying additional requirements for the retention of a record subject to the agency's jurisdiction.

§ 13.   Admissibility in Evidence.

In a proceeding, evidence of a record or signature may not be excluded solely because it is in electronic form.

§ 14.   Automated Transaction.

In an automated transaction, the following rules apply:

(1)   A contract may be formed by the interaction of electronic agents of the parties, even if no individual was aware of or reviewed the electronic agents' actions or the resulting terms and agreements.

(2)   A contract may be formed by the interaction of an electronic agent and an individual, acting on the individual's own behalf or for another person, including by an interaction in which the individual performs actions that the individual is free to refuse to perform and which the individual knows or has reason to know will cause the electronic agent to complete the transaction or performance.

(3)   The terms of the contract are determined by the substantive law applicable to it.

Comment

1.   This section confirms that contracts can be formed by machines functioning as electronic agents for parties to a transaction. It negates any claim that lack of human intent, at the time of contract formation, prevents contract formation. When machines are involved, the requisite intention flows from the programing and use of the machine. As in other cases, these are salutary provisions consistent with the fundamental purpose of the Act to remove barriers to electronic transactions while leaving the substantive law, e.g., law of mistake, law of contract formation, unaffected to the greatest extent possible.

2.   The process in paragraph (2) validates an anonymous click-through transaction. It is possible that an anonymous click-through process may simply result in no recognizable legal relationship, e.g., A goes to a person's website and acquires access without in any way identifying herself, or otherwise indicating agreement or assent to any limitation or obligation, and the owner's site grants A access. In such a case no legal relationship has been created.

On the other hand it may be possible that A's actions indicate agreement to a particular term. For example, A goes to a website and is confronted by an initial screen which advises her that the information at this site is proprietary, that A may use the information for her own personal purposes, but that, by clicking below, A agrees that any other use without the site owner's permission is prohibited. If A clicks "agree" and downloads the information and then uses the information for other, prohibited purposes, should not A be bound by the click? It seems the answer properly should be, and would be, yes.

If the owner can show that the only way A could have obtained the information was from his website, and that the process to access the subject information required that A must have clicked the "I agree" button after having the ability to see the conditions on use, A has performed actions which A was free to refuse, which A knew would cause the site to grant her access, i.e., "complete the transaction." The terms of the resulting contract will be determined under general contract principles, but will include the limitation on A's use of the information, as a condition precedent to granting her access to the information.

3. In the transaction set forth in Comment 2, the record of the transaction also will include an electronic signature. By clicking "I agree" A adopted a process with the intent to "sign," i.e., bind herself to a legal obligation, the resulting record of the transaction. If a "signed writing" were required under otherwise applicable law, this transaction would be enforceable. If a "signed writing" were not required, it may be sufficient to establish that the electronic record is attributable to A under Section 9. Attribution may be shown in any manner reasonable including showing that, of necessity, A could only have gotten the information through the process at the website.

§ 15. Time and Place of Sending and Receipt.

(a) Unless otherwise agreed between the sender and the recipient, an electronic record is sent when it:

(1) is addressed properly or otherwise directed properly to an information processing system that the recipient has designated or uses for the purpose of receiving electronic records or information of the type sent and from which the recipient is able to retrieve the electronic record;

(2) is in a form capable of being processed by that system; and

(3) enters an information processing system outside the control of the sender or of a person that sent the electronic record on behalf of the sender or enters a region of the information processing system designated or used by the recipient which is under the control of the recipient.

(b) Unless otherwise agreed between a sender and the recipient, an electronic record is received when:

(1) it enters an information processing system that the recipient has designated or uses for the purpose of receiving electronic records or information of the type sent and from which the recipient is able to retrieve the electronic record; and

(2) it is in a form capable of being processed by that system.

(c) Subsection (b) applies even if the place the information processing system is located is different from the place the electronic record is deemed to be received under subsection (d).

(d) Unless otherwise expressly provided in the electronic record or agreed between the sender and the recipient, an electronic record is deemed to be sent from the sender's place of business and to be received at the recipient's place of business. For purposes of this subsection, the following rules apply:

(1) If the sender or recipient has more than one place of business, the place of business of that person is the place having the closest relationship to the underlying transaction.

(2) If the sender or the recipient does not have a place of business, the place of business is the sender's or recipient's residence, as the case may be.

(e) An electronic record is received under subsection (b) even if no individual is aware of its receipt.

(f) Receipt of an electronic acknowledgment from an information processing system described in subsection (b) establishes that a record was received but, by itself, does not establish that the content sent corresponds to the content received.

(g) If a person is aware that an electronic record purportedly sent under subsection (a), or purportedly received under subsection (b), was not actually sent or received, the legal effect of the sending or receipt is determined by other applicable law. Except to the extent permitted by the other law, the requirements of this subsection may not be varied by agreement.

Comment

1.   This section provides default rules regarding when and from where an electronic record is sent and when and where an electronic record is received. This section does not address the efficacy of the record that is sent or received. That is, whether a record is unintelligible or unusable by a recipient is a separate issue from whether that record was sent or received. The effectiveness of an illegible record, [and] whether it binds any party, are questions left to other law.

2.   Subsection (a) furnishes rules for determining when an electronic record is sent. The effect of the sending and its import are determined by other law once it is determined that a sending has occurred.

In order to have a proper sending, the subsection requires that information be properly addressed or otherwise directed to the recipient. In order to send within the meaning of this section, there must be specific information which will direct the record to the intended recipient. Although mass electronic sending is not precluded, a general broadcast message, sent to systems rather than individuals, would not suffice as a sending.

The record will be considered sent once it leaves the control of the sender, or comes under the control of the recipient. Records sent through e-mail or the internet will pass through many different server systems. Accordingly, the critical element when more than one system is involved is the loss of control by the sender.

However, the structure of many message delivery systems is such that electronic records may actually never leave the control of the sender. For example, within a university or corporate setting, e-mail sent within the system to another faculty member is technically not out of the sender's control since it never leaves the organization's server. Accordingly, to qualify as a sending, the e-mail must arrive at a point where the recipient has control. This section does not address the effect of an electronic record that is thereafter "pulled back," e.g., removed from a mailbox. The analog in the paper world would be removing a letter from a person's mailbox. As in the case of providing information electronically under Section 8, the recipient's ability to receive a message should be judged from the perspective of whether the sender has done any action which would preclude retrieval. This is especially the case in regard to sending, since the sender must direct the record to a system designated or used by the recipient.

3.   Subsection (b) provides simply that when a record enters the system which the recipient has designated or uses and to which it has access, in a form capable of being processed by that system, it is received. Keying receipt to a system accessible by the recipient removes the potential for a recipient leaving messages with a server or other service in order to avoid receipt. However, the section does not resolve the issue of how the sender proves the time of receipt.

To assure that the recipient retains control of the place of receipt, subsection (b) requires that the system be specified or used by the recipient, and that the system be used or designated for the type of record being sent. Many people have multiple e-mail addresses for different purposes. Subsection (b) assures that recipients can designate the e-mail address or system to be used in a particular transaction. For example, the recipient retains the ability to designate a home e-mail for personal matters, work e-mail for official business, or a separate organizational e-mail solely for the business purposes of that organization. If A sends B a notice at his home which relates to business, it may not be deemed received if B designated his business address as the sole address for business purposes. Whether actual knowledge upon seeing it at home would qualify as receipt is determined under the otherwise applicable substantive law.

4.   Subsections (c) and (d) provide default rules for determining where a record will be considered to have been sent or received. The focus is on the place of business of the recipient and not the physical location of the information processing system, which may bear absolutely no relation to the transaction between the parties. It is not uncommon for users of electronic commerce to communicate from one State to another without knowing the location of information systems through which communication is operated. In addition, the location of certain communication systems may change without either of the parties being aware of the change. Accordingly, where the place of sending or receipt is an issue under other applicable law, e.g.,

conflict of laws issues, tax issues, the relevant location should be the location of the sender or recipient and not the location of the information processing system.

Subsection (d) assures individual flexibility in designating the place from which a record will be considered sent or at which a record will be considered received. Under subsection (d) a person may designate the place of sending or receipt unilaterally in an electronic record. This ability, as with the ability to designate by agreement, may be limited by otherwise applicable law to places having a reasonable relationship to the transaction.

5.   Subsection (e) makes clear that receipt is not dependent on a person having notice that the record is in the person's system. Receipt occurs when the record reaches the designated system whether or not the recipient ever retrieves the record. The paper analog is the recipient who never reads a mail notice.

6.   Subsection (f) provides legal certainty regarding the effect of an electronic acknowledgment. It only addresses the fact of receipt, not the quality of the content, nor whether the electronic record was read or "opened."

7.   Subsection (g) limits the parties' ability to vary the method for sending and receipt provided in subsections (a) and (b), when there is a legal requirement for the sending or receipt. As in other circumstances where legal requirements derive from other substantive law, to the extent that the other law permits variation by agreement, this Act does not impose any additional requirements, and provisions of this Act may be varied to the extent provided in the other law.

ELECTRONIC SIGNATURES IN GLOBAL AND NATIONAL COMMERCE ACT

(2000)

[Congress enacted the Electronic Signatures in Global and National Commerce Act ("E-Sign") in 2000. Its purpose is much like that of the Uniform Electronic Transactions Act ("UETA")—to facilitate contracting using electronic records, including electronic contracts, and electronic signatures. E-Sign prevents challenges to the legal effect, validity, or enforceability of contracts that are based only on their electronic form. As indicated in the annotation to UETA in this pamphlet, above, E-Sign applies very broadly to "any transaction in or affecting interstate or foreign commerce." 15 U.S.C. § 7001(a). Consequently, Congress considered whether, as a federal statute, E-Sign should pre-empt UETA and similar state statutes. E-Sign provides that it does not pre-empt UETA if UETA is enacted in its original version (1999), or a state enacts a similar statute. 15 U.S.C. § 7002(a). By superseding state statutes of frauds for many transactions, E-Sign was another important step in modernizing and making uniform the law governing many contracts, including international contracts, to which U.S. law applies. (*See also* the United Nations Convention on the Use of Electronic Communications in International Contracts, below.)

[E-Sign and UETA each addresses some issues that the other does not, and they treat a few issues differently. For example, E-Sign contains special provisions to protect consumers. *See* 15 U.S.C. § 7001(c). Consequently, E-Sign and UETA are both important parts of the law governing contracts.]

Table of Contents

---

§ 7001. General Rule of Validity.

(a) **In General.** Notwithstanding any statute, regulation, or other rule of law (other than this title and title II), with respect to any transaction in or affecting interstate or foreign commerce—

(1) a signature, contract, or other record relating to such transaction may not be denied legal effect, validity, or enforceability solely because it is in electronic form; and

(2) a contract relating to such transaction may not be denied legal effect, validity, or enforceability solely because an electronic signature or electronic record was used in its formation.

(b) **Preservation of Rights and Obligations.** This title does not—

(1) limit, alter, or otherwise affect any requirement imposed by a statute, regulation, or rule of law relating to the rights and obligations of persons under such statute, regulation, or rule of law other than a requirement that contracts or other records be written, signed, or in nonelectronic form; or

(2) require any person to agree to use or accept electronic records or electronic signatures, other than a governmental agency with respect to a record other than a contract to which it is a party.

(c) **Consumer Disclosures.**

(1) **Consent to Electronic Records.** Notwithstanding subsection (a), if a statute, regulation, or other rule of law requires that information relating to a transaction or transactions in or affecting interstate or foreign commerce be provided or made available to a consumer in writing, the use of an electronic record to provide or make available (whichever is required) such information satisfies the requirement that such information be in writing if—

(A) the consumer has affirmatively consented to such use and has not withdrawn such consent;

(B) the consumer, prior to consenting, is provided with a clear and conspicuous statement—

(i) informing the consumer of (I) any right or option of the consumer to have the record provided or made available on paper or in nonelectronic form, and (II) the right of the consumer to withdraw the consent to have the record provided or made available in an electronic form and of any conditions, consequences (which may include termination of the parties' relationship), or fees in the event of such withdrawal;

(ii) informing the consumer of whether the consent applies (I) only to the particular transaction which gave rise to the obligation to provide the record, or (II) to identified categories of records that may be provided or made available during the course of the parties' relationship;

(iii) describing the procedures the consumer must use to withdraw consent as provided in clause (i) and to update information needed to contact the consumer electronically; and

(iv) informing the consumer (I) how, after the consent, the consumer may, upon request, obtain a paper copy of an electronic record, and (II) whether any fee will be charged for such copy;

(C) the consumer—

(i) prior to consenting, is provided with a statement of the hardware and software requirements for access to and retention of the electronic records; and

(ii) consents electronically, or confirms his or her consent electronically, in a manner that reasonably demonstrates that the consumer can access information in the electronic form that will be used to provide the information that is the subject of the consent; and

(D) after the consent of a consumer in accordance with subparagraph (A), if a change in the hardware or software requirements needed to access or retain electronic records creates a material risk that the consumer will not be able to access or retain a subsequent electronic record that was the subject of the consent, the person providing the electronic record—

(i) provides the consumer with a statement of (I) the revised hardware and software requirements for access to and retention of the electronic records, and (II) the right to withdraw consent without the imposition of any fees for such withdrawal and without the imposition of any condition or consequence that was not disclosed under subparagraph (B)(i); and

(ii) again complies with subparagraph (C).

(2) **Other Rights.**

(A) **Preservation of Consumer Protections.** Nothing in this title affects the content or timing of any disclosure or other record required to be provided or made available to any consumer under any statute, regulation, or other rule of law.

(B) **Verification or Acknowledgment.** If a law that was enacted prior to this Act expressly requires a record to be provided or made available by a specified method that requires verification or acknowledgment of receipt, the record may be provided or made available electronically only if the method used provides verification or acknowledgment of receipt (whichever is required).

(3) **Effect of Failure to Obtain Electronic Consent or Confirmation of Consent.** The legal effectiveness, validity, or enforceability of any contract executed by a consumer shall not be denied solely because of the failure to obtain electronic consent or confirmation of consent by that consumer in accordance with paragraph (1)(C)(ii).

(4) **Prospective Effect.** Withdrawal of consent by a consumer shall not affect the legal effectiveness, validity, or enforceability of electronic records provided or made available to that consumer in accordance with paragraph (1) prior to implementation of the consumer's withdrawal of consent. A consumer's withdrawal of consent shall be effective within a reasonable period of time after receipt of the withdrawal by the provider of the record. Failure to comply with paragraph (1)(D) may, at the election of the consumer, be treated as a withdrawal of consent for purposes of this paragraph.

(5) **Prior Consent.** This subsection does not apply to any records that are provided or made available to a consumer who has consented prior to the effective date of this title to receive such records in electronic form as permitted by any statute, regulation, or other rule of law.

(6) **Oral Communications.** An oral communication or a recording of an oral communication shall not qualify as an electronic record for purposes of this subsection except as otherwise provided under applicable law. . . .

(e) **Accuracy and Ability to Retain Contracts and Other Records.** Notwithstanding subsection (a), if a statute, regulation, or other rule of law requires that a contract or other record relating to a transaction in or affecting interstate or foreign commerce be in writing, the legal effect, validity, or enforceability of an electronic record of such contract or other record may be denied if such electronic record is not in a form that is capable of being retained and accurately reproduced for later reference by all parties or persons who are entitled to retain the contract or other record. . . .

(h) **Electronic Agents.** A contract or other record relating to a transaction in or affecting interstate or foreign commerce may not be denied legal effect, validity, or enforceability solely because its formation, creation, or delivery involved the action of one or more electronic agents so long as the action of any such electronic agent is legally attributable to the person to be bound.

§ 7002. Exemption to Preemption.

(a) **In General.** A State statute, regulation, or other rule of law may modify, limit, or supersede the provisions of section 101 with respect to State law only if such statute, regulation, or rule of law—

(1) constitutes an enactment or adoption of the Uniform Electronic Transactions Act as approved and recommended for enactment in all the States by the National Conference of Commissioners on Uniform State Laws in 1999, except that any exception to the scope of such Act enacted by a State under section 3(b)(4) of such Act shall be preempted to the extent such exception is inconsistent with this title or title II, or would not be permitted under paragraph (2)(A)(ii) of this subsection; or

(2)(A) specifies the alternative procedures or requirements for the use or acceptance (or both) of electronic records or electronic signatures to establish the legal effect, validity, or enforceability of contracts or other records, if—

    (i) such alternative procedures or requirements are consistent with this title and title II; and

    (ii) such alternative procedures or requirements do not require, or accord greater legal status or effect to, the implementation or application of a specific technology or technical specification for performing the functions of creating, storing, generating, receiving, communicating, or authenticating electronic records or electronic signatures; and

(B) if enacted or adopted after the date of the enactment of this Act, makes specific reference to this Act. . . .

(c) **Prevention of Circumvention**. Subsection (a) does not permit a State to circumvent this title or title II through the imposition of nonelectronic delivery methods under section 8(b)(2) of the Uniform Electronic Transactions Act.

§ 7003. Specific Exceptions.

(a) **Excepted Requirements.** The provisions of section 101 shall not apply to a contract or other record to the extent it is governed by—

(1) a statute, regulation, or other rule of law governing the creation and execution of wills, codicils, or testamentary trusts;

(2) a State statute, regulation, or other rule of law governing adoption, divorce, or other matters of family law; or

(3) the Uniform Commercial Code, as in effect in any State, other than sections 1–107 and 1–206 and Articles 2 and 2A. . . .

§ 7006. Definitions.

For purposes of this title:

(1) **Consumer.** The term "consumer" means an individual who obtains, through a transaction, products or services which are used primarily for personal, family, or household purposes, and also means the legal representative of such an individual.

(2) **Electronic.** The term "electronic" means relating to technology having electrical, digital, magnetic, wireless, optical, electromagnetic, or similar capabilities.

(3) **Electronic Agent.** The term "electronic agent" means a computer program or an electronic or other automated means used independently to initiate an action or respond to electronic records or performances in whole or in part without review or action by an individual at the time of the action or response.

(4) **Electronic Record.** The term "electronic record" means a contract or other record created, generated, sent, communicated, received, or stored by electronic means.

(5) **Electronic Signature.** The term "electronic signature" means an electronic sound, symbol, or process, attached to or logically associated with a contract or other record and executed or adopted by a person with the intent to sign the record.

(6) **Federal Regulatory Agency.** The term "Federal regulatory agency" means an agency, as that term is defined in section 552(f) of title 5, United States Code.

(7) **Information.** The term "information" means data, text, images, sounds, codes, computer programs, software, databases, or the like.

(8) **Person.** The term "person" means an individual, corporation, business trust, estate, trust, partnership, limited liability company, association, joint venture, governmental agency, public corporation, or any other legal or commercial entity.

(9) **Record.** The term "record" means information that is inscribed on a tangible medium or that is stored in an electronic or other medium and is retrievable in perceivable form.

(10) **Requirement.** The term "requirement" includes a prohibition.

(11) **Self-Regulatory Organization.**—The term "self-regulatory organization" means an organization or entity that is not a Federal regulatory agency or a State, but that is under the supervision of a Federal regulatory agency and is authorized under Federal law to adopt and administer rules applicable to its members that are enforced by such organization or entity, by a Federal regulatory agency, or by another self-regulatory organization.

(12) **State.** The term "State" includes the District of Columbia and the territories and possessions of the United States.

(13) **Transaction.** The term "transaction" means an action or set of actions relating to the conduct of business, consumer, or commercial affairs between two or more persons, including any of the following types of conduct—

    (A)   the sale, lease, exchange, licensing, or other disposition of (i) personal property, including goods and intangibles, (ii) services, and (iii) any combination thereof; and

    (B)   the sale, lease, exchange, or other disposition of any interest in real property, or any combination thereof. . . .

AMERICAN LAW INSTITUTE PRINCIPLES OF THE LAW OF SOFTWARE CONTRACTS

As Adopted and Promulgated
by
THE AMERICAN LAW INSTITUTE AT WASHINGTON D.C.
May 19, 2009

[Unlike the American Law Institute's ("ALI's") restatements of the law, its more recently developed "Principles" series does not purport to state the rules and standards of existing law. Instead, the Principles aim to make the law better by advising courts, legislatures, and governmental agencies about what the law should be. Accordingly, like the Restatements, the Principles are not binding until some law-making institution adopts one or more of them. However, the ALI is a highly respected organization. Its works go through an extremely thorough process of development, in which eminent professors of law, judges, and practicing lawyers participate. Its restatements of the law have been influential. Consequently, the ALI hopes that its Principles series will also guide the development of the law, especially where the law needs modernization.

[The Principles of the Law of Software Contracts ("PLSC") addresses the law that should apply to contracting in one specific, rapidly changing technological environment. These Principles apply broadly to agreements for the transfer of software for a consideration, including sales, leases, licenses, and sharing arrangements. PLSC § 1.06. Some provisions concern issues that some courts have addressed, such as contracting over the Internet when a transferee signifies agreement by clicking on a button placed ahead of a standard form contract's terms. *Id.* at § 2.02(c)(3). Other provisions concern issues not yet adjudicated or otherwise decided.

[The future influence of the PLSC must be considered cloudy. Other major efforts to introduce new law governing software and similar new-technology contracts have been so controversial that the efforts failed. Two examples are the National Conference of Commissioners on Uniform State Law's Uniform Computer Information Act (2002) (enacted by only two states) and the amendments to Article 2 of the Uniform Commercial Code (2003) (not enacted by any state). The latter failed mainly because the text left it unclear whether the amended Article 2 would apply to software and similar contracts when the software was not in a tangible form, such as a computer disc.]

TABLE OF CONTENTS

CHAPTER 1. DEFINITIONS, SCOPE, AND GENERAL TERMS

TOPIC 1. DEFINITIONS

CHAPTER 4. REMEDIES

CHAPTER 1

DEFINITIONS, SCOPE, AND GENERAL TERMS

TOPIC 1. DEFINITIONS

§ 1.01. Definitions.

As used in these Principles

(a) Access Agreement

An "access agreement" is an agreement that authorizes the user of software to access the provider's software via a data-transmission system, such as the Internet, or via a private network or another intermediary now known or hereafter developed.

(b) Agreement

An "agreement" is the bargain of the parties in fact as found in their language or other circumstances, including course of performance, course of dealing, or usage of trade.

(c) Computer

A "computer" is an electronic device that processes information and follows instructions to accomplish a result.

(d) Consumer Agreement

A "consumer agreement" is an agreement for the transfer of software or access to software primarily for personal, family, or household purposes.

(e) Contract

A "contract" is the total legal obligation that results from the parties' agreement, these Principles, and any other applicable law.

(f) Digital Content

"Digital content" consists of "digital art" or a "digital database."

(1) "Digital art" is literary and artistic information stored electronically, such as music, photographs, motion pictures, books, newspapers, and other images and sounds.

(2) A "digital database" is a compilation of facts arranged in a systematic manner and stored electronically. A digital database does not include digital art.

(g) Digital-Content Player

A "digital-content player" consists of software that renders digital content visible, audible, or otherwise perceivable.

(h) Electronic

"Electronic" means technology having electrical, digital, magnetic, wireless, optical, electromagnetic, or similar capabilities.

(i) Record

A "record" is information that is inscribed on a tangible medium or that is stored in an electronic or other medium and is retrievable in perceivable form.

(j)   Software

    (1)   "Software" consists of statements or instructions that are executed by a computer to produce a certain result.

    (2)   Software does not include digital content, but does include a digital-content player.

(k)   Standard Form and Standard Term

    (1)   A "standard form" is a record regularly used to embody terms of agreements of the same type.

    (2)   A "standard term" is a term appearing in a standard form and relating to a particular matter.

(*l*)   Standard-Form Transfer of Generally Available Software

A "standard-form transfer of generally available software" is a transfer using a standard form of

    (1)   a small number of copies of software to an end user; or

    (2)   the right to access software to a small number of end users if the software is generally available to the public under substantially the same standard terms.

(m)   Transfer

A "transfer" is a conveyance of rights in software or an authorization to access software, including by way of sale, license, lease, or access agreement.

(n)   Transferor and Transferee

    (1)   Except where otherwise provided, a "transferor" is a party who, pursuant to an agreement with the transferee, has transferred or has agreed to transfer software.

    (2)   Except where otherwise provided, a "transferee" is party who, pursuant to an agreement with the transferor, has received or has agreed to receive rights in or access to software.

TOPIC 2. SCOPE

§ 1.06. Scope; Generally.

    (a)   These Principles apply to agreements for the transfer of software for a consideration. Software agreements include agreements to sell, lease, license, access, or otherwise transfer or share software.

    (b)   These Principles do not apply to

    (1)   the transfer of any disk, CD-ROM, or other tangible medium that stores the software, or

    (2)   the transfer of a security interest in software.

§ 1.07. Scope; Embedded Software.

    (a)   Subject to § 1.06, these Principles apply to agreements for the transfer of software embedded in goods if a reasonable transferor would believe the transferee's predominant purpose for engaging in the transfer is to obtain the software.

    (b)   These Principles apply to agreements for the transfer of embedded software only if these Principles applied to the transfer of the embedded software being upgraded or replaced.

§ 1.08. Scope; Mixed Transfers Including Non-Embedded Software.

(a) For purposes of this section,

    (1) "goods" include any embedded software, and

    (2) A "mixed transfer" constitutes a single transaction that consists of the transfer of non-embedded software and any combination of goods, digital content, and services.

(b) Subject to § 1.06, in the case of an agreement for a mixed transfer, these Principles apply to the transfer of the non-embedded software unless the transfer also includes digital content or services and a reasonable transferor would believe the transferee's predominant purpose for engaging in the transfer is to obtain the digital content or services.

§ 1.09. Enforcement of Terms under Federal Intellectual Property Law.

A term of an agreement is unenforceable if it (a) conflicts with a mandatory rule of federal intellectual property law; or (b) conflicts impermissibly with the purposes and policies of federal intellectual property law; or (c) would constitute federal intellectual property misuse in an infringement proceeding.

§ 1.10. Public Policy.

A term of an agreement is unenforceable if the interest in enforcement of the term is clearly outweighed in the circumstances by a public policy against its enforcement.

§ 1.11. Unconscionability.

(a) If the court as a matter of law finds the agreement of any term of the agreement to have been unconscionable at the time it was made, the court may refuse to enforce the agreement, or it may enforce the remainder of the agreement without the unconscionable term, or it may so limit the application of any unconscionable term to avoid any unconscionable result.

(b) When it is claimed or appears to the court that the agreement or any term thereof may be unconscionable, the parties shall be afforded a reasonable opportunity to present evidence as to its commercial setting, purpose, and effect to aid the court in making the determination.

§ 1.12. Relation to Outside Law.

These Principles should be considered in the context of other applicable law.

TOPIC 3. GENERAL TERMS

§ 1.13. Choice of Law in Standard-Form Transfers of Generally Available Software.

(a) The parties to a standard-form transfer of generally available software may by agreement select the law of a domestic or foreign jurisdiction to govern their rights and duties with respect to an issue in contract if their transaction bears a reasonable relationship to the selected jurisdiction. However, if application of the selected law to an issue would lead to a result that is repugnant to public policy as expressed in the law of the jurisdiction that would otherwise govern under subsection (b), then the law of the jurisdiction chosen by subsection (b) governs with respect to that issue.

(b) In the absence of an enforceable agreement on choice of law, the rights and duties of the parties to a standard-form transfer of generally available software with respect to an issue in contract are determined

    (1) in the case of a consumer agreement, by the law of the jurisdiction where the consumer is located; and

(2) in all other cases, by the law of the jurisdiction where the transferor is located.

(c) For purposes of subsection (b):

(1) an individual is located at the individual's principal residence.

(2) an organization that has only one place of business is located at its place of business.

(3) an organization that has more than one place of business is located at its chief executive office.

(4) an organization that does not have a physical place of business is located at its place of incorporation or primary registration.

§ 1.14. Forum-Selection Clauses.

The parties may by agreement choose an exclusive forum unless the choice is unfair or unreasonable. A forum choice may be unfair or unreasonable if:

(a) the forum is unreasonably inconvenient for a party;

(b) the agreement as to the forum was obtained by misrepresentation, duress, the abuse of economic power, or other unconscionable means;

(c) the forum does not have power under its domestic law to entertain the action or to award remedies otherwise available; or

(d) enforcement of the forum-selection clause would be repugnant to public policy as expressed in the law of the forum in which suit is brought.

CHAPTER 2

FORMATION AND ENFORCEMENT

TOPIC 1. FORMATION GENERALLY

§ 2.01. Formation, Generally.

(a)   Subject to § 2.02, a contract may be formed in any manner sufficient to show an agreement, including by offer and acceptance and by conduct.

(b)   A contract may be formed under subsection (a) even though

(1)   one or more terms are left open, if there is a reasonably certain basis for granting an appropriate remedy in the event of a breach; or

(2)   the parties' records are different. In such a case, the terms of the contract are

(A)   terms, whether in a record or not, to which both parties agree;

(B)   terms that appear in the records of both parties; and

(C)   terms supplied by these Principles or other law.

TOPIC 2. STANDARD-FORM TRANSFERS OF GENERALLY AVAILABLE SOFTWARE; ENFORCEMENT OF THE STANDARD FORM

§ 2.02. Standard-Form Transfers of Generally Available Software: Enforcement of the Standard Form.

(a)   This Section applies to standard-form transfers of generally available software as defined in § 1.01(1).

(b)   A transferee adopts a standard form as a contract when a reasonable transferor would believe the transferee intends to be bound to the form.

(c)   A transferee will be deemed to have adopted a standard form as a contract if

(1)   the standard form is reasonably accessible electronically prior to initiation of the transfer at issue;

(2)   upon initiating the transfer, the transferee has reasonable notice of and access to the standard form before payment or, if there is no payment, before completion of the transfer;

(3)   in the case of an electronic transfer of software, the transferee signifies agreement at the end of or adjacent to the electronic standard form, or in the case of a standard form printed on or attached to packaged software or separately wrapped from the software, the transferee does not exercise the opportunity to return the software unopened for a full refund within a reasonable time after the transfer; and

(4)   the transferee can store and reproduce the standard form if presented electronically.

(d)   Subject to § 1.10 (public policy), § 1.11 (unconscionability), and other invalidating defenses supplied by these Principles or outside law, a standard term is enforceable if reasonably comprehensible.

(e)   If a transferee asserts that it did not adopt a standard form as a contract under subsection (b) or asserts a failure of the transferor to comply with subsection (c) or (d), the transferor has the burden of production and persuasion on the issue of compliance with the subsections.

TOPIC 3. CONTRACT MODIFICATION

§ 2.03. Contract Modification.

(a) Subject to subsection (c), an agreement modifying a contract is enforceable without consideration and may be formed in any manner sufficient to show an agreement, including by offer and acceptance and by conduct.

(b) In the case of an electronic transfer of software, a transferee will be deemed to have agreed to a modification of the transferee receives reasonable electronic notice of the modification and the transferee signifies agreement to the modification electronically at the end of or adjacent to the electronic notice.

(c) An agreement modifying a contract is not enforceable if

(1) A party agrees to the modification as a result of fraud, duress, or another invalidating cause, or

(2) The contract being modified is in a record that includes a no-oral-modification or other clause excluding modification except by an authenticated record, and the modifications oral or unauthenticated by the party contesting the modification, unless the other party has reasonably relied on a waiver of the no-oral-modification or other clause.

(d) Subject to subsection (a) through (c), the parties may agree in their contract to procedures for unmodifying it. However, in the case of a standard-form transfer of generally available software, mere notice of a material modification sent by one party is insufficient to prove agreement by the other party, even if the original contract authorizes this manner of modifying the contract.]

CHAPTER 3

PERFORMANCE

TOPIC 1. INDEMNIFICATION AND WARRANTIES

§ 3.01. Implied Indemnification Against Infringement.

(a)   Except as provided in (d) or as excluded or modified under (e), a transferor that deals in software of the kind transferred or holds itself out by occupation as having knowledge or skill peculiar to the software, and that receives money or a right to payment of a monetary obligation in exchange for the software, must indemnify and hold the transferee harmless against any claim of a third party based on infringement of an intellectual property or like right which right exists at the time of transfer and is based on the laws of the United States or a State thereof. The transferor must pay those costs and damages incurred by the transferee that are specifically attributable to such claim or those costs and damages agreed to in a monetary settlement of such claim.

(b)   If a court enjoins the transferee's use of the software or holds the software infringing or otherwise in violation of a like right under subsection (a), the transferor may be liable for damages under § 4.05 and must at its own expense and on reasonable notice from the transferee of its desire for a remedy provide the transferee with one of the following remedies as the transferor chooses:

(1)   procure for the transferee at no cost to the transferee the continued right to use the software under the terms of the applicable agreement;

(2)   replace or modify the software with non-infringing software of substantially equivalent functionality; or

(3)   cancel the applicable agreement and refund to the transferee the fees actually paid by the transferee for the infringing components of the software. If the infringement renders the software substantially unusable, the transferor must refund the entire fee. In either case, the transferor must also reimburse the transferee for incidental expenses incurred in replacing the software, but the transferor may deduct from the amounts due to the transferee under this section a reasonable allowance for the period of time the transferee used the software.

(c)   The indemnification law of the state whose law applies to the agreement under § 1.13 or under otherwise applicable law applies to the duty of indemnification of subsection (a).

(d)   Unless otherwise agreed, a transferor has no obligations under subsections (a) and (b) if

(1)   the transferee uses or modifies the software in a manner not in accordance with the terms of the agreement where such use or modification gives rise to the claim; or

(2)   the infringement arises from the transferor's compliance with (i) transferee-provided functional specifications; and (ii) a transferee-provided method or process for implementation of those specifications, unless the transferor knows of potential infringement or a claim of infringement at the time of transfer and does not notify the transferee that compliance with the specifications and method or process may result in an infringement.

(e)   Indemnification under subsection (a) and the duties of subsection (b) may be excluded or modified

(1)   if the exclusion or modification is in a record, is conspicuous, and uses language that gives the transferee reasonable notice of the modification or notice that the transferor has no obligation to indemnify the transferee; or

(2)   by course of performance, course of dealing, or usage of trade.

§ 3.02. Express Quality Warranties.

(a)   In this Section "transferee" includes both an "immediate transferee" that enters an agreement with the transferor and a "remote transferee" that receives the software or access to the software in the normal chain of distribution.

(b)   Except as provided in subsection (d), the transferor creates an express warranty to the transferee as follows:

(1)   An affirmation of fact or promise made by the transferor to the transferee, including by advertising or by a record packaged with or accompanying the software, that relates to the software and on which a reasonable transferee could rely creates an express warranty that the software will conform to the affirmation of fact or promise.

(2)   Any description of the software made by the transferor to the transferee on which a reasonable transferee could rely creates an express warranty that the software will conform to the description.

(3)   Any demonstration of software shown by the transferor to the transferee on which a reasonable transferee could rely creates an express warranty that the software will conform to the demonstration.

(c)   A transferor can create an express warranty without using formal words, such as "warrant" or "guarantee," or without intending to create an express warranty. However, a mere opinion or commendation of the software does not create an express warranty.

(d)   A distributor or dealer that merely transfers software covered by a warranty in a record made by another party, which warranty identifies the maker of the record as the warrantor, is not liable for breach of the warranty. The distributor or dealer is liable for any express warranties of its own or if it adopts the maker's warranty.

§ 3.03. Implied Warranty of Merchantability.

(a)   Unless excluded or modified, a transferor that deals in software of the kind transferred or that holds itself out by occupation as having knowledge or skill peculiar to the software warrants to the transferee that the software is merchantable.

(b)   Merchantable software at minimum must

(1)   pass without objection in the trade under the contract description; and

(2)   be fit for the ordinary purposes for which such software is used; and

(3)   be adequately packaged and labeled.

§ 3.04. Implied Warranty of Fitness for a Particular Purpose.

(a)   Unless excluded or modified, if a transferor at the time of contracting has reason to know any particular purpose for which the transferee requires the software and the transferee relies on the transferor's skill or judgment to select, develop, or furnish the software, the transferor warrants that the software is fit for the transferee's purpose.

(b)   Unless excluded or modified, if an agreement requires a transferor to provide or select a system of hardware and software and the transferor at the time of contracting has reason to know that the transferee is relying on the skill or judgment of the transferor to select the components of the system, the transferor warrants that the software provided or selected will function together with the hardware as a system.

§ 3.05. Other Implied Quality Warranties.

(a) Unless modified or excluded, implied warranties may arise from course of dealing or usage of trade.

(b) A transferor that receives money or a right to payment of a monetary obligation in exchange for the software warrants to any party in the normal chain of distribution that the software contains no material hidden defects of which the transferor was aware at the time of the transfer. This warranty may not be excluded. In addition, this warranty does not displace an action for misrepresentation or its remedies.

§ 3.06. Disclaimer of Express and Implied Quality Warranties.

A statement intending to exclude or modify an express quality warranty is unenforceable if a reasonable transferee would not expect the exclusion or modification.

(a) Unless the circumstances suggest otherwise, all implied quality warranties other than the warranty of no material hidden defects (§ 3.05(b)) are excluded by language in a record communicated to the transferee such as "as is," "with all faults," or other language that a reasonable transferee would believe excludes all implied quality warranties.

(b) The implied warranty of merchantability is excluded if the exclusion is in a record communicated to the transferee, is conspicuous, and mentions "merchantability."

(c) The implied warranty of fitness for a particular purpose is excluded if the exclusion is in a record communicated to the transferee, is conspicuous, and mentions "fitness for a particular purpose."

(d) If before entering an agreement a transferee has tested the software as fully as desired or unreasonably has refused to test it, there are no implied quality warranties with regard to defects that a test should have or would have revealed.

(e) An implied quality warranty other than the warranty of no material hidden defects (§ 3.05(b)) may be excluded or modified by course performance, course dealing, or usage of trade.

(f) Remedies for breach of quality warranties may be limited in accordance with § 4.01 of these Principles.

§ 3.07. Third-Party Beneficiaries of Warranty.

(a) A transferor's warranty extends to any person for whose benefit the transferor intends to supply the software if the person uses the software in a manner contemplated or that should have been contemplated by the transferor.

(b) A transferor's warranty to a consumer extends to the consumer's immediate family, household members, or guests if the transferor reasonably should expect such persons to use the software.

(c) Except as provided in (b), a contractual term that excludes or limits the third parties to which a warranty extends is enforceable.

(d) An exclusion or modification of a warranty that is effective against the transferee is also effective against third parties to which the warranty extends under this Section.

TOPIC 2. PAROL-EVIDENCE RULE AND INTERPRETATION

§ 3.08. Integration, Ambiguity, and Parol Evidence.

(a) A full integration constitutes a record or records intended by the parties as a complete and exclusive statement of the terms of an agreement. A partial integration constitutes a record or records intended by the parties as the complete and exclusive statement of one or more terms of an agreement.

(b) The court should determine whether a record is fully integrated, partially integrated, or not integrated prior to applying subsections (e) and (f). In making this determination, the court should consider all credible and relevant extrinsic evidence, including evidence of agreements and negotiations prior to or contemporaneous with the adoption of the record.

(c) If the transfer is a standard-form transfer of generally available software, a term in a record indicating that the record is fully integrated or partially integrated should be probative but not conclusive on the issue.

(d) The court should determine whether a term in a record is ambiguous prior to applying subsections (e) and (f). In making this determination, the court should consider all credible and relevant extrinsic evidence, including evidence of agreements and negotiations prior to or contemporaneous with the adoption of the record. If a term or terms is ambiguous, extrinsic evidence is admissible to prove the meaning of the term or terms.

(e) Unambiguous terms set forth in a fully integrated record may not be contradicted by evidence of any prior agreement or of a contemporaneous oral agreement, but may be explained by evidence of a course of performance, course of dealing, or usage of trade.

(f) Unambiguous terms set forth in a partially integrated record may not be contradicted by evidence of prior or contemporaneous oral conflicting terms, but may be explained by evidence of course of performance, course of dealing, usage of trade, or consistent additional terms.

(g) Notwithstanding subsections (e) and (f),

    (1) evidence is admissible to prove

        (A) illegality, fraud, duress, mistake, or other invalidating causes; and

        (B) independent agreements; and

    (2) evidence of course of performance, course of dealing, and usage of trade is admissible to supplement a record.

§ 3.09. General Principles of Interpretation.

(a) Words or conduct should be interpreted in accordance with the meaning intended by both parties. Subject to § 3.10, if the parties disagree over that meaning, words or conduct should be interpreted reasonably in light of all of the circumstances.

(b) In determining a reasonable interpretation of the words or conduct, significant factors include:

    (1) each party's purpose or purposes in making the contract;

    (2) any course of performance, course of dealing, or usage of trade; and

    (3) the language of the entire agreement.

§ 3.10. Whose Meaning Prevails.

(a) If the parties disagree over the meaning of words or conduct, the meaning intended by one of them should be enforced if at the time the parties made the agreement that party did not know or have reason to know any different meaning intended by the other party, and the other party knew or had reason to know the meaning intended by the first party.

(b) The parties have not made an enforceable agreement if

    (1) the parties disagree over the meaning of a fundamental term or terms;

    (2) the term or terms is ambiguous; and

    (3) neither party knew or should have known of the other's meaning.

(c)   In all other cases of disagreement as to the meaning of a term or terms, § 3.09 applies.

TOPIC 3. BREACH

§ 3.11. Breach and Material Breach.

(a)   A breach occurs if a party without legal excuse fails to perform an obligation as required by the agreement.

(b)   An uncured breach, whether or not material, entitles the aggrieved party to remedies.

(c)   In determining whether a breach is material, significant factors include:

    (1)   the terms of the agreement;

    (2)   usage of trade, course of dealing, and course of performance;

    (3)   the extent to which the aggrieved party will be deprived of the benefit reasonably expected;

    (4)   the extent to which the aggrieved party can be adequately compensated for the part of the benefit deprived;

    (5)   the degree of harm or likely harm to the aggrieved party; and

    (6)   the extent to which the behavior of the party failing to perform or to offer to perform departs from standards of good faith and fair dealing.

(d)   Notwithstanding subsection (c) or any provision to the contrary in the agreement, a material breach occurs if:

    (1)   the transferor breaches the warranty of § 3.05(b);

    (2)   a limited remedy fails of its essential purpose under § 4.01; or

    (3)   the transferor breaches the agreement by failing to comply with § 4.03.

(e)   The cumulative effect of nonmaterial breaches may be material.

§ 3.12. Cure of Breach.

(a)   Unless otherwise agreed, a party in breach of contract may, on seasonable notice to the aggrieved party and at its own expense, cure the breach by making a conforming performance if:

    (1)   the time for performance has not yet expired and the conforming performance occurs within the time for performance; or

    (2)   the breaching party had reasonable grounds to believe the nonconforming performance would be acceptable with or without money allowance and provides a conforming performance within a further reasonable time after performance was due; or

    (3)   the breaching party seasonably notifies the aggrieved party of its intent to cure and promptly provides a conforming performance before the aggrieved party cancels under § 4.04.

(b)   If a breaching party fails to cure a material breach, the aggrieved party's obligation to perform any remaining duties is suspended except with respect to restrictions on the use of the software. The aggrieved party also may cancel under § 4.04.

(c)   A party may not cancel or refuse to perform because of a breach that has been seasonably cured under subsection (a).

(d)   The cumulative effect of repeated attempts to cure may be a material breach.

CHAPTER 4

REMEDIES

TOPIC 1. AGREEMENTS WITH RESPECT TO REMEDY

§ 4.01. Contractual Modification or Limitation of Remedy.

(a)   Subject to the provisions of subsections (b) and (c) of this Section, § 4.02 (liquidation and limitation of damages), § 4.03(e) (unauthorized automated disablement), and except for damages for breach of the warranty of § 3.05(b) (no material hidden defects),

(1)   the agreement may provide for remedies in addition to or in substitution for those provided in these Principles and may limit or alter the measure of damages recoverable under these Principles, as by limiting the transferee's remedy to return of the software and repayment of the price or to repair and replacement of nonconforming software; and

(2)   resort to a remedy as provided is optional unless the remedy is expressly agreed to be exclusive, in which case it is the sole remedy.

(b)   If circumstances cause an exclusive or limited remedy to fail of its essential purpose, the aggrieved party may recover a remedy as provided in these Principles or applicable outside law.

(c)   Subject to the provisions of § 4.03(e) (unauthorized automated disablement), and except for damages for breach of the warranty of § 3.05(b) (no material hidden defects), consequential damages may be limited or excluded unless the limitation or exclusion is unconscionable at the time of contracting or operates in an unconscionable way. This rule applies even if circumstances cause an exclusive or limited remedy to fail of its essential purpose under subsection (b). Limitation of consequential damages for personal injury in the case of consumer software is prima facie unconscionable but limitation of consequential damages where the loss is commercial is not.

§ 4.02. Liquidation and Limitation of Damages.

(a)   Damages for breach by either party may be liquidated in the agreement but only at an amount that is reasonable in light of the anticipated or actual harm caused by the breach, the difficulties of proof of loss, and the inconvenience or nonfeasibility of otherwise obtaining an adequate remedy. Section 4.01 determines the enforceability of a term that limits but does not liquidate damages.

(b)   If a term liquidating damages is unenforceable under this Section, the aggrieved party may recover a remedy as provided in these Principles, except as limited by other terms of the agreement.

§ 4.03. Use of Automated Disablement to Impair Use.

(a)   "Automated disablement" means the use of electronic means to disable or materially impair the functionality of software.

(b)   A transferor may not use automated disablement if the process results in the loss of rights granted in the agreement or the loss of use of other software or digital content.

(c)   Notwithstanding anything to the contrary in the agreement, a transferor may not use automated disablement as a remedy for breach if the agreement is a standard-form transfer of generally available software or if the transaction is a consumer agreement.

(d)   Subject to subsection (c), if the transferor has a right to cancel under § 4.04, it may do so using automated disablement only if such authorization is provided for in the agreement and under the following circumstances:

(1) the term authorizing automated disablement is conspicuous; and

(2) the transferor provides timely notice of the breach and its intent to use automated disablement and provides the transferee with a reasonable opportunity to cure the breach and the transferee has not so cured; and

(3) the transferor has obtained a court order permitting it to use automated disablement.

(e) A transferee may recover direct, incidental, and consequential damages caused by use of automated disablement in violation of this Section notwithstanding any agreement to the contrary.

(f) Obligations of the transferor and rights of the transferee under this Section may not be waived.

TOPIC 2. REMEDIES IN THE ABSENCE OF AGREEMENT

§ 4.04. Cancellation.

(a) An aggrieved party may cancel a contract on a material breach of the whole contract if the breach has not been cured under § 3.12 or waived.

(b) Cancellation is not effective unless the canceling party gives reasonable notice of cancellation to the party in breach.

(c) Except as otherwise provided in the agreement, upon effective cancellation by the transferor:

(1) of an access contract, any rights of access are discontinued; and

(2) all rights of the transferee in the software provided under the agreement terminate and the transferee must destroy any physical copies of the software or seasonably return them to the transferor, delete all electronic copies on its systems, and refuse delivery of any physical copies.

(d) Except as otherwise provided in the agreement, upon cancellation by either party, all executory obligations of both parties are discharged except those based on a previous breach or performance or those that the parties agreed would survive termination or cancellation.

(e) A cancellation is ineffective if it fails to meet the standard of subsection (a) or the requirements of subsection (b).

§ 4.05. Expectation Damages.

Unless otherwise agreed, damages under these Principles should put the aggrieved party in as good a position as if the other party had fully performed. Damages for lost expectancy include direct, incidental, and consequential damages, less expenses saved in consequence of the breach.

§ 4.06. Specific Performance.

(a) Specific performance may be decreed when the software to be transferred is unique, or in other proper circumstances. Specific performance is not available if it would require the performance of personal services or if an award of damages would be adequate to protect the expectation interest of the transferee.

(b) The decree for specific performance may include such terms and conditions as to payment of the price, damages, confidentiality, and rights in the software as the court may deem just.

(c) An aggrieved transferor who does not cancel may be entitled to a decree requiring adherence to the terms of the agreement as against a breaching transferee, but not if the decree would require the performance of personal services or if an award of damages would be adequate to protect the expectation interest of the transferor.

PART VIII
INTERNATIONAL CONTRACT LAW

UNITED NATIONS CONVENTION ON CONTRACTS FOR THE INTERNATIONAL SALE OF GOODS

(1980)

[In 1969, the United Nations Commission on International Trade Law (UNCITRAL) appointed a working group to prepare a draft of an international convention (treaty) on the sale of goods. The United States was an active participant in the working group. The ultimate result was the Convention for the International Sale of Goods (the CISG), which was adopted in 1980, and came into force in 1988 when it had been ratified by the requisite ten countries.]

The CISG aims to do for international sales of goods essentially what Article 2 of the Uniform Commercial Code did for sales within the U.S. Prior to adoption of the CISG, the parties could agree on which nation's law would apply to their contract by including a choice-of-law provision in the contract. Many contracts, however, did not contain such provisions, and the courts of some nations were (and continue to be) more likely than others to give choice-of-law provisions full effect. In either case, the law that determined the applicable law was (and, for other kinds of international contracts, is) vague and undependable. Moreover, different nations' laws can differ dramatically, especially when different legal traditions shaped them. The result of these complications was considerable uncertainty in the law, which discouraged contracting by making it more costly.

[The CISG's principal purpose is to establish a uniform law and to reduce legal uncertainties for international sales of goods. Because it is an international treaty, it is binding only on Contracting States—those that have ratified, accepted, approved, or acceded to the treaty. CISG, Art. 99(1). As of May 1, 2017, there were more than 80 Contracting States, including the United States and most other major trading nations.

[Following the Senate's advice and consent, the U.S. ratified the CISG in 1986 (subject to certain reservations). It then became part of the "supreme law of the land," pre-empting inconsistent state contract law. U.S. Const., Art. VI(2). Until 2008, it was settled that this treaty is "self-executing;" therefore, federal and state courts applied it as domestic law even though Congress had not acted to make it domestic law. In that year, the U.S. Supreme Court narrowed the self-executing treaty doctrine in a way that unsettles this issue. Medellin v. Texas, 128 S.Ct. 1346, 1368–69 (2008).

[Although in form the CISG is an international treaty, in substance it is a code, much like Article 2 of the UCC. Article 2 governs contracts for the sale of goods between a seller and a buyer in the United States. The CISG governs contracts for the sale of goods (with certain exclusions, such as consumer contracts) between parties who have their places of business in two different countries, both of which have ratified the CISG. Accordingly, if, for example, a United States seller with its place of business in New York enters into a contract for the sale of goods to a buyer with its place of business in France (one of the countries that has ratified the CISG), then unless the parties otherwise provide, the contract is governed by the provisions of the CISG. However, under CISG Article 6 the parties to a contract that would otherwise fall within the CISG may exclude the application of the CISG to the contract or, with certain exceptions, derogate from or vary the effect of any CISG provisions.[1]

[Like the UCC, the CISG does not govern the issue whether a contract is substantively valid; that is, it does not govern matters such as fraud, capacity, duress, mistake, legality, or the like. However, the CISG does govern whether a contract satisfies requisite formal requirements, such as whether a contract is required to be in writing, and also governs matters such as whether a contract was formed and whether a contract is sufficiently definite to be enforceable.]

---

[1]   The CISG is potentially applicable to international sale-of-goods contracts even though one of the parties resides in a country that has not ratified the Convention. However, when the United States ratified the CISG it filed a "reservation" under which it does not adhere to that portion of the CISG that makes the CISG applicable in such cases. Accordingly, the CISG is not applicable to a contract for the sale of goods between a firm with its place of business in the United States and a firm with its place of business in a country that has not ratified the CISG.

CONVENTION ON CONTRACTS FOR THE INTERNATIONAL SALE OF GOODS

THE STATES PARTIES TO THIS CONVENTION

BEARING IN MIND the broad objectives in the resolutions adopted by the sixth special session of the General Assembly of the United Nations on the establishment of a New International Economic Order,

CONSIDERING that the development of international trade on the basis of equality and mutual benefit is an important element in promoting friendly relations among States,

BEING OF THE OPINION that the adoption of uniform rules which govern contracts for the international sale of goods and take into account the different social, economic and legal systems would contribute to the removal of legal barriers in international trade and promote the development of international trade,

HAVE AGREED as follows:

PART I. SPHERE OF APPLICATION AND GENERAL PROVISIONS

CHAPTER I. SPHERE OF APPLICATION

Article 1

(1)   This Convention applies to contracts of sale of goods between parties whose places of business are in different States:

(a)   when the States are Contracting States; or

(b)   when the rules of private international law lead to the application of the law of a Contracting State.

(2)   The fact that the parties have their places of business in different States is to be disregarded whenever this fact does not appear either from the contract or from any dealings between, or from information disclosed by, the parties at any time before or at the conclusion of the contract.

(3)   Neither the nationality of the parties nor the civil or commercial character of the parties or of the contract is to be taken into consideration in determining the application of this Convention.

[The United States has declared a reservation under Article 95, and therefore is not bound by Article 1(1)(b).]

Article 2

This Convention does not apply to sales:

(a)   of goods bought for personal, family or household use, unless the seller, at any time before or at the conclusion of the contract, neither knew nor ought to have known that the goods were bought for any such use;

(b)   by auction;

(c)   on execution or otherwise by authority of law;

(d)   of stocks, shares, investment securities, negotiable instruments or money;

(e)   of ships, vessels, hovercraft or aircraft;

(f)   of electricity.

Article 3

(1)   Contracts for the supply of goods to be manufactured or produced are to be considered sales unless the party who orders the goods undertakes to supply a substantial part of the materials necessary for such manufacture or production.

(2)   This Convention does not apply to contracts in which the preponderant part of the obligations of the party who furnishes the goods consists in the supply of labour or other services.

Article 4

This Convention governs only the formation of the contract of sale and the rights and obligations of the seller and the buyer arising from such a contract. In particular, except as otherwise expressly provided in this Convention, it is not concerned with:

(a)   the validity of the contract or of any of its provisions or of any usage;

(b)   the effect which the contract may have on the property in the goods sold.

Article 5

This Convention does not apply to the liability of the seller for death or personal injury caused by the goods to any person.

Article 6

The parties may exclude the application of this Convention or, subject to Article 12, derogate from or vary the effect of any of its provisions.

CHAPTER II. GENERAL PROVISIONS

Article 7

(1)   In the interpretation of this Convention, regard is to be had to its international character and to the need to promote uniformity in its application and the observance of good faith in international trade.

(2)   Questions concerning matters governed by this Convention which are not expressly settled in it are to be settled in conformity with the general principles on which it is based or, in the absence of such principles, in conformity with the law applicable by virtue of the rules of private international law.

Article 8

(1)   For the purposes of this Convention statements made by and other conduct of a party are to be interpreted according to his intent where the other party knew or could not have been unaware what that intent was.

(2)   If the preceding paragraph is not applicable, statements made by and other conduct of a party are to be interpreted according to the understanding that a reasonable person of the same kind as the other party would have had in the same circumstances.

(3)   In determining the intent of a party or the understanding a reasonable person would have had, due consideration is to be given to all relevant circumstances of the case including the negotiations, any practices which the parties have established between themselves, usages and any subsequent conduct of the parties.

Article 9

(1)   The parties are bound by any usage to which they have agreed and by any practices which they have established between themselves.

(2)   The parties are considered, unless otherwise agreed, to have impliedly made applicable to their contract or its formation a usage of which the parties knew or ought to have known and which in international trade is widely known to, and regularly observed by, parties to contracts of the type involved in the particular trade concerned.

Article 10

For the purposes of this Convention:

(a)   if a party has more than one place of business, the place of business is that which has the closest relationship to the contract and its performance, having regard to the circumstances known to or contemplated by the parties at any time before or at the conclusion of the contract;

(b)   if a party does not have a place of business, reference is to be made to his habitual residence.

Article 11

A contract of sale need not be concluded in or evidenced by writing and is not subject to any other requirement as to form. It may be proved by any means, including witnesses.

Article 12

Any provision of article 11, article 29 or Part II of this Convention that allows a contract of sale or its modification or termination by agreement or any offer, acceptance or other indication of intention to be made in any form other than in writing does not apply where any party has his place of business in a Contracting State which has made a declaration under article 96 of this Convention. The parties may not derogate from or vary the effect of this article.

Article 13

For the purposes of this Convention "writing" includes telegram and telex.

PART II. FORMATION OF THE CONTRACT

Article 14

(1)   A proposal for concluding a contract addressed to one or more specific persons constitutes an offer if it is sufficiently definite and indicates the intention of the offeror to be bound in case of acceptance. A proposal is sufficiently definite if it indicates the goods and expressly or implicitly fixes or makes provision for determining the quantity and the price.

(2)   A proposal other than one addressed to one or more specific persons is to be considered merely as an invitation to make offers, unless the contrary is clearly indicated by the person making the proposal.

Article 15

(1)   An offer becomes effective when it reaches the offeree.

(2)   An offer, even if it is irrevocable, may be withdrawn if the withdrawal reaches the offeree before or at the same time as the offer.

Article 16

(1)   Until a contract is concluded an offer may be revoked if the revocation reaches the offeree before he has dispatched an acceptance.

(2)   However, an offer cannot be revoked:

(a)   if it indicates, whether by stating a fixed time for acceptance or otherwise, that it is irrevocable; or

(b)   if it was reasonable for the offeree to rely on the offer as being irrevocable and the offeree has acted in reliance on the offer.

Article 17

An offer, even if it is irrevocable, is terminated when a rejection reaches the offeror.

Article 18

(1)   A statement made by or other conduct of the offeree indicating assent to an offer is an acceptance. Silence or inactivity does not in itself amount to acceptance.

(2)   An acceptance of an offer becomes effective at the moment the indication of assent reaches the offeror. An acceptance is not effective if the indication of assent does not reach the offeror within the time he has fixed or, if no time is fixed, within a reasonable time, due account being taken of the circumstances of the transaction, including the rapidity of the means of communication employed by the offeror. An oral offer must be accepted immediately unless the circumstances indicate otherwise.

(3)   However, if, by virtue of the offer or as a result of practices which the parties have established between themselves or of usage, the offeree may indicate assent by performing an act, such as one relating to the dispatch of the goods or payment of the price, without notice to the offeror, the acceptance is effective at the moment the act is performed, provided that the act is performed within the period of time laid down in the preceding paragraph.

Article 19

(1)   A reply to an offer which purports to be an acceptance but contains additions, limitations or other modifications is a rejection of the offer and constitutes a counter-offer.

(2)   However, a reply to an offer which purports to be an acceptance but contains additional or different terms which do not materially alter the terms of the offer constitutes an acceptance, unless the offeror, without undue delay, objects orally to the discrepancy or dispatches a notice to that effect. If he does not so object, the terms of the contract are the terms of the offer with the modifications contained in the acceptance.

(3)   Additional or different terms relating, among other things, to the price, payment, quality and quantity of the goods, place and time of delivery, extent of one party's liability to the other or the settlement of disputes are considered to alter the terms of the offer materially.

Article 20

(1)   A period of time for acceptance fixed by the offeror in a telegram or a letter begins to run from the moment the telegram is handed in for dispatch or from the date shown on the letter or, if no such date is shown, from the date shown on the envelope. A period of time for acceptance fixed by the offeror by telephone, telex or other means of instantaneous communication, begins to run from the moment that the offer reaches the offeree.

(2)   Official holidays or non-business days occurring during the period for acceptance are included in calculating the period. However, if a notice of acceptance cannot be delivered at the address of the offeror on the last day of the period because that day falls on an official holiday or a non-business

day at the place of business of the offeror, the period is extended until the first business day which follows.

Article 21

(1)   A late acceptance is nevertheless effective as an acceptance if without delay the offeror orally so informs the offeree or dispatches a notice to that effect.

(2)   If a letter or other writing containing a late acceptance shows that it has been sent in such circumstances that if its transmission had been normal it would have reached the offeror in due time, the late acceptance is effective as an acceptance unless, without delay, the offeror orally informs the offeree that he considers his offer as having lapsed or dispatches a notice to that effect.

Article 22

An acceptance may be withdrawn if the withdrawal reaches the offeror before or at the same time as the acceptance would have become effective.

Article 23

A contract is concluded at the moment when an acceptance of an offer becomes effective in accordance with the provisions of this Convention.

Article 24

For the purposes of this Part of the Convention, an offer, declaration of acceptance or any other indication of intention "reaches" the addressee when it is made orally to him or delivered by any other means to him personally, to his place of business or mailing address or, if he does not have a place of business or mailing address, to his habitual residence.

PART III. SALE OF GOODS

CHAPTER I. GENERAL PROVISIONS

Article 25

A breach of contract committed by one of the parties is fundamental if it results in such detriment to the other party as substantially to deprive him of what he is entitled to expect under the contract, unless the party in breach did not foresee and a reasonable person of the same kind in the same circumstances would not have foreseen such a result.

Article 26

A declaration of avoidance of the contract is effective only if made by notice to the other party.

Article 27

Unless otherwise expressly provided in this Part of the Convention, if any notice, request or other communication is given or made by a party in accordance with this Part and by means appropriate in the circumstances, a delay or error in the transmission of the communication or its failure to arrive does not deprive that party of the right to rely on the communication.

Article 28

If, in accordance with the provisions of this Convention, one party is entitled to require performance of any obligation by the other party, a court is not bound to enter a judgment for specific performance unless the court would do so under its own law in respect of similar contracts of sale not governed by this Convention.

Article 29

(1)   A contract may be modified or terminated by the mere agreement of the parties.

(2)   A contract in writing which contains a provision requiring any modification or termination by agreement to be in writing may not be otherwise modified or terminated by agreement. However, a party may be precluded by his conduct from asserting such a provision to the extent that the other party has relied on that conduct.

CHAPTER II. OBLIGATIONS OF THE SELLER

Article 30

The seller must deliver the goods, hand over any documents relating to them and transfer the property in the goods, as required by the contract and this Convention.

SECTION I.

DELIVERY OF THE GOODS AND HANDING OVER OF DOCUMENTS

Article 31

If the seller is not bound to deliver the goods at any other particular place, his obligation to deliver consists:

(a)   if the contract of sale involves carriage of the goods—in handing the goods over to the first carrier for transmission to the buyer;

(b)   if, in cases not within the preceding subparagraph, the contract relates to specific goods, or unidentified goods to be drawn from a specific stock or to be manufactured or produced, and at the time of the conclusion of the contract the parties knew that the goods were at, or were to be manufactured or produced at, a particular place—in placing the goods at the buyer's disposal at that place;

(c)   in other cases—in placing the goods at the buyer's disposal at the place where the seller had his place of business at the time of the conclusion of the contract.

Article 32

(1)   If the seller, in accordance with the contract or this Convention, hands the goods over to a carrier and if the goods are not clearly identified to the contract by markings on the goods, by shipping documents or otherwise, the seller must give the buyer notice of the consignment specifying the goods.

(2)   If the seller is bound to arrange for carriage of the goods, he must make such contracts as are necessary for carriage to the place fixed by means of transportation appropriate in the circumstances and according to the usual terms for such transportation.

(3)   If the seller is not bound to effect insurance in respect of the carriage of the goods, he must, at the buyer's request, provide him with all available information necessary to enable him to effect such insurance.

Article 33

The seller must deliver the goods:

(a)   if a date is fixed by or determinable from the contract, on that date;

(b)   if a period of time is fixed by or determinable from the contract, at any time within that period unless circumstances indicate that the buyer is to choose a date; or

(c)   in any other case, within a reasonable time after the conclusion of the contract.

Article 34

If the seller is bound to hand over documents relating to the goods, he must hand them over at the time and place and in the form required by the contract. If the seller has handed over documents before that time, he may, up to that time, cure any lack of conformity in the documents, if the exercise of this right does not cause the buyer unreasonable inconvenience or unreasonable expense. However, the buyer retains any right to claim damages as provided for in this Convention.

SECTION II.

CONFORMITY OF THE GOODS AND THIRD PARTY CLAIMS

Article 35

(1)   The seller must deliver goods which are of the quantity, quality and description required by the contract and which are contained or packaged in the manner required by the contract.

(2)   Except where the parties have agreed otherwise, the goods do not conform with the contract unless they;

(a)   are fit for the purposes for which goods of the same description would ordinarily be used;

(b)   are fit for any particular purpose expressly or impliedly made known to the seller at the time of the conclusion of the contract, except where the circumstances show that the buyer did not rely, or that it was unreasonable for him to rely, on the seller's skill and judgement;

(c)   possess the qualities of goods which the seller has held out to the buyer as a sample or model;

(d)   are contained or packaged in the manner usual for such goods or, where there is no such manner, in a manner adequate to preserve and protect the goods.

(3)   The seller is not liable under subparagraphs (a) to (d) of the preceding paragraph for any lack of conformity of the goods if at the time of the conclusion of the contract the buyer knew or could not have been unaware of such lack of conformity.

Article 36

(1)   The seller is liable in accordance with the contract and this Convention for any lack of conformity which exists at the time when the risk passes to the buyer, even though the lack of conformity becomes apparent only after that time.

(2)   The seller is also liable for any lack of conformity which occurs after the time indicated in the preceding paragraph and which is due to a breach of any of his obligations, including a breach of any guarantee that for a period of time the goods will remain fit for their ordinary purpose or for some particular purpose or will retain specified qualities or characteristics.

Article 37

If the seller has delivered goods before the date for delivery, he may, up to that date, deliver any missing part or make up any deficiency in the quantity of the goods delivered, or deliver goods in replacement of any non-conforming goods delivered or remedy any lack of conformity in the goods delivered, provided that the exercise of this right does not cause the buyer unreasonable inconvenience or unreasonable expense. However, the buyer retains any right to claim damages as provided for in this Convention.

Article 38

(1)   The buyer must examine the goods, or cause them to be examined, within as short a period as is practicable in the circumstances.

(2)   If the contract involves carriage of the goods, examination may be deferred until after the goods have arrived at their destination.

(3)   If the goods are redirected in transit or redispatched by the buyer without a reasonable opportunity for examination by him and at the time of the conclusion of the contract the seller knew or ought to have known of the possibility of such redirection or redispatch, examination may be deferred until after the goods have arrived at the new destination.

Article 39

(1)   The buyer loses the right to rely on a lack of conformity of the goods if he does not give notice to the seller specifying the nature of the lack of conformity within a reasonable time after he has discovered it or ought to have discovered it.

(2)   In any event, the buyer loses the right to rely on a lack of conformity of the goods if he does not give the seller notice thereof at the latest within a period of two years from the date on which the goods were actually handed over to the buyer, unless this time-limit is inconsistent with a contractual period of guarantee.

Article 40

The seller is not entitled to rely on the provisions of articles 38 and 39 if the lack of conformity relates to facts of which he knew or could not have been unaware and which he did not disclose to the buyer.

Article 41

The seller must deliver goods which are free from any right or claim of a third party, unless the buyer agreed to take the goods subject to that right or claim. However, if such right or claim is based on industrial property or other intellectual property, the seller's obligation is governed by article 42.

Article 42

(1)   The seller must deliver goods which are free from any right or claim of a third party based on industrial property or other intellectual property, of which at the time of the conclusion of the contract the seller knew or could not have been unaware, provided that the right or claim is based on industrial property or other intellectual property:

(a)   under the law of the State where the goods will be resold or otherwise used, if it was contemplated by the parties at the time of the conclusion of the contract that the goods would be resold or otherwise used in that State; or

(b)   in any other case, under the law of the State where the buyer has his place of business.

(2)   The obligation of the seller under the preceding paragraph does not extend to cases where:

(a)   at the time of the conclusion of the contract the buyer knew or could not have been unaware of the right or claim; or

(b)   the right or claim results from the seller's compliance with technical drawings, designs, formulae or other such specifications furnished by the buyer.

Article 43

(1)   The buyer loses the right to rely on the provisions of article 41 or article 42 if he does not give notice to the seller specifying the nature of the right or claim of the third party within a reasonable time after he has become aware or ought to have become aware of the right or claim.

(2)   The seller is not entitled to rely on the provisions of the preceding paragraph if he knew of the right or claim of the third party and the nature of it.

Article 44

Notwithstanding the provisions of paragraph (1) of article 39 and paragraph (1) of article 43, the buyer may reduce the price in accordance with article 50 or claim damages, except for loss of profit, if he has a reasonable excuse for his failure to give the required notice.

SECTION III.

REMEDIES FOR BREACH OF CONTRACT BY THE SELLER

Article 45

(1)   If the seller fails to perform any of his obligations under the contract or this Convention, the buyer may:

(a)   exercise the rights provided in articles 46 to 52;

(b)   claim damages as provided in articles 74 to 77.

(2)   The buyer is not deprived of any right he may have to claim damages by exercising his right to other remedies.

(3)   No period of grace may be granted to the seller by a court or arbitral tribunal when the buyer resorts to a remedy for breach of contract.

Article 46

(1)   The buyer may require performance by the seller of his obligations unless the buyer has resorted to a remedy which is inconsistent with this requirement.

(2)   If the goods do not conform with the contract, the buyer may require delivery of substitute goods only if the lack of conformity constitutes a fundamental breach of contract and a request for substitute goods is made either in conjunction with notice given under article 39 or within a reasonable time thereafter.

(3)   If the goods do not conform with the contract, the buyer may require the seller to remedy the lack of conformity by repair, unless this is unreasonable having regard to all the circumstances. A request for repair must be made either in conjunction with notice given under article 39 or within a reasonable time thereafter.

Article 47

(1)   The buyer may fix an additional period of time of reasonable length for performance by the seller of his obligations.

(2)   Unless the buyer has received notice from the seller that he will not perform within the period so fixed, the buyer may not, during that period, resort to any remedy for breach of contract. However, the buyer is not deprived thereby of any right he may have to claim damages for delay in performance.

Article 48

(1)   Subject to article 49, the seller may, even after the date for delivery, remedy at his own expense any failure to perform his obligations, if he can do so without unreasonable delay and without causing the buyer unreasonable inconvenience or uncertainty of reimbursement by the seller of expenses advanced by the buyer. However, the buyer retains any right to claim damages as provided for in this Convention.

(2)   If the seller requests the buyer to make known whether he will accept performance and the buyer does not comply with the request within a reasonable time, the seller may perform within the time indicated in his request. The buyer may not, during that period of time, resort to any remedy which is inconsistent with performance by the seller.

(3)   A notice by the seller that he will perform within a specified period of time is assumed to include a request, under the preceding paragraph, that the buyer make known his decision.

(4)   A request or notice by the seller under paragraph (2) or (3) of this article is not effective unless received by the buyer.

Article 49

(1)   The buyer may declare the contract avoided:

(a)   if the failure by the seller to perform any of his obligations under the contract or this Convention amounts to a fundamental breach of contract; or

(b)   in case of non-delivery, if the seller does not deliver the goods within the additional period of time fixed by the buyer in accordance with paragraph (1) of article 47 or declares that he will not deliver within the period so fixed.

(2)   However, in cases where the seller has delivered the goods, the buyer loses the right to declare the contract avoided unless he does so:

(a)   in respect of late delivery, within a reasonable time after he has become aware that delivery has been made;

(b)   in respect of any breach other than late delivery, within a reasonable time:

(i)   after he knew or ought to have known of the breach;

(ii)   after the expiration of any additional period of time fixed by the buyer in accordance with paragraph (1) of article 47, or after the seller has declared that he will not perform his obligations within such an additional period; or

(iii)   after the expiration of any additional period of time indicated by the seller in accordance with paragraph (2) of article 48, or after the buyer has declared that he will not accept performance.

Article 50

If the goods do not conform with the contract and whether or not the price has already been paid, the buyer may reduce the price in the same proportion as the value that the goods actually delivered had at the time of the delivery bears to the value that conforming goods would have had at that time. However, if the seller remedies any failure to perform his obligations in accordance with article 37 or article 48 or if the buyer refuses to accept performance by the seller in accordance with those articles, the buyer may not reduce the price.

Article 51

(1)   If the seller delivers only a part of the goods or if only a part of the goods delivered is in conformity with the contract, articles 46 to 50 apply in respect of the part which is missing or which does not conform.

(2)   The buyer may declare the contract avoided in its entirety only if the failure to make delivery completely or in conformity with the contract amounts to a fundamental breach of the contract.

Article 52

(1)   If the seller delivers the goods before the date fixed, the buyer may take delivery or refuse to take delivery.

(2)   If the seller delivers a quantity of goods greater than that provided for in the contract, the buyer may take delivery or refuse to take delivery of the excess quantity. If the buyer takes delivery of all or part of the excess quantity, he must pay for it at the contract rate.

CHAPTER III. OBLIGATIONS OF THE BUYER

Article 53

The buyer must pay the price for the goods and take delivery of them as required by the contract and this Convention.

SECTION I.

PAYMENT OF THE PRICE

Article 54

The buyer's obligation to pay the price includes taking such steps and complying with such formalities as may be required under the contract or any laws and regulations to enable payment to be made.

Article 55

Where a contract has been validly concluded but does not expressly or implicitly fix or make provision for determining the price, the parties are considered, in the absence of any indication to the contrary, to have impliedly made reference to the price generally charged at the time of the conclusion of the contract for such goods sold under comparable circumstances in the trade concerned.

Article 56

If the price if fixed according to the weight of the goods, in case of doubt it is to be determined by the net weight.

Article 57

(1)   If the buyer is not bound to pay the price at any other particular place, he must pay it to the seller:

(a)   at the seller's place of business; or

(b)   if the payment is to be made against the handing over of the goods or of documents, at the place where the handing over takes place.

(2)   The seller must bear any increase in the expenses incidental to payment which is caused by a change in his place of business subsequent to the conclusion of the contract.

Article 58

(1)   If the buyer is not bound to pay the price at any other specific time, he must pay it when the seller places either the goods or documents controlling their disposition at the buyer's disposal in accordance with the contract and this Convention. The seller may make such payment a condition for handing over the goods or documents.

(2)   If the contract involves carriage of the goods, the seller may dispatch the goods on terms whereby the goods, or documents controlling their disposition, will not be handed over to the buyer except against payment of the price.

(3)   The buyer is not bound to pay the price until he has had an opportunity to examine the goods, unless the procedures for delivery or payment agreed upon by the parties are inconsistent with his having such an opportunity.

Article 59

The buyer must pay the price on the date fixed by or determinable from the contract and this Convention without the need for any request or compliance with any formality on the part of the seller.

SECTION II.

TAKING DELIVERY

Article 60

The buyer's obligation to take delivery consists:

(a)   in doing all the acts which could reasonably be expected of him in order to enable the seller to make delivery; and

(b)   in taking over the goods.

SECTION III.

REMEDIES FOR BREACH OF CONTRACT BY THE BUYER

Article 61

(1)   If the buyer fails to perform any of his obligations under the contract or this Convention, the seller may:

(a)   exercise the rights provided in articles 62 to 65;

(b)   claim damages as provided in articles 74 to 77.

(2)   The seller is not deprived of any right he may have to claim damages by exercising his right to other remedies.

(3)   No period of grace may be granted to the buyer by a court or arbitral tribunal when the seller resorts to a remedy for breach of contract.

Article 62

The seller may require the buyer to pay the price, take delivery or perform his other obligations, unless the seller has resorted to a remedy which is inconsistent with this requirement.

Article 63

(1)   The seller may fix an additional period of time of reasonable length for performance by the buyer of his obligations.

(2)   Unless the seller has received notice from the buyer that he will not perform within the period so fixed, the seller may not, during that period, resort to any remedy for breach of contract. However, the seller is not deprived thereby of any right he may have to claim damages for delay in performance.

Article 64

(1)   The seller may declare the contract avoided:

(a)   if the failure by the buyer to perform any of his obligations under the contract or this Convention amounts to a fundamental breach of contract; or

(b)   if the buyer does not, within the additional period of time fixed by the seller in accordance with paragraph (1) of article 63, perform his obligation to pay the price or take delivery of the goods, or if he declares that he will not do so within the period so fixed.

(2)   However, in cases where the buyer has paid the price, the seller loses the right to declare the contract avoided unless he does so:

(a)   in respect of late performance by the buyer, before the seller has become aware that performance has been rendered; or

(b)   in respect of any breach other than late performance by the buyer, within a reasonable time:

(i)   after the seller knew or ought to have known of the breach; or

(ii)   after the expiration of any additional period of time fixed by the seller in accordance with paragraph (1) of article 63, or after the buyer has declared that he will not perform his obligations within such an additional period.

Article 65

(1)   If under the contract the buyer is to specify the form, measurement or other features of the goods and he fails to make such specification either on the date agreed upon or within a reasonable time after receipt of a request from the seller, the seller may, without prejudice to any other rights he may have, make the specification himself in accordance with the requirements of the buyer that may be known to him.

(2)   If the seller makes the specification himself, he must inform the buyer of the details thereof and must fix a reasonable time within which the buyer may make a different specification. If, after receipt of such a communication, the buyer fails to do so within the time so fixed, the specification made by the seller is binding.

CHAPTER IV. PASSING OF RISK

Article 66

Loss of or damage to the goods after the risk has passed to the buyer does not discharge him from his obligation to pay the price, unless the loss or damage is due to an act or omission of the seller.

Article 67

(1)   If the contract of sale involves carriage of the goods and the seller is not bound to hand them over at a particular place, the risk passes to the buyer when the goods are handed over to the first carrier for transmission to the buyer in accordance with the contract of sale. If the seller is bound to hand the goods over to a carrier at a particular place, the risk does not pass to the buyer until the goods are handed over to the carrier at that place. The fact that the seller is authorized to retain documents controlling the disposition of the goods does not affect the passage of the risk.

(2)   Nevertheless, the risk does not pass to the buyer until the goods are clearly identified to the contract, whether by markings on the goods, by shipping documents, by notice given to the buyer or otherwise.

Article 68

The risk in respect of goods sold in transit passes to the buyer from the time of the conclusion of the contract. However, if the circumstances so indicate, the risk is assumed by the buyer from the time the goods were handed over to the carrier who issued the documents embodying the contract of carriage. Nevertheless, if at the time of the conclusion of the contract of sale the seller knew or ought to have known that the goods had been lost or damaged and did not disclose this to the buyer, the loss or damage is at the risk of the seller.

Article 69

(1)   In cases not within articles 67 and 68, the risk passes to the buyer when he takes over the goods or, if he does not do so in due time, from the time when the goods are placed at his disposal and he commits a breach of contract by failing to take delivery.

(2)   However, if the buyer is bound to take over the goods at a place other than a place of business of the seller, the risk passes when delivery is due and the buyer is aware of the fact that the goods are placed at his disposal at that place.

(3)   If the contract relates to goods not then identified, the goods are considered not to be placed at the disposal of the buyer until they are clearly identified to the contract.

Article 70

If the seller had committed a fundamental breach of contract, articles 67, 68 and 69 do not impair the remedies available to the buyer on account of the breach.

CHAPTER V. PROVISIONS COMMON TO THE OBLIGATIONS OF THE SELLER AND OF THE BUYER

Section I.

Anticipatory Breach and Instalment Contracts

Article 71

(1)   A party may suspend the performance of his obligations if, after the conclusion of the contract, it becomes apparent that the other party will not perform a substantial part of his obligations as a result of:

(a)   a serious deficiency in his ability to perform or in his creditworthiness; or

(b)   his conduct in preparing to perform or in performing the contract.

(2)   If the seller has already dispatched the goods before the grounds described in the preceding paragraph become evident, he may prevent the handing over of the goods to the buyer even though the buyer holds a document which entitles him to obtain them. The present paragraph relates only to the rights in the goods as between the buyer and the seller.

(3)   A party suspending performance, whether before or after dispatch of the goods, must immediately give notice of the suspension to the other party and must continue with performance if the other party provides adequate assurance of his performance.

Article 72

(1) If prior to the date for performance of the contract it is clear that one of the parties will commit a fundamental breach of contract, the other party may declare the contract avoided.

(2) If time allows, the party intending to declare the contract avoided must give reasonable notice to the other party in order to permit him to provide adequate assurance of his performance.

(3) The requirements of the preceding paragraph do not apply if the other party has declared that he will not perform his obligations.

Article 73

(1) In the case of a contract for delivery of goods by instalments, if the failure of one party to perform any of his obligations in respect of any instalment constitutes a fundamental breach of contract with respect to that instalment, the other party may declare the contract avoided with respect to that instalment.

(2) If one party's failure to perform any of his obligations in respect of any instalment gives the other party good grounds to conclude that a fundamental breach of contract will occur with respect to future instalments, he may declare the contract avoided for the future, provided that he does so within a reasonable time.

(3) A buyer who declares the contract avoided in respect of any delivery may, at the same time, declare it avoided in respect of deliveries already made or of future deliveries if, by reason of their interdependence, those deliveries could not be used for the purpose contemplated by the parties at the time of the conclusion of the contract.

SECTION II.

DAMAGES

Article 74

Damages for breach of contract by one party consist of a sum equal to the loss, including loss of profit, suffered by the other party as a consequence of the breach. Such damages may not exceed the loss which the party in breach foresaw or ought to have foreseen at the time of the conclusion of the contract, in the light of the facts and matters of which he then knew or ought to have known, as a possible consequence of the breach of contract.

Article 75

If the contract is avoided and if, in a reasonable manner and within a reasonable time after avoidance, the buyer has bought goods in replacement or the seller has resold the goods, the party claiming damages may recover the difference between the contract price and the price in the substitute transaction as well as any further damages recoverable under article 74.

Article 76

(1) If the contract is avoided and there is a current price for the goods, the party claiming damages may, if he has not made a purchase or resale under article 75, recover the difference between the price fixed by the contract and the current price at the time of avoidance as well as any further damages recoverable under article 74. If, however, the party claiming damages has avoided the contract after taking over the goods, the current price at the time of such taking over shall be applied instead of the current price at the time of avoidance.

(2) For the purpose of the preceding paragraph, the current price is the price prevailing at the place where delivery of the goods should have been made or, if there is no current price at that place,

the price at such other place as serves as a reasonable substitute, making due allowance for differences in the cost of transporting the goods.

Article 77

A party who relies on a breach of contract must take such measures as are reasonable in the circumstances to mitigate the loss, including loss of profit, resulting from the breach. If he fails to take such measures, the party in breach may claim a reduction in the damages in the amount by which the loss should have been mitigated.

SECTION III.

INTEREST

Article 78

If a party fails to pay the price or any other sum that is in arrears, the other party is entitled to interest on it, without prejudice to any claim for damages recoverable under article 74.

SECTION IV.

EXEMPTIONS

Article 79

(1)   A party is not liable for a failure to perform any of his obligations if he proves that the failure was due to an impediment beyond his control and that he could not reasonably be expected to have taken the impediment into account at the time of the conclusion of the contract or to have avoided or overcome it or its consequences.

(2)   If the party's failure is due to the failure by a third person whom he has engaged to perform the whole or a part of the contract, that party is exempt from liability only if:

(a)   he is exempt under the preceding paragraph; and

(b)   the person whom he has so engaged would be so exempt if the provisions of that paragraph were applied to him.

(3)   The exemption provided by this article has effect for the period during which the impediment exists.

(4)   The party who fails to perform must give notice to the other party of the impediment and its effects on his ability to perform. If the notice is not received by the other party within a reasonable time after the party who fails to perform knew or ought to have known of the impediment, he is liable for damages resulting from such non-receipt.

(5)   Nothing in this article prevents either party from exercising any right other than to claim damages under this Convention.

Article 80

A party may not rely on a failure of the other party to perform, to the extent that such failure was caused by the first party's act or omission.

SECTION V.

EFFECTS OF AVOIDANCE

Article 81

(1)   Avoidance of the contract releases both parties from their obligations under it, subject to any damages which may be due. Avoidance does not affect any provision of the contract for the settlement

of disputes or any other provision of the contract governing the rights and obligations of the parties consequent upon the avoidance of the contract.

(2)   A party who has performed the contract either wholly or in part may claim restitution from the other party of whatever the first party has supplied or paid under the contract. If both parties are bound to make restitution, they must do so concurrently.

Article 82

(1)   The buyer loses the right to declare the contract avoided or to require the seller to deliver substitute goods if it is impossible for him to make restitution of the goods substantially in the condition in which he received them.

(2)   The preceding paragraph does not apply:

(a)   if the impossibility of making restitution of the goods or of making restitution of the goods substantially in the condition in which the buyer received them is not due to his act or omission;

(b)   if the goods or part of the goods have perished or deteriorated as a result of the examination provided for in article 38; or

(c)   if the goods or part of the goods have been sold in the normal course of business or have been consumed or transformed by the buyer in the course of normal use before he discovered or ought to have discovered the lack of conformity.

Article 83

A buyer who has lost the right to declare the contract avoided or to require the seller to deliver substitute goods in accordance with article 82 retains all other remedies under the contract and this Convention.

Article 84

(1)   If the seller is bound to refund the price, he must also pay interest on it, from the date on which the price was paid.

(2)   The buyer must account to the seller for all benefits which he has derived from the goods or part of them:

(a)   if he must make restitution of the goods or part of them; or

(b)   if it is impossible for him to make restitution of all or part of the goods or to make restitution of all or part of the goods substantially in the condition in which he received them, but he has nevertheless declared the contract avoided or required the seller to deliver substitute goods.

SECTION VI.

PRESERVATION OF THE GOODS

Article 85

If the buyer is in delay in taking delivery of the goods or, where payment of the price and delivery of the goods are to be made concurrently, if he fails to pay the price, and the seller is either in possession of the goods or otherwise able to control their disposition, the seller must take such steps as are reasonable in the circumstances to preserve them. He is entitled to retain them until he has been reimbursed his reasonable expenses by the buyer.

Article 86

(1)   If the buyer has received the goods and intends to exercise any right under the contract or this Convention to reject them, he must take such steps to preserve them as are reasonable in the circumstances. He is entitled to retain them until he has been reimbursed his reasonable expenses by the seller.

(2)   If goods dispatched to the buyer have been placed at his disposal at their destination and he exercises the right to reject them, he must take possession of them on behalf of the seller, provided that this can be done without payment of the price and without unreasonable inconvenience or unreasonable expense. This provision does not apply if the seller or a person authorized to take charge of the goods on his behalf is present at the destination. If the buyer takes possession of the goods under this paragraph, his rights and obligations are governed by the preceding paragraph.

Article 87

A party who is bound to take steps to preserve the goods may deposit them in a warehouse of a third person at the expense of the other party provided that the expense incurred is not unreasonable.

Article 88

(1)   A party who is bound to preserve the goods in accordance with article 85 or 86 may sell them by any appropriate means if there has been an unreasonable delay by the other party in taking possession of the goods or in taking them back or in paying the price or the cost of preservation, provided that reasonable notice of the intention to sell has been given to the other party.

(2)   If the goods are subject to rapid deterioration or their preservation would involve unreasonable expense, a party who is bound to preserve the goods in accordance with article 85 or 86 must take reasonable measures to sell them. To the extent possible he must give notice to the other party of his intention to sell.

(3)   A party selling the goods has the right to retain out of the proceeds of sale an amount equal to the reasonable expenses of preserving the goods and of selling them. He must account to the other party for the balance.

PART IV. FINAL PROVISIONS

Article 89

The Secretary-General of the United Nations is hereby designated as the depositary for this Convention.

Article 90

This Convention does not prevail over any international agreement which has already been or may be entered into and which contains provisions concerning the matters governed by this Convention, provided that the parties have their places of business in States parties to such agreement.

Article 91

(1)   This Convention is open for signature at the concluding meeting of the United Nations Conference on Contracts for the International Sale of Goods and will remain open for signature by all States at the Headquarters of the United Nations, New York until 30 September 1981.

(2)   This Convention is subject to ratification, acceptance or approval by the signatory States.

(3)   This Convention is open for accession by all States which are not signatory States as from the date it is open for signature.

(4)   Instruments of ratification, acceptance, approval and accession are to be deposited with the Secretary-General of the United Nations.

Article 92

(1)   A Contracting State may declare at the time of signature, ratification, acceptance, approval or accession that it will not be bound by Part II of this Convention or that it will not be bound by Part III of this Convention.

(2)   A Contracting State which makes a declaration in accordance with the preceding paragraph in respect of Part II or Part III of this Convention is not to be considered a Contracting State within paragraph (1) of article 1 of this Convention in respect of matters governed by the Part to which the declaration applies.

Article 93

(1)   If a Contracting State has two or more territorial units in which, according to its constitution, different systems of law are applicable in relation to the matters dealt with in this Convention, it may, at the time of signature, ratification, acceptance, approval or accession, declare that this Convention is to extend to all its territorial units or only to one or more of them, and may amend its declaration by submitting another declaration at any time.

(2)   These declarations are to be notified to the depositary and are to state expressly the territorial units to which the Convention extends.

(3)   If, by virtue of a declaration under this article, this Convention extends to one or more but not all of the territorial units of a Contracting State, and if the place of business of a party is located in that State, this place of business, for the purposes of this Convention, is considered not to be in a Contracting State, unless it is in a territorial unit to which the Convention extends.

(4)   If a Contracting State makes no declaration under paragraph (1) of this article, the Convention is to extend to all territorial units of that State.

Article 94

(1)   Two or more Contracting States which have the same or closely related legal rules on matters governed by this Convention may at any time declare that the Convention is not to apply to contracts of sale or to their formation where the parties have their places of business in those States. Such declarations may be made jointly or by reciprocal unilateral declarations.

(2)   A Contracting State which has the same or closely related legal rules on matters governed by this Convention as one or more non-Contracting States may at any time declare that the Convention is not to apply to contracts of sale or to their formation where the parties have their places of business in those States.

(3)   If a State which is the object of a declaration under the preceding paragraph subsequently becomes a Contracting State, the declaration made will, as from the date on which the Convention enters into force in respect of the new Contracting State, have the effect of a declaration made under paragraph (1), provided that the new Contracting State joins in such declaration or makes a reciprocal unilateral declaration.

Article 95

Any State may declare at the time of the deposit of its instrument of ratification, acceptance, approval or accession that it will not be bound by subparagraph (1)(b) of article 1 of this Convention.

[The United States has declared a reservation to CISG under Article 95].

Article 96

A Contracting State whose legislation requires contracts of sale to be concluded in or evidenced by writing may at any time make a declaration in accordance with article 12 that any provision of article 11, article 29, or Part II of this Convention, that allows a contract of sale or its modification or termination by agreement or any offer, acceptance, or other indication of intention to be made in any form other than in writing, does not apply where any party has his place of business in that State.

Article 97

(1) Declarations made under this Convention at the time of signature are subject to confirmation upon ratification, acceptance or approval.

(2) Declarations and confirmations of declarations are to be in writing and be formally notified to the depositary.

(3) A declaration takes effect simultaneously with the entry into force of this Convention in respect of the State concerned. However, a declaration of which the depositary receives formal notification after such entry into force takes effect on the first day of the month following the expiration of six months after the date of its receipt by the depositary. Reciprocal unilateral declarations under article 94 take effect on the first day of the month following the expiration of six months after the receipt of the latest declaration by the depositary.

(4) Any State which makes a declaration under this Convention may withdraw it at any time by a formal notification in writing addressed to the depositary. Such withdrawal is to take effect on the first day of the month following the expiration of six months after the date of the receipt of the notification by the depositary.

(5) A withdrawal of a declaration made under article 94 renders inoperative, as from the date on which the withdrawal takes effect, any reciprocal declaration made by another State under that article.

Article 98

No reservations are permitted except those expressly authorized in this Convention.

Article 99

(1) This Convention enters into force, subject to the provisions of paragraph (6) of this article, on the first day of the month following the expiration of twelve months after the date of deposit of the tenth instrument of ratification, acceptance, approval or accession, including an instrument which contains a declaration made under article 92.

(2) When a State ratifies, accepts, approves or accedes to this Convention after the deposit of the tenth instrument of ratification, acceptance, approval or accession, this Convention, with the exception of the Part excluded, enters into force in respect of that State, subject to the provisions of paragraph (6) of this article, on the first day of the month following the expiration of twelve months after the date of the deposit of its instrument of ratification, acceptance, approval or accession.

(3) A State which ratifies, accepts, approves or accedes to this Convention and is a party to either or both the Convention relating to a Uniform Law on the Formation of Contracts for the International Sale of Goods done at The Hague on 1 July 1964 (1964 Hague Formation Convention) and the Convention relating to a Uniform Law on the International Sale of Goods done at The Hague on 1 July 1964 (1964 Hague Sales Convention) shall at the same time denounce, as the case may be, either or both the 1964 Hague Sales Convention and the 1964 Hague Formation Convention by notifying the Government of the Netherlands to that effect.

(4) A State party to the 1964 Hague Sales Convention which ratifies, accepts, approves or accedes to the present Convention and declares or has declared under article 92 that it will not be

bound by Part II of this Convention shall at the time of ratification, acceptance, approval or accession denounce the 1964 Hague Sales Convention by notifying the Government of the Netherlands to that effect.

(5)   A State party to the 1964 Hague Formation Convention which ratifies, accepts, approves or accedes to the present Convention and declares or has declared under article 92 that it will not be bound by Part III of this Convention shall at the time of ratification, acceptance, approval or accession denounce the 1964 Hague Formation Convention by notifying the Government of the Netherlands to that effect.

(6)   For the purpose of this article, ratifications, acceptances, approvals and accessions in respect of this Convention by States parties to the 1964 Hague Formation Convention or to the 1964 Hague Sales Convention shall not be effective until such denunciations as may be required on the part of those States in respect of the latter two Conventions have themselves become effective. The depositary of this Convention shall consult with the Government of the Netherlands, as the depositary of the 1964 Convention, so as to ensure necessary co-ordination in this respect.

Article 100

(1)   This Convention applies to the formation of a contract only when the proposal for concluding the contract is made on or after the date when the Convention enters into force in respect of the Contracting States referred to in subparagraph (1)(a) or the Contracting State referred to in subparagraph (1)(b) of article 1.

(2)   This Convention applies only to contracts concluded on or after the date when the Convention enters into force in respect of the Contracting States referred to in subparagraph (1)(a) or the Contracting State referred to in subparagraph (1)(b) of article 1.

Article 101

(1)   A Contracting State may denounce this Convention, or Part II or Part III of the Convention, by a formal notification in writing addressed to the depositary.

(2)   The denunciation takes effect on the first day of the month following the expiration of twelve months after the notification is received by the depositary. Where a longer period for the denunciation to take effect is specified in the notification, the denunciation takes effect upon the expiration of such longer period after the notification is received by the depositary.

UNITED NATIONS CONVENTION ON THE USE OF ELECTRONIC COMMUNICATIONS IN INTERNATIONAL CONTRACTS

(2005)

(Excerpts)

[Like the U.S. Electronic Signatures in Global and National Commerce Act ("E-Sign") and the Uniform Electronic Transactions Act ("UETA"), both included in Part V of this pamphlet, the United Nations Convention on the Use of Electronic Communications in International Contracts ("CUECIC") aims to enhance legal certainty and commercial predictability. It applies when parties make international contracts using electronic means. Primarily, it prevents such a contract from being held invalid or unenforceable solely because the parties made it in electronic form. The CUECIC thereby displaces such laws as statutes of frauds. CUECIC, Arts. 8.1, 9. The CUECIC entered into force on March 1, 2013 when three States had ratified, accepted, approved, or acceded to it. As of May 1, 2017, only seven states had done so.]

Chapter I
Sphere of application

Article 1
Scope of application

1. This Convention applies to the use of electronic communications in connection with the formation or performance of a contract between parties whose places of business are in different States.

2. The fact that the parties have their places of business in different States is to be disregarded whenever this fact does not appear either from the contract or from any dealings between the parties or from information disclosed by the parties at any time before or at the conclusion of the contract.

3. Neither the nationality of the parties nor the civil or commercial character of the parties or of the contract is to be taken into consideration in determining the application of this Convention.

Article 2
Exclusions

1. This Convention does not apply to electronic communications relating to any of the following:

(a) Contracts concluded for personal, family or household purposes;

(b) (i) Transactions on a regulated exchange; (ii) foreign exchange transactions; (iii) inter-bank payment systems, inter-bank payment agreements or clearance and settlement systems relating to securities or other financial assets or instruments; (iv) the transfer of security rights in sale, loan or holding of or agreement to repurchase securities or other financial assets or instruments held with an intermediary.

2. This Convention does not apply to bills of exchange, promissory notes, consignment notes, bills of lading, warehouse receipts or any transferable document or instrument that entitles the bearer or beneficiary to claim the delivery of goods or the payment of a sum of money.

UNITED NATIONS CONVENTION ON THE USE OF ELECTRONIC COMMUNICATIONS

Article 3
Party autonomy

The parties may exclude the application of this Convention or derogate from or vary the effect of any of its provisions.

Chapter II
General provisions

Article 4
Definitions

For the purposes of this Convention:

(a) "Communication" means any statement, declaration, demand, notice or request, including an offer and the acceptance of an offer, that the parties are required to make or choose to make in connection with the formation or performance of a contract;

(b) "Electronic communication" means any communication that the parties make by means of data messages;

(c) "Data message" means information generated, sent, received or stored by electronic, magnetic, optical or similar means, including, but not limited to, electronic data interchange, electronic mail, telegram, telex or telecopy;

(d) "Originator" of an electronic communication means a party by whom, or on whose behalf, the electronic communication has been sent or generated prior to storage, if any, but it does not include a party acting as an intermediary with respect to that electronic communication;

(e) "Addressee" of an electronic communication means a party who is intended by the originator to receive the electronic communication, but does not include a party acting as an intermediary with respect to that electronic communication;

(f) "Information system" means a system for generating, sending, receiving, storing or otherwise processing data messages;

(g) "Automated message system" means a computer program or an electronic or other automated means used to initiate an action or respond to data messages or performances in whole or in part, without review or intervention by a natural person each time an action is initiated or a response is generated by the system;

(h) "Place of business" means any place where a party maintains a non-transitory establishment to pursue an economic activity other than the temporary provision of goods or services out of a specific location.

Article 5
Interpretation

1. In the interpretation of this Convention, regard is to be had to its international character and to the need to promote uniformity in its application and the observance of good faith in international trade.

2. Questions concerning matters governed by this Convention which are not expressly settled in it are to be settled in conformity with the general principles on which it is based or, in the absence of such principles, in conformity with the law applicable by virtue of the rules of private international law.

Article 6
Location of the parties

1.   For the purposes of this Convention, a party's place of business is presumed to be the location indicated by that party, unless another party demonstrates that the party making the indication does not have a place of business at that location.

2.   If a party has not indicated a place of business and has more than one place of business, then the place of business for the purposes of this Convention is that which has the closest relationship to the relevant contract, having regard to the circumstances known to or contemplated by the parties at any time before or at the conclusion of the contract.

3.   If a natural person does not have a place of business, reference is to be made to the person's habitual residence.

4.   A location is not a place of business merely because that is: (a) where equipment and technology supporting an information system used by a party in connection with the formation of a contract are located; or (b) where the information system may be accessed by other parties.

5.   The sole fact that a party makes use of a domain name or electronic mail address connected to a specific country does not create a presumption that its place of business is located in that country.

Article 7
Information requirements

Nothing in this Convention affects the application of any rule of law that may require the parties to disclose their identities, places of business or other information, or relieves a party from the legal consequences of making inaccurate, incomplete or false statements in that regard.

Chapter III
Use of electronic communications in international contracts

Article 8
Legal recognition of electronic communications

1.   A communication or a contract shall not be denied validity or enforceability on the sole ground that it is in the form of an electronic communication.

2.   Nothing in this Convention requires a party to use or accept electronic communications, but a party's agreement to do so may be inferred from the party's conduct.

Article 9
Form requirements

1.   Nothing in this Convention requires a communication or a contract to be made or evidenced in any particular form.

2.   Where the law requires that a communication or a contract should be in writing, or provides consequences for the absence of a writing, that requirement is met by an electronic communication if the information contained therein is accessible so as to be useable for subsequent reference.

3.   Where the law requires that a communication or a contract should be signed by a party, or provides consequences for the absence of a signature, that requirement is met in relation to an electronic communication if:

    (a)   A method is used to identify the party and to indicate that party's intention in respect of the information contained in the electronic communication; and

    (b)   The method used is either:

(i)   As reliable as appropriate for the purpose for which the electronic communication was generated or communicated, in the light of all the circumstances, including any relevant agreement; or

(ii)   Proven in fact to have fulfilled the functions described in subparagraph (a) above, by itself or together with further evidence.

4.   Where the law requires that a communication or a contract should be made available or retained in its original form, or provides consequences for the absence of an original, that requirement is met in relation to an electronic communication if:

(a)   There exists a reliable assurance as to the integrity of the information it contains from the time when it was first generated in its final form, as an electronic communication or otherwise; and

(b)   Where it is required that the information it contains be made available, that information is capable of being displayed to the person to whom it is to be made available.

5.   For the purposes of paragraph 4(a):

(a)   The criteria for assessing integrity shall be whether the information has remained complete and unaltered, apart from the addition of any endorsement and any change that arises in the normal course of communication, storage and display; and

(b)   The standard of reliability required shall be assessed in the light of the purpose for which the information was generated and in the light of all the relevant circumstances.

Article 10
Time and place of dispatch and receipt of electronic communications

1.   The time of dispatch of an electronic communication is the time when it leaves an information system under the control of the originator or of the party who sent it on behalf of the originator or, if the electronic communication has not left an information system under the control of the originator or of the party who sent it on behalf of the originator, the time when the electronic communication is received.

2.   The time of receipt of an electronic communication is the time when it becomes capable of being retrieved by the addressee at an electronic address designated by the addressee. The time of receipt of an electronic communication at another electronic address of the addressee is the time when it becomes capable of being retrieved by the addressee at that address and the addressee becomes aware that the electronic communication has been sent to that address. An electronic communication is presumed to be capable of being retrieved by the addressee when it reaches the addressee's electronic address.

3.   An electronic communication is deemed to be dispatched at the place where the originator has its place of business and is deemed to be received at the place where the addressee has its place of business, as determined in accordance with article 6.

4.   Paragraph 2 of this article applies notwithstanding that the place where the information system supporting an electronic address is located may be different from the place where the electronic communication is deemed to be received under paragraph 3 of this article.

Article 11
Invitations to make offers

A proposal to conclude a contract made through one or more electronic communications which is not addressed to one or more specific parties, but is generally accessible to parties making use of information systems, including proposals that make use of interactive applications for the placement of orders through such information systems, is to be considered as an invitation to make offers, unless it clearly indicates the intention of the party making the proposal to be bound in case of acceptance.

Article 12
Use of automated message systems for contract formation

A contract formed by the interaction of an automated message system and a natural person, or by the interaction of automated message systems, shall not be denied validity or enforceability on the sole ground that no natural person reviewed or intervened in each of the individual actions carried out by the automated message systems or the resulting contract.

Article 13
Availability of contract terms

Nothing in this Convention affects the application of any rule of law that may require a party that negotiates some or all of the terms of a contract through the exchange of electronic communications to make available to the other party those electronic communications which contain the contractual terms in a particular manner, or relieves a party from the legal consequences of its failure to do so.

Article 14
Error in electronic communications

1.   Where a natural person makes an input error in an electronic communication exchanged with the automated message system of another party and the automated message system does not provide the person with an opportunity to correct the error, that person, or the party on whose behalf that person was acting, has the right to withdraw the portion of the electronic communication in which the input error was made if:

(a)   The person, or the party on whose behalf that person was acting, notifies the other party of the error as soon as possible after having learned of the error and indicates that he or she made an error in the electronic communication; and

(b)   The person, or the party on whose behalf that person was acting, has not used or received any material benefit or value from the goods or services, if any, received from the other party.

2.   Nothing in this article affects the application of any rule of law that may govern the consequences of any error other than as provided for in paragraph 1. . . .

THE UNIDROIT PRINCIPLES OF INTERNATIONAL COMMERCIAL CONTRACTS*

(2016)

[The International Institute for the Unification of Private Law ("UNIDROIT") is an independent intergovernmental organization located in Rome. Sixty-three member States—from all regions of the world—support it. UNIDROIT's principal purposes include promoting the modernization, harmonization, and uniformity of commercial law internationally. It furthers these purposes by, among other things, developing and publishing collections of principles on private law topics. In 1971, the governing council of the Institute determined to include a codification of the law of contracts in its program. A Working Group consisting of academics, judges, and civil servants was created in 1980. The members of the Working Group were of different nationalities, but sat in their personal capacities, not to express the views of their governments. The result was the UNIDROIT Principles of International Commercial Contracts, which was first published in 1994 and has since been revised. The goal of the UNIDROIT Principles is to set forth general rules for international commercial contracts. The Principles are intended to enunciate communal principles and rules of existing legal systems, and to select the solutions that are best adapted to the special requirements of international commercial contracts. In preparing the Principles, particular attention was paid to recent codifications of contract and commercial law, including the UCC, the Restatement Second of Contracts, the Netherlands Civil Code, the 1985 Foreign Economic Contract law of the People's Republic of China, the Draft New Civil Code of Quebec, and the United Nations Convention on Contracts for the International Sale of Goods.

[As such, the UNIDROIT Principles, much like the American Law Institute's Restatements, offers general principles and rules that are not binding law in any State. The Preamble to the UNIDROIT Principles states that the general rules for international contracts stated therein *shall* be applied when the parties to an international commercial contract have agreed that these principles and rules shall govern their contract and *may* be applied (1) when the parties have not agreed on the governing law; (2) when the parties have agreed that general principles of law or the *lex mercatoria* shall govern; (3) to interpret or supplement international uniform-law instruments; and (4) to interpret or supplement domestic contract law when an international commercial contract is involved. Because the Principles stem from an internationally negotiated blend of common law, civil law, and other legal traditions, and are supportive of evolving international contracting practices, they have a distinctive international character.]

PREAMBLE**

(Purpose of the Principles)

These Principles set forth general rules for international commercial contracts.

They shall be applied when the parties have agreed that their contract be governed by them.

---

*   Copyright UNIDROIT 2016—The complete version of the UNIDROIT Principles contains not only the black-letter rules reproduced herein, but also detailed comments on each article and, where appropriate, illustrations, which are to be seen as an integral part of the Principles. This complete version, which is published in English, French, German, Italian and Spanish, may be ordered directly from UNIDROIT, Via Panisperna, 28, 00184 Rome, Italy—Fax: +39 6/6994 1394.

**   Parties wishing to provide that their agreement be governed by the Principles might use one of the *Model Clauses for the Use of the UNIDROIT Principles* ((see http://www.unidroit.org/instruments/commercial-contracts/upicc-model-clauses).

They may be applied when the parties have agreed that their contract be governed by general principles of law, the *lex mercatoria* or the like.

They may be applied when the parties have not chosen any law to govern their contract.

They may be used to interpret or supplement international uniform law instruments.

They may be used to interpret or supplement domestic law.

They may serve as a model for national and international legislators.

CHAPTER 1—GENERAL PROVISIONS

ARTICLE 1.1

(Freedom of contract)

The parties are free to enter into a contract and to determine its content.

ARTICLE 1.2

(No form required)

Nothing in these Principles requires a contract, statement or any other act to be made in or evidenced by a particular form. It may be proved by any means, including witnesses.

ARTICLE 1.3

(Binding character of contract)

A contract validly entered into is binding upon the parties. It can only be modified or terminated in accordance with its terms or by agreement or as otherwise provided in these Principles.

ARTICLE 1.4

(Mandatory rules)

Nothing in these Principles shall restrict the application of mandatory rules, whether of national, international or supranational origin, which are applicable in accordance with the relevant rules of private international law.

ARTICLE 1.5

(Exclusion or modification by the parties)

The parties may exclude the application of these Principles or derogate from or vary the effect of any of their provisions, except as otherwise provided in the Principles.

ARTICLE 1.6

(Interpretation and supplementation of the Principles)

(1)   In the interpretation of these Principles, regard is to be had to their international character and to their purposes including the need to promote uniformity in their application.

(2)   Issues within the scope of these Principles but not expressly settled by them are as far as possible to be settled in accordance with their underlying general principles.

ARTICLE 1.7

(Good faith and fair dealing)

(1)   Each party must act in accordance with good faith and fair dealing in international trade.

(2)   The parties may not exclude or limit this duty.

ARTICLE 1.8

(Inconsistent Behaviour)

A party cannot act inconsistently with an understanding it has caused the other party to have and upon which that other party reasonably has acted in reliance to its detriment.

ARTICLE 1.9

(Usages and practices)

(1)   The parties are bound by any usage to which they have agreed and by any practices which they have established between themselves.

(2)   The parties are bound by a usage that is widely known to and regularly observed in international trade by parties in the particular trade concerned except where the application of such a usage would be unreasonable.

ARTICLE 1.10

(Notice)

(1)   Where notice is required it may be given by any means appropriate to the circumstances.

(2)   A notice is effective when it reaches the person to whom it is given.

(3)   For the purpose of paragraph (2) a notice "reaches" a person when given to that person orally or delivered at that person's place of business or mailing address.

(4)   For the purpose of this article "notice" includes a declaration, demand, request or any other communication of intention.

ARTICLE 1.11

(Definitions)

In these Principles

—"court" includes an arbitral tribunal;

—where a party has more than one place of business the relevant "place of business" is that which has the closest relationship to the contract and its performance, having regard to the circumstances known to or contemplated by the parties at any time before or at the conclusion of the contract;

—"long-term contract" refers to a contract which is to be performed over a period of time and which normally involves, to a varying degree, complexity of the transaction and an ongoing relationship between the parties;

—"obligor" refers to the party who is to perform an obligation and "obligee" refers to the party who is entitled to performance of that obligation.

—"writing" means any mode of communication that preserves a record of the information contained therein and is capable of being reproduced in tangible form. . . .

CHAPTER 2—FORMATION . . .

SECTION 1: FORMATION

ARTICLE 2.1.1

(Manner of formation)

A contract may be concluded either by the acceptance of an offer or by conduct of the parties that is sufficient to show agreement.

ARTICLE 2.1.2

(Definition of offer)

A proposal for concluding a contract constitutes an offer if it is sufficiently definite and indicates the intention of the offeror to be bound in case of acceptance.

ARTICLE 2.1.3

(Withdrawal of offer)

(1)   An offer becomes effective when it reaches the offeree.

(2)   An offer, even if it is irrevocable, may be withdrawn if the withdrawal reaches the offeree before or at the same time as the offer.

ARTICLE 2.1.4

(Revocation of offer)

(1)   Until a contract is concluded an offer may be revoked if the revocation reaches the offeree before it has dispatched an acceptance.

(2)   However, an offer cannot be revoked

(a)   if it indicates, whether by stating a fixed time for acceptance or otherwise, that it is irrevocable; or

(b)   if it was reasonable for the offeree to rely on the offer as being irrevocable and the offeree has acted in reliance on the offer.

ARTICLE 2.1.5

(Rejection of offer)

An offer is terminated when a rejection reaches the offeror.

ARTICLE 2.1.6

(Mode of acceptance)

(1)   A statement made by or other conduct of the offeree indicating assent to an offer is an acceptance. Silence or inactivity does not in itself amount to acceptance.

(2)   An acceptance of an offer becomes effective when the indication of assent reaches the offeror.

(3)   However, if, by virtue of the offer or as a result of practices which the parties have established between themselves or of usage, the offeree may indicate assent by performing an act without notice to the offeror, the acceptance is effective when the act is performed.

ARTICLE 2.1.7

(Time of acceptance)

An offer must be accepted within the time the offeror has fixed or, if no time is fixed, within a reasonable time having regard to the circumstances, including the rapidity of the means of communication employed by the offeror. An oral offer must be accepted immediately unless the circumstances indicate otherwise.

ARTICLE 2.1.8

(Acceptance within a fixed period of time)

A period of acceptance fixed by the offeror begins to run from the time that the offer is dispatched. A time indicated in the offer is deemed to be the time of dispatch unless the circumstances indicate otherwise.

ARTICLE 2.1.9

(Late acceptance. Delay in transmission)

(1) A late acceptance is nevertheless effective as an acceptance if without undue delay the offeror so informs the offeree or gives notice to that effect.

(2) If a communication containing a late acceptance shows that it has been sent in such circumstances that if its transmission had been normal it would have reached the offeror in due time, the late acceptance is effective as an acceptance unless, without undue delay, the offeror informs the offeree that it considers the offer as having lapsed.

ARTICLE 2.1.10

(Withdrawal of acceptance)

An acceptance may be withdrawn if the withdrawal reaches the offeror before or at the same time as the acceptance would have become effective.

ARTICLE 2.1.11

(Modified acceptance)

(1) A reply to an offer which purports to be an acceptance but contains additions, limitations or other modifications is a rejection of the offer and constitutes a counter-offer.

(2) However, a reply to an offer which purports to be an acceptance but contains additional or different terms which do not materially alter the terms of the offer constitutes an acceptance, unless the offeror, without undue delay, objects to the discrepancy. If the offeror does not object, the terms of the contract are the terms of the offer with the modifications contained in the acceptance.

ARTICLE 2.1.12

(Writings in confirmation)

If a writing which is sent within a reasonable time after the conclusion of the contract and which purports to be a confirmation of the contract contains additional or different terms, such terms become part of the contract, unless they materially alter the contract or the recipient, without undue delay, objects to the discrepancy.

ARTICLE 2.1.13

*(Conclusion of contract dependent on agreement on
specific matters or in a particular form)*

When in the course of negotiations one of the parties insists that the contract is not concluded until there is agreement on specific matters or in a particular form, no contract is concluded before agreement is reached on those matters or in that form.

ARTICLE 2.1.14

(Contract with terms deliberately left open)

(1)   If the parties intend to conclude a contract, the fact that they intentionally leave a term to be agreed upon in further negotiations or to be determined by one of the parties or a third person does not prevent a contract from coming into existence.

(2)   The existence of the contract is not affected by the fact that subsequently

(a)   the parties reach no agreement on the term;

(b)   the party who is to determine the term does not do so; or

(c)   the third person does not determine the term,

provided that there is an alternative means of rendering the term definite that is reasonable in the circumstances, having regard to the intention of the parties.

ARTICLE 2.1.15

(Negotiations in bad faith)

(1)   A part is free to negotiate and is not liable for failure to reach an agreement.

(2)   However, a party who negotiates or breaks off negotiations in bad faith is liable for the losses caused to the other party.

(3)   It is bad faith, in particular, for a party to enter into or continue negotiations when intending not to reach an agreement with the other party.

ARTICLE 2.1.16

(Duty of confidentiality)

Where information is given as confidential by one party in the course of negotiations, the other party is under a duty not to disclose that information or to use it improperly for its own purposes, whether or not a contract is subsequently concluded. Where appropriate, the remedy for breach of that duty may include compensation based on the benefit received by the other party.

ARTICLE 2.1.17

(Merger clauses)

A contract in writing which contains a clause indicating that the writing completely embodies the terms on which the parties have agreed cannot be contradicted or supplemented by evidence of prior statements or agreements. However, such statements or agreements may be used to interpret the writing.

ARTICLE 2.1.18

(Modification in a particular form)

A contract in writing which contains a clause requiring any modification or termination by agreement to be in a particular form may not be otherwise modified or terminated. However, a party may be precluded by its conduct from asserting such a clause to the extent that the other party has reasonably acted in reliance on that conduct.

ARTICLE 2.1.19

(Contracting under standard terms)

(1)   Where one party or both parties use standard terms in concluding a contract, the general rules on formation apply, subject to Articles 2.1.20–2.1.22.

(2)   Standard terms are provisions which are prepared in advance for general and repeated use by one party and which are actually used without negotiation with the other party.

ARTICLE 2.1.20

(Surprising terms)

(1)   No term contained in standard terms which is of such a character that the other party could not reasonably have expected it, is effective unless it has been expressly accepted by that party.

(2)   In determining whether a term is of such a character regard shall be had to its content, language and presentation.

ARTICLE 2.1.21

(Conflict between standard terms and non-standard terms)

In case of conflict between a standard term and a term which is not a standard term the latter prevails.

ARTICLE 2.1.22

(Battle of forms)

Where both parties use standard terms and reach agreement except on those terms, a contract is concluded on the basis of the agreed terms and of any standard terms which are common in substance unless one party clearly indicates in advance, or later and without undue delay informs the other party, that it does not intend to be bound by such a contract. . . .

CHAPTER 3—VALIDITY

SECTION 1: GENERAL PROVISIONS

ARTICLE 3.1.1

(Matters not covered)

This Chapter does not deal with lack of capacity.

. . .

1.   No need for consideration

In common law systems, "consideration" is traditionally seen as a prerequisite for the validity or enforceability of a contract, as well as for the modification or termination of a contract by the parties.

However, in commercial dealings this requirement is of minimal practical importance since in that context obligations are almost always undertaken by both parties. It is for this reason that Article 29(1) CISG dispenses with the requirement of consideration in relation to the modification and termination by the parties of contracts for the international sale of goods. The fact that this Article extends this approach to the conclusion, modification and termination by the parties of international commercial contracts in general can only bring about greater certainty and reduce litigation.

2.   No need for *cause*

This Article also excludes the requirement of "*cause*" which exists in some civil law systems and is in certain respects functionally similar to the common law "consideration".

. . .

ARTICLE 3.1.3

(Initial impossibility)

(1)   The mere fact that at the time of the conclusion of the contract the performance of the obligation assumed was impossible does not affect the validity of the contract.

(2)   The mere fact that at the time of the conclusion of the contract a party was not entitled to dispose of the assets to which the contract relates does not affect the validity of the contract.

ARTICLE 3.1.4

(Mandatory character of the provisions)

The provisions on fraud, threat, gross disparity and illegality contained in this Chapter are mandatory.

SECTION 2: GROUNDS FOR AVOIDANCE

ARTICLE 3.2.1

(Definition of mistake)

Mistake is an erroneous assumption relating to facts or to law existing when the contract was concluded.

ARTICLE 3.2.2

(Relevant mistake)

(1)   A party may only avoid the contract for mistake if, when the contract was concluded, the mistake was of such importance that a reasonable person in the same situation as the party in error would only have concluded the contract on materially different terms or would not have concluded it at all if the true state of affairs had been known, and

(a)   the other party made the same mistake, or caused the mistake, or knew or ought to have known of the mistake and it was contrary to reasonable commercial standards of fair dealing to leave the mistaken party in error; or

(b)   the other party had not at the time of avoidance reasonably acted in reliance on the contract.

(2)   However, a party may not avoid the contract if

(a)   it was grossly negligent in committing the mistake; or

(b)   the mistake relates to a matter in regard to which the risk of mistake was assumed or, having regard to the circumstances, should be borne by the mistaken party.

ARTICLE 3.2.3

(Error in expression or transmission)

An error occurring in the expression or transmission of a declaration is considered to be a mistake of the person from whom the declaration emanated.

ARTICLE 3.2.4

(Remedies for non-performance)

A party is not entitled to avoid the contract on the ground of mistake if the circumstances on which that party relies afford, or could have afforded, a remedy for non-performance.

ARTICLE 3.2.5

(Fraud)

A party may avoid the contract when it has been led to conclude the contract by the other party's fraudulent representation, including language or practices, or fraudulent non-disclosure of circumstances which, according to reasonable commercial standards of fair dealing, the latter party should have disclosed.

ARTICLE 3.2.6

(Threat)

A party may avoid the contract when it has been led to conclude the contract by the other party's unjustified threat which, having regard to the circumstances, is so imminent and serious as to leave the first party no reasonable alternative. In particular, a threat is unjustified if the act or omission with which a party has been threatened is wrongful in itself, or it is wrongful to use it as a means to obtain the conclusion of the contract. . . .

ARTICLE 3.2.8

(Third persons)

(1) Where fraud, threat, gross disparity or a party's mistake is imputable to, or is known or ought to be known by, a third person for whose acts the other party is responsible, the contract may be avoided under the same conditions as if the behaviour or knowledge had been that of the party itself.

ARTICLE 3.2.9

(Confirmation)

If the party entitled to avoid the contract expressly or impliedly confirms the contract after the period of time for giving notice of avoidance has begun to run, avoidance of the contract is excluded.

ARTICLE 3.2.10

(Loss of right to avoid)

(1) If a party is entitled to avoid the contract for mistake but the other party declares itself willing to perform or performs the contract as it was understood by the party entitled to avoidance, the contract is considered to have been concluded as the latter party understood it. The other party must make such a declaration or render such performance promptly after having been informed of the manner in which the party entitled to avoidance had understood the contract and before that party has reasonably acted in reliance on a notice of avoidance.

(2)   After such a declaration or performance the right to avoidance is lost and any earlier notice of avoidance is ineffective.

ARTICLE 3.2.11

(Notice of avoidance)

The right of a party to avoid the contract is exercised by notice to the other party.

ARTICLE 3.2.12

(Time limits)

(1)   Notice of avoidance shall be given within a reasonable time, having regard to the circumstances, after the avoiding party knew or could not have been unaware of the relevant facts or became capable of acting freely.

(2)   Where an individual term of the contract may be avoided by a party under Article 3.2.7, the period of time for giving notice of avoidance begins to run when that term is asserted by the other party.

ARTICLE 3.2.13

(Partial avoidance)

Where a ground of avoidance affects only individual terms of the contract, the effect of avoidance is limited to those terms unless, having regard to the circumstances, it is unreasonable to uphold the remaining contract.

ARTICLE 3.2.14

(Retroactive effect of avoidance)

Avoidance takes effect retroactively.

ARTICLE 3.2.15

(Restitution)

(1)   On avoidance either party may claim restitution of whatever it has supplied under the contract, or the part of it avoided, provided that such party concurrently makes restitution of whatever it has received under the contract, or the part of it avoided.

(2)   If restitution in kind is not possible or appropriate, an allowance has to be made in money whenever reasonable.

(3)   The recipient of the performance does not have to make an allowance in money if the impossibility to make restitution in kind is attributable to the other party.

(4)   Compensation may be claimed for expenses reasonably required to preserve or maintain the performance received.

ARTICLE 3.2.16

(Damages)

Irrespective of whether or not the contract has been avoided, the party who knew or ought to have known of the ground for avoidance is liable for damages so as to put the other party in the same position in which it would have been if it had not concluded the contract.

ARTICLE 3.2.17

(Unilateral declarations)

The provisions of this Chapter apply with appropriate adaptations to any communication of intention addressed by one party to the other.

SECTION 3: ILLEGALITY

ARTICLE 3.3.1

(Contracts infringing mandatory rules)

(1)   Where a contract infringes a mandatory rule, whether of national, international or supranational origin, applicable under Article 1.4 of these Principles, the effects of that infringement upon the contract are the effects, if any, expressly prescribed by that mandatory rule.

(2)   Where the mandatory rule does not expressly prescribe the effects of an infringement upon a contract, the parties have the right to exercise such remedies under the contract as in the circumstances are reasonable.

(3)   In determining what is reasonable regard is to be had in particular to:

    (a)   the purpose of the rule which has been infringed;

    (b)   the category of persons for whose protection the rule exists;

    (c)   any sanction that may be imposed under the rule infringed;

    (d)   the seriousness of the infringement;

    (e)   whether one or both parties knew or ought to have known of the infringement;

    (f)   whether the performance of the contract necessitates the infringement; and

    (g)   the parties' reasonable expectations.

ARTICLE 3.3.2

(Restitution)

(1)   Where there has been performance under a contract infringing a mandatory rule under Article 3.3.1, restitution may be granted where this would be reasonable in the circumstances.

(2)   In determining what is reasonable, regard is to be had, with the appropriate adaptations, to the criteria referred to in Article 3.3.1(3).

(3)   If restitution is granted, the rules set out in Article 3.2.15 apply with appropriate adaptations.

CHAPTER 4—INTERPRETATION

ARTICLE 4.1

(Intention of the parties)

(1)   A contract shall be interpreted according to the common intention of the parties.

(2)   If such an intention cannot be established, the contract shall be interpreted according to the meaning that reasonable persons of the same kind as the parties would give to it in the same circumstances.

ARTICLE 4.2

(Interpretation of statements and other conduct)

(1)   The statements and other conduct of a party shall be interpreted according to that party's intention if the other party knew or could not have been unaware of that intention.

(2)   If the preceding paragraph is not applicable, such statements and other conduct shall be interpreted according to the meaning that a reasonable person of the same kind as the other party would give to it in the same circumstances.

ARTICLE 4.3

(Relevant circumstances)

In applying Articles 4.1 and 4.2, regard shall be had to all the circumstances, including

(a)   preliminary negotiations between the parties;

(b)   practices which the parties have established between themselves;

(c)   the conduct of the parties subsequent to the conclusion of the contract;

(d)   the nature and purpose of the contract;

(e)   the meaning commonly given to terms and expressions in the trade concerned;

(f)   usages.

ARTICLE 4.4

(Reference to contract or statement as a whole)

Terms and expressions shall be interpreted in the light of the whole contract or statement in which they appear.

ARTICLE 4.5

(All terms to be given effect)

Contract terms shall be interpreted so as to give effect to all the terms rather than to deprive some of them of effect.

ARTICLE 4.6

(Contra proferentem rule)

If contract terms supplied by one party are unclear, an interpretation against that party is preferred.

ARTICLE 4.7

(Linguistic discrepancies)

Where a contract is drawn up in two or more language versions which are equally authoritative there is, in case of discrepancy between the versions, a preference for the interpretation according to a version in which the contract was originally drawn up.

ARTICLE 4.8

(Supplying an omitted term)

(1) Where the parties to a contract have not agreed with respect to a term which is important for a determination of their rights and duties, a term which is appropriate in the circumstances shall be supplied.

(2) In determining what is an appropriate term regard shall be had, among other factors, to

    (a) the intention of the parties;

    (b) the nature and purpose of the contract;

    (c) good faith and fair dealing;

    (d) reasonableness.

CHAPTER 5—CONTENT AND THIRD PARTY RIGHTS

SECTION 1: CONTENT

ARTICLE 5.1.1

(Express and implied obligations)

The contractual obligations of the parties may be express or implied.

ARTICLE 5.1.2

(Implied obligations)

Implied obligations stem from

(a) the nature and purpose of the contract;

(b) practices established between the parties and usages;

(c) good faith and fair dealing;

(d) reasonableness.

ARTICLE 5.1.3

(Co-operation between the parties)

Each party shall co-operate with the other party when such co-operation may reasonably be expected for the performance of that party's obligations.

ARTICLE 5.1.4

(Duty to achieve a specific result; Duty of best efforts)

(1) To the extent that an obligation of a party involves a duty to achieve a specific result, that party is bound to achieve that result.

(2) To the extent that an obligation of a party involves a duty of best efforts in the performance of an activity, that party is bound to make such efforts as would be made by a reasonable person of the same kind in the same circumstances.

ARTICLE 5.1.5

(Determination of kind of duty involved)

In determining the extent to which an obligation of a party involves a duty of best efforts in the performance of an activity or a duty to achieve a specific result, regard shall be had, among other factors, to

(a)   the way in which the obligation is expressed in the contract;

(b)   the contractual price and other terms of the contract;

(c)   the degree of risk normally involved in achieving the expected result;

(d)   the ability of the other party to influence the performance of the obligation.

ARTICLE 5.1.6

(Determination of quality of performance)

Where the quality of performance is neither fixed by, nor determinable from, the contract a party is bound to render a performance of a quality that is reasonable and not less than average in the circumstances.

ARTICLE 5.1.7

(Price determination)

(1)   Where a contract does not fix or make provision for determining the price, the parties are considered, in the absence of any indication to the contrary, to have made reference to the price generally charged at the time of the conclusion of the contract for such performance in comparable circumstances in the trade concerned or, if no such price is available, to a reasonable price.

(2)   Where the price is to be determined by one party and that determination is manifestly unreasonable, a reasonable price shall be substituted notwithstanding any contract term to the contrary.

(3)   Where the price is to be fixed by one party or a third person, and that party or the third person cannot or will not do so, the price shall be a reasonable price.

(4)   Where the price is to be fixed by reference to factors which do not exist or have ceased to exist or to be accessible, the nearest equivalent factor shall be treated as a substitute.

ARTICLE 5.1.8

(Termination of a contract for an indefinite period)

A contract for an indefinite period may be ended by either party by giving notice a reasonable time in advance. As to the effects of termination in general, and as to restitution, the provisions in Articles 7.3.5 and 7.3.7 apply.

ARTICLE 5.1.9

(Release by agreement)

(1)   An obligee may release its right by agreement with the obligor.

(2)   An offer to release a right gratuitously shall be deemed accepted if the obligor does not reject the offer without delay after having become aware of it.

SECTION 2: THIRD PARTY RIGHTS

ARTICLE 5.2.1

(Contracts in favour of third parties)

(1)   The parties (the "promisor" and the "promisee") may confer by express or implied agreement a right on a third party (the "beneficiary").

(2)   The existence and content of the beneficiary's right against the promisor are determined by the agreement of the parties and are subject to any conditions or other limitations under the agreement.

ARTICLE 5.2.2

(Third party identifiable)

The beneficiary must be identifiable with adequate certainty by the contract but need not be in existence at the time the contract is made.

ARTICLE 5.2.3

(Exclusion and limitation clauses)

The conferment of rights in the beneficiary includes the right to invoke a clause in the contract which excludes or limits the liability of the beneficiary.

ARTICLE 5.2.4

(Defences)

The promisor may assert against the beneficiary all defences which the promisor could assert against the promisee.

ARTICLE 5.2.5

(Revocation)

The parties may modify or revoke the rights conferred by the contract on the beneficiary until the beneficiary has accepted them or reasonably acted in reliance on them.

ARTICLE 5.2.6

(Renunciation)

The beneficiary may renounce a right conferred on it.

CHAPTER 6—PERFORMANCE

SECTION 1: PERFORMANCE IN GENERAL

ARTICLE 6.1.1

(Time of performance)

A party must perform its obligations:

(a)   if a time is fixed by or determinable from the contract, at that time;

(b)   if a period of time is fixed by or determinable from the contract, at any time within that period unless circumstances indicate that the other party is to choose a time;

(c)   in any other case, within a reasonable time after the conclusion of the contract.

ARTICLE 6.1.2

(Performance at one time or in instalments)

In cases under Article 6.1.1(b) or (c), a party must perform its obligations at one time if that performance can be rendered at one time and the circumstances do not indicate otherwise.

ARTICLE 6.1.3

(Partial performance)

(1)   The obligee may reject an offer to perform in part at the time performance is due, whether or not such offer is coupled with an assurance as to the balance of the performance, unless the obligee has no legitimate interest in so doing.

(2)   Additional expenses caused to the obligee by partial performance are to be borne by the obligor without prejudice to any other remedy.

ARTICLE 6.1.4

(Order of performance)

(1)   To the extent that the performances of the parties can be rendered simultaneously, the parties are bound to render them simultaneously unless the circumstances indicate otherwise.

(2)   To the extent that the performance of only one party requires a period of time, that party is bound to render its performance first, unless the circumstances indicate otherwise.

ARTICLE 6.1.5

(Earlier performance)

(1)   The obligee may reject an earlier performance unless it has no legitimate interest in so doing.

(2)   Acceptance by a party of an earlier performance does not affect the time for the performance of its own obligations if that time has been fixed irrespective of the performance of the other party's obligations.

(3)   Additional expenses caused to the obligee by earlier performance are to be borne by the obligor, without prejudice to any other remedy.

ARTICLE 6.1.6

(Place of performance)

(1)   If the place of performance is neither fixed by, nor determinable from, the contract, a party is to perform:

(a)   a monetary obligation, at the obligee's place of business;

(b)   any other obligation, at its own place of business.

(2)   A party must bear any increase in the expenses incidental to performance which is caused by a change in its place of business subsequent to the conclusion of the contract.

ARTICLE 6.1.7

(Payment by [check] or other instrument)

(1)   Payment may be made in any form used in the ordinary course of business at the place for payment.

(2)　However, an obligee who accepts, either by virtue of paragraph (1) or voluntarily, a [check], any other order to pay or a promise to pay, is presumed to do so only on condition that it will be [honored].

ARTICLE 6.1.8

(Payment by funds transfer)

(1)　Unless the obligee has indicated a particular account, payment may be made by a transfer to any of the financial institutions in which the obligee has made it known that it has an account.

(2)　In case of payment by a transfer the obligation of the obligor is discharged when the transfer to the obligee's financial institution becomes effective.

ARTICLE 6.1.9

(Currency of payment)

(1)　If a monetary obligation is expressed in a currency other than that of the place for payment, it may be paid by the obligor in the currency of the place for payment unless

    (a)　that currency is not freely convertible; or

    (b)　the parties have agreed that payment should be made only in the currency in which the monetary obligation is expressed.

(2)　If it is impossible for the obligor to make payment in the currency in which the monetary obligation is expressed, the obligee may require payment in the currency of the place for payment, even in the case referred to in paragraph (1)(b).

(3)　Payment in the currency of the place for payment is to be made according to the applicable rate of exchange prevailing there when payment is due.

(4)　However, if the obligor has not paid at the time when payment is due, the obligee may require payment according to the applicable rate of exchange prevailing either when payment is due or at the time of actual payment.

ARTICLE 6.1.10

(Currency not expressed)

Where a monetary obligation is not expressed in a particular currency, payment must be made in the currency of the place where payment is to be made.

ARTICLE 6.1.11

(Costs of performance)

Each party shall bear the costs of performance of its obligations.

ARTICLE 6.1.12

(Imputation of payments)

(1)　An obligor owing several monetary obligations to the same obligee may specify at the time of payment the debt to which it intends the payment to be applied. However, the payment discharges first any expenses, then interest due and finally the principal.

(2)　If the obligor makes no such specification, the obligee may, within a reasonable time after payment, declare to the obligor the obligation to which it imputes the payment, provided that the obligation is due and undisputed.

(3)   In the absence of imputation under paragraphs (1) or (2), payment is imputed to that obligation which satisfies one of the following criteria and in the order indicated:

    (a)   an obligation which is due or which is the first to fall due;

    (b)   the obligation for which the obligee has least security;

    (c)   the obligation which is the most burdensome for the obligor;

    (d)   the obligation which has arisen first.

If none of the preceding criteria applies, payment is imputed to all the obligations proportionally.

ARTICLE 6.1.13

(Imputation of non-monetary obligations)

Article 6.1.12 applies with appropriate adaptations to the imputation of performance of non-monetary obligations.

ARTICLE 6.1.14

(Application for public permission)

Where the law of a State requires a public permission affecting the validity of the contract or its performance and neither that law nor the circumstances indicate otherwise

    (a)   if only one party has its place of business in that State, that party shall take the measures necessary to obtain the permission;

    (b)   in any other case the party whose performance requires permission shall take the necessary measures.

ARTICLE 6.1.15

(Procedure in applying for permission)

(1)   The party required to take the measures necessary to obtain the permission shall do so without undue delay and shall bear any expenses incurred.

(2)   That party shall whenever appropriate give the other party notice of the grant or refusal of such permission without undue delay.

ARTICLE 6.1.16

(Permission neither granted nor refused)

(1)   If, notwithstanding the fact that the party responsible has taken all measures required, permission is neither granted nor refused within an agreed period or, where no period has been agreed, within a reasonable time from the conclusion of the contract, either party is entitled to terminate the contract.

(2)   Where the permission affects some terms only, paragraph (1) does not apply if, having regard to the circumstances, it is reasonable to uphold the remaining contract even if the permission is refused.

ARTICLE 6.1.17

(Permission refused)

(1)   The refusal of a permission affecting the validity of the contract renders the contract void. If the refusal affects the validity of some terms only, only such terms are void if, having regard to the circumstances, it is reasonable to uphold the remaining contract.

(2)   Where the refusal of a permission renders the performance of the contract impossible in whole or in part, the rules on non-performance apply.

SECTION 2: HARDSHIP

ARTICLE 6.2.1

(Contract to be observed)

Where the performance of a contract becomes more onerous for one of the parties, that party is nevertheless bound to perform its obligations subject to the following provisions on hardship.

ARTICLE 6.2.2

(Definition of hardship)

There is hardship where the occurrence of events fundamentally alters the equilibrium of the contract either because the cost of a party's performance has increased or because the value of the performance a party receives has diminished, and

(a)   the events occur or become known to the disadvantaged party after the conclusion of the contract;

(b)   the events could not reasonably have been taken into account by the disadvantaged party at the time of the conclusion of the contract;

(c)   the events are beyond the control of the disadvantaged party; and

(d)   the risk of the events was not assumed by the disadvantaged party.

ARTICLE 6.2.3

(Effects of hardship)

(1)   In case of hardship the disadvantaged party is entitled to request renegotiations. The request shall be made without undue delay and shall indicate the grounds on which it is based.

(2)   The request for renegotiation does not in itself entitle the disadvantaged party to withhold performance.

(3)   Upon failure to reach agreement within a reasonable time either party may resort to the court.

(4)   If the court finds hardship it may, if reasonable,

(a)   terminate the contract at a date and on terms to be fixed; or

(b)   adapt the contract with a view to restoring its equilibrium.

CHAPTER 7—NON-PERFORMANCE

SECTION 1: NON-PERFORMANCE IN GENERAL

ARTICLE 7.1.1

(Non-performance defined)

Non-performance is failure by a party to perform any of its obligations under the contract, including defective performance or late performance.

ARTICLE 7.1.2

(Interference by the other party)

A party may not rely on the non-performance of the other party to the extent that such non-performance was caused by the first party's act or omission or by another event as to which the first party bears the risk.

ARTICLE 7.1.3

(Withholding performance)

(1)   Where the parties are to perform simultaneously, either party may withhold performance until the other party tenders its performance.

(2)   Where the parties are to perform consecutively, the party that is to perform later may withhold its performance until the first party has performed.

ARTICLE 7.1.4

(Cure by non-performing party)

(1)   The non-performing party may, at its own expense, cure any non-performance, provided that

(a)   without undue delay, it gives notice indicating the proposed manner and timing of the cure;

(b)   cure is appropriate in the circumstances;

(c)   the aggrieved party has no legitimate interest in refusing cure; and

(d)   cure is effected promptly.

(2)   The right to cure is not precluded by notice of termination.

(3)   Upon effective notice of cure, rights of the aggrieved party that are inconsistent with the non-performing party's performance are suspended until the time for cure has expired.

(4)   The aggrieved party may withhold performance pending cure.

(5)   Notwithstanding cure, the aggrieved party retains the right to claim damages for delay as well as for any harm caused or not prevented by the cure.

ARTICLE 7.1.5

(Additional period for performance)

(1)   In a case of non-performance the aggrieved party may by notice to the other party allow an additional period of time for performance.

(2)   During the additional period the aggrieved party may withhold performance of its own reciprocal obligations and may claim damages but may not resort to any other remedy. If it receives notice from the other party that the latter will not perform within that period, or if upon expiry of that period due performance has not been made, the aggrieved party may resort to any of the remedies that may be available under this Chapter.

(3)   Where in a case of delay in performance which is not fundamental the aggrieved party has given notice allowing an additional period of time of reasonable length, it may terminate the contract at the end of that period. If the additional period allowed is not of reasonable length it shall be extended to a reasonable length. The aggrieved party may in its notice provide that if the other party fails to perform within the period allowed by the notice the contract shall automatically terminate.

(4)   Paragraph (3) does not apply where the obligation which has not been performed is only a minor part of the contractual obligation of the non-performing party.

ARTICLE 7.1.6

(Exemption clauses)

A clause which limits or excludes one party's liability for non-performance or which permits one party to render performance substantially different from what the other party reasonably expected may not be invoked if it would be grossly unfair to do so, having regard to the purpose of the contract.

ARTICLE 7.1.7

(Force majeure)

(1)   Non-performance by a party is excused if that party proves that the non-performance was due to an impediment beyond its control and that it could not reasonably be expected to have taken the impediment into account at the time of the conclusion of the contract or to have avoided or overcome it or its consequences.

(2)   When the impediment is only temporary, the excuse shall have effect for such period as is reasonable having regard to the effect of the impediment on the performance of the contract.

(3)   The party who fails to perform must give notice to the other party of the impediment and its effect on its ability to perform. If the notice is not received by the other party within a reasonable time after the party who fails to perform knew or ought to have known of the impediment, it is liable for damages resulting from such non-receipt.

(4)   Nothing in this article prevents a party from exercising a right to terminate the contract or to withhold performance or request interest on money due.

SECTION 2: RIGHT TO PERFORMANCE

ARTICLE 7.2.1

(Performance of monetary obligation)

Where a party who is obliged to pay money does not do so, the other party may require payment.

ARTICLE 7.2.2

(Performance of non-monetary obligation)

Where a party who owes an obligation other than one to pay money does not perform, the other party may require performance, unless

(a)   performance is impossible in law or in fact;

(b)   performance or, where relevant, enforcement is unreasonably burdensome or expensive;

(c)   the party entitled to performance may reasonably obtain performance from another source;

(d)   performance is of an exclusively personal character; or

(e)   the party entitled to performance does not require performance within a reasonable time after it has, or ought to have, become aware of the non-performance.

ARTICLE 7.2.3

(Repair and replacement of defective performance)

The right to performance includes in appropriate cases the right to require repair, replacement, or other cure of defective performance. The provisions of Articles 7.2.1 and 7.2.2 apply accordingly.

ARTICLE 7.2.4

(Judicial penalty)

(1)   Where the court orders a party to perform, it may also direct that this party pay a penalty if it does not comply with the order.

(2)   The penalty shall be paid to the aggrieved party unless mandatory provisions of the law of the forum provide otherwise. Payment of the penalty to the aggrieved party does not exclude any claim for damages.

ARTICLE 7.2.5

(Change of remedy)

(1)   An aggrieved party who has required performance of a non-monetary obligation and who has not received performance within a period fixed or otherwise within a reasonable period of time may invoke any other remedy.

(2)   Where the decision of a court for performance of a non-monetary obligation cannot be enforced, the aggrieved party may invoke any other remedy.

SECTION 3: TERMINATION

ARTICLE 7.3.1

(Right to terminate the contract)

(1)   A party may terminate the contract where the failure of the other party to perform an obligation under the contract amounts to a fundamental non-performance.

(2)   In determining whether a failure to perform an obligation amounts to a fundamental non-performance regard shall be had, in particular, to whether

(a)   the non-performance substantially deprives the aggrieved party of what it was entitled to expect under the contract unless the other party did not foresee and could not reasonably have foreseen such result;

(b)   strict compliance with the obligation which has not been performed is of essence under the contract;

(c)   the non-performance is intentional or reckless;

(d)   the non-performance gives the aggrieved party reason to believe that it cannot rely on the other party's future performance;

(e)   the non-performing party will suffer disproportionate loss as a result of the preparation or performance if the contract is terminated.

(3)   In the case of delay the aggrieved party may also terminate the contract if the other party fails to perform before the time allowed it under Article 7.1.5 has expired.

ARTICLE 7.3.2

(Notice of termination)

(1)   The right of a party to terminate the contract is exercised by notice to the other party.

(2)   If performance has been offered late or otherwise does not conform to the contract the aggrieved party will lose its right to terminate the contract unless it gives notice to the other party within a reasonable time after it has or ought to have become aware of the offer or of the non-conforming performance.

ARTICLE 7.3.3

(Anticipatory non-performance)

Where prior to the date for performance by one of the parties it is clear that there will be a fundamental non-performance by that party, the other party may terminate the contract.

ARTICLE 7.3.4

(Adequate assurance of due performance)

A party who reasonably believes that there will be a fundamental non-performance by the other party may demand adequate assurance of due performance and may meanwhile withhold its own performance. Where this assurance is not provided within a reasonable time the party demanding it may terminate the contract.

ARTICLE 7.3.5

(Effects of termination in general)

(1)   Termination of the contract releases both parties from their obligation to effect and to receive future performance.

(2)   Termination does not preclude a claim for damages for non-performance.

(3)   Termination does not affect any provision in the contract for the settlement of disputes or any other term of the contract which is to operate even after termination.

ARTICLE 7.3.6

(Restitution with respect to contracts to be performed at one time)

(1)   On termination of a contract to be performed at one time either party may claim restitution of whatever it has supplied under the contract, provided that such party concurrently makes restitution of whatever it has received under the contract.

(2)   If restitution in kind is not possible or appropriate, an allowance has to be made in money whenever reasonable.

(3)   The recipient of the performance does not have to make an allowance in money if the impossibility to make restitution in kind is attributable to the other party.

(4)   Compensation may be claimed for expenses reasonably required to preserve or maintain the performance received.

ARTICLE 7.3.7

(Restitution with respect to long-term contracts)

(1)   On termination of a long-term contract restitution can only be claimed for the period after termination has taken effect, provided the contract is divisible.

(2)   As far as restitution has to be made, the provisions of Article 7.3.6 apply.

SECTION 4: DAMAGES

ARTICLE 7.4.1

(Right to damages)

Any non-performance gives the aggrieved party a right to damages either exclusively or in conjunction with any other remedies except where the non-performance is excused under these Principles.

ARTICLE 7.4.2

(Full compensation)

(1)   The aggrieved party is entitled to full compensation for harm sustained as a result of the non-performance. Such harm includes both any loss which it suffered and any gain of which it was deprived, taking into account any gain to the aggrieved party resulting from its avoidance of cost or harm.

(2)   Such harm may be non-pecuniary and includes, for instance, physical suffering or emotional distress.

ARTICLE 7.4.3

(Certainty of harm)

(1)   Compensation is due only for harm, including future harm, that is established with a reasonable degree of certainty.

(2)   Compensation may be due for the loss of a chance in proportion to the probability of its occurrence.

(3)   Where the amount of damages cannot be established with a sufficient degree of certainty, the assessment is at the discretion of the court.

ARTICLE 7.4.4

(Foreseeability of harm)

The non-performing party is liable only for harm which it foresaw or could reasonably have foreseen at the time of the conclusion of the contract as being likely to result from its non-performance.

ARTICLE 7.4.5

(Proof of harm in case of replacement transaction)

Where the aggrieved party has terminated the contract and has made a replacement transaction within a reasonable time and in a reasonable manner it may recover the difference between the contract price and the price of the replacement transaction as well as damages for any further harm.

ARTICLE 7.4.6

(Proof of harm by current price)

(1)   Where the aggrieved party has terminated the contract and has not made a replacement transaction but there is a current price for the performance contracted for, it may recover the difference between the contract price and the price current at the time the contract is terminated as well as damages for any further harm.

(2)   Current price is the price generally charged for goods delivered or services rendered in comparable circumstances at the place where the contract should have been performed or, if there is

no current price at that place, the current price at such other place that appears reasonable to take as a reference.

ARTICLE 7.4.7

(Harm due in part to aggrieved party)

Where the harm is due in part to an act or omission of the aggrieved party or to another event as to which that party bears the risk, the amount of damages shall be reduced to the extent that these factors have contributed to the harm, having regard to the conduct of each of the parties.

ARTICLE 7.4.8

(Mitigation of harm)

(1) The non-performing party is not liable for harm suffered by the aggrieved party to the extent that the harm could have been reduced by the latter party's taking reasonable steps.

(2) The aggrieved party is entitled to recover any expenses reasonably incurred in attempting to reduce the harm.

ARTICLE 7.4.9

(Interest for failure to pay money)

(1) If a party does not pay a sum of money when it falls due the aggrieved party is entitled to interest upon that sum from the time when payment is due to the time of payment whether or not the non-payment is excused.

(2) The rate of interest shall be the average bank short-term lending rate to prime borrowers prevailing for the currency of payment at the place for payment, or where no such rate exists at that place, then the same rate in the State of the currency of payment. In the absence of such a rate at either place the rate of interest shall be the appropriate rate fixed by the law of the State of the currency of payment.

(3) The aggrieved party is entitled to additional damages if the non-payment caused it a greater harm.

ARTICLE 7.4.10

(Interest on damages)

Unless otherwise agreed, interest on damages for non-performance of non-monetary obligations accrues as from the time of non-performance.

ARTICLE 7.4.11

(Manner of monetary redress)

(1) Damages are to be paid in a lump sum. However, they may be payable in instalments where the nature of the harm makes this appropriate.

(2) Damages to be paid in instalments may be indexed.

ARTICLE 7.4.12

(Currency in which to assess damages)

Damages are to be assessed either in the currency in which the monetary obligation was expressed or in the currency in which the harm was suffered, whichever is more appropriate.

ARTICLE 7.4.13

(Agreed payment for non-performance)

(1)   Where the contract provides that a party who does not perform is to pay a specified sum to the aggrieved party for such non-performance, the aggrieved party is entitled to that sum irrespective of its actual harm.

(2)   However, notwithstanding any agreement to the contrary the specified sum may be reduced to a reasonable amount where it is grossly excessive in relation to the harm resulting from the non-performance and to the other circumstances. . . .

CHAPTER 9—ASSIGNMENT OF RIGHTS, TRANSFER OF OBLIGATIONS, ASSIGNMENT OF CONTRACTS

SECTION 1: ASSIGNMENT OF RIGHTS

ARTICLE 9.1.1

(Definitions)

"Assignment of a right" means the transfer by agreement from one person (the "assignor") to another person (the "assignee"), including transfer by way of security, of the assignor's right to payment of a monetary sum or other performance from a third person ("the obligor").

ARTICLE 9.1.2

(Exclusions)

This Section does not apply to transfers made under the special rules governing the transfers:

(a)   of instruments such as negotiable instruments, documents of title or financial instruments, or

(b)   of rights in the course of transferring a business.

ARTICLE 9.1.3

(Assignability of non-monetary rights)

A right to non-monetary performance may be assigned only if the assignment does not render the obligation significantly more burdensome.

ARTICLE 9.1.4

(Partial assignment)

(1)   A right to the payment of a monetary sum may be assigned partially.

(2)   A right to other performance may be assigned partially only if it is divisible, and the assignment does not render the obligation significantly more burdensome.

ARTICLE 9.1.5

(Future rights)

A future right is deemed to be transferred at the time of the agreement, provided the right, when it comes into existence, can be identified as the right to which the assignment relates.

ARTICLE 9.1.6

(Rights assigned without individual specification)

A number of rights may be assigned without individual specification, provided such rights can be identified as rights to which the assignment relates at the time of the assignment or when they come into existence.

ARTICLE 9.1.7

(Agreement between assignor and assignee sufficient)

(1)   A right is assigned by mere agreement between the assignor and the assignee, without notice to the obligor.

(2)   The consent of the obligor is not required unless the obligation in the circumstances is of an essentially personal character.

ARTICLE 9.1.8

(Obligor's additional costs)

The obligor has a right to be compensated by the assignor or the assignee for any additional costs caused by the assignment.

ARTICLE 9.1.9

(Non-assignment clauses)

(1)   The assignment of a right to the payment of a monetary sum is effective notwithstanding an agreement between the assignor and the obligor limiting or prohibiting such an assignment. However, the assignor may be liable to the obligor for breach of contract.

(2)   The assignment of a right to other performance is ineffective if it is contrary to an agreement between the assignor and the obligor limiting or prohibiting the assignment. Nevertheless, the assignment is effective if the assignee, at the time of the assignment, neither knew nor ought to have known of the agreement. The assignor may then be liable to the obligor for breach of contract.

ARTICLE 9.1.10

(Notice to the obligor)

(1)   Until the obligor receives a notice of the assignment from either the assignor or the assignee, it is discharged by paying the assignor.

(2)   After the obligor receives such a notice, it is discharged only by paying the assignee.

ARTICLE 9.1.11

(Successive assignments)

If the same right has been assigned by the same assignor to two or more successive assignees, the obligor is discharged by paying according to the order in which the notices were received.

ARTICLE 9.1.12

(Adequate proof of assignment)

(1)   If notice of the assignment is given by the assignee, the obligor may request the assignee to provide within a reasonable time adequate proof that the assignment has been made.

(2)   Until adequate proof is provided, the obligor may withhold payment.

(3)   Unless adequate proof is provided, notice is not effective.

(4)   Adequate proof includes, but is not limited to, any writing emanating from the assignor and indicating that the assignment has taken place.

ARTICLE 9.1.13

(Defences and rights of set-off)

(1)   The obligor may assert against the assignee all defences that the obligor could assert against the assignor.

(2)   The obligor may exercise against the assignee any right of set-off available to the obligor against the assignor up to the time notice of assignment was received.

ARTICLE 9.1.14

(Rights related to the right assigned)

The assignment of a right transfers to the assignee:

(a)   all the assignor's rights to payment or other performance under the contract in respect of the right assigned, and

(b)   all rights securing performance of the right assigned.

ARTICLE 9.1.15

(Undertakings of the assignor)

The assignor undertakes towards the assignee, except as otherwise disclosed to the assignee, that:

(a)   the assigned right exists at the time of the assignment, unless the right is a future right;

(b)   the assignor is entitled to assign the right;

(c)   the right has not been previously assigned to another assignee, and it is free from any right or claim from a third party;

(d)   the obligor does not have any defences;

(e)   neither the obligor nor the assignor has given notice of set-off concerning the assigned right and will not give any such notice;

(f)   the assignor will reimburse the assignee for any payment received from the obligor before notice of the assignment was given.

SECTION 2: TRANSFER OF OBLIGATIONS

ARTICLE 9.2.1

(Modes of transfer)

An obligation to pay money or render other performance may be transferred from one person (the "original obligor") to another person (the "new obligor") either

(a)   by an agreement between the original obligor and the new obligor subject to Article 9.2.3, or

(b)   by an agreement between the obligee and the new obligor, by which the new obligor assumes the obligation.

ARTICLE 9.2.2

(Exclusion)

This Section does not apply to transfers of obligations made under the special rules governing transfers of obligations in the course of transferring a business.

ARTICLE 9.2.3

(Requirement of obligee's consent to transfer)

The transfer of an obligation by an agreement between the original obligor and the new obligor requires the consent of the obligee.

ARTICLE 9.2.4

(Advance consent of obligee)

(1) The obligee may give its consent in advance.

(2) If the obligee has given its consent in advance, the transfer of the obligation becomes effective when a notice of the transfer is given to the obligee or when the obligee acknowledges it.

ARTICLE 9.2.5

(Discharge of original obligor)

(1) The obligee may discharge the original obligor.

(2) The obligee may also retain the original obligor as an obligor in case the new obligor does not perform properly.

(3) Otherwise the original obligor and the new obligor are jointly and severally liable.

ARTICLE 9.2.6

(Third party performance)

(1) Without the obligee's consent, the obligor may contract with another person that this person will perform the obligation in place of the obligor, unless the obligation in the circumstances has an essentially personal character.

(2) The obligee retains its claim against the obligor.

ARTICLE 9.2.7

(Defences and rights of set-off)

(1) The new obligor may assert against the obligee all defences which the original obligor could assert against the obligee.

(2) The new obligor may not exercise against the obligee any right of set-off available to the original obligor against the obligee.

ARTICLE 9.2.8

(Rights related to the obligation transferred)

(1) The obligee may assert against the new obligor all its rights to payment or other performance under the contract in respect of the obligation transferred.

(2)   If the original obligor is discharged under Article 9.2.5(1), a security granted by any person other than the new obligor for the performance of the obligation is discharged, unless that other person agrees that it should continue to be available to the obligee.

(3)   Discharge of the original obligor also extends to any security of the original obligor given to the obligee for the performance of the obligation, unless the security is over an asset which is transferred as part of a transaction between the original obligor and the new obligor.

SECTION 3: ASSIGNMENT OF CONTRACTS

ARTICLE 9.3.1

(Definitions)

"Assignment of a contract" means the transfer by agreement from one person (the "assignor") to another person (the "assignee") of the assignor's rights and obligations arising out of a contract with another person (the "other party").

ARTICLE 9.3.2

(Exclusion)

This Section does not apply to the assignment of contracts made under the special rules governing transfers of contracts in the course of transferring a business.

ARTICLE 9.3.3

(Requirement of consent of the other party)

The assignment of a contract requires the consent of the other party.

ARTICLE 9.3.4

(Advance consent of the other party)

(1)   The other party may give its consent in advance.

(2)   If the other party has given its consent in advance, the assignment of the contract becomes effective when a notice of the assignment is given to the other party or when the other party acknowledges it.

ARTICLE 9.3.5

(Discharge of the assignor)

(1)   The other party may discharge the assignor.

(2)   The other party may also retain the assignor as an obligor in case the assignee does not perform properly.

(3)   Otherwise the assignor and the assignee are jointly and severally liable.

ARTICLE 9.3.6

(Defences and rights of set-off)

(1)   To the extent that the assignment of a contract involves an assignment of rights, Article 9.1.13 applies accordingly.

(2)   To the extent that the assignment of a contract involves a transfer of obligations, Article 9.2.7 applies accordingly.

ARTICLE 9.3.7

(Rights transferred with the contract)

(1) To the extent that the assignment of a contract involves an assignment of rights, Article 9.1.14 applies accordingly.

(2) To the extent that the assignment of a contract involves a transfer of obligations, Article 9.2.8 applies accordingly. . . .

THE PRINCIPLES OF EUROPEAN CONTRACT LAW

(2002)

(Excerpts)

[In 1982, the European Commission directed its Commission on European Contract Law ("CECL") to begin the process of creating a modern and uniform contract law among the member States of what is now the European Union ("EU"). The goal was to develop a common body of contract law that harmonizes the member States' often-inconsistent domestic laws, as required for the proper functioning of their common market. Without such a trans-European body of law, a contract made within the European common market would be governed by the law of one nation on the basis of choice-of-law principles and the contractual designation, if any, of that nation's law. With such a body of law, the European Commission hoped, the flow of goods and services within the European common market would be facilitated.

[Though progress was slow, a revised text of the Principles of European Contract Law ("PECL") was published in 2002. The PECL deals mainly with issues that affect international commercial contracts, but they are intended to apply to other contracts as well. When formulating them, the CECL drew on the contract laws of the EU member States, and non-EU sources such as the United Nations Convention on Contracts for the International Sale of Goods and the American Law Institute's Restatement (Second) of Contracts, both of which are included in this pamphlet above. The PECL is not binding on anyone; instead, the CECL hopes, it will serve as the first draft of part of an eventual European Civil Code, which would address contract law as well as many other topics.

[The EU has issued Directives (laws) on several specific topics within contract law. Two of them, which affect consumer contracts, are included in this pamphlet below.]

CHAPTER 1. GENERAL PROVISIONS

CHAPTER 2. FORMATION

CHAPTER 3. AUTHORITY OF AGENTS

CHAPTER 4. VALIDITY

CHAPTER 1—GENERAL PROVISIONS*

Section 1: Scope of the Principles

Article 1.101. Application of the Principles

(1)   These Principles are intended to be applied as general rules of contract law in the European Union.

(2)   These Principles will apply when the parties have agreed to incorporate them into their contract or that their contract is to be governed by them.

(3)   These Principles may be applied when the parties:

(a)   have agreed that their contract is to be governed by "general principles of law", the "lex mercatoria" or the like; or

(b)   have not chosen any system or rules of law to govern their contract.

(4)   These Principles may provide a solution to the issue raised where the system or rules of law applicable do not do so.

Article 1.102. Freedom of Contract

(1)   Parties are free to enter into a contract and to determine its contents, subject to the requirements of good faith and fair dealing, and the mandatory rules established by these Principles.

(2)   The parties may exclude the application of any of the Principles or derogate from or vary their effects, except as otherwise provided by these Principles.

Article 1.103. Mandatory Law

(1)   Where the law otherwise applicable so allows, the parties may choose to have their contract governed by the Principles, with the effect that national mandatory rules are not applicable.

(2)   Effect should nevertheless be given to those mandatory rules of national, supranational and international law which, according to the relevant rules of private international law, are applicable irrespective of the law governing the contract.

Article 1.104. Application to Questions of Consent

(1)   The existence and validity of the agreement of the parties to adopt or incorporate these Principles shall be determined by these Principles.

(2)   Nevertheless, a party may rely upon the law of the country in which it has its habitual residence to establish that it did not consent if it appears from the circumstances that it would not be reasonable to determine the effect of the party's conduct in accordance with these Principles.

Article 1.105. Usages and Practices

(1)   The parties are bound by any usage to which they have agreed and by any practice they have established between themselves.

(2)   The parties are bound by a usage which would be considered generally applicable by persons in the same situation as the parties, except where the application of such usage would be unreasonable.

---

*   For ease of reading, where the English and American spelling of words used in the Principles of European Contract Law differ, American spellings have been substituted for the English spellings. For example, "favor" has been substituted for "favour" and "authorized" has been substituted for "authorised". (Footnote by ed.)

Article 1.106. Interpretation and Supplementation

(1)   These Principles should be interpreted and developed in accordance with their purposes. In particular, regard should be had to the need to promote good faith and fair dealing, certainty in contractual relationships and uniformity of application.

(2)   Issues within the scope of these Principles but not expressly settled by them are so far as possible to be settled in accordance with the ideas underlying the Principles. Failing this, the legal system applicable by virtue of the rules of private international law is to be applied.

Article 1.107. Application of the Principles by Way of Analogy

These Principles apply with appropriate modifications to agreements to modify or end a contract, to unilateral promises and to other statements and conduct indicating intention.

Section 2: General Duties

Article 1.201. Good Faith and Fair Dealing

(1)   Each party must act in accordance with good faith and fair dealing.

(2)   The parties may not exclude or limit this duty.

Article 1.202. Duty to Co-operate

Each party owes to the other a duty to co-operate in order to give full effect to the contract.

Section 3: Terminology and Other Provisions

Article 1.301. Meaning of Terms

In these Principles, except where the context otherwise requires:

(1)   'act' includes omission;

(2)   'court' includes arbitral tribunal;

(3)   an 'intentional' act includes an act done recklessly;

(4)   'non-performance' denotes any failure to perform an obligation under the contract, whether or not excused, and includes delayed performance, defective performance and failure to co-operate in order to give full effect to the contract.

(5)   a matter is 'material' if it is one which a reasonable person in the same situation as one party ought to have known would influence the other party in its decision whether to contract on the proposed terms or to contract at all;

(6)   'written' statements include communications made by telegram, telex, telefax and electronic mail and other means of communication capable of providing a readable record of the statement on both sides

Article 1.302. Reasonableness

Under these Principles reasonableness is to be judged by what persons acting in good faith and in the same situation as the parties would consider to be reasonable. In particular, in assessing what is reasonable the nature and purpose of the contract, the circumstances of the case and the usages and practices of the trades or professions involved should be taken into account.

Article 1.303. Notice

(1)   Any notice may be given by any means, whether in writing or otherwise, appropriate to the circumstances.

(2)   Subject to paragraphs (4) and (5), any notice becomes effective when it reaches the addressee.

(3)   A notice reaches the addressee when it is delivered to it or to its place of business or mailing address, or, if it does not have a place of business or mailing address, to its habitual residence.

(4)   If one party gives notice to the other because of the other's non-performance or because such non-performance is reasonably anticipated by the first party, and the notice is properly dispatched or given, a delay or inaccuracy in the transmission of the notice or its failure to arrive does not prevent it from having effect. The notice shall have effect from the time at which it would have arrived in normal circumstances.

(5)   A notice has no effect if a withdrawal of it reaches the addressee before or at the same time as the notice.

(6)   In this Article, 'notice' includes the communication of a promise, statement, offer, acceptance, demand, request or other declaration.

Article 1.304. Computation of Time

(1)   A period of time set by a party in a written document for the addressee to reply or take other action begins to run from the date stated as the date of the document. If no date is shown, the period begins to run from the moment the document reaches the addressee.

(2)   Official holidays and official non-working days occurring during the period are included in calculating the period. However, if the last day of the period is an official holiday or official non-working day at the address of the addressee, or at the place where a prescribed act is to be performed, the period is extended until the first following working day in that place.

(3)   Periods of time expressed in days, weeks, months or years shall begin at 00.00 on the next day and shall end at 24.00 on the last day of the period; but any reply that has to reach the party which set the period must arrive, or other act which is to be done must be completed, by the normal close of business in the relevant place on the last day of the period.

Article 1.305. Imputed Knowledge and Intention

If any person who with a party's assent was involved in making a contract, or who was entrusted with performance by a party or performed with its assent:

(a)   knew or foresaw a fact, or ought to have known or foreseen it; or

(b)   acted intentionally or with gross negligence, or not in accordance with good faith and fair dealing, this knowledge, foresight or behaviour is imputed to the party itself.

CHAPTER 2—FORMATION

Section 1: General Provisions

Article 2.101. Conditions for the Conclusion of a Contract

(1)   A contract is concluded if:

(a)   the parties intend to be legally bound, and

(b)   they reach a sufficient agreement without any further requirement.

(2)   A contract need not be concluded or evidenced in writing nor is it subject to any other requirement as to form. The contract may be proved by any means, including witnesses.

Article 2.102. Intention

The intention of a party to be legally bound by contract is to be determined from the party's statements or conduct as they were reasonably understood by the other party.

Article 2.103. Sufficient Agreement

(1)   There is sufficient agreement if the terms:

    (a)   have been sufficiently defined by the parties so that the contract can be enforced, or

    (b)   can be determined under these Principles.

(2)   However, if one of the parties refuses to conclude a contract unless the parties have agreed on some specific matter, there is no contract unless agreement on that matter has been reached.

Article 2.104. Terms Not Individually Negotiated

(1)   Contract terms which have not been individually negotiated may be invoked against a party which did not know of them only if the party invoking them took reasonable steps to bring them to the other party's attention before or when the contract was concluded.

(2)   Terms are not brought appropriately to a party's attention by a mere reference to them in a contract document, even if that party signs the document.

Article 2.105. Merger Clause

(1)   If a written contract contains an individually negotiated clause stating that the writing embodies all the terms of the contract (a merger clause), any prior statements, undertakings or agreements which are not embodied in the writing do not form part of the contract.

(2)   If the merger clause is not individually negotiated it will only establish a presumption that the parties intended that their prior statements, undertakings or agreements were not to form part of the contract. This rule may not be excluded or restricted.

(3)   The parties' prior statements may be used to interpret the contract. This rule may not be excluded or restricted except by an individually negotiated clause.

(4)   A party may by its statements or conduct be precluded from asserting a merger clause to the extent that the other party has reasonably relied on them.

Article 2.106. Written Modification Only

(1)   A clause in a written contract requiring any modification or ending by agreement to be made in writing establishes only a presumption that an agreement to modify or end the contract is not intended to be legally binding unless it is in writing.

(2)   A party may by its statements or conduct be precluded from asserting such a clause to the extent that the other party has reasonably relied on them.

Article 2.107. Promises Binding Without Acceptance

A promise which is intended to be legally binding without acceptance is binding.

Section 2: Offer and Acceptance

Article 2.201. Offer

(1)   A proposal amounts to an offer if:

    (a)   it is intended to result in a contract if the other party accepts it, and

    (b)   it contains sufficiently definite terms to form a contract.

(2)   An offer may be made to one or more specific persons or to the public.

(3)   A proposal to supply goods or services at stated prices made by a professional supplier in a public advertisement or a catalogue, or by a display of goods, is presumed to be an offer to sell or supply at that price until the stock of goods, or the supplier's capacity to supply the service, is exhausted.

Article 2.202. Revocation of an Offer

(1)   An offer may be revoked if the revocation reaches the offeree before it has dispatched its acceptance or, in cases of acceptance by conduct, before the contract has been concluded under Article 2.205(2) or (3).

(2)   An offer made to the public can be revoked by the same means as were used to make the offer.

(3)   However, a revocation of an offer is ineffective if:

    (a)   the offer indicates that it is irrevocable; or

    (b)   it states a fixed time for its acceptance; or

    (c)   it was reasonable for the offeree to rely on the offer as being irrevocable and the offeree has acted in reliance on the offer.

Article 2.203. Rejection

When a rejection of an offer reaches the offeror, the offer lapses.

Article 2.204. Acceptance

(1)   Any form of statement or conduct by the offeree is an acceptance if it indicates assent to the offer.

(2)   Silence or inactivity does not in itself amount to acceptance.

Article 2.205. Time of Conclusion of the Contract

(1)   If an acceptance has been dispatched by the offeree the contract is concluded when the acceptance reaches the offeror.

(2)   In case of acceptance by conduct, the contract is concluded when notice of the conduct reaches the offeror.

(3)   If by virtue of the offer, of practices which the parties have established between themselves, or of a usage, the offeree may accept the offer by performing an act without notice to the offeror, the contract is concluded when the performance of the act begins.

Article 2.206. Time Limit for Acceptance

In order to be effective, acceptance of an offer must reach the offeror within the time fixed by it.

(1)   In order to be effective, acceptance of an offer must reach the offeror within the time fixed by it.

(2)   If no time has been fixed by the offeror acceptance must reach it within a reasonable time.

(3)   In the case of an acceptance by an act of performance under art. 2.205 (3), that act must be performed within the time for acceptance fixed by the offeror or, if no such time is fixed, within a reasonable time.

Article 2.207. Late Acceptance

(1)   A late acceptance is nonetheless effective as an acceptance if without delay the offeror informs the offeree that he treats it as such.

(2)   If a letter or other writing containing a late acceptance shows that it has been sent in such circumstances that if its transmission had been normal it would have reached the offeror in due time, the late acceptance is effective as an acceptance unless, without delay, the offeror informs the offeree that it considers its offer as having lapsed.

Article 2.208. Modified Acceptance

(1)   A reply by the offeree which states or implies additional or different terms which would materially alter the terms of the offer is a rejection and a new offer.

(2)   A reply which gives a definite assent to an offer operates as an acceptance even if it states or implies additional or different terms, provided these do not materially alter the terms of the offer. The additional or different terms then become part of the contract.

(3)   However, such a reply will be treated as a rejection of the offer if:

(a)   the offer expressly limits acceptance to the terms of the offer; or

(b)   the offeror objects to the additional or different terms without delay; or

(c)   the offeree makes its acceptance conditional upon the offeror's assent to the additional or different terms, and the assent does not reach the offeree within a reasonable time.

Article 2.209. Conflicting General Conditions

(1)   If the parties have reached agreement except that the offer and acceptance refer to conflicting general conditions of contract, a contract is nonetheless formed. The general conditions form part of the contract to the extent that they are common in substance.

(2)   However, no contract is formed if one party:

(a)   has indicated in advance, explicitly, and not by way of general conditions, that it does not intend to be bound by a contract on the basis of paragraph (1); or

(b)   without delay, informs the other party that it does not intend to be bound by such contract.

(3)   General conditions of contract are terms which have been formulated in advance for an indefinite number of contracts of a certain nature, and which have not been individually negotiated between the parties.

Article 2.210. Professional's Written Confirmation

If professionals have concluded a contract but have not embodied it in a final document, and one without delay sends the other a writing which purports to be a confirmation of the contract but which contains additional or different terms, such terms will become part of the contract unless:

(a)   the terms materially alter the terms of the contract, or

(b)   the addressee objects to them without delay.

Article 2.211. Contracts Not Concluded Through Offer and Acceptance

The rules in this section apply with appropriate adaptations even though the process of conclusion of a contract cannot be analyzed into offer and acceptance.

Section 3: Liability for Negotiations

Article 2.301. Negotiations Contrary to Good Faith

(1)   A party is free to negotiate and is not liable for failure to reach an agreement.

(2)   However, a party who has negotiated or broken off negotiations contrary to good faith and fair dealing is liable for the losses caused to the other party.

(3)   It is contrary to good faith and fair dealing, in particular, for a party to enter into or continue negotiations with no real intention of reaching an agreement with the other party.

Article 2.302. Breach of Confidentiality

If confidential information is given by one party in the course of negotiations, the other party is under a duty not to disclose that information or use it for its own purposes whether or not a contract is subsequently concluded. The remedy for breach of this duty may include compensation for loss suffered and restitution of the benefit received by the other party.

CHAPTER 3—AUTHORITY OF AGENTS

Section 1: General Provisions

Article 3.101. Scope of the Chapter

(1)   This Chapter governs the authority of an agent or other intermediary to bind its principal in relation to a contract with a third party.

(2)   This Chapter does not govern an agent's authority bestowed by law or the authority of an agent appointed by a public or judicial authority.

(3)   This Chapter does not govern the internal relationship between the agent or intermediary and its principal.

Article 3.102. Categories of Representation

(1)   Where an agent acts in the name of a principal, the rules on direct representation apply (Section 2). It is irrelevant whether the principal's identity is revealed at the time the agent acts or is to be revealed later.

(2)   Where an intermediary acts on instructions and on behalf of, but not in the name of, a principal, or where the third party neither knows nor has reason to know that the intermediary acts as an agent, the rules on indirect representation apply (Section 3).

Section 2: Direct Representation

Article 3.201. Express, Implied and Apparent Authority

· (1)   The principal's grant of authority to an agent to act in its name may be express or may be implied from the circumstances.

(2)   The agent has authority to perform all acts necessary in the circumstances to achieve the purposes for which the authority was granted.

(3)   A person is to be treated as having granted authority to an apparent agent if the person's statements or conduct induce the third party reasonably and in good faith to believe that the apparent agent has been granted authority for the act performed by it.

Article 3.202. Agent Acting in Exercise of Its Authority

Where an agent is acting within its authority as defined by Article 3.201, its acts bind the principal and the third party directly to each other. The agent itself is not bound to the third party.

Article 3.203. Unidentified Principal

If an agent enters into a contract in the name of a principal whose identity is to be revealed later, but fails to reveal that identity within a reasonable time after a request by the third party, the agent itself is bound by the contract.

Article 3.204. Agent Acting Without or Outside Its Authority

(1)   Where a person acting as an agent acts without authority or outside the scope of its authority, its acts are not binding upon the principal and the third party.

(2)   Failing ratification by the principal according to Article 3.207, the agent is liable to pay the third party such damages as will place the third party in the same position as if the agent had acted with authority. This does not apply if the third party knew or could not have been unaware of the agent's lack of authority.

Article 3.205. Conflict of Interest

(1)   If a contract concluded by an agent involves the agent in a conflict of interest of which the third party knew or could not have been unaware, the principal may avoid the contract according to the provisions of Articles 4.112 to 4.116.

(2)   There is presumed to be a conflict of interest where:

(a)   the agent also acted as agent for the third party; or

(b)   the contract was with itself in its personal capacity.

(3)   However, the principal may not avoid the contract:

(a)   if it had consented to, or could not have been unaware of, the agent's so acting; or

(b)   if the agent had disclosed the conflict of interest to it and it had not objected within a reasonable time.

Article 3.206. Subagency

An agent has implied authority to appoint a subagent to carry out tasks which are not of a personal character and which it is not reasonable to expect the agent to carry out itself. The rules of this Section apply to the subagency; acts of the subagent which are within its and the agent's authority bind the principal and the third party directly to each other.

Article 3.207. Ratification by Principal

(1)   Where a person acting as an agent acts without authority or outside its authority, the principal may ratify the agent's acts.

(2)   Upon ratification, the agent's acts are considered as having been authorized, without prejudice to the rights of other persons.

Article 3.208. Third Party's Right With Respect
to Confirmation of Authority

Where the statements or conduct of the principal gave the third party reason to believe that an act performed by the agent was authorized, but the third party is in doubt about the authorization, it may send a written confirmation to the principal or request ratification from it. If the principal does not object or answer the request without delay, the agent's act is treated as having been authorized.

Article 3.209. Duration of Authority

(1)   An agent's authority continues until the third party knows or ought to know that:

(a)   the agent's authority has been brought to an end by the principal, the agent, or both; or

(b)   the acts for which the authority had been granted have been completed, or the time for which it had been granted has expired; or

(c)   the agent has become insolvent or, where a natural person, has died or become incapacitated; or

(d)   the principal has become insolvent.

(2)   The third party is considered to know that the agent's authority has been brought to an end under paragraph(1)(a) above if this has been communicated or publicized in the same manner in which the authority was originally communicated or publicized.

(3)   However, the agent remains authorized for a reasonable time to perform those acts which are necessary to protect the interests of the principal or its successors.

Section 3: Indirect Representation

Article 3.301. Intermediaries Not Acting in the Name of a Principal

(1)   Where an intermediary acts:

(a)   on instructions and on behalf, but not in the name, of a principal, or

(b)   on instructions from a principal but the third party does not know and has no reason to know this,

the intermediary and the third party are bound to each other.

(2)   The principal and the third party are bound to each other only under the conditions set out in Articles 3.302 to 3.304.

Article 3.302. Intermediary's Insolvency or Fundamental
Non-performance to Principal

If the intermediary becomes insolvent, or if it commits a fundamental non-performance towards the principal, or if prior to the time for performance it is clear that there will be a fundamental non-performance:

(a)   on the principal's demand, the intermediary shall communicate the name and address of the third party to the principal; and

(b)   the principal may exercise against the third party the rights acquired on the principal's behalf by the intermediary, subject to any defences which the third party may set up against the intermediary.

Article 3.303. Intermediary's Insolvency or Fundamental Non-performance to Third Party

If the intermediary becomes insolvent, or if it commits a fundamental non-performance towards the third party, or if prior to the time for performance it is clear that there will be a fundamental non-performance:

(a)   on the third party's demand, the intermediary shall communicate the name and address of the principal to the third party; and

(b)   the third party may exercise against the principal the rights which the third party has against the intermediary, subject to any defences which the intermediary may set up against the third party and those which the principal may set up against the intermediary.

Article 3.304. Requirement of Notice

The rights under Articles 3.302 and 3.303 may be exercised only if notice of intention to exercise them is given to the intermediary and to the third party or principal, respectively. Upon receipt of the notice, the third party or the principal is no longer entitled to render performance to the intermediary.

CHAPTER 4—VALIDITY

Article 4.101. Matters Not Covered

This chapter does not deal with invalidity arising from illegality, immorality or lack of capacity.

Article 4.102. Initial Impossibility

A contract is not invalid merely because at the time it was concluded performance of the obligation assumed was impossible, or because a party was not entitled to dispose of the assets to which the contract relates.

Article 4.103. Fundamental Mistake as to Facts or Law

(1)   A party may avoid a contract for mistake of fact or law existing when the contract was concluded if:

(a)   (i)   the mistake was caused by information given by the other party; or

(ii)   the other party knew or ought to have known of the mistake and it was contrary to good faith and fair dealing to leave the mistaken party in error; or

(iii)   the other party made the same mistake,

and

(b)   the other party knew or ought to have known that the mistaken party, had it known the truth, would not have entered the contract or would have done so only on fundamentally different terms.

(2)   However a party may not avoid the contract if:

(a)   in the circumstances its mistake was inexcusable, or

(b)   the risk of the mistake was assumed, or in the circumstances should be borne, by it.

Article 4.104. Inaccuracy in Communication

An inaccuracy in the expression or transmission of a statement is to be treated as a mistake of the person who made or sent the statement and Article 4.103 applies.

Article 4.105. Adaptation of Contract

(1)   If a party is entitled to avoid the contract for mistake but the other party indicates that it is willing to perform, or actually does perform, the contract as it was understood by the party entitled to avoid it, the contract is to be treated as if it had been concluded as that party understood it. The other party must indicate its willingness to perform, or render such performance, promptly after being informed of the manner in which the party entitled to avoid it understood the contract and before that party acts in reliance on any notice of avoidance.

(2)   After such indication or performance the right to avoid is lost and any earlier notice of avoidance is ineffective.

(3)   Where both parties have made the same mistake, the court may at the request of either party bring the contract into accordance with what might reasonably have been agreed had the mistake not occurred.

Article 4.106. Incorrect Information

A party who has concluded a contract relying on incorrect information given it by the other party may recover damages in accordance with Article 4.117(2) and (3) even if the information does not give rise to a fundamental mistake under Article 4.103, unless the party who gave the information had reason to believe that the information was correct.

Article 4.107. Fraud

(1)   A party may avoid a contract when it has been led to conclude it by the other party's fraudulent representation, whether by words or conduct, or fraudulent non-disclosure of any information which in accordance with good faith and fair dealing it should have disclosed.

(2)   A party's representation or non-disclosure is fraudulent if it was intended to deceive.

(3)   In determining whether good faith and fair dealing required that a party disclose particular information, regard should be had to all the circumstances, including:

   (a)   whether the party had special expertise;

   (b)   the cost to it of acquiring the relevant information;

   (c)   whether the other party could reasonably acquire the information for itself; and

   (d)   the apparent importance of the information to the other party.

Article 4.108. Threats

A party may avoid a contract when it has been led to conclude it by the other party's imminent and serious threat of an act:

   (a)   which is wrongful in itself, or

   (b)   which it is wrongful to use as a means to obtain the conclusion of the contract,

unless in the circumstances the first party had a reasonable alternative.

Article 4.109. Excessive Benefit or Unfair Advantage

(1)   A party may avoid a contract if, at the time of the conclusion of the contract:

   (a)   it was dependent on or had a relationship of trust with the other party, was in economic distress or had urgent needs, was improvident, ignorant, inexperienced or lacking in bargaining skill, and

(b)   the other party knew or ought to have known of this and, given the circumstances and purpose of the contract, took advantage of the first party's situation in a way which was grossly unfair or took an excessive benefit.

(2)   Upon the request of the party entitled to avoidance, a court may if it is appropriate adapt the contract in order to bring it into accordance with what might have been agreed had the requirements of good faith and fair dealing been followed.

(3)   A court may similarly adapt the contract upon the request of a party receiving notice of avoidance for excessive benefit or unfair advantage, provided that this party informs the party which gave the notice promptly after receiving it and before that party has acted in reliance on it.

Article 4.110. Unfair Terms Not Individually Negotiated

(1)   A party may avoid a term which has not been individually negotiated if, contrary to the requirements of good faith and fair dealing, it causes a significant imbalance in the parties' rights and obligations arising under the contract to the detriment of that party, taking into account the nature of the performance to be rendered under the contract, all the other terms of the contract and the circumstances at the time the contract was concluded.

(2)   This Article does not apply to:

(a)   a term which defines the main subject matter of the contract, provided the term is in plain and intelligible language; or to

(b)   the adequacy in value of one party's obligations compared to the value of the obligations of the other party.

Article 4.111. Third Persons

(1)   Where a third person for whose acts a party is responsible, or who with a party's assent is involved in the making of a contract:

(a)   causes a mistake by giving information, or knows of or ought to have known of a mistake,

(b)   gives incorrect information,

(c)   commits fraud,

(d)   makes a threat, or

(e)   takes excessive benefit or unfair advantage,

remedies under this Chapter will be available under the same conditions as if the behavior or knowledge had been that of the party itself.

(2)   Where any other third person:

(a)   gives incorrect information,

(b)   commits fraud,

(c)   makes a threat, or

(d)   takes excessive benefit or unfair advantage,

remedies under this Chapter will be available if the party knew or ought to have known of the relevant facts, or at the time of avoidance it has not acted in reliance on the contract.

Article 4.112. Notice of Avoidance

Avoidance must be by notice to the other party.

Article 4.113. Time Limits

(1)   Notice of avoidance must be given within a reasonable time, with due regard to the circumstances, after the avoiding party knew or ought to have known of the relevant facts or became capable of acting freely.

(2)   However, a party may avoid an individual term under Article 4.110 if it gives notice of avoidance within a reasonable time after the other party has invoked the term.

Article 4.114. Confirmation

If the party which is entitled to avoid a contract confirms it, expressly or impliedly, after it knows of the ground for avoidance, or becomes capable of acting freely, avoidance of the contract is excluded.

Article 4.115. Effect of Avoidance

On avoidance either party may claim restitution of whatever it has supplied under the contract, provided it makes concurrent restitution of whatever it has received. If restitution cannot be made in kind for any reason, a reasonable sum must be paid for what has been received.

Article 4.116. Partial Avoidance

If a ground of avoidance affects only particular terms of a contract, the effect of an avoidance is limited to those terms unless, giving due consideration to all the circumstances of the case, it is unreasonable to uphold the remaining contract.

Article 4.117. Damages

(1)   A party which avoids a contract under this Chapter may recover from the other party damages so as to put the avoiding party as nearly as possible into the same position as if it had not concluded the contract, provided that the other party knew or ought to have known of the mistake, fraud, threat or taking of excessive benefit or unfair advantage.

(2)   If a party has the right to avoid a contract under this Chapter, but does not exercise its right or has lost its right under the provisions of Articles 4.113 or 4.114, it may recover, subject to paragraph (1), damages limited to the loss caused to it by the mistake, fraud, threat or taking of excessive benefit or unfair advantage. The same measure of damages shall apply when the party was misled by incorrect information in the sense of Article 4.106.

(3)   In other respects, the damages shall be in accordance with the relevant provisions of Chapter 9, Section 5, with appropriate adaptations.

Article 4.118. Exclusion or Restriction of Remedies

(1)   Remedies for fraud, threats and excessive benefit or unfair advantage-taking, and the right to avoid an unfair term which has not been individually negotiated, cannot be excluded or restricted.

(2)   Remedies for mistake and incorrect information may be excluded or restricted unless the exclusion or restriction is contrary to good faith and fair dealing.

Article 4.119. Remedies for Non-performance

A party which is entitled to a remedy under this Chapter in circumstances which afford that party a remedy for non-performance may pursue either remedy.

CHAPTER 5—INTERPRETATION

Article 5.101. General Rules of Interpretation

(1)   A contract is to be interpreted according to the common intention of the parties even if this differs from the literal meaning of the words.

(2)   If it is established that one party intended the contract to have a particular meaning, and at the time of the conclusion of the contract the other party could not have been unaware of the first party's intention, the contract is to be interpreted in the way intended by the first party.

(3)   If an intention cannot be established according to (1) or (2), the contract is to be interpreted according to the meaning that reasonable persons of the same kind as the parties would give to it in the same circumstances.

Article 5.102. Relevant Circumstances

In interpreting the contract, regard shall be had, in particular, to:

(a)   the circumstances in which it was concluded, including the preliminary negotiations;

(b)   the conduct of the parties, even subsequent to the conclusion of the contract;

(c)   the nature and purpose of the contract;

(d)   the interpretation which has already been given to similar clauses by the parties and the practices they have established between themselves;

(e)   the meaning commonly given to terms and expressions in the branch of activity concerned and the interpretation similar clauses may already have received;

(f)   usages; and

(g)   good faith and fair dealing

Article 5.103. Contra Proferentem Rule

Where there is doubt about the meaning of a contract term not individually negotiated, an interpretation of the term against the party who supplied it is to be preferred.

Article 5.104. Preference to Negotiated Terms

Terms which have been individually negotiated take preference over those which are not.

Article 5.105. Reference to Contract as a Whole

Terms are to be interpreted in the light of the whole contract in which they appear.

Article 5.106. Terms to Be Given Effect

An interpretation which renders the terms of the contract lawful, or effective, is to be preferred to one which would not.

Article 5.107. Linguistic Discrepancies

Where a contract is drawn up in two or more language versions none of which is stated to be authoritative, there is, in case of discrepancy between the versions, a preference for the interpretation according to the version in which the contract was originally drawn up.

CHAPTER 6—CONTENTS AND EFFECTS

Article 6.101. Statements Giving Rise to Contractual Obligations

(1)   A statement made by one party before or when the contract is concluded is to be treated as giving rise to a contractual obligation if that is how the other party reasonably understood it in the circumstances, taking into account:

    (a)   the apparent importance of the statement to the other party;

    (b)   whether the party was making the statement in the course of business; and

    (c)   the relative expertise of the parties.

(2)   If one of the parties is a professional supplier who gives information about the quality or use of services or goods or other property when marketing or advertising them or otherwise before the contract for them is concluded, the statement is to be treated as giving rise to a contractual obligation unless it is shown that the other party knew or could not have been unaware that the statement was incorrect.

(3)   Such information and other undertakings given by a person advertising or marketing services, goods or other property for the professional supplier, or by a person in earlier links of the business chain, are to be treated as giving rise to a contractual obligation on the part of the professional supplier unless it did not know and had no reason to know of the information or undertaking.

Article 6.102. Implied Terms

In addition to the express terms, a contract may contain implied terms which stem from

    (a)   the intention of the parties,

    (b)   the nature and purpose of the contract, and

    (c)   good faith and fair dealing.

Article 6.103. Simulation

When the parties have concluded an apparent contract which was not intended to reflect their true agreement, as between the parties the true agreement prevails.

Article 6.104. Determination of Price

Where the contract does not fix the price or the method of determining it, the parties are to be treated as having agreed on a reasonable price.

Article 6.105. Unilateral Determination by a Party

Where the price or any other contractual term is to be determined by one party whose determination is grossly unreasonable, then notwithstanding any provision to the contrary, a reasonable price or other term shall be substituted.

Article 6.106. Determination by a Third Person

(1)   Where the price or any other contractual term is to be determined by a third person, and it cannot or will not do so, the parties are presumed to have empowered the court to appoint another person to determine it.

(2)   If a price or other term fixed by a third person is grossly unreasonable, a reasonable price or term shall be substituted.

Article 6.107. Reference to a Non-Existent Factor

Where the price or any other contractual term is to be determined by reference to a factor which does not exist or has ceased to exist or to be accessible, the nearest equivalent factor shall be substituted.

Article 6.108. Quality of Performance

If the contract does not specify the quality, a party must tender performance of at least average quality.

Article 6.109. Contract for an Indefinite Period

A contract for an indefinite period may be ended by either party by giving notice of reasonable length.

Article 6.110. Stipulation in Favor of a Third Party

(1) A third party may require performance of a contractual obligation when its right to do so has been expressly agreed upon between the promisor and the promisee, or when such agreement is to be inferred from the purpose of the contract or the circumstances of the case. The third party need not be identified at the time the agreement is concluded.

(2) If the third party renounces the right to performance the right is treated as never having accrued to it.

(3) The promisee may by notice to the promisor deprive the third party of the right to performance unless:

(a) the third party has received notice from the promisee that the right has been made irrevocable, or

(b) the promisor or the promisee has received notice from the third party that the latter accepts the right.

Article 6.111. Change of Circumstances

(1) A party is bound to fulfil its obligations even if performance has become more onerous, whether because the cost of performance has increased or because the value of the performance it receives has diminished.

(2) If, however, performance of the contract becomes excessively onerous because of a change of circumstances, the parties are bound to enter into negotiations with a view to adapting the contract or terminating it, provided that:

(a) the change of circumstances occurred after the time of conclusion of the contract,

(b) the possibility of a change of circumstances was not one which could reasonably have been taken into account at the time of conclusion of the contract, and

(c) the risk of the change of circumstances is not one which, according to the contract, the party affected should be required to bear.

(3) If the parties fail to reach agreement within a reasonable period, the court may:

(a) end the contract at a date and on terms to be determined by the court; or

(b) adapt the contract in order to distribute between the parties in a just and equitable manner the losses and gains resulting from the change of circumstances.

In either case, the court may award damages for the loss suffered through a party refusing to negotiate or breaking off negotiations contrary to good faith and fair dealing.

THE PRINCIPLES OF EUROPEAN CONTRACT LAW

CHAPTER 7—PERFORMANCE

Article 7.101. Place of Performance

(1)   If the place of performance of a contractual obligation is not fixed by or determinable from the contract it shall be:

(a)   in the case of an obligation to pay money, the creditor's place of business at the time of the conclusion of the contract;

(b)   in the case of an obligation other than to pay money, the debtor's place of business at the time of conclusion of the contract.

(2)   If a party has more than one place of business, the place of business for the purpose of the preceding paragraph is that which has the closest relationship to the contract, having regard to the circumstances known to or contemplated by the parties at the time of conclusion of the contract.

(3)   If a party does not have a place of business its habitual residence is to be treated as its place of business.

Article 7.102. Time of Performance

A party has to effect its performance:

(1)   if a time is fixed by or determinable from the contract, at that time;

(2)   if a period of time is fixed by or determinable from the contract, at any time within that period unless the circumstances of the case indicate that the other party is to choose the time;

(3)   in any other case, within a reasonable time after the conclusion of the contract.

Article 7.103. Early Performance

(1)   A party may decline a tender of performance made before it is due except where acceptance of the tender would not unreasonably prejudice its interests.

(2)   A party's acceptance of early performance does not affect the time fixed for the performance of its own obligation.

Article 7.104. Order of Performance

To the extent that the performances of the parties can be rendered simultaneously, the parties are bound to render them simultaneously unless the circumstances indicate otherwise.

Article 7.105. Alternative Performance

(1)   Where an obligation may be discharged by one of alternative performances, the choice belongs to the party which is to perform, unless the circumstances indicate otherwise.

(2)   If the party which is to make the choice fails to do so by the time required by the contract, then:

(a)   if the delay in choosing is fundamental, the right to choose passes to the other party;

(b)   if the delay is not fundamental, the other party may give a notice fixing an additional period of reasonable length in which the party to choose must do so. If the latter fails to do so, the right to choose passes to the other party.

Article 7.106. Performance by a Third Person

(1)   Except where the contract requires personal performance the creditor cannot refuse performance by a third person if:

(a)   the third person acts with the assent of the debtor; or

(b)   the third person has a legitimate interest in performance and the debtor has failed to perform or it is clear that it will not perform at the time performance is due.

(2)   Performance by the third person in accordance with paragraph (1) discharges the debtor.

Article 7.107. Form of Payment

(1)   Payment of money due may be made in any form used in the ordinary course of business.

(2)   A creditor which, pursuant to the contract or voluntarily, accepts a check or other order to pay or a promise to pay is presumed to do so only on condition that it will be honored. The creditor may not enforce the original obligation to pay unless the order or promise is not honored.

Article 7.108. Currency of Payment

(1)   The parties may agree that payment shall be made only in a specified currency.

(2)   In the absence of such agreement, a sum of money expressed in a currency other than that of the place where payment is due may be paid in the currency of that place according to the rate of exchange prevailing there at the time when payment is due.

(3)   If, in a case falling within the preceding paragraph, the debtor has not paid at the time when payment is due, the creditor may require payment in the currency of the place where payment is due according to the rate of exchange prevailing there either at the time when payment is due or at the time of actual payment.

Article 7.109. Appropriation of Performance

(1)   Where a party has to perform several obligations of the same nature and the performance tendered does not suffice to discharge all of the obligations, then subject to paragraph (4) the party may at the time of its performance declare to which obligation the performance is to be appropriated.

(2)   If the performing party does not make such a declaration, the other party may within a reasonable time appropriate the performance to such obligation as it chooses. It shall inform the performing party of the choice. However, any such appropriation to an obligation which:

(a)   is not yet due, or

(b)   is illegal, or

(c)   is disputed,

is invalid.

(3)   In the absence of an appropriation by either party, and subject to paragraph (4), the performance is appropriated to that obligation which satisfies one of the following criteria in the sequence indicated:

(a)   the obligation which is due or is the first to fall due;

(b)   the obligation for which the creditor has the least security;

(c)   the obligation which is the most burdensome for the debtor

(d)   the obligation which has arisen first.

If none of the preceding criteria applies, the performance is appropriated proportionately to all obligations.

(4)   In the case of a monetary obligation, a payment by the debtor is to be appropriated, first, to expenses, secondly, to interest, and thirdly, to principal, unless the creditor makes a different appropriation.

Article 7.110. Property Not Accepted

(1)   A party who is left in possession of tangible property other than money because of the other party's failure to accept or retake the property must take reasonable steps to protect and preserve the property.

(2)   The party left in possession may discharge its duty to deliver or return:

(a)   by depositing the property on reasonable terms with a third person to be held to the order of the other party, and notifying the other party of this; or

(b)   by selling the property on reasonable terms after notice to the other party, and paying the net proceeds to that party.

(3)   Where, however, the property is liable to rapid deterioration or its preservation is unreasonably expensive, the party must take reasonable steps to dispose of it. It may discharge its duty to deliver or return by paying the net proceeds to the other party.

(4)   The party left in possession is entitled to be reimbursed or to retain out of the proceeds of sale any expenses reasonably incurred.

Article 7.111. Money Not Accepted

Where a party fails to accept money properly tendered by the other party, that party may after notice to the first party discharge its obligation to pay by depositing the money to the order of the first party in accordance with the law of the place where payment is due.

Article 7.112. Costs of Performance

Each party shall bear the costs of performance of its obligations.

CHAPTER 8—NON-PERFORMANCE AND REMEDIES IN GENERAL

Article 8.101. Remedies Available

(1)   Whenever a party does not perform an obligation under the contract and the non-performance is not excused under Article 8.108, the aggrieved party may resort to any of the remedies set out in Chapter 9.

(2)   Where a party's non-performance is excused under Article 8.108, the aggrieved party may resort to any of the remedies set out in Chapter 9 except claiming performance and damages.

(3)   A party may not resort to any of the remedies set out in Chapter 9 to the extent that its own act caused the other party's non-performance.

Article 8.102. Cumulation of Remedies

Remedies which are not incompatible may be cumulated. In particular, a party is not deprived of its right to damages by exercising its right to any other remedy.

Article 8.103. Fundamental Non-Performance

A non-performance of an obligation is fundamental to the contract if:

(a)   strict compliance with the obligation is of the essence of the contract; or

(b)   the non-performance substantially deprives the aggrieved party of what it was entitled to expect under the contract, unless the other party did not foresee and could not reasonably have foreseen that result; or

(c)   the non-performance is intentional and gives the aggrieved party reason to believe that it cannot rely on the other party's future performance.

Article 8.104. Cure by Non-Performing Party

A party whose tender of performance is not accepted by the other party because it does not conform to the contract may make a new and conforming tender where the time for performance has not yet arrived or the delay would not be such as to constitute a fundamental non-performance.

Article 8.105. Assurance of Performance

(1)   A party which reasonably believes that there will be a fundamental non-performance by the other party may demand adequate assurance of due performance and meanwhile may withhold performance of its own obligations so long as such reasonable belief continues.

(2)   Where this assurance is not provided within a reasonable time, the party demanding it may terminate the contract if it still reasonably believes that there will be a fundamental non-performance by the other party and gives notice of termination without delay.

Article 8.106. Notice Fixing Additional Period for Performance

(1)   In any case of non-performance the aggrieved party may by notice to the other party allow an additional period of time for performance.

(2)   During the additional period the aggrieved party may withhold performance of its own reciprocal obligations and may claim damages, but it may not resort to any other remedy. If it receives notice from the other party that the latter will not perform within that period, or if upon expiry of that period due performance has not been made, the aggrieved party may resort to any of the remedies that may be available under chapter 9.

(3)   If in a case of delay in performance which is not fundamental the aggrieved party has given a notice fixing an additional period of time of reasonable length, it may terminate the contract at the end of the period of notice. The aggrieved party may in its notice provide that if the other party does not perform within the period fixed by the notice the contract shall terminate automatically. If the period stated is too short, the aggrieved party may terminate, or, as the case may be, the contract shall terminate automatically, only after a reasonable period from the time of the notice.

Article 8.107. Performance Entrusted to Another

A party which entrusts performance of the contract to another person remains responsible for performance.

Article 8.108. Excuse Due to an Impediment

(1)   A party's non-performance is excused if it proves that it is due to an impediment beyond its control and that it could not reasonably have been expected to take the impediment into account at the time of the conclusion of the contract, or to have avoided or overcome the impediment or its consequences.

(2)   Where the impediment is only temporary the excuse provided by this Article has effect for the period during which the impediment exists. However, if the delay amounts to a fundamental non-performance, the creditor may treat it as such.

(3)   The non-performing party must ensure that notice of the impediment and of its effect on its ability to perform is received by the other party within a reasonable time after the non-performing party knew or ought to have known of these circumstances. The other party is entitled to damages for any loss resulting from the non-receipt of such notice.

Article 8.109. Clause Excluding or Restricting Remedies

Remedies for non-performance may be excluded or restricted unless it would be contrary to good faith and fair dealing to invoke the exclusion or restriction.

CHAPTER 9—PARTICULAR REMEDIES FOR NON-PERFORMANCE

Section 1: Right to Performance

Article 9.101. Monetary Obligations

(1)   The creditor is entitled to recover money which is due.

(2)   Where the creditor has not yet performed its obligation and it is clear that the debtor will be unwilling to receive performance, the creditor may nonetheless proceed with its performance and may recover any sum due under the contract unless:

    (a)   it could have made a reasonable substitute transaction without significant effort or expense; or

    (b)   performance would be unreasonable in the circumstances.

Article 9.102. Non-Monetary Obligations

(1)   The aggrieved party is entitled to specific performance of an obligation other than one to pay money, including the remedying of a defective performance.

(2)   Specific performance cannot, however, be obtained where:

    (a)   performance would be unlawful or impossible; or

    (b)   performance would cause the debtor unreasonable effort or expense; or

    (c)   the performance consists [of] the provision of services or work of a personal character or depends upon a personal relationship, or

    (d)   the aggrieved party may reasonably obtain performance from another source.

(3)   The aggrieved party will lose the right to specific performance if it fails to seek it within a reasonable time after it has or ought to have become aware of the non-performance.

Article 9.103. Damages Not Precluded

The fact that a right to performance is excluded under this Section does not preclude a claim for damages.

Section 2: Withholding Performance

Article 9.201. Right to Withhold Performance

(1)   A party which is to perform simultaneously with or after the other party may withhold performance until the other has tendered performance or has performed. The first party may withhold the whole of its performance or a part of it as may be reasonable in the circumstances.

(2)   A party may similarly withhold performance for as long as it is clear that there will be a non-performance by the other party when the other party's performance becomes due.

Section 3: Termination of the Contract

Article 9.301. Right to Terminate the Contract

(1)   A party may terminate the contract if the other party's non-performance is fundamental.

(2)   In the case of delay the aggrieved party may also terminate the contract under Article 8.106(3).

Article 9.302. Contract to be Performed in Parts

If the contract is to be performed in separate parts and in relation to a part to which a counter-performance can be apportioned, there is a fundamental non-performance, the aggrieved party may exercise its right to terminate under this Section in relation to the part concerned. It may terminate the contract as a whole only if the non-performance is fundamental to the contract as a whole.

Article 9.303. Notice of Termination

(1)   A party's right to terminate the contract is to be exercised by notice to the other party.

(2)   The aggrieved party loses its right to terminate the contract unless it gives notice within a reasonable time after it has or ought to have become aware of the non-performance.

(3)   (a)   When performance has not been tendered by the time it was due, the aggrieved party need not give notice of termination before a tender has been made. If a tender is later made it loses its right to terminate if it does not give such notice within a reasonable time after it has or ought to have become aware of the tender.

(b)   If, however, the aggrieved party knows or has reason to know that the other party still intends to tender within a reasonable time, and the aggrieved party unreasonably fails to notify the other party that it will not accept performance, it loses its right to terminate if the other party in fact tenders within a reasonable time.

(4)   If a party is excused under Article 8.108 through an impediment which is total and permanent, the contract is terminated automatically and without notice at the time the impediment arises.

Article 9.304. Anticipatory Non-Performance

Where prior to the time for performance by a party it is clear that there will be a fundamental non-performance by it, the other party may terminate the contract.

Article 9.305. Effects of Termination in General

(1)   Termination of the contract releases both parties from their obligation to effect and to receive future performance, but, subject to Articles 9.306 to 9.308, does not affect the rights and liabilities that have accrued up to the time of termination.

(2)   Termination does not affect any provision of the contract for the settlement of disputes or any other provision which is to operate even after termination.

Article 9.306. Property Reduced in Value

A party which terminates the contract may reject property previously received from the other party if its value to the first party has been fundamentally reduced as a result of the other party's non-performance.

Article 9.307. Recovery of Money Paid

On termination of the contract a party may recover money paid for a performance which it did not receive or which it properly rejected.

Article 9.308. Recovery of Property

On termination of the contract a party which has supplied property which can be returned and for which it has not received payment or other counter-performance may recover the property.

Article 9.309. Recovery for Performance That Cannot Be Returned

On termination of the contract a party which has rendered a performance which cannot be returned and for which it has not received payment or other counter-performance may recover a reasonable amount for the value of the performance to the other party.

Section 4: Price Reduction

Article 9.401. Right to Reduce Price

(1)   A party which accepts a tender of performance not conforming to the contract may reduce the price. This reduction shall be proportionate to the decrease in the value of the performance at the time this was tendered compared to the value which a conforming tender would have had at that time.

(2)   A party which is entitled to reduce the price under the preceding paragraph and which has already paid a sum exceeding the reduced price may recover the excess from the other party.

(3)   A party which reduces the price cannot also recover damages for reduction in the value of the performance but remains entitled to damages for any further loss it has suffered so far as these are recoverable under Section 5 of this Chapter.

Section 5: Damages and Interest

Article 9.501. Right to Damages

(1)   The aggrieved party is entitled to damages for loss caused by the other party's non-performance which is not excused under Article 8.108.

(2)   The loss for which damages are recoverable includes:

(a)   non-pecuniary loss; and

(b)   future loss which is reasonably likely to occur.

Article 9.502. General Measure of Damages

The general measure of damages is such sum as will put the aggrieved party as nearly as possible into the position in which it would have been if the contract had been duly performed. Such damages cover the loss which the aggrieved party has suffered and the gain of which it has been deprived.

Article 9.503. Foreseeability

The non-performing party is liable only for loss which it foresaw or could reasonably have foreseen at the time of conclusion of the contract as a likely result of its non-performance, unless the non-performance was intentional or grossly negligent.

Article 9.504. Loss Attributable to Aggrieved Party

The non-performing party is not liable for loss suffered by the aggrieved party to the extent that the aggrieved party contributed to the non-performance or its effects.

Article 9.505. Reduction of Loss

(1) The non-performing party is not liable for loss suffered by the aggrieved party to the extent that the aggrieved party could have reduced the loss by taking reasonable steps.

(2) The aggrieved party is entitled to recover any expenses reasonably incurred in attempting to reduce the loss.

Article 9.506. Substitute Transaction

Where the aggrieved party has terminated the contract and has made a substitute transaction within a reasonable time and in a reasonable manner, it may recover the difference between the contract price and the price of the substitute transaction as well as damages for any further loss so far as these are recoverable under this Section.

Article 9.507. Current Price

Where the aggrieved party has terminated the contract and has not made a substitute transaction but there is a current price for the performance contracted for, it may recover the difference between the contract price and the price current at the time the contract is terminated as well as damages for any further loss so far as these are recoverable under this Section.

Article 9.508. Delay in Payment of Money

(1) If payment of a sum of money is delayed, the aggrieved party is entitled to interest on that sum from the time when payment is due to the time of payment at the average commercial bank short-term lending rate to prime borrowers prevailing for the contractual currency of payment at the place where payment is due.

(2) The aggrieved party may in addition recover damages for any further loss so far as these are recoverable under this Section.

Article 9.509. Agreed Payment for Non-Performance

(1) Where the contract provides that a party which fails to perform is to pay a specified sum to the aggrieved party for such non-performance, the aggrieved party shall be awarded that sum irrespective of its actual loss.

(2) However, despite any agreement to the contrary the specified sum may be reduced to a reasonable amount where it is grossly excessive in relation to the loss resulting from the non-performance and the other circumstances.

Article 9.510. Currency by Which Damages to be Measured

Damages are to be measured by the currency which most appropriately reflects the aggrieved party's loss.

CHAPTER 10—PLURALITY OF PARTIES*

---

*   Omitted.

CHAPTER 11—ASSIGNMENT OF CLAIMS

Section 1: General Principles

Article 11.101. Scope of Chapter

(1)   This Chapter applies to the assignment by agreement of a right to performance ("claim") under an existing or future contract.

(2)   Except where otherwise stated or the context otherwise requires, this Chapter also applies to the assignment by agreement of other transferable claims.

(3)   This Chapter does not apply:

(a)   to the transfer of a financial instrument or investment security where, under the law otherwise applicable, such transfer must be by entry in a register maintained by or for the issuer; or

(b)   to the transfer of a bill of exchange or other negotiable instrument or of a negotiable security or a document of title to goods where, under the law otherwise applicable, such transfer must be by delivery (with any necessary endorsement).

(4)   In this Chapter "assignment" includes an assignment by way of security.

(5)   This Chapter also applies, with appropriate adaptations, to the granting by agreement of a right in security over a claim otherwise than by assignment.

Article 11.102. Contractual Claims Generally Assignable

(1)   Subject to Articles 11.301 and 11.302, a party to a contract may assign a claim under it.

(2)   A future claim arising under an existing or future contract may be assigned if at the time when it comes into existence, or at such other time as the parties agree, it can be identified as the claim to which the assignment relates.

Article 11.103. Partial Assignment

A claim which is divisible may be assigned in part, but the assignor is liable to the debtor for any increased costs which the debtor thereby incurs.

Article 11.104. Form of Assignment

An assignment need not be in writing and is not subject to any other requirement as to form. It may be proved by any means, including witnesses.

Section 2: Effects of Assignment As Between Assignor and Assignee

Article 11.201. Rights Transferred to Assignee

(1)   The assignment of a claim transfers to the assignee:

(a)   all the assignor's rights to performance in respect of the claim assigned; and

(b)   all accessory rights securing such performance.

(2)   Where the assignment of a claim under a contract is associated with the substitution of the assignee as debtor in respect of any obligation owed by the assignor under the same contract, this Article takes effect subject to Article 12.201.

Article 11.202. When Assignment Takes Effect

(1)   An assignment of an existing claim takes effect at the time of the agreement to assign or such later time as the assignor and assignee agree.

(2)   An assignment of a future claim is dependent upon the assigned claim coming into existence but thereupon takes effect from the time of the agreement to assign or such later time as the assignor and assignee agree.

Article 11.203. Preservation of Assignee's Rights Against Assignor

An assignment is effective as between the assignor and assignee, and entitles the assignee to whatever the assignor receives from the debtor, even if it is ineffective against the debtor under Article 11.301 or 11.302.

Article 11.204. Undertakings by Assignor

By assigning or purporting to assign a claim the assignor undertakes to the assignee that:

(a)   at the time when the assignment is to take effect the following conditions will be satisfied except as otherwise disclosed to the assignee:

(i)   the assignor has the right to assign the claim;

(ii)   the claim exists and the assignee's rights are not affected by any defences or rights (including any right of set-off) which the debtor might have against the assignor; and

(iii)   the claim is not subject to any prior assignment or right in security in favor of any other party or to any other encumbrance;

(b)   the claim and any contract under which it arises will not be modified without the consent of the assignee unless the modification is provided for in the assignment agreement or is one which is made in good faith and is of a nature to which the assignee could not reasonably object; and

(c)   the assignor will transfer to the assignee all transferable rights intended to secure performance which are not accessory rights.

Section 3: Effects of Assignment As Between Assignee and Debtor

Article 11.301. Contractual Prohibition of Assignment

(1)   An assignment which is prohibited by or is otherwise not in conformity with the contract under which the assigned claim arises is not effective against the debtor unless:

(a)   the debtor has consented to it; or

(b)   the assignee neither knew nor ought to have known of the non-conformity; or

(c)   the assignment is made under a contract for the assignment of future rights to payment of money.

(2)   Nothing in the preceding paragraph affects the assignor's liability for the non-conformity.

Article 11.302. Other Ineffective Assignments

An assignment to which the debtor has not consented is ineffective against the debtor so far as it relates to a performance which the debtor, by reason of the nature of the performance or the relationship of the debtor and the assignor, could not reasonably be required to render to anyone except the assignor.

Article 11.303. Effect on Debtor's Obligation

(1)   Subject to Articles 11.301, 11.302, 11.307 and 11.308, the debtor is bound to perform in favor of the assignee if and only if the debtor has received a notice in writing from the assignor or the assignee which reasonably identifies the claim which has been assigned and requires the debtor to give performance to the assignee.

(2)   However, if such notice is given by the assignee, the debtor may within a reasonable time request the assignee to provide reliable evidence of the assignment, pending which the debtor may withhold performance.

(3)   Where the debtor has acquired knowledge of the assignment otherwise than by a notice conforming to paragraph (1), the debtor may either withhold performance from or give performance to the assignee.

(4)   Where the debtor gives performance to the assignor, the debtor is discharged if and only if the performance is given without knowledge of the assignment.

Article 11.304. Protection of Debtor

A debtor who performs in favor of a person identified as assignee in a notice of assignment under Article 11.303 is discharged unless the debtor could not have been unaware that such person was not the person entitled to performance.

Article 11.305. Competing Demands

A debtor who has received notice of two or more competing demands for performance may discharge liability by conforming to the law of the due place of performance, or, if the performances are due in different places, the law applicable to the claim.

Article 11.306. Place of Performance

(1)   Where the assigned claim relates to an obligation to pay money at a particular place, the assignee may require payment at any place within the same country or, if that country is a Member State of the European Union, at any place within the European Union, but the assignor is liable to the debtor for any increased costs which the debtor incurs by reason of any change in the place of performance.

(2)   Where the assigned claim relates to a non-monetary obligation to be performed at a particular place, the assignee may not require performance at any other place.

Article 11.307. Defences and Rights of Set-Off

(1)   The debtor may set up against the assignee all substantive and procedural defences to the assigned claim which the debtor could have used against the assignor.

(2)   The debtor may also assert against the assignee all rights of set-off which would have been available against the assignor under Chapter 13 in respect of any claim against the assignor:

(a)   existing at the time when a notice of assignment, whether or not conforming to Article 11.303(1), reaches the debtor; or

(b)   closely connected with the assigned claim.

Article 11.308. Unauthorized Modification Not Binding on Assignee

A modification of the claim made by agreement between the assignor and the debtor, without the consent of the assignee, after a notice of assignment, whether or not conforming to Article 11.303(1), reaches the debtor does not affect the rights of the assignee against the debtor unless the modification is provided for in the assignment agreement or is one which is made in good faith and is of a nature to which the assignee could not reasonably object.

Section 4: Order of Priority between Assignee and Competing Claimants

Article 11.401. Priorities

(1)   Where there are successive assignments of the same claim, the assignee whose assignment is first notified to the debtor has priority over any earlier assignee if at the time of the later assignment the assignee under that assignment neither knew nor ought to have known of the earlier assignment.

(2)   Subject to paragraph (1), the priority of successive assignments, whether of existing or future claims, is determined by the order in which they are made.

(3)   The assignee's interest in the assigned claim has priority over the interest of a creditor of the assignor who attaches that claim, whether by judicial process or otherwise, after the time the assignment has taken effect under Article 11.202.

(4)   In the event of the assignor's bankruptcy, the assignee's interest in the assigned claim has priority over the interest of the assignor's insolvency administrator and creditors, subject to any rules of the law applicable to the bankruptcy relating to:

(a)   publicity required as a condition of such priority;

(b)   the ranking of claims; or

(c)   the avoidance or ineffectiveness of transactions in the bankruptcy proceedings.

CHAPTER 12—SUBSTITUTION OF NEW DEBTOR: TRANSFER OF CONTRACT

Section 1: Substitution of New Debtor

Article 12.101. Substitution; General Rules

(1)   A third person may undertake with the agreement of the debtor and the creditor to be substituted as debtor, with the effect that the original debtor is discharged.

(2)   A creditor may agree in advance to a future substitution. In such a case the substitution takes effect only when the creditor is given notice by the new debtor of the agreement between the new and the original debtor.

Article 12.102. Effects of Substitution on Defences and Securities

(1)   The new debtor cannot invoke against the creditor any rights or defences arising from the relationship between the new debtor and the original debtor.

(2)   The discharge of the original debtor also extends to any security of the original debtor given to the creditor for the performance of the obligation, unless the security is over an asset which is transferred to the new debtor as part of a transaction between the original and the new debtor.

(3)   Upon discharge of the original debtor, a security granted by any person other than the new debtor for the performance of the obligation is released, unless that other person agrees that it should continue to be available to the creditor.

(4)   The new debtor may invoke against the creditor all defences which the original debtor could have invoked against the creditor.

Section 2: Transfer of Contract

Article 12.201. Transfer of Contract

(1)   A party to a contract may agree with a third person that that person is to be substituted as the contracting party. In such a case the substitution takes effect only where, as a result of the other party's assent, the first party is discharged.

(2)   To the extent that the substitution of the third person as a contracting party involves a transfer of rights to performance ("claims"), the provisions of Chapter 11 apply; to the extent that obligations are transferred, the provisions of Section 1 of this Chapter apply.

CHAPTER 13—SET-OFF*

CHAPTER 14—PRESCRIPTION

Section 1: General Provision

Article 14.101. Claims Subject to Prescription

A right to performance of an obligation ("claim") is subject to prescription by the expiry of a period of time in accordance with these Principles.

Section 2: Periods of Prescription and Their Commencement

Article 14.201. General Period

The general period of prescription is three years.

Article 14.202. Period for a Claim Established by Legal Proceedings

(1)   The period of prescription for a claim established by judgment is ten years.

(2)   The same applies to a claim established by an arbitral award or other instrument which is enforceable as if it were a judgment. . . .

Section 4: Renewal of Periods

Article 14.401. Renewal by Acknowledgement

(1)   If the debtor acknowledges the claim, vis-à-vis the creditor, by part payment, payment of interest, giving of security, or in any other manner, a new period of prescription begins to run.

(2)   The new period is the general period of prescription. . . .

Section 6: Modification by Agreement

Article 14.601. Agreements Concerning Prescription

(1)   The requirements for prescription may be modified by agreement between the parties, in particular by either shortening or lengthening the periods of prescription.

(2)   The period of prescription may not, however, be reduced to less than one year or extended to more than thirty years after the time of commencement set out in Article 14.203.

---

*   Omitted.

CHAPTER 15—ILLEGALITY

Article 15.101. Contracts Contrary to Fundamental Principles

A contract is of no effect to the extent that it is contrary to principles recognized as fundamental in the laws of the Member States of the European Union.

Article 15.102. Contracts Infringing Mandatory Rules

(1)   Where a contract infringes a mandatory rule of law applicable under Article 1.103 of these Principles, the effects of that infringement upon the contract are the effects, if any, expressly prescribed by that mandatory rule.

(2)   Where the mandatory rule does not expressly prescribe the effects of an infringement upon a contract, the contract may be declared to have full effect, to have some effect, to have no effect, or to be subject to modification.

(3)   A decision reached under paragraph (2) must be an appropriate and proportional response to the infringement, having regard to all relevant circumstances, including:

(a)   the purpose of the rule which has been infringed;

(b)   the category of persons for whose protection the rule exists;

(c)   any sanction that may be imposed under the rule infringed;

(d)   the seriousness of the infringement;

(e)   whether the infringement was intentional; and

(f)   the closeness of the relationship between the infringement and the contract.

Article 15.103. Partial Ineffectiveness

(1)   If only part of a contract is rendered ineffective under Articles 15.101 or 15.102, the remaining part continues in effect unless, giving due consideration to all the circumstances of the case, it is unreasonable to uphold it.

(2)   Articles 15.104 and 15.105 apply, with appropriate adaptations, to a case of partial ineffectiveness.

Article 15.104. Restitution

(1)   When a contract is rendered ineffective under Articles 15.101 or 15.102, either party may claim restitution of whatever that party has supplied under the contract, provided that, where appropriate, concurrent restitution is made of whatever has been received.

(2)   When considering whether to grant restitution under paragraph (1), and what concurrent restitution, if any, would be appropriate, regard must be had to the factors referred to in Article 15.102(3).

(3)   An award of restitution may be refused to a party who knew or ought to have known of the reason for the ineffectiveness.

(4)   If restitution cannot be made in kind for any reason, a reasonable sum must be paid for what has been received.

Article 15.105. Damages

(1)   A party to a contract which is rendered ineffective under Articles 15.101 or 15.102 may recover from the other party damages putting the first party as nearly as possible into the same

position as if the contract had not been concluded, provided that the other party knew or ought to have known of the reason for the ineffectiveness.

(2)   When considering whether to award damages under paragraph (1), regard must be had to the factors referred to in Article 15.102(3).

(3)   An award of damages may be refused where the first party knew or ought to have known of the reason for the ineffectiveness.

CHAPTER 16—CONDITIONS

Article 16.101. Types of Condition

A contractual obligation may be made conditional upon the occurrence of an uncertain future event, so that the obligation takes effect only if the event occurs (suspensive condition) or comes to an end if the event occurs (resolutive condition).

Article 16.102. Interference With Conditions

(1)   If fulfillment of a condition is prevented by a party, contrary to duties of good faith and fair dealing or co-operation, and if fulfillment would have operated to that party's disadvantage, the condition is deemed to be fulfilled.

(2)   If fulfillment of a condition is brought about by a party, contrary to duties of good faith and fair dealing or co-operation, and if fulfillment operates to that party's advantage, the condition is deemed not to be fulfilled.

Article 16.103. Effect of Conditions

(1)   Upon fulfillment of a suspensive condition, the relevant obligation takes effect unless the parties otherwise agree.

(2)   Upon fulfillment of a resolutive condition, the relevant obligation comes to an end unless the parties otherwise agree.

. . .

CHAPTER 17—CAPITALISATION OF INTEREST*

---

*   Omitted.

EUROPEAN COMMUNITY COUNCIL DIRECTIVE 93/13/EEC OF 5 APRIL 1993 ON UNFAIR TERMS IN CONSUMER CONTRACTS

[The Directive on Unfair Terms in Consumer Contracts ("DUTCC") is law within the European Union ("EU") (formerly called the "European Community"). Its general thrust is comparable to the part of U.S. contract law's unconscionability doctrine that is widely known as "substantive unconscionability." Prior to its adoption, the EU's member States each had domestic laws that protected consumers. These laws differed in many respects, including in their definitions of "unfairness" (or the equivalent) and in the consequences they prescribed when a contract or term was unfair. The European Commission believed that these differences made consumers in one member State wary of contracting with parties elsewhere in the EU. To facilitate contracting in the EU's common market, the Commission developed the DUTCC to harmonize the laws of the member States and thereby increase consumer confidence in the fairness of contracting with parties elsewhere in the EU. The DUTCC, however, also applies to contracts between a seller or supplier and a consumer when both are in one member State.

[In 2015, the European Parliament and the Council adopted a Consumer Rights Directive. It will be found below in this pamphlet. This Directive, 2011/83/EC, does not supersede 93/13/EEC.]

Article 1

1.   The purpose of this Directive is to approximate the laws, regulations and administrative provisions of the Member States relating to unfair terms in contracts concluded between a seller or supplier and a consumer.

2.   The contractual terms which reflect mandatory statutory or regulatory provisions and the provisions or principles of international conventions to which the Member States or the Community are party, particularly in the transport area, shall not be subject to the provisions of this Directive.

Article 2

For the purposes of this Directive:

(a)   "unfair terms" means the contractual terms defined in Article 3;

(b)   "consumer" means any natural person who, in contracts covered by this Directive, is acting for purposes which are outside his trade, business or profession;

(c)   "seller or supplier" means any natural or legal person who, in contracts covered by this Directive, is acting for purposes relating to his trade, business or profession, whether publicly owned or privately owned.

Article 3

1.   A contractual term which has not been individually negotiated shall be regarded as unfair if, contrary to the requirement of good faith, it causes a significant imbalance in the parties' rights and obligations arising under the contract, to the detriment of the consumer.

2.   A term shall always be regarded as not individually negotiated where it has been drafted in advance and the consumer has therefore not been able to influence the substance of the term, particularly in the context of a pre-formulated standard contract.

The fact that certain aspects of a term or one specific term have been individually negotiated shall not exclude the application of this Article to the rest of a contract if an overall assessment of the contract indicates that it is nevertheless a pre-formulated standard contract.

Where any seller or supplier claims that a standard term has been individually negotiated, the burden of proof in this respect shall be incumbent on him.

3.   The Annex shall contain an indicative and non-exhaustive list of the terms which may be regarded as unfair.

Article 4

1.   Without prejudice to Article 7, the unfairness of a contractual term shall be assessed, taking into account the nature of the goods or services for which the contract was concluded and by referring, at the time of conclusion of the contract, to all the circumstances attending the conclusion of the contract and to all the other terms of the contract or of another contract on which it is dependent.

2.   Assessment of the unfair nature of the terms shall relate neither to the definition of the main subject matter of the contract nor to the adequacy of the price and remuneration, on the one hand, as against the services or goods supplied in exchange, on the other, in so far as these terms are in plain intelligible language.

Article 5

In the case of contracts where all or certain terms offered to the consumer are in writing, these terms must always be drafted in plain, intelligible language. Where there is doubt about the meaning of a term, the interpretation most favourable to the consumer shall prevail. This rule on interpretation shall not apply in the context of the procedures laid down in Article 7(2).

Article 6

1.   Member States shall lay down that unfair terms used in a contract concluded with a consumer by a seller or supplier shall, as provided for under their national law, not be binding on the consumer and that the contract shall continue to bind the parties upon those terms if it is capable of continuing in existence without the unfair terms.

2.   Member States shall take the necessary measures to ensure that the consumer does not lose the protection granted by this Directive by virtue of the choice of the law of a non-Member country as the law applicable to the contract if the latter has a close connection with the territory of the Member States.

Article 7

1.   Member States shall ensure that, in the interests of consumers and of competitors, adequate and effective means exist to prevent the continued use of unfair terms in contracts concluded with consumers by sellers or suppliers.

2.   The means referred to in paragraph 1 shall include provisions whereby persons or organizations, having a legitimate interest under national law in protecting consumers, may take action according to the national law concerned before the courts or before competent administrative bodies for a decision as to whether contractual terms drawn up for general use are unfair, so that they can apply appropriate and effective means to prevent the continued use of such terms.

3.   With due regard for national laws, the legal remedies referred to in paragraph 2 may be directed separately or jointly against a number of sellers or suppliers from the same economic sector or their associations which use or recommend the use of the same general contractual terms or similar terms.

Article 8

Member States may adopt or retain the most stringent provisions compatible with the Treaty in the area covered by this Directive, to ensure a maximum degree of protection for the consumer. . . .

Article 9

The Commission shall present a report to the European Parliament and to the Council concerning the application of this Directive five years at the latest after the date in Article 10(1).

Article 10

1.   Member States shall bring into force the laws, regulations and administrative provisions necessary to comply with this Directive no later than 31 December 1994. They shall forthwith inform the Commission thereof.

These provisions shall be applicable to all contracts concluded after 31 December 1994.

2.   When Member States adopt these measures, they shall contain a reference to this Directive or shall be accompanied by such reference on the occasion of their official publication. The methods of making such a reference shall be laid down by the Member States.

3.   Member States shall communicate the main provisions of national law which they adopt in the field covered by this Directive to the Commission.

Article 11

This Directive is addressed to the Member States. . . .

ANNEX

TERMS REFERRED TO IN ARTICLE 3(3)

1.   Terms which have the object or effect of:

(a)   excluding or limiting the legal liability of a seller or supplier in the event of the death of a consumer or personal injury to the latter resulting from an act or omission of that seller or supplier;

(b)   inappropriately excluding or limiting the legal rights of the consumer vis-à-vis the seller or supplier or another party in the event of total or partial non-performance or inadequate performance by the seller or supplier of any of the contractual obligations, including the option of offsetting a debt owed to the seller or supplier against any claim which the consumer may have against him;

(c)   making an agreement binding on the consumer whereas provision of services by the seller or supplier is subject to a condition whose realization depends on his own will alone;

(d)   permitting the seller or supplier to retain sums paid by the consumer where the latter decides not to conclude or perform the contract, without providing for the consumer to receive compensation of an equivalent amount from the seller or supplier where the latter is the party cancelling the contract;

(e)   requiring any consumer who fails to fulfil his obligation to pay a disproportionately high sum in compensation;

(f)   authorizing the seller or supplier to dissolve the contract on a discretionary basis where the same facility is not granted to the consumer, or permitting the seller or supplier to retain the sums paid for services not yet supplied by him where it is the seller or supplier himself who dissolves the contract;

(g)   enabling the seller or supplier to terminate a contract of indeterminate duration without reasonable notice except where there are serious grounds for doing so;

(h)   automatically extending a contract of fixed duration where the consumer does not indicate otherwise, when the deadline fixed for the consumer to express this desire not to extend the contract is unreasonably early;

(i)   irrevocably binding the consumer to terms with which he had no real opportunity of becoming acquainted before the conclusion of the contract;

(j)   enabling the seller or supplier to alter the terms of the contract unilaterally without a valid reason which is specified in the contract;

(k)   enabling the seller or supplier to alter unilaterally without a valid reason any characteristics of the product or service to be provided;

(*l*)   providing for the price of goods to be determined at the time of delivery or allowing a seller of goods or supplier of services to increase their price without in both cases giving the consumer the corresponding right to cancel the contract if the final price is too high in relation to the price agreed when the contract was concluded;

(m)   giving the seller or supplier the right to determine whether the goods or services supplied are in conformity with the contract, or giving him the exclusive right to interpret any term of the contract;

(n)   limiting the seller's or supplier's obligation to respect commitments undertaken by his agents or making his commitments subject to compliance with a particular formality;

(o)   obliging the consumer to fulfil all his obligations where the seller or supplier does not perform his;

(p)   giving the seller or supplier the possibility of transferring his rights and obligations under the contract, where this may serve to reduce the guarantees for the consumer, without the latter's agreement;

(q)   excluding or hindering the consumer's right to take legal action or exercise any other legal remedy, particularly by requiring the consumer to take disputes exclusively to arbitration not covered by legal provisions, unduly restricting the evidence available to him or imposing on him a burden of proof which, according to the applicable law, should lie with another party to the contract.

2.   Scope of subparagraphs (g), (j), and (*l*)

(a)   Subparagraph (g) is without hindrance to terms by which a supplier of financial services reserves the right to terminate unilaterally a contract of indeterminate duration without notice where there is a valid reason, provided that the supplier is required to inform the other contracting party or parties thereof immediately.

(b)   Subparagraph (j) is without hindrance to terms under which a supplier of financial services reserves the right to alter the rate of interest payable by the consumer or due to the latter, or the amount of other charges for financial services without notice where there is a valid reason, provided that the supplier is required to inform the other contracting party or parties thereof at the earliest opportunity and that the latter are free to dissolve the contract immediately.

Subparagraph (j) is also without hindrance to terms under which a seller or supplier reserves the right to alter unilaterally the conditions of a contract of indeterminate duration, provided that he is required to inform the consumer with reasonable notice and that the consumer is free to dissolve the contract.

(c)   Subparagraphs (g), (j) and (*l*) do not apply to:

— transactions in transferable securities, financial instruments and other products or services where the price is linked to fluctuations in a stock exchange quotation or index or a financial market rate that the seller or supplier does not control;

— contracts for the purchase or sale of foreign currency, traveller's cheques or international money orders denominated in foreign currency;

(d)   Subparagraph (*l*) is without hindrance to price-indexation clauses, where lawful, provided that the method by which prices vary is explicitly described.

DIRECTIVE 2005/29/EC OF
THE EUROPEAN PARLIAMENT AND
OF THE COUNCIL OF 11 MAY 2005

[Known as the "Unfair Commercial Practices Directive" ("UCPD"), this Directive aims to harmonize the laws of the member States of the European Union ("EU") that police unfair commercial practices disadvantaging consumers. Like the EU's Directive on Unfair Terms in Consumer Contracts ("DUTCC"), included in this pamphlet above, the purpose of such harmonization is to facilitate contracting in the EU's common market by increasing consumer confidence in the fairness of contracts with parties in other member States. The UCPD differs from the DUTCC because the latter concerns a contract's terms whereas the former concerns contracting practices. So, for example, UCPD prohibits practices that mislead consumers or are so aggressive as to cause a consumer to make a contract he or she otherwise would not have made. UCPD, Arts. 6–9. The UCPD is comparable to the part of U.S. contract law's unconscionability doctrine that is widely known as "procedural unconscionability."]

CHAPTER 1

GENERAL PROVISIONS

Article 1

Purpose

The purpose of this Directive is to contribute to the proper functioning of the internal market and achieve a high level of consumer protection by approximating the laws, regulations and administrative provisions of the Member States on unfair commercial practices harming consumers' economic interests.

Article 2

Definitions

For the purposes of this Directive:

(a) 'consumer' means any natural person who, in commercial practices covered by this Directive, is acting for purposes which are outside his trade, business, craft or profession;

(b) 'trader' means any natural or legal person who, in commercial practices covered by this Directive, is acting for purposes relating to his trade, business, craft or profession and anyone acting in the name of or on behalf of a trader;

(c) 'product' means any goods or service including immovable property, rights and obligations;

(d) 'business-to-consumer commercial practices' (hereinafter also referred to as commercial practices) means any act, omission, course of conduct or representation, commercial communication including advertising and marketing, by a trader, directly connected with the promotion, sale or supply of a product to consumers;

(e) 'to materially distort the economic behaviour of consumers' means using a commercial practice to appreciably impair the consumer's ability to make an informed decision, thereby causing the consumer to take a transactional decision that he would not have taken otherwise;

(f) 'code of conduct' means an agreement or set of rules not imposed by law, regulation or administrative provision of a Member State which defines the behaviour of traders who undertake to be bound by the code in relation to one or more particular commercial practices or business sectors;

(g) 'code owner' means any entity, including a trader or group of traders, which is responsible for the formulation and revision of a code of conduct and/or for monitoring compliance with the code by those who have undertaken to be bound by it;

(h) 'professional diligence' means the standard of special skill and care which a trader may reasonably be expected to exercise towards consumers, commensurate with honest market practice and/or the general principle of good faith in the trader's field of activity;

(i) 'invitation to purchase' means a commercial communication which indicates characteristics of the product and the price in a way appropriate to the means of the commercial communication used and thereby enables the consumer to make a purchase;

(j) 'undue influence' means exploiting a position of power in relation to the consumer so as to apply pressure, even without using or threatening to use physical force, in a way which significantly limits the consumer's ability to make an informed decision;

(k) 'transactional decision' means any decision taken by a consumer concerning whether, how and on what terms to purchase, make payment in whole or in part for, retain or dispose of a product or to exercise a contractual right in relation to the product, whether the consumer decides to act or to refrain from acting;

(l) 'regulated profession' means a professional activity or a group of professional activities, access to which or the pursuit of which, or one of the modes of pursuing which, is conditional, directly or indirectly, upon possession of specific professional qualifications, pursuant to laws, regulations or administrative provisions.

Article 3

Scope

1.   This Directive shall apply to unfair business-to-consumer commercial practices, as laid down in Article 5, before, during and after a commercial transaction in relation to a product.

2.   This Directive is without prejudice to contract law and, in particular, to the rules on the validity, formation or effect of a contract.

3.   This Directive is without prejudice to Community or national rules relating to the health and safety aspects of products.

4.   In the case of conflict between the provisions of this Directive and other Community rules regulating specific aspects of unfair commercial practices, the latter shall prevail and apply to those specific aspects.

5.   For a period of six years from 12 June 2007, Member States shall be able to continue to apply national provisions within the field approximated by this Directive which are more restrictive or prescriptive than this Directive and which implement directives containing minimum harmonisation clauses. These measures must be essential to ensure that consumers are adequately protected against unfair commercial practices and must be proportionate to the attainment of this objective. . . .

6.   Member States shall notify the Commission without delay of any national provisions applied on the basis of paragraph 5.

7.   This Directive is without prejudice to the rules determining the jurisdiction of the courts.

8.   This Directive is without prejudice to any conditions of establishment or of authorisation regimes, or to the deontological codes of conduct or other specific rules governing regulated professions in order to uphold high standards of integrity on the part of the professional, which Member States may, in conformity with Community law, impose on professionals.

9. In relation to 'financial services', as defined in Directive 2002/65/EC, and immovable property, Member States may impose requirements which are more restrictive or prescriptive than this Directive in the field which it approximates.

10. This Directive shall not apply to the application of the laws, regulations and administrative provisions of Member States relating to the certification and indication of the standard of fineness of articles of precious metal.

Article 4

Internal market

Member States shall neither restrict the freedom to provide services nor restrict the free movement of goods for reasons falling within the field approximated by this Directive.

CHAPTER 2

UNFAIR COMMERCIAL PRACTICES

Article 5

Prohibition of unfair commercial practices

1. Unfair commercial practices shall be prohibited.

2. A commercial practice shall be unfair if:

(a) it is contrary to the requirements of professional diligence, and

(b) it materially distorts or is likely to materially distort the economic behaviour with regard to the product of the average consumer whom it reaches or to whom it is addressed, or of the average member of the group when a commercial practice is directed to a particular group of consumers.

3. Commercial practices which are likely to materially distort the economic behaviour only of a clearly identifiable group of consumers who are particularly vulnerable to the practice or the underlying product because of their mental or physical infirmity, age or credulity in a way which the trader could reasonably be expected to foresee, shall be assessed from the perspective of the average member of that group. This is without prejudice to the common and legitimate advertising practice of making exaggerated statements or statements which are not meant to be taken literally.

4. In particular, commercial practices shall be unfair which:

(a) are misleading as set out in Articles 6 and 7, or

(b) are aggressive as set out in Articles 8 and 9.

5. Annex I contains the list of those commercial practices which shall in all circumstances be regarded as unfair. The same single list shall apply in all Member States and may only be modified by revision of this Directive.

Section 1

Misleading commercial practices

Article 6

Misleading actions

1. A commercial practice shall be regarded as misleading if it contains false information and is therefore untruthful or in any way, including overall presentation, deceives or is likely to deceive the

average consumer, even if the information is factually correct, in relation to one or more of the following elements, and in either case causes or is likely to cause him to take a transactional decision that he would not have taken otherwise:

(a) the existence or nature of the product;

(b) the main characteristics of the product, such as its availability, benefits, risks, execution, composition, accessories, after-sale customer assistance and complaint handling, method and date of manufacture or provision, delivery, fitness for purpose, usage, quantity, specification, geographical or commercial origin or the results to be expected from its use, or the results and material features of tests or checks carried out on the product;

(c) the extent of the trader's commitments, the motives for the commercial practice and the nature of the sales process, any statement or symbol in relation to direct or indirect sponsorship or approval of the trader or the product;

(d) the price or the manner in which the price is calculated, or the existence of a specific price advantage;

(e) the need for a service, part, replacement or repair;

(f) the nature, attributes and rights of the trader or his agent, such as his identity and assets, his qualifications, status, approval, affiliation or connection and ownership of industrial, commercial or intellectual property rights or his awards and distinctions;

(g) the consumer's rights, including the right to replacement or reimbursement under Directive 1999/44/EC of the European Parliament and of the Council of 25 May 1999 on certain aspects of the sale of consumer goods and associated guarantees, or the risks he may face.

2.   A commercial practice shall also be regarded as misleading if, in its factual context, taking account of all its features and circumstances, it causes or is likely to cause the average consumer to take a transactional decision that he would not have taken otherwise, and it involves:

(a) any marketing of a product, including comparative advertising, which creates confusion with any products, trade marks, trade names or other distinguishing marks of a competitor;

(b) non-compliance by the trader with commitments contained in codes of conduct by which the trader has undertaken to be bound, where:

(i) the commitment is not aspirational but is firm and is capable of being verified, and

(ii) the trader indicates in a commercial practice that he is bound by the code.

Article 7

Misleading omissions

1.   A commercial practice shall be regarded as misleading if, in its factual context, taking account of all its features and circumstances and the limitations of the communication medium, it omits material information that the average consumer needs, according to the context, to take an informed transactional decision and thereby causes or is likely to cause the average consumer to take a transactional decision that he would not have taken otherwise.

2.   It shall also be regarded as a misleading omission when, taking account of the matters described in paragraph 1, a trader hides or provides in an unclear, unintelligible, ambiguous or untimely manner such material information as referred to in that paragraph or fails to identify the commercial intent of the commercial practice if not already apparent from the context, and where, in either case, this causes or is likely to cause the average consumer to take a transactional decision that he would not have taken otherwise.

3.   Where the medium used to communicate the commercial practice imposes limitations of space or time, these limitations and any measures taken by the trader to make the information

available to consumers by other means shall be taken into account in deciding whether information has been omitted.

4.   In the case of an invitation to purchase, the following information shall be regarded as material, if not already apparent from the context:

(a)   the main characteristics of the product, to an extent appropriate to the medium and the product;

(b)   the geographical address and the identity of the trader, such as his trading name and, where applicable, the geographical address and the identity of the trader on whose behalf he is acting;

(c)   the price inclusive of taxes, or where the nature of the product means that the price cannot reasonably be calculated in advance, the manner in which the price is calculated, as well as, where appropriate, all additional freight, delivery or postal charges or, where these charges cannot reasonably be calculated in advance, the fact that such additional charges may be payable;

(d)   the arrangements for payment, delivery, performance and the complaint handling policy, if they depart from the requirements of professional diligence;

(e)   for products and transactions involving a right of withdrawal or cancellation, the existence of such a right.

5.   Information requirements established by Community law in relation to commercial communication including advertising or marketing . . . shall be regarded as material.

Section 2

Aggressive commercial practices

Article 8

Aggressive commercial practices

A commercial practice shall be regarded as aggressive if, in its factual context, taking account of all its features and circumstances, by harassment, coercion, including the use of physical force, or undue influence, it significantly impairs or is likely to significantly impair the average consumer's freedom of choice or conduct with regard to the product and thereby causes him or is likely to cause him to take a transactional decision that he would not have taken otherwise.

Article 9

Use of harassment, coercion and undue influence

In determining whether a commercial practice uses harassment, coercion, including the use of physical force, or undue influence, account shall be taken of:

(a)   its timing, location, nature or persistence;

(b)   the use of threatening or abusive language or behaviour;

(c)   the exploitation by the trader of any specific misfortune or circumstance of such gravity as to impair the consumer's judgement, of which the trader is aware, to influence the consumer's decision with regard to the product;

(d)   any onerous or disproportionate non-contractual barriers imposed by the trader where a consumer wishes to exercise rights under the contract, including rights to terminate a contract or to switch to another product or another trader;

(e)   any threat to take any action that cannot legally be taken. . . .

DIRECTIVE 2005/29/EC OF
THE EUROPEAN PARLIAMENT

ANNEX I

COMMERCIAL PRACTICES WHICH ARE IN ALL
CIRCUMSTANCES CONSIDERED UNFAIR

Misleading commercial practices

1. Claiming to be a signatory to a code of conduct when the trader is not.

2. Displaying a trust mark, quality mark or equivalent without having obtained the necessary authorisation.

3. Claiming that a code of conduct has an endorsement from a public or other body which it does not have.

4. Claiming that a trader (including his commercial practices) or a product has been approved, endorsed or authorised by a public or private body when he/it has not or making such a claim without complying with the terms of the approval, endorsement or authorisation.

5. Making an invitation to purchase products at a specified price without disclosing the existence of any reasonable grounds the trader may have for believing that he will not be able to offer for supply or to procure another trader to supply, those products or equivalent products at that price for a period that is, and in quantities that are, reasonable having regard to the product, the scale of advertising of the product and the price offered (bait advertising).

6. Making an invitation to purchase products at a specified price and then:

   (a) refusing to show the advertised item to consumers; or

   (b) refusing to take orders for it or deliver it within a reasonable time; or

   (c) demonstrating a defective sample of it, with the intention of promoting a different product (bait and switch)

7. Falsely stating that a product will only be available for a very limited time, or that it will only be available on particular terms for a very limited time, in order to elicit an immediate decision and deprive consumers of sufficient opportunity or time to make an informed choice.

8. Undertaking to provide after-sales service to consumers with whom the trader has communicated prior to a transaction in a language which is not an official language of the Member State where the trader is located and then making such service available only in another language without clearly disclosing this to the consumer before the consumer is committed to the transaction.

9. Stating or otherwise creating the impression that a product can legally be sold when it cannot.

10. Presenting rights given to consumers in law as a distinctive feature of the trader's offer.

11. Using editorial content in the media to promote a product where a trader has paid for the promotion without making that clear in the content or by images or sounds clearly identifiable by the consumer (advertorial). This is without prejudice to Council Directive 89/552/EEC.

12. Making a materially inaccurate claim concerning the nature and extent of the risk to the personal security of the consumer or his family if the consumer does not purchase the product.

13. Promoting a product similar to a product made by a particular manufacturer in such a manner as deliberately to mislead the consumer into believing that the product is made by that same manufacturer when it is not.

14. Establishing, operating or promoting a pyramid promotional scheme where a consumer gives consideration for the opportunity to receive compensation that is derived primarily from the introduction of other consumers into the scheme rather than from the sale or consumption of products.

15. Claiming that the trader is about to cease trading or move premises when he is not.

16. Claiming that products are able to facilitate winning in games of chance.

17. Falsely claiming that a product is able to cure illnesses, dysfunction or malformations.

18. Passing on materially inaccurate information on market conditions or on the possibility of finding the product with the intention of inducing the consumer to acquire the product at conditions less favourable than normal market conditions.

19. Claiming in a commercial practice to offer a competition or prize promotion without awarding the prizes described or a reasonable equivalent.

20. Describing a product as 'gratis', 'free', 'without charge' or similar if the consumer has to pay anything other than the unavoidable cost of responding to the commercial practice and collecting or paying for delivery of the item.

21. Including in marketing material an invoice or similar document seeking payment which gives the consumer the impression that he has already ordered the marketed product when he has not.

22. Falsely claiming or creating the impression that the trader is not acting for purposes relating to his trade, business, craft or profession, or falsely representing oneself as a consumer.

23. Creating the false impression that after-sales service in relation to a product is available in a Member State other than the one in which the product is sold.

Aggressive commercial practices

24. Creating the impression that the consumer cannot leave the premises until a contract is formed.

25. Conducting personal visits to the consumer's home ignoring the consumer's request to leave or not to return except in circumstances and to the extent justified, under national law, to enforce a contractual obligation.

26. Making persistent and unwanted solicitations by telephone, fax, e-mail or other remote media except in circumstances and to the extent justified under national law to enforce a contractual obligation. . . .

27. Requiring a consumer who wishes to claim on an insurance policy to produce documents which could not reasonably be considered relevant as to whether the claim was valid, or failing systematically to respond to pertinent correspondence, in order to dissuade a consumer from exercising his contractual rights.

28. Including in an advertisement a direct exhortation to children to buy advertised products or persuade their parents or other adults to buy advertised products for them. This provision is without prejudice to Article 16 of Directive 89/552/EEC on television broadcasting.

29. Demanding immediate or deferred payment for or the return or safekeeping of products supplied by the trader, but not solicited by the consumer except where the product is a substitute supplied in conformity with Article 7(3) of Directive 97/7/EC (inertia selling).

30. Explicitly informing a consumer that if he does not buy the product or service, the trader's job or livelihood will be in jeopardy.

31. Creating the false impression that the consumer has already won, will win, or will on doing a particular act win, a prize or other equivalent benefit, when in fact either:

DIRECTIVE 2005/29/EC OF
THE EUROPEAN PARLIAMENT

— there is no prize or other equivalent benefit, or

— taking any action in relation to claiming the prize or other equivalent benefit is subject to the consumer paying money or incurring a cost. . . .

DIRECTIVE 2011/83/EU OF THE EUROPEAN PARLIAMENT AND OF THE COUNCIL OF 25 OCTOBER 2011

[Directive 2011/83/EU, the "Consumer Rights Directive," was adopted by the European Parliament and the Council of the European Union and became effective on December 13, 2011. Its purpose is to implement a part of the Treaty on the Functioning of the European Union, which provides that the EU should contribute to a high level of consumer protection. This Directive applies to "distance" and "off-premises" contracts as defined in the Directive, Article 2, Sections (7) and (8), which would include contracts between traders and consumers made door-to-door or over the Internet. It is up to Member States of the EU to enforce the directive, as provided in Article 23 below.

[The excerpted provisions focus on a consumer's "right of withdrawal," which empowers a consumer to cancel a covered contract within two weeks from, for example, taking delivery of goods, without giving any reason. The closest counterpart in U.S. law is the Federal Trade Commission's regulation providing for a "cooling off" period of three days following the making of a contract between a buyer and a door-to-door salesman. It is included in this book below. Clearly, the EU Directive is more protective of consumers.]

CHAPTER 1

SUBJECT MATTER, DEFINITIONS AND SCOPE

Article 1

Subject matter

The purpose of this Directive is, through the achievement of a high level of consumer protection, to contribute to the proper functioning of the internal market by approximating certain aspects of the laws, regulations and administrative provisions of the Member States concerning contracts concluded between consumers and traders.

Article 2

Definitions

For the purpose of this Directive, the following definitions shall apply:

(1) 'consumer' means any natural person who, in contracts covered by this Directive, is acting for purposes which are outside his trade, business, craft or profession;

(2) 'trader' means any natural person or any legal person, irrespective of whether privately or publicly owned, who is acting, including through any other person acting in his name or on his behalf, for purposes relating to his trade, business, craft or profession in relation to contracts covered by this directive;

. . .

(7) 'distance contract' means any contract concluded between the trader and the consumer under an organized distance sales or service-provision scheme without the simultaneous physical presence of the trader and the consumer, with the exclusive use of one or more means of distance communication up to and including the time at which the contract is conducted;

(8) 'off-premises contract' means any contract between the trader and the consumer;

 (a) concluded in the simultaneous physical presence of the trader and the consumer, in a place which is not the business premises of the trader;

(b) for which an offer was made by the consumer in the same circumstances as referred to in point (a);

(c) concluded on the business premises of the trader or through any means of distance communication immediately after the consumer was personally and individually addressed in a place which is not the business premises of the trader in the simultaneous physical presence of the trader and the consumer, or

(d) concluded during an excursion organized by the trader with the aim or effect of promoting and selling goods or services to the consumer;

(9) 'business premises' means:

(a) any immovable retail premises where the trader carries out his activity on a permanent basis; or

(b) any movable retail premises where the trader carries out his activity on a usual basis;

(10) 'durable medium' means any instrument which enables the consumer or the trader to store information addressed personally to him in a way accessible for future reference for a period of time adequate for the purposes of the information and which allows the unchanged reproduction of the information stored;

(11) 'digital content' means data which are produced and supplied in digital form;

. . .

Article 3

Scope

1.   This Directive shall apply, under the conditions and to the extent set out in its provisions, to any contact concluded between a trader and a consumer. . . .

. . .

Article 4

Level of harmonization

Member States shall not maintain or introduce, in their national law, provisions diverging from those laid down in this Directive, including more or less stringent provisions to ensure a different level of consumer protection, unless otherwise provided for in this Directive.

. . .

CHAPTER III

CONSUMER INFORMATION AND RIGHT OF WITHDRAWAL
FOR DISTANCE AND OFF-PREMISES CONTRACTS

Article 6

Information requirements for distance and off-premises contracts

1.   Before the consumer is bound by a distance or off-premises contract, or any corresponding offer, the trader shall provide the consumer with the following information in a clear and comprehensible manner;

(a) the main characteristics of the goods or services, to the extent appropriate to the medium and to the goods or services;

(b) the identity of the trader, such as his trading name;

(c)   the geographical address at which the trader is established and the trader's telephone number, fax number and e-mail address, where available, to enable the consumer to contact the trader quickly and communicate with him efficiently and, where applicable, the geographical address and identity of the trader on whose behalf he is acting;

(d)   if different from the address provided in accordance with point (c), the geographical address of the place of business of the trader, and, where applicable, that of the trader on whose behalf he is acting, where the consumer can address any complaints;

(e)   the total price of the goods or services inclusive of taxes, or where the nature of the goods or services is such that the price cannot reasonably be calculated in advance, the manner in which the price is to be calculated, as well as, where applicable, all additional freight, delivery or postal charges and any other costs or, where those charges cannot reasonably be calculated in advance, the fact that such additional charges may be payable. In the case of a contract of indeterminate duration or a contract containing a subscription, the total price shall include the total costs per billing period. Where such contracts are charged at a fixed rate, the total price shall also mean the total monthly costs. Where the total costs cannot be reasonably calculated in advance, the manner in which the price is to be calculated shall be provided;

(f)   the cost of using the means of distance communication for the conclusion of the contract where that cost is calculated other than at the basic rate;

(g)   the arrangements for payment, delivery, performance, the time by which the trader undertakes to deliver the goods or to perform the services and, where applicable, the trader's complaint handling policy;

(h)   where a right of withdrawal exists, the conditions, time limit and procedures for exercising that right in accordance with Article 11(1), as well as the model withdrawal form set out in Annex 1(B);

(i)   where applicable, that the consumer will have to bear the cost of returning the goods in case of withdrawal and, for distance contracts, if the goods, by their nature, cannot normally be returned by post, the cost of returning the goods;

(j)   that, if the consumer exercises the right of withdrawal after having made a request in accordance with Article 7(3) or Article 8(8), the consumer shall be liable to pay the trader reasonable costs in accordance with Article 14(3);

(k)   where a right of withdrawal is not provided for in accordance with Article 16, the information that the consumer will not benefit from a right of withdrawal or, where applicable, the circumstances under which the consumer loses his right of withdrawal;

(l)   a reminder of the existence of a legal guarantee of conformity for goods;

(m)   where applicable, the existence and the conditions of [after-sale] customer assistance, after-sales services and commercial guarantees;

(n)   the existence of relevant codes of conduct, . . . and how copies of them can be obtained, where applicable;

(o)   the duration of the contract, where applicable, or, if the contract is of indeterminate duration or is to be extended automatically, the conditions for terminating the contract;

(p)   where applicable, the minimum duration of the consumer's obligations under the contract;

(q)   where applicable, the existence and the conditions of deposits or other financial guarantees to be paid or provided by the consumer at the request of the trader;

(r)   where applicable, the functionality, including applicable technical protection measures, of digital content;

(s)   where applicable, any relevant interoperability of digital content with hardware and software that the trader is aware of or can reasonably be expected to have been aware of;

(t)   where applicable, the possibility of having recourse to an out-of-court complaint and redress mechanism, to which the trader is subject, and the methods for having access to it.

. . .

5.   The information referred to in paragraph 1 shall form an integral part of the distance or off-premises contract and shall not be altered unless the contracting parties expressly agree otherwise.

. . .

Article 7

Formal requirements for off-premises contracts

1.   With respect to off-premises contracts, the trader shall give the information provided for in Article 6(1) to the consumer on paper or, if the consumer agrees, on another durable medium. That information shall be legible and in plain, intelligible language.

. . .

Article 8

Formal requirements for distance contracts

1.   With respect to distance contracts, the trader shall give the information provided for in Article 6(1) or make that information available to the consumer in a way appropriate to the means of distance communication used in plain and intelligible language. In so far as that information is provided on a durable medium, it shall be legible.

2.   If a distance contract to be concluded by electronic means places the consumer under an obligation to pay, the trader shall make the consumer aware in a clear and prominent manner, and directly before the consumer places his order, of the information provided for in points (a), (e), (o) and (p) of Article 6(1).

The trader shall ensure that the consumer, when placing his order, explicitly acknowledges that the order implies an obligation to pay. If placing an order entails activating a button or a similar function, the button or similar function shall be labelled in an easily legible manner only with the words 'order with obligation to pay' or a corresponding unambiguous formulation indicating that placing the order entails an obligation to pay the trader. If the trader has not complied with this subparagraph, the consumer shall not be bound by the contract or order.

3.   Trading websites shall indicate clearly and legibly at the latest at the beginning of the ordering process whether any delivery restrictions apply and which means of payment are accepted.

4.   If the contract is concluded through a means of distance communication which allows limited space or time to display the information, the trader shall provide, on that particular means prior to the conclusion of such a contract, at least the pre-contractual information regarding the main characteristics of the goods or services, the identity of the trader, the total price, the right of withdrawal, the duration of the contract and, if the contract is of indeterminate duration, the conditions for terminating the contract, as referred to in points (a), (b), (e), (h) and (o) of Article 6(1). The other information referred to in Article 6(1) shall be provided by the trader to the consumer in an appropriate way in accordance with paragraph 1 of this Article.

5.   Without prejudice to paragraph 4, if the trader makes a telephone call to the consumer with a view to concluding a distance contract, he shall, at the beginning of the conversation with the consumer, disclose his identity and, where applicable, the identity of the person on whose behalf he makes that call, and the commercial purpose of the call.

6.   Where a distance contract is to be concluded by telephone, Member States may provide that the trader has to confirm the offer to the consumer who is bound only once he has signed the offer or has sent his written consent. Member States may also provide that such confirmations have to be made on a durable medium.

7.   The trader shall provide the consumer with the confirmation of the contract concluded, on a durable medium within a reasonable time after the conclusion of the distance contract, and at the latest at the time of the delivery of the goods or before the performance of the service begins. . . .

. . .

Article 9

Right of withdrawal

1.   Save where the exceptions provided for in Article 16 apply, the consumer shall have a period of 14 days to withdraw from a distance or off-premises contract, without giving any reason, and without incurring any costs other than those provided for in Article 13(2) and Article 14.

2.   Without prejudice to Article 10, the withdrawal period referred to in paragraph 1 of this Article shall expire after 14 days from:

. . .

(b)   in the case of sales contracts, the day on which the consumer or a third party other than the carrier and indicated by the consumer acquires physical possession of the good or;

   (i)   in the case of multiple goods ordered by the consumer in one order and delivered separately, the day on which the consumer or a third party other than the carrier and indicated by the consumer acquires physical possession of the last good;

   (ii)   in the case of delivery of a good consisting of multiple lots or pieces, the day on which the consumer or a third party other than the carrier indicated by the consumer acquires physical possession of the last lot or piece;

   (iii) in the case of contracts for regular delivery of goods during defined period of time, the day on which the consumer or a third party other than the carrier and indicated by the consumer acquires physical possession of the first good. . . .

. . .

Article 10

Omission of information on the right of withdrawal

1.   If the trader has not provided the consumer with the information on the right of withdrawal as required by point (h) of Article 6(1), the withdrawal period shall expire 12 months from the end of the initial withdrawal period, as determined in accordance with Article 9(2).

2.   If the trader has provided the consumer with the information provided for in paragraph 1 of this Article within 12 months from the day referred to in Article 9(2), the withdrawal period shall expire 14 days after the day upon which the consumer receives that information.

Article 11

Exercise of the right of withdrawal

1.   Before the expiry of the withdrawal period, the consumer shall inform the trader of his decision to withdraw from the contract. . . .

. . .

2.   The consumer shall have exercised his right of withdrawal within the withdrawal period referred to in Article 9(2) and Article 10 if the communication concerning the exercise of the right of withdrawal is sent by the consumer before that period has expired.

3.   The trader may, in addition to the possibilities referred to in paragraph 1, give the option to the consumer to electronically fill in and submit either the model withdrawal form set out in Annex 1(B) or any other unequivocal statement on the trader's website. In those cases the trader shall communicate to the consumer an acknowledgement of receipt of such a withdrawal on a durable medium without delay.

4.   The burden of proof of exercising the right of withdrawal in accordance with this Article shall be on the consumer.

Article 12

Effects of withdrawal

The exercise of the right of withdrawal shall terminate the obligations of the parties:

(a)   to perform the distance or off-premises contract; or

(b)   to conclude the distance or off-premises contract, in cases where an offer was made by the consumer.

Article 13

Obligations of the trader in the event of withdrawal

1.   The trader shall reimburse all payments received from the consumer, including, if applicable, the costs of delivery without undue delay and in any event not later than 14 days from the day on which he is informed of the consumer's decision to withdraw from the contract in accordance with Article 11.

The trader shall carry out the reimbursement referred to in the first subparagraph using the same means of payment as the consumer used for the initial transaction, unless the consumer has expressly agreed otherwise and provided that the consumer does not incur any fees as a result of such reimbursement.

2.   Notwithstanding paragraph 1, the trader shall not be required to reimburse the supplementary costs, if the consumer has expressly opted for a type of delivery other than the least expensive type of standard delivery offered by the trader.

3.   Unless the trader has offered to collect the goods himself, with regard to sales contracts, the trader may withhold the reimbursement until he has received the goods back, or until the consumer has supplied evidence of having sent back the goods, whichever is the earliest.

Article 14

Obligations of the consumer in the event of withdrawal

1.   Unless the trader has offered to collect the goods himself, the consumer shall send back the goods or hand them over to the trader or to a person authorized by the trader to receive the goods, without undue delay and in any event not later than 14 days from the day of which he has communicated his decision to withdraw from the contract to the trader in accordance with Article 11. The deadline shall be met if the consumer sends back the goods before the period of 14 days has expired.

The consumer shall only bear the direct cost of returning the goods unless the trader has agreed to bear them or the trader failed to inform the consumer that the consumer has to bear them.

In the case of off-premises contracts where the goods have been delivered to the consumer's home at the time of the conclusion of the contract, the trader shall at his own expense collect the goods if, by their nature, those goods cannot normally be returned by post.

2.   The consumer shall only be liable for any diminished value of the goods resulting from the handling of the goods other than what is necessary to establish the nature, characteristics and functioning of the goods. The consumer shall in any event not be liable for diminished value of the goods where the trader has failed to provide notice of the right of withdrawal in accordance with point (h) of Article 6(1).

3.   Where a consumer exercises the right of withdrawal after having made a request in accordance with Article 7(3) or Article 8(8), the consumer shall pay to the trader an amount which is in proportion to what has been provided until the time the consumer has informed the trader of the exercise of the right of withdrawal, in comparison with the full coverage of the contract. The proportionate amount to be paid by the consumer to the trader shall be calculated on the basis of the total price agreed in the contract. If the total price is excessive, the proportionate amount shall be calculated on the basis of the market value of what has been provided.

4.   The consumer shall bear no cost for:

(a)   the performance of services or the supply of water, gas or electricity, where they are not put up for sale in a limited volume or set quantity, or of district heating, in full or in part, during the withdrawal period, where:

   (i)   the trader has failed to provide information in accordance with points (h) or (j) of Article 6(1); or

   (ii)   the consumer has not expressly requested performance to begin during the withdrawal period in accordance with Article 7(3) and Article 8(8); or

(b)   the supply, in full or in part, of digital content which is not supplied on a tangible medium where:

   (i)   the consumer has not given his prior express consent to the beginning of the performance before the end of the 14-day period referred to in Article 9;

   (ii)   the consumer has not acknowledged that he loses his right of withdrawal when giving his consent; or

   (iii) the trader has failed to provide confirmation in accordance with Article 7(2) or Article 8(7).

5.   Except as provided for in Article 13(2) and in this Article the consumer shall not incur any liability as a consequence of the exercise of the right of withdrawal.

. . .

CHAPTER V

GENERAL PROVISIONS

Article 23

Enforcement

1.   Member States shall ensure that adequate and effective means exist to ensure compliance with this Directive.

2.   The means referred to in paragraph 1 shall include provisions whereby one or more of the following bodies, as determined by national law, may take action under national law before the courts

or before the competent administrative bodies to ensure that the national provisions transposing this Directive are applied:

    (a)   public bodies or their representatives;

    (b)   consumer organizations having a legitimate interest in protecting consumers;

    (c)   professional organizations having a legitimate interest in acting.

Article 24

Penalties

1.   Member States shall lay down the rules on penalties applicable to infringements of the national provisions adopted pursuant to this Directive and shall take all measures necessary to ensure that they are implemented. The penalties provided for must be effective, proportionate and dissuasive.

STANDARD CONTRACTS LAW 5743–1982 (ISRAEL)

[The Israeli Standard Contracts Law was enacted in 1982 "to protect customers against prejudicial conditions in standard contracts." Standard Contracts Law § 1. It establishes a tribunal to review a consumer contract to determine whether it gives a supplier an unfair advantage. Suppliers may apply to the tribunal for a certification that their contracts pass muster. If a contract passes muster, it is protected from claims that it is unfairly advantageous to the supplier for a period of five years, whether proceedings are brought before the tribunal or a court. It does not preclude claims under other Israeli laws, such as a claim that a contract is unenforceable because it is against public policy. The following is an unofficial translation.]

CHAPTER ONE: BASIC PROVISIONS

Objective

1. The objective of this Law is to protect customers against prejudicial conditions in standard contracts.

Definitions

2. In this Law—

    "standard contract"—the text of a contract, in which all or some of the conditions were determined in advance by one party, to be used as conditions in many contracts between that party and an indefinite number of unidentified persons;

    "condition"—a stipulation in a standard contract, including a stipulation referred to in it and also every other stipulation that is part of the contract, but exclusive of any stipulation on which the supplier and the customer agreed specially for purposes of a specific contract;

    "supplier"—whoever proposes that a contract with him shall be according to a standard contract and it does not matter whether he is the one who gives or receives a certain thing;

    "customer"—a person to whom a supplier proposes that a contract between them shall be according to a standard contract and it does not matter whether he is the one who gives or receives a certain thing;

    "Tribunal"—the Standard Contracts Tribunal set up under this Law.

Prejudicial conditions and there [sic] annulment

3. A Court and the Tribunal shall, according to the provisions of this Law, annul or change any condition of a standard contract that—taking the totality of the contract's conditions and other circumstances into account—imposes a prejudicial condition on customers or gives the supplier an unfair advantage that is likely to result in harm to customers

Presumptions

4. The presumption is that the following conditions are prejudicial:

    (1) a condition that fully or partly relieves the supplier of a responsibility he would have to bear under any statute, if not for that condition, or that unreasonably restricts the responsibility he would have to bear by virtue of the contract, if not for that condition;

    (2) a condition that gives the supplier an unreasonable right to cancel, suspend or defer performance of the contract or to alter his substantive obligations under the contract;

    (3) a condition that gives the supplier the right to transfer his responsibility to a third party;

    (4) a condition that gives the supplier the right to determine or to change—at his sole discretion and after the contract was concluded—a price or other substantive obligation

imposed on the customer, except when the change arises out of factors that the supplier does not control;

(5) a condition that unreasonably requires the customer to resort to the supplier or to some other person or otherwise limits the customer's freedom to enter or not to enter into contracts with others;

(6) a condition that denies or limits a right or remedy statutorily available to the customer, unreasonably restricts a right or remedy available to him by virtue of the contract or makes it conditional on giving notice in an unreasonable form or within an unreasonable time or on any other unreasonable requirement;

(7) a condition that imposes on the customer a burden of proof that he would not have to bear, if not for that condition;

(8) a condition that denies or limits the customer's right to present certain arguments to judicial authorities or that determines that any controversy between the supplier and the customer be heard by arbitration;

(9) a condition that stipulates a statutory provision on the place of jurisdiction or gives the supplier the exclusive right to choose the place of jurisdiction or of arbitration where a dispute is to be heard;

(10) a condition that prescribes that a dispute be referred to arbitration when the supplier has greater influence than the customer on the conditions of the arbitration, including selection of the arbitrator, the place of arbitration, conditions under which the arbitration shall proceed; how the arbitration shall be conducted and law procedures at the arbitration, all even if the supplier proved that bringing the controversy to arbitration by itself, as said in paragraph (8), is not discriminatory;

(11) a condition that prescribes the linkage of a price or other payment under the contract to any index, so that its decrease or increase will not benefit the customer.

Void conditions in a standard contract

5. (a) A condition in a standard contract that denies or restricts the customer's right to apply to judicial authorities is void.

(b) A condition in a standard contract that wholly or partly exempts the supplier from liability for bodily harm or for a malicious act that he bears under a statute is void.

CHAPTER TWO: STANDARD CONTRACTS TRIBUNAL

The Tribunal and its members

6. (a) A Standard Contracts Tribunal is hereby set up. . . .

CHAPTER FOUR: ANNULMENT OF A PREJUDICIAL CONDITION

Petition to a Tribunal to annul a prejudicial condition

16. (a) The Attorney General or his representative, the Consumer Protection and Fair Trade Commissioner under the Consumer Protection Law 5741–1981, any customers' organization and public authority designated in regulations, as well as a customers' organization approved by the Minister of Justice for a particular matter may apply to the Tribunal for the annulment of a prejudicial condition in a standard contract. . . .

Annulment and change of a condition by the Tribunal

17. (a) If the Tribunal concluded that a condition is prejudicial, it shall annul it or change it to the extent necessary in order to eliminate the prejudice involved. . . .

Annulment and change of conditions by Court

19. (a) If in a proceeding between a supplier and a customer the Court concluded that a condition is prejudicial, it shall annul the condition in the contract between them or change it to the extent necessary in order to eliminate the prejudice. . . .

PART IX

MISCELLANEOUS STATUTES, DIRECTIVES, AND ADMINISTRATIVE REGULATIONS

MAGNUSON-MOSS WARRANTY ACT

(1975)

(Excerpts)

[The Magnuson-Moss Warranty Act ("MMWA"), codified at 15 U.S.C. §§ 2301 *et seq.*, primarily regulates written warranties on consumer products sold to consumers, and authorizes the Federal Trade Commission to implement the Act by promulgating additional rules of law. (These rules are in this pamphlet, below.) The MMWA aims to protect consumers by, among other things, preventing deception and requiring warrantors to disclose a written warranty's terms and conditions "fully and conspicuously in simple and readily understood language." 15 U.S.C § 2302(a). The MMWA applies to transactions that affect interstate commerce. The MMWA, and the FTC's implementing rules, establish a floor for consumer protection insofar as they provide it; consequently, they neither displace other federal consumer protection laws nor pre-empt state laws providing greater protections to consumers. 15 U.S.C § 2311(b). Article 2 of the Uniform Commercial Code also governs warranties in contracts for the sale of goods to consumers, as well as those in contracts for the sale of goods to merchants. *See* UCC §§ 2–312—2–318.]

TITLE I. CONSUMER PRODUCT WARRANTIES

Table of Contents

---

§ 101. Definitions. [15 U.S.C.A. § 2301]

For the purposes of this title:

(1) The term "consumer product" means any tangible personal property which is distributed in commerce and which is normally used for personal, family, or household purposes (including any such property intended to be attached to or installed in any real property without regard to whether it is so attached or installed).

(2) The term "Commission" means the Federal Trade Commission.

(3) The term "consumer" means a buyer (other than for purposes of resale) of any consumer product, any person to whom such product is transferred during the duration of an implied or written warranty (or service contract) applicable to the product, and any other person who is entitled by the terms of such warranty (or service contract) or under applicable State law to

enforce against the warrantor (or service contractor) the obligations of the warranty (or service contract).

(4) The term "supplier" means any person engaged in the business of making a consumer product directly or indirectly available to consumers.

(5) The term "warrantor" means any supplier or other person who gives or offers to give a written warranty or who is or may be obligated under an implied warranty.

(6) The term "written warranty" means—

(A) any written affirmation of fact or written promise made in connection with the sale of a consumer product by a supplier to a buyer which relates to the nature of the material or workmanship and affirms or promises that such material or workmanship is defect free or will meet a specified level of performance over a specified period of time, or

(B) any undertaking in writing in connection with the sale by a supplier of a consumer product to refund, repair, replace, or take other remedial action with respect to such product in the event that such product fails to meet the specifications set forth in the undertaking,

which written affirmation, promise, or undertaking becomes part of the basis of the bargain between a supplier and a buyer for purposes other than resale of such product.

(7) The term "implied warranty" means an implied warranty arising under State law (as modified by sections 108 and 104(a)) in connection with the sale by a supplier of a consumer product.

(8) The term "service contract" means a contract in writing to perform, over a fixed period of time or for a specified duration, services relating to the maintenance or repair (or both) of a consumer product.

(9) The term "reasonable and necessary maintenance" consists of those operations (A) which the consumer reasonably can be expected to perform or have performed and (B) which are necessary to keep any consumer product performing its intended function and operating at a reasonable level of performance.

(10) The term "remedy" means whichever of the following actions the warrantor elects:

(A) repair,

(B) replacement, or

(C) refund;

except that the warrantor may not elect refund unless (i) the warrantor is unable to provide replacement and repair is not commercially practicable or cannot be timely made, or (ii) the consumer is willing to accept such refund.

(11) The term "replacement" means furnishing a new consumer product which is identical or reasonably equivalent to the warranted consumer product.

(12) The term "refund" means refunding the actual purchase price (less reasonable depreciation based on actual use where permitted by rules of the Commission).

(13) The term "distributed in commerce" means sold in commerce, introduced or delivered for introduction into commerce, or held for sale or distribution after introduction into commerce.

(14) The term "commerce" means trade, traffic, commerce, or transportation—

(A) between a place in a State and any place outside thereof, or

(B) which affects trade, traffic, commerce, or transportation described in subparagraph (A).

(15) The term "State" means a State, the District of Columbia, the Commonwealth of Puerto Rico, the Virgin Islands, Guam, the Canal Zone, or American Samoa. The term "State law" includes a law of the United States applicable only to the District of Columbia or only to a territory or possession of the United States; and the term "Federal law" excludes any State law.

§ 102. Warranty Provisions. [15 U.S.C.A. § 2302]

(a) In order to improve the adequacy of information available to consumers, prevent deception, and improve competition in the marketing of consumer products, any warrantor warranting a consumer product to a consumer by means of a written warranty shall, to the extent required by rules of the Commission, fully and conspicuously disclose in simple and readily understood language the terms and conditions of such warranty. Such rules may require inclusion in the written warranty of any of the following items among others:

(1) The clear identification of the names and addresses of the warrantors.

(2) The identity of the party or parties to whom the warranty is extended.

(3) The products or parts covered.

(4) A statement of what the warrantor will do in the event of a defect, malfunction, or failure to conform with such written warranty—at whose expense—and for what period of time.

(5) A statement of what the consumer must do and expenses he must bear.

(6) Exceptions and exclusions from the terms of the warranty.

(7) The step-by-step procedure which the consumer should take in order to obtain performance of any obligation under the warranty, including the identification of any person or class of persons authorized to perform the obligations set forth in the warranty.

(8) Information respecting the availability of any informal dispute settlement procedure offered by the warrantor and a recital, where the warranty so provides, that the purchaser may be required to resort to such procedure before pursuing any legal remedies in the courts.

(9) A brief, general description of the legal remedies available to the consumer.

(10) The time at which the warrantor will perform any obligations under the warranty.

(11) The period of time within which, after notice of a defect, malfunction, or failure to conform with the warranty, the warrantor will perform any obligations under the warranty.

(12) The characteristics or properties of the products, or parts thereof, that are not covered by the warranty.

(13) The elements of the warranty in words or phrases which would not mislead a reasonable, average consumer as to the nature or scope of the warranty.

(b)(1)(A) The Commission shall prescribe rules requiring that the terms of any written warranty on a consumer product be made available to the consumer (or prospective consumer) prior to the sale of the product to him.

(B) The Commission may prescribe rules for determining the manner and form in which information with respect to any written warranty of a consumer product shall be clearly and conspicuously presented or displayed so as not to mislead the reasonable, average consumer, when such information is contained in advertising, labeling, point-of-sale material, or other representations in writing.

(2) Nothing in this title (other than paragraph (3) of this subsection) shall be deemed to authorize the Commission to prescribe the duration of written warranties given or to require that a consumer product or any of its components be warranted.

(3) The Commission may prescribe rules for extending the period of time a written warranty or service contract is in effect to correspond with any period of time in excess of a reasonable period (not less than 10 days) during which the consumer is deprived of the use of such consumer product by reason of failure of the product to conform with the written warranty or by reason of the failure of the warrantor (or service contractor) to carry out such warranty (or service contract) within the period specified in the warranty (or service contract).

(c) No warrantor of a consumer product may condition his written or implied warranty of such product on the consumer's using, in connection with such product, any article or service (other than article or service provided without charge under the terms of the warranty) which is identified by brand, trade, or corporate name; except that the prohibition of this subsection may be waived by the Commission if—

(1) the warrantor satisfies the Commission that the warranted product will function properly only if the article or service so identified is used in connection with the warranted product, and

(2) the Commission finds that such a waiver is in the public interest.

The Commission shall identify in the Federal Register, and permit public comment on, all applications for waiver of the prohibition of this subsection, and shall publish in the Federal Register its disposition of any such application, including the reasons therefor.

(d) The Commission may by rule devise detailed substantive warranty provisions which warrantors may incorporate by reference in their warranties.

(e) The provisions of this section apply only to warranties which pertain to consumer products actually costing the consumer more than $5.

§ 103. Designation of Warranties. [15 U.S.C.A. § 2303]

(a) Any warrantor warranting a consumer product by means of a written warranty shall clearly and conspicuously designate such warranty in the following manner, unless exempted from doing so by the Commission pursuant to subsection (c) of this section:

(1) If the written warranty meets the Federal minimum standards for warranty set forth in section 104 of this Act, then it shall be conspicuously designated a "full (statement of duration) warranty".

(2) If the written warranty does not meet the Federal minimum standards for warranty set forth in section 104 of this Act, then it shall be conspicuously designated a "limited warranty".

(b) Sections 102, 103, and 104 shall not apply to statements or representations which are similar to expressions of general policy concerning customer satisfaction and which are not subject to any specific limitations.

(c) In addition to exercising the authority pertaining to disclosure granted in section 102 of this Act, the Commission may by rule determine when a written warranty does not have to be designated either "full (statement of duration)" or "limited" in accordance with this section.

(d) The provisions of subsections (a) and (c) of this section apply only to warranties which pertain to consumer products actually costing the consumer more than $10 and which are not designated "full (statement of duration) warranties".

§ 104. Federal Minimum Standards for Warranty. [15 U.S.C.A. § 2304]

(a) In order for a warrantor warranting a consumer product by means of a written warranty to meet the Federal minimum standards for warranty—

(1)   such warrantor must as a minimum remedy such consumer product within a reasonable time and without charge, in the case of a defect, malfunction, or failure to conform with such written warranty;

(2)   notwithstanding section 108(b), such warrantor may not impose any limitation on the duration of any implied warranty on the product;

(3)   such warrantor may not exclude or limit consequential damages for breach of any written or implied warranty on such product, unless such exclusion or limitation conspicuously appears on the face of the warranty; and

(4)   if the product (or a component part thereof) contains a defect or malfunction after a reasonable number of attempts by the warrantor to remedy defects or malfunctions in such product, such warrantor must permit the consumer to elect either a refund for, or replacement without charge of, such product or part (as the case may be). The Commission may by rule specify for purposes of this paragraph, what constitutes a reasonable number of attempts to remedy particular kinds of defects or malfunctions under different circumstances. If the warrantor replaces a component part of a consumer product, such replacement shall include installing the part in the product without charge.

(b)(1) In fulfilling the duties under subsection (a) respecting a written warranty, the warrantor shall not impose any duty other than notification upon any consumer as a condition of securing remedy of any consumer product which malfunctions, is defective, or does not conform to the written warranty, unless the warrantor has demonstrated in a rulemaking proceeding, or can demonstrate in an administrative or judicial enforcement proceeding (including private enforcement), or in an informal dispute settlement proceeding, that such a duty is reasonable.

(2)   Notwithstanding paragraph (1), a warrantor may require, as a condition to replacement of, or refund for, any consumer product under subsection (a), that such consumer product shall be made available to the warrantor free and clear of liens and other encumbrances, except as otherwise provided by rule or order of the Commission in cases in which such a requirement would not be practicable.

(3)   The Commission may, by rule define in detail the duties set forth in section 104(a) of this Act and the applicability of such duties to warrantors of different categories of consumer products with "full (statement of duration)" warranties.

(4)   The duties under subsection (a) extend from the warrantor to each person who is a consumer with respect to the consumer product.

(c)   The performance of the duties under subsection (a) of this section shall not be required of the warrantor if he can show that the defect, malfunction, or failure of any warranted consumer product to conform with a written warranty, was caused by damage (not resulting from defect or malfunction) while in the possession of the consumer, or unreasonable use (including failure to provide reasonable and necessary maintenance).

(d)   For purposes of this section and of section 102(c), the term "without charge" means that the warrantor may not assess the consumer for any costs the warrantor or his representatives incur in connection with the required remedy of a warranted consumer product. An obligation under subsection (a)(1)(A) to remedy without charge does not necessarily require the warrantor to compensate the consumer for incidental expenses; however, if any incidental expenses are incurred because the remedy is not made within a reasonable time or because the warrantor imposed an unreasonable duty upon the consumer as a condition of securing remedy, then the consumer shall be entitled to recover reasonable incidental expenses which are so incurred in any action against the warrantor.

(e)   If a supplier designates a warranty applicable to a consumer product as a "full (statement of duration)" warranty, then the warranty on such product shall, for purposes of any action under section 110(d) or under any State law, be deemed to incorporate at least the minimum requirements of this section and rules prescribed under this section.

§ 105. Full and Limited Warranting of a Consumer Product. [15 U.S.C.A. § 2305]

Nothing in this title shall prohibit the selling of a consumer product which has both full and limited warranties if such warranties are clearly and conspicuously differentiated.

§ 106. Service Contracts. [15 U.S.C.A. § 2306]

(a)   The Commission may prescribe by rule the manner and form in which the terms and conditions of service contracts shall be fully, clearly, and conspicuously disclosed.

(b)   Nothing in this title shall be construed to prevent a supplier or warrantor from entering into a service contract with the consumer in addition to or in lieu of a written warranty if such contract fully, clearly, and conspicuously discloses its terms and conditions in simple and readily understood language.

§ 107. Designation of Representatives. [15 U.S.C.A. § 2307]

Nothing in this title shall be construed to prevent any warrantor from designating representatives to perform duties under the written or implied warranty: *Provided*, That such warrantor shall make reasonable arrangements for compensation of such designated representatives, but no such designation shall relieve the warrantor of his direct responsibilities to the consumer or make the representative a cowarrantor.

§ 108. Limitation on Disclaimer of Implied Warranties. [15 U.S.C.A. § 2308]

(a)   No supplier may disclaim or modify (except as provided in subsection (b)) any implied warranty to a consumer with respect to such consumer product if (1) such supplier makes any written warranty to the consumer with respect to such consumer product, or (2) at the time of sale, or within 90 days thereafter, such supplier enters into a service contract with the consumer which applies to such consumer product.

(b)   For purposes of this title (other than section 104(a)(2)), implied warranties may be limited in duration to the duration of a written warranty of reasonable duration, if such limitation is conscionable and is set forth in clear and unmistakable language and prominently displayed on the face of the warranty.

(c)   A disclaimer, modification, or limitation made in violation of this section shall be ineffective for purposes of this title and State law.

§ 109. Commission Rules. [15 U.S.C.A. § 2309]

(a)   Any rule prescribed under this title shall be prescribed in accordance with section 553 of title 5, United States Code; except that the Commission shall give interested persons an opportunity for oral presentations of data, views, and arguments, in addition to written submissions. A transcript shall be kept of any oral presentation. Any such rule shall be subject to judicial review under section 18(e) of the Federal Trade Commission Act (as amended by section 202 of this Act) in the same manner as rules prescribed under section 18(a)(1)(B) of such Act, except that section 18(e)(3)(B) of such Act shall not apply.

(b)   The Commission shall initiate within one year after the date of enactment of this Act a rulemaking proceeding dealing with warranties and warranty practices in connection with the sale of used motor vehicles; and, to the extent necessary to supplement the protections offered the consumer by this title, shall prescribe rules dealing with such warranties and practices. In prescribing rules under this subsection, the Commission may exercise any authority it may have under this title, or other law, and in addition it may require disclosure that a used motor vehicle is sold without any warranty and specify the form and content of such disclosure.

§ 110. Remedies. [15 U.S.C.A. § 2310]

(a)(1) Congress hereby declares it to be its policy to encourage warrantors to establish procedures whereby consumer disputes are fairly and expeditiously settled through informal dispute settlement mechanisms.

(2)   The Commission shall prescribe rules setting forth minimum requirements for any informal dispute settlement procedure which is incorporated into the terms of a written warranty to which any provision of this title applies. Such rules shall provide for participation in such procedure by independent or governmental entities.

(3)   One or more warrantors may establish an informal dispute settlement procedure which meets the requirements of the Commission's rules under paragraph (2). If—

(A)   a warrantor establishes such a procedure,

(B)   such procedure, and its implementation, meets the requirements of such rules, and

(C)   he incorporates in a written warranty a requirement that the consumer resort to such procedure before pursuing any legal remedy under this section respecting such warranty,

then (i) the consumer may not commence a civil action (other than a class action) under subsection (d) of this section unless he initially resorts to such procedure; and (ii) a class of consumers may not proceed in a class action under subsection (d) except to the extent the court determines necessary to establish the representative capacity of the named plaintiffs, unless the named plaintiffs (upon notifying the defendant that they are named plaintiffs in a class action with respect to a warranty obligation) initially resort to such procedure. In the case of such a class action which is brought in a district court of the United States, the representative capacity of the named plaintiffs shall be established in the application of rule 23 of the Federal Rules of Civil Procedure. In any civil action arising out of a warranty obligation and relating to a matter considered in such a procedure, any decision in such procedure shall be admissible in evidence.

(4)   The Commission on its own initiative may, or upon written complaint filed by any interested person shall, review the bona fide operation of any dispute settlement procedure resort to which is stated in a written warranty to be a prerequisite to pursuing a legal remedy under this section. If the Commission finds that such procedure or its implementation fails to comply with the requirements of the rules under paragraph (2), the Commission may take appropriate remedial action under any authority it may have under this title or any other provision of law.

(5)   Until rules under paragraph (2) take effect, this subsection shall not affect the validity of any informal dispute settlement procedure respecting consumer warranties, but in any action under subsection (d), the court may invalidate any such procedure if it finds that such procedure is unfair.

(b)   It shall be a violation of section 5(a)(1) of the Federal Trade Commission Act (15 U.S.C. 45(a)(1)) for any person to fail to comply with any requirement imposed on such person by this title (or a rule thereunder) or to violate any prohibition contained in this title (or a rule thereunder).

(c)(1)   The district courts of the United States shall have jurisdiction of any action brought by the Attorney General (in his capacity as such), or by the Commission by any of its attorneys designated by it for such purpose, to restrain (A) any warrantor from making a deceptive warranty with respect to a consumer product, or (B) any person from failing to comply with any requirement imposed on such person by or pursuant to this title or from violating any prohibition contained in this title. Upon proper showing that, weighing the equities and considering the Commission's or Attorney General's likelihood of ultimate success, such action would be in the public interest and after notice to the defendant, a temporary restraining order or preliminary injunction may be granted without bond. In the case of an action brought by the Commission, if a complaint under section 5 of the Federal Trade Commission Act is not filed within such period (not exceeding 10 days) as may be specified by the court after the issuance of the temporary restraining order or preliminary injunction, the order or injunction shall be dissolved by the court and be of no further force and effect. Any suit shall be brought in the district in which such person resides or transacts business. Whenever it appears to the court that the ends of justice require that other persons should be parties in the action, the court may cause them to be summoned whether or not they reside in the district in which the court is held, and to that end process may be served in any district.

(2)　For the purposes of this subsection, the term "deceptive warranty" means (A) a written warranty which (i) contains an affirmation, promise, description, or representation which is either false or fraudulent, or which, in light of all of the circumstances, would mislead a reasonable individual exercising due care; or (ii) fails to contain information which is necessary in light of all of the circumstances, to make the warranty not misleading to a reasonable individual exercising due care; or (B) a written warranty created by the use of such terms as "guaranty" or "warranty", if the terms and conditions of such warranty so limit its scope and application as to deceive a reasonable individual.

(d)(1)　Subject to subsections (a)(3) and (e), a consumer who is damaged by the failure of a supplier, warrantor, or service contractor to comply with any obligation under this title, or under a written warranty, implied warranty, or service contract, may bring suit for damages and other legal and equitable relief—

(A)　in any court of competent jurisdiction in any State or the District of Columbia; or

(B)　in an appropriate district court of the United States, subject to paragraph (3) of this subsection.

(2)　If a consumer finally prevails in any action brought under paragraph (1) of this subsection, he may be allowed by the court to recover as part of the judgment a sum equal to the aggregate amount of cost and expenses (including attorneys' fees based on actual time expended) determined by the court to have been reasonably incurred by the plaintiff for or in connection with the commencement and prosecution of such action, unless the court in its discretion shall determine that such an award of attorneys' fees would be inappropriate.

(3)　No claim shall be cognizable in a suit brought under paragraph (1)(B) of this subsection—

(A)　if the amount in controversy of any individual claim is less than the sum or value of $25;

(B)　if the amount in controversy is less than the sum or value of $50,000 (exclusive of interests and costs) computed on the basis of all claims to be determined in this suit; or

(C)　if the action is brought as a class action, and the number of named plaintiffs is less than one hundred.

(e)　No action (other than a class action or an action respecting a warranty to which subsection (a)(3) applies) may be brought under subsection (d) for failure to comply with any obligation under any written or implied warranty or service contract, and a class of consumers may not proceed in a class action under such subsection with respect to such a failure except to the extent the court determines necessary to establish the representative capacity of the named plaintiffs, unless the person obligated under the warranty or service contract is afforded a reasonable opportunity to cure such failure to comply. In the case of such a class action (other than a class action respecting a warranty to which subsection (a)(3) applies) brought under subsection (d) for breach of any written or implied warranty or service contract, such reasonable opportunity will be afforded by the named plaintiffs and they shall at that time notify the defendant that they are acting on behalf of the class. In the case of such a class action which is brought in a district court of the United States, the representative capacity of the named plaintiffs shall be established in the application of rule 23 of the Federal Rules of Civil Procedure.

(f)　For purposes of this section, only the warrantor actually making a written affirmation of fact, promise, or undertaking shall be deemed to have created a written warranty, and any rights arising thereunder may be enforced under this section only against such warrantor and no other person.

§ 111. Effect on Other Laws. [15 U.S.C.A. § 2311]

(a)(1)　Nothing contained in this title shall be construed to repeal, invalidate, or supersede the Federal Trade Commission Act (15 U.S.C. 41 et seq.) or any statute defined therein as an Antitrust Act.

(2)　Nothing in this title shall be construed to repeal, invalidate, or supersede the Federal Seed Act (7 U.S.C. 1551–1611) and nothing in this title shall apply to seed for planting.

(b)(1)　Nothing in this title shall invalidate or restrict any right or remedy of any consumer under State law or any other Federal law.

(2)　Nothing in this title (other than sections 108 and 104(a)(2) and (4)) shall (A) affect the liability of, or impose liability on, any person for personal injury, or (B) supersede any provision of State law regarding consequential damages for injury to the person or other injury.

(c)(1)　Except as provided in subsection (b) and in paragraph (2) of this subsection, a State requirement—

(A)　which relates to labeling or disclosure with respect to written warranties or performance thereunder;

(B)　which is within the scope of an applicable requirement of sections 102, 103, and 104 (and rules implementing such sections), and

(C)　which is not identical to a requirement of section 102, 103, or 104 (or a rule thereunder),

shall not be applicable to written warranties complying with such sections (or rules thereunder).

(2)　If, upon application of an appropriate State agency, the Commission determines (pursuant to rules issued in accordance with section 109) that any requirement of such State covering any transaction to which this title applies (A) affords protection to consumers greater than the requirements of this title and (B) does not unduly burden interstate commerce, then such State requirement shall be applicable (notwithstanding the provisions of paragraph (1) of this subsection) to the extent specified in such determination for so long as the State administers and enforces effectively any such greater requirement.

(d)　This title (other than section 102(c)) shall be inapplicable to any written warranty the making or content of which is otherwise governed by Federal law. If only a portion of a written warranty is so governed by Federal law, the remaining portion shall be subject to this title.

§ 112. Effective Date. [15 U.S.C.A. § 2312]

(a)　Except as provided in subsection (b) of this section, this title shall take effect 6 months after the date of its enactment but shall not apply to consumer products manufactured prior to such date.

(b)　Section 102(a) shall take effect 6 months after the final publication of rules respecting such section; except that the Commission, for good cause shown, may postpone the applicability of such sections until one year after such final publication in order to permit any designated classes of suppliers to bring their written warranties into compliance with rules promulgated pursuant to this title.

(c)　The Commission shall promulgate rules for initial implementation of this title as soon as possible after the date of enactment of this Act but in no event later than one year after such date.

FEDERAL TRADE COMMISSION, TRADE REGULATION RULES: RULES, REGULATIONS, STATEMENTS AND INTERPRETATIONS UNDER THE MAGNUSON-MOSS WARRANTY ACT

(1977)

[The Magnuson-Moss Warranty Act ("MMWA"), in this pamphlet above, authorized the Federal Trade Commission ("FTC") to promulgate rules to implement its provisions. The FTC's implementing Rules, Regulations, Statements and Interpretations, 16 C.F.R. Parts 700–703, follows. As implementing rules, they pursue the same goals as the MMWA, but go into considerably more detail. When promulgated in accordance with federal administrative law, such rules are law. Like the MMWA, these rules neither displace other federal consumer-protection laws nor pre-empt state laws providing greater protections to consumers. 15 U.S.C § 2311(b).]

TITLE 16. COMMERCIAL PRACTICES

REGULATIONS

PART 700. INTERPRETATIONS OF MAGNUSON-MOSS WARRANTY ACT

PART 701. DISCLOSURE OF WRITTEN CONSUMER PRODUCT WARRANTY TERMS AND CONDITIONS

PART 702. PRE-SALE AVAILABILITY OF WRITTEN WARRANTY TERMS

PART 703. INFORMAL DISPUTE SETTLEMENT PROCEDURES

PART 700

INTERPRETATIONS OF MAGNUSON-MOSS WARRANTY ACT

§ 700.1   Products Covered.

(a)   The Act applies to written warranties on tangible personal property which is normally used for personal, family, or household purposes. This definition includes property which is intended to be attached to or installed in any real property without regard to whether it is so attached or installed. This means that a product is a "consumer product" if the use of that type of product is not uncommon. The percentage of sales or the use to which a product is put by any individual buyer is not determinative. For example, products such as automobiles and typewriters which are used for both personal and commercial purposes come within the definition of consumer product. Where it is unclear whether a particular product is covered under the definition of consumer product, any ambiguity will be resolved in favor of coverage.

(b)   Agricultural products such as farm machinery, structures and implements used in the business or occupation of farming are not covered by the Act where their personal, family, or household use is uncommon. However, those agricultural products normally used for personal or household gardening (for example, to produce goods for personal consumption, and not for resale) are consumer products under the Act.

(c)   The definition of "Consumer product" limits the applicability of the Act to personal property, "including any such property intended to be attached to or installed in any real property without regard to whether it is so attached or installed." This provision brings under the Act separate items of equipment attached to real property, such as air conditioners, furnaces, and water heaters.

(d)   The coverage of separate items to equipment attached to real property includes, but is not limited to, appliances and other thermal, mechanical, and electrical equipment. (It does not extend to the wiring, plumbing, ducts and other items which are integral component parts of the structure.) State law would classify many such products as fixtures to, and therefore a part of, realty. The statutory definition is designed to bring such products under the Act regardless of whether they may be considered fixtures under state law.

(e)   The coverage of building materials which are not separate items of equipment is based on the nature of the purchase transaction. An analysis of the transaction will determine whether the goods are real or personal property. The numerous products which go into the construction of a consumer dwelling are all consumer products when sold "over the counter," as by hardware and building supply retailers. This is also true where a consumer contracts for the purchase of such materials in connection with the improvement, repair, or modification of a home (for example, paneling, dropped ceilings, siding, roofing, storm windows, remodeling). However, where such products are at the time of sale integrated into the structure of a dwelling they are not consumer products as they cannot be practically distinguished from realty. Thus, for example, the beams, wallboard, wiring, plumbing, windows, roofing, and other structural components of a dwelling are not consumer products when they are sold as part of real estate covered by a written warranty.

(f)　In the case where a consumer contracts with a builder to construct a home, a substantial addition to a home, or other realty (such as a garage or an in-ground swimming pool) the building materials to be used are not consumer products. Although the materials are separately identifiable at the time the contract is made, it is the intention of the parties to contract for the construction of realty which will integrate the component materials. Of course, as noted above, any separate items of equipment to be attached to such realty are consumer products under the Act.

(g)　Certain provisions of the Act apply only to products actually costing the consumer more than a specified amount. Section 103 applies to consumer products actually costing the consumer more than $10, excluding tax. The $10 minimum will be interpreted to include multiple-packaged items which may individually sell for less than $10, but which have been packaged in a manner that does not permit breaking the package to purchase an item or items at a price less than $10. Thus, a written warranty on a dozen items packaged and priced for sale at $12 must be designated, even though identical items may be offered in smaller quantities at under $10. This interpretation applies in the same manner to the minimum dollar limits in section 102 and rules promulgated under that section.

(h)　Warranties or replacement parts and components used to repair consumer products are covered; warranties on services are not covered. Therefore, warranties which apply solely to a repairer's workmanship in performing repairs are not subject to the Act. Where a written agreement warrants both the parts provided to effect a repair and the workmanship in making that repair, the warranty must comply with the Act and the rules thereunder.

(i)　The Act covers written warranties on consumer products "distributed in commerce" as that term is defined in section 101(3). Thus, by its terms the Act arguably applies to products exported to foreign jurisdictions. However, the public interest would not be served by the use of Commission resources to enforce the Act with respect to such products. Moreover, the legislative intent to apply the requirements of the Act to such products is not sufficiently clear to justify such an extraordinary result. The Commission does not contemplate the enforcement of the Act with respect to consumer products exported to foreign jurisdictions. Products exported for sale at military post exchanges remain subject to the same enforcement standards as products sold within the United States, its territories and possessions.

§ 700.2　Date of Manufacture.

Section 112 of the Act provides that the Act shall apply only to those consumer products manufactured after July 4, 1975. When a consumer purchases repair of a consumer product the date of manufacture of any replacement parts used is the measuring date for determining coverage under the Act. The date of manufacture of the consumer product being repaired is in this instance not relevant. Where a consumer purchases or obtains on an exchange basis a rebuilt consumer product, the date that the rebuilding process is completed determines the Act's applicability.

§ 700.3　Written Warranty.

(a)　The Act imposes specific duties and liabilities on suppliers who offer written warranties on consumer products. Certain representations, such as energy efficiency ratings for electrical appliances, care labeling of wearing apparel, and other product information disclosures may be express warranties under the Uniform Commercial Code. However, these disclosures alone are not written warranties under this Act. Section 101(6) provides that a written affirmation of fact or a written promise of a specified level of performance must relate to a specified period of time in order to be considered a "written warranty."[1] A product information disclosure without a specified time period to which the

---

[1]　A "written warranty" is also created by a written affirmation of fact or a written promise that the product is defect free, or by a written undertaking of remedial action within the meaning of § 101(6)(B).

disclosure relates is therefore not a written warranty. In addition, section 111(d) exempts from the Act (except section 102(c)) any written warranty the making or content of which is required by federal law. The Commission encourages the disclosure of product information which is not deceptive and which may benefit consumers, and will not construe the Act to impede information disclosure in product advertising or labeling.

(b)   Certain terms, or conditions, of sale of a consumer product may not be "written warranties" as that term is defined in Section 101(6), and should not be offered or described in a manner that may deceive consumers as to their enforceability under the Act. For example, a seller of consumer products may give consumers an unconditional right to revoke acceptance of goods within a certain number of days after delivery without regard to defects or failure to meet a specified level of performance. Or a seller may permit consumers to return products for any reason for credit toward purchase of another item. Such terms of sale taken alone are not written warranties under the Act. Therefore, suppliers should avoid any characterization of such terms of sale as warranties. The use of such terms as "free trial period" and "trade-in credit policy" in this regard would be appropriate. Furthermore, such terms of sale should be stated separately from any written warranty. Of course, the offering and performance of such terms of sale remain subject to section 5 of the Federal Trade Commission Act, 15 U.S.C. 45.

(c)   The Magnuson-Moss Warranty Act generally applies to written warranties covering consumer products. Many consumer products are covered by warranties which are neither intended for, nor enforceable by, consumers. A common example is a warranty given by a component supplier to a manufacturer of consumer products. (The manufacturer may, in turn, warrant these components to consumers.) The component supplier's warranty is generally given solely to the product manufacturer, and is neither intended to be conveyed to the consumer nor brought to the consumer's attention in connection with the sale. Such warranties are not subject to the Act, since a written warranty under section 101(6) of the Act must become "part of the basis of the bargain between a supplier and a buyer for purposes other than resale." However, the Act applies to a component supplier's warranty in writing which is given to the consumer. An example is a supplier's written warranty to the consumer covering a refrigerator that is sold installed in a boat or recreational vehicle. The supplier of the refrigerator relies on the boat or vehicle assembler to convey the written agreement to the consumer. In this case, the supplier's written warranty is to a consumer, and is covered by the Act.

§ 700.4   Parties "Actually Making" a Written Warranty.

Section 110(f) of the Act provides that only the supplier "actually making" a written warranty is liable for purposes of FTC and private enforcement of the Act. A supplier who does no more than distribute or sell a consumer product covered by a written warranty offered by another person or business and which identifies that person or business as the warrantor is not liable for failure of the written warranty to comply with the Act or rules thereunder. However, other actions and written and oral representations of such a supplier in connection with the offer or sale of a warranted product may obligate that supplier under the Act. If under state law the supplier is deemed to have "adopted" the written affirmation of fact, promise, or undertaking, the supplier is also obligated under the Act. Suppliers are advised to consult state law to determine those actions and representations which may make them co-warrantors, and therefore obligated under the warranty of the other person or business.

§ 700.5   Expressions of General Policy.

(a)   Under section 103(b), statements or representations of general policy concerning customer satisfaction which are not subject to any specific limitation need not be designated as full or limited warranties, and are exempt from the requirements of sections 102, 103, and 104 of the Act and rules thereunder. However, such statements remain subject to the enforcement provisions of section 110 of the Act, and to section 5 of the Federal Trade Commission Act, 15 U.S.C. 45.

(b)   The section 103(b) exemption applies only to general policies not to those which are limited to specific consumer products manufactured or sold by the supplier offering such a policy. In addition, to qualify for an exemption under section 103(b) such policies may not be subject to any specific limitations. For example, policies which have an express limitation of duration or a limitation of the amount to be refunded are not exempted. This does not preclude the imposition of reasonable limitations based on the circumstances in each instance a consumer seeks to invoke such an agreement. For instance, a warrantor may refuse to honor such an expression of policy where a consumer has used a product for 10 years without previously expressing any dissatisfaction with the product. Such a refusal would not be a specific limitation under this provision.

§ 700.6   Designation of Warranties.

(a)   Section 103 of the Act provides that written warranties on consumer products manufactured after July 4, 1975, and actually costing the consumer more than $10, excluding tax, must be designated either "Full (statement of duration) Warranty" or "Limited Warranty". Warrantors may include a statement of duration in a limited warranty designation. The designation or designations should appear clearly and conspicuously as a caption, or prominent title, clearly separated from the text of the warranty. The full (statement of duration) warranty and limited warranty are the exclusive designations permitted under the Act, unless a specific exception is created by rule.

(b)   Section 104(b)(4) states that "the duties under subsection (a) (of section 104) extend from the warrantor to each person who is a consumer with respect to the consumer product." Section 101(3) defines a consumer as "a buyer (other than for purposes of resale) of any consumer product, any person to whom such product is transferred during the duration of an implied or written warranty (or service contract) applicable to the product . . . ." Therefore, a full warranty may not expressly restrict the warranty rights of a transferee during its stated duration. However, where the duration of a full warranty is defined solely in terms of first purchaser ownership there can be no violation of section 104(b)(4), since the duration of the warranty expires, by definition, at the time of transfer. No rights of a subsequent transferee are cut off as there is no transfer of ownership "during the duration of (any) warranty." Thus, these provisions do not preclude the offering of a full warranty with its duration determined exclusively by the period during which the first purchaser owns the product, or uses it in conjunction with another product. For example, an automotive battery or muffler warranty may be designated as "full warranty for as long as you own your car." Because this type of warranty leads the consumer to believe that proof of purchase is not needed so long as he or she owns the product a duty to furnish documentary proof may not be reasonably imposed on the consumer under this type of warranty. The burden is on the warrantor to prove that a particular claimant under this type of warranty is not the original purchaser or owner of the product. Warrantors or their designated agents may, however, ask consumers to state or affirm that they are the first purchaser of the product.

§ 700.7   Use of Warranty Registration Cards.

(a)   Under section 104(b)(1) of the Act a warrantor offering a full warranty may not impose on consumers any duty other than notification of a defect as a condition of securing remedy of the defect or malfunction, unless such additional duty can be demonstrated by the warrantor to be reasonable. Warrantors have in the past stipulated the return of a "warranty registration" or similar card. By "warranty registration card" the Commission means a card which must be returned by the consumer shortly after purchase of the product and which is stipulated or implied in the warranty to be a condition precedent to warranty coverage and performance.

(b)   A requirement that the consumer return a warranty registration card or a similar notice as a condition of performance under a full warranty is an unreasonable duty. Thus, a provision such as, "This warranty is void unless the warranty registration card is returned to the warrantor" is not permissible in a full warranty, nor is it permissible to imply such a condition in a full warranty.

(c)   This does not prohibit the use of such registration cards where a warrantor suggests use of the card as one possible means of proof of the date the product was purchased. For example, it is permissible to provide in a full warranty that a consumer may fill out and return a card to place on file proof of the date the product was purchased. Any such suggestion to the consumer must include notice that failure to return the card will not affect rights under the warranty, so long as the consumer can show in a reasonable manner the date the product was purchased. Nor does this interpretation prohibit a seller from obtaining from purchasers at the time of sale information requested by the warrantor.

§ 700.8   Warrantor's Decision as Final.

A warrantor shall not indicate in any written warranty or service contract either directly or indirectly that the decision of the warrantor, service contractor, or any designated third party is final or binding in any dispute concerning the warranty or service contract. Nor shall a warrantor or service contractor state that it alone shall determine what is a defect under the agreement. Such statements are deceptive since section 110(d) of the Act gives state and federal courts jurisdiction over suits for breach of warranty and service contract.

§ 700.9   Duty to Install Under a Full Warranty.

Under section 101(a)(1) of the Act, the remedy under a full warranty must be provided to the consumer without charge. If the warranted product has utility only when installed, a full warranty must provide such installation without charge regardless of whether or not the consumer originally paid for installation by the warrantor or his agent. However, this does not preclude the warrantor from imposing on the consumer a duty to remove, return, or reinstall where such duty can be demonstrated by the warrantor to meet the standard of reasonableness under section 104(b)(1).

§ 700.10   Section 102(c).

(a)   Section 102(c) prohibits tying arrangements that condition coverage under a written warranty on the consumer's use of an article or service identified by brand, trade, or corporate name unless that article or service is provided without charge to the consumer.

(b)   Under a limited warranty that provides only for replacement of defective parts and no portion of labor charges, section 102(c) prohibits a condition that the consumer use only service (labor) identified by the warrantor to install the replacement parts. A warrantor or his designated representative may not provide parts under the warranty in a manner which impedes or precludes the choice by the consumer of the person or business to perform necessary labor to install such parts.

(c)   No warrantor may condition the continued validity of a warranty on the use of only authorized repair service and/or authorized replacement parts for non-warranty service and maintenance. For example, provisions such as, "This warranty is void if service is performed by anyone other than an authorized 'ABC' dealer and all replacement parts must be genuine 'ABC' parts," and the like, are prohibited where the service or parts are not covered by the warranty. These provisions violate the Act in two ways. First, they violate the section 102(c) ban against tying arrangements. Second, such provisions are deceptive under section 110 of the Act, because a warrantor cannot, as a matter of law, avoid liability under a written warranty where a defect is unrelated to the use by a consumer of "unauthorized" articles or service. This does not preclude a warrantor from expressly excluding liability for defects or damage caused by such "unauthorized" articles or service; nor does it preclude the warrantor from denying liability where the warrantor can demonstrate that the defect or damage was so caused.

§ 700.11   Written Warranty, Service Contract, and Insurance Distinguished for Purposes of Compliance Under the Act.

(a)   The Act recognizes two types of agreements which may provide similar coverage of consumer products, the written warranty, and the service contract. In addition, other agreements may meet the statutory definitions of either "written warranty" or "service contract," but are sold and regulated under state law as contracts of insurance. One example is the automobile breakdown insurance policies sold in many jurisdictions and regulated by the state as a form of casualty insurance. The McCarran-Ferguson Act, 15 U.S.C. 1011 et seq., precludes jurisdiction under federal law over "the business of insurance" to the extent an agreement is regulated by state law as insurance. Thus, such agreements are subject to the Magnuson-Moss Warranty Act only to the extent they are not regulated in a particular state as the business of insurance.

(b) "Written warranty" and "service contract" are defined in sections 101(6) and 101(8) of the Act, respectively. A written warranty must be "part of the basis of the bargain." This means that it must be conveyed at the time of sale of the consumer product and the consumer must not give any consideration beyond the purchase price of the consumer product in order to benefit from the agreement. It is not a requirement of the Act that an agreement obligate a supplier of the consumer product to a written warranty, but merely that it be part of the basis of the bargain between a supplier and a consumer. This contemplates written warranties by third-party non-suppliers.

(c) A service contract under the Act must meet the definitions of section 101(8). An agreement which would meet the definition of written warranty in section 101(6)(A) or (B) but for its failure to satisfy the basis of the bargain test is a service contract. For example, an agreement which calls for some consideration in addition to the purchase price of the consumer product, or which is entered into at some date after the purchase of the consumer product to which it applies, is a service contract. An agreement which relates only to the performance of maintenance and/or inspection services and which is not an undertaking, promise, or affirmation with respect to a specified level of performance, or that the product is free of defects in materials or workmanship, is a service contract. An agreement to perform periodic cleaning and inspection of a product over a specified period of time, even when offered at the time of sale and without charge to the consumer, is an example of such a service contract.

§ 700.12   Effective Date of 16 CFR, Parts 701 and 702.

The Statement of Basis and Purpose of the final rules promulgated on December 31, 1975, provides that Parts 701 and 702 will become effective one year after the date of promulgation, December 31, 1976. The Commission intends this to mean that these rules apply only to written warranties on products manufactured after December 31, 1976.

PART 701

DISCLOSURE OF WRITTEN CONSUMER PRODUCT
WARRANTY TERMS AND CONDITIONS

§ 701.1   Definitions.

(a) "The Act" means the Magnuson-Moss Warranty Federal Trade Commission Improvement Act, 15 U.S.C. 2301, et seq.

(b) "Consumer product" means any tangible personal property which is distributed in commerce and which is normally used for personal, family, or household purposes (including any such property intended to be attached to or installed in any real property without regard to whether it is so attached or installed). Products which are purchased solely for commercial or industrial use are excluded solely for purposes of this Part.

(c) "Written warranty" means—(1) any written affirmation of fact or written promise made in connection with the sale of a consumer product by a supplier to a buyer which relates to the nature of the material or workmanship and affirms or promises that such material or workmanship is defect free or will meet a specified level of performance over a specified period of time, or

(2) any undertaking in writing in connection with the sale by a supplier of a consumer product to refund, repair, replace, or take other remedial action with respect to such product in the event that such product fails to meet the specifications set forth in the undertaking, which

written affirmation, promise or undertaking becomes part of the basis of the bargain between a supplier and a buyer for purposes other than resale of such product.

(d) "Implied warranty" means an implied warranty arising under State law (as modified by secs. 104(a) and 108 of the Act) in connection with the sale by a supplier of a consumer product.

(e) "Remedy" means whichever of the following actions the warrantor elects:

(1) repair,

(2) replacement, or

(3) refund; except that the warrantor may not elect refund unless:

(i) the warrantor is unable to provide replacement and repair is not commercially practicable or cannot be timely made, or

(ii) the consumer is willing to accept such refund.

(f) "Supplier" means any person engaged in the business of making a consumer product directly or indirectly available to consumers.

(g) "Warrantor" means any supplier or other person who gives or offers to give a written warranty.

(h) "Consumer" means a buyer (other than for purposes of resale or use in the ordinary course of the buyer's business) of any consumer product, any person to whom such product is transferred during the duration of an implied or written warranty applicable to the product, and any other such person who is entitled by the terms of such warranty or under applicable State law to enforce against the warrantor the obligations of the warranty.

(i) "On the face of the warranty" means—(1) where the warranty is a single sheet with printing on both sides of the sheet or where the warranty is comprised of more than one sheet, the page on which the warranty text begins;

(2) where the warranty is included as part of a larger document, such as a use and care manual, the page in such document on which the warranty text begins.

§ 701.2   Scope.

The regulations in this part establish requirements for warrantors for disclosing the terms and conditions of written warranties on consumer products actually costing the consumer more than $15.00.

§ 701.3   Written Warranty Terms.

(a) Any warrantor warranting to a consumer by means of a written warranty a consumer product actually costing the consumer more than $15.00 shall clearly and conspicuously disclose in a single document in simple and readily understood language, the following items of information: (1) The identity of the party or parties to whom the written warranty is extended, if the enforceability of the written warranty is limited to the original consumer purchaser or is otherwise limited to persons other than every consumer owner during the term of the warranty;

(2) A clear description and identification of products, or parts, or characteristics, or components or properties covered by and where necessary for clarification, excluded from the warranty;

(3) A statement of what the warrantor will do in the event of a defect, malfunction or failure to conform with the written warranty, including the items or services the warrantor will pay for or provide, and, where necessary for clarification, those which the warrantor will not pay for or provide;

(4)   The point in time or event on which the warranty term commences, if different from the purchase date, and the time period or other measurement of warranty duration;

(5)   A step-by-step explanation of the procedure which the consumer should follow in order to obtain performance of any warranty obligation, including the persons or class of persons authorized to perform warranty obligations. This includes the name(s) of the warrantor(s), together with: the mailing addresses of the warrantor(s), and/or the name or title and the address of any employee or department of the warrantor responsible for the performance of warranty obligations, and/or a telephone number which consumers may use without charge to obtain information on warranty performance;

(6)   Information respecting the availability of an informal dispute settlement mechanism elected by the warrantor in compliance with Part 703 of this subchapter;

(7)   Any limitations on the duration of implied warranties, disclosed on the face of the warranty as provided in Section 108 of the Act, accompanied by the following statement:

Some states do not allow limitations on how long an implied warranty lasts, so the above limitation may not apply to you.

(8)   Any exclusions of or limitations on relief such as incidental or consequential damages, accompanied by the following statement, which may be combined with the statement required in sub-paragraph (7) above:

Some states do not allow the exclusion or limitation of incidental or consequential damages, so the above limitation or exclusion may not apply to you.

(9)   A statement in the following language:

This warranty gives you specific legal rights, and you may also have other rights which vary from state to state.

(b)   Paragraph (a)(1)–(9) of this Section shall not be applicable with respect to statements of general policy on emblems, seals or insignias issued by third parties promising replacement or refund if a consumer product is defective, which statements contain no representation or assurance of the quality or performance characteristics of the product; provided that (1) the disclosures required by paragraph (a)(1)–(9) are published by such third parties in each issue of a publication with a general circulation, and (2) such disclosures are provided free of charge to any consumer upon written request.

§ 701.4   Owner Registration Cards.

When a warrantor employs any card such as an owner's registration card, a warranty registration card, or the like, and the return of such card is a condition precedent to warranty coverage and performance, the warrantor shall disclose this fact in the warranty. If the return of such card reasonably appears to be a condition precedent to warranty coverage and performance, but is not such a condition, that fact shall be disclosed in the warranty.

PART 702

PRE-SALE AVAILABILITY OF WRITTEN WARRANTY TERMS

§ 702.1   Definitions.

(a)   "The Act" means the Magnuson-Moss Warranty Federal Trade Commission Improvement Act, 15 U.S.C. 2301, et seq.

(b)   "Consumer product" means any tangible personal property which is distributed in commerce and which is normally used for personal, family, or household purposes (including any such property intended to be attached to or installed in any real property without regard to whether it is so attached or installed). Products which are purchased solely for commercial or industrial use are excluded solely for purposes of this Part.

(c) "Written warranty" means—(1) any written affirmation of fact or written promise made in connection with the sale of a consumer product by a supplier to a buyer which relates to the nature of the material or workmanship and affirms or promises that such material or workmanship is defect free or will meet a specified level of performance over a specified period of time, or

(2) any undertaking in writing in connection with the sale by a supplier of a consumer product to refund, repair, replace, or take other remedial action with respect to such product in the event that such product fails to meet the specifications set forth in the undertaking, which written affirmation, promise or undertaking becomes part of the basis of the bargain between a supplier and a buyer for purposes other than resale of such product.

(d) "Warrantor" means any supplier or other person who gives or offers to give a written warranty.

(e) "Seller" means any person who sells or offers for sale for purposes other than resale or use in the ordinary course of the buyer's business any consumer product.

(f) "Supplier" means any person engaged in the business of making a consumer product directly or indirectly available to consumers.

§ 702.2   Scope.

The regulations in this part establish requirements for sellers and warrantors for making the terms of any written warranty on a consumer product available to the consumer prior to sale.

§ 702.3   Pre-Sale Availability of Written Warranty Terms.

The following requirements apply to consumer products actually costing the consumer more than $15.00:

(a) *Duties of seller.* Except as provided in paragraphs (c) through (d) of this section, the seller of a consumer product with a written warranty shall make a text of the warranty readily available for examination by the prospective buyer by:

(1) Displaying it in close proximity to the warranted product, or

(2) Furnishing it upon request prior to sale and placing signs reasonably calculated to elicit the prospective buyer's attention in prominent locations in the store or department advising such prospective buyers of the availability of warranties upon request.

(b) *Duties of the warrantor.* (1) A warrantor who gives a written warranty warranting to a consumer a consumer product actually costing the consumer more than $15.00 shall:

(i) Provide sellers with warranty materials necessary for such sellers to comply with the requirements set forth in paragraph (a) of this section, by the use of one or more by the following means:

(A) Providing a copy of the written warranty with every warranted consumer product; and/or

(B) Providing a tag, sign, sticker, label, decal or other attachment to the product, which contains the full text of the written warranty; and/or

(C) Printing on or otherwise attaching the text of the written warranty to the package, carton, or other container if that package, carton or other container is normally used for display purposes. If the warrantor elects this option a copy of the written warranty must also accompany the warranted product; and/or

(D) Providing a notice, sign, or poster disclosing the text of a consumer product warranty.

If the warrantor elects this option, a copy of the written warranty must also accompany each warranted product.

(ii) Provide catalog, mail order, and door-to-door sellers with copies of written warranties necessary for such sellers to comply with the requirements set forth in paragraphs (c) and (d) of this section.

(2) Sub-paragraph (1) of this paragraph (b) shall not be applicable with respect to statements of general policy on emblems, seals or insignias issued by third parties promising replacement or refund if a consumer product is defective, which statements contain no representation or assurance of the quality or performance characteristics of the product; provided that (i) the disclosures required by 701.3(a)(1)–(9) are published by such third parties in each issue of a publication with a general circulation, and (ii) such disclosures are provided free of charge to any consumer upon written request.

(c) *Catalog and Mail Order Sales.* (1) For purposes of this paragraph:

(i) "Catalog or mail order sales", means any offer for sale, or any solicitation for an order for a consumer product with a written warranty, which includes instructions for ordering the product which do not require a personal visit to the seller's establishment.

(ii) "Close conjunction" means on the page containing the description of the warranted product, or on the page facing that page.

(2) Any seller who offers for sale to consumers consumer products with written warranties by means of a catalog or mail order solicitation shall:

(i) clearly and conspicuously disclose in such catalog or solicitation in close conjunction to the description of warranted product, or in an information section of the catalog or solicitation clearly referenced, including a page number, in close conjunction to the description of the warranted product, *either*:

(A) the full text of the written warranty; or

(B) that the written warranty can be obtained free upon specific written request, and the address where such warranty can be obtained. If this option is elected, such seller shall promptly provide a copy of any written warranty requested by the consumer.

(d) *Door-to-door sales.* (1) For purposes of this paragraph:

(i) "Door-to-door sale" means a sale of consumer products in which the seller or his representative personally solicits the sale, including those in response to or following an invitation by a buyer, and the buyer's agreement to offer to purchase is made at a place other than the place of business of the seller.

(ii) "Prospective buyer" means an individual solicited by a door-to-door seller to buy a consumer product who indicates sufficient interest in that consumer product or maintains sufficient contact with the seller for the seller reasonably to conclude that the person solicited is considering purchasing the product.

(2) Any seller who offers for sale to consumers consumer products with written warranties by means of door-to-door sales shall, prior to the consummation of the sale, disclose the fact that the sales representative has copies of the warranties for the warranted products being offered for sale, which may be inspected by the prospective buyer at any time during the sales presentation. Such disclosure shall be made orally and shall be included in any written materials shown to prospective buyers.

PART 703

INFORMAL DISPUTE SETTLEMENT PROCEDURES

§ 703.1 Definitions.

(a) "The Act" means the Magnuson-Moss Warranty—Federal Trade Commission Improvement Act, 15 U.S.C. 2301, et seq.

(b) "Consumer product" means any tangible personal property which is distributed in commerce and which is normally used for personal, family, or household purposes (including any such property intended to be attached to or installed in any real property without regard to whether it is so attached or installed).

(c) "Written warranty" means:

(1) Any written affirmation of fact or written promise made in connection with the sale of a consumer product by a supplier to a buyer which relates to the nature of the material or workmanship and affirms or promises that such material or workmanship is defect free or will meet a specified level of performance over a specified period of time, or

(2) Any undertaking in writing in connection with the sale by a supplier of a consumer product to refund, repair, replace, or take other remedial action with respect to such product in the event that such product fails to meet the specifications set forth in the undertaking, which written affirmation, promise or undertaking becomes part of the basis of the bargain between a supplier and a buyer for purposes other than resale of such product.

(d) "Warrantor" means any person who given or offers to give a written warranty which incorporates an informal dispute settlement mechanism.

(e) "Mechanism" means an informal dispute settlement procedure which is incorporated into the terms of a written warranty to which any provision of Title I of the Act applies, as provided in Section 110 of the Act.

(f) "Members" means the person or persons within a Mechanism actually deciding disputes.

(g) "Consumer" means a buyer (other than for purposes of resale) of any consumer product, any person to whom such product is transferred during the duration of a written warranty applicable to the product, and any other person who is entitled by the terms of such warranty or under applicable state law to enforce against the warrantor the obligations of the warranty.

(h) "On the face of the warranty" means:

(1) If the warranty is a single sheet with printing on both sides of the sheet, or if the warranty is comprised of more than one sheet, the page on which the warranty text begins;

(2) If the warranty is included as part of a longer document, such as a use and care manual, the page in such document on which the warranty text begins.

§ 703.2 Duties of Warrantor.

(a) The warrantor shall not incorporate into the terms of a written warranty a Mechanism that fails to comply with the requirements contained in §§ 703.3–703.8 of this part. This paragraph shall not prohibit a warrantor from incorporating into the terms of a written warranty the step-by-step procedure which the consumer should take in order to obtain performance of any obligation under the warranty as described in section 102(a)(7) of the Act and required by Part 701 of this subchapter.

(b) The warrantor shall disclose clearly and conspicuously at least the following information on the face of the written warranty:

(1) A statement of the availability of the informal dispute settlement mechanism;

(2)   The name and address of the Mechanism, or the name and a telephone number of the Mechanism which consumers may use without charge;

(3)   A statement of any requirement that the consumer resort to the Mechanism before exercising rights or seeking remedies created by Title I of the Act; together with the disclosure that if a consumer chooses to seek redress by pursuing rights and remedies not created by Title I of the Act, resort to the Mechanism would not be required by any provision of the Act; and

(4)   A statement, if applicable, indicating where further information on the Mechanism can be found in materials accompanying the product, as provided in § 703.2(c) of this section.

(c)   The warrantor shall include in the written warranty or in a separate section of materials accompanying the product, the following information:

(1)   Either (i) a form addressed to the Mechanism containing spaces requesting the information which the Mechanism may require for prompt resolution of warranty disputes; or (ii) a telephone number of the Mechanism which consumers may use without charge;

(2)   The name and address of the Mechanism;

(3)   A brief description of Mechanism procedures;

(4)   The time limits adhered to by the Mechanism; and

(5)   The types of information which the Mechanism may require for prompt resolution of warranty disputes.

(d)   The warrantor shall take steps reasonably calculated to make consumers aware of the Mechanism's existence at the time consumers experience warranty disputes. Nothing contained in paragraphs (b), (c), or (d) of this section shall limit the warrantor's option to encourage consumers to seek redress directly from the warrantor as long as the warrantor does not expressly require consumers to seek redress directly from the warrantor. The warrantor shall proceed fairly and expeditiously to attempt to resolve all disputes submitted directly to the warrantor.

(e)   Whenever a dispute is submitted directly to the warrantor, the warrantor shall, within a reasonable time, decide whether, and to what extent, it will satisfy the consumer, and inform the consumer of its decision. In its notification to the consumer of its decision, the warrantor shall include the information required in § 703.2(b) and (c) of this section.

(f)   The warrantor shall: (1) Respond fully and promptly to reasonable requests by the Mechanism for information relating to disputes;

(2)   Upon notification of any decision of the Mechanism that would require action on the part of the warrantor, immediately notify the Mechanism whether, and to what extent, warrantor will abide by the decision; and

(3)   Perform any obligations it has agreed to.

(g)   The warrantor shall act in good faith in determining whether, and to what extent, it will abide by a Mechanism decision.

(h)   The warrantor shall comply with any reasonable requirements imposed by the Mechanism to fairly and expeditiously resolve warranty disputes.

§ 703.3   Mechanism Organization.

(a)   The Mechanism shall be funded and competently staffed at a level sufficient to ensure fair and expeditious resolution of all disputes, and shall not charge consumers any fee for use of the Mechanism.

(b)   The warrantor and the sponsor of the Mechanism (if other than the warrantor) shall take all steps necessary to ensure that the Mechanism, and its members and staff, are sufficiently insulated from the warrantor and the sponsor, so that the decisions of the members and the performance of the staff are not influenced by either the warrantor or the sponsor. Necessary steps shall include, at a minimum, committing funds in advance, basing personnel decisions solely on merit, and not assigning conflicting warrantor or sponsor duties to Mechanism staff persons.

(c) The Mechanism shall impose any other reasonable requirements necessary to ensure that the members and staff act fairly and expeditiously in each dispute.

§ 703.4   Qualification of Members.

(a) No member deciding a dispute shall be: (1) A party to the dispute, or an employee or agent of a party other than for purposes of deciding disputes; or

(2) A person who is or may become a party in any legal action, including but not limited to class actions, relating to the product or complaint in dispute, or an employee or agent of such person other than for purposes of deciding disputes. For purposes of this paragraph (a) a person shall not be considered a "party" solely because he or she acquires or owns an interest in a party solely for investment, and the acquisition or ownership of an interest which is offered to the general public shall be prima facie evidence of its acquisition or ownership solely for investment.

(b) When one or two members are deciding a dispute, all shall be persons having no direct involvement in the manufacture, distribution, sale or service of any product. When three or more members are deciding a dispute, at least two-thirds shall be persons having no direct involvement in the manufacture, distribution, sale or service of any product. "Direct involvement" shall not include acquiring or owning an interest solely for investment, and the acquisition or ownership of an interest which is offered to the general public shall be prima facie evidence of its acquisition or ownership solely for investment. Nothing contained in this section shall prevent the members from consulting with any persons knowledgeable in the technical, commercial or other areas relating to the product which is the subject of the dispute.

(c) Members shall be persons interested in the fair and expeditious settlement of consumer disputes.

§ 703.5   Operation of the Mechanism.

(a) The Mechanism shall establish written operating procedures which shall include at least those items specified in paragraphs (b) through (j) of this section. Copies of the written procedures shall be made available to any person upon request.

(b) Upon notification of a dispute, the Mechanism shall immediately inform both the warrantor and the consumer of receipt of the dispute.

(c) The Mechanism shall investigate, gather and organize all information necessary for a fair and expeditious decision in each dispute. When any evidence gathered by or submitted to the Mechanism raises issues relating to the number of repair attempts, the length of repair periods, the possibility of unreasonable use of the product, or any other issues relevant in light of Title I of the Act (or rules thereunder), including issues relating to consequential damages, or any other remedy under the Act (or rules thereunder), the Mechanism shall investigate these issues. When information which will or may be used in the decision, submitted by one party, or a consultant under § 703.4(b) of this part, or any other source tends to contradict facts submitted by the other party, the Mechanism shall clearly, accurately, and completely disclose to both parties the contradictory information (and its source) and shall provide both parties an opportunity to explain or rebut the information and to submit additional materials. The Mechanism shall not require any information not reasonably necessary to decide the dispute.

(d) If the dispute has not been settled, the Mechanism shall, as expeditiously as possible but at least within 40 days of notification of the dispute, except as provided in paragraph (e) of this section:

(1)   Render a fair decision based on the information gathered as described in paragraph (c) of this section, and on any information submitted at an oral presentation which conforms to the requirements of paragraph (f) of this section (A decision shall include any remedies appropriate under the circumstances, including repair, replacement, refund, reimbursement for expenses, compensation for damages, and any other remedies available under the written warranty or the Act (or rules thereunder); and a decision shall state a specified reasonable time for performance);

(2)   Disclose to the warrantor its decision and the reasons therefor;

(3)   If the decision would require action on the part of the warrantor, determine whether, and to what extent, warrantor will abide by its decision; and

(4)   Disclose to the consumer its decision, the reasons therefor, warrantor's intended actions (if the decision would require action on the part of the warrantor), and the information described in paragraph (g) of this section. For purposes of this paragraph (d) a dispute shall be deemed settled when the Mechanism has ascertained from the consumer that:

(i)   The dispute has been settled to the consumer's satisfaction; and

(ii)   the settlement contains a specified reasonable time for performance.

(e)   The Mechanism may delay the performance of its duties under paragraph (d) of this section beyond the 40 day time limit;

(1)   Where the period of delay is due solely to failure of a consumer to provide promptly his or her name and address, brand name and model number of the product involved, and a statement as to the nature of the defect or other complaint; or

(2)   For a 7 day period in those cases where the consumer has made no attempt to seek redress directly from the warrantor.

(f)   The Mechanism may allow an oral presentation by a party to a dispute (or a party's representative) only if: (1) Both warrantor and consumer expressly agree to the presentation;

(2)   Prior to agreement the Mechanism fully discloses to the consumer the following information:

(i)   That the presentation by either party will take place only if both parties so agree, but that if they agree, and one party fails to appear at the agreed upon time and place, the presentation by the other party may still be allowed;

(ii)   That the members will decide the dispute whether or not an oral presentation is made;

(iii)   The proposed date, time and place for the presentation; and

(iv)   A brief description of what will occur at the presentation including, if applicable, parties' rights to bring witnesses and/or counsel; and

(3)   Each party has the right to be present during the other party's oral presentation. Nothing contained in this paragraph (b) of this section shall preclude the Mechanism from allowing an oral presentation by one party, if the other party fails to appear at the agreed upon time and place, as long as all of the requirements of this paragraph have been satisfied.

(g)   The Mechanism shall inform the consumer, at the time of disclosure required in paragraph (d) of this section that:

(1)   If he or she is dissatisfied with its decision or warrantor's intended actions, or eventual performance, legal remedies, including use of small claims court, may be pursued;

(2)   The Mechanism's decision is admissible in evidence as provided in section 110(a)(3) of the Act; and

(3)   The consumer may obtain, at reasonable cost, copies of all Mechanism records relating to the consumer's dispute.

(h)   If the warrantor has agreed to perform any obligations, either as part of a settlement agreed to after notification to the Mechanism of the dispute or as a result of a decision under paragraph (d) of this section, the Mechanism shall ascertain from the consumer within 10 working days of the date for performance whether performance has occurred.

(i)   A requirement that a consumer resort to the Mechanism prior to commencement of an action under section 110(d) of the Act shall be satisfied 40 days after notification to the Mechanism of the dispute or when the Mechanism completes all of its duties under paragraph (d) of this section, whichever occurs sooner. Except that, if the Mechanism delays performance of its paragraph (d) of this section duties as allowed by paragraph (e) of this section, the requirement that the consumer initially resort to the Mechanism shall not be satisfied until the period of delay allowed by paragraph (e) of this section has ended.

(j)   Decisions of the Mechanism shall not be legally binding on any person. However, the warrantor shall act in good faith, as provided in § 703.2(g) of this part. In any civil action arising out of a warranty obligation and relating to a matter considered by the Mechanism, any decision of the Mechanism shall be admissible in evidence, as provided in section 110(a)(3) of the Act.

§ 703.6   Recordkeeping.

(a)   The Mechanism shall maintain records on each dispute referred to it which shall include:

(1)   Name, address and telephone number of the consumer;

(2)   Name, address, telephone number and contact person of the warrantor;

(3)   Brand name and model number of the product involved;

(4)   The date of receipt of the dispute and the date of disclosure to the consumer of the decision;

(5)   All letters or other written documents submitted by either party;

(6)   All other evidence collected by the Mechanism relating to the dispute, including summaries of relevant and material portions of telephone calls and meetings between the Mechanism and any other person (including consultants described in § 703.4(b) of this part);

(7)   A summary of any relevant and material information presented by either party at an oral presentation;

(8)   The decision of the members including information as to date, time and place of meeting, and the identity of members voting; or information on any other resolution;

(9)   A copy of the disclosure to the parties of the decision;

(10) A statement of the warrantor's intended action(s);

(11) Copies of follow-up letters (or summaries of relevant and material portions of follow-up telephone calls) to the consumer, and responses thereto; and

(12) Any other documents and communications (or summaries of relevant and material portions of oral communications) relating to the dispute.

(b)   The Mechanism shall maintain an index of each warrantor's disputes grouped under brand name and subgrouped under product model.

(c)   The Mechanism shall maintain an index for each warrantor as will show:

(1)   All disputes in which the warrantor has promised some performance (either by settlement or in response to a Mechanism decision) and has failed to comply; and

(2)   All disputes in which the warrantor has refused to abide by a Mechanism decision.

(d)   The Mechanism shall maintain an index as will show all disputes delayed beyond 40 days.

(e)   The Mechanism shall compile semi-annually and maintain statistics which show the number and percent of disputes in each of the following categories:

(1)   Resolved by staff of the Mechanism and warrantor has complied;

(2)   Resolved by staff of the Mechanism, time for compliance has occurred, and warrantor has not complied;

(3)   Resolved by staff of the Mechanism and time for compliance has not yet occurred;

(4)   Decided by members and warrantor has complied;

(5)   Decided by members, time for compliance has occurred, and warrantor has not complied;

(6)   Decided by members and time for compliance has not yet occurred;

(7)   Decided by members adverse to the consumer;

(8)   No jurisdiction;

(9)   Decision delayed beyond 40 days under § 703.5(e)(1) of this part;

(10)   Decision delayed beyond 40 days under § 703.5(e)(2) of this part;

(11)   Decision delayed beyond 40 days for any other reason; and

(12)   Pending decision.

(f)   The Mechanism shall retain all records specified in paragraphs (a) through (e) of this section for at least 4 years after final disposition of the dispute.

§ 703.7   Audits.

(a)   The Mechanism shall have an audit conducted at least annually, to determine whether the Mechanism and its implementation are in compliance with this part. All records of the Mechanism required to be kept under § 703.6 of this part shall be available for audit.

(b)   Each audit provided for in paragraph (a) of this section shall include at a minimum the following:

(1)   Evaluation of warrantors' efforts to make consumers aware of the Mechanism's existence as required in § 703.2(d) of this part;

(2)   Review of the indexes maintained pursuant to § 703.6(b), (c), and (d) of this part; and

(3)   Analysis of a random sample of disputes handled by the Mechanism to determine the following:

(i)   Adequacy of the Mechanism's complaint and other forms, investigation, mediation and follow-up efforts, and other aspects of complaint handling; and

(ii)   Accuracy of the Mechanism's statistical compilations under § 703.6(e) of this part. (For purposes of this subparagraph "analysis" shall include oral or written contact with the consumers involved in each of the disputes in the random sample.)

(c)   A report of each audit under this section shall be submitted to the Federal Trade Commission, and shall be made available to any person at reasonable cost. The Mechanism may direct its auditor to delete names of parties to disputes, and identity of products involved, from the audit report.

(d) Auditors shall be selected by the Mechanism. No auditor may be involved with the Mechanism as a warrantor, sponsor or member, or employee or agent thereof, other than for purposes of the audit.

§ 703.8   Openness of Records and Proceedings.

(a) The statistical summaries specified in § 703.6(e) of this part shall be available to any person for inspection and copying.

(b) Except as provided under paragraphs (a) and (e) of this section, and paragraph (c) of § 703.7 of this part, all records of the Mechanism may be kept confidential, or made available only on such terms and conditions, or in such form, as the Mechanism shall permit.

(c) The policy of the Mechanism with respect to records made available at the Mechanism's option shall be set out in the procedures under § 703.5(a) of this part; the policy shall be applied uniformly to all requests for access to or copies of such records.

(d) Meetings of the members to hear and decide disputes shall be open to observers on reasonable and nondiscriminatory terms. The identity of the parties and products involved in disputes need not be disclosed at meetings.

(e) Upon request the Mechanism shall provide to either party to a dispute:

(1) Access to all records relating to the dispute; and

(2) Copies of any records relating to the dispute, at reasonable cost.

(f) The Mechanism shall make available to any person upon request, information relating to the qualifications of Mechanism staff and members.

FEDERAL TRADE COMMISSION, TRADE REGULATION RULES: RULE CONCERNING COOLING-OFF PERIOD FOR SALES MADE AT HOMES OR AT CERTAIN OTHER LOCATIONS

(1995)

[In 1972, the Federal Trade Commission ("FTC") promulgated rules to restrain the overly aggressive sales practices of some door-to-door salesmen. These rules became effective as law in 1974, and the FTC adopted a few amendments in 1995. *See* 16 C.F.R. Part 429. These rules generally allow a buyer to cancel a contract within three days after making it with a door-to-door salesman. They do not preempt state laws concerning door-to-door sales unless the state laws are inconsistent with, or provide less protection to buyers than, these rules.]

---

§ 429.1 The Rule.

In connection with any door-to-door sale, it constitutes an unfair and deceptive act or practice for any seller to:

(a) Fail to furnish the buyer with a fully completed receipt or copy of any contract pertaining to such sale at the time of its execution, which is in the same language, e.g., Spanish, as that principally used in the oral sales presentation and which shows the date of the transaction and contains the name and address of the seller, and in immediate proximity to the space reserved in the contract for the signature of the buyer or on the front page of the receipt if a contract is not used and in boldface type of a minimum size of 10 points, a statement in substantially the following form:

"YOU, THE BUYER, MAY CANCEL THIS TRANSACTION AT ANY TIME PRIOR TO MIDNIGHT OF THE THIRD BUSINESS DAY AFTER THE DATE OF THIS TRANSACTION. SEE THE ATTACHED NOTICE OF CANCELLATION FORM FOR AN EXPLANATION OF THIS RIGHT."

(b) Fail to furnish each buyer, at the time he signs the door-to-door sales contract or otherwise agrees to buy consumer goods or services from the seller, a completed form in duplicate, captioned "NOTICE OF CANCELLATION", which shall be attached to the contract or receipt and easily detachable, and which shall contain in ten point bold face type the following information and statements in the same language, e.g., Spanish, as that used in the contract:

NOTICE OF CANCELLATION

(enter DATE OF TRANSACTION)

(Date)

YOU MAY CANCEL THIS TRANSACTION, WITHOUT ANY PENALTY OR OBLIGATION, WITHIN THREE BUSINESS DAYS FROM THE ABOVE DATE.

IF YOU CANCEL, ANY PROPERTY TRADED IN, ANY PAYMENTS MADE BY YOU UNDER THE CONTRACT OR SALE, AND ANY NEGOTIABLE INSTRUMENT EXECUTED BY YOU WILL BE RETURNED WITHIN 10 BUSINESS DAYS FOLLOWING RECEIPT BY THE SELLER OF YOUR CANCELLATION NOTICE, AND ANY SECURITY INTEREST ARISING OUT OF THE TRANSACTION WILL BE CANCELED.

IF YOU CANCEL, YOU MUST MAKE AVAILABLE TO THE SELLER AT YOUR RESIDENCE, IN SUBSTANTIALLY AS GOOD CONDITION AS WHEN RECEIVED, ANY GOODS DELIVERED

TO YOU UNDER THIS CONTRACT OR SALE; OR YOU MAY IF YOU WISH, COMPLY WITH THE INSTRUCTIONS OF THE SELLER REGARDING THE RETURN SHIPMENT OF THE GOODS AT THE SELLER'S EXPENSE AND RISK.

IF YOU DO MAKE THE GOODS AVAILABLE TO THE SELLER AND THE SELLER DOES NOT PICK THEM UP WITHIN 20 DAYS OF THE DATE OF YOUR NOTICE OF CANCELLATION, YOU MAY RETAIN OR DISPOSE OF THE GOODS WITHOUT ANY FURTHER OBLIGATION. IF YOU FAIL TO MAKE THE GOODS AVAILABLE TO THE SELLER, OR IF YOU AGREE TO RETURN THE GOODS TO THE SELLER AND FAIL TO DO SO, THEN YOU REMAIN LIABLE FOR PERFORMANCE OF ALL OBLIGATIONS UNDER THE CONTRACT.

TO CANCEL THIS TRANSACTION, MAIL OR DELIVER A SIGNEDAND DATED COPY OF THIS CANCELLATION NOTICE OR ANY OTHER WRITTEN NOTICE, OR SEND A TELEGRAM, TO _____, AT_____ NOT LATER THAN

[Name of seller]   [Address of seller's place of business]

MIDNIGHT OF _____.

[Date]

I HEREBY CANCEL THIS TRANSACTION.

_____   _____

(Date)   (Buyer's Signature)

(c)   Fail, before furnishing copies of the "Notice of Cancellation" to the buyer, to complete both copies by entering the name of the seller, the address of the seller's place of business, the date of the transaction, and the date, not earlier than the third business day following the date of the transaction, by which the buyer may give notice of cancellation.

(d)   Include in any door-to-door contract or receipt any confession of judgment or any waiver of any of the rights to which the buyer is entitled under this section including specifically his right to cancel the sale in accordance with the provisions of this section.

(e)   Fail to inform each buyer orally, at the time he signs the contract or purchases the goods or services, of his right to cancel.

(f)   Misrepresent in any manner the buyer's right to cancel.

(g)   Fail or refuse to honor any valid notice of cancellation by a buyer and within 10 business days after the receipt of such notice, to (i) refund all payments made under the contract or sale; (ii) return any goods or property traded in, in substantially as good condition as when received by the seller; (iii) cancel and return any negotiable instrument executed by the buyer in connection with the contract or sale and take any action necessary or appropriate to terminate promptly any security interest created in the transaction.

(h)   Negotiate, transfer, sell, or assign any note or other evidence of indebtedness to a finance company or other third party prior to midnight of the fifth business day following the day the contract was signed or the goods or services were purchased.

(i)   Fail, within 10 business days of receipt of the buyer's notice of cancellation, to notify him whether the seller intends to repossess or to abandon any shipped or delivered goods.

Note 1: *Definitions.* For the purposes of the section the following definitions shall apply:

(a) *Door-to-door sale.* A sale, lease, or rental of consumer goods or services with a purchase price of $25 or more, whether under single or multiple contracts, in which the seller or his representative personally solicits the sale, including those in response to or following an invitation by the buyer, and the buyer's agreement or offer to purchase is made at a place other than the place of business of the seller. The term "door-to-door sale" does not include a transaction:

(1) Made pursuant to prior negotiations in the course of a visit by the buyer to a retail business establishment having a fixed permanent location where the goods are exhibited or the services are offered for sale on a continuing basis; or

(2) In which the consumer is accorded the right of rescission by the provisions of the Consumer Credit Protection Act (15 U.S.C. 1635) or regulations issued pursuant thereto; or

(3) In which the buyer has initiated the contact and the goods or services are needed to meet a bona fide immediate personal emergency of the buyer, and the buyer furnishes the seller with a separate dated and signed personal statement in the buyer's handwriting describing the situation requiring immediate remedy and expressly acknowledging and waiving the right to cancel the sale within 3 business days; or

(4) Conducted and consummated entirely by mail or telephone; and without any other contact between the buyer and the seller or its representative prior to delivery of the goods or performance of the services; or

(5) In which the buyer has initiated the contact and specifically requested the seller to visit his home for the purpose of repairing or performing maintenance upon the buyer's personal property. If in the course of such a visit, the seller sells the buyer the right to receive additional services or goods other than replacement parts necessarily used in performing the maintenance or in making the repairs, the sale of those additional goods or services would not fall within this exclusion; or

(6) Pertaining to the sale or rental of real property, to the sale of insurance or to the sale of securities or commodities by a broker-dealer registered with the Securities and Exchange Commission.

(b) *Consumer goods or services.* Goods or services purchased, leased, or rented primarily for personal, family, or household purposes, including courses of instruction or training regardless of the purpose for which they are taken.

(c) *Seller.* Any person, partnership, corporation, or association engaged in the door-to-door sale of consumer goods or services.

(d) *Place of business.* The main or permanent branch office or local address of a seller.

(e) *Purchase price.* The total price paid or to be paid for the consumer goods or services, including all interest and service charges.

(f) *Business day.* Any calendar day except Sunday, or the following business holidays: New Year's Day, Washington's Birthday, Memorial Day, Independence Day, Labor Day, Columbus Day, Veterans' Day, Thanksgiving Day, and Christmas Day.

Note 2: *Effect on State laws and municipal ordinances.*

(a) The Commission is cognizant of the significant burden imposed upon door-to-door sellers by the various and often inconsistent State laws which provide the buyer with the right to cancel door-to-door sales transactions. However, it does not believe that this constitutes sufficient justification for preempting all of the provisions of such laws or of the ordinances of the political subdivisions of the various States. The record in the proceedings supports the view that the joint and coordinated efforts of both the Commission and State and local officials are required to insure that a consumer who has purchased from a door-to-door seller something he does not want, does not need, or cannot afford, is accorded a unilateral right to rescind, without penalty, his agreement to purchase the goods or services.

(b)   This section will not be construed to annul, or exempt any seller from complying with the laws of any State, or with the ordinances of political subdivisions thereof, regulating door-to-door sales, except to the extent that such laws or ordinances, if they permit door-to-door selling, are directly inconsistent with the provisions of this section. Such laws or ordinances which do not accord the buyer, with respect to the particular transaction, a right to cancel a door-to-door sale which is substantially the same or greater than that provided in this section, or which permit the imposition of any fee or penalty on the buyer for the exercise of such right, or which do not provide for giving the buyer notice of his right to cancel the transaction in substantially the same form and manner provided for in this section, are among those which will be considered directly inconsistent.

FEDERAL TRADE COMMISSION, TRADE REGULATION RULES: RETAIL FOOD STORE ADVERTISING AND MARKETING PRACTICES

(1989)

(Excerpts)

[The Federal Trade Commission's ("FTC's") rules on Retail Food Store Advertising and Marketing Practices, first promulgated in 1971, were amended in 1989. 16 C.F.R. Part 424. Subject to specified exceptions, they require retail food stores to have adequate stock to meet reasonable demand for items advertised for sale at specified prices. These rules apply to acts or practices in or affecting interstate commerce. The FTC can enforce these rules by ordering violators to cease and desist, or by obtaining injunctions, civil money penalties, or restitution for the victim in the federal courts. 15 U.S.C. § 45. The Uniform Deceptive Trade Practices Act, in this pamphlet below, pursues similar goals with respect to a broader range of advertising practices.]

Sec.

---

§ 424.1   Unfair or Deceptive Acts or Practices.

In connection with the sale or offering for sale by retail food stores of food, grocery products or other merchandise to consumers in or affecting commerce as "commerce" is defined in section 4 of the Federal Trade Commission Act, 15 U.S.C. 44, it is an unfair or deceptive act or practice in violation of section 5(a)(1) of the Federal Trade Commission Act, 15 U.S.C. 45(a)(1), to offer any such products for sale at a stated price, by means of an advertisement disseminated in an area served by any stores which are covered by the advertisement, if those stores do not have the advertised products in stock and readily available to customers during the effective period of the advertisement, unless the advertisement clearly and adequately discloses that supplies of the advertised products are limited or the advertised products are available only at some outlets.

§ 424.2   Defenses.

No violation of § 424.1 shall be found if:

(a)   The advertised products were ordered in adequate time for delivery in quantities sufficient to meet reasonably anticipated demand;

(b)   The food retailer offers a "raincheck" for the advertised products;

(c)   The food retailer offers at the advertised price or at a comparable price reduction a similar product that is at least comparable in value to the advertised product; or

(d)   The food retailer offers other compensation at least equal to the advertised value.

FEDERAL TRADE COMMISSION, TRADE REGULATION RULES: PRESERVATION OF CONSUMERS' CLAIMS AND DEFENSES

(1975)

(Excerpts)

[Generally speaking, a party with rights under a contract (the "creditor") may transfer ("assign") its rights to a third party (the "assignee"), who then may enforce the rights against the other party to the original contract (the "debtor"). Before the Federal Trade Commission promulgated its rules on the Preservation of Consumers' Claims and Defenses, 16 C.F.R. § 433 (1975), the assignee might take such rights free of any claims or defenses (such as breach of warranty) that the debtor had against the creditor. The FTC rules changed the law by requiring credit contracts and purchase-money loans involving consumers to contain standardized terms that preserve the debtor's claims and defenses when the creditor assigns its rights to a third party. These rules are law. They apply to acts or practices in or affecting interstate commerce.]

Sec.

§ 433.1   Definitions . . .

(c)   *Creditor.* A person who, in the ordinary course of business, lends purchase money or finances the sale of goods or services to consumers on a deferred payment basis; *Provided,* such person is not acting, for the purposes of a particular transaction, in the capacity of a credit card issuer.

(d) *Purchase money loan.*   A cash advance which is received by a consumer in return for a "Finance Charge" within the meaning of the Truth in Lending Act and Regulation Z, which is applied, in whole or substantial part, to a purchase of goods or services from a seller who (1) refers consumers to the creditor or (2) is affiliated with the creditor by common control, contract, or business arrangement.[*]

(e) *Financing a sale.*   Extending credit to a consumer in connection with a "Credit Sale" within the meaning of the Truth in Lending Act and Regulation Z. . . .[**]

(i)   *Consumer credit contract.*   Any instrument which evidences or embodies a debt arising from a "Purchase Money Loan" transaction or a "financed sale" as defined in paragraphs (d) and (e) of this section. . . .

§ 433.2   Preservation of Consumers' Claims and Defenses, Unfair or Deceptive Acts or Practices.

In connection with any sale or lease of goods or services to consumers, in or affecting commerce as "commerce" is defined in the Federal Trade Commission Act, it is an unfair or deceptive act or practice within the meaning of Section 5 of that Act for a seller, directly or indirectly, to:

---

[*]   Regulation Z is set forth at 12 C.F.R. § 226.1 et seq. Section 226.4 of Reg. Z defines "finance charge" to mean "the cost of consumer credit as a dollar amount." (Footnote by ed.)

[**]   Regulation Z defines "credit sale" to mean "a sale in which the seller is a creditor."

(a)   Take or receive a consumer credit contract which fails to contain the following provision in at least ten point, bold face, type:

NOTICE

ANY HOLDER OF THIS CONSUMER CREDIT CONTRACT IS SUBJECT TO ALL CLAIMS AND DEFENSES WHICH THE DEBTOR COULD ASSERT AGAINST THE SELLER OF GOODS OR SERVICES OBTAINED PURSUANT HERETO OR WITH THE PROCEEDS HEREOF. RECOVERY HEREUNDER BY THE DEBTOR SHALL NOT EXCEED AMOUNTS PAID BY THE DEBTOR HEREUNDER.

or,

(b)   Accept, as full or partial payment for such sale or lease, the proceeds of any purchase money loan (as purchase money loan is defined herein), unless any consumer credit contract made in connection with such purchase money loan contains the following provision in at least ten point, bold face, type:

NOTICE

ANY HOLDER OF THIS CONSUMER CREDIT CONTRACT IS SUBJECT TO ALL CLAIMS AND DEFENSES WHICH THE DEBTOR COULD ASSERT AGAINST THE SELLER OF GOODS OR SERVICES OBTAINED WITH THE PROCEEDS HEREOF. RECOVERY HEREUNDER BY THE DEBTOR SHALL NOT EXCEED AMOUNTS PAID BY THE DEBTOR HEREUNDER. . . .

CONSUMER REVIEW FAIRNESS ACT OF 2016

[The Consumer Review Fairness Act of 2016, Public Law 114–258, 130 Stat. 1355, aims to protect consumers from non-disparagement clauses in form contracts for the sale of goods or services. Such clauses have interfered with some consumers' efforts to post reviews of good and services on the internet or elsewhere. To simplify, the Act renders non-disparagement clauses void from the inception of a form contract. Many consumers benefit from crowd-sourcing reviews of products or services. This Act seeks to curtail non-disparagement clauses to preserve the credibility and value of online consumer reviews.]

SECTION 1. SHORT TITLE.

This Act may be cited as the "Consumer Review Fairness Act of 2016".

SEC. 2. CONSUMER REVIEW PROTECTION.

(a) DEFINITIONS.—In this section:

(1) COMMISSION.—The term "Commission" means the Federal Trade Commission.

(2) COVERED COMMUNICATION.—The term "covered communication" means a written, oral, or pictorial review, performance assessment of, or other similar analysis of, including by electronic means, the goods, services, or conduct of a person by an individual who is party to a form contract with respect to which such person is also a party.

(3) FORM CONTRACT.—

(A) IN GENERAL.—Except as provided in subparagraph (B), the term "form contract" means a contract with standardized terms—

(i) used by a person in the course of selling or leasing the person's goods or services; and

(ii) imposed on an individual without a meaningful opportunity for such individual to negotiate the standardized terms.

(B) EXCEPTION.—The term "form contract" does not include an employer-employee or independent contractor contract.

(4) PICTORIAL.—The term "pictorial" includes pictures, photographs, video, illustrations, and symbols.

(b) INVALIDITY OF CONTRACTS THAT IMPEDE CONSUMER REVIEWS.—

(1) IN GENERAL.—Except as provided in paragraphs (2) and (3), a provision of a form contract is void from the inception of such contract if such provision—

(A) prohibits or restricts the ability of an individual who is a party to the form contract to engage in a covered communication;

(B) imposes a penalty or fee against an individual who is a party to the form contract for engaging in a covered communication; or

(C) transfers or requires an individual who is a party to the form contract to transfer to any person any intellectual property rights in review or feedback content, with the exception of a non-exclusive license to use the content, that the individual may have in any otherwise lawful covered communication about such person or the goods or services provided by such person.

(2)   RULE OF CONSTRUCTION.—Nothing in paragraph (1) shall be construed to affect—

(A)   any duty of confidentiality imposed by law (including agency guidance);

(B)   any civil cause of action for defamation, libel, or slander, or any similar cause of action;

(C)   any party's right to remove or refuse to display publicly on an Internet website or webpage owned, operated, or otherwise controlled by such party any content of a covered communication that—

(i)   contains the personal information or likeness of another person, or is libelous, harassing, abusive, obscene, vulgar, sexually explicit, or is inappropriate with respect to race, gender, sexuality, ethnicity, or other intrinsic characteristic;

(ii)   is unrelated to the goods or services offered by or available at such party's Internet website or webpage; or

(iii)   is clearly false or misleading; or

(D)   a party's right to establish terms and conditions with respect to the creation of photographs or video of such party's property when those photographs or video are created by an employee or independent contractor of a commercial entity and solely intended for commercial purposes by that entity.

(3)   EXCEPTIONS.—Paragraph (1) shall not apply to the extent that a provision of a form contract prohibits disclosure or submission of, or reserves the right of a person or business that hosts online consumer reviews or comments to remove—

(A)   trade secrets or commercial or financial information obtained from a person and considered privileged or confidential;

(B)   personnel and medical files and similar information the disclosure of which would constitute a clearly unwarranted invasion of personal privacy;

(C)   records or information compiled for law enforcement purposes, the disclosure of which would constitute a clearly unwarranted invasion of personal privacy;

(D)   content that is unlawful or otherwise meets the requirements of paragraph (2)(C); or

(E)   content that contains any computer viruses, worms, or other potentially damaging computer code, processes, programs, applications, or files.

(c)   PROHIBITION.—It shall be unlawful for a person to offer a form contract containing a provision described as void in subsection (b).

(d)   ENFORCEMENT BY COMMISSION.—

(1)   UNFAIR OR DECEPTIVE ACTS OR PRACTICES.—A violation of subsection (c) by a person with respect to which the Commission is empowered under section 5(a)(2) of the Federal Trade Commission Act (15 U.S.C. 45(a)(2)) shall be treated as a violation of a rule defining an unfair or deceptive act or practice prescribed under section 18(a)(1)(B) of the Federal Trade Commission Act (15 U.S.C. 57a(a)(1)(B)).

(2)   POWERS OF COMMISSION.—

(A)   IN GENERAL.—The Commission shall enforce this section in the same manner, by the same means, and with the same jurisdiction, powers, and duties as though all applicable terms and provisions of the Federal Trade Commission Act (15 U.S.C. 41 et seq.) were incorporated into and made a part of this Act.

(B)   PRIVILEGES AND IMMUNITIES.—Any person who violates this section shall be subject to the penalties and entitled to the privileges and immunities provided in the Federal Trade Commission Act (15 U.S.C. 41 et seq.).

(e) ENFORCEMENT BY STATES.—

(1) AUTHORIZATION.—Subject to paragraph (2), in any case in which the attorney general of a State has reason to believe that an interest of the residents of the State has been or is threatened or adversely affected by the engagement of any person subject to subsection (c) in a practice that violates such subsection, the attorney general of the State may, as parens patriae, bring a civil action on behalf of the residents of the State in an appropriate district court of the United States to obtain appropriate relief.

(2) RIGHTS OF FEDERAL TRADE COMMISSION.—

(A) NOTICE TO FEDERAL TRADE COMMISSION.—

(i) IN GENERAL.—Except as provided in clause (iii), the attorney general of a State shall notify the Commission in writing that the attorney general intends to bring a civil action under paragraph (1) before initiating the civil action against a person described in subsection (d)(1).

(ii) CONTENTS.—The notification required by clause (i) with respect to a civil action shall include a copy of the complaint to be filed to initiate the civil action.

(iii) EXCEPTION.—If it is not feasible for the attorney general of a State to provide the notification required by clause (i) before initiating a civil action under paragraph (1), the attorney general shall notify the Commission immediately upon instituting the civil action.

(B) INTERVENTION BY FEDERAL TRADE COMMISSION.—The Commission may—

(i) intervene in any civil action brought by the attorney general of a State under paragraph (1) against a person described in subsection (d)(1); and

(ii) upon intervening—

(I) be heard on all matters arising in the civil action; and

(II) file petitions for appeal of a decision in the civil action.

(3) INVESTIGATORY POWERS.—Nothing in this subsection may be construed to prevent the attorney general of a State from exercising the powers conferred on the attorney general by the laws of the State to conduct investigations, to administer oaths or affirmations, or to compel the attendance of witnesses or the production of documentary or other evidence.

(4) PREEMPTIVE ACTION BY FEDERAL TRADE COMMISSION.—If the Federal Trade Commission institutes a civil action or an administrative action with respect to a violation of subsection (c), the attorney general of a State may not, during the pendency of such action, bring a civil action under paragraph (1) against any defendant named in the complaint of the Commission for the violation with respect to which the Commission instituted such action.

(5) VENUE; SERVICE OF PROCESS.—

(A) VENUE.—Any action brought under paragraph (1) may be brought in—

(i) the district court of the United States that meets applicable requirements relating to venue under section 1391 of title 28, United States Code; or

(ii) another court of competent jurisdiction.

(B) SERVICE OF PROCESS.—In an action brought under paragraph (1), process may be served in any district in which the defendant—

(i) is an inhabitant; or

(ii) may be found.

(6) ACTIONS BY OTHER STATE OFFICIALS.—

(A) IN GENERAL.—In addition to civil actions brought by attorneys general under paragraph (1), any other consumer protection officer of a State who is authorized by the State to do so may bring a civil action under paragraph (1), subject to the same requirements and limitations that apply under this subsection to civil actions brought by attorneys general.

(B) SAVINGS PROVISION.—Nothing in this subsection may be construed to prohibit an authorized official of a State from initiating or continuing any proceeding in a court of the State for a violation of any civil or criminal law of the State.

(f) EDUCATION AND OUTREACH FOR BUSINESSES.—Not later than 60 days after the date of the enactment of this Act, the Commission shall commence conducting education and outreach that provides businesses with non-binding best practices for compliance with this Act.

(g) RELATION TO STATE CAUSES OF ACTION.—Nothing in this section shall be construed to affect any cause of action brought by a person that exists or may exist under State law.

(h) SAVINGS PROVISION.—Nothing in this section shall be construed to limit, impair, or supersede the operation of the Federal Trade Commission Act or any other provision of Federal law.

(i) EFFECTIVE DATES.—This section shall take effect on the date of the enactment of this Act, except that—

(1) subsections (b) and (c) shall apply with respect to contracts in effect on or after the date that is 90 days after the date of the enactment of this Act; and

(2) subsections (d) and (e) shall apply with respect to contracts in effect on or after the date that is 1 year after the date of the enactment of this Act.

POSTAL REORGANIZATION ACT: MAILING OF UNORDERED MERCHANDISE

(1971)

[Prior to enactment of this part of the Postal Reorganization Act ("PRA"), 39 U.S.C. § 3009, an offeror could mail unordered merchandise to an offeree on terms specified by the offeror, and if the offeree acted inconsistently with the offeror's continued ownership, as by using or keeping the merchandise, a contract was formed, requiring the offeree to pay for the merchandise. Restatement (Second) of Contracts § 69(2) (1981). The PRA changed this law by making the mailing of unordered merchandise an "unfair method of competition and an unfair trade practice." 39 U.S.C. § 3009(a). Consequently, the Federal Trade Commission Act, 15 U.S.C. § 45, empowered the Federal Trade Commission to enforce this statute by ordering violators to cease and desist, or by obtaining injunctions, civil money penalties, or restitution for the offeree in the federal courts. Moreover, the offeree may do anything with the goods, including using them, without liability to the offeror.]

§ 3009. Mailing of Unordered Merchandise.

(a)   Except for (1) free samples clearly and conspicuously marked as such, and (2) merchandise mailed by a charitable organization soliciting contributions, the mailing of unordered merchandise or of communications prohibited by subsection (c) of this section constitutes an unfair method of competition and an unfair trade practice in violation of section 45(a)(1) of title 15.

(b)   Any merchandise mailed in violation of subsection (a) of this section, or within the exceptions contained therein, may be treated as a gift by the recipient, who shall have the right to retain, use, discard, or dispose of it in any manner he sees fit without any obligation whatsoever to the sender. All such merchandise shall have attached to it a clear and conspicuous statement informing the recipient that he may treat the merchandise as a gift to him and has the right to retain, use, discard, or dispose of it in any manner he sees fit without any obligation whatsoever to the sender.

(c)   No mailer of any merchandise mailed in violation of subsection (a) of this section, or within the exceptions contained therein, shall mail to any recipient of such merchandise a bill for such merchandise or any dunning communications.

(d)   For the purposes of this section, "unordered merchandise" means merchandise mailed without the prior expressed request or consent of the recipient.

BANKRUPTCY CODE

(As amended, 2010)

[The core purpose of bankruptcy law is to allow a debtor to file for bankruptcy when its debts exceed its ability to repay them, and there is little prospect that the debtor will be able to emerge from this deficit. The bankrupt must turn over most of her assets to a court-appointed trustee for the benefit of her creditors. The bankruptcy proceeding results in a discharge of most of the debtor's obligations to pay its creditors, and the creditors get a percentage of the amounts of the debts, depending on the value of the debtor's remaining assets. The discharge, it is hoped, will give the debtor a "fresh start" so that he or she can become a productive member of society again, or can restructure or wind up a business.

[One provision of a complicated federal statute, the Bankruptcy Code,11 U.S.C. § 524, modifies an exception to the common law requirement of consideration in contract law. The common law allowed a creditor to enforce a debtor's promise to pay a debt that had been discharged in bankruptcy even when no new consideration supported enforcement of the new promise. Restatement (Second) of Contracts § 83 (1981). Section 524 makes it more difficult for a creditor to enforce such a promise by protecting a debtor from further improvidence or a creditor's predatory conduct. This section does not, however, require new consideration supporting the post-discharge promise.]

§ 524. Effect of Discharge.

(a)   A discharge in a case under this title—

(1)   voids any judgment at any time obtained, to the extent that such judgment is a determination of the personal liability of the debtor with respect to any debt discharged under section 727, 944, 1141, 1228, or 1328 of this title, whether or not discharge of such debt is waived;

(2)   operates as an injunction against the commencement or continuation of an action, the employment of process, or an act, to collect, recover or offset any such debt as a personal liability of the debtor, whether or not discharge of such debt is waived; and

(3)   operates as an injunction against the commencement or continuation of an action, the employment of process, or an act, to collect or recover from, or offset against, property of the debtor of the kind specified in section 541(a)(2) of this title that is acquired after the commencement of the case, on account of any allowable community claim, except a community claim that is excepted from discharge under section 523, 1228(a)(1), or 1328(a)(1), or that would be so excepted, determined in accordance with the provisions of sections 523(c) and 523(d) of this title, in a case concerning the debtor's spouse commenced on the date of the filing of the petition in the case concerning the debtor, whether or not discharge of the debt based on such community claim is waived.

. . .

(c)   An agreement between a holder of a claim and the debtor, the consideration for which, in whole or in part, is based on a debt that is dischargeable in a case under this title is enforceable only to any extent enforceable under applicable nonbankruptcy law, whether or not discharge of such debt is waived, only if—

(1)   such agreement was made before the granting of the discharge . . .;

(2)   the debtor received the disclosures described in subsection (k) [omitted] at or before the time at which the debtor signed the agreement;

(3)   such agreement has been filed with the court and, if applicable, accompanied by a declaration or an affidavit of the attorney that represented the debtor during the course of negotiating an agreement under this subsection, which states that—

(A) such agreement represents a fully informed and voluntary agreement by the debtor;

(B) such agreement does not impose an undue hardship on the debtor or a dependent of the debtor; and

(C) the attorney fully advised the debtor of the legal effect and consequences of—

(i) an agreement of the kind specified in this subsection; and

(ii) any default under such an agreement;

(4) the debtor has not rescinded such agreement at any time prior to discharge or within sixty days after such agreement is filed with the court, whichever occurs later, by giving notice of rescission to the holder of such claim;

(5) the provisions of subsection (d) of this section have been complied with; and

(6)(A) in a case concerning an individual who was not represented by an attorney during the course of negotiating an agreement under this subsection, the court approves such agreement as—

(i) not imposing an undue hardship on the debtor or a dependent of the debtor; and

(ii) in the best interest of the debtor.

(B) Subparagraph (A) shall not apply to the extent that such debt is a consumer debt secured by real property.

(d) In a case concerning an individual, when the court has determined whether to grant or not to grant a discharge under section 727, 1141, 1228, or 1328 of this title, the court may hold a hearing at which the debtor shall appear in person. At any such hearing, the court shall inform the debtor that a discharge has been granted or the reason why a discharge has not been granted. If a discharge has been granted and if the debtor desires to make an agreement of the kind specified in subsection (c) of this section and was not represented by an attorney during the course of negotiating such agreement, then the court shall hold a hearing at which the debtor shall appear in person and at such hearing the court shall—

(1) inform the debtor—

(A) that such an agreement is not required under this title, under nonbankruptcy law, or under any agreement not made in accordance with the provisions of subsection (c) of this section; and

(B) of the legal effect and consequences of—

(i) an agreement of the kind specified in subsection (c) of this section; and

(ii) a default under such an agreement; and

(2) determine whether the agreement that the debtor desires to make complies with the requirements of subsection (c)(6) of this section, if the consideration for such agreement is based in whole or in part on a consumer debt that is not secured by real property of the debtor.

(e) Except as provided in subsection (a)(3) of this section, discharge of a debt of the debtor does not affect the liability of any other entity on, or the property of any other entity for, such debt.

(f) Nothing contained in subsection (c) or (d) of this section prevents a debtor from voluntarily repaying any debt. . . .

UNIFORM CONSUMER CREDIT CODE

(1974)

(Excerpts)

[The National Conference of Commissioners on Uniform State Laws (now the Uniform Law Commission) proposed the Uniform Consumer Credit Code ("U3C") in 1968, as a consumer protection law. In 1974, the Commission proposed substantial amendments, largely due to the emergence of bank credit cards distributed extensively on a nationwide basis. As of May 1, 2011, only 11 states had enacted the U3C, some in its 1968 version and others in its 1974 version. However, a federal statute, and the Federal Reserve Board's implementing rules, now regulate many aspects of consumer credit contracts. See the Truth in Lending Act, as amended by the Credit Card Accountability Responsibility and Disclosure Act of 2009 (also known as the "Credit CARD Act of 2009"), 15 U.S.C. § 1601 *et seq.*; 12 C.F.R. Part 226. The U3C's provision on unconscionability is still significant for contract law.]

---

§ 1.301   [General Definitions] . . .

. . .

(12) "Consumer credit sale":

(a) Except as provided in paragraph (b), "consumer credit sale" means a sale of goods, services, or an interest in land in which:

(i)   credit is granted either pursuant to a seller credit card or by a seller who regularly engages as a seller in credit transactions of the same kind;

(ii) the buyer is a person other than an organization;

(iii) the goods, services, or interest in land are purchased primarily for a personal, family, household, or agricultural purpose;

(iv) the debt is payable in instalments or a finance charge is made; and

(v)   with respect to a sale of goods or services, the amount financed does not exceed $25,000.

(b) A "consumer credit sale" does not include . . .

(ii) . . . a sale of an interest in land if the finance charge does not exceed 12 per cent. . . .

(13) "Consumer credit transaction" means a consumer credit sale or consumer loan. . . .

§ 5.108   [Unconscionability; Inducement by Unconscionable Conduct . . .]

(1) With respect to . . . a consumer credit transaction, if the court as a matter of law finds:

(a) the agreement or transaction to have been unconscionable at the time it was made, or to have been induced by unconscionable conduct, the court may refuse to enforce the agreement; or

(b) any term or part of the agreement or transaction to have been unconscionable at the time it was made, the court may refuse to enforce the agreement, enforce the remainder of the

493

agreement without the unconscionable term or part, or so limit the application of any unconscionable term or part as to avoid any unconscionable result. . . .

(4) In applying subsection (1), consideration shall be given to each of the following factors, among others, as applicable. . . .

(b) . . . knowledge by the seller . . . at the time of the sale . . . of the inability of the consumer to receive substantial benefits from the property or services sold or leased;

(c) . . . gross disparity between the price of the property or services sold . . . and the value of the property or services measured by the price at which similar property or services are readily obtainable in credit transactions by like consumers. . . .

(e) the fact that the seller, lessor, or lender has knowingly taken advantage of the inability of the consumer or debtor reasonably to protect his interests by reason of physical or mental infirmities, ignorance, illiteracy, inability to understand the language of the agreement, or similar factors. . . .

Comment . . .

4. [Subsection (4) lists] a number of specific factors to be considered on the issue of unconscionability. It is impossible to anticipate all of the factors and considerations which may support a conclusion of unconscionability in a given instance so the listing is not exclusive. The following are illustrative of individual transactions which would entitle a consumer to relief under this section. . . .

Under subsection (4)(b), a sale to a Spanish speaking laborer-bachelor of an English language encyclopedia set, or the sale of two expensive vacuum cleaners to two poor families sharing the same apartment and one rug;

Under subsection (4)(c), a home solicitation sale of a set of cookware or flatware to a housewife for $375 in an area where a set of comparable quality is readily available on credit in stores for $125 or less;

Under subsection (4)(e), a sale of goods on terms known by the seller to be disadvantageous to the consumer where the written agreement is in English, the consumer is literate only in Spanish, the transaction was negotiated orally in Spanish by the seller's salesman, and the written agreement was neither translated nor explained to the consumer, but the mere fact a consumer has little education and cannot read or write and must sign with an "X" is not itself determinative of unconscionability. . . .

TRUTH IN LENDING: REGULATION Z

(2011)

(Excerpts)

["Regulation Z" implements the Federal Truth in Lending Act, which is contained in Title I of the Consumer Credit Protection Act, as amended (15 U.S.C. § 1601 *et seq.*), and other statutes not relevant here. It was promulgated by the federal Bureau of Consumer Financial Protection and became effective on December 31, 2011. As excerpted, it (1) requires an issuer of credit cards to consider a consumer's "independent ability to make the required minimum periodic payments" under the credit card agreement (12 C.F.R. § 1026.51(a)); (2) prohibits an issuer from opening a credit card account for consumers under the age of 21 unless the consumer has submitted a written application agreement (12 C.F.R. § 1026.51(b); (3) requires an issuer to make extensive and detailed disclosures of the contract terms to consumers (12 C.F.R. §§ 1026.60, 1026.6); and (4) regulates credit card issuers in other ways (12 C.F.R. §§ 1026.53, 1026.55)]

Sec.

---

§ 1026.6   Account Opening Disclosures . . .

(b)   Rules affecting open-end (not home-secured) plans. The requirements of paragraph (b) of this section apply to plans other than home-equity plans subject to the requirements of § 1026.40.

(1)   Form of disclosures; tabular format for open-end (not home-secured) plans. Creditors must provide the account-opening disclosures specified in paragraph (b) (2)(i) through (b)(2)(v) (except for (b)(2)(i)(D)(2)) and (b)(2)(vii) through (b)(2) (xiv) of this section in the form of a table with the headings, content, and format substantially similar to any of the applicable tables in G–17 in Appendix G.

(i)   Highlighting. In the table, any annual percentage rate required to be disclosed pursuant to paragraph (b)(2)(i) of this section; any introductory rate permitted to be disclosed pursuant to paragraph (b)(2)(i)(B) or required to be disclosed under paragraph (b)(2)(i)(F) of this section, any rate that will apply after a premium initial rate expires permitted to be disclosed pursuant to paragraph (b)(2)(i)(C) or required to be disclosed pursuant to paragraph (b)(2)(i)(F), and any fee or percentage amounts or maximum limits on fee amounts disclosed pursuant to paragraphs (b)(2)(ii), (b)(2)(iv), (b)(2)(vii) through (b)(2)(xii) of this section must be disclosed in bold text. However, bold text shall not be used for: The amount of any periodic fee disclosed pursuant to paragraph (b)(2) of this section that is not an annualized amount; and other annual percentage rates or fee amounts disclosed in the table.

(ii)   Location. Only the information required or permitted by paragraphs (b)(2)(i) through (v) (except for (b)(2)(i)(D)(2)) and (b)(2)(vii) through (xiv) of this section shall be in the table. Disclosures required by paragraphs (b)(2)(i)(D)(2), (b)(2)(i) (D)(3), (b)(2)(vi), and (b)(2)(xv) of this section shall be placed directly below the table. Disclosures required by paragraphs (b)(3) through (5) of this section that are not otherwise required to be in the table and other information may be presented with the account agreement or account-opening disclosure statement, provided such information appears outside the required table. . . .

(2)   Required disclosures for account-opening table for open-end (not home-secured) plans. A creditor shall disclose the items in this section, to the extent applicable:

(i)   Annual percentage rate. Each periodic rate that may be used to compute the finance charge, on an outstanding balance for purchases, a cash advance, or a balance transfer, expressed as an annual percentage rate (as determined by § 1026.14(b)). When more man one rate applies for a category of transactions, the range of balances to which each rate is applicable shall also be disclosed. The annual percentage rate for purchases disclosed pursuant to this paragraph shall be in at least 16-point type, except for the following: A penalty rate that may apply upon the occurrence of one or more specific events.

(A)   Variable-rate information. If a rate disclosed under paragraph (b)(2)(i) of this section is a variable rate, the creditor shall also disclose the fact that the rate may vary and how the rate is determined. In describing how the applicable rate will be determined, the creditor must identify the type of index or formula that is used in setting the rate. The value of the index and the amount of the margin that are used to calculate the variable rate shall not be disclosed in the table. A disclosure of any applicable limitations on rate increases or decreases shall not be included in the table.

(B)   Discounted initial rates. If the initial rate is an introductory rate, as that term is defined in § 1026.16(g)(2)(ii), the creditor must disclose the rate that would otherwise apply to the account pursuant to paragraph (b)(2)(i) of this section. Where the rate is not tied to an index or formula, the creditor must disclose the rate that will apply after the introductory rate expires. In a variable-rate account, the creditor must disclose a rate based on the applicable index or formula in accordance with the accuracy requirements of paragraph (b)(4)(ii)(G) of this section. Except as provided in paragraph (b)(2)(i)(F) of this section, the creditor is not required to, but may disclose in the table the introductory rate along with the rate that would otherwise apply to the account if the creditor also discloses the time period during which the introductory rate will remain in effect, and uses the term "introductory" or "intro" in immediate proximity to the introductory rate.

(C)   Premium initial rate. If the initial rate is temporary and is higher than the rate that will apply after the temporary rate expires, the creditor must disclose the premium initial rate pursuant to paragraph (b)(2)(i) of this section. Consistent with paragraph (b)(2)(i) of this section, the premium initial rate for purchases must be in at least 16-point type. Except as provided in paragraph (b)(2)(i)(F) of this section, the creditor is not required to, but may disclose in the table the rate that will apply after the premium initial rate expires if the creditor also discloses the time period during which the premium initial rate will remain in effect. If the creditor also discloses in the table the rate that will apply after the premium initial rate for purchases expires, that rate also must be in at least 16-point type.

(D)   Penalty rates.

(1)   In general. Except as provided in paragraph (b)(2)(i)(D)(2) and (b) (2)(i)(D)(3) of this section, if a rate may increase as a penalty for one or more events specified in the account agreement, such as a late payment or an extension of credit that exceeds the credit limit, the creditor must disclose pursuant to paragraph (b)(2)(i) of this section the increased rate that may apply, a brief description of the event or events that may result in the increased rate, and a brief description of how long the increased rate will remain in effect. If more than one penalty rate may apply, the creditor at its option may disclose the highest rate that could apply, instead of disclosing the specific rates or the range of rates that could apply.

(2) *Introductory rates.* If the creditor discloses in the table an introductory rate, as that term is defined in § 1026.16(g)(2)(ii), creditors must briefly disclose directly beneath the table the circumstances under which the introductory rate may be revoked, and the rate that will apply after the introductory rate is revoked.

(3) *Employee preferential rates.* If a creditor discloses in the table a preferential annual percentage rate for which only employees of the creditor, employees of a third party, or other individuals with similar affiliations with the creditor or third party, such as executive officers, directors, or principal shareholders are eligible, the creditor must briefly disclose directly beneath the table the circumstances under which such preferential rate may be revoked, and the rate that will apply after such preferential rate is revoked. . . .

(F) *Credit card accounts under an open-end (not home-secured) consumer credit plan.* Notwithstanding paragraphs (b)(2)(i)(B) and (b)(2)(i)(C) of this section, for credit card accounts under an open-end (not home-secured) plan, issuers must disclose in the table:

(1) Any introductory rate as that term is defined in § 1026,16(g)(2)(ii) that would apply to the account, consistent with the requirements of paragraph (b)(2)(i)(B) of this section, and

(2) Any rate that would apply upon the expiration of a premium initial rate, consistent with the requirements of paragraph (b)(2)(i)(C) of this section.

(ii) *Fees for issuance or availability.*

(A) Any annual or other periodic fee that may be imposed for the issuance or availability of an open-end plan, including any fee based on account activity or inactivity; how frequently it will be imposed; and the annualized amount of the fee.

(B) Any non-periodic fee that relates to opening the plan. A creditor must disclose that the fee is a one-time fee.

(iii) *Fixed finance charge; minimum interest charge.* Any fixed finance charge and a brief description of the charge. Any minimum interest charge if it exceeds $1.00 that could be imposed during a billing cycle, and a brief description of the charge. The $1.00 threshold amount shall be adjusted periodically by the Bureau to reflect changes in the Consumer Price Index. The Bureau shall calculate each year a price level adjusted minimum interest charge using the Consumer Price Index in effect on the June 1 of that year. When the cumulative change in the adjusted minimum value derived from applying the annual Consumer Price level to the current minimum interest charge threshold has risen by a whole dollar, the minimum interest charge will be increased by $1.00. The creditor may, at its option, disclose in the table minimum interest charges below this threshold.

(iv) *Transaction charges.* Any transaction charge imposed by the creditor for use of the open-end plan for purchases.

(v) *Grace period.* The date by which or the period within which any credit extended may be repaid without incurring a finance charge due to a periodic interest rate and any conditions on the availability of the grace period. If no grace period is provided, that fact must be disclosed. If the length of the grace period varies, the creditor may disclose the range of days, the minimum number of days, or the average number of the days in the grace period, if the disclosure is identified as a range, minimum, or average. In disclosing in the tabular format a grace period that applies to all features on the account, the phrase "How to Avoid Paying Interest" shall be used as the heading for the row describing the grace period. If a grace period is not offered on all features of the account, in disclosing this fact in the tabular format, the phrase "Paying Interest" shall be used as the heading for the row describing this fact.

(vi) Balance computation method. The name of the balance computation method listed in § 1026.60(g) that is used to determine the balance on which the finance charge is computed for each feature, or an explanation of the method used if it is not listed, along with a statement that an explanation of the method(s) required by paragraph (b)(4)(i)(D) of this section is provided with the account-opening disclosures. In determining which balance computation method to disclose, the creditor shall assume that credit extended will not be repaid within any grace period, if any.

(vii) Cash advance fee. Any fee imposed for an extension of credit in the form of cash or its equivalent.

(viii) Late payment fee. Any fee imposed for a late payment.

(ix) Over-the-limit fee. Any fee imposed for exceeding a credit limit.

(x) Balance transfer fee. Any fee imposed to transfer an outstanding balance.

(xi) Returned-payment fee. Any fee imposed by the creditor for a returned payment.

(xii) Required insurance, debt cancellation or debt suspension coverage.

(A) A fee for insurance described in § 1026.4(b)(7) or debt cancellation or suspension coverage described in § 1026.4(b)(10), if the insurance, or debt cancellation or suspension coverage is required as part of the plan; and

(B) A cross reference to any additional information provided about the insurance or coverage, as applicable.

(xiii) Available credit. If a creditor requires fees for the issuance or availability of credit described in paragraph (b)(2)(ii) of this section, or requires a security deposit for such credit, and the total amount of those required fees and/or security deposit that will be imposed and charged to the account when the account is opened is 15 percent or more of the minimum credit limit for the plan, a creditor must disclose the available credit remaining after these fees or security deposit are debited to the account The determination whether the 15 percent threshold is met must be based on the minimum credit limit for the plan. However, the disclosure provided under this paragraph must be based on the actual initial credit limit provided on the account. In determining whether the 15 percent threshold test is met, the creditor must only consider fees for issuance or availability of credit, or a security deposit, that are required. If fees for issuance or availability are optional, these fees should not be considered in determining whether the disclosure must be given. Nonetheless, if the 15 percent threshold test is met, the creditor in providing the disclosure must disclose the amount of available credit calculated by excluding those optional fees, and the available credit including those optional fees. The creditor shall also disclose that the consumer has the right to reject the plan and not be obligated to pay those fees or any other fee or charges until the consumer has used the account or made a payment on the account after receiving a periodic statement. This paragraph does not apply with respect to fees or security deposits that are not debited to the account. . . .

§ 1026.51   Ability to Pay.

(a) General rule.

(1)(i) Consideration of ability to pay. A card issuer must not open a credit card account for a consumer under an open-end (not home-secured) consumer credit plan, or increase any credit limit applicable to such account, unless the card issuer considers the consumer's independent ability to make the required minimum periodic payments under the terms of the account based on the consumer's income or assets and current obligations.

(ii) Reasonable policies and procedures. Card issuers must establish and maintain reasonable written policies and procedures to consider a consumer's independent income or assets and current obligations. Reasonable policies and procedures to consider a consumer's independent ability to make the required payments include the consideration of at least one of the following: The ratio of debt obligations to income; the ratio of debt obligations to assets; or the income the consumer will have after paying debt obligations. It would be unreasonable for a card issuer to not review any information about a consumer's income, assets, or current obligations, or to issue a credit card to a consumer who does not have any independent income or assets.

(2)   Minimum periodic payments.

(i)   Reasonable method. For purposes of paragraph (a)(1) of this section, a card issuer must use a reasonable method for estimating the minimum periodic payments the consumer would be required to pay under the terms of the account.

(ii)   Safe harbor. A card issuer complies with paragraph (a)(2)(i) of this section if it estimates required minimum periodic payments using the following method:

(A)   The card issuer assumes utilization, from the first day of the billing cycle, of the full credit line that the issuer is considering offering to the consumer; and

(B)   The card issuer uses a minimum payment formula employed by the issuer for the product the issuer is considering offering to the consumer or, in the case of an existing account, the minimum payment formula that currently applies to that account, provided that;

(1)   If the applicable minimum payment formula includes interest charges, the card issuer estimates those charges using an interest rate that the issuer is considering offering to the consumer for purchases or, in the case of an existing account, the interest rate that currently applies to purchases; and

(2)   If the applicable minimum payment formula includes mandatory fees, the card issuer must assume that such fees have been charged to the account.

(b)   Rules affecting young consumers.

(1)   Applications from young consumers. A card issuer may not open a credit card account under an open-end (not home-secured) consumer credit plan for a consumer less than 21 years old, unless the consumer has submitted a written application and the card issuer has:

(i)   Financial information indicating the consumer has an independent ability to make the required minimum periodic payments on the proposed extension of credit in connection with the account, consistent with paragraph (a) of this section; or

(ii)   (A)   A signed agreement of a cosigner, guarantor, or joint applicant who is at least 21 years old to be either secondarily liable for any debt on the account incurred by the consumer before the consumer has attained the age of 21 or jointly liable with the consumer for any debt on the account, and

(B)   Financial information indicating such cosigner, guarantor, or joint applicant has the independent ability to make the required minimum periodic payments on such debts, consistent with paragraph (a) of this section.

(2)   Credit line increases for young consumers. If a credit card account has been opened pursuant to paragraph (b)(l)(ii) of this section, no increase in the credit limit may be made on such account before the consumer attains the age of 21 unless the cosigner, guarantor, or joint accountholder who assumed liability at account opening agrees in writing to assume liability on the increase.

§ 1026.53   Allocation of Payments.

(a)   General rule. Except as provided in paragraph (b) of this section, when a consumer makes a payment in excess of the required minimum periodic payment for a credit card account under an open-end (not home-secured) consumer credit plan, the card issuer must allocate the excess amount first to the balance with the highest annual percentage rate and any remaining portion to the other balances in descending order based on the applicable annual percentage rate. . . .

§ 1026.55 Limitations on Increasing Annual Percentage Rates, Fees, and Charges.

(a) General rule. Except as provided in paragraph (b) of this section, a card issuer must not increase an annual percentage rate or a fee or charge required to be disclosed under § 1026.6(b)(2)(ii), (b)(2)(iii), or (b)(2)(xii) on a credit card account under an open-end (not home-secured) consumer credit plan.

(b) Exceptions. A card issuer may increase an annual percentage rate or a fee or charge required to be disclosed under § 1026.6(b)(2)(H), (b)(2)(iii), or (b)(2)(xii) pursuant to an exception set forth in this paragraph even if that increase would not be permitted under a different exception.

(1) Temporary rate, fee, or charge exception. A card issuer may increase an annual percentage rate or a fee or charge required to be disclosed under § 1026.6(b)(2)(ii), (b)(2)(iii), or (b)(2)(xii) upon the expiration of a specified period of six months or longer, provided that:

(i) Prior to the commencement of that period, the card issuer disclosed in writing to the consumer, in a clear and conspicuous manner, the length of the period and the annual percentage rate, fee, or charge that would apply after expiration of the period; and

(ii) Upon expiration of the specified period:

(A) The card issuer must not apply an annual percentage rate, fee, or charge to transactions that occurred prior to the period that exceeds the annual percentage rate, fee, or charge that applied to those transactions prior to the period;

(B) If the disclosures required by paragraph (b)(*l*)(i) of this section are provided pursuant to § 1026.9(c), the card issuer must not apply an annual percentage rate, fee, or charge to transactions that occurred within 14 days after provision of the notice that exceeds the annual percentage rate, fee, or charge that applied to that category of transactions prior to provision of the notice; and

(C) The card issuer must not apply an annual percentage rate, fee, or charge to transactions that occurred during the period that exceeds the increased annual percentage rate, fee, or charge disclosed pursuant to paragraph (b)(*l*)(i) of this section.

(2) Variable rate exception. A card issuer may increase an annual percentage rate when:

(i) The annual percentage rate varies according to an index that is not under the card issuer's control and is available to the general public; and

(ii) The increase in the annual percentage rate is due to an increase in the index.

(3) *Advance notice exception.* A card issuer may increase an annual percentage rate or a fee or charge required to be disclosed under § 1026.6(b)(2)(ii), (b)(2)(iii), or (b)(2)(xii) after complying with the applicable notice requirements in § 1026.9(b), (c), or (g), provided that:

(i) If a card issuer discloses an increased annual percentage rate, fee, or charge pursuant to § 1026.9(b), the card issuer must not apply that rate, fee, or charge to transactions that occurred prior to provision of the notice;

(ii) If a card issuer discloses an increased annual percentage rate, fee, or charge pursuant to § 1026.9(c) or (g), the card issuer must not apply that rate, fee, or charge to transactions that occurred prior to or within 14 days after provision of the notice; and

(iii) This exception does not permit a card issuer to increase an annual percentage rate or a fee or charge required to be disclosed under § 1026.6(b)(2)(ii), (iii), or (xii) during the first year after the account is opened, while the account is closed, or while the card issuer does not permit the consumer to use the account for new transactions. For purposes of this paragraph, an account is considered open no earlier than the date on which the account may first be used by the consumer to engage in transactions.

(4)　*Delinquency exception.* A card issuer may increase an annual percentage rate or a fee or charge required to be disclosed under § 1026.6(b)(2)(ii), (b)(2)(iii), or (b)(2)(xii) due to the card issuer not receiving the consumer's required minimum periodic payment within 60 days after the due date for that payment, provided that:

(i)　The card issuer must disclose in a clear and conspicuous manner in the notice of the increase pursuant to § 1026.9(c) or (g):

(A)　A statement of the reason for the increase; and

(B)　That the increased annual percentage rate, fee, or charge will cease to apply if the card issuer receives six consecutive required minimum periodic payments on or before the payment due date beginning with the first payment due following the effective date of the increase; and

(ii)　If the card issuer receives six consecutive required minimum periodic payments on or before the payment due date beginning with the first payment due following the effective date of the increase, the card issuer must reduce any annual percentage rate, fee, or charge increased pursuant to this exception to the annual percentage rate, fee, or charge that applied prior to the increase with respect to transactions that occurred prior to or within 14 days after provision of the § 1026.9(c) or (g) notice.

(5)　Workout and temporary hardship arrangement exception. A card issuer may increase an annual percentage rate or a fee or charge required to be disclosed under § 1026.6(b)(2)(ii), (b)(2)(iii), or (b)(2)(xii) due to the consumer's completion of a workout or temporary hardship arrangement or the consumer's failure to comply with the terms of such an arrangement, provided that:

(i)　Prior to commencement of the arrangement (except as provided in § 1026.9(c) (2)(v)(D)), the card issuer has provided the consumer with a clear and conspicuous written disclosure of the terms of the arrangement (including any increases due to the completion or failure of the arrangement); and

(ii)　Upon the completion or failure of the arrangement, the card issuer must not apply to any transactions that occurred prior to commencement of the arrangement an annual percentage rate, fee, or charge that exceeds the annual percentage rate, fee, or charge that applied to those transactions prior to commencement of the arrangement. . . .

§ 1026.57　Reporting and Marketing Rules for College Student Open-End Credit.

(a)　Definitions.

(1)　College student credit card. The term "college student credit card" as used in this section means a credit card issued under a credit card account under an open-end (not home-secured) consumer credit plan to any college student.

(2)　College student. The term "college student" as used in this section means a consumer who is a full-time or part-time student of an institution of higher education.

(3)　Institution of higher education. The term "institution of higher education" as used in this section has the same meaning as in sections 101 and 102 of the Higher Education Act of 1965 (20 U.S.C. 1001 and 1002).

(4)　Affiliated organization. The term "affiliated organization" as used in this section means an alumni organization or foundation affiliated with or related to an institution of higher education.

(5)   College credit card agreement. The term "college credit card agreement" as used in this section means any business, marketing or promotional agreement between a card issuer and an institution of higher education or an affiliated organization in connection with which college student credit cards are issued to college students currently enrolled at that institution.

(b)   Public disclosure of agreements. An institution of higher education shall publicly disclose any contract or other agreement made with a card issuer or creditor for the purpose of marketing a credit card.

(c)   Prohibited inducements. No card issuer or creditor may offer a college student any tangible item to induce such student to apply for or open an open-end consumer credit plan offered by such card issuer or creditor, if such offer is made:

(1)   On the campus of an institution of higher education;

(2)   Near the campus of an institution of higher education; or

(3)   At an event sponsored by or related to an institution of higher education.

. . .

§ 1026.60   Credit and Charge Card Applications and Solicitations.

(a)   General rules. The card issuer shall provide the disclosures required under this section on or with a solicitation or an application to open a credit or charge card account.

(1)   Definition of solicitation. For purposes of this section, the term solicitation means an offer by the card issuer to open a credit or charge card account that does not require the consumer to complete an application. A "firm offer of credit" as defined in section 603(1) of the Fair Credit Reporting Act (15 U.S.C. 1681a(1)) for a credit or charge card is a solicitation for purposes of this section.

(2)   Form of disclosures; tabular format.

(i)   The disclosures in paragraphs (b)(1) through (5) (except for (b)(*l*)(iv)(B)) and (b)(7) through (15) of this section made pursuant to paragraph (c), (d)(2), (e)(1) or (f) of this section generally shall be in the form of a table with headings, content, and format substantially similar to any of the applicable tables found in G–10 in Appendix G to this part.

(ii)   The table described in paragraph (a)(2)(i) of this section shall contain only the information required or permitted by this section. Other information may be presented on or with an application or solicitation, provided such information appears outside the required table.

(iii)   Disclosures required by paragraphs (b)(1)(iv)(B), (b)(*l*)(iv)(C) and (b)(6) of this section must be placed directly beneath the table.

(iv)   When a tabular format is required, any annual percentage rate required to be disclosed pursuant to paragraph (b)(1) of this section, any introductory rate required to be disclosed pursuant to paragraph (b)(*l*)(ii) of this section, any rate that will apply after a premium initial rate expires required to be disclosed under paragraph (b)(*l*)(iii) of this section, and any fee or percentage amounts or maximum limits on fee amounts disclosed pursuant to paragraphs (b)(2), (b)(4), (b)(8) through (b)(13) of this section must be disclosed in bold text. However, bold text shall not be used for: The amount of any periodic fee disclosed pursuant to paragraph (b)(2) of this section that is not an annualized amount; and other annual percentage rates or fee amounts disclosed in the table.

(v)   For an application or a solicitation that is accessed by the consumer in electronic form, the disclosures required under this section may be provided to the consumer in electronic form on or with the application or solicitation.

(vi) (A) Except as provided in paragraph (a)(2)(vi)(B) of this section, the table described in paragraph (a)(2)(i) of this section must be provided in a prominent location on or with an application or a solicitation.

(B) If the table described in paragraph (a)(2)(i) of this section is provided electronically, it must be provided in close proximity to the application or solicitation.

(3) *Fees based on a percentage.* If the amount of any fee required to be disclosed under this section is determined on the basis of a percentage of another amount, the percentage used and the identification of the amount against which the percentage is applied may be disclosed instead of the amount of the fee.

(4) *Fees that vary by state.* Card issuers that impose fees referred to in paragraphs (b)(8) through (12) of this section that vary by state may, at the issuer's option, disclose in the table required by paragraph (a)(2)(i) of this section: The specific fee applicable to the consumer's account; or the range of the fees, if the disclosure includes a statement that the amount of the fee varies by state and refers the consumer to a disclosure provided with the table where the amount of the fee applicable to the consumer's account is disclosed. A card issuer may not list fees for multiple states in the table.

(5) *Exceptions.* This section does not apply to:

(i) Home-equity plans accessible by a credit or charge card that are subject to the requirements of § 1026.40;

(ii) Overdraft lines of credit tied to asset accounts accessed by check-guarantee cards or by debit cards;

(iii) Lines of credit accessed by check-guarantee cards or by debit cards that can be used only at automated teller machines;

(iv) Lines of credit accessed solely by account numbers;

(v) Additions of a credit or charge card to an existing open-end plan;

(vi) General purpose applications unless the application, or material accompanying it, indicates that it can be used to open a credit or charge card account; or

(vii) Consumer-initiated requests for applications.

(b) *Required disclosures.* The card issuer shall disclose the items in this paragraph on or with an application or a solicitation in accordance with the requirements of paragraphs (c), (d), (e)(1) or (f) of this section. A credit card issuer shall disclose all applicable items in this paragraph except for paragraph (b)(7) of this section. A charge card issuer shall disclose the applicable items in paragraphs (b)(2), (4), (7) through (12), and (15) of this section.

(1) *Annual percentage rate.* Each periodic rate that may be used to compute the finance charge on an outstanding balance for purchases, a cash advance, or a balance transfer, expressed as an annual percentage rate (as determined by § 1026.14(b)). When more than one rate applies for a category of transactions, the range of balances to which each rate is applicable shall also be disclosed. The annual percentage rate for purchases disclosed pursuant to this paragraph shall be in at least 16-point type, except for the following: Oral disclosures of the annual percentage rate for purchases; or a penalty rate that may apply upon the occurrence of one or more specific events.

(i) *Variable rate information.* If a rate disclosed under paragraph (b)(1) of this section is a variable rate, the card issuer shall also disclose the fact that the rate may vary and how the rate is determined. In describing how the applicable rate will be determined, the card issuer must identify the type of index or formula that is used in setting the rate. The value of the index and the amount of the margin that are used to calculate the variable rate shall not be disclosed in the table. A disclosure of any applicable limitations on rate increases shall not be included in the table.

(ii) Discounted initial rate. If the initial rate is an introductory rate, as that term is defined in § 1026.16(g)(2)(ii), the card issuer must disclose in the table the introductory rate, the time period during which the introductory rate will remain in effect, and must use the term "introductory" or "intro" in immediate proximity to the introductory rate. The card issuer also must disclose the rate that would otherwise apply to the account pursuant to paragraph (b)(1) of this section. Where the rate is not tied to an index or formula, the card issuer must disclose the rate that will apply after the introductory rate expires. In a variable-rate account, the card issuer must disclose a rate based on the applicable index or formula in accordance with the accuracy requirements set forth in paragraphs (c)(2), (d)(3), or (e)(4) of this section, as applicable.

(iii) Premium initial rate. If the initial rate is temporary and is higher than the rate that will apply after the temporary rate expires, the card issuer must disclose the premium initial rate pursuant to paragraph (b)(1) of this section and the time period during which the premium initial rate will remain in effect. Consistent with paragraph (b)(1) of this section, the premium initial rate for purchases must be in at least 16-point type. The issuer must also disclose in the table the rate that will apply after the premium initial rate expires, in at least 16-point type.

(iv) Penalty rates.

    (A) In general. Except as provided in paragraph (b)(*l*)(iv)(B) and (C) of this section, if a rate may increase as a penalty for one or more events specified in the account agreement, such as a late payment or an extension of credit that exceeds the credit limit, the card issuer must disclose pursuant to this paragraph (b)(1) the increased rate that may apply, a brief description of the event or events that may result in the increased rate, and a brief description of how long the increased rate will remain in effect.

    (B) Introductory rates. If the issuer discloses an introductory rate, as that term is defined in § 1026.16(g)(2)(ii), in the table or in any written or electronic promotional materials accompanying applications or solicitations subject to paragraph (c) or (e) of this section, the issuer must briefly disclose directly beneath the table the circumstances, if any, under which the introductory rate may be revoked, and the type of rate that will apply after the introductory rate is revoked.

    (C) Employee preferential rates. If a card issuer discloses in the table a preferential annual percentage rate for which only employees of the card issuer, employees of a third party, or other individuals with similar affiliations with the card issuer or third party, such as executive officers, directors, or principal shareholders are eligible, the card issuer must briefly disclose directly beneath the table the circumstances under which such preferential rate may be revoked, and the rate that will apply after such preferential rate is revoked.

(v) Rates that depend on consumer's creditworthiness: If a rate cannot be determined at the time disclosures are given because the rate depends, at least in part, on a later determination of the consumer's creditworthiness, the card issuer must disclose the specific rates or the range of rates that could apply and a statement that the rate for which the consumer may qualify at account opening will depend on the consumer's creditworthiness, and other factors if applicable. If the rate that depends, at least in part, on a later determination of the consumer's creditworthiness is a penalty rate, as described in paragraph (b)(*l*)(iv) of this section, the card issuer at its option may disclose the highest rate that could apply, instead of disclosing the specific rates or the range of rates that could apply.

(vi)   APRs that vary by state. Issuers imposing annual percentage rates that vary by state may, at the issuer's option, disclose in the table: the specific annual percentage rate applicable to the consumer's account; or the range of the annual percentage rates, if the disclosure includes a statement that the annual percentage rate varies by state and refers the consumer to a disclosure provided with the table where the annual percentage rate applicable to the consumer's account is disclosed, A card issuer may not list annual percentage rates for multiple states in the table.

(2)   Fees for issuance or availability.

(i)   Any annual or other periodic fee that may be imposed for the issuance or availability of a credit or charge card, including any fee based on account activity or inactivity; how frequently it will be imposed; and the annualized amount of the fee.

(ii)   Any non-periodic fee that relates to opening an account. A card issuer must disclose that the fee is a one-time fee.

(3)   Fixed finance charge; minimum interest charge. Any fixed finance charge and a brief description of the charge. Any minimum interest charge if it exceeds $1.00 that could be imposed during a billing cycle, and a brief description of the charge. The $ 1.00 threshold amount shall be adjusted periodically by the Bureau to reflect changes in the Consumer Price Index. The Bureau shall calculate each year a price level adjusted minimum interest charge using the Consumer Price Index in effect on June 1 of that year. When the cumulative change in the adjusted minimum value derived from applying the annual Consumer Price level to the current minimum interest charge threshold has risen by a whole dollar, the minimum interest charge will be increased by $1.00. The issuer may, at its option, disclose in the table minimum interest charges below this threshold.

(4)   Transaction charges. Any transaction charge imposed by the card issuer for the use of the card for purchases.

(5)   Grace period. The date by which or the period within which any credit extended for purchases may be repaid without incurring a finance charge due to a periodic interest rate and any conditions on the availability of the grace period. If no grace period is provided, that fact must be disclosed. If the length of the grace period varies, the card issuer may disclose the range of days, the minimum number of days, or the average number of days in the grace period, if the disclosure is identified as a range, minimum, or average. In disclosing in the tabular format a grace period that applies to all types of purchases, the phrase "How to Avoid Paying Interest on Purchases" shall be used as the heading for the row describing the grace period. If a grace period is not offered on all types of purchases, in disclosing this fact in the tabular format, the phrase "Paying Interest" shall be used as the heading for the row describing this fact.

(6)   Balance computation method. The name of the balance computation method listed in paragraph (g) of this section that is used to determine the balance for purchases on which the finance charge is computed, or an explanation of the method used if it is not listed. In determining which balance computation method to disclose, the card issuer shall assume that credit extended for purchases will not be repaid within the grace period, if any.

(7)   Statement on charge card payments. A statement that charges incurred by use of the charge card are due when the periodic statement is received.

(8)   Cash advance fee. Any fee imposed for an extension of credit in the form of cash or its equivalent.

(9)   Late payment fee. Any fee imposed for a late payment. . . .

(c)   Direct mail and electronic applications and solicitations.

    (1)   General. The card issuer shall disclose the applicable items in paragraph (b) of this section on or with an application or solicitation that is mailed to consumers or provided to consumers in electronic form.

    (2)   Accuracy.

        (i)   Disclosures in direct mail applications and solicitations must be accurate as of the time the disclosures are mailed. An accurate variable annual percentage rate is one in effect within 60 days before mailing.

        (ii)   Disclosures provided in electronic form must be accurate as of the time they are sent, in the case of disclosures sent to a consumer's email address, or as of the time they are viewed by the public, in the case of disclosures made available at a location such as a card issuer's Web site. An accurate variable annual percentage rate provided in electronic form is one in effect within 30 days before it is sent to a consumer's email address, or viewed by the public, as applicable. . . .

(e)   Applications and solicitations made available to general public. The card issuer shall provide disclosures, to the extent applicable, on or with an application or solicitation that is made available to the general public, including one contained in a catalog, magazine, or other generally available publication. The disclosures shall be provided in accordance with paragraph (e)(1) or (e)(2) of this section.

    (1)   Disclosure of required credit information. The card issuer may disclose in a prominent location on the application or solicitation the following:

        (i)   The applicable information in paragraph (b) of this section;

        (ii)   The date the required information was printed, including a statement that the required information was accurate as of that date and is subject to change after that date; and

        (iii)   A statement that the consumer should contact the card issuer for any change in the required information since it was printed, and a toll-free telephone number or a mailing address for that purpose.

    (2)   No disclosure of credit information. If none of the items in paragraph (b) of this section is provided on or with the application or solicitation, the card issuer may state in a prominent location on the application or solicitation the following:

        (i)   There are costs associated with the use of the card; and

        (ii)   The consumer may contact the card issuer to request specific information about the costs, along with a toll-tree telephone number and a mailing address for that purpose.

    (3)   Prompt response to requests for information. Upon receiving a request for any of the information referred to in this paragraph, the card issuer shall promptly and fully disclose the information requested.

    (4)   Accuracy. The disclosures given pursuant to paragraph (e)(1) of this section must be accurate as of the date of printing. A variable annual percentage rate is accurate if it was in effect within 30 days before printing.

(f)   In-person applications and solicitations. A card issuer shall disclose the information in paragraph (b) of this section, to the extent applicable, on or with an application or solicitation that is initiated by the card issuer and given to the consumer in person. A card issuer complies with the requirements of this paragraph if the issuer provides disclosures in accordance with paragraph (c)(1) or (e)(1) of this section. . . .

UNITED STATES ARBITRATION ACT

(1925)

[Arbitration is a private dispute settlement procedure that is an alternative to litigating contract and other disputes in courts. It is available to parties when they agree to arbitrate a dispute between them, as by including an arbitration clause in their contract. Prior to enactment of the United States Arbitration Act (better known as the "Federal Arbitration Act" or "FAA"), 9 U.S.C. §§ 1 *et seq.*, courts often refused to enforce pre-dispute agreements to arbitrate on the ground that enforcement would "oust the courts of jurisdiction." The FAA changes that approach by requiring the courts to enforce written agreements to arbitrate, "save upon such grounds as exist at law or in equity for the revocation of any contract." *Id.* § 2. State contract law determines whether such grounds exist. The FAA governs enforcement and other matters pertaining to arbitration. Thus, it requires courts to enforce valid agreements to arbitrate by issuing stays of litigation and/or orders compelling arbitration. It also makes arbitration awards enforceable as though they were judicial judgments. The FAA applies to all transactions affecting interstate or foreign commerce, and it preempts inconsistent state arbitration law. Both federal and state courts must apply the FAA.]

CHAPTER 1. GENERAL PROVISIONS

CHAPTER 2. CONVENTION ON THE RECOGNITION AND ENFORCEMENT OF FOREIGN ARBITRAL AWARDS

Chapter 1. General Provisions

§ 1. "Maritime Transactions" and "Commerce" Defined; Exceptions to Operation of Title.

"Maritime transactions", as herein defined, means charter parties, bills of lading of water carriers, agreements relating to wharfage, supplies furnished vessels or repairs to vessels, collisions, or any other matters in foreign commerce which, if the subject of controversy, would be embraced within admiralty jurisdiction; "commerce", as herein defined, means commerce among the several States or with foreign nations, or in any Territory of the United States or in the District of Columbia, or between any such Territory and another, or between any such Territory and any State or foreign nation, or between the District of Columbia and any State or Territory or foreign nation, but nothing herein contained shall apply to contracts of employment of seamen, railroad employees, or any other class of workers engaged in foreign or interstate commerce.

§ 2. Validity, Irrevocability, and Enforcement of Agreements to Arbitrate.

A written provision in any maritime transaction or a contract evidencing a transaction involving commerce to settle by arbitration a controversy thereafter arising out of such contract or transaction, or the refusal to perform the whole or any part thereof, or an agreement in writing to submit to arbitration an existing controversy arising out of such a contract, transaction, or refusal, shall be valid, irrevocable, and enforceable, save upon such grounds as exist at law or in equity for the revocation of any contract.

§ 3. Stay of Proceedings Where Issue Therein Referable to Arbitration.

If any suit or proceeding be brought in any of the courts of the United States upon any issue referable to arbitration under an agreement in writing for such arbitration, the court in which such suit is pending, upon being satisfied that the issue involved in such suit or proceeding is referable to arbitration under such an agreement, shall on application of one of the parties stay the trial of the action until such arbitration has been had in accordance with the terms of the agreement, providing the applicant for the stay is not in default in proceeding with such arbitration.

§ 4. Failure to Arbitrate Under Agreement; Petition to United States Court Having Jurisdiction for Order to Compel Arbitration; Notice and Service Thereof; Hearing and Determination.

A party aggrieved by the alleged failure, neglect, or refusal of another to arbitrate under a written agreement for arbitration may petition any United States district court which, save for such agreement, would have jurisdiction under Title 28, in a civil action or in admiralty of the subject matter of a suit arising out of the controversy between the parties, for an order directing that such arbitration proceed in the manner provided for in such agreement. Five days' notice in writing of such application shall be served upon the party in default. Service thereof shall be made in the manner provided by the Federal Rules of Civil Procedure. The court shall hear the parties, and upon being satisfied that the making of the agreement for arbitration or the failure to comply therewith is not in issue, the court shall make an order directing the parties to proceed to arbitration in accordance with the terms of the agreement. The hearing and proceedings, under such agreement, shall be within the district in which the petition for an order directing such arbitration is filed. If the making of the arbitration agreement or the failure, neglect, or refusal to perform the same be in issue, the court shall proceed summarily to the trial thereof. If no jury trial be demanded by the party alleged to be in default, or if the matter in dispute is within admiralty jurisdiction, the court shall hear and determine such issue. Where such an issue is raised, the party alleged to be in default may, except in cases of admiralty, on or before the return day of the notice of application, demand a jury trial of such issue, and upon such demand the court shall make an order referring the issue or issues to a jury in the manner provided by the Federal Rules of Civil Procedure, or may specially call a jury for that purpose. If the jury find that no agreement in writing for arbitration was made or that there is no default in proceeding thereunder, the proceeding shall be dismissed. If the jury find that an agreement for arbitration was made in writing and that there is a default in proceeding thereunder, the court shall make an order summarily directing the parties to proceed with the arbitration in accordance with the terms thereof.

§ 5.   Appointment of Arbitrators or Umpire.

If in the agreement provision be made for a method of naming or appointing an arbitrator or arbitrators or an umpire, such method shall be followed; but if no method be provided therein, or if a method be provided and any party thereto shall fail to avail himself of such method, or if for any other reason there shall be a lapse in the naming of an arbitrator or arbitrators or umpire, or in filling a vacancy, then upon the application of either party to the controversy the court shall designate and appoint an arbitrator or arbitrators or umpire, as the case may require, who shall act under the said agreement with the same force and effect as if he or they had been specifically named therein; and unless otherwise provided in the agreement the arbitration shall be by a single arbitrator.

§ 6.   Application Heard as Motion.

Any application to the court hereunder shall be made and heard in the manner provided by law for the making and hearing of motions, except as otherwise herein expressly provided.

§ 7.   Witnesses Before Arbitrators; Fees; Compelling Attendance.

The arbitrators selected either as prescribed in this title or otherwise, or a majority of them, may summon in writing any person to attend before them or any of them as a witness and in a proper case to bring with him or them any book, record, document, or paper which may be deemed material as evidence in the case. The fees for such attendance shall be the same as the fees of witnesses before masters of the United States courts. Said summons shall issue in the name of the arbitrator or arbitrators, or a majority of them, and shall be signed by the arbitrators, or a majority of them, and shall be directed to the said person and shall be served in the same manner as subpoenas to appear and testify before the court; if any person or persons so summoned to testify shall refuse or neglect to obey said summons, upon petition the United States district court for the district in which such arbitrators, or a majority of them, are sitting may compel the attendance of such person or persons before said arbitrator or arbitrators, or punish said person or persons for contempt in the same manner provided by law for securing the attendance of witnesses or their punishment for neglect or refusal to attend in the courts of the United States.

§ 8.   Proceedings Begun by Libel in Admiralty and Seizure of Vessel or Property.

If the basis of jurisdiction be a cause of action otherwise justiciable in admiralty, then, notwithstanding anything herein to the contrary, the party claiming to be aggrieved may begin his proceeding hereunder by libel and seizure of the vessel or other property of the other party according to the usual course of admiralty proceedings, and the court shall then have jurisdiction to direct the parties to proceed with the arbitration and shall retain jurisdiction to enter its decree upon the award.

§ 9.   Award of Arbitrators; Confirmation; Jurisdiction; Procedure.

If the parties in their agreement have agreed that a judgment of the court shall be entered upon the award made pursuant to the arbitration, and shall specify the court, then at any time within one year after the award is made any party to the arbitration may apply to the court so specified for an order confirming the award, and thereupon the court must grant such an order unless the award is vacated, modified, or corrected as prescribed in sections 10 and 11 of this title. If no court is specified in the agreement of the parties, then such application may be made to the United States court in and for the district within which such award was made. Notice of the application shall be served upon the adverse party, and thereupon the court shall have jurisdiction of such party as though he had appeared generally in the proceeding. If the adverse party is a resident of the district within which the award was made, such service shall be made upon the adverse party or his attorney as prescribed by law for service of notice of motion in an action in the same court. If the adverse party shall be a nonresident, then the notice of the application shall be served by the marshal of any district within which the adverse party may be found in like manner as other process of the court.

§ 10.   Same; Vacation; Grounds; Rehearing.

(a) In any of the following cases the United States court in and for the district wherein the award was made may make an order vacating the award upon the application of any party to the arbitration—

     (1) where the award was procured by corruption, fraud, or undue means;

     (2) where there was evident partiality or corruption in the arbitrators, or either of them;

     (3) where the arbitrators were guilty of misconduct in refusing to postpone the hearing, upon sufficient cause shown, or in refusing to hear evidence pertinent and material to the controversy; or of any other misbehavior by which the rights of any party have been prejudiced; or

     (4) where the arbitrators exceeded their powers, or so imperfectly executed them that a mutual, final, and definite award upon the subject matter submitted was not made.

(b) If an award is vacated and the time within which the agreement required the award to be made has not expired, the court may, in its discretion, direct a rehearing by the arbitrators.

(c) The United States district court for the district wherein an award was made that was issued pursuant to section 580 of title 5 may make an order vacating the award upon the application of a person, other than a party to the arbitration, who is adversely affected or aggrieved by the award, if the use of arbitration or the award is clearly inconsistent with the factors set forth in section 572 of title 5.

§ 11.   Same; Modification or Correction; Grounds; Order.

In either of the following cases the United States court in and for the district wherein the award was made may make an order modifying or correcting the award upon the application of any party to the arbitration—

(a) Where there was an evident material miscalculation of figures or an evident material mistake in the description of any person, thing, or property referred to in the award.

(b) Where the arbitrators have awarded upon a matter not submitted to them, unless it is a matter not affecting the merits of the decision upon the matter submitted.

(c) Where the award is imperfect in matter of form not affecting the merits of the controversy.

The order may modify and correct the award, so as to effect the intent thereof and promote justice between the parties.

§ 12.   Notice of Motions to Vacate or Modify; Service; Stay of Proceedings.

Notice of a motion to vacate, modify, or correct an award must be served upon the adverse party or his attorney within three months after the award is filed or delivered. If the adverse party is a resident of the district within which the award was made, such service shall be made upon the adverse party or his attorney as prescribed by law for service of notice of motion in an action in the same court. If the adverse party shall be a nonresident then the notice of the application shall be served by the marshal of any district within which the adverse party may be found in like manner as other process of the court. For the purposes of the motion any judge who might make an order to stay the proceedings in an action brought in the same court may make an order, to be served with the notice of motion, staying the proceedings of the adverse party to enforce the award.

§ 13.   Papers Filed With Order on Motions; Judgment; Docketing; Force and Effect; Enforcement.

The party moving for an order confirming, modifying, or correcting an award shall, at the time such order is filed with the clerk for the entry of judgment thereon, also file the following papers with the clerk:

(a) The agreement; the selection or appointment, if any, of an additional arbitrator or umpire; and each written extension of the time, if any, within which to make the award.

(b) The award.

(c) Each notice, affidavit, or other paper used upon an application to confirm, modify, or correct the award, and a copy of each order of the court upon such an application.

The judgment shall be docketed as if it was rendered in an action.

The judgment so entered shall have the same force and effect, in all respects, as, and be subject to all the provisions of law relating to, a judgment in an action; and it may be enforced as if it had been rendered in an action in the court in which it is entered.

§ 14.   Contracts Not Affected.

This title shall not apply to contracts made prior to January 1, 1926.

§ 15.   Inapplicability of the Act of State Doctrine.

Enforcement of arbitral agreements, confirmation of arbitral awards, and execution upon judgments based on orders confirming such awards shall not be refused on the basis of the Act of State doctrine.

§ 16.   Appeals.

(a) An appeal may be taken from—

    (1) an order—

    (A)   refusing a stay of any action under section 3 of this title,

    (B)   denying a petition under section 4 of this title to order arbitration to proceed,

    (C)   denying an application under section 206 of this title to compel arbitration,

    (D)   confirming or denying confirmation of an award or partial award, or

    (E)   modifying, correcting, or vacating an award;

  (2)   an interlocutory order granting, continuing, or modifying an injunction against an arbitration that is subject to this title; or

  (3)   a final decision with respect to an arbitration that is subject to this title.

  (b)   Except as otherwise provided in section 1292(b) of title 28, an appeal may not be taken from an interlocutory order—

  (1)   granting a stay of any action under section 3 of this title;

  (2)   directing arbitration to proceed under section 4 of this title;

  (3)   compelling arbitration under section 206 of this title; or

  (4)   refusing to enjoin an arbitration that is subject to this title.

Chapter 2. Convention on the Recognition and Enforcement of Foreign Arbitral Awards

§ 201. Enforcement of Convention.

The Convention on the Recognition and Enforcement of Foreign Arbitral Awards of June 10, 1958, shall be enforced in United States courts in accordance with this chapter.

§ 202. Agreement or Award Falling Under the Convention.

An arbitration agreement or arbitral award arising out of a legal relationship, whether contractual or not, which is considered as commercial, including a transaction, contract, or agreement described in section 2 of this title, falls under the Convention. An agreement or award arising out of such a relationship which is entirely between citizens of the United States shall be deemed not to fall under the Convention unless that relationship involves property located abroad, envisages performance or enforcement abroad, or has some other reasonable relation with one or more foreign states. For the purpose of this section a corporation is a citizen of the United States if it is incorporated or has its principal place of business in the United States.

§ 203. Jurisdiction; Amount in Controversy.

An action or proceeding falling under the Convention shall be deemed to arise under the laws and treaties of the United States. The district courts of the United States (including the courts enumerated in section 460 of title 28) shall have original jurisdiction over such an action or proceeding, regardless of the amount in controversy.

§ 204. Venue.

An action or proceeding over which the district courts have jurisdiction pursuant to section 203 of this title may be brought in any such court in which save for the arbitration agreement an action or proceeding with respect to the controversy between the parties could be brought, or in such court for the district and division which embraces the place designated in the agreement as the place of arbitration if such place is within the United States.

§ 205. Removal of Cases From State Courts.

Where the subject matter of an action or proceeding pending in a State court relates to an arbitration agreement or award falling under the Convention, the defendant or the defendants may, at any time before the trial thereof, remove such action or proceeding to the district court of the United States for the district and division embracing the place where the action or proceeding is pending. The procedure for removal of causes otherwise provided by law shall apply, except that the ground for removal provided in this section need not appear on the face of the complaint but may be shown in the petition for removal. For the purposes of Chapter 1 of this title any action or proceeding removed under this section shall be deemed to have been brought in the district court to which it is removed.

§ 206. Order to Compel Arbitration; Appointment of Arbitrators.

A court having jurisdiction under this chapter may direct that arbitration be held in accordance with the agreement at any place therein provided for, whether that place is within or without the United States. Such court may also appoint arbitrators in accordance with the provisions of the agreement.

§ 207. Award of Arbitrators; Confirmation; Jurisdiction; Proceeding.

Within three years after an arbitral award falling under the Convention is made, any party to the arbitration may apply to any court having jurisdiction under this chapter for an order confirming the award as against any other party to the arbitration. The court shall confirm the award unless it finds one of the grounds for refusal or deferral of recognition or enforcement of the award specified in the said Convention.

§ 208. Chapter 1; Residual Application.

Chapter 1 applies to actions and proceedings brought under this chapter to the extent that chapter is not in conflict with this chapter or the Convention as ratified by the United States.

Chapter 3. Inter-American Convention on
International Commercial Arbitration

§ 301. Enforcement of Convention.

The Inter-American Convention on International Commercial Arbitration of January 30, 1975, shall be enforced in United States courts in accordance with this chapter.

§ 302. Incorporation by Reference.

Sections 202, 203, 204, 205, and 207 of this title shall apply to this chapter as if specifically set forth herein, except that for the purposes of this chapter "the Convention" shall mean the Inter-American Convention.

§ 303. Order to Compel Arbitration; Appointment of Arbitrators; Locale.

(a) A court having jurisdiction under this chapter may direct that arbitration be held in accordance with the agreement at any place therein provided for, whether that place is within or without the United States. The court may also appoint arbitrators in accordance with the provisions of the agreement.

(b) In the event the agreement does not make provision for the place of arbitration or the appointment of arbitrators, the court shall direct that the arbitration shall be held and the arbitrators be appointed in accordance with Article 3 of the Inter-American Convention.

§ 304. Recognition and Enforcement of Foreign Arbitral Decisions and Awards; Reciprocity.

Arbitral decisions or awards made in the territory of a foreign State shall, on the basis of reciprocity, be recognized and enforced under this chapter only if that State has ratified or acceded to the Inter-American Convention.

§ 305. Relationship Between the Inter-American Convention and the Convention on the Recognition and Enforcement of Foreign Arbitral Awards of June 10, 1958.

When the requirements for application of both the Inter-American Convention and the Convention on the Recognition and Enforcement of Foreign Arbitral Awards of June 10, 1958, are met, determination as to which Convention applies shall, unless otherwise expressly agreed, be made as follows:

(1) If a majority of the parties to the arbitration agreement are citizens of a State or States that have ratified or acceded to the Inter-American Convention and are member States of the Organization of American States, the Inter-American Convention shall apply.

(2) In all other cases the Convention on the Recognition and Enforcement of Foreign Arbitral Awards of June 10, 1958, shall apply.

§ 306. Applicable Rules of Inter-American Commercial Arbitration Commission.

(a) For the purposes of this chapter the rules of procedure of the Inter-American Commercial Arbitration Commission referred to in Article 3 of the Inter-American Convention shall, subject to subsection (b) of this section, be those rules as promulgated by the Commission on July 1, 1988.

(b) In the event the rules of procedure of the Inter-American Commercial Arbitration Commission are modified or amended in accordance with the procedures for amendment of the rules of that Commission, the Secretary of State, by regulation in accordance with section 553 of title 5, consistent with the aims and purposes of this Convention, may prescribe that such modifications or amendments shall be effective for purposes of this chapter.

§ 307. Chapter 1; Residual Application.

Chapter 1 applies to actions and proceedings brought under this chapter to the extent chapter 1 is not in conflict with this chapter or the Inter-American Convention as ratified by the United States.

PART X
SAMPLE CONTRACTS

AMERICAN INSTITUTE OF ARCHITECTS
SAMPLE FORM CONTRACTS

ꭗAIA Document A101™ – 2017

Standard Form of Agreement Between Owner and Contractor where the basis of payment is a Stipulated Sum

AGREEMENT made as of the _____ day of _____ in the year _____
(In words, indicate day, month and year.)

BETWEEN the Owner:
(Name, legal status, address and other information)

and the Contractor:
(Name, legal status, address and other information)

for the following Project:
(Name, location and detailed description)

The Architect:
(Name, legal status, address and other information)

This document has important legal consequences. Consultation with an attorney is encouraged with respect to its completion or modification.

The parties should complete A101™–2017, Exhibit A, Insurance and Bonds, contemporaneously with this Agreement.

AIA Document A201™–2017, General Conditions of the Contract for Construction, is adopted in this document by reference. Do not use with other general conditions unless this document is modified.

The Owner and Contractor agree as follows.

Init.

/

1

TABLE OF ARTICLES

ARTICLE 1   THE CONTRACT DOCUMENTS
The Contract Documents consist of this Agreement, Conditions of the Contract (General, Supplementary, and other Conditions), Drawings, Specifications, Addenda issued prior to execution of this Agreement, other documents listed in this Agreement, and Modifications issued after execution of this Agreement, all of which form the Contract, and are as fully a part of the Contract as if attached to this Agreement or repeated herein. The Contract represents the entire and integrated agreement between the parties hereto and supersedes prior negotiations, representations, or agreements, either written or oral. An enumeration of the Contract Documents, other than a Modification, appears in Article 9.

ARTICLE 2   THE WORK OF THIS CONTRACT
The Contractor shall fully execute the Work described in the Contract Documents, except as specifically indicated in the Contract Documents to be the responsibility of others.

ARTICLE 3   DATE OF COMMENCEMENT AND SUBSTANTIAL COMPLETION
§ 3.1 The date of commencement of the Work shall be:
(Check one of the following boxes.)

☐ The date of this Agreement.

☐ A date set forth in a notice to proceed issued by the Owner.

☐ Established as follows:
(Insert a date or a means to determine the date of commencement of the Work.)

If a date of commencement of the Work is not selected, then the date of commencement shall be the date of this Agreement.

§ 3.2 The Contract Time shall be measured from the date of commencement of the Work.

§ 3.3 Substantial Completion
§ 3.3.1 Subject to adjustments of the Contract Time as provided in the Contract Documents, the Contractor shall achieve Substantial Completion of the entire Work:
(Check one of the following boxes and complete the necessary information.)

☐ Not later than   (   ) calendar days from the date of commencement of the Work.

☐ By the following date:

§ 3.3.2 Subject to adjustments of the Contract Time as provided in the Contract Documents, if portions of the Work are to be completed prior to Substantial Completion of the entire Work, the Contractor shall achieve Substantial Completion of such portions by the following dates:

Portion of Work   **Substantial Completion Date**

§ 3.3.3 If the Contractor fails to achieve Substantial Completion as provided in this Section 3.3, liquidated damages, if any, shall be assessed as set forth in Section 4.5.

ARTICLE 4   CONTRACT SUM
§ 4.1 The Owner shall pay the Contractor the Contract Sum in current funds for the Contractor's performance of the Contract. The Contract Sum shall be   ($), subject to additions and deductions as provided in the Contract Documents.

§ 4.2 Alternates
§ 4.2.1 Alternates, if any, included in the Contract Sum:

Item   **Price**

§ 4.2.2 Subject to the conditions noted below, the following alternates may be accepted by the Owner following execution of this Agreement. Upon acceptance, the Owner shall issue a Modification to this Agreement.
(Insert below each alternate and the conditions that must be met for the Owner to accept the alternate.)

Item   **Price**   **Conditions for Acceptance**

§ 4.3 Allowances, if any, included in the Contract Sum:
(Identify each allowance.)

Item   **Price**

§ 4.4 Unit prices, if any:
(Identify the item and state the unit price and quantity limitations, if any, to which the unit price will be applicable.)

Item   **Units and Limitations**   **Price per Unit ($0.00)**

§ 4.5 Liquidated damages, if any:
(Insert terms and conditions for liquidated damages, if any.)

§ 4.6 Other:
(Insert provisions for bonus or other incentives, if any, that might result in a change to the Contract Sum.)

Init.

/

3

ARTICLE 5 PAYMENTS
§ 5.1 Progress Payments
§ 5.1.1 Based upon Applications for Payment submitted to the Architect by the Contractor and Certificates for Payment issued by the Architect, the Owner shall make progress payments on account of the Contract Sum to the Contractor as provided below and elsewhere in the Contract Documents.

§ 5.1.2 The period covered by each Application for Payment shall be one calendar month ending on the last day of the month, or as follows:

§ 5.1.3 Provided that an Application for Payment is received by the Architect not later than the   day of a month, the Owner shall make payment of the amount certified to the Contractor not later than the   day of the month. If an Application for Payment is received by the Architect after the application date fixed above, payment of the amount certified shall be made by the Owner not later than   (   ) days after the Architect receives the Application for Payment.
(Federal, state or local laws may require payment within a certain period of time.)

§ 5.1.4 Each Application for Payment shall be based on the most recent schedule of values submitted by the Contractor in accordance with the Contract Documents. The schedule of values shall allocate the entire Contract Sum among the various portions of the Work. The schedule of values shall be prepared in such form, and supported by such data to substantiate its accuracy, as the Architect may require. This schedule of values shall be used as a basis for reviewing the Contractor's Applications for Payment.

§ 5.1.5 Applications for Payment shall show the percentage of completion of each portion of the Work as of the end of the period covered by the Application for Payment.

§ 5.1.6 In accordance with AIA Document A201™–2017, General Conditions of the Contract for Construction, and subject to other provisions of the Contract Documents, the amount of each progress payment shall be computed as follows:

§ 5.1.6.1 The amount of each progress payment shall first include:
.1   That portion of the Contract Sum properly allocable to completed Work;
.2   That portion of the Contract Sum properly allocable to materials and equipment delivered and suitably stored at the site for subsequent incorporation in the completed construction, or, if approved in advance by the Owner, suitably stored off the site at a location agreed upon in writing; and
.3   That portion of Construction Change Directives that the Architect determines, in the Architect's professional judgment, to be reasonably justified.

§ 5.1.6.2 The amount of each progress payment shall then be reduced by:
.1   The aggregate of any amounts previously paid by the Owner;
.2   The amount, if any, for Work that remains uncorrected and for which the Architect has previously withheld a Certificate for Payment as provided in Article 9 of AIA Document A201–2017;
.3   Any amount for which the Contractor does not intend to pay a Subcontractor or material supplier, unless the Work has been performed by others the Contractor intends to pay;
.4   For Work performed or defects discovered since the last payment application, any amount for which the Architect may withhold payment, or nullify a Certificate of Payment in whole or in part, as provided in Article 9 of AIA Document A201–2017; and
.5   Retainage withheld pursuant to Section 5.1.7.

§ 5.1.7 Retainage
§ 5.1.7.1 For each progress payment made prior to Substantial Completion of the Work, the Owner may withhold the following amount, as retainage, from the payment otherwise due:
(Insert a percentage or amount to be withheld as retainage from each Application for Payment. The amount of retainage may be limited by governing law.)

§ 5.1.7.1.1 The following items are not subject to retainage:
(Insert any items not subject to the withholding of retainage, such as general conditions, insurance, etc.)

§ 5.1.7.2 Reduction or limitation of retainage, if any, shall be as follows:
(If the retainage established in Section 5.1.7.1 is to be modified prior to Substantial Completion of the entire Work, including modifications for Substantial Completion of portions of the Work as provided in Section 3.3.2, insert provisions for such modifications.)

§ 5.1.7.3 Except as set forth in this Section 5.1.7.3, upon Substantial Completion of the Work, the Contractor may submit an Application for Payment that includes the retainage withheld from prior Applications for Payment pursuant to this Section 5.1.7. The Application for Payment submitted at Substantial Completion shall not include retainage as follows:
(Insert any other conditions for release of retainage upon Substantial Completion.)

§ 5.1.8 If final completion of the Work is materially delayed through no fault of the Contractor, the Owner shall pay the Contractor any additional amounts in accordance with Article 9 of AIA Document A201–2017.

§ 5.1.9 Except with the Owner's prior approval, the Contractor shall not make advance payments to suppliers for materials or equipment which have not been delivered and stored at the site.

§ 5.2 Final Payment
§ 5.2.1 Final payment, constituting the entire unpaid balance of the Contract Sum, shall be made by the Owner to the Contractor when
 .1 the Contractor has fully performed the Contract except for the Contractor's responsibility to correct Work as provided in Article 12 of AIA Document A201–2017, and to satisfy other requirements, if any, which extend beyond final payment; and
 .2 a final Certificate for Payment has been issued by the Architect.

§ 5.2.2 The Owner's final payment to the Contractor shall be made no later than 30 days after the issuance of the Architect's final Certificate for Payment, or as follows:

§ 5.3 Interest
Payments due and unpaid under the Contract shall bear interest from the date payment is due at the rate stated below, or in the absence thereof, at the legal rate prevailing from time to time at the place where the Project is located.
(Insert rate of interest agreed upon, if any.)

_____ %

ARTICLE 6   DISPUTE RESOLUTION
§ 6.1 Initial Decision Maker
The Architect will serve as the Initial Decision Maker pursuant to Article 15 of AIA Document A201–2017, unless the parties appoint below another individual, not a party to this Agreement, to serve as the Initial Decision Maker.
(If the parties mutually agree, insert the name, address and other contact information of the Initial Decision Maker, if other than the Architect.)

§ 6.2 Binding Dispute Resolution
For any Claim subject to, but not resolved by, mediation pursuant to Article 15 of AIA Document A201–2017, the method of binding dispute resolution shall be as follows:
(Check the appropriate box.)

☐   Arbitration pursuant to Section 15.4 of AIA Document A201–2017

☐   Litigation in a court of competent jurisdiction

☐   Other *(Specify)*

If the Owner and Contractor do not select a method of binding dispute resolution, or do not subsequently agree in writing to a binding dispute resolution method other than litigation, Claims will be resolved by litigation in a court of competent jurisdiction.

ARTICLE 7   TERMINATION OR SUSPENSION
§ 7.1 The Contract may be terminated by the Owner or the Contractor as provided in Article 14 of AIA Document A201–2017.

§ 7.1.1 If the Contract is terminated for the Owner's convenience in accordance with Article 14 of AIA Document A201–2017, then the Owner shall pay the Contractor a termination fee as follows:
(Insert the amount of, or method for determining, the fee, if any, payable to the Contractor following a termination for the Owner's convenience.)

§ 7.2 The Work may be suspended by the Owner as provided in Article 14 of AIA Document A201–2017.

ARTICLE 8   MISCELLANEOUS PROVISIONS
§ 8.1 Where reference is made in this Agreement to a provision of AIA Document A201–2017 or another Contract Document, the reference refers to that provision as amended or supplemented by other provisions of the Contract Documents.

§ 8.2 The Owner's representative:
(Name, address, email address, and other information)

§ 8.3 The Contractor's representative:
(Name, address, email address, and other information)

§ 8.4 Neither the Owner's nor the Contractor's representative shall be changed without ten days' prior notice to the other party.

§ 8.5 Insurance and Bonds

§ 8.5.1 The Owner and the Contractor shall purchase and maintain insurance as set forth in AIA Document A101™–2017, Standard Form of Agreement Between Owner and Contractor where the basis of payment is a Stipulated Sum, Exhibit A, Insurance and Bonds, and elsewhere in the Contract Documents.

§ 8.5.2 The Contractor shall provide bonds as set forth in AIA Document A101™–2017 Exhibit A, and elsewhere in the Contract Documents.

§ 8.6 Notice in electronic format, pursuant to Article 1 of AIA Document A201–2017, may be given in accordance with AIA Document E203™–2013, Building Information Modeling and Digital Data Exhibit, if completed, or as otherwise set forth below:
(If other than in accordance with AIA Document E203–2013, insert requirements for delivering notice in electronic format such as name, title, and email address of the recipient and whether and how the system will be required to generate a read receipt for the transmission.)

§ 8.7 Other provisions:

ARTICLE 9 ENUMERATION OF CONTRACT DOCUMENTS

§ 9.1 This Agreement is comprised of the following documents:

   .1   AIA Document A101™–2017, Standard Form of Agreement Between Owner and Contractor
   .2   AIA Document A101™–2017, Exhibit A, Insurance and Bonds
   .3   AIA Document A201™–2017, General Conditions of the Contract for Construction
   .4   AIA Document E203™–2013, Building Information Modeling and Digital Data Exhibit, dated as indicated below:
       (Insert the date of the E203-2013 incorporated into this Agreement.)

   .5   Drawings

Number	Title	Date

   .6   Specifications

Section	Title	Date	Pages

   .7   Addenda, if any:

Number	Date	Pages

Portions of Addenda relating to bidding or proposal requirements are not part of the Contract Documents unless the bidding or proposal requirements are also enumerated in this Article 9.

   .8   Other Exhibits:
       (Check all boxes that apply and include appropriate information identifying the exhibit where required.)

       ☐ AIA Document E204™–2017, Sustainable Projects Exhibit, dated as indicated below:
          (Insert the date of the E204-2017 incorporated into this Agreement.)

Init.

/

7

☐ The Sustainability Plan:

Title   **Date**   **Pages**

☐ Supplementary and other Conditions of the Contract:

Document   **Title**   **Date**   **Pages**

.9   Other documents, if any, listed below:
(List here any additional documents that are intended to form part of the Contract Documents. AIA Document A201™–2017 provides that the advertisement or invitation to bid, Instructions to Bidders, sample forms, the Contractor's bid or proposal, portions of Addenda relating to bidding or proposal requirements, and other information furnished by the Owner in anticipation of receiving bids or proposals, are not part of the Contract Documents unless enumerated in this Agreement. Any such documents should be listed here only if intended to be part of the Contract Documents.)

This Agreement entered into as of the day and year first written above.

OWNER *(Signature)*   **CONTRACTOR** *(Signature)*

(Printed name and title)   *(Printed name and title)*

AIA Document A101™ – 2017 Exhibit A

Insurance and Bonds

This Insurance and Bonds Exhibit is part of the Agreement, between the Owner and the
Contractor, dated the _____ day of _____ in the year _____
(In words, indicate day, month and year.)

for the following PROJECT:
(Name and location or address)

THE OWNER:
(Name, legal status and address)

THE CONTRACTOR:
(Name, legal status and address)

This document has important legal
consequences. Consultation with
an attorney is encouraged with
respect to its completion or
modification.

This document is intended to be
used in conjunction with AIA
Document A201™–2017, General
Conditions of the Contract for
Construction. Article 11 of
A201™–2017 contains additional
insurance provisions.

TABLE OF ARTICLES

A.1   GENERAL

A.2   OWNER'S INSURANCE

A.3   CONTRACTOR'S INSURANCE AND BONDS

A.4   SPECIAL TERMS AND CONDITIONS

ARTICLE A.1 GENERAL
The Owner and Contractor shall purchase and maintain insurance, and provide bonds, as set forth in this Exhibit. As
used in this Exhibit, the term General Conditions refers to AIA Document A201™–2017, General Conditions of the
Contract for Construction.

ARTICLE A.2 OWNER'S INSURANCE
§ A.2.1 General
Prior to commencement of the Work, the Owner shall secure the insurance, and provide evidence of the coverage,
required under this Article A.2 and, upon the Contractor's request, provide a copy of the property insurance policy or
policies required by Section A.2.3. The copy of the policy or policies provided shall contain all applicable conditions,
definitions, exclusions, and endorsements.

§ A.2.2 Liability Insurance
The Owner shall be responsible for purchasing and maintaining the Owner's usual general liability insurance.

§ A.2.3 Required Property Insurance
§ A.2.3.1 Unless this obligation is placed on the Contractor pursuant to Section A.3.3.2.1, the Owner shall purchase and
maintain, from an insurance company or insurance companies lawfully authorized to issue insurance in the jurisdiction
where the Project is located, property insurance written on a builder's risk "all-risks" completed value or equivalent
policy form and sufficient to cover the total value of the entire Project on a replacement cost basis. The Owner's

property insurance coverage shall be no less than the amount of the initial Contract Sum, plus the value of subsequent Modifications and labor performed and materials or equipment supplied by others. The property insurance shall be maintained until Substantial Completion and thereafter as provided in Section A.2.3.1.3, unless otherwise provided in the Contract Documents or otherwise agreed in writing by the parties to this Agreement. This insurance shall include the interests of the Owner, Contractor, Subcontractors, and Sub-subcontractors in the Project as insureds. This insurance shall include the interests of mortgagees as loss payees.

§ A.2.3.1.1 Causes of Loss. The insurance required by this Section A.2.3.1 shall provide coverage for direct physical loss or damage, and shall not exclude the risks of fire, explosion, theft, vandalism, malicious mischief, collapse, earthquake, flood, or windstorm. The insurance shall also provide coverage for ensuing loss or resulting damage from error, omission, or deficiency in construction methods, design, specifications, workmanship, or materials. Sub-limits, if any, are as follows:
(Indicate below the cause of loss and any applicable sub-limit.)

Cause of Loss	Sub-Limit

§ A.2.3.1.2 Specific Required Coverages. The insurance required by this Section A.2.3.1 shall provide coverage for loss or damage to falsework and other temporary structures, and to building systems from testing and startup. The insurance shall also cover debris removal, including demolition occasioned by enforcement of any applicable legal requirements, and reasonable compensation for the Architect's and Contractor's services and expenses required as a result of such insured loss, including claim preparation expenses. Sub-limits, if any, are as follows:
(Indicate below type of coverage and any applicable sub-limit for specific required coverages.)

Coverage	Sub-Limit

§ A.2.3.1.3 Unless the parties agree otherwise, upon Substantial Completion, the Owner shall continue the insurance required by Section A.2.3.1 or, if necessary, replace the insurance policy required under Section A.2.3.1 with property insurance written for the total value of the Project that shall remain in effect until expiration of the period for correction of the Work set forth in Section 12.2.2 of the General Conditions.

§ A.2.3.1.4 Deductibles and Self-Insured Retentions. If the insurance required by this Section A.2.3 is subject to deductibles or self-insured retentions, the Owner shall be responsible for all loss not covered because of such deductibles or retentions.

§ A.2.3.2 Occupancy or Use Prior to Substantial Completion. The Owner's occupancy or use of any completed or partially completed portion of the Work prior to Substantial Completion shall not commence until the insurance company or companies providing the insurance under Section A.2.3.1 have consented in writing to the continuance of coverage. The Owner and the Contractor shall take no action with respect to partial occupancy or use that would cause cancellation, lapse, or reduction of insurance, unless they agree otherwise in writing.

§ A.2.3.3 Insurance for Existing Structures
If the Work involves remodeling an existing structure or constructing an addition to an existing structure, the Owner shall purchase and maintain, until the expiration of the period for correction of Work as set forth in Section 12.2.2 of the General Conditions, "all-risks" property insurance, on a replacement cost basis, protecting the existing structure against direct physical loss or damage from the causes of loss identified in Section A.2.3.1, notwithstanding the undertaking of the Work. The Owner shall be responsible for all co-insurance penalties.

§ A.2.4 Optional Extended Property Insurance.
The Owner shall purchase and maintain the insurance selected and described below.
(Select the types of insurance the Owner is required to purchase and maintain by placing an X in the box(es) next to the description(s) of selected insurance. For each type of insurance selected, indicate applicable limits of coverage or other conditions in the fill point below the selected item.)

☐ **§ A.2.4.1 Loss of Use, Business Interruption, and Delay in Completion Insurance,** to reimburse the Owner for loss of use of the Owner's property, or the inability to conduct normal operations due to a covered cause of loss.

☐ **§ A.2.4.2 Ordinance or Law Insurance,** for the reasonable and necessary costs to satisfy the minimum requirements of the enforcement of any law or ordinance regulating the demolition, construction, repair, replacement or use of the Project.

☐ **§ A.2.4.3 Expediting Cost Insurance,** for the reasonable and necessary costs for the temporary repair of damage to insured property, and to expedite the permanent repair or replacement of the damaged property.

☐ **§ A.2.4.4 Extra Expense Insurance,** to provide reimbursement of the reasonable and necessary excess costs incurred during the period of restoration or repair of the damaged property that are over and above the total costs that would normally have been incurred during the same period of time had no loss or damage occurred.

☐ **§ A.2.4.5 Civil Authority Insurance,** for losses or costs arising from an order of a civil authority prohibiting access to the Project, provided such order is the direct result of physical damage covered under the required property insurance.

☐ **§ A.2.4.6 Ingress/Egress Insurance,** for loss due to the necessary interruption of the insured's business due to physical prevention of ingress to, or egress from, the Project as a direct result of physical damage.

☐ **§ A.2.4.7 Soft Costs Insurance,** to reimburse the Owner for costs due to the delay of completion of the Work, arising out of physical loss or damage covered by the required property insurance: including construction loan fees; leasing and marketing expenses; additional fees, including those of architects, engineers, consultants, attorneys and accountants, needed for the completion of the construction, repairs, or reconstruction; and carrying costs such as property taxes, building permits, additional interest on loans, realty taxes, and insurance premiums over and above normal expenses.

§ A.2.5 Other Optional Insurance.
The Owner shall purchase and maintain the insurance selected below.
(Select the types of insurance the Owner is required to purchase and maintain by placing an X in the box(es) next to the description(s) of selected insurance.)

☐ **§ A.2.5.1 Cyber Security Insurance** for loss to the Owner due to data security and privacy breach, including costs of investigating a potential or actual breach of confidential or private information.
(Indicate applicable limits of coverage or other conditions in the fill point below.)

☐ **§ A.2.5.2 Other Insurance**
(List below any other insurance coverage to be provided by the Owner and any applicable limits.)

Coverage   Limits

ARTICLE A.3   CONTRACTOR'S INSURANCE AND BONDS
§ A.3.1 General
§ A.3.1.1 Certificates of Insurance. The Contractor shall provide certificates of insurance acceptable to the Owner evidencing compliance with the requirements in this Article A.3 at the following times: (1) prior to commencement of the Work; (2) upon renewal or replacement of each required policy of insurance; and (3) upon the Owner's written request. An additional certificate evidencing continuation of commercial liability coverage, including coverage for completed operations, shall be submitted with the final Application for Payment and thereafter upon renewal or replacement of such coverage until the expiration of the periods required by Section A.3.2.1 and Section A.3.3.1. The certificates will show the Owner as an additional insured on the Contractor's Commercial General Liability and excess or umbrella liability policy or policies.

§ A.3.1.2 Deductibles and Self-Insured Retentions. The Contractor shall disclose to the Owner any deductible or self-insured retentions applicable to any insurance required to be provided by the Contractor.

§ A.3.1.3 Additional Insured Obligations. To the fullest extent permitted by law, the Contractor shall cause the commercial general liability coverage to include (1) the Owner, the Architect, and the Architect's consultants as additional insureds for claims caused in whole or in part by the Contractor's negligent acts or omissions during the Contractor's operations; and (2) the Owner as an additional insured for claims caused in whole or in part by the Contractor's negligent acts or omissions for which loss occurs during completed operations. The additional insured coverage shall be primary and non-contributory to any of the Owner's general liability insurance policies and shall apply to both ongoing and completed operations. To the extent commercially available, the additional insured coverage shall be no less than that provided by Insurance Services Office, Inc. (ISO) forms CG 20 10 07 04, CG 20 37 07 04, and, with respect to the Architect and the Architect's consultants, CG 20 32 07 04.

§ A.3.2 Contractor's Required Insurance Coverage
§ A.3.2.1 The Contractor shall purchase and maintain the following types and limits of insurance from an insurance company or insurance companies lawfully authorized to issue insurance in the jurisdiction where the Project is located. The Contractor shall maintain the required insurance until the expiration of the period for correction of Work as set forth in Section 12.2.2 of the General Conditions, unless a different duration is stated below:
(If the Contractor is required to maintain insurance for a duration other than the expiration of the period for correction of Work, state the duration.)

§ A.3.2.2 Commercial General Liability
§ A.3.2.2.1 Commercial General Liability insurance for the Project written on an occurrence form with policy limits of not less than _____ ($__) each occurrence, _____ ($__) general aggregate, and _____ ($__) aggregate for products-completed operations hazard, providing coverage for claims including
- .1 damages because of bodily injury, sickness or disease, including occupational sickness or disease, and death of any person;
- .2 personal injury and advertising injury;
- .3 damages because of physical damage to, or destruction of, tangible property, including the loss of use of such property;
- .4 bodily injury or property damage arising out of completed operations; and
- .5 the Contractor's indemnity obligations under Section 3.18 of the General Conditions.

§ A.3.2.2.2 The Contractor's Commercial General Liability policy under this Section A.3.2.2 shall not contain an exclusion or restriction of coverage for the following:

   .1   Claims by one insured against another insured, if the exclusion or restriction is based solely on the fact that the claimant is an insured, and there would otherwise be coverage for the claim.

   .2   Claims for property damage to the Contractor's Work arising out of the products-completed operations hazard where the damaged Work or the Work out of which the damage arises was performed by a Subcontractor.

   .3   Claims for bodily injury other than to employees of the insured.

   .4   Claims for indemnity under Section 3.18 of the General Conditions arising out of injury to employees of the insured

   .5   Claims or loss excluded under a prior work endorsement or other similar exclusionary language.

   .6   Claims or loss due to physical damage under a prior injury endorsement or similar exclusionary language.

   .7   Claims related to residential, multi-family, or other habitational projects, if the Work is to be performed on such a project.

   .8   Claims related to roofing, if the Work involves roofing.

   .9   Claims related to exterior insulation finish systems (EIFS), synthetic stucco or similar exterior coatings or surfaces, if the Work involves such coatings or surfaces.

   .10   Claims related to earth subsidence or movement, where the work involves such hazards.

   .11   Claims related to explosion, collapse, and underground hazards, where the Work involves such hazards.

§ A.3.2.3 Automobile Liability covering vehicles owned, and non-owned vehicles used, by the Contractor, with policy limits of not less than _____ ($__) per accident, for bodily injury, death of any person, and property damage arising out of the ownership, maintenance and use of those motor vehicles along with any other statutorily required automobile coverage.

§ A.3.2.4 The Contractor may achieve the required limits and coverage for Commercial General Liability and Automobile Liability through a combination of primary and excess or umbrella liability insurance, provided such primary and excess or umbrella insurance policies result in the same or greater coverage as the coverages required under Section A.3.2.2 and A.3.2.3, and in no event shall any excess or umbrella liability insurance provide narrower coverage than the primary policy. The excess policy shall not require the exhaustion of the underlying limits only through the actual payment by the underlying insurers.

§ A.3.2.5 Workers' Compensation at statutory limits.

§ A.3.2.6 Employers' Liability with policy limits not less than _____ ($__) each accident, _____ ($__) each employee, and _____ ($__) policy limit.

§ A.3.2.7 Jones Act, and the Longshore & Harbor Workers' Compensation Act, as required, if the Work involves hazards arising from work on or near navigable waterways, including vessels and docks

§ A.3.2.8 If the Contractor is required to furnish professional services as part of the Work, the Contractor shall procure Professional Liability insurance covering performance of the professional services, with policy limits of not less than _____ ($__) per claim and _____ ($__) in the aggregate.

§ A.3.2.9 If the Work involves the transport, dissemination, use, or release of pollutants, the Contractor shall procure Pollution Liability insurance, with policy limits of not less than _____ ($__) per claim and _____ ($__) in the aggregate.

§ A.3.2.10 Coverage under Sections A.3.2.8 and A.3.2.9 may be procured through a Combined Professional Liability and Pollution Liability insurance policy, with combined policy limits of not less than _____ ($__) per claim and _____ ($__) in the aggregate.

§ A.3.2.11 Insurance for maritime liability risks associated with the operation of a vessel, if the Work requires such activities, with policy limits of not less than _____ ($__) per claim and _____ ($__) in the aggregate.

§ A.3.2.12 Insurance for the use or operation of manned or unmanned aircraft, if the Work requires such activities, with policy limits of not less than _____ ($__) per claim and _____ ($__) in the aggregate.

Init.

/

5

§ A.3.3 Contractor's Other Insurance Coverage

§ A.3.3.1 Insurance selected and described in this Section A.3.3 shall be purchased from an insurance company or insurance companies lawfully authorized to issue insurance in the jurisdiction where the Project is located. The Contractor shall maintain the required insurance until the expiration of the period for correction of Work as set forth in Section 12.2.2 of the General Conditions, unless a different duration is stated below:

(If the Contractor is required to maintain any of the types of insurance selected below for a duration other than the expiration of the period for correction of Work, state the duration.)

§ A.3.3.2 The Contractor shall purchase and maintain the following types and limits of insurance in accordance with Section A.3.3.1.

(Select the types of insurance the Contractor is required to purchase and maintain by placing an X in the box(es) next to the description(s) of selected insurance. Where policy limits are provided, include the policy limit in the appropriate fill point.)

☐ **§ A.3.3.2.1** Property insurance of the same type and scope satisfying the requirements identified in Section A.2.3, which, if selected in this section A.3.3.2.1, relieves the Owner of the responsibility to purchase and maintain such insurance except insurance required by Section A.2.3.1.3 and Section A.2.3.3. The Contractor shall comply with all obligations of the Owner under Section A.2.3 except to the extent provided below. The Contractor shall disclose to the Owner the amount of any deductible, and the Owner shall be responsible for losses within the deductible. Upon request, the Contractor shall provide the Owner with a copy of the property insurance policy or policies required. The Owner shall adjust and settle the loss with the insurer and be the trustee of the proceeds of the property insurance in accordance with Article 11 of the General Conditions unless otherwise set forth below.

(Where the Contractor's obligation to provide property insurance differs from the Owner's obligations as described under Section A.2.3, indicate such differences in the space below. Additionally, if a party other than the Owner will be responsible for adjusting and settling a loss with the insurer and acting as the trustee of the proceeds of property insurance in accordance with Article 11 of the General Conditions, indicate the responsible party below.)

☐ **§ A.3.3.2.2 Railroad Protective Liability Insurance**, with policy limits of not less than _____ ($__) per claim and _____ ($__) in the aggregate, for Work within fifty (50) feet of railroad property.

☐ **§ A.3.3.2.3 Asbestos Abatement Liability Insurance**, with policy limits of not less than _____ ($__) per claim and _____ ($__) in the aggregate, for liability arising from the encapsulation, removal, handling, storage, transportation, and disposal of asbestos-containing materials.

☐ **§ A.3.3.2.4** Insurance for physical damage to property while it is in storage and in transit to the construction site on an "all-risks" completed value form.

☐ **§ A.3.3.2.5** Property insurance on an "all-risks" completed value form, covering property owned by the Contractor and used on the Project, including scaffolding and other equipment.

☐ **§ A.3.3.2.6 Other Insurance**

(List below any other insurance coverage to be provided by the Contractor and any applicable limits.)

Coverage   Limits

§ A.3.4 Performance Bond and Payment Bond
The Contractor shall provide surety bonds, from a company or companies lawfully authorized to issue surety bonds in the jurisdiction where the Project is located, as follows:
(Specify type and penal sum of bonds.)

Type	Penal Sum ($0.00)
Payment Bond	
Performance Bond	

Payment and Performance Bonds shall be AIA Document A312™, Payment Bond and Performance Bond, or contain provisions identical to AIA Document A312™, current as of the date of this Agreement.

ARTICLE A.4   SPECIAL TERMS AND CONDITIONS
Special terms and conditions that modify this Insurance and Bonds Exhibit, if any, are as follows:

Init.

/

7

▲AIA® Document A312™ – 2010

Performance Bond

CONTRACTOR:
(Name, legal status and address)

SURETY:
(Name, legal status and principal place of business)

OWNER:
(Name, legal status and address)

CONSTRUCTION CONTRACT
Date:

Amount:

Description:
(Name and location)

BOND
Date:
(Not earlier than Construction Contract Date)

Amount:

Modifications to this Bond: ☐ None   ☐ See Section 16

CONTRACTOR AS PRINCIPAL
Company: *(Corporate Seal)*

SURETY
Company: *(Corporate Seal)*

Signature: _____
Name
and Title:

Signature: _____
Name
and Title:

(Any additional signatures appear on the last page of this Performance Bond.)

(FOR INFORMATION ONLY — Name, address and telephone)
AGENT or BROKER:

OWNER'S REPRESENTATIVE:
(Architect, Engineer or other party:)

This document has important legal consequences. Consultation with an attorney is encouraged with respect to its completion or modification.

Any singular reference to Contractor, Surety, Owner or other party shall be considered plural where applicable.

AIA Document A312–2010 combines two separate bonds, a Performance Bond and a Payment Bond, into one form. This is not a single combined Performance and Payment Bond.

AIA Document A312™ – 2010. The American Institute of Architects.

061110

1

§ 1 The Contractor and Surety, jointly and severally, bind themselves, their heirs, executors, administrators, successors and assigns to the Owner for the performance of the Construction Contract, which is incorporated herein by reference.

§ 2 If the Contractor performs the Construction Contract, the Surety and the Contractor shall have no obligation under this Bond, except when applicable to participate in a conference as provided in Section 3.

§ 3 If there is no Owner Default under the Construction Contract, the Surety's obligation under this Bond shall arise after

.1   the Owner first provides notice to the Contractor and the Surety that the Owner is considering declaring a Contractor Default. Such notice shall indicate whether the Owner is requesting a conference among the Owner, Contractor and Surety to discuss the Contractor's performance. If the Owner does not request a conference, the Surety may, within five (5) business days after receipt of the Owner's notice, request such a conference. If the Surety timely requests a conference, the Owner shall attend. Unless the Owner agrees otherwise, any conference requested under this Section 3.1 shall be held within ten (10) business days of the Surety's receipt of the Owner's notice. If the Owner, the Contractor and the Surety agree, the Contractor shall be allowed a reasonable time to perform the Construction Contract, but such an agreement shall not waive the Owner's right, if any, subsequently to declare a Contractor Default;

.2   the Owner declares a Contractor Default, terminates the Construction Contract and notifies the Surety; and

.3   the Owner has agreed to pay the Balance of the Contract Price in accordance with the terms of the Construction Contract to the Surety or to a contractor selected to perform the Construction Contract.

§ 4 Failure on the part of the Owner to comply with the notice requirement in Section 3.1 shall not constitute a failure to comply with a condition precedent to the Surety's obligations, or release the Surety from its obligations, except to the extent the Surety demonstrates actual prejudice.

§ 5 When the Owner has satisfied the conditions of Section 3, the Surety shall promptly and at the Surety's expense take one of the following actions:

§ 5.1 Arrange for the Contractor, with the consent of the Owner, to perform and complete the Construction Contract;

§ 5.2 Undertake to perform and complete the Construction Contract itself, through its agents or independent contractors;

§ 5.3 Obtain bids or negotiated proposals from qualified contractors acceptable to the Owner for a contract for performance and completion of the Construction Contract, arrange for a contract to be prepared for execution by the Owner and a contractor selected with the Owner's concurrence, to be secured with performance and payment bonds executed by a qualified surety equivalent to the bonds issued on the Construction Contract, and pay to the Owner the amount of damages as described in Section 7 in excess of the Balance of the Contract Price incurred by the Owner as a result of the Contractor Default; or

§ 5.4 Waive its right to perform and complete, arrange for completion, or obtain a new contractor and with reasonable promptness under the circumstances:

.1   After investigation, determine the amount for which it may be liable to the Owner and, as soon as practicable after the amount is determined, make payment to the Owner; or

.2   Deny liability in whole or in part and notify the Owner, citing the reasons for denial.

§ 6 If the Surety does not proceed as provided in Section 5 with reasonable promptness, the Surety shall be deemed to be in default on this Bond seven days after receipt of an additional written notice from the Owner to the Surety demanding that the Surety perform its obligations under this Bond, and the Owner shall be entitled to enforce any remedy available to the Owner. If the Surety proceeds as provided in Section 5.4, and the Owner refuses the payment or the Surety has denied liability, in whole or in part, without further notice the Owner shall be entitled to enforce any remedy available to the Owner.

§ 7 If the Surety elects to act under Section 5.1, 5.2 or 5.3, then the responsibilities of the Surety to the Owner shall not be greater than those of the Contractor under the Construction Contract, and the responsibilities of the Owner to the Surety shall not be greater than those of the Owner under the Construction Contract. Subject to the commitment by the Owner to pay the Balance of the Contract Price, the Surety is obligated, without duplication, for

.1   the responsibilities of the Contractor for correction of defective work and completion of the Construction Contract;

.2   additional legal, design professional and delay costs resulting from the Contractor's Default, and resulting from the actions or failure to act of the Surety under Section 5; and

.3   liquidated damages, or if no liquidated damages are specified in the Construction Contract, actual damages caused by delayed performance or non-performance of the Contractor.

§ 8 If the Surety elects to act under Section 5.1, 5.3 or 5.4, the Surety's liability is limited to the amount of this Bond.

§ 9 The Surety shall not be liable to the Owner or others for obligations of the Contractor that are unrelated to the Construction Contract, and the Balance of the Contract Price shall not be reduced or set off on account of any such unrelated obligations. No right of action shall accrue on this Bond to any person or entity other than the Owner or its heirs, executors, administrators, successors and assigns.

§ 10 The Surety hereby waives notice of any change, including changes of time, to the Construction Contract or to related subcontracts, purchase orders and other obligations.

§ 11 Any proceeding, legal or equitable, under this Bond may be instituted in any court of competent jurisdiction in the location in which the work or part of the work is located and shall be instituted within two years after a declaration of Contractor Default or within two years after the Contractor ceased working or within two years after the Surety refuses or fails to perform its obligations under this Bond, whichever occurs first. If the provisions of this Paragraph are void or prohibited by law, the minimum period of limitation available to sureties as a defense in the jurisdiction of the suit shall be applicable.

§ 12 Notice to the Surety, the Owner or the Contractor shall be mailed or delivered to the address shown on the page on which their signature appears.

§ 13 When this Bond has been furnished to comply with a statutory or other legal requirement in the location where the construction was to be performed, any provision in this Bond conflicting with said statutory or legal requirement shall be deemed deleted herefrom and provisions conforming to such statutory or other legal requirement shall be deemed incorporated herein. When so furnished, the intent is that this Bond shall be construed as a statutory bond and not as a common law bond.

§ 14 Definitions
§ 14.1 Balance of the Contract Price. The total amount payable by the Owner to the Contractor under the Construction Contract after all proper adjustments have been made, including allowance to the Contractor of any amounts received or to be received by the Owner in settlement of insurance or other claims for damages to which the Contractor is entitled, reduced by all valid and proper payments made to or on behalf of the Contractor under the Construction Contract.

§ 14.2 Construction Contract. The agreement between the Owner and Contractor identified on the cover page, including all Contract Documents and changes made to the agreement and the Contract Documents.

§ 14.3 Contractor Default. Failure of the Contractor, which has not been remedied or waived, to perform or otherwise to comply with a material term of the Construction Contract.

§ 14.4 Owner Default. Failure of the Owner, which has not been remedied or waived, to pay the Contractor as required under the Construction Contract or to perform and complete or comply with the other material terms of the Construction Contract.

§ 14.5 Contract Documents. All the documents that comprise the agreement between the Owner and Contractor.

§ 15 If this Bond is issued for an agreement between a Contractor and subcontractor, the term Contractor in this Bond shall be deemed to be Subcontractor and the term Owner shall be deemed to be Contractor.

Init.

/

AIA Document A312™ – 2010. The American Institute of Architects.

3

§ 16 Modifications to this bond are as follows:

(Space is provided below for additional signatures of added parties, other than those appearing on the cover page.)

CONTRACTOR AS PRINCIPAL		SURETY	
Company:	*(Corporate Seal)*	Company:	*(Corporate Seal)*

Signature: _____   Signature: _____
Name and Title: Name and Title:
Address   Address

CAUTION: You should sign an original AIA Contract Document, on which this text appears in RED. An original assures that changes will not be obscured.

AIA Document A312™ – 2010. The American Institute of Architects.

Init.

/

4

AIA Document A312™ – 2010

Payment Bond

CONTRACTOR:
(Name, legal status and address)

SURETY:
(Name, legal status and principal place of business)

OWNER:
(Name, legal status and address)

CONSTRUCTION CONTRACT
Date:

Amount:

Description:
(Name and location)

BOND
Date:
(Not earlier than Construction Contract Date)

Amount:

Modifications to this Bond: ☐ None ☐ See Section 18

This document has important legal consequences. Consultation with an attorney is encouraged with respect to its completion or modification.

Any singular reference to Contractor, Surety, Owner or other party shall be considered plural where applicable.

AIA Document A312–2010 combines two separate bonds, a Performance Bond and a Payment Bond, into one form. This is not a single combined Performance and Payment Bond.

CONTRACTOR AS PRINCIPAL
Company: *(Corporate Seal)*

SURETY
Company: *(Corporate Seal)*

Signature: _____
Name   Nam
and Title:

Signature: _____
e
and Title:

(Any additional signatures appear on the last page of this Payment Bond.)

(FOR INFORMATION ONLY — Name, address and telephone)
AGENT or BROKER:

OWNER'S REPRESENTATIVE:
(Architect, Engineer or other party:)

§ 1 The Contractor and Surety, jointly and severally, bind themselves, their heirs, executors, administrators, successors and assigns to the Owner to pay for labor, materials and equipment furnished for use in the performance of the Construction Contract, which is incorporated herein by reference, subject to the following terms.

§ 2 If the Contractor promptly makes payment of all sums due to Claimants, and defends, indemnifies and holds harmless the Owner from claims, demands, liens or suits by any person or entity seeking payment for labor, materials or equipment furnished for use in the performance of the Construction Contract, then the Surety and the Contractor shall have no obligation under this Bond.

§ 3 If there is no Owner Default under the Construction Contract, the Surety's obligation to the Owner under this Bond shall arise after the Owner has promptly notified the Contractor and the Surety (at the address described in Section 13) of claims, demands, liens or suits against the Owner or the Owner's property by any person or entity seeking payment for labor, materials or equipment furnished for use in the performance of the Construction Contract and tendered defense of such claims, demands, liens or suits to the Contractor and the Surety.

§ 4 When the Owner has satisfied the conditions in Section 3, the Surety shall promptly and at the Surety's expense defend, indemnify and hold harmless the Owner against a duly tendered claim, demand, lien or suit.

§ 5 The Surety's obligations to a Claimant under this Bond shall arise after the following:

§ 5.1 Claimants, who do not have a direct contract with the Contractor,

    .1   have furnished a written notice of non-payment to the Contractor, stating with substantial accuracy the amount claimed and the name of the party to whom the materials were, or equipment was, furnished or supplied or for whom the labor was done or performed, within ninety (90) days after having last performed labor or last furnished materials or equipment included in the Claim; and

    .2   have sent a Claim to the Surety (at the address described in Section 13).

§ 5.2 Claimants, who are employed by or have a direct contract with the Contractor, have sent a Claim to the Surety (at the address described in Section 13).

§ 6 If a notice of non-payment required by Section 5.1.1 is given by the Owner to the Contractor, that is sufficient to satisfy a Claimant's obligation to furnish a written notice of non-payment under Section 5.1.1.

§ 7 When a Claimant has satisfied the conditions of Sections 5.1 or 5.2, whichever is applicable, the Surety shall promptly and at the Surety's expense take the following actions:

§ 7.1 Send an answer to the Claimant, with a copy to the Owner, within sixty (60) days after receipt of the Claim, stating the amounts that are undisputed and the basis for challenging any amounts that are disputed; and

§ 7.2 Pay or arrange for payment of any undisputed amounts.

§ 7.3 The Surety's failure to discharge its obligations under Section 7.1 or Section 7.2 shall not be deemed to constitute a waiver of defenses the Surety or Contractor may have or acquire as to a Claim, except as to undisputed amounts for which the Surety and Claimant have reached agreement. If, however, the Surety fails to discharge its obligations under Section 7.1 or Section 7.2, the Surety shall indemnify the Claimant for the reasonable attorney's fees the Claimant incurs thereafter to recover any sums found to be due and owing to the Claimant.

§ 8 The Surety's total obligation shall not exceed the amount of this Bond, plus the amount of reasonable attorney's fees provided under Section 7.3, and the amount of this Bond shall be credited for any payments made in good faith by the Surety.

§ 9 Amounts owed by the Owner to the Contractor under the Construction Contract shall be used for the performance of the Construction Contract and to satisfy claims, if any, under any construction performance bond. By the Contractor furnishing and the Owner accepting this Bond, they agree that all funds earned by the Contractor in the performance of the Construction Contract are dedicated to satisfy obligations of the Contractor and Surety under this Bond, subject to the Owner's priority to use the funds for the completion of the work.

§ 10 The Surety shall not be liable to the Owner, Claimants or others for obligations of the Contractor that are unrelated to the Construction Contract. The Owner shall not be liable for the payment of any costs or expenses of any Claimant under this Bond, and shall have under this Bond no obligation to make payments to, or give notice on behalf of, Claimants or otherwise have any obligations to Claimants under this Bond.

§ 11 The Surety hereby waives notice of any change, including changes of time, to the Construction Contract or to related subcontracts, purchase orders and other obligations.

§ 12 No suit or action shall be commenced by a Claimant under this Bond other than in a court of competent jurisdiction in the state in which the project that is the subject of the Construction Contract is located or after the expiration of one year from the date (1) on which the Claimant sent a Claim to the Surety pursuant to Section 5.1.2 or 5.2, or (2) on which the last labor or service was performed by anyone or the last materials or equipment were furnished by anyone under the Construction Contract, whichever of (1) or (2) first occurs. If the provisions of this Paragraph are void or prohibited by law, the minimum period of limitation available to sureties as a defense in the jurisdiction of the suit shall be applicable.

§ 13 Notice and Claims to the Surety, the Owner or the Contractor shall be mailed or delivered to the address shown on the page on which their signature appears. Actual receipt of notice or Claims, however accomplished, shall be sufficient compliance as of the date received.

§ 14 When this Bond has been furnished to comply with a statutory or other legal requirement in the location where the construction was to be performed, any provision in this Bond conflicting with said statutory or legal requirement shall be deemed deleted herefrom and provisions conforming to such statutory or other legal requirement shall be deemed incorporated herein. When so furnished, the intent is that this Bond shall be construed as a statutory bond and not as a common law bond.

§ 15 Upon request by any person or entity appearing to be a potential beneficiary of this Bond, the Contractor and Owner shall promptly furnish a copy of this Bond or shall permit a copy to be made.

§ 16 Definitions
§ 16.1 Claim. A written statement by the Claimant including at a minimum:
    .1   the name of the Claimant;
    .2   the name of the person for whom the labor was done, or materials or equipment furnished;
    .3   a copy of the agreement or purchase order pursuant to which labor, materials or equipment was furnished for use in the performance of the Construction Contract;
    .4   a brief description of the labor, materials or equipment furnished;
    .5   the date on which the Claimant last performed labor or last furnished materials or equipment for use in the performance of the Construction Contract;
    .6   the total amount earned by the Claimant for labor, materials or equipment furnished as of the date of the Claim;
    .7   the total amount of previous payments received by the Claimant; and
    .8   the total amount due and unpaid to the Claimant for labor, materials or equipment furnished as of the date of the Claim.

§ 16.2 Claimant. An individual or entity having a direct contract with the Contractor or with a subcontractor of the Contractor to furnish labor, materials or equipment for use in the performance of the Construction Contract. The term Claimant also includes any individual or entity that has rightfully asserted a claim under an applicable mechanic's lien or similar statute against the real property upon which the Project is located. The intent of this Bond shall be to include without limitation in the terms "labor, materials or equipment" that part of water, gas, power, light, heat, oil, gasoline, telephone service or rental equipment used in the Construction Contract, architectural and engineering services required for performance of the work of the Contractor and the Contractor's subcontractors, and all other items for which a mechanic's lien may be asserted in the jurisdiction where the labor, materials or equipment were furnished.

§ 16.3 Construction Contract. The agreement between the Owner and Contractor identified on the cover page, including all Contract Documents and all changes made to the agreement and the Contract Documents.

§ 16.4 Owner Default. Failure of the Owner, which has not been remedied or waived, to pay the Contractor as required under the Construction Contract or to perform and complete or comply with the other material terms of the Construction Contract.

§ 16.5 Contract Documents. All the documents that comprise the agreement between the Owner and Contractor.

§ 17 If this Bond is issued for an agreement between a Contractor and subcontractor, the term Contractor in this Bond shall be deemed to be Subcontractor and the term Owner shall be deemed to be Contractor.

§ 18 Modifications to this bond are as follows:

(Space is provided below for additional signatures of added parties, other than those appearing on the cover page.)

| **CONTRACTOR AS PRINCIPAL** | | **SURETY** | |
| Company: | *(Corporate Seal)* | Company: | *(Corporate Seal)* |

Signature: _____   Signature: _____
Name and Title: Name and Title:
Address   Address

CAUTION: You should sign an original AIA Contract Document, on which this text appears in RED. An original assures that changes will not be obscured.

AIA Document A312™ – 2010. The American Institute of Architects.

Init.

/

8